Developmental Disorders of Language Learning and Cognition

Developmental Disorders of Language Learning and Cognition

Charles Hulme and Margaret J. Snowling

A John Wiley & Sons, Ltd., Publication

Blackwell Publishing was acquired by John Wiley & Sons in February 2007. Blackwell's publishing program has been merged with Wiley's global Scientific, Technical, and Medical business to form Wiley-Blackwell.

Registered Office
John Wiley & Sons Ltd, The Atrium, Southern Gate, Chichester, West Sussex, PO19 8SQ, United Kingdom

Editorial Offices
350 Main Street, Malden, MA 02148-5020, USA
9600 Garsington Road, Oxford, OX4 2DQ, UK
The Atrium, Southern Gate, Chichester, West Sussex, PO19 8SQ, UK

For details of our global editorial offices, for customer services, and for information about how to apply for permission to reuse the copyright material in this book please see our website at www.wiley.com/wiley-blackwell.

Library of Congress Cataloging-in-Publication Data

Hulme, Charles.
  Developmental disorders of language learning and cognition / Charles Hulme and Margaret J. Snowling.
    p. cm.
  Includes bibliographical references and index.
  ISBN 978-0-631-20611-8 (hardcover : alk. paper) – ISBN 978-0-631-20612-5 (pbk. : alk. paper)
1. Developmental disabilities. 2. Language disorders in children. 3. Cognition disorders in children.
I. Snowling, Margaret J. II. Title.
  RJ506.D47H85 2009
  618.92′855–dc22

                              2008044391

A catalogue record for this book is available from the British Library

Set in 10/13pt Sabon
by SPi Publisher Services, Pondicherry, India
Printed and bound in Singapore by C.O.S. Printers Pte Ltd

9   2015

Contents

List of Plates

List of Figures

List of Boxes

Acknowledgments

We are indebted to a huge number of friends and colleagues who helped and supported us during the time it has taken to write this book. Many collaborators, old and new, provided critical comments on the manuscript at various stages, notably Paula Clarke, Debbie Gooch, Sue Leekam, Helen Likierman, Valerie Muter, Kate Nation, Linda Pring, Silke Goebel, David Sugden and Eric Taylor. We were also extremely lucky that two of the most eminent scholars in the field, Dorothy Bishop and Michael Rutter, each read the entire manuscript and provided incisive and challenging comments. Our illustrator Dean Chesher did a fantastic job, always remaining positive and calm in the face of the many requests we made for amendments to the figures. We are grateful to members of our research group in the Centre for Reading and Language who either commented on chapters or helped in the final stages of revising them: Leesa Clarke, Piers Dawes, Fiona Duff, Lorna Hamilton, Becky Larkin, Emma Hayiou-Thomas, Lisa Henderson, Sophie Brigstocke and Emma Truelove. We also thank several graduate students who helped us to identify glossary terms: Nabilah Halah, Anna Jordan, Maria Markogiannaki, Silvana Mengoni, Zoi Pappa, Noah Wang. Our thanks also go to Susannah Witts and Geraldine Collins for administrative support and Peter Bailey, Kim Manderson, John Hobcraft, Anne Hillairet de Boisferon and Cathy Price for assistance at various stages. Several chapters of the book were written while MJS was in receipt of a British Academy Research Readership. We also acknowledge the support of the British Academy, ESRC, Nuffield Foundation, The Health Foundation and the Wellcome Trust for supporting our research at various stages in the book's preparation. Finally, Gerry Tehan and Bill Lovegrove kindly hosted our study visit to the University of Southern Queensland in 2006 which was very helpful to us while writing this book. Our thanks to all these people for their help, support and friendship.

1
Understanding Developmental Cognitive Disorders

John, Peter, and Ann are three 7-year-old children. John's parents and teachers have concerns about his progress in learning to read. John is generally bright and understands concepts well. Formal testing showed that he had a high IQ (120) with somewhat higher scores on the performance than the verbal scales of the test. John could only read a few simple words on a single word-reading test – a level of performance equivalent to a typical 5½-year-old child. John does not know the names or sounds of several letters of the alphabet. Verbally John is a good communicator, though he does show occasional word-finding problems and occasionally mispronounces long words. John is a child with dyslexia.

Peter is also a bright little boy (IQ 110, but with markedly lower scores on the performance than the verbal subtests). He has made a very good start with learning to read, and on the same test given to Peter he read as many words correctly as an average 8-year-old child. Peter has severe problems with games and sport at school, particularly with ball games. He is notably ill-coordinated and frequently drops and spills things. He has very serious difficulties with drawing and copying, and his handwriting is poorly formed and difficult to read. Peter has developmental coordination disorder.

Ann is a socially withdrawn child. She avoids interacting with other children in school whenever she can. She is sometimes observed rocking repetitively and staring out of the classroom window. Ann's communication skills are very poor, and she appears to have quite marked difficulties understanding what is said to her, particularly if what is said is at all abstract. When an attempt was made to give Ann a formal IQ test, testing was discontinued because she refused to cooperate. The few items she did complete suggested she would obtain a very low IQ score. Ann is fascinated by cars and will spend many hours cutting out pictures of them to add to her collection. Ann is a child with autism.

These three cases of 7-year-old children illustrate some of the varied cognitive problems that can be observed in children. In this book we will attempt to provide a broad survey of the major forms of cognitive disorder found in children, and lay out a theoretical framework for how these disorders can best be understood.

Understanding these disorders, in turn, holds prospects for how best to treat them. Our approach to these disorders is from a developmental perspective, by which we mean that a satisfactory understanding of these disorders needs to be informed by knowledge of how these skills typically develop. Most of the explanations we consider in the book will focus on the cognitive level: a functional level dealing with how the brain typically learns and performs the skills in question. Wherever possible, however, we will relate these cognitive explanations to what is known about the biological (genetic and neural) mechanisms involved in development. The interplay between genetic, neural, and cognitive explanations for behavioral development is currently an area of intense activity and excitement.

Some Terminology for Classifying Cognitive Disorders

In this book we will consider a wide range of developmental disorders that affect language, learning, and cognition. The disorders considered include those affecting language, reading, arithmetic, motor skills, attention, and social interaction (autism spectrum disorders). There are a number of features that are shared by the disorders we will discuss: they all occur quite commonly and have serious consequences for education, and thereafter for well-being in adulthood. There is also good evidence that all these disorders reflect the effects of genetic and environmental influences on the developing brain and mind.

To begin with it is important to distinguish between specific (or restricted) difficulties and general difficulties. Specific difficulties involve disorders where there is a deficit in just one or a small number of skills, with typical functioning in other areas. General difficulties involve impairments in most, if not all, cognitive functions. Terminology in this field differs between the UK and the USA; we will consider both here, but we will use primarily British terminology in later sections of the book.

In the UK a selective difficulty in acquiring a skill is referred to as a "specific learning difficulty." The term learning difficulty makes it clear that skills must be learned; specific means that the difficulty occurs in a restricted domain. Dyslexia is one of the best known and best understood examples of a specific learning difficulty. Children with dyslexia have specific difficulties in learning to read and to spell, but they have no particular difficulty in understanding concepts and may have talents in many other areas such as science, sport, and art. In the USA (following DSM-IV, the *Diagnostic and Statistical Manual of Mental Disorders* of the American Psychiatric Association) such specific difficulties are called learning disorders.

Specific learning difficulties can be contrasted with general learning difficulties (or, in US terminology, mental retardation). General learning difficulties involve difficulties in acquiring a wide range of skills. People with the chromosomal abnormality of Down syndrome, for example, usually have general learning difficulties and typically have problems in mastering all academic skills and with understanding in most domains. In this book we will focus upon specific learning difficulties.

In practice, the distinction between specific and general learning difficulties is often based on the results of a standardized IQ test. IQ tests (or measures of general intelligence) are highly predictive of variations in attainment in all manner of settings. The average IQ for the population is 100 (with a standard deviation of 15 points). In the UK people with IQ scores between 50 and 70 are referred to as having moderate learning difficulties, and people with IQ scores below 50 are said to have severe learning difficulties. US terminology distinguishes between mild (50–70), moderate (40–50), severe (25–40), and profound (IQ below 20) mental retardation. Often the diagnosis of a specific learning difficulty is made only in cases where the child achieves an IQ score in the average range (perhaps an IQ of 85 or above).

Operationally the distinction between specific and general learning difficulties is therefore quite clear: children with specific learning difficulties typically have average or near to average IQ scores, while children with general learning difficulties have IQ scores below 70. Conceptually, however, the distinction is probably a bit more slippery. It is important to appreciate that there is a continuum running from the highly restricted deficits found in some children (e.g., a child with a severe but isolated problem with arithmetic), to more general difficulties (e.g., a child with severe language difficulties who has difficulties both with understanding speech and expressing himself in speech), to very general difficulties (a child with an IQ of 40, who is likely to have problems in reading and spelling, as well as spoken language, together with a range of other problems including problems of perception, motor control, and general conceptual understanding). One aim of this book is to convey an appreciation of how studies of children with different types of learning difficulties have contributed to an understanding of how a range of different brain systems are involved in learning. The range of learning difficulties that occurs ultimately helps us to understand how the developing mind is organized and how the skills that are impaired in some children are typically acquired.

Levels of Explanation in Studies of Developmental Cognitive Disorders

What form of explanation can we hope to achieve for developmental cognitive disorders? It is important to distinguish between the different levels of explanation that are possible. Morton and Frith (1995) have laid out very clearly the logic and importance of distinguishing the different levels of explanation that are needed for understanding developmental disorders. They show how it is essential to consider three major levels of explanation: biological, cognitive, and behavioral. At each of these levels underlying processes (in the child) interact with a range of environmental influences to determine the observed outcome.

We can illustrate the role of different levels of explanation with reference to conduct disorder, a disorder of socio-emotional development that we will not deal with further in this book. Conduct disorder is a disorder where there have been advances in understanding at several different levels recently (Viding & Frith, 2006) and it is therefore a good example to illustrate the different levels of explanation involved in the study of developmental disorders. Conduct disorder is defined in DSM-IV as persistent antisocial behavior that deviates from age-appropriate social norms and violates the basic rights of others (American Psychiatric Association, 1994); alternative terms sometimes used for this disorder include antisocial behavior and conduct problems. A model for one aspect of conduct disorder – reactive aggression – proposed by Viding and Frith (2006) is shown in Figure 1.1 below.

This model represents processes operating at the biological, cognitive, and behavioral levels of explanation. It appears that at the biological level specific differences in genes that regulate the action of the neurotransmitter serotonin are important in giving rise to a predisposition to commit acts of violence. More specifically, different variants (alleles) of a gene coding for monoamine oxidase inhibitor A (MAOA) have been identified, with either high (MAOA-H) or low activity (MAOA-L). Research has suggested that having the MAOA-L gene may predispose an individual to display violent behavior but only if they experience maltreatment in childhood (Caspi et al., 2002). (This is a very important finding since it provides an example of gene–environment interaction; neither having the gene nor being maltreated alone may be sufficient but both factors together give a greatly increased risk of developing

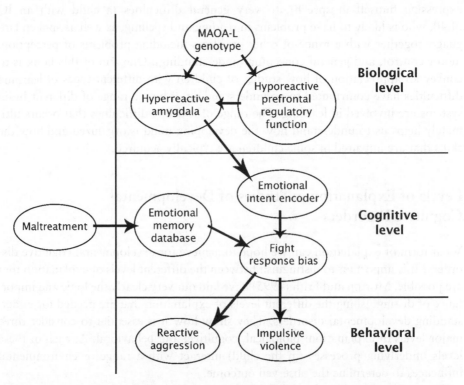

Figure 1.1   A causal model of the potential gene–brain–cognition–behavior pathways from MAOA-L to reactive aggression. (Adapted from Viding, E. & Frith, U. Genes for violence lurk in the brain. Commentary. *Proceedings for the National Academy of Sciences, 103,* 6085–6086. Copyright (2006) National Academy of Sciences, USA.)

conduct disorder.) These genetic and environmental risk factors in turn appear to operate on the development of brain systems concerned with the regulation of emotion. In particular it is thought that the MAOA-L gene may be associated with the development of hyperresponsivity of the amygdala during emotional arousal coupled with diminished responsivity of areas of the prefrontal cortex that normally play a role in regulating such emotional responses. This pattern of brain dysfunction might be seen as providing the biological basis for reacting excessively emotionally and violently when provoked by certain environmental conditions (in everyday terminology, losing control or "losing it" when provoked).

Viding and Frith suggest that these brain differences express themselves at the cognitive level via a mechanism called an emotional intent encoder, which in turn is associated with a bias to fight. Interestingly, in this model, Viding and Frith explicitly propose that the interactive effects of childhood maltreatment operate at a cognitive level by leading to the creation of many emotionally charged memory representations. This is an interesting and testable hypothesis, but of course such effects may also operate at a biological level as well as, or instead of, at the cognitive level.

The final level in the model is the behavioral level, where the fight response bias mechanism may lead to reactive aggression (fighting when provoked) as well as impulsive violence.

A complete explanation of any disorder will involve at least three levels of description. For one aspect of conduct disorder – reactive aggression – genes appear to contribute powerfully to the risk of developing the disorder in interaction with specific environmental experiences (maltreatment) in childhood. It appears that these genetic effects in turn affect the development of brain circuits concerned with the experience and regulation of emotion, perhaps particularly anger, which, in interaction with memories of previous experiences associated with violence, may lead to a bias toward fighting (rather than running away or being afraid). At a behavioral level, this bias toward a fight response may lead to the observed profile of responding violently when provoked and occasionally committing unprovoked, impulsive acts of violence.

Morton and Frith (1995; Morton 2004) argue that it is useful to make explicit diagrams of these sorts of theoretical explanations, using an approach they term causal modeling. The Viding and Frith diagram (Figure 1.1) is an example. It is important to note that the arrows in such a diagram represent hypothetical causal links. According to this model, a genetic difference causes a brain difference (abnormality), which in turn causes cognitive (emotional) deficits, which in turn cause the observed behavioral patterns (a propensity to violence). Note that within this framework environmental effects can be thought of as operating at each level. So, for example, a virus or early brain injury might also lead to the brain abnormality underlying the emotion control problem, and the effects of positive experiences (a nurturant nonaggressive parental style) might prevent the development of the emotion regulation deficits. Some forms of treatment (teaching anger management strategies) might also have effects on the behavioral level (inhibiting violent outbursts) without having a direct effect on the cognitive level (the person may still feel angry and feel the urge to lash out, but develop ways of controlling such feelings).

It is important to emphasize that all three levels of description are useful, and each helps us to understand the disorder. While links can and should be made between these different levels of explanation, we cannot reduce or replace one level of explanation with a lower level. The cognitive level of explanation (emotion encoding) cannot be replaced by a neural explanation (problems with the amygdala). We would note here that we have followed Morton and Frith's terminology by referring to the level between the brain and behavior as "cognitive." This might seem too narrow a term because cognition essentially refers to thought processes. We will stick with this term for the moment, though in some of the disorders we consider later (as well as in the case of conduct disorder) this terminology might usefully be broadened to consider other forms of mental processes, particularly emotional and motivational processes, that probably cannot simply be reduced to cognition. The point, however, is that we need a level of "mind" or "mental process" as an intervening level of explanation between brain and behavior. We would also argue, in light of recent advances in our understanding of developmental disorders, that the causal model presented in Figure 1.1 is too unidirectional to capture the truly interactive nature of development. It is also necessary to postulate causal arrows running "backwards" from lower levels to upper levels. This at first seems counterintuitive, but some examples help to explain why it is necessary.

Can changes at the behavioral level alter things at the cognitive level? Almost certainly yes. If we take the example of teaching anger management strategies mentioned above, it may be that such training will work by modifying the cognitive mechanisms associated with emotional encoding; seeing a person grin could be interpreted simply as showing that they were happy rather than indicating they are intending to insult you. Do such changes at the cognitive level depend upon changes in underlying brain mechanisms? Again it would seem likely that they do. Connections between nerve cells may be modified by experience and this in turn will result in lasting structural and functional changes in the circuits responsible for encoding and regulating emotion.

Finally, and perhaps most surprisingly, we can consider whether changes at the behavioral and cognitive levels can affect things at the genetic level. Most people would probably doubt this proposition. Our genetic makeup is fixed (we inherit our DNA at conception and experiences are not going to alter it), this is true, but there is evidence that experiences can alter the way genes are expressed. Genes (genes are sequences of base pairs in DNA) do not regulate development directly. Rather, genes control the production of messenger RNA (mRNA), and mRNA in turn controls the production of proteins in cells. Furthermore, mRNA molecules degrade quickly so that if more of a protein is needed the cells concerned have to keep manufacturing more mRNA. Changes in the rate at which a gene produces mRNA will therefore result in changes in the rate at which the protein coded is produced in a cell. The levels of regulation in cells, as currently conceptualized by molecular biologists, are shown in Figure 1.2. Once again, in this diagram there are different levels of explanation: the genome (the genes that consist of sequences of base pairs in DNA), the transcriptome (the mRNA produced under the control of the base sequences in the DNA), the proteome (the proteins produced under the control of mRNA), the

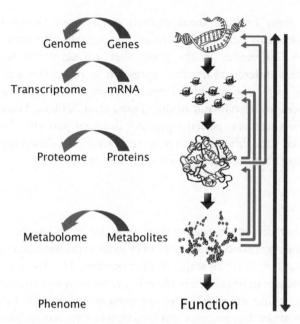

Figure 1.2   Diagram showing the complexities of genetic mechanisms. There are potentially numerous interactions at each level, as well as bidirectional influences between levels. All these parameters may differ between different developmental stages or in different tissues of the body. (With kind permission from Springer Science and Business Media. *Metabolomics*, Metabolomics – the way forward, 1, 2005, p. 2, Goodacre, R., fig.a.)

metabolome (the products of proteins and other chemicals created by metabolism in the cell), and the phenome (the functioning of the cell within its environment in the body).

As shown in Figure 1.2, there are bidirectional arrows connecting these different levels (not a one-way arrow flowing from DNA to Function). One of the ways in which experiences may affect the expression of the genome is through the operation of control genes. Such control genes exist to control the operation of other genes by switching these other genes on or off (i.e., making genes either produce or stop producing mRNA). It now appears that such control genes may cause other genes to be switched off in response to changes in the internal and external environment. One remarkable example of such effects is shown by the observation that tweaking a rat's whiskers may cause changes in gene expression in the animal's sensory cortex (Mack & Mack, 1992). Similarly, when a songbird hears their species' song this experience may operate to change the expression of genes in the brain (Mello, Vicario, & Clayton, 1992). Thus, we need to accept that environmental effects may result in changes in the way genes are expressed. Such changes in gene expression may in turn result in long-lasting changes in the neural structures whose development is partly under genetic control (see Plomin, DeFries, McClearn, & Rutter, 1997, for more details).

In line with these findings from animals it has been shown that in human monozygotic (identical) twin pairs there are measurable differences in patterns of gene expression (differences in the genes that are active or being expressed). Furthermore, these differences in gene expression increase with age and tend to be greater for twin pairs who have lived apart for longer and who have experienced greater differences in lifestyle and health (Fraga et al., 2005). These effects clearly suggest that differences in experience produce different patterns of gene expression in people and that such differences may be responsible for differences in health and brain development that may have effects on behavior.

Summary

We hope that our discussion makes clear that the environment affects how our genetic makeup is expressed. The patterns of gene expression in cells will differ in different tissues and at different stages of development. The tissues most relevant for explaining differences in behavior are those in the nervous and endocrine (hormonal) systems. The most important point for the present argument is to appreciate that experiences may affect the processes involved in gene expression. Viewed in this way, the genome is not fixed in the way it operates throughout development. Rather, the genome receives signals from the environment that can turn genes on or off in different tissues of the body (including the brain). This means that differences in our experiences may well affect how genes that play a role in controlling brain development are expressed.

For most of this book we will be concentrating on explanations for developmental disorders that seek to relate observed impairments at the behavioral level to deficits at the cognitive level. We believe that such cognitive explanations are important and valid in their own right. A cognitive explanation of a disorder is essentially a functional explanation, couched in terms of how a particular skill is learned and performed, and in what ways this typical functioning is disturbed. Such an explanation is satisfying in its own right, and also has practical importance, in that it relates closely (though always indirectly) to how we can best assess and treat a disorder. This is not to say that biological levels of explanation are not also important. We will, where appropriate, cite evidence about the biological mechanisms underlying the cognitive level of explanation, particularly where such biological evidence places constraints on the types of cognitive explanation that are most viable. As has already been made clear from the brief account of research on conduct disorder above, there are two levels of biological mechanism that may be particularly relevant to the study of developmental cognitive disorders: genetic and brain mechanisms. We will consider very briefly the way in which these mechanisms are studied.

Genetic Mechanisms

There are two levels at which the genetic basis of a disorder can be studied. Population genetic studies examine the patterns of inheritance of a disorder across individuals.

Molecular genetic studies go beyond this and identify certain genes (DNA sequences) or gene markers that are associated with the development of a disorder. Both of these levels of analysis have been applied in the case of conduct disorder.

Population genetic studies relate variations in genetic association to degrees of similarity in the phenotype (observed characteristics). Basically, if a characteristic is inherited, people who are genetically similar to each other should also be similar to each other in that characteristic. One of the ways to get such evidence is from studies of twins. These studies make use of the fact that there are two different types of twin. Identical or monozygotic (MZ) twins develop from a single fertilized egg. Nonidentical (sometimes referred to as fraternal) or dizygotic (DZ) twins occur when two different fertilized eggs implant in the womb at the same time. MZ twins effectively share all their genetic material, whereas DZ twins will only share on average the same degree of genetic similarity to each other as any other pair of siblings. (DZ twins should, on average, share 50% of their segregating or polymorphic genes. These segregating genes are the coding sequences of DNA that differ between people and contribute to individual differences. Such segregating genes only account for a tiny proportion of our DNA: indeed it has been suggested that human beings share 98% of their genetic code with chimpanzees.) Twin studies often involve making comparisons between how frequently a disorder occurs in pairs of MZ and DZ twins. If both twins in a pair share the same condition, they are said to be concordant. Concordance rates should be higher in MZ, than DZ, twin pairs if genetic factors are important.

Concordance rates are only really useful when studying characteristics that are either present or absent. For example, if breast cancer were influenced by genetic factors, we would expect that the risk of pairs of MZ twins both contracting the disease would be higher than for pairs of DZ twins. However, as we shall see later in the book, for many cognitive disorders it is difficult to set precise cut-offs for whether a person has, or has not, got a disorder. This is because the disorders are best described as dimensional (so that individuals can have a disorder to varying degrees). Because of this we need a method of studying the degree of similarity between pairs of twins when the measures are quantitative dimensions rather than categories. Such a method was developed by DeFries and Fulker (1985). This method basically uses a form of regression equation to assess the influence of genetic factors on a characteristic. If genes are important in determining a continuous characteristic (such as height), MZ twins should be more similar to each other on that characteristic than DZ twins.

The degree of genetic influence on the development of a characteristic is expressed in terms of a heritability estimate. Heritability is concerned with quantifying the extent to which differences among people in a population reflect genetic differences. A heritability estimate of 0 would mean that genetic differences played no role in explaining the differences among people in a characteristic, while a heritability estimate of 1.0 would mean that genetic differences accounted entirely for the differences observed. In practice heritability estimates are usually intermediate in size but it is common for developmental disorders to show substantial heritability, meaning that genetic influences are important for their development. To return to the case of conduct disorder, there is good evidence that genetic factors are important for its development. For example, Blonigen et al. (2005) reported a heritability estimate of approximately 50 for a measure of impulsive antisociality in a large twin sample, meaning that some 50% of the differences between people on this measure reflected genetic differences between people in the sample studied.

Molecular genetic studies try to identify the specific genes that may be responsible for the development of a disorder. Modern techniques allow the sequence of base pairs in an individual's DNA to be "read off" quite rapidly. The problem then becomes one of sifting the huge amount of data generated. It would not be appropriate to go into the details of these methods here. However, the basic approach is to try to identify DNA sequences that are shared by close relatives who both display a disorder but are not shared by other close relatives who do not have the disorder. Such studies involve sifting huge amounts of data and, rather than identifying specific genes, quite large DNA sequences (consisting of potentially many genes) may be identified. A group of genes that can be shown to correlate with the development of a complex quantitative trait (such as reading ability) is referred to as a quantitative trait locus (QTL). However, in some cases specific candidate genes have been identified that appear to be causally related to the development of a disorder. In the example of conduct disorder described above, one of the variants (alleles) of a gene coding for low activity of the monoamine oxidase inhibitor A (MAOA-L) appears to predispose an individual to display violent behavior (but only if they experience maltreatment in childhood).

The Causes of Development – Nature Working with Nurture

One of the oldest and most central debates in developmental psychology is about the role of genes (nature) and environment (nurture) as determinants of development. As we will see later in the book, there is overwhelming evidence that genetic factors are powerful influences on the origins of many developmental disorders. We take this conclusion to be established beyond any reasonable doubt. This is not the same as saying the disorders are innate, however.

Innate is defined in the *Shorter Oxford English Dictionary* as "Existing in a person (or organism) from birth ... inborn ... of qualities ... (especially mental) opposite of acquired ..." It is important to appreciate that the idea embodied in this definition is totally at variance with current thinking in genetics and developmental biology. The critical point is that genes contain information that serves to direct development, but all development takes place in an environment and information from the environment interacts with the genetic "blueprint" in complex ways. Development results from the interaction of genetic and environmental inputs – an idea referred to as epigenesis. Furthermore, according to the idea of "probabilistic epigenesis" (Gottlieb, 1992; Johnson, 1997), there may be bidirectional influences between different levels so that, for example, genes that help to specify aspects of physical development (including brain development) can in turn be reciprocally influenced by the structures they have helped to produce (see Figure 1.3). Similarly, and perhaps more obviously,

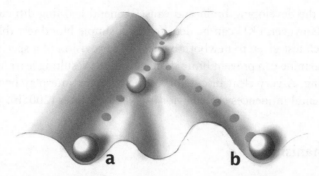

Figure 1.3 Waddington's epigenetic landscape is a metaphor for how gene regulation processes modulate development. Each of the marbles rolling down the hill represents a cell and different grooves in the landscape represent different trajectories that will result in different developmental courses and so different "end states" for a cell. Differences in the environment will play a role in determining the trajectory taken by a given cell. At a higher level we could think of the marbles representing whole organisms and again the end points of development will depend on both genetic and environmental influences.

learning (an influence from the environment) operates to modify structures in the brain that developed under genetic control and in turn may influence subsequent learning.

Development has to be seen as an extremely complex process that is characterized by change and interaction. All of the cognitive disorders we will consider in this book depend upon functional brain systems (brain systems that are defined by what they do) and it is simply not sensible to view these systems as arising directly and invariantly from information coded in the genes. In practice, performing any cognitive activity will depend upon one or more brain circuits, which comprise complex assemblies of many thousands of nerve cells communicating information between each other. Such brain circuits will develop under some degree of genetic influence but also as a product of learning from interactions with the environment.

Genes code for the production of proteins, which in turn have complex and at least partially indirect effects on the way physical structures such as the brain develop. Furthermore, as we have already noted, experiences may serve to switch on, or switch off, genes that are involved in controlling structural and functional aspects of brain development. In short, functional brain systems (brain circuits) develop as a result of complex interactions between genetic information and a range of environmental influences (where the environment includes many physical influences on development, such as temperature, nutrition, toxins, and radiation, as well as psychological experiences).

An acceptance that some aspect of development is under genetic influences does nothing to negate the importance of the environment. In relation to developmental disorders this can be illustrated by a well-known example. Phenylketonuria (PKU) is a genetic disorder that is controlled by a single gene. Children who inherit two such recessive alleles of this gene are unable to metabolize phenylalanine (an amino acid present in many foods) and this results in a build-up of this substance in the body that damages the developing brain and causes general learning difficulties (mental retardation). However, PKU can be detected by a simple blood test (blood is taken in the heel prick test given to newborn babies) and provision of a special diet that is low in phenylalanine can prevent brain damage and the resulting learning difficulties from developing. A very clear discussion of the complex interplay between genetic and environmental influences on behavior is given by Rutter (2005b).

Brain Mechanisms

Genetic differences between people, in concert with environmental influences, determine the course of development, including development of the brain (epigenesis). In relation to developmental cognitive disorders it is likely that the problems we observe in different children will reflect both structural and functional differences in brain organization. In the last 20 years or so there has been an explosion of research concerned with understanding the relationships between brain, behavior, and cognition. Most of this research has focused on brain function, though it is also the case that some important work continues to examine the possible relationships between structural brain abnormalities and various forms of learning difficulties (Leonard, Eckert, Given, Berninger, & Eden, 2006)

   Our ability to study the functional organization and operation of the brain while we are thinking has been transformed by the advent of brain imaging techniques. Positron emission tomography (PET) and functional magnetic resonance imaging (fMRI) are two techniques that have been used to study the patterns of neural activation occurring during ongoing cognitive tasks. Both PET and fMRI detect changes in blood flow in specific regions of the brain that arise during the performance of a task. When a brain region does work, it requires metabolic energy, which in turn requires extra oxygen and thus extra blood flow. Both of these techniques provide evidence for fairly slow-acting changes in brain activity and usually depend on averaging measurements from a number of trials in an experiment. However, the techniques give quite precise information about localization in the brain. The other methodological wrinkle is that we need to have a "baseline" against which to measure any putative increase in activation in a specific task. This therefore involves subtracting the levels of activation seen in a specific task from levels of activation seen in a similar task, preferably in a task that involves everything apart from the one component of an experimental task that we are particularly interested in. So, for example, activation might be compared in a condition where a subject sees and silently reads a sequence of words, and in another condition where exactly the same words are presented as pictures to be silently named. Areas of the brain that show increases in activation in the reading condition, compared to the picture condition, presumably are somehow specifically involved in processing written words (orthographic processing) and translating from orthography (print) to phonology (speech sounds). Details of the subtraction methodology become complicated, but the point is that imaging studies always involve some sort of inference to be made based on a comparison between closely matched tasks.

Electroencephalography (EEG) and magnetoencephalography (MEG) are two techniques that give better temporal (time-based) information about patterns of brain activity but poorer information about the localization of activity. EEG involves attaching electrodes to the scalp and measuring differences in voltage between the electrodes and how these voltage differences change across time. The timing of these voltage changes, which reflect patterns of firing from large sets of neurons in the brain, can be measured with millisecond (0.001 s) accuracy. One particularly useful EEG technique is event-related potentials (ERPs). To measure ERPs, EEG recordings are taken in response to a particular stimulus (or set of stimuli) and the results are averaged over many trials to identify consistent patterns of activity. MEG is a methodologically superior technique to EEG that also measures changes in neural activity in the brain. MEG measures the magnetic fields produced by the electrical activity in the brain by using superconducting quantum interference devices (SQUIDs), which are housed in a helmet-like enclosure that fits around the head (see Plate 1). Like EEG, MEG yields quite precise information about the timing of neural responses to stimuli, but it gives relatively crude information about the localization of activity in the brain. It seems likely that MEG will become a very valuable technique for studying brain activity, and combining MEG with fMRI recordings in the same individual provides the possibility of getting both localization and temporal information about patterns of brain activity.

Separable Systems in the Mind – Modularity and Development

Subsequent chapters in this book will consider what we know about the nature, origins, and treatments for a variety of developmental cognitive disorders. The fact that there is a wide range of somewhat specific developmental disorders (some children have difficulties with language, while other children have difficulties with the control of movement, for example) supports the idea that the mind has different systems (or modules) that are responsible for different functions (language and motor control in the case just cited).

The idea that the mind is a modular system (a system composed of separable subsystems) has a very long history that can be traced back at least as far as the ancient Greek philosophers (Arbib, Caplan, & Marshall, 1982). A slightly more recent, but now discredited, modular approach was represented in Gall's pseudo-scientific phrenology (see Figure 1.4). According to Gall the relative size of different brain regions (measured by feeling the shape of the skull!) could be used to infer characteristics of people, such as their "acquisitiveness" or "secretiveness." The idea of modularity has been brought to prominence in modern psychology by the work of Fodor (1983) and Marr (1983).

Studies of cognition in adults, and particularly studies in adult cognitive neuropsychology, have been dominated by an approach that sees the mind as a modular system. Cognitive neuropsychology seeks to develop theories about how the mind typically operates, by studying the disorders in mental (cognitive) processes that

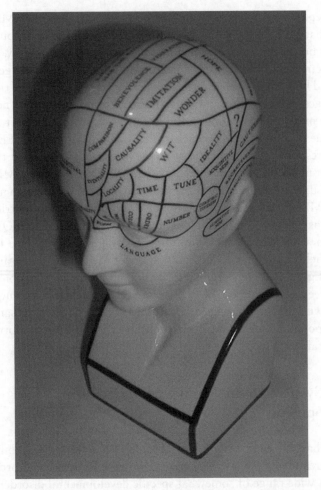

Figure 1.4   A phrenological head showing areas labeled with their supposed functions.

arise as a result of brain damage (see Shallice, 1988). A modular view sees the mind as composed of separate systems or modules, just as we might think of our bodies as being composed of different systems such as the circulatory, respiratory, and digestive systems. An analogy to convey the concept of modularity can be given by considering a computer (see Figure 1.5). A desktop computer usually consists of a number of interconnected components, some of which are physically separate (the monitor, key-board) while others may be housed in the same box (the processor, hard disk, CD drive, sound card, video card, etc.). Problems in such a system can be easily identified, and rectified, by isolating or swapping components. To take a trivial example, if the monitor does not work, this may be due to a number of components (the monitor itself, the cable connecting it to the computer, or perhaps the video card inside the computer that generates the signals to control the monitor). By testing each of these components sequentially we can gradually identify the component that is causing the fault in such a system (though often such a process can be time consuming and frustrating!).

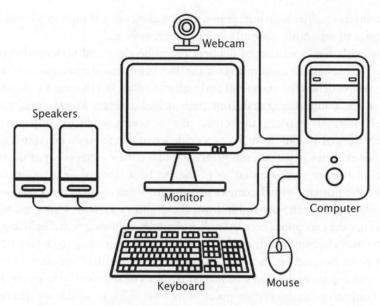

Figure 1.5 A computer as an example of a modular system.

In some ways, the studies we describe later can be thought of as analogous to this process of finding a fault in a computer system. If, for example, children with dyslexia perform tasks requiring them to isolate individual sounds in words very poorly, but perform as well as other children on analogous tasks requiring them to isolate shapes in complex visual displays, we might infer that the brain systems dealing with speech sounds are impaired in children with dyslexia, while other brain systems dealing with the perception of complex visual patterns are intact. We will, however, spend a great deal of time showing how understanding disorders of the developing mind is a much more complicated process than locating a fault in a computer system.

Cognitive neuropsychology in adults has made enormous progress by adopting an approach that seeks to understand the effects of brain damage as arising from impairments to separable cognitive systems that can be damaged independently as a result of brain injury. At the simplest level, modularity simply amounts to the claim that the mind consists of separate subsystems. To take an obvious example, there are separate systems responsible for vision and hearing in the brain. Damage to the primary visual cortex (at the back of the head, in the occipital lobe) results in areas of blindness, while damage to the primary auditory cortex (at the side of the head, in the temporal lobe) results in difficulties in discriminating the frequency of sounds (Tramo, Shah, & Braida, 2002). In these cases no one would wish to argue with the proposition that separate brain systems are responsible for the senses of hearing and vision, and that it is possible to get impairments in vision, without impairments in hearing, and vice versa. This, in the parlance of cognitive neuropsychology, would be an example of a double dissociation: patients with damage to the primary visual cortex have problems with vision, but hear normally; patients with damage to the primary auditory cortex have problems with hearing, but see normally. Double dissociations have often been interpreted as providing critical support for modularity: the existence of separable, neurally independent, systems.

This example has been chosen deliberately to be clear and noncontroversial. We will make the reasonable assumption for the time being that the two patients described showed massive deficits on the visual and auditory tasks, but that each was completely normal on the nonimpaired task (one patient had a severe visual impairment, but completely normal hearing; the other had a severe auditory impairment, but completely normal vision). In such cases evidence of this sort can be related to a variety of other evidence (e.g., that the primary visual cortex receives input from cells in the retina of the eye, and stimulation of the eye by a flash of light results in neural activity in the primary visual cortex) to support a theory that the visual system is functionally and neurally separable from the auditory system. However, such very clear cases are the exception, even in studies of adults following focal brain lesions, and such distinctions become much harder to make once we move on to consider "higher" cognitive processes such as memory. Furthermore, as we shall see later, in studies of children with cognitive disorders such clear patterns of selective impairment are quite unusual (and this is an interesting point in its own right, to which we will return).

In reality the logic and practice of seeking to establish the existence of separate cognitive systems by looking for double dissociations is both controversial and complex and has been debated extensively (e.g., Coltheart & Davies, 2003; Dunn & Kirsner, 1988; 2003; Gurd & Marshall, 2003; Jones, 1983; Van Orden, Pennington, & Stone, 2001). There are both logical and statistical issues at stake in the debate about this issue. Logically, it seems reasonable to conclude that any given pattern of double dissociation might in principle be open to a variety of theoretical interpretations. Claims about separable processes will always depend upon having a clear theory about the processes concerned and finding converging evidence to support the idea of their separability (as in the case of converging evidence for the role of the visual cortex in vision described above).

At another level there are also purely statistical or methodological issues about how we need to measure behavior in order to establish dissociations between tasks (which is a prerequisite for trying to infer that the tasks depend upon dissociable mechanisms). In a typical case, the process of establishing an impairment in one domain, but not another, amounts to identifying what Chapman and Chapman (1973) referred to as a differential deficit. As these authors pointed out, identifying differential deficits depends critically upon the statistical properties of the measures used. In particular, the greater the true score (or reliable) variance in a test, the easier it will be to show that a clinical group is impaired on that test. True score variance increases as the reliability and the variance (the range of scores) of a test increase. The reliability of a test refers to the extent to which measurement is subject to error. The variance in scores from a test will vary with the relative difficulty of the test for the sample of people it is used with: the variance in test scores will decrease when tests are either too hard (tendency toward a floor effect) or too easy (tendency toward a ceiling effect). The statistical methods needed to identify differential deficits are well understood, though in practice these methods can be onerous and are rarely followed rigorously.

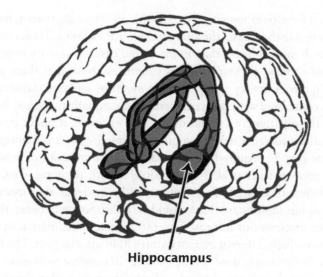

Hippocampus

Figure 1.6　The hippocampus: a bilateral mid-brain structure that plays a critical role in memory function. Patient HM suffered bilateral damage to the hippocampus following brain surgery to relieve intractable epilepsy.

A much more severe limitation on the use of double dissociations comes from the sorts of inferences that we wish to draw from observing dissociations. In practice all we observe directly are dissociations on tasks (we observe that Patient A is bad on Task 1, but fine on Task 2, and that Patient B is bad on Task 2, but fine on Task 1). However, the interpretations that we are interested in involve theoretical systems (modules). Sometimes inferences from tasks to hypothetical processes seem straightforward enough. In the example given above (observing one patient fail to report flashes of light presented to certain parts of their visual field, and another patient with problems in identifying sounds) it seems safe enough to infer that they suffer impairments to the visual and auditory systems, respectively (and this assertion relates to a wide range of other evidence and theory). However, once we leave the study of "peripheral" sensory systems and move on to study "higher" mental processes, the inferences required become considerably more complex.

This difficulty of identifying separable higher mental processes can be illustrated with a justly famous example. Some adult patients have been identified who have particular difficulties with the immediate, verbatim recall of spoken lists of words while their memory for information from the past is preserved (KF, a patient studied by Warrington & Shallice, 1969). These problems have been interpreted as evidence for an impairment to a short-term memory system (a system holding information in conscious awareness for a second or two) with no impairment to a separate long-term memory store (a system that holds a vast amount of information for extended periods of time). In contrast, other patients (e.g., HM; Scoville & Milner, 1957; HM had bilateral damage to the hippocampus; see Figure 1.6) have been described who have great difficulties in remembering events from the past but are relatively good at the verbatim recall of lists of words, and this has been interpreted as evidence for an impairment in a long-term memory system with an intact short-term memory store. However, note that in these cases the inferences from the observed tasks to hypothetical systems are much more indirect than in the earlier cases of sensory impairments.

Observations of these patients' deficits cannot establish that there are separable short- and long-term memory systems. There might be separate memory systems for immediate, as contrasted with delayed, memory but equally there may be other ways of explaining these patterns of impairments. For example, it might be that patients such as KF suffer problems in maintaining information in a phonological (sound-based) code (as may be required for immediate verbatim recall of arbitrary lists of words) while patients such as HM have problems with recalling semantic information (the meanings of events). This would still be evidence that memory is not a unitary process, but in this case there would be a distinction between the codes representing different classes of information, rather than a distinction in terms of the time period over which different memory stores hold information. The best interpretation of these dissociations need not be a matter of concern to us now. The point of importance is that the observation of a dissociation in performance on different tasks may be amenable to a variety of different theoretical interpretations (in terms of the underlying psychological systems, or modules, involved).

We now need to consider what precisely (or at least more precisely) we mean by modularity in psychology. Our example of a computer system is a useful intuitive starting point. A modern computer is a modular system in the sense that different components are specialized to perform different functions (such as the monitor, keyboard, CD drive, processor, sound card, and video card). Unfortunately, even with modern technologies such as brain imaging techniques it is not possible to identify separate components in the brain directly. Fodor (1983) set out to develop a theory about what cognitive modules are like. Fodor listed a number of features that he believed typically, but not necessarily, characterized modules. He suggested that modules tended to be "domain specific," meaning a given module only takes a restricted range of inputs (perhaps one module exists that "computes" the identity of letters, while another module "computes" the identity of spoken words). The first hypothetical module in this case would only take a restricted set of visual information as input (color and brightness would be irrelevant) while the second module would only take a restricted range of auditory information as input. This is analogous to the case of the sound card and video card in our computer example: the sound card plays no role in dealing with information going to the monitor, and the video card plays no role in dealing with audio signals going to the speakers.

Modules also, according to Fodor, display "informational encapsulation," which means that higher "conscious" levels of the system have limited access to the processes operating in the modules. Modules also tend to be "computationally autonomous," meaning that they do not share general-purpose resources such as attention. These three properties bring with them a benefit: modules, according to Fodor, operate quickly and effortlessly.

Fodor also suggested that modules were likely to be innate. (The suggestion that anything is "innate" is an idea that we have already rejected above.) We will not dwell on the details of Fodor's characterization of modules, which have been the subject of extensive debate and criticism. The general point, however, is clear. Fodor was suggesting that there is a set of relatively independent, innate, fast-acting systems in the mind that carry on doing their work without the need for conscious attention or effort. Fodor also suggested that the evidence for modular organization was clearest in the case of input and output systems. He suggested that there were also "central systems," such as those responsible for reasoning and problem solving, that probably were not modular. These central systems were, he suggested, very hard to understand, precisely because they were nonmodular. In fact, Fodor (2000, 2005) has gone on to argue that the view that much of mental life can be explained in terms of a large set of modules ("massive modularity") is misguidedly optimistic. In his view the need for nonmodular systems underlying higher-level cognitive processes, and how such nonmodular systems can be conceptualized, remains a major challenge for theories in cognitive psychology.

In practice psychologists have generally been happy (perhaps too happy in Fodor's view) to assume that the mind consists of many separate but highly interactive systems. Indeed without this assumption, or some version of it, the task of trying to understand the mind seems impossibly complex. As Fodor argued, this idea is generally easiest to grasp in relation to the most peripheral input or output systems (it seems obvious in the example above that different systems underlie vision and hearing) but becomes more difficult to pin down as we move to more "central" processes (how many different memory systems are there?). Psychologists typically seek converging evidence from different sources to support or refute theories about the number of separable modules that underlie particular skills or tasks. One particularly important source of evidence for separate processes (but not the only one) comes from demonstrations of separate impairments (people may be blind, but not deaf, and vice versa).

In summary, in studies of adults a common working assumption is that there are separate modules or subsystems in the mind that perform different functions. Theories are often expressed in terms of boxes and arrows diagrams, or more rarely as computer programmes that attempt to implement the processes represented in such separate boxes.

The Need to Relate Developmental Disorders to Patterns of Typical Development

How are we going to understand disorders of cognitive development? A number of different approaches have been adopted, one of which is to relate developmental disorders to patterns of impairment seen in adults following brain damage (Temple, 1997). In our view this approach is misguided because it is based on a view that the cognitive modules seen in adults are essentially innate. Our view, in contrast, would be that the only way to understand developmental disorders is to relate them to studies of typical development. If we want to understand the reading problems seen in children with developmental dyslexia we need to do this by relating the problems seen in these children to patterns of typical development. A theory of reading development needs to specify how typically developing children learn to read. A theory of developmental

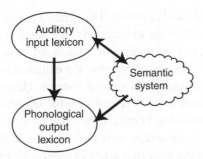

Figure 1.7   Modular systems underlying the comprehension and production of spoken words in adults. Our ability to comprehend and produce spoken words appears to depend upon at least three separable systems dealing with the recognition (auditory input lexicon), production (phonological output lexicon), and meaning of words (semantic system).

dyslexia would then specify how and why the processes that are involved in typical reading development are impaired in children with developmental dyslexia.

If we accept arguments from adult neuropsychology and cognitive psychological theories of normal adult cognition that the mind is to some degree a modular system, we can then ask how such modules develop. One view, which Fodor favored, was that many modules are under strong genetic control, that is, we are born genetically programmed for the brain to develop certain specialized systems, given only certain rudimentary inputs. It seems plausible that this is true for some systems. Again, sensory systems such as vision seem plausible candidates for being under strong genetic control. However, there are plenty of modules postulated by psychologists that almost certainly are not under direct genetic control: the systems underlying reading and writing would be good examples. Reading and writing are very recently acquired skills in evolutionary terms and almost certainly reflect the fact that the brain can create modules by a process of learning. In fact, as Bishop (1997a) has pointed out, many of the properties of "modules" proposed by Fodor (such as speed and autonomy of operation) are plausibly seen as properties of cognitive systems that have benefited from extensive practice (think of skilled typing, or riding a bike, for example). No one is born with an innate "typing" module, but skilled typists can type at a remarkable speed, often with seemingly little cognitive effort.

Some have argued that a good starting point for studies of cognitive impairments in children is with a model of the adult "modular" system (Temple, 1997), but one of the simplest things that can be said about development is that it involves change. Typically developing children show large changes in the course of acquiring certain skills such as language or reading and writing. To take a concrete example, there would be fairly wide agreement that in an adult we can distinguish at least three separate systems involved in dealing with individual spoken words: a system for recognizing the sound structure of spoken words, a system for saying words, and a semantic system that deals with the meanings of the words that we hear or need to say. This idea is illustrated in Figure 1.7.

The auditory input lexicon holds representations of the words we know and can recognize when we hear them, the phonological output lexicon holds representations of words that we know in a form suitable for controlling how we say them, and the semantic system holds information about the meanings of words. A typically developing child learns to say their first words at around 12 months of age, and thereafter rapidly expands their expressive vocabulary over an extended period of development. Arguably, the typical 8-month-old has none of the ovals illustrated in Figure 1.7 in their mind, the typical 2-year-old has perhaps small-scale versions of all three systems, and the typical 10-year-old has something that is a very close approximation to the adult system. In our view then, it is not useful to start with an adult model and ask how it is impaired in a child who has severe problems in learning language. Rather, we would argue that developmental disorders require a developmental approach to understanding them, that is, we must start with theories and models of how, in a typically developing child, certain skills are acquired. The proper form of explanation for developmental disorders will be to specify how, and in what ways, the typical developmental path is disturbed. Although adult models may provide a very useful description of what typically arises as a result of development, such models say little about how systems develop. In this book we will take a developmental approach. For each of the disorders we consider, we will evaluate how current knowledge of the disorder may be interpreted in terms of theoretical accounts of typical development.

It will be clear from this that the challenges in understanding developmental disorders are considerable. In the case of adult disorders, we need to understand how damage to the brain results in a particular pattern of impairments. In terms of a cognitive model we need to relate the pattern of impairment to a static adult model of cognitive function. For developmental disorders the task is considerably more complex. This complexity arises from the fact that the developing cognitive systems we are studying change as children develop. A theoretical explanation of a cognitive disorder therefore needs to specify how impairments in a given process arise, and how this affects the development of other systems. Development involves change, and an abnormality of development means that the rate and pattern of change with age are modified. Furthermore, deficits in one area may have diverse knock-on effects on other aspects of development because different systems interact during development.

We might illustrate this complicated idea most simply by considering a sensory impairment such as deafness. Congenital deafness in childhood can have very damaging effects on oral language development, and speech skills will usually be severely impaired. Deaf children typically show grave deficits in a number of aspects of oral language development, including impairments in phonology (mastering the sound system of language) and syntax (grammar). These difficulties in a congenitally deaf child need to be understood in terms of how typical oral language development depends on our experience of hearing and producing speech. The effects of acquired deafness in adulthood are quite different, however. In this case, language skills that have been learnt previously remain intact although the comprehension of speech is obviously compromised by problems in hearing. This example conveys directly, we hope, how a problem early in development may be expected to have consequences that are both more diverse and possibly more severe than a corresponding problem that only occurs in adulthood after cognitive development is complete.

In summary, we believe some version of the idea of modularity (in a weak sense, meaning only that the mind consists of partially independent systems) is correct. However, we would reject explicitly the suggestion that most cognitive modules are "innate." Rather, there is overwhelming evidence that cognitive systems depend upon extensive amounts of learning for their development. At a broader level we also believe that part of what occurs in development (and development here would include learning new skills, such as typing, in adulthood) is a gradual increase in "modularity" (Hulme & Snowling, 1992; Karmiloff-Smith, 1992). When a skill is in an early phase of development many systems (including, in Fodor's terms, central systems such as thinking and problem solving) may be involved in its performance. As learning proceeds we suppose that neural circuits become established that enable the skill to be performed efficiently, effortlessly, and with less need for central control (think of learning to type or to ride a bike). Hence modules consist of established neural circuits that depend upon learning for their development. Such learning does not arise from a state of equipotentiality (from a brain where all structures are general purpose) and we accept that there are genetic and neural constraints on the development of the brain circuits (or modules) that underlie skilled cognitive tasks such as language, arithmetic, and motor skills.

The timing of development

Development involves change over time, and younger children are less accomplished in many different cognitive domains than older children. Developmental disorders are typically characterized by slow rates of development, either in a specific domain (specific learning difficulties such as dyslexia or mathematics disorder) or more generally across many domains (general learning difficulties or mental retardation).

A great deal of time has been spent discussing the extent to which different developmental disorders reflect delay (slow development) or deviance (abnormal development). Most of the disorders we will discuss seem best characterized in terms of a delay, at least early in development. For example, it is not that children with mathematics disorder are completely unable to perform arithmetic, it is just that their arithmetic performance tends to be slow and error prone, like much younger typically developing children. One of the main tasks in studying developmental disorders therefore is to explain the delays in development seen in such disorders: What process or processes are not working properly to result in such slow rates of development?

If development is slow it could be that problems will ensue because of critical periods in development. The idea of a critical period is that there may be a particular period of development when the child is prepared to learn a skill and that if learning does not occur during this period it will become difficult or impossible to compensate for this later in development. This idea is closely linked to notions of neural plasticity. Up to some point in development neural changes associated with particular forms of learning may occur easily but thereafter there is a gradual reduction in neural plasticity.

There is ample evidence from studies of animals for critical periods in development. One striking example is in studies of birdsong learning (for a review see

Brainerd & Doupe, 2002). Marler (1970), for example, showed that white-crowned male sparrows only learn their species-typical song adequately if they hear their own species' song during an early sensitive period between the age of 10 and 50 days. If learning is delayed beyond this point, mastery of the song will always remain impaired.

It is easy to see analogies between birds learning to sing their species-specific song and children learning to understand and produce their native language. It is probably no coincidence, therefore, that in developmental psychology the notion of a critical period has received most attention in relation to language learning. The idea of a critical period for learning language is closely allied to the idea that humans have an innate propensity to learn language. Lenneberg (1967) for example suggested that language learning needed to be completed by puberty, though others have suggested that the critical period for easy and complete mastery of language may be as early as before 5 years of age (Krashen, 1973). Pinker (1994) asserted that the acquisition of language is guaranteed for children up to the age of 6, is steadily compromised from then until shortly after puberty, and is rare thereafter. The evidence for a critical period (or, in a weaker form, a sensitive period) is not strong. Studies of children who have experienced severe deprivation in early childhood may in some cases show persistent problems with language, but in such cases it is hard to rule out the fact that these children had congenital abnormalities (Skuse, 1993). Other evidence comes from studies of second language learning, and it has been suggested that while adult second language learners may become perfectly proficient in their use of syntax, typically these people retain a persistent foreign accent in the second language, suggesting that the critical age for mastering the phonological system may be earlier than for syntax.

While the critical period hypothesis for language learning is probably too strong it does seem plausible that there may be a gradual decline with age in the ease with which we learn language and other cognitive skills. In studies of developmental cognitive disorders we are typically dealing with an impairment in the rate at which basic learning mechanisms operate. It may be in some cases that such a limitation in the rate of learning is further compromised by a gradual reduction in neural plasticity as children get older, though to date evidence for this idea is limited.

In summary, the most striking characteristic of the disorders we will consider in this book is that they typically involve slower rates of development in certain key areas. So, for example, a child with dyslexia may only learn to read slowly and with difficulty, while a child with mathematics disorder will show a similar pattern in relation to learning to perform arithmetic. However, the patterns of reading and arithmetic performance seen in such children usually resemble those seen in younger typically developing children: such patterns are described as delayed rather than deviant. It is possible that in some cases delays in the development of certain processes may result in deviant patterns of development in later developing processes. Such instances are probably rare and we will not discuss this issue further here. The most striking pattern that characterizes most developmental cognitive disorders is a delay in the rate at which particular skills develop.

Categorical versus Dimensional Views of Developmental Disorders

If most disorders we are dealing with reflect delays in development, this leads directly to questions of diagnosis. A delay in development represents a quantitative difference between children and in this view it is natural to view disorders in dimensional terms. In this view children with mathematics disorder simply represent the bottom end of a distribution of children in terms of their mathematical skills. At first sight this view seems at odds with using categorical labels for these disorders. Instead of talking about mathematics disorder, perhaps we should refer to children with weak mathematical skills? The arguments about the usefulness of categorical labels in diagnosis are complex. Although we do subscribe to a dimensional view of the disorders we will be discussing in this book, we will typically use categorical labels to refer to affected children. This is partly just to aid communication: It is often easier to use a categorical label (children with dyslexia) than a dimensional expression (children with severe and specific problems in learning to read words).

The use of categorical labels for the extremes of continuously distributed differences among people is not confined to the area of developmental cognitive disorders. Think of medical conditions such as obesity or hypertension. There are large differences in weight and blood pressure between people in the general population (and incidentally these tend to correlate or be associated with each other). However, if weight or blood pressure becomes too high it may pose significant risk for other aspects of health. Nevertheless, exactly where we decide to put the cut-off between hypertension and "normal" blood pressure is to some extent arbitrary. The same is true of the disorders that we will be discussing in this book. We see these disorders as the extreme end of normal variations in skills in the population. However, diagnostic labels for disorders aid communication and can be useful in conveying the nature of the difficulties children experience and for guiding educational management and intervention policies.

Methods of Study in Developmental Cognitive Disorders

There are a number of methodological approaches that have been used to study developmental cognitive disorders. We will consider these approaches and their merits and weaknesses briefly.

Group versus case studies

In adult neuropsychology the detailed study of single cases has been particularly influential, arguably more influential than studies of groups of patients (Ellis & Young 1988; Shallice, 1988). In studies of developmental disorders both group and case studies have been used, but there is little doubt that group studies have been more important. It is therefore worth considering briefly the strengths and weaknesses of single case studies and group studies.

In adult cognitive neuropsychology the study of single patients has for many years been the dominant approach. The attraction of single case studies in adult neuropsychology is easy to understand and probably arises from the fact that some of the patterns of deficit seen in adults following brain damage can be extreme and remarkable. However, pure cases with theoretically interesting deficits do not walk into the clinic every day, so it becomes important to make the most of those rare cases that are available to study. There is no doubt that case studies of cognitive deficits following brain damage in adults have contributed powerfully to the development of theories of cognitive function (Shallice, 1988)

However, even if several patients exist with similar deficits, averaging the results from different patients may be dangerous because the group average may not be representative of any single patient in a group. This line of argument led Caramazza (1986) to argue that the study of single cases was the only valid basis for making theoretical claims in neuropsychology (cf. Shallice, 1988). This, to many people, seems to be going a little far; surely ten nearly identical patients are more convincing than just one? The basic idea, however, that carefully documented dissociations from single case studies provide strong evidence for the existence of separable systems has been widely accepted in adult neuropsychology.

In studies of developmental disorders single case studies have been used occasionally (e.g. Hulme & Snowling 1992; Pitchford, Funnell, de Haan, & Morgan, 2007; Temple & Marshall, 1983) but the dominant approach has certainly been to study groups of children. The reason for this, as Bishop (1997) has said so clearly, is that the aims of adult cognitive neuropsychology as compared to studies of developmental cognitive disorders have been quite different. Adult cognitive neuropsychology has been concerned predominantly with trying to make inferences about the structure of the mind from the patterns of impairment found after brain damage. This is captured very succinctly by the title of Tim Shallice's (1988) book *From Neuropsychology to Mental Structure*, which gives an excellent review of this area. The critical type of evidence for this enterprise comes from finding dissociations. Clear, theoretically interesting, dissociations only occur rarely in patients, but logically clear dissociations between different functions in well-documented cases are very persuasive. For these reasons single case studies have become the method of choice in adult cognitive neuropsychology.

Studies of cognitive impairments in children have not, however, been particularly concerned with identifying separate systems in the developing mind (though as we shall see in later chapters the occurrence of specific learning difficulties certainly provides evidence that we can identify separable systems that develop somewhat independently of each other). Rather, the major aim of those studying developmental disorders has been to understand the disorders themselves: their origin, developmental trajectories, and possible treatments. As Bishop (1997) has noted, a critical aim in studies of developmental disorders is to make generalizations about the patterns of deficit that characterize a particular disorder in order to identify its causes. In developmental dyslexia, for example (see Chapter 2), there is very strong evidence that the primary cause of most of these children's problems in learning to recognize printed words is a deficit in phonological (speech sound) skills. Such a conclusion (a generalization about a group of children with a particular disorder) can only be reached by studying groups of children.

It is important to note that here we are making a claim based on an association or correlation: Reading problems in children with dyslexia are associated with phonological difficulties. This association does not prove that the reading problems in dyslexia are caused by the phonological difficulties, though this is a plausible theory, as we will see later. In adult neuropsychology, researchers have been very wary of interpreting patterns of associated deficits as evidence for the organization of mental processes or structures. The fact that two deficits commonly occur in patients who have had strokes does not mean that these deficits are functionally related. The association may arise just because the brain regions that are involved in these two functions are close together and therefore liable to be damaged at the same time. One example of this comes from a disorder referred to as "Gerstmann syndrome," which has been described in both adult (acquired) and developmental forms (see Shallice, 1988). Patients with acquired Gertsmann syndrome show a striking cluster of deficits including difficulties with arithmetic, spelling, right–left disorientation, and finger agnosia (problems in identifying the relative position of fingers by touch alone). Various theories were developed to account for the functional relationship between these different symptoms but it is now generally accepted that the symptoms seen in Gerstmann syndrome cluster together merely because they all depend upon damage to anatomically adjacent brain systems in the left parietal cortex.

As we shall see in later chapters, studies of developmental disorders are replete with similar examples of associations leading theorists up blind allies. If we find that a certain disorder is associated with a particular cognitive deficit that does not mean we have found the cause of the disorder. Given that many associations occur, we will consider later in the chapter how we can try to determine which associated deficits may play a causal role in accounting for a disorder.

Longitudinal versus cross-sectional studies

Another critical methodological issue in studies of development is the distinction between cross-sectional and longitudinal studies. Cross-sectional studies look at children at one point in time. Most of the studies we will deal with in this book (whether case studies or group studies) are cross-sectional in design. Cross-sectional studies provide a "snap-shot" of development frozen at one point in development (or several, if different age groups are considered in a single study). Longitudinal studies in contrast assess the same children over a number of occasions and thus allow us to track how changes in one skill may relate to changes in another. Longitudinal studies have some very important advantages over cross-sectional studies but they are time consuming, expensive and difficult to conduct. For these reasons longitudinal studies are usually only conducted when a number of cross-sectional studies have already identified some useful hypotheses that need to be tested in a longitudinal design.

One important advantage of longitudinal studies relates to how we interpret correlations (which is dealt with below). Most of the evidence we have about developmental disorders comes from correlations. So, for example, we may observe that a group of children with dyslexia perform worse than typically developing children on several measures of speech (phonological) skills. This group difference amounts to a correlation; children with dyslexia also have poor phonological skills, and typically developing children have better reading skills and better phonological skills. Correlation does not demonstrate cause. Logically, there are three interpretations of such a correlation: (1) poor phonology causes poor reading, (2) poor reading causes poor phonology, or, most worryingly, (3) both things depend on something else we have not measured (e.g., general intelligence, motivation to complete the tests, language skills, the ability to attend).

Longitudinal studies allow us to assess correlations between measures taken at different points in time. Logically there is an asymmetry between correlations from measurements taken at different points in time. If a prior condition (phonology at Time 1) correlates with a later condition (reading at Time 2), the later condition cannot cause the earlier condition but clearly the earlier condition might cause the later condition. Longitudinal studies therefore help us to get a better handle on the direction of causation (but they are still open to objection (3) above; the only way round this is to conduct an intervention study).

The choice of comparison or control groups

In both cross-sectional and longitudinal studies (involving either groups or single cases) the aim is to identify the cognitive deficits that characterize a given disorder. The most widely used study design in this area is one where a group of children with a disorder is compared at one point in time to a group of children without the disorder. This type of design is called a case–control study in medicine. The question then becomes how to select the "control" children to compare to the clinical "cases." Different comparison or control groups give us different types of information. The usual approach is to try to control for differences by matching the clinical cases to the control children on one or more variables. Given that on most tasks there are large increases in performance associated with increasing age, a common practice has been to select typically developing children of the same age as the clinical cases (a chronological age or CA control group). It would be common when doing this to try to match for other variables as well, such as the school(s) the children were attending, their gender, their scores on an IQ test, and other variables that might seem relevant to how well children would do on the experimental task being used. Comparison with a CA control group establishes if a clinical group has deficits on a task in relation to their age; if they do not we might conclude that the disorder is not associated with any difficulties on such a task. However, if a clinical group does differ from a CA control group on a given task (or set of tasks), this is really just the starting point for exploring whether such a deficit might be a plausible cause of a disorder. One obvious problem with such a finding is that the difference might be a product of the disorder rather than a cause (children with mathematics disorder might perform badly on a number judgment task simply as a consequence of their limited skills in, or experience of, mathematics for example).

One approach to reducing such problems of interpretation is to choose a younger typically developing control group of children who are matched for performance in the area of interest (perhaps reading ability as assessed by a well-standardized test of reading ability if we were studying children with dyslexia). This sort of comparison group is referred to as an ability-matched control group (in this case a reading ability or reading-age-matched group). This also is an informative comparison group and was first used to our knowledge in studies of children with spelling difficulties by Frank (1936).

One advantage of an ability-matched control group is that it eliminates absolute levels of performance on the task used to identify the clinical group (say, reading ability) as an explanation for differences on another task (say, speech perception). In other words, if children with dyslexia are worse on a measure of speech perception than younger control children whose absolute level of reading skill is the same as theirs, this difference cannot simply be a product of differences in reading skill. Conversely, a difference between children with dyslexia and a CA control group may always be explained away in terms of the difference being the product of a certain level of reading ability. While this is true, using an ability-matched control group usually means that there are large differences in chronological age (with the clinical group being older) and this may mean that deficits in the clinical group are unlikely to show up in such a comparison. If deficits do show up in an ability-matched design, this indicates that the clinical group are performing even more poorly than younger typically developing children, and this in turn suggests that the deficit is a severe one that we should consider seriously as a possible cause of the disorder. It is useful to have both CA-matched and ability-matched control groups to compare to a clinical group as each provides different information about the extent of difficulties shown by the clinical group.

Establishing the Causes of Developmental Disorders

The issue of how we can identify the causes of developmental disorders is really at the heart of this book, and we should consider this issue directly before we go further. A starting point for identifying a cause is to look for correlations. Though, as almost every introductory statistics text will tell you, correlation does not prove causation, the presence of a correlation is the usual starting point that makes us consider whether there is a causal relationship between two variables.

It may help to make this clear by looking at a well-established causal relationship from medicine. In the 1950s people asked whether smoking causes lung cancer. It was observed using case–control studies that there was an association (correlation) between smoking and lung cancer, with people who smoked being more likely to develop lung cancer than nonsmokers (Doll & Hill, 1950, 1954). However, a correlation is ambiguous because it might depend upon a third variable. It might be, for example, that a genetic difference between people causes both a greater propensity to smoke and a susceptibility to lung cancer. A very good way of expressing ideas about possible causal theories is in terms of path diagrams. Path diagrams, and the

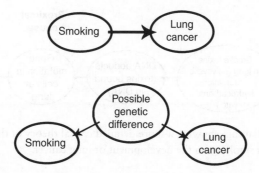

Figure 1.8 Two alternative causal theories of the association between smoking and lung cancer. According to the first theory, smoking is a cause of lung cancer (and therefore persuading people not to smoke will reduce the risk of developing lung cancer). According to the second theory, smoking is not a cause of lung cancer (and therefore persuading people not to smoke will have no effect on the risk of developing lung cancer). The first theory is (probably) the correct one!

statistical techniques associated with them, arose early in the last century in studies of genetics by Sewall Wright (1920, 1921). In a path diagram single-headed arrows are used to express hypothetical causal relationships. These two alternative causal theories are expressed in path diagrams in Figure 1.8.

In fact, in the case of lung cancer further studies have filled in a detailed causal theory of how cigarette smoke causes lung cancer by inducing damage to the DNA in cells in the lining of the lung (Hecht, 1999). A simplified version of this causal theory is shown in the form of a path diagram in Figure 1.9. The details of this theory, and the evidence that supports it, need not detain us here. However, there is one aspect of this diagram that is useful in refining our discussion of what is a cause. The path diagram for lung cancer in Figure 1.9 shows a chain of causes, with certain constituents of tobacco smoke (including polycyclic aromatic hydrocarbons) leading to mutations in critical genes in cells of the lung. In terms of the theory shown here, cigarette smoke would be a *distal* cause of lung cancer while the gene mutations in the lung tissue produced by constituents of the smoke would be the *proximal* cause of lung cancer. It is clear that the terms proximal (immediate) and distal (distant) cause are relative terms that can change as theories develop. What appears to be the proximal cause of something in an early stage of theory development may become less proximal as further steps in a causal chain are uncovered and understood.

How, logically, do we move beyond correlations to prove what causes an illness or a disorder? This is a difficult question at the heart of scientific and philosophical inquiry that we will not try to solve here; see Pearl (2000) and Shipley (2000) for excellent, if technical, discussions of causality. We will, however, lay out some of the steps that we believe are useful in thinking about this critical issue.

Cause or causation is used to refer to a relationship between events. Informally, if every time a white billiard ball hits a red ball the red ball moves, we might say that being struck by the white ball causes the red ball to move. Traditionally, in philosophy it

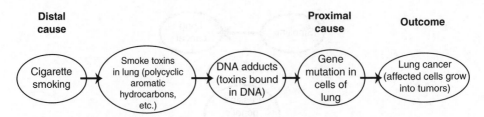

Figure 1.9   A path diagram showing a more detailed causal theory of the processes that mediate the effects of smoking on the development of lung cancer.

was common to distinguish between necessary and sufficient causes. If something is a necessary and sufficient cause this implies certainty (every time A happens B will follow). However, causes could be necessary (we need A for B to happen) but not sufficient (sometimes when A happens B does not follow, perhaps because other factors are involved and are needed in addition to A to make B happen).

One problem with the use of the word cause is that in everyday speech "cause" often seems to be associated with this idea of a necessary and sufficient cause (i.e. with certainty of outcome). If smoking causes cancer anyone who has ever smoked should die of lung cancer. This is obviously not true. In fact current ideas about causality are framed in terms of probabilities, not certainties. Whenever we speak about causes in this book we will be talking probabilistically: Smoking we believe does cause lung cancer, but not in a deterministic fashion. Causes are things that increase the likelihood of an outcome: Smoking makes it more likely you will develop lung cancer. Furthermore, typically there are a number of causes operating to produce an outcome. Those different causes may sometimes operate independently (if smoking 10 cigarettes a day increases the chances of getting lung cancer by 10%, having a gene that makes you susceptible to lung cancer might also increase the chances of lung cancer by 10%; having both might then give a person a 20% increase in the likelihood of getting lung cancer). However, it is likely that often causes interact with each other, in which case, for example, having both smoking (10% increase in risk alone) and a susceptibility gene (10% increase in risk alone) might produce a 50% increase in risk of cancer. We saw earlier an example (in conduct disorder) where genetic and environmental causes interact in the genesis of the propensity to behave violently: Having a specific gene and being maltreated as a child both independently give a small increase in risk, but having both factors together gives a greatly increased risk of violent behavior.

Understanding that causes operate probabilistically means that a whole set of statistical techniques used to measure the association or correlation between variables is critical to assessing causes. Correlation and related techniques give us a way of expressing the strength of association between possible causes and their outcomes. In recent years huge strides have been made in philosophy and statistical methods for expressing and evaluating causal theories (see Pearl, 2000; Shipley, 2000). These advances give us a whole battery of conceptual and statistical tools to try to pin down causes. Sewall Wright who invented path analysis referred to it as "causal

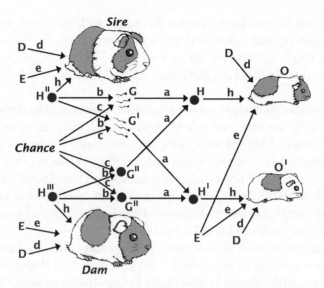

Figure 1.10 A reproduction of one of Sewall Wright's earliest path diagrams (Wright, 1920) showing the effects of genetic and environmental influences on the pattern of coat color seen in guinea pigs.

analysis." Wright was a geneticist and his first paper to use path analysis (Wright, 1920) was concerned with the role of genetic and environmental influences on variations in coat color in guinea pigs. Wright's first path diagram is reproduced in Figure 1.10.

There was no doubt for Wright (1920) that he was studying causal relationships: "In a broad sense the peculiarities of an individual are entirely determined by heredity and environment" (p. 328). Based on logic and theory he postulated genetic and environmental influences on the characteristics of animals born to parents who differed on the same characteristics. His insight was that it was useful to represent proposed causal relationships between things that could be measured in the form of a path diagram. In such a diagram measured variables (that stand as proxies for underlying hypothetical mechanisms) are connected by single-headed arrows to represent causal connections. Wright's further insight was that, once such a diagram was constructed, measures of the correlations between variables could be used to estimate the strength of the proposed causal relationships, and that the strength of compound (indirect) causal paths could be calculated by simple rules (the strength of a compound path depends upon the product of the component paths).

Path diagrams are examples of what are now referred to in mathematics as directed graphs (directed graphs contain one-headed arrows, and arrows point from causes to consequences in path diagrams). Directed graphs, coupled with methods for translating them into quantifiable predictions using notions about probability distributions, give us a language for constructing and testing causal theories. Path diagrams are useful partly because they make such theories explicit and easy to understand and partly because they then link in to a powerful set of statistical techniques for testing our ideas about causes. (It should be noted that Morton and Frith's causal modeling framework for developmental disorders, with its use of arrows to link biological, cognitive, and behavioral levels of explanation, can be seen as direct application of Wright's (1920) idea of path analysis. The distinctive thing about their framework is that an explicit distinction is made between different levels of explanation.)

When is a correlation likely to represent a cause? Causes need to come before their consequences (after cannot cause before). This is called antecedence or the "logic of causal order" (Davis, 1985). If we notice a negative correlation between the amount of television watched as a college student and becoming President of the USA (people who become President did not watch much television as students), we might think that not watching television at college was a cause of later political success. But it could not be the other way round (becoming President could not cause differences in television watching earlier in life!) (Davis, 1985).

The idea that causes must precede their consequences is why longitudinal studies are so important in trying to understand development and developmental disorders. The causes of a disorder should be observable before other symptoms of the disorder have developed, and correlations between possible causes of a disorder early in life and symptoms of the disorder measured later in life will help us to develop theories of what causes the disorder to develop. If phonological difficulties cause dyslexia, we need to show that such difficulties pre-date these children's reading difficulties (ideally we would want to show that phonological problems in young children, before they start to learn to read, predict the later development of reading problems when the children get to school).

We can try to home in on plausible causes by asking a large number of further questions once the issue of antecedence has been established (that the putative cause pre-dates the development of the disorder):

1 Universality? Does the deficit occur in all (or most) children with the disorder?
2 Power? Do variations in the severity of the deficit tend to correlate with the severity of the disorder?
3 Specificity? Is the deficit specific to the disorder, or is it also found in other diverse disorders (if a deficit occurs in many diverse disorders, it is implausible that it is a cause of any of them – because a cause should result in the same deficit in all affected children – unless such a cause is simply a contributor to many disorders that operates in conjunction with separate causes for each disorder)?
4 Theoretical plausibility? Finally, if a deficit does correlate strongly and selectively with one disorder we need to develop a theory of how a deficit in one skill (e.g., phonology) can lead to a deficit in the development of another skill (e.g., reading).

These arguments lay out how we can try to strengthen our belief in certain correlates of a disorder being causes of that disorder. Ultimately, however, no amount of correlational evidence can demonstrate a causal relationship. However, what can help a lot is having an explicit and detailed theory. Belief in causes depends a great deal on having a plausible mechanism that might explain an observed correlation (look back at the theory linking smoking to lung cancer). Saying we have identified a "cause" of a disorder is always a theoretical statement and such statements are always provisional in science.

Can we ever prove that a certain deficit is the cause of a disorder? "Prove" is another very difficult word (just as difficult as cause). The traditional answer is that to prove that a variable is a cause we need to be able to manipulate it and observe a change in the outcome. This is the great insight (one of the great insights) of Sir Ronald Fisher (after whom the *F* ratio in statistics is named). Fisher (1926) described the principles of the randomized experiment in his book *The Design of Experiments*. Fisher worked in agriculture and we can use an agricultural example to illustrate the idea of a randomized experiment. Suppose we want to determine if fertilizer causes an increased crop yield from potato plants. We take a field and divide it into plots (say, 50 plots), we then at random apply fertilizer to half of those plots, wait for the crop to grow, and at harvest time weigh the potatoes from the 25 plots that received the fertilizer and the 25 plots that did not. There could of course be many differences between different parts of a field that might influence how well the potatoes would grow (differences in moisture and sunlight for example and perhaps differences between the potato seeds that were planted) but the process of randomization effectively serves to eliminate (or at least drastically reduce) the influence of such pre-existing differences on the outcome. The logic of random assignment is that it makes pre-existing differences between different plots or plants unlikely as explanations for the outcome of an experiment. The beauty of random assignment is that we do not need to know what these pre-existing differences are because by using a random process any such differences should all balance out.

To go back to the smoking example, and to dispense with all ethical considerations, if we wanted to prove that smoking causes cancer we could do the following experiment. Take a large group of people. Randomly assign them to two groups. Force one group to smoke cigarettes every day and ensure the other group did not smoke and lived in a smoke-free environment. We would wait several years and observe how many people in each group develop lung cancer. Random assignment of people to groups is essential here because it should eliminate pre-existing differences between the people that might influence the outcome. If we just asked for volunteers to smoke that would be hopeless, because only the reckless people (who for other reasons might be likely to contract cancer) would volunteer to be in the smoking group. Random assignment to groups is generally considered the best way for demonstrating causes in experimental sciences such as biology and psychology.

However, the notion of random assignment immediately runs into difficulties in relation to establishing the causes of cognitive disorders (as in many areas in biology and psychology). Given that the hypothetical causes of developmental cognitive disorders are typically properties of the child (their genes and brain systems that have developed under genetic influence), we cannot use random assignment to establish a causal link. By definition, we cannot randomly assign some children to have a certain genetic makeup, or to have a particular highly circumscribed cognitive deficit that we might believe is the cause of a developmental disorder. Such a procedure is logically impossible to implement (which may be just as well because, if it could be done, it would certainly be unethical). In this sense our room for maneuver in testing the causes of developmental disorders is severely limited. There is, however, one version of a randomized experimental design for testing causes that we can use – it involves intervening to try to remediate a cognitive deficit.

Intervention studies as a way of establishing the causes of a disorder

Let us suppose that we have developed a causal theory about a cognitive deficit that we believe is a critical cause of the symptoms displayed in a disorder. (Much of the rest of this book is devoted to sifting evidence relevant to assessing the plausibility of theories of this type). If a potential cognitive deficit is identified we can then try to develop an intervention (usually a form of education or training) to cure (or at least ameliorate) the cognitive deficit. We can then randomly assign children diagnosed as having the disorder to either receive the intervention or to receive another form of intervention that targets another area of cognitive function. If such an intervention study "works" in the sense of producing improvements in the putative cause of the disorder coupled with a reduction in the frequency or severity of the symptoms of disorder, we have found good evidence for a cause (at a cognitive level) of the disorder.

This might seem a little circumspect, which is intended. Evaluating whether such an intervention works is a complicated process. There are two important aspects to evaluating if such an intervention has worked. First, the intervention should produce an improvement in the symptoms of the disorder. Second, ideally we should be able to relate the degree to which the intervention has improved the symptoms of the disorder to the degree to which the targeted cognitive deficit has improved. (If we believe that the reading difficulties of children with dyslexia depend upon a phonological deficit, then we should be able to improve these children's reading skills by training phonology, and the extent to which their reading skills improve should relate to how much of an improvement in phonological skills the training program has brought about.) These requirements are an ideal, and in practice there are many complications in conducting and evaluating such intervention studies. Nevertheless such intervention studies are potentially of enormous theoretical importance; they get us as close to establishing the causes of a disorder as we can. Such studies are also of great practical importance because if they work they lead directly to practical recommendations about how to treat or prevent the development of a disorder.

A final word on causes: The importance of theories

Even in the case of a successful intervention study (or set of such studies) we always need to be careful about claiming to have "proved" a cause. Causes ultimately depend upon a theory: a model of how things operate. These theories depend upon processes that can never be directly observed but must instead be inferred from observations, and the way we make our observations and analyze the data from them typically involves numerous untested assumptions. According to Karl Popper (1980), in science we never prove something. What we do is develop theories to explain our observations. Any good theory is testable, and can therefore be disproved or refuted by further observations. This is the spirit in which we should approach the testing of theories about the causes of developmental disorders. We observe the disorder and measure things about it. We formulate theories about the causes of the disorder in the ways we have outlined. Good theories will give an explicit statement about how and why a disorder develops. Further studies of the disorder will in turn test predictions from the theory and likely refine, alter, and sometimes even refute it. In Popper's terms all we ever have are conjectures and refutations (theories and problems for these theories). No amount of positive evidence (supported predictions) ever proves a theory. But negative evidence (unsupported predictions) may lead to a theory being abandoned or changed. In practice no single study or observation is ever water-tight, which is why in science we place such importance on the notion of replication. If a whole series of studies carried out in slightly different ways, by different people, fail to uphold a critical prediction of a theory, that theory is weakened and may be modified, or eventually be abandoned, in the light of accumulated negative evidence. Science is a sifting of evidence in which we try to get closer and closer to an approximation of the truth about how things work. The "truth" here is always an abstract model or theory of how things operate. Based on an explicit theory we accumulate and sift through evidence trying to evaluate in diverse ways the adequacy of the theory. This sifting of evidence may not be too dissimilar to the weighing up of evidence in a court of law to arrive at a judgment about the probable guilt or innocence of a defendant (Rapport & Wright, 1963).

Comorbidity and Separating Causes from Correlates

We need to be clear that many problems that occur commonly in a cognitive disorder may not be the cause of that disorder. It is now well established that different developmental disorders often tend to co-occur in the same child – this is referred to as "comorbidity" (Angold, Costello, & Erkanli, 1999). Caron and Rutter (1991) showed that comorbidity between many developmental disorders occurs much more frequently than expected by chance, given the rate of occurrence of the different disorders in the population. Getting accurate estimates of the true rates of comorbidity is difficult because it depends upon having representative samples of the population (such samples require epidemiological studies in which we assess many children who are selected to a truly representative sample of children in the population at large). So, for example, if we believe that motor impairments tend to co-occur with reading problems, we could test all the children referred for reading problems to a clinic to assess both their reading and motor skills. This would not allow us to get an accurate assessment of true comorbidity, however, because the children referred to the clinic are unlikely to be truly representative of all children with reading problems (perhaps having both a reading and motor disorder makes it more likely that the child will be referred to the clinic).

Comorbidities may arise for different reasons in different disorders. In some disorders, it is plausible to argue that one disorder may cause another. So, for example, having attention deficit hyperactivity disorder (ADHD) early in life may put children at risk of developing conduct disorder later in life. In this example, perhaps a fundamental problem in inhibiting or regulating behavior shows different manifestations at different stages of development. In other cases, such as the comorbidity between reading difficulties and motor impairments, it seems unlikely that there is any direct causal link at the cognitive level between these two disorders; both problems may simply reflect the fact that brain development has gone awry with diverse effects on cognitive development. So, in this case, we would argue that problems with balance and motor coordination are unlikely to tap a cause of problems in learning to read. We will say much more about comorbidities between different disorders in the chapters that follow and return to the issue in Chapter 9.

Summary and Conclusions

In this book we will review what we know about a range of developmental disorders. We will consider a wide range of disorders including reading disorders, language disorders, arithmetic disorders, motor disorders, and autism spectrum disorders. This chapter has outlined a number of key conceptual issues that lie at the heart of studies of developmental cognitive disorders. We have argued that such disorders can only be understood in the context of a developmental theory of how the cognitive processes concerned typically operate, and by inference how those developmental processes are delayed or disordered in some children. As we shall see, most developmental disorders seem best characterized in terms of delays to typical developmental processes. This leads us to see such disorders as dimensional: The children identified are simply at the bottom end of a continuum of normal variation in the population. Nevertheless, diagnostic labels can be useful in communicating the form of difficulties experienced by different groups of children. Finally, the process of trying to understand the causes of developmental disorders is highly complex and depends critically upon having explicit theories of the nature of each disorder and the causal processes operating at different levels to generate the behavioral profile seen. Such causal theories can be tested in a variety of ways, but two of the most powerful forms of evidence come from longitudinal and intervention studies. We have introduced the idea of path diagrams as ways of representing causal theories, and we will use such diagrams in different chapters to represent different theories about the origins of the disorders we discuss.

2
Reading Disorders I: Developmental Dyslexia

Of all the cognitive deficits that occur in children, reading disorders are the most studied and best understood. Studies in this area serve as a model for the approaches that we outlined in Chapter 1, and illustrate nearly all the methodological and theoretical points that were made in that chapter.

When we consider reading skills it is important to distinguish between reading accuracy and reading comprehension. We typically assess reading accuracy by asking children to read words aloud. Tests of reading accuracy usually consist of lists of unrelated words that are graded in difficulty from easy to hard. In contrast, reading comprehension is usually measured by giving children passages to read (either aloud or silently) and then asking them questions to assess what they have understood.

In this chapter we will focus on dyslexia, which is probably the best understood of all specific cognitive impairments that occur in childhood. Dyslexia is a disorder in which children find it very difficult to read accurately and with fluency. Chapter 3 will deal with reading comprehension impairment, which can be thought of as the "mirror image" of dyslexia. Children with reading comprehension impairment can decode words adequately but have great trouble in understanding the meaning of what they read.

Reading Disorders in Children: Definitions and Prevalence

The *Diagnostic and Statistical Manual of Mental Disorders* (DSM-IV; American Psychiatric Association, 2004) classifies a person as having reading disorder when their "reading achievement, as measured by individually administered standardized tests of reading accuracy or comprehension, is substantially below that expected given the person's chronological age, measured intelligence, and age-appropriate education." A number of points are raised by this definition. First, note that the definition refers to both reading accuracy and comprehension, but as we have already hinted reading comprehension impairment is quite distinct from dyslexia. Second, the definition is explicitly a developmental definition, and states that reading needs to be below the level expected for a person's age and education. Learning to read takes many years of practice and instruction, so we do not expect a 6-year-old to be a proficient reader, and we expect the average 10-year-old to be a much better reader than the average 6-year-old. Third, the definition also acknowledges the importance of education. Children are taught to read at school and if a child has not been given adequate teaching then this may be a sufficient explanation for poor reading skills. Finally, the last point made by the definition, that reading should be below the level expected in relation to a child's intelligence, has proved a matter of considerable controversy. This idea is referred to as a discrepancy definition (the reading level is discrepant from the level expected for a child's IQ and age).

At first blush the idea that reading depends on intelligence (IQ) seems eminently reasonable. Surely, bright children will learn to read more easily than less bright children, just as they learn other things more easily? This idea, however, depends on a strong theoretical assumption that often has not been made explicit (that varia-tions in IQ are a cause of variations in the ease with which children learn to read) and this assumption is, at best, unproven (Stanovich & Siegel, 1994). The correlation between IQ and reading accuracy ranges from about .3 to .6, which, although far from massive, does suggest that somewhere between 10 and 30% of the differences in reading ability amongst children might be explicable in terms of IQ. This correlation between reading ability and IQ guided studies of large representative samples of children (epidemiological studies) that had the aim of describing the nature and prevalence of reading problems in the child population. One of the first and most influential epidemiological studies of reading ability was carried out on the Isle of Wight (Rutter & Yule, 1975). In this study, measures of reading ability, IQ, and a number of other variables were taken from all children on the island between the ages of 9 and 11 years. Rutter and Yule distinguished between specific reading retardation (children whose reading ability was below the level predicted for their age and IQ – dyslexia) and reading backwardness (children whose reading was below the level predicted for their age, ignoring IQ).

Of course, the prevalence of dyslexia using a definition such as that of specific reading retardation depends on how far below expectation a child needs to be before being labeled as dyslexic. If we simply assume that all scores (reading, age, and IQ) are distributed normally then 2.28% of children should score more than 2 standard errors of measurement below their "predicted" reading score (the statistics behind this claim need not detain us). Using this cut-off Yule, Rutter, Berger, and Thompson (1974) reported rates of specific reading retardation (using a test of reading accuracy) ranging from 3.1% among children in the Isle of Wight to 6.3% in an Inner London Borough. Other, more recent studies have suggested rather lower rates of reading problems and a recent American study (S. Shaywitz, Escobar, Shaywitz, Fletcher, & Makugh, 1992) using a less stringent cut-off point of 1.5 standard errors of measurement reported prevalence rates of 5.6% in first grade, 7% in third grade, and 5.4% in fifth grade.

In all these studies, reading problems are defined in terms of a discrepancy between a child's reading score and that expected for their age and IQ. But what evidence is there that IQ is important? This question really revolves around whether children with specific reading difficulties (poor reading in relation to age and IQ) are different to children with general reading problems associated with low general cognitive ability.

Current evidence suggests that these two groups of children differ much less than many experts would have expected. Perhaps the most critical question to ask is whether classifying children as having *specific* reading difficulties / dyslexia rather than as having more general reading difficulties has implications for how they will make progress in learning to read.

In one of the first studies to address this question, Rutter and Yule (1975) reported that over a 4- to 5-year period children diagnosed as having specific reading difficulties actually made less progress in learning to read than those with general reading problems (and perhaps most interestingly there was the opposite pattern for arithmetic, with the children with specific difficulties making more progress). However, the prospects for children with dyslexia may have improved since then and more recent studies have failed to show an effect of IQ differences at least as far as gains in reading accuracy are concerned (Hatcher & Hulme, 1999; Share, McGee, McKenzie, Williams, & Silva, 1987; B. Shaywitz, Fletcher, Holahan, & Shaywitz, 1992).

In summary, IQ certainly correlates with children's reading accuracy. However, IQ does not explain well the problems some 3–6% of children have in learning to read. From an educational perspective there is no evidence that children who have word-level (decoding) reading problems will vary in their responsiveness to teaching according to their IQ level, and theoretically there is no reason to believe that the causes of word recognition difficulties in reading are different in children with low, rather than high, IQ.

In terms of giving a useful definition of dyslexia, the definition of reading disorder offered by DSM-IV is not very helpful because it conflates problems of reading accuracy (dyslexia) with problems of reading comprehension. A more useful definition, and one that anticipates much of the evidence we will cover in this chapter, is given by Lyon, Shaywitz, and Shaywitz (2003): "Dyslexia is a specific learning disability that is of neurobiological origin. It is characterized by difficulties with accurate and/or fluent word recognition and by poor spelling...These difficulties typically result from a deficit of the phonological component of language..." (adapted from *http://www.interdys.org/FAQWhatIs.htm*).

This definition retains an emphasis on a discrepancy between reading and IQ (hence the term specific learning disability). Although the usefulness of a reading/IQ discrepancy for diagnosis has been hotly debated, in terms of research practice the use of IQ discrepancy-defined groups has been, and remains, the usual approach when studying dyslexia. This is a cautious research strategy; by selecting groups of poor readers with at least average IQ, the hope is to exclude more general learning problems and so maximize the chances of establishing the cognitive deficits that are the causes of reading problems. We shall see shortly that this research agenda has been pursued with considerable success.

Summary   measured

Dyslexia can be operationally defined as a problem in learning to recognize printed words at a level appropriate for a child's age. It is in fact quite a common disorder affecting around 3–6% of children, with more boys than girls affected (Rutter et al., 2004). As we shall see, in most cases dyslexia appears to depend on problems of phonology (skills in dealing with speech sounds). However, in addition, social factors play a key role in determining the risk for reading disability (Rutter & Maughan, 2005; Yule et al., 1974).

The persistence of dyslexia

There are now several studies that have examined the profile of difficulties shown by children with dyslexia when they reach adulthood. Although many such children who have received appropriate help develop reasonable levels of reading accuracy, reading speed (or fluency) appears more difficult to remediate, and spelling skills typically remain impaired (Bruck, 1990; Maughan & Hagell, 1996). Indeed, in a follow-up of children with specific reading difficulties from the Isle of Wight study when they were in their mid-40s, it was reported that 80% of these people had spelling scores at least two standard deviations below the population average (Rutter, Kim-Cohen, & Maughan, 2006). Thus, like many developmental disorders considered in this book, it appears that dyslexia persists into adulthood, though it appears to have a range of different manifestations in adult life that are, as yet, poorly understood.

Comorbidities between dyslexia and other disorders

Comorbidity is a term used to refer to the co-occurrence of different disorders. Dyslexia has been reported to occur together with language impairment, attention deficit hyperactivity disorder, and developmental coordination disorder (Catts, Adlof, Hogan, & Ellis Weismer 2005; Kadesjo & Gillberg, 2001; Kaplan, Wilson, Dewey, & Crawford, 1998; Willcutt & Pennington, 2000) as well as with difficulties in mathematical cognition. Moreover it is not unusual for more than two of these disorders to co-occur, especially in referred samples. As yet, the frequency of such comorbidities is not established and their causes and consequences is the subject of ongoing research (see Chapter 9 for discussion).

The Normal Development of Literacy: A Theoretical Framework

Studies of normal development and studies of developmental disorders can inform each other. A central claim of this book is that any proper understanding of a developmental disorder must be couched in terms of a model of normal development. To understand dyslexia is to be able to say how reading development in dyslexia goes awry in comparison to normal development. A better understanding of dyslexia will in turn help to refine and constrain theories of normal development because individuals who show striking failures of development help to sharpen our appreciation of the processes underlying normal development. With this in mind, we will consider the normal development of reading, to inform our later explanations of dyslexia.

Proponents	Gough & Hillinger (1980)	Mason (1980)	Marsh et al. (1980)	Chall (1983)	Frith (1985)	Ehri (1998)	Stuart & Coltheart (1988)	Seymour & Duncan (2001)	
Number of developmental periods	2	3	4	5	3	4	2	4	
1. Pre-reading	Cue reading	Contextual dependency	Rote, linguistic guessing	Stage 0: Letters/ book exposure	Logographic	Pre-alphabetic	Partial orthographic	Pre-literacy	
2. Early reading		Visual recognition	Discrimination, net guessing	Memory & contextual guessing		Partial alphabetic		Dual foundation	
3. Decoding	Cipher reading	Letter sound analysis	Sequential decoding	Stage 1: Decoding attending to letters/ sounds	Alphabetic	Full alphabetic	Complete orthographic	Logographic	Alphabetic
4. Fluent reading			Hierarchical decoding	Stage 2: Fluency, consolidation	Orthographic	Consolidated alphabetic, automaticity		Orthographic	
								Morphographic	

Figure 2.1   Stage models of reading development. (From Ehri, L. C. (2005). Development of sight word reading: Phrases and findings. In Snowling, M. J. and Hulme, C. (Eds) *The Science of Reading: A Handbook* (pp. 135–154). Oxford, Blackwell.)

How do children learn to read?

A number of theories propose that reading development proceeds in a series of stages or phases (Ehri, 2005, for a review). Although there are differences between different models (see Figure 2.1 by way of illustration), we describe here in outline the sequence of development culled from stage models.

Children begin the process of learning to read by making quite arbitrary associations between printed words and pronunciations. This visual approach to reading is limited and children soon show evidence of coming to understand the systematic relationships between the letter sequences in printed words and the sounds that the letters represent. As reading skill develops, reading becomes more rapid and less effortful and appears to depend upon sophisticated representations of the relationships between print, sound, and meaning, at a number of different levels.

At the earliest point in development, referred to as the logographic stage (Frith, 1985), the child appears to be attaching a label (the word's name) to a string of letters, without any proper appreciation of how the letters in a word map on to its pronunciation. At this stage, reading errors come predominantly from the set of words the child has been taught, with a tendency for them to preserve word length. For example, Seymour and Elder (1986) reported a child reading policeman as "children" saying, "I know it's that one because it is a long one." They also noted confusion between words with salient features in common. One child read smaller as "yellow" (both share a double l) and another read stop as "lost" (both share the cluster st though not in the same position).

One important difference between stage theories concerns how early, and in what way, children come to start using phonological information in learning to recognize words. (see Box 2.1). According to Ehri (1992), as soon as the young child has some

Box 2.1   The nature of phonological skills

"Phonological skills" is a blanket term used by psychologists to refer to skills that involve dealing with speech sounds. An important distinction in relation to reading development is between implicit and explicit phonological processing. Implicit phonological processing skills are those that are automatically engaged, for example in verbal short-term memory tasks. Such implicit phonological tasks can be contrasted with explicit phonological tasks, usually referred to as phonological awareness or phonological sensitivity tasks. These explicit tasks require the child to reflect upon and manipulate the speech sounds in words.

The most common tasks used to tap implicit phonological processing in studies of reading development are verbal short-term memory and rapid automatized naming (RAN) tasks. In verbal short-term memory tasks, participants usually listen to a string of numbers (digit span) or words (word span) and then repeat these items in the order of presentation. Two short-term memory phenomena provide evidence that the task engages phonological codes. The first is the "phonological confusability" effect, the finding that the recall of word lists is better when the items in the list are phonologically distinct than when there is overlap, and the second is the word length effect, the finding that more short than long words can be recalled in order. In the RAN task the participant is presented with a matrix of objects, colors, letters, or digits and is required to name the items as quickly as possible. This task requires rapid retrieval of the phonological forms (the names) of the items in the matrix.

There are robust correlations between performance on implicit phonological processing task and reading skills. However there are generally stronger relationships between reading and explicit phonological awareness. It is widely held that the development of phonological awareness proceeds from large to small units. Thus, children first become sensitive to the syllable structure of words and only later become aware of intrasyllabic units. English has a complex syllable structure. All syllables contain a vowel; simple CVC syllables comprise an onset (the consonant before the vowel) and a rime (the technical term used to describe the unit comprising the vowel and the final consonant or coda). In turn, rime units can be segmented into phoneme units, namely the vowel and the coda. In more complex syllables (see below), both the onset and the coda may include consonant clusters. The difficulty of a phonological awareness task will depend on a number of factors including the size of the phonological unit and the nature of the manipulation that is required. Generally tasks involving the manipulation of larger units (e.g., syllables or rime units) are easier than tasks involving smaller units (phonemes). Tasks involving the deletion or transposition of sounds within words are typically harder than tasks requiring judgments about the similarity between sounds in words.

Box 2.1   *(cont'd)*

Syllable		CRUST		
Onset – rime		CR	UST	
Onset – vowel – coda		CR	U	ST
Phoneme	C R	U S T		

basic letter–sound and letter–name knowledge (at the age of 5 years or so), this starts to influence the process of learning associations between letter strings in words and their pronunciations. The use of letter–sound relationships in reading gradually becomes more and more explicit and systematic and children enter an alphabetic stage where they read using phonological strategies. Simple alphabetic strategies involve using letter–sound correspondences (sometimes described as "phonic strategies") to decipher print and, depending on how they have been taught, children can sometimes be heard to sound out and blend unknown words (CAT, > /k/, /ae/, /t/ > "cat"). As children consolidate this alphabetic stage, the application of letter–sound knowledge becomes progressively more automated and less effortful and the orthographic representations that underpin word recognition become more fully specified (the orthographic stage of reading development).

Stage models of reading provide descriptions of the way in which children's reading changes with age but they do not provide a mechanistic account of how these developmental changes come about; nor do they permit consideration of individual differences in the rate or course of development. A powerful way to investigate the role of different cognitive skills in learning to read is to conduct longitudinal studies (see Box 2.2). In these studies children are studied over a number of years, preferably beginning before they have started reading. If we can find measures of cognitive skills in prereaders that predict children's progress in learning to read, this may give us clues to the causes of variations in reading development.

Bradley and Bryant (1983) conducted a highly influential study that examined the relationship between early phonological skills and later reading achievement. The study involved some 400 children who were followed between the ages of 4 and 8 years. There was a strong relationship between the children's phonological awareness assessed on tasks tapping rhyme and alliteration skills at 4 years and their reading and spelling skills at 8, even when the effects of IQ, memory, and social class were controlled. Similar findings were reported by Lundberg, Olofsson, and Wall (1980) from a study conducted in Denmark where, at the time, reading instruction did not begin until the age of 7 years. These two studies were the starting point for a now voluminous literature showing the strong relationship between phonological awareness prior to reading instruction and later reading achievement (see Bowey, 2005, for a review).

If we accept that phonological skills and learning to read are intimately related, a more specific question is whether different levels of phonological representation are particularly crucial. Words consist of syllables (*Butterfly* has three syllables). Spoken syllables in turn can be segmented at different levels. A monosyllabic word such as *Spring* consists

Box 2.2 A longitudinal study of normal reading development

Muter, Hulme, Snowling, and Stevenson (2004) conducted a study in which 90 children were given a wide range of measures just after they entered school and then they were retested 1 and 2 years later (at the start of their second and third year in school). At school entry the children were assessed on a range of measures of rhyme and phoneme manipulation skills as well as on measures of vocabulary, reading, and letter knowledge. Rhyme skills were assessed by three tasks: rhyme detection (this is a CAT, which of these three words "fish, gun, hat" rhymes with cat) rhyme production (the word is "day," tell me as many words as you can that rhyme with "day"), and rhyme oddity (the words are "sand, hand, bank," which word does not rhyme with the others?). Phoneme skills were assessed with two tests: phoneme deletion (the word is "tin," "tin without the /t/ says....[in]") and phoneme completion (here the examiner said the beginning of a word and the child had to complete it by giving the final (missing) sound; given a picture of a gate the examiner would say "the word is /geɪ/" and the child would respond with a sound to complete the word "/t/"). In all these tests, pictures of the words were shown to the child. Children's letter knowledge (how many letters could the children give the name or sound for), reading skills (reading aloud lists of simple words), and vocabulary knowledge (selecting the correct picture from one of four pictures that represented a spoken word) were also assessed.

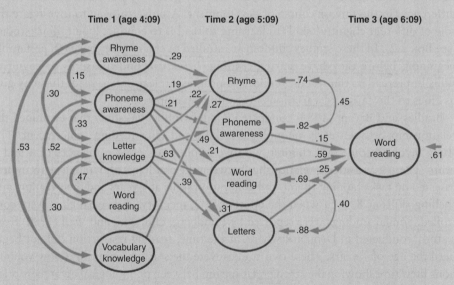

Longitudinal predictors of word recognition from age 4 to 6 years. (Muter, V., Hulme, C., Snowling, M. J., Stevenson, J. Phonemes, rimes, vocabulary and grammatical skills as foundations of early reading development, *Developmental Psychology*, 40, p. 674, 2004, published by American Psychological Association and adapted with permission.)

Box 2.2   (*cont'd*)

The main results from this study are shown in the path diagram. Following the conventions for path diagrams, the arrows from the measures at Time 1 to the measures at Time 2 represent the statistically significant relationships between these measures, and the numbers above the arrows indicate the relative strength of these relationships. As can be seen there were only two predictors of reading skills at Time 2; these were children's ability to manipulate phonemes in spoken words and their letter knowledge (and these same variables then continue to predict variations in reading skills at Time 3). This study gives strong support to the idea that phoneme manipulation ability and letter knowledge are two critical foundations for children learning to recognize words in reading.

of an onset /spr/ and a rime /ɪŋ/. At a finer level syllables can be divided into individual phonemes /s/p/r/ɪ/ŋ/. Goswami and Bryant (1990) proposed that rhyming skills were the precursors of reading development (in children learning English) and argued that the first links that children make in learning to read are between large units (onsets and rimes) and groups of letters, with the development of links between phonemes and graphemes being a second step. A number of studies have now tested this idea but have come down in favor of an alternative view, notably that rhyme and phoneme segmentation skills are relatively independent of each other and that initial phoneme segmentation ability is a far better predictor of children's subsequent progress in learning to read than is rime (Hulme, et al., 2002; Muter, Hulme, Snowling, & Stevenson, 2004).

Together, these studies converge with others in the literature (Byrne, 1998) in demonstrating that phoneme awareness and letter knowledge are critical foundations for the development of reading skills in children just entering school. Children who have some ability to manipulate phonemes in spoken words when they enter school and who have good knowledge of the sounds of letters make much better progress in learning to read than children for whom either of these skills is weak.

But to what extent do the findings we have discussed regarding learning to read apply to languages other than English? For children learning to read English, a major problem is the irregular relationship between letters and sounds. English is referred to as an irregular, opaque, or deep orthography (the relationships between spelling (orthography) and sound are not straightforward, as illustrated by words such as *colonel* and *yacht*). Many other European languages such as Czech, German, and Italian have much more transparent orthographies with letters generally corresponding to single phonemes. We therefore need to consider whether learning to read in English draws on rather different underlying cognitive skills to learning to read in other languages.

Learning to read in different alphabetic languages

Although rather few studies have made direct comparisons between readers of different orthographies using the same stimuli, there is now substantial evidence that children learn to read and spell more quickly in transparent writing systems than in opaque systems such as English (Seymour, 2005).

One of the first studies to demonstrate differences between children learning to read in opaque and transparent orthographies was conducted by Oney and Goldman (1984), who compared the reading skills of children learning to read in English (American) and Turkish. Turkish is a transparent orthography containing consistent letter–sound correspondences and therefore provides an interesting comparison with the opaque orthography of English. These researchers investigated nonword as well as word reading. While words can be read from memory by directly accessing ortho-graphic representations (memorized spelling patterns), nonword reading provides a relatively pure test of decoding ability. Oney and Goldman (1984) reported that both decoding accuracy and speed were better among children learning to read in Turkish than English.

Wimmer and Goswami (1994) used a similar technique to investigate the influ-ence of orthographic consistency on reading development in English- and German-speaking children. In this study, children were asked to read numerals (1, 3, 5), number words (ten, seven) and nonwords derived from the number words by chang-ing the onset of the syllable (e.g. sen, feven). There were no group differences in the speed or accuracy with which numerals and number words could be read, but there was a group difference in nonword reading: German children, who had learned the transparent language, made fewer errors and read the nonwords faster (see also Frith, Wimmer, & Landerl, 1998, who noted that English children have particular difficulty reading vowels that are represented inconsistently in the English orthography).

Caravolas, Volin, and Hulme (2005) made a direct comparison between the pre-dictors of reading development in Czech (a highly transparent orthography) and English using carefully equated measures in the two languages. Reading in both lan-guages was assessed by a test of reading fluency (the rate of reading aloud a list of unrelated words) since in the regular Czech orthography all children would be able to read aloud with near perfect accuracy. Spelling accuracy was also assessed. In both languages the predictors of variations in reading fluency were identical (pho-neme awareness and coding – a speeded copying test), indicating that even in a transparent orthography variation in a child's ability to isolate phonemes in speech is a critical determinant of individual differences in reading ability (see Patel, Snowling, & De Jong, 2004, for a Dutch–English comparison). Phoneme awareness (along with reading ability and vocabulary) was also a predictor of spelling in both languages.

Thus it seems that the ease with which children learn to read in different languages varies according to the transparency of the mappings between letters and sounds in the orthography. In transparent orthographies, where these mappings are straight-forward, children learn to read more easily. However, variations in the rate of learn-ing to read are predicted by variations in children's ability to manipulate phonemes in speech in transparent orthographies just as in an opaque orthography such as English. Moreover, there is a reciprocal relationship between phonological aware-ness and the development of literacy in alphabetic writing systems. Morais, Cary, Alegria, and Bertelson (1979) showed that illiterate adults performed less well on

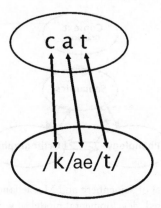

Figure 2.2 A simple diagram of the letter string CAT with arrows from the letters to the phonemes in the spoken word /k/ /æ/ /t/.

phoneme awareness tasks than people who had been taught to read, suggesting that people's awareness of phonemes improves as a result of learning to read and spell. In line with this view, phoneme awareness appears to develop more quickly in readers of transparent languages, along with their reading skills, than in readers of English and other less transparent languages (notably Chinese, a nonalphabetic language; Read, Zhang, Nie, & Ding 1986).

In summary, children need to be able to make connections between strings of letters in printed words and the sounds (phonemes) for which those letters stand in the spoken word (Figure 2.2).

This process of learning mappings between letters and sounds has interactive effects: Developing reading skills may depend upon incomplete, nascent phoneme-level representations of speech, but learning to recognize words in reading in turn facilitates the further refinement of the phonemic representations of speech.

Connectionist models of learning to read

As we have seen, there are specific cognitive requisites for learning to read but quintessentially it can be thought of as a process of learning. In recent years, the process of learning to read has been simulated in connectionist models that provide explicit theories of how children learn to map speech onto orthographic strings during reading development. Connectionist models are mechanistic models, implemented as computer programs. Their essential feature is that representations of words are not holistic (global representations) but are distributed across many simple processing elements in input and output systems. The input system can be thought of as representing words in their orthographic or printed form and is implemented as a set of orthographic units coding the letters and their position in printed words. Correspondingly, the output system represents words in their phonological or spoken form as a set of phonological units coding the phonological features of word pronunciations. Patterns of activation across these input and output units gradually

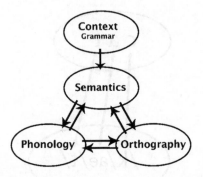

Figure 2.3   The Triangle model of Seidenberg and McClelland (1989). (Seidenberg, M. S. and McClelland, J., A distributed, developmental model of word recognition, *Psychological Review*, 96, p. 526, 1989, published by American Psychological Association and adapted with permission.)

become associated with each other as a function of learning, just as during reading acquisition children gradually learn the associations between letter strings in written words and their pronunciations.

The most influential connectionist model of reading development was proposed by Seidenberg and McClelland (1989; see Figure 2.3), referred to here as SM89. This "Triangle" model contains sets of representations dealing with orthographic (print), phonological (speech sound), and semantic (meaning) information, interconnected by sets of hidden units. The sets of hidden units give the model flexibility and allow it to learn complex sets of interdependencies between inputs and outputs.

The part of the model first implemented was a network with orthographic input and phonological output units connected by a set of hidden units (the so-called phonological pathway). Before "training" the model had essentially weak and random connections between the orthographic and phonological units, via the hidden units. Arguably, this beginning state is like that of the child when first approaching the task of reading. Training the model involved so-called supervised learning using a mathematical procedure (the generalized delta rule); the details need not bother us here. Essentially, on each training trial the computer presents the network with an input (a set of letters) and the network sends what can be thought of as feedback–activation from the activated input units to the hidden units and then on to the output units (this pattern of activity on the output units corresponds to the model's "pronunciation" of the printed word presented). At the start of training this output pattern will be random, and bear no systematic relationship to the correct pattern. The output pattern is then compared to the desired, or ideal, output pattern and the strengths of the connections between the output and input units (via the hidden units) are adjusted over many learning trials to bring them closer to the desired pattern. At the end of the training the model will "pronounce" nearly all the words on which it has been trained correctly (though there will likely be some small degree of error); the model has abstracted the relationships that exist between input and output representations in the set of words on which it is trained.

After training on a large corpus of nearly all English single-syllable words the SM89 model simulated several aspects of human word recognition. Perhaps the most important observation for present purposes was that after training the model could generalize (from knowledge embodied in the connections between input and output units) to words it had not been explicitly taught to read. That is, when presented with a novel string of letters, the model will generate a plausible pronunciation for that string. This can be likened to the developing reader's growing capacity to read new words that they have not seen before (though it has to be said that the ability of the SM89 model to read nonwords was not as good as that of a typical skilled adult reader of English; Besner, Twilley, McCann, & Seergobin, 1990).

A development of the SM89 model implemented to improve its generalization was proposed by Plaut, McClelland, Seidenberg, and Patterson (1996). Essentially, Plaut et al. (1996) adopted forms of representation in their new model corresponding to phonemes and graphemes and this allowed them to overcome the earlier model's problems with generalization (i.e. reading nonwords). When tested on nonword reading, the Plaut et al. (1996) model outperformed SM89, with performance approximating that of adult readers. Just as children learn to read most effectively when they come to the task with well-specified phonological representations (Snowling & Hulme, 1994), generalization within the connectionist architecture was better when training began with well-structured input and output representations (see also Harm & Seidenberg, 1999; Hulme, Quinlan, Bolt, & Snowling, 1995).

Another limitation of the SM89 model was that it did not deal with meaning. Plaut, et al. (1996) attempted to improve their model of reading by implementing a semantic pathway. In addition to the phonological pathway of connections between orthography and phonology, the Plaut et al. model contained a semantic pathway mapping orthography to phonology via semantic representations. Plaut et al.'s semantic units did not attempt to encode word meanings. Rather, the simulation involved training a network in which a semantic pathway provided additional activation to the phoneme units. An effect of combining semantic and phonological influences in the model was to increase the rate of learning, particularly for exception words (words like *yacht* that do not conform to the rules of pronunciation in English). In the later stages of training, Plaut et al. (1996) showed that the two pathways became highly specialized, so that the semantic pathway began to deal primarily with the pronunciation of exception words while the phonological pathway continued to be involved in the pronunciation of words (and nonwords) with consistent pronunciations.

The Triangle model (Plaut et al., 1996) provides a good framework for considering both the interaction of phonological and semantic skills during the course of reading development and individual differences in reading and its disorders (Plaut, 1997; Snowling & Hulme, 2006). According to this model the process of learning to read consists of creating mappings between orthography and phonology (the phonological pathway), and between orthography and phonology via semantics (the semantic pathway). Within each representational system in the triangle (orthography, phonology, semantics) we can think of words as being represented in terms of patterns of activation present on primitive features (these might be, for example, primitive line segments of letters, or features of how sounds in words are articulated, such as place or voicing). From a connectionist perspective, the child learning to read creates patterns of association (or mappings) that embody the relationships between spelling and sound, and spelling and meaning. In this view there is no need to postulate distinct phases or stages of development, but different stage-like behaviors may emerge as a consequence of different levels of training of such a "network". Moreover, such a system may display "rule-like" behavior without having any explicit representation of rules. It appears, as we will see later, that for children with dyslexia this phonological pathway does not develop as it should because of an underlying weakness in the phonological system.

The Pattern of Reading Impairment in Dyslexia

According to the models of reading development outlined above, phonological skills are critical for learning to read. In the Triangle model, learning to read is a process of creating mappings between orthography and phonology (the phonological pathway) and from orthography to phonology via semantics (the semantic pathway). If children with dyslexia have problems in the representation of phonology this would clearly be expected to impair the phonological pathway and, less obviously, might also delay the development of the semantic pathway (because learning the associations between semantic and phonological representations may be hindered by the phonological problems in dyslexia).

Clinically, the pattern of reading problems seen in English-speaking children with dyslexia is consistent with this idea. One of the first signs of dyslexia is a problem learning letter names and sounds. The ability to learn letters can be thought of as a form of paired-associate learning that depends upon creating associations between visual forms (of the letter) and new phonological forms (names or sounds). The bulk of evidence from studies of paired-associate learning suggests it is the verbal aspect of the process that creates problems for children with dyslexia, that is, a deficit in phonological learning (Vellutino, 1979).

Beyond letter learning, children with dyslexia typically have marked problems in reading isolated single words, where context and meaning can be of little help, and rather less severe problems in reading prose. Surprisingly it is often the case that the child with dyslexia may struggle with reading a passage aloud but show reasonable understanding by relying on well-developed language comprehension skills. Typically children with dyslexia will find learning to spell even more difficult than learning to read. Whereas reading can proceed on the basis of partial cues, spelling requires full information.

One of the most direct ways of investigating the development of decoding skills is to look at how well a child can read nonwords. A typically developing 7-year-old child will have no difficulty pronouncing nonwords such as pim or zot that they have never seen before. Children with dyslexia have problems in reading nonwords in comparison to younger children matched for reading age (Rack, Snowling, & Olson, 1992). Van Ijzendoorn and Bus (1994) conducted a meta-analysis and showed that the nonword reading deficit was moderate in size (Cohen's *d* =0.48; based on a total sample size of 1183 children). (See Box 2.3 for an explanation of effect size as used in this meta-analysis.)

Are there Different Types of Dyslexia in Childhood?

So far we have not referred to individual differences among children with dyslexia. Are all children with dyslexia the same, or are there different types of dyslexia? There have been many attempts to find so-called subtypes of dyslexia and many of these have been based upon the patterns of reading difficulties the children show. It has been suggested that children with dyslexia may be classified as phonological or surface dyslexics.

Phonological dyslexia is the pattern we have described above in which children experience severe nonword reading difficulties. Children with phonological dyslexia appear to have marked problems in using "phonic" reading strategies (sounding out unfamiliar words), while their use of lexical strategies (recognizing familiar words) is comparatively normal. Surface dyslexia is a term used to describe a different reading pattern. These children may read nonwords relatively accurately (but often slowly) and they find regular words (words like *camel* that can be sounded out using spelling–sound rules) easier to read than exception words (words like *yacht* that violate spelling–sound rules). Children with surface dyslexia have been described as often making regularization errors with exception words, that is, pronouncing them incorrectly as if they do follow spelling–sound rules (Coltheart, Masterson, Byng, Prior, & Riddoch, 1983). In other words, surface dyslexia is a pattern of reading that suggests overreliance on a phonological strategy; it is as if these children are locked in to using a letter–sound strategy slavishly and inflexibly. To identify how common these putative subtypes of dyslexia are, studies have been conducted with groups of children with dyslexia. Castles and Coltheart (1993) came up with an ingenious way of performing this classification. They suggested that nonword reading could be used as a measure of a child's phonological reading skills, and that exception word reading could be used as a measure of lexical reading skills (by lexical reading skills we mean the stored knowledge of words that a child has acquired; exception words are used for this because, arguably, they cannot be decoded using knowledge of spelling–sound correspondences; if you do not recognize the word *yacht* it will be difficult to work out how it is pronounced).

Castles and Coltheart (1993) then went on to use regression to predict nonword reading from exception word reading in a sample of normal children, and conversely to predict exception word reading from nonword reading in these same children. They then superimposed the scores for the children with dyslexia on these two plots. In such plots, children with dyslexia whose nonword reading fell below the level expected from their exception word reading ability, but whose exception word reading predicted from nonword reading was within normal limits, were classified as showing phonological dyslexia. Conversely, children with dyslexia whose exception word reading fell below the level expected for their nonword reading ability, but

Box 2.3   Effect sizes and meta-analysis

When we are considering findings from quantitative studies an important issue concerns the relative size of different effects. This is referred to as effect size in statistics and the basic idea is simple. Suppose we wanted to compare the differences in height and weight between samples of men drawn from the populations of two cities. We find the following figures for the two cities (City A: average height 175 cm, average weight 91 kg; City B: average height 173 cm, average weight 71 kg).

The men in City A are taller and heavier than the men in City B. The question, however, is how to compare these figures for height and weight in terms that make them comparable. Is the 2 cm difference in height smaller, bigger, or about the same as the 20 kg difference in weight? To make this comparison we need to express these differences in relation to the degree of variability in each of the measures. The measure of variability that we will use is the standard deviation of each measure. We can divide the difference in height by the standard deviation for height (this measure then gives us Cohen's *d*, the size of an effect in standard deviation or *z*-score units) and the same can be done for weight.

Let us suppose that the standard deviation of height in this population is 11 cm and the standard deviation of weight is 19 kg (these figures have been chosen to be roughly correct for 18-year-old males in Britain). So the difference in height relative to the variability of height is 2/11 = 0.18 (Cohen's *d* = 0.18) ; and for weight the corresponding figure is 20/19 = 1.05 (Cohen's *d* = 1.05). These figures show that the difference in weight for men in the two cities (1.05 standard deviation units) is much larger than the difference in height (0.18 standard deviation units).

Cohen (1988) suggested that in studies that are typical of psychology, effect sizes of 0.2 or less were small, effect sizes around 0.5 were medium, and effect sizes of 0.8 or above were large. As psychologists we are probably most familiar with IQ as a measure. IQ is measured on a scale where the population average is 100 with a standard deviation of 15. This means that in terms of Cohen's *d* a difference in IQ of 3 points would be a small effect (*d* = 3/15 = 0.20), a difference of 8 points would be a medium effect (*d* = 8/15 = 0.53), and a difference of 12 points would be a large effect (*d* = 12/15 = 0.8).

There are other measures of effect size that can be used, but in this book, where we are typically interested in the difference in means between two groups, Cohen's *d* is the most obvious one to use, and one that is very easy to understand. When we discuss differences in the average level of performance between clinical and control groups of children we will often use this measure of effect size to convey the magnitude of a given effect.

One other important feature of effect sizes is that they give a way of combining information from many different studies, using a technique called meta-analysis. So for example, van Ijzendoorn and Bus (1994) found many studies that had

Box 2.3   *(cont'd)*

examined how well children with dyslexia could read nonwords but the different studies had used many different tests of nonword reading ability. However, given that each study reports the mean and the standard deviation for the nonword reading scores for the dyslexic and control children, they could calculate an effect size for each study and then average the effect sizes from the different studies to get an average effect size. Combining effect sizes in this way (usually giving a greater weight to the estimates of effect size from studies with large samples) gives us a powerful way of combining the results from different studies.

whose nonword reading predicted from exception word reading was within normal limits, were classified as showing surface dyslexia. Thus, in this scheme, children with phonological dyslexia have problems in nonword reading in the presence of adequate exception word reading, while children with surface dyslexia have problems with exception word reading but adequate nonword reading.

One important problem with this study, however, was that the data for normally developing children came from children whose reading skills were much better than those of the children with dyslexia (Snowling, Bryant, & Hulme, 1996). This research strategy has been criticized on the grounds that it creates problems for the interpretation of group effects. Essentially, by comparing children who differ in levels of reading achievement, it is not possible to judge whether apparent group differences between good and poor readers are a cause of their reading problem or a consequence of different amounts of reading experience. To get around this problem, a common strategy is to compare children with dyslexia, not only with children of the same age who are normal readers but also with younger children matched for reading age (RA controls).

Two studies following on from Castles and Coltheart (1993) used this technique to compare children with dyslexia with younger RA controls (Manis, Seidenberg, Doi, McBride-Chang, & Petersen, 1996; Stanovich, Siegel, & Gottardo, 1997). These studies produced much weaker evidence for subtypes of dyslexia: Stanovich et al. showed that 17/68 children with dyslexia showed the phonological pattern but only 1/68 showed the surface pattern. Similar results were also obtained in the study by Manis et al. Most interestingly, in both studies it was the children classified as having phonological dyslexia who tended to show significant deficits on tests of phonological ability.

In our view it is better to move away from using the phonological and surface subtype labels since these are just behavioral descriptions of patterns of reading impairment that are not in fact stable over time (Manis & Bailey, 2001). The results described above might be better thought of in terms of continuous variations in the skills that underlie reading development. As Griffiths and Snowling (2002) showed, children with the most severe phonological difficulties will tend to show the most severe nonword reading difficulties. The surface dyslexic pattern seems in contrast to be associated with much milder phonological difficulties. Mild phonological difficulties, possibly coupled with being taught with an emphasis on "phonics" and low levels of print experience, may lead to a surface dyslexic pattern in which the child laboriously tries to sound out every unknown word. It is important to emphasize that the reading patterns that are used to "diagnose" surface and phonological dyslexia are concerned with children's attempts to read aloud words (or nonwords) they do not know. However, all these children with dyslexia show poor word recognition skills in relation to their age, and these problems are manifested in problems in reading both irregular and regular words. Testing nonword reading gives us a tool to examine how well a child's phonological reading system is working and it is clear that a significant proportion of children with dyslexia show nonword reading problems that are even more severe than expected for their overall level of reading skill. These children appear to be those with the most severe phonological difficulties.

Dyslexia in Different Languages

As we saw earlier there is evidence that children find it easier to learn to read in languages such as Czech and German with regular sound–spelling correspondences than in English, which has somewhat irregular sound–spelling correspondences. We might expect that the problem of dyslexia would be less severe in regular writing systems than in an irregular writing system such as English. There is some evidence in support of this idea. It has been claimed that among German-speaking children with dyslexia early difficulties with phoneme awareness are overcome by the second year in school (Wimmer, 1996) and that in terms of reading accuracy they may be no worse than CA controls, although they do appear to read more slowly and many have spelling difficulties (Landerl & Wimmer, 2000; Wimmer, 1996). However, Caravolas et al. (2005) compared the cognitive deficits found in groups of English and Czech children with dyslexia using more sensitive (and more difficult) measures of phoneme awareness than those used by Wimmer and his colleagues in studies of German. Caravolas et al. found that in both Czech and English the children with dyslexia showed severe problems in manipulating phonemes in spoken words. These findings suggest that problems in phoneme manipulation skills are a core deficit in children with dyslexia in both regular and irregular orthographies (see Caravolas, 2005, for a review). In Chinese, where phoneme level skills are less important, the picture is somewhat different. However it is worth noting that poor rapid naming skills characterize children with dyslexia in Chinese who have difficulty in establishing character–sound connections, which depend on phonological learning.

Cognitive Explanations of Developmental Dyslexia

With these ideas about normal reading development, and the pattern of reading difficulties shown by children with dyslexia as background, we are now ready to consider some of the possible cognitive causes of dyslexia. If we accept the triangle model as a metaphor for learning to read single words, then problems with the creation of any of the three classes of representation embodied in the model might be involved: problems with phonological (sound), orthographic (print) or semantic (meaning) representations, or problems in creating appropriate linkages between these classes of representation. These three representational systems (or modules to use Fodor's term) all develop quite gradually. The phonological and semantic systems are both components of oral language and typically these systems, and the linkages between them, are quite well developed by the time a child goes to school (see Chapter 4). The phonological system allows a child to perceive the sound structure of spoken words, and to produce those sound structures when speaking. The semantic system allows a child to access the meanings of words they hear and to express the meanings they want to convey using appropriate words in speech. Both systems therefore participate in language comprehension and production. According to some models, the phonological system used in speech perception may be separable from the phonological system required for speech production.

In contrast to the phonological and semantic systems, the orthographic system is something that only develops as a result of learning to read. The development of this system depends critically upon the ability to map the speech sounds of spoken words onto the visual representations of printed words. Satisfactory development of orthographic representations therefore depends not only on language skills but also upon sensitivity to the graphic features of letters and the ability to parse letter strings, together referred to as graphemic parsing skills.

By far the best developed theory of dyslexia is that it arises from a phonological deficit. This dominant phonological deficit theory of dyslexia attributes the child's reading difficulties to an inability to establish the phonological pathway in the triangle model. Here we will present this theory in some detail, and we will only consider alternative theories (for which the evidence is much weaker) very briefly.

Dyslexia as a phonological deficit

It may be useful to start by drawing the phonological deficit theory of dyslexia in a path diagram (see Figure 2.4). This is a very simple causal theory stating that problems with phonology that pre-date reading are a cause of later reading problems. Though this theory could be refined and developed in various ways, representing the

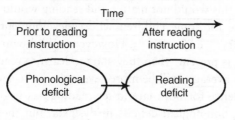

Figure 2.4 Path model showing the primary cause of dyslexia.

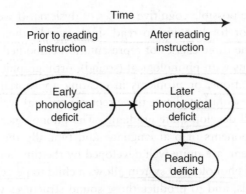

Figure 2.5   Elaborated path model showing causes of dyslexia.

bare-bones of this theory is a useful place to start. Such a theory makes at least two strong claims:

1 Children who become dyslexic will show a phonological deficit before they begin to learn to read.
2 The severity of the phonological deficit will predict variations in the severity of the reading deficit.

We should note that the version of this theory we are advocating sees the phonological deficit persisting through time. It is the phonological deficit present at the time the child is learning to read that is the proximal cause of reading difficulties. The important point, however, is that the cause (a phonological deficit) pre-dates the consequence (a reading problem). We can represent this slightly elaborated theory as in Figure 2.5.

In this slightly elaborated theory, the later phonological deficit is shown as persisting at the time that reading emerges (the underlying phonological deficit is acting forward in time to cause problems in learning to read). This theory makes an additional and highly specific prediction which is that the early phonological deficit affects later reading ability through a mediated relationship. That is, the effects of the early phonological deficit are entirely mediated by (operate through) its effects on the later phonological deficit. It is the later phonological deficit that is the immediate cause of the reading problem. (We can test such mediated relationships statistically, but that is not important in the current context.) What this means is really very simple: If a child had a phonological deficit early in life that was remedied before they started reading, this would not matter and reading would develop normally (as seems to be the case for some children whose developmental speech difficulties resolve by school entry; see Chapter 4). However, a child who has a persisting phonological deficit that is present when they start to learn to read will develop a reading problem that, on average, will be more severe the more severe the phonological deficit. There is evidence for both late (after reading has begun) and early (before reading has begun) phonological deficits in dyslexia, but there is much more evidence concerning the late deficits. We will consider this evidence first.

Phonological deficits in school-age children with dyslexia

Before considering evidence for phonological deficits in children with dyslexia, a couple of methodological points are worth reiterating. First, the studies we will summarize typically involve groups of children with moderate to severe reading problems but normal IQ. This is a conservative strategy; if we find cognitive deficits in people with reading problems who have average IQ, then the deficit cannot simply be due to some general intellectual impairment and might therefore be a possible cause of the reading problem. Second, these studies often compare children with dyslexia to normally developing children of the same age and IQ (a chronological-age (CA)-matched design), and sometimes also to younger normally developing children whose reading skills are at the same absolute level (the reading-age (RA)-matched design). The logic here is that if children with dyslexia perform more poorly on a task than younger children who have the same level of reading skill, then the difference cannot be explained in terms of reading ability or experience. This is particularly important with tasks where it could be the case that learning to read improves the skill in question, which is the case for almost all measures of phonological ability given the evidence we have considered earlier that there is a reciprocal relationship between phonological and reading skills. It is useful to consider evidence for phonological deficits in dyslexia under two broad headings: phonological awareness and phonological processing. In the literature, this difference has also been referred to as explicit versus implicit phonology.

Phonological awareness in dyslexia

Phonological awareness tasks measure children's ability to make explicit judgments about the sound structure of spoken words. One of the first studies to show that children with dyslexia are poor at these sorts of task was that of Bradley and Bryant (1978), who compared a group of 12-year-old children with dyslexia with a group of younger RA-matched children. In this study, children heard a sequence of four words and simply had to select the word that did not rhyme, or did not begin with the same sound, as the other three words. The children with dyslexia were worse at this task than the RA controls, and were also worse at generating words to rhyme with a target word. Subsequent studies have confirmed this pattern of impairments in phonological awareness tasks in children and adults with dyslexia compared to RA controls (Bruck, 1990; Manis, Custodio, & Szeszulski, 1993).

There is evidence, as we saw earlier, that for normally developing children awareness of phonemes seems to be much more strongly related to reading than is awareness of larger phonological units such as rimes. We might expect, therefore, that children with dyslexia would show even greater deficits on measures of phoneme awareness than on measures of rime awareness. This turns out to be the case. Swan and Goswami (1997a) compared children with dyslexia with a group of CA and younger RA controls. The children with dyslexia were worse than the CA control group, but comparable to RA controls, on tests of syllable segmentation and onset–rime similarity. However, they were actually significantly worse than the RA controls on a phonemic awareness task. The same pattern was found by Windfuhr and Snowling

(2001). Thus in children with dyslexia, as in normally developing children, the ability to analyze speech at the phonemic level appears to be particularly closely related to the ability to learn to read.

Phonological processing in dyslexia

Phonological processing tasks require the child to use speech, without necessarily reflecting upon the structure of spoken words. Typical examples of tasks that psychologists have used to investigate phonological processing include repeating a word or nonword, naming a picture, or remembering a list of words. Children with dyslexia show difficulties on all these simple tasks.

Nonword repetition   One of the simplest procedures we can use to assess a child's phonological abilities is to ask them to repeat a spoken word or nonword. Snowling (1981) compared the ability of children with dyslexia with a group of RA controls, some 4 years younger, to repeat polysyllabic words (e.g., pedestrian, magnificent) and nonwords derived from the same words (kebestrian, bagmivishent). The children with dyslexia had no difficulty repeating the words but were worse than the RA controls at repeating the nonwords.

In a further study Snowling, Goulandris, Bowlby, and Howell (1986) examined the repetition of nonwords, low-frequency words, and high-frequency words by children with dyslexia and CA and RA controls. To examine the possible importance of perceptual factors, the words and nonwords were presented in varying degrees of noise (noise masking). Both the children with dyslexia and the controls were affected by the noise masking, to a similar degree, suggesting that any difficulty in repetition could not be attributed to problems in perception. Most importantly, however, the children with dyslexia repeated fewer nonwords correctly than both the CA and RA controls. With low-frequency words the children with dyslexia showed milder difficulties, being worse than the CA controls, but similar to the RA controls.

A parsimonious account of these findings is that children with dyslexia have particular difficulties in setting up the speech motor programs that are necessary to articulate a novel item (see also Hulme & Snowling, 1992). Furthermore, it is plausible that the speech production problems revealed in nonword repetition tasks are fundamental to explaining a wide range of difficulties in children with dyslexia. In fact nonword repetition ability in normally developing children has been shown to be a good predictor of vocabulary acquisition (Baddeley, Gathercole, & Papagno, 1998) and of foreign language learning (Service, 1992). Clinically, there is a strong association between dyslexia and subtle speech problems, including mispronouncing unusual words, word-finding problems, and malapropisms (interchanging a word with a similar sound for the intended word). People with dyslexia also often complain of difficulties in learning foreign languages. The speech production problems underlying nonword repetition problems may well delay the learning of spoken vocabulary and one of the consistent findings from population surveys is that children with reading difficulties are slow to learn to speak. These problems of learning may also compromise the quality of representations for spoken words that are stored in memory, and this in turn may result in difficulties in tasks such as naming, to which we will now turn.

Naming difficulties Confrontation naming, which involves asking someone to name a picture, provides a simple way of assessing a child's language skills. Snowling, van Wagtendonk, and Stafford (1988) gave 11-year-old children with dyslexia a picture naming test and compared their performance with that of an age-matched and a younger comparison group. The children with dyslexia named fewer pictures than CA controls but were comparable to the younger children of roughly similar reading skill. In a second study each child with dyslexia was individually matched with a normal reader for their ability to define spoken words. This arguably gives a measure of the size of a child's vocabulary. The children were then given two other tasks: a confrontation-naming test (as before) and a test requiring the child to choose a picture that corresponded to a spoken word. These two tests give measures of closely related but different aspects of vocabulary knowledge. Confrontation naming gives a measure of expressive vocabulary (how many words can a child successfully produce) while matching a spoken word to a picture gives a measure of receptive vocabulary. The results were very clear; the children with dyslexia showed deficits on confrontation naming (expressive vocabulary) but were normal on the word/picture-matching task (receptive vocabulary).

These naming difficulties in dyslexia are consistent with the idea that semantic information (word meanings) is adequately represented in memory but that phonological information (word sounds) is poorly represented. Further evidence that is consistent with this idea comes from a study by Swan and Goswami (1997b). Here a group of children with dyslexia together with RA and CA controls were given a difficult naming task. The children with dyslexia performed even more poorly on this task than the RA controls and only did as well as generally poor readers of low IQ. Importantly, however, the children with dyslexia were able to define many of the words they had been unable to produce as names to the pictures, indicating that they had effective semantic representations of the words.

A different way of assessing naming problems is by using tests of rapid automatized naming (RAN; Denckla & Rudel, 1976). Denckla and Rudel gave children cards with 50 (10 rows of 5) common items (letters, digits, color patches) to name as quickly as possible. This study, together with many subsequent ones, showed that on average children with dyslexia are slower on such tests than typically developing readers of the same age (Wolf & Bowers, 1999), and that these problems persist into adulthood (Pennington, van Orden, Smith, Green, & Haith, 1990). The precise nature and best theoretical explanation for these RAN deficits in children with dyslexia is currently the subject of much research.

One simple view would be that slow naming on the RAN task is just another indicator, along with failures to name objects with long low-frequency names correctly, of an underlying deficit in phonological representations (Snowling & Hulme, 1994; Wagner, Torgesen, & Rashotte, 1994). If the phonological forms of words are stored inefficiently in memory, it may take longer to retrieve them when they are needed. Another view is that RAN deficits may be part of a difficulty with a timing mechanism (Wolf & Bowers, 1999). There are certainly other possibilities as well: The

RAN task demands rapid articulation and sustained concentration, and both of these might be weaker in children with reading problems. For present purposes we simply note that studies of RAN provide evidence, from another very simple task, suggestive of underlying phonological problems in dyslexia.

Short-term memory   Although children with dyslexia have been reported to show normal visual memory, verbal short-term memory tasks are an area of difficulty for them (Hulme, 1981; Shankweiler, Liberman, Mark, Fowler, & Fischer, 1979). In a typical verbal short-term memory task, the person hears a spoken list of words and simply has to repeat these words in the same order as they are presented. This task will obviously tap the adequacy of speech perception and production mechanisms (amongst other processes) and we know that people place very heavy reliance on a phonological code for the completion of such tasks (Crowder, 1978). Evidence for the importance of phonological coding comes from the observation that it is much harder to remember sequences of items that sound similar to each other than sequences that sound dissimilar (the phonological similarity effect; Conrad, 1964) and it is harder to remember sequences of long words than short words (the word length effect; Baddeley, Thomson, & Buchanan, 1975). It appears that children with dyslexia, like normal readers, place heavy reliance on the same phonological code in these tasks but that this code operates less efficiently (Hall, Ewing, Tinzmann, & Wilson, 1981; Johnston, Rugg, & Scott, 1987).

The effects of word length on short-term memory take a highly specific form. Longer words take longer to articulate and there is a strong relationship between the rate at which people can articulate words of different lengths and their memory for these words (Baddeley et al., 1975). It also appears that, developmentally, differences in short-term memory performance are closely paralleled by changes in maximal articulation. Figure 2.6 shows the results of an experiment with children ranging

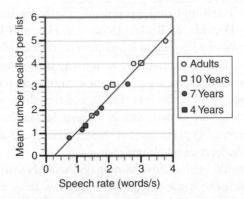

Figure 2.6   The relationship between speech rate and memory span across development. For each age group, three symbols are shown representing the results from one-, two- and three- syllable words. (Reprinted from *Journal of Experimental Child Psychology*, 38, Hulme, C., Thomson, N., Muir, C., and Lawrence, A. L. Speech rate and the development of short term memory span, pp. 241–253, copyright (1984), with permission from Elsevier.)

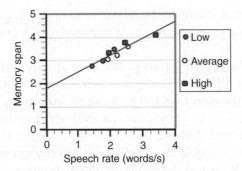

Figure 2.7   The relationship between speech rate and memory span in children of low, average, and high reading ability. (Reprinted from *Journal of Experimental Child Psychology*, 58, McDougall, S., Hulme, C., Ellis, A. W., and Monk, A. Learning to read: The role of short-term memory and phonological skills, p. 120, copyright (1994), with permission from Elsevier.)

in age from 4 to 11 years as well as adults (Hulme, Thomson, Muir, & Lawrence, 1984). In this study, participants were given lists of one-, two- and three- syllable words to remember that were selected from pictures in young children's books; they were also asked to repeat aloud these same words as quickly as they could. It is clear that both the differences in memory between words of different lengths and the differences in memory performance with age are closely paralleled by differences in articulation rate. These results show that there is a close association between speech production processes and short-term memory processes.

McDougall, Hulme, Ellis, and Monk (1994) used the relationship between word length and articulation rate to explore the origins of memory differences in children who differed in reading ability. This study did not involve children with dyslexia, but a fairly large sample (90) of children who differed widely in reading ability. The children were simply divided into three groups according to reading ability, and the poor readers were selected in such a way that they had similar, though less severe, reading problems to those seen in dyslexia. The results of this study (shown in Figure 2.7) are remarkably clear. The poor readers have substantially lower memory spans (memory span is the longest list a subject can recall correctly) than the average and good readers, but the differences between groups in memory span are exactly paralleled by differences in speech rate. In fact if differences in speech rate between the groups are controlled for statistically, differences in recall are eliminated.

The best theoretical account of the relationship between word length, speech rate, and memory performance is currently the subject of debate. For present purposes it is worth considering that it might be that those individuals who can articulate words more quickly also have better developed phonological representations of those words. The findings of McDougall et al. (1994) demonstrate clearly that the short-term memory difficulties of poor readers are intimately related to problems in speech processing mechanisms (as indexed by slow rates of articulation). In short, there seems to be a basic inefficiency in the operation of this phonological code in children with dyslexia that might tentatively be related to an underlying problem with speech production mechanisms that also results in impaired speech rate.

Phonological paired-associate learning We have already seen that children with dyslexia find naming difficult. Naming is a memory retrieval task in which we use the visual stimulus (the object we see) as a cue to retrieve the name of that object from memory. Difficulties in naming provide evidence that this retrieval process is inefficient in children with dyslexia.

We can look at these problems in a different way, by examining the process of learning new names. Learning the names of objects is an example of visual–verbal paired-associate learning. In paired-associate learning we have to learn that a particular stimulus (the picture) is associated with a particular response (the name). We know from many experiments that children with dyslexia find paired-associate learning difficult when a verbal response is required, but that they perform normally if they have to learn to associate two visual nonverbal forms (Vellutino, Scanlon, & Spearing, 1995). Children with dyslexia also find it difficult to learn to associate nonsense names with unusual animals (Wimmer, Mayringer, & Landerl, 1998) or with abstract shapes (Windfuhr, 1998). It is plausible to see these difficulties in verbal paired-associate learning as another reflection of problems with the representation of phonological information in children with dyslexia. However, Hulme, Goetz, Gooch, Adams, and Snowling (2007) showed, in a large sample of normally developing children, that visual–phonological paired-associate learning and phoneme awareness were statistically independent predictors of variations in reading skill. This suggests that there may be something tapped by measures of phonological learning that is not simply reducible to phonological skills per se.

Are phonological deficits present before reading development begins?

The phonological deficit found in children with dyslexia is present before reading begins (and hence cannot be a consequence of the reading impairment). Evidence for this comes from longitudinal studies of children selected for being at risk of dyslexia (because of a family history of the disorder). In the first study of this type, Scarborough (1990) reported data from 34 at-risk children. The analyses compared the performance of 20/32 of the at-risk children who went on to develop reading problems with the 12/32 at-risk children who became normal readers. The at-risk children who became dyslexic showed problems with pronunciation in spontaneous speech at 2.5 years, had problems with receptive vocabulary and object naming at 3 years, and at 5 years (before they started school) had weaknesses in letter knowledge, phoneme awareness, and object naming. This study shows that, as well as having phonological difficulties well before they learn to read, children with dyslexia show signs of some broader language weaknesses (such as shorter utterances and lower syntactic complexity) in the preschool years.

Convergent findings have since been observed in a number of other studies. Pennington and Lefly (2001) followed the progress of 67 children at high risk of dyslexia and 57 controls considered to be at low risk, from before entry to kindergarten when the children were 5 years old to the summer after second grade. They found an increased risk of dyslexia in affected families: 34% of the high-risk group were diagnosed as "reading disabled" in second grade, compared to only 6% of the low-risk (control) group. Children who became reading disabled showed deficits on tests of speech perception, verbal short-term memory, rapid serial naming, and phonological awareness at all testing points relative to controls and to high-risk unimpaired children.

Similar results were reported by Snowling, Gallagher, and Frith (2003), who followed 56 children at high risk of reading difficulties from just before their fourth birthday until 8 years of age. The children who went on to become dyslexic experienced delayed early language development at 3 years 9 months (Gallagher, Frith, & Snowling, 2000), with weaknesses in object naming, letter knowledge, and nonword repetition; at 6 years they had persisting oral language impairments and phonological awareness was poorly developed. In contrast, the high-risk unimpaired group was not distinguishable from controls on oral language tests. In similar vein, Hindson et al. (2005) compared the cognitive, language, and preliteracy skills of preschool children who were either at family risk of dyslexia or not. The at-risk group showed lower scores on a wide range of phonological and language measures, including phoneme awareness, rhyme awareness, letter knowledge, verbal memory, articulation rate, and vocabulary knowledge.

It seems safe to conclude that children with dyslexia display a phonological deficit before they have begun to learn to read. In contrast to findings from laboratory studies, children from family samples also appear to show some broader (nonphonological) language weaknesses in the preschool years. Arguably in family samples, oral language difficulties affect reading development via delayed phonological skills. Within this model, phonological deficits are mediators of poor reading (Figure 2.8).

Is the phonological deficit the product of a speech perception deficit?

The evidence so far shows that children with dyslexia perform poorly on a variety of tasks that tap phonological (speech processing) skills. We have argued that these

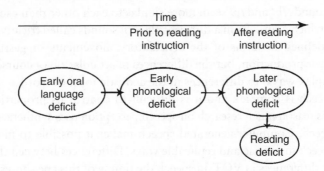

Figure 2.8 Path diagram showing phonological deficits as mediators of poor reading.

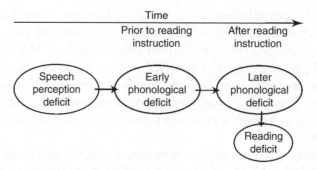

Figure 2.9   Path diagram showing a possible causal role of speech perception deficits in the development of reading problems.

phonological problems seem to reflect a problem with speech production rather than speech perception. It remains the case, however, that problems of perception and production are hard to separate, and it is always possible that subtle problems in the perception of speech, could lead to problems with speech production. In fact it is possible that problems with the perception of speech might lead to problems in creating adequate phonological representations. We might represent that theory as in Figure 2.9. Within this theory, again phonological deficits mediate the impact of speech perception on reading. Evidence directly relevant to this causal theory is limited, though a number of studies have examined speech perception in school-age children with dyslexia.

Speech can be analyzed as units of different sizes. A fundamental unit is the phoneme. A phoneme is defined as the smallest unit of sound that signals a difference in meaning. So, for example, *pin* and *bin* are two words that differ only in the first phoneme, and the initial sounds in these two words are represented as /p / and /b/. In fact phonemes themselves can be considered to be composed of even smaller parts, perhaps analogously to the way atoms can be considered to consist of subatomic particles. In the case of the initial phonemes (or obstruents) in *pin* and *bin* the sounds /p / and /b/ differ by only one phonetic feature; this feature is voice onset time (VOT), the time between lip closure and the onset of vocal cord vibration. (Intuitively, the similarity between these sounds is probably obvious when you say the words *pin* and *bin*; the sounds /b/ and /p/ seem more similar to each other than each is to the /s/ sound in *sin*, which comes from a different class of sounds called fricatives.) Phonetic features are defined in terms of the articulatory movements or gestures that are involved in their production, but the differences in articulation of course correspond (often in complex ways) to differences in the acoustic form of words.

Natural speech is complex and it is difficult to control its properties in experiments. For this reason much research on speech perception uses synthetic or computer-generated speech. Computer-generated speech makes it possible to manipulate the features of speech in precise and replicable ways. Differences between the sounds /p/ and /b/ reflect differences in VOT. In speech the timing of this cue shows more or less continuous variation. Consonant phonemes cannot be produced or perceived in

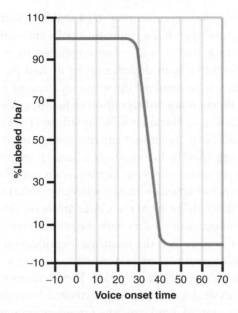

Figure 2.10 Graph showing categorical perception for [ba] versus [pa].

the absence of a vowel and therefore consonants are placed in a syllable with a vowel when we ask people to make judgments. So, for example, we might present to people two synthesized syllables /ba/ and /pa/ (these sound like *bah* and *pah*). However, if the cue of VOT is continuously varied in such a pair of syllables we do not perceive a continuously varying signal that gradually sounds less like /pa/ and more like /ba/. Instead we perceive either the syllable /pa/ or /ba/ (see Figure 2.10). This is referred to as categorical perception (we perceive sounds as belonging to one or other category, while being relatively insensitive to differences between sounds within a category; this is clearly adaptive, because we want our speech perception module to recognize the spoken words we hear in an unambiguous way).

Several studies have now investigated the perception of synthetic and natural speech stimuli in children with dyslexia. Evidence from several studies shows that children with dyslexia on average have mild difficulties on speech perception tasks (Chiappe, Chiappe, & Siegel, 2001; de Weirdt, 1988; Reed, 1989). However, there is accumulating evidence that these group differences might be attributable to a subgroup of children in the sample who show speech perception deficits. Manis et al. (1997) examined the perception of synthetic stop consonants (/b/ and /p/) in 12-year-old children with dyslexia. Overall, the performance of children with dyslexia was more error prone and they were more likely to identify clear instances of /p/ as /b/ and vice versa; this particular difficulty might plausibly be related to a difficulty in attaching the appropriate "labels" to the different stimuli rather than to a problem with speech perception per se. Manis et al. went on to show that among the children with dyslexia only 7/25 had difficulties on the speech perception task, and these children also showed severe phoneme awareness difficulties.

Adlard and Hazan (1998) reported that 4/13 children with dyslexia had quite severe problems on natural speech discrimination tasks and with a difficult synthetic speech identification task (sue – zoo) when compared to younger RA controls. It appears that these children with dyslexia probably had the most severe phonological difficulties – they were amongst the worst on a test of nonword reading and two of the group had severe nonword repetition difficulties. A similar pattern to this was also found by Masterson, Hazan, and Wijayatilake (1995).

However, a subtly different conclusion emerges from a study by Joanisse, Manis, Keating, and Seidenberg (2000). In this study a large group of 137 children with reading difficulties were given phoneme identification tests involving voice onset time (dug – tug) and place of articulation (spy – sky). Somwhat surprisingly, the poor readers as a group did not differ from the CA controls on these speech perception measures and, furthermore, poor readers with the most severe phonological difficulties were not the most impaired on the phoneme identification measures. However, a small subgroup of nine poor readers performed at a lower level than younger RA controls on the phoneme identification tasks. These children were referred to as "language impaired" dyslexics and were characterized by poor vocabulary knowledge and low scores on a test of word structure tapping grammatical skill. Regression analyses showed that, among the children with dyslexia, performance on a word structure test (tapping morphology) was a strong predictor of speech perception ability (phoneme identification) while tests of phonological skills (phoneme deletion and nonword reading) were not. The findings from this study suggest that the speech perception problems that are sometimes, but not always, found in children with dyslexia may relate to broader oral language difficulties that occur in a minority of these children, rather than being tied specifically to phonological difficulties.

It is perhaps important to emphasize that experiments such as these, with difficult discriminations and many trials, are very demanding of attention in young children. Children may do badly on such tasks because they find it difficult to maintain attention even though their perceptual abilities are actually fine. A different, and perhaps better, way of investigating speech perception comes from the gating task (Grosjean, 1980). Here children hear progressively longer snippets of recordings of single words and the task is simply to say what the word is. Typically, people can identify a word before they have heard all of it, and more familiar (high-frequency) words are identified more easily. Some studies have found that children with dyslexia typically recognize words in gating tasks as well as age-matched controls (Elliott, Scholl, Grant, & Hammer, 1990; Griffiths, & Snowling, 2001). However, a slightly more complex pattern of results was reported by Bruno et al. (2007), who performed a gating task with a group of children with dyslexia and age-matched controls. As in previous studies these authors found no difference in the accuracy of performance on the gating task between the children with dyslexia and controls. However, they also scored responses in the gating task for whether the child responded with an item from the correct category (defined as a word that ended in the same category of consonant (nasal, lateral, or oral stop consonant) as the target word). On this score, the children with dyslexia performed less well than the age-matched control children. These responses, it was argued, reflected how well children could use information from coarticulation to identify the likely terminal consonant in the word (coarticulation refers to the fact that the way a vowel is articulated will differ depending upon the consonant that follows it). In regression analyses, it was shown that a measure of phoneme and syllable deletion was related to the category gating scores, but that gating was not a predictor of reading ability once the effect of phoneme and syllable deletion was accounted for. It was argued that these results support the theory that children with dyslexia have poor representations of the phonological forms of words (and that these difficulties with phonological representations account for their difficulty in arriving at the best "category" of response in the gating task).

It seems from the studies considered so far that any problems in speech perception in children with dyslexia are certainly less marked than the problems shown on phonological output tasks such as nonword repetition and confrontation naming. Recently, a variant of the hypothesis that speech perception difficulties might be a cause of dyslexia has been proposed by Serniclaes, Van Heghe, Mousty, Carré, and Sprenger-Charolles (2004). They propose that children with dyslexia display an "allophonic mode of speech perception." Allophones are variants of the same phoneme that normal listeners would categorize as belonging to the same phoneme category. Normal listeners are relatively insensitive to differences between allophones but are correspondingly highly sensitive to differences between different phonemes. Serniclaes et al. suggested that children with dyslexia show greater sensitivity to allophones and a reduced sensitivity to differences between speech sounds that cross a phoneme boundary.

To test this idea they compared a group of 18 (9-year-old) children with dyslexia to a group of normally developing children of the same age. The task involved children listening to pairs of syllables that differed in voice onset time (VOT) and deciding if each pair was the same or different; different pairs of syllables varied in the degree of difference in VOT. The expectation for normal listeners is that people should show increased sensitivity to pairs of syllables that cross the phoneme boundary, and this was found for the control children. The children with dyslexia, in contrast, showed a flatter function, with the suggestion of reduced sensitivity at the phoneme boundary and slightly enhanced sensitivity at another point within a phoneme category. Levels of performance on the speech discrimination task were very low, however, suggesting that the task may have been too difficult for all the participants (including some adults who were tested).

In summary, it appears that problems on speech perception tasks in children with dyslexia are relatively mild in comparison to the problems shown on other phonological tasks, and some studies report that only a small minority of children with dyslexia show such impairments. Most studies in this area say little about what differentiates those children with dyslexia who have speech perception impairments from the majority whose speech perception appears normal. However, the study by Joanisse et al. makes quite a convincing case that the speech perception problems found in children with reading difficulties might actually be a manifestation of broader oral language problems that are found in only a minority of children with reading difficulties. (In this view speech perception problems are not a cause of the phonological and reading problems seen in most children with dyslexia, though they may contribute to the phonological difficulties in a subgroup of children with dyslexia who also have broader (nonphonological) language difficulties.) We badly need more studies that explore this issue, using broader and more inclusive assessments of different oral language skills and preferably following children longitudinally to explore whether the patterns of association between different impairments change with age.

An important study that moves us some way toward this goal was reported by Boada and Pennington (2006), who set out to test the segmental hypothesis of dyslexia. According to the segmental hypothesis (Fowler, 1991), the cause of reading problems can be traced to poorly specified phonological representations that, in turn, compromise reading development, a view with which we have sympathy (Snowling, 2000; Snowling & Hulme, 1994). In order to test this hypothesis, Boada and Pennington (2006) used three tasks designed to assess implicit phonological processing in dyslexia and also measured speech perception, explicit phonological awareness, nonword repetition, and rapid automatized naming (RAN) for colors and objects. In addition, to assess the hypothesis that language-impaired children with dyslexia might show more severe impairments, particularly speech perception deficits, they included groups of children with dyslexia only (RD) and children with dyslexia who also had a history of speech-language difficulty (RD+LD) according to parental report (it should be noted at the outset that this way of differentiating the two groups was not validated in terms of concurrent language performance and therefore could be regarded as less than ideal).

These two groups of poor readers were compared with an age-matched (CA control) and a younger typically developing (RA control) group of readers, matched on performance IQ, gender, and socio-economic status. ADHD symptoms were also measured by parent report.

There were three tasks measuring implicit phonology. Perhaps the one to yield the clearest results was the syllable similarity task, in which children heard triads of words, two sharing the first phoneme (e.g., bis, bun) and two sharing syllable structure (e.g., bis, dis). Each word in each triad was associated with a small toy animal and the child's task was to learn the names of the animals. On each training trial the child repeated the word as the toy was shown and on each learning trial the child responded by pointing to indicate the toy that went with the name (e.g., which one is "dis"?). These trials were alternated up to six times. For children who learned the names to the criterion there was a delay of 2 min in which the child named letters or numbers and then they were asked to name the animals again and once more after 30 s.

There was no difference between the RD and RD + LD groups on this or on any of the implicit phonology tasks, therefore the data were pooled. The main variable of interest was the proportion of confusion errors on the learning trials that shared the first phoneme with the target name, compared with the proportion that shared its syllable structure. The assumption was that children who make relatively more phonemic errors have more mature segmental memory representations (Treiman & Breaux, 1982). In fact, the RD groups made more syllabic structure confusions than phonemic errors when compared to the CA controls. The RA controls showed less mature performance than the CA controls and made similar numbers of both types of error during learning; however, after the delay they made more phoneme errors than the RD group.

These findings (together with others reported) show that children with dyslexia have problems on implicit phonological tasks, which in turn suggest that they have poorly specified or nonsegmental (not phonemically organized) phonological representations. Perhaps most importantly, it was found that the measures of implicit phonology correlated with measures of phoneme awareness but that the measures of implicit phonology accounted for additional variance in reading ability after controlling for phoneme awareness and a range of other cognitive skills.

Phonological impairments in children with dyslexia: A summary

The evidence reviewed shows that children with dyslexia have problems on a variety of phonological tasks and that some of these problems are present before they have started learning to read. Phonological deficits appear to be more clearly in evidence on tasks tapping phonological output (e.g., memory or naming) than phonological input (speech perception) processes. The dominant theory at the present time is that the core deficit in dyslexia is a deficit in the way spoken words are represented in the brain (the phonological representations hypothesis). Recent evidence, particularly regarding individual differences in the phonological processes that are affected, makes it likely that this deficit in phonological representations may be the outcome of a number of different developmental trajectories. For example, the speech perception deficits found in some children with dyslexia, possibly associated with oral language deficits, are a plausible cause of phonological deficits. For other children, the cause may be related to a difficulty in establishing articulatory motor programs for new words. Furthermore, the systems responsible for speech perception and speech production are likely to have a highly interactive relationship during development. Deficits in speech perception early in development might have knock-on effects on the development of speech output systems, and vice versa. In this view, although speech perception difficulties may be largely resolved by the age when they are typically investigated in children with dyslexia, it is still possible that these problems are important in explaining the development of some of the other phonological deficits found in people with dyslexia through adult life. Longitudinal studies are badly needed to test alternative causal models of the relationships among different speech processing (phonological) skills and reading attainments.

Are phonological impairments in dyslexia caused by auditory perceptual problems?

Another theory regarding the cause of the phonological difficulties seen in children with dyslexia is that these are the consequence of a problem with basic auditory perceptual mechanisms (Tallal, 1980). The same hypothesis has also been proposed as an explanation for the language-learning problems of children with specific language impairment (SLI) and we will consider this in Chapter 4. The hypothesis

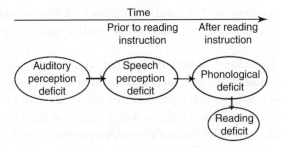

Figure 2.11   Path diagram showing a possible causal role of an auditory perceptual deficit in the development of reading problems.

originally proposed by Tallal (Tallal 1980; Tallal & Piercy 1973) was that the language-learning difficulties found in dyslexia and SLI arose from a slow rate of auditory processing, which in turn led to problems in perceiving rapid auditory changes that are critical for identifying consonant sounds in speech.

This hypothesis, that dyslexia is caused by a problem in rapid auditory temporal processing, is shown in path diagram form in Figure 2.11. As can be seen, the hypothesis clearly predicts that variations in auditory perception should predict variations in both speech perception and phonological skills.

Tallal and Piercy (1973) developed a task called the Auditory Repetition Task (ART) to test their theory. In the ART, the child listens to two complex tones that differ in pitch, separated by a gap that varied in duration (the interstimulus interval or ISI). The child has to copy the order of the tones by pressing one of two response keys in turn (the child is first trained to associate each of the two complex tones with a response key). Tallal and Piercy reported that SLI children found this task more difficult than typically developing children of the same age, but only when there was a relatively short gap between the two successive tones (ISI < 150 ms).

Tallal (1980) reported that ART performance was poor relative to that of controls for 9 of the 20 reading-impaired children in her study, and that ART scores were correlated with nonword reading ability ($r = .81$). Tallal speculated that the problems on ART shown by some of the children with dyslexia may have been related to problems in oral language skills rather than reading problems. In a subsequent study Tallal and Stark (1982) studied a group of children with dyslexia selected for normal oral language abilities. In this group they found no problems on the ART in relation to normal control children. This finding suggests strongly that the problems with the ART sometimes found in samples of children with dyslexia are actually associated with oral language difficulties, rather than being a specific correlate of reading problems (this is the same pattern as described for measures of speech perception earlier).

In line with this suggestion three other studies have failed to find evidence for problems on rapid auditory temporal processing difficulties in children with dyslexia. Nittrouer (1999) found that good and poor readers did not differ in performance on an ART-like task, nor did the poor readers show impairments in a speech perception task requiring the use of brief formant transitions to cue a phonemic contrast involving manner of articulation. Marshall, Snowling, and Bailey (2001) found no differences between children with dyslexia and RA controls in mean ART performance, although there was a small subgroup of children with dyslexia (24%) whose ART performance was outside the normal range. These children also tended to take longer to reach the criterion in a tone identification and response mapping pretest, suggesting that verbal labeling skill rather than simply efficiency in rapid auditory processing is important for ART performance. Finally, Bretherton and Holmes (2003) examined performance on the ART in a group of dyslexic children and a group of age-matched control children (aged 10–12 years old). There was no evidence of selective problems on the ART at rapid rates in the dyslexic group (as postulated by Tallal's theory) and performance on the ART was not predictive of variations in phonological awareness or reading skills in these groups of children. Overall these studies fail to provide support for the idea that the phonological deficits seen in dyslexic children can be traced to a basic problem with rapid auditory temporal processing.

Heath, Hogben, and Clark (1999) performed a direct test of whether problems on the ART are linked to reading problems or oral language problems. They selected a group of children with dyslexia with normal oral language skills, a group of children with dyslexia with poor oral language skills, and group of control children of the same age. The experiment involved extensive practice followed by a procedure whereby the ISI between pairs of tones was systematically varied across a large number of trials to obtain a reliable estimate of a child's threshold on the ART (i.e., the smallest ISI at which the child could reliably judge the order of the two tones). There was no statistically reliable difference on the ART between the control children and the children with dyslexia and normal language skills. However, the controls were reliably better on this task than the children with dyslexia and language impairments. The children with dyslexia and normal language skills showed a very wide range of performance on the ART. Further exploration of this group showed that those children with the weakest language skills were the worst on the ART (there was a correlation of −.62 between language scores (on the Clinical Evaluation of Language Fundamentals, CELF) and the ART in this group). A subgroup of children with dyslexia with better oral language skills (9/16) was identical to the controls on the ART. This study shows clearly that problems on the ART are associated with oral language difficulties in children, but not with dyslexia. There were only weak correlations between ART thresholds and a measure of nonword reading in the whole sample, suggesting that this measure is only weakly associated with children's phonological skills.

In summary, it seems that a deficit in rapid auditory perceptual skills cannot account for the phonological impairments found in children with dyslexia. When problems on these tasks do occur in samples of children with dyslexia they appear to be restricted to a subgroup of children who show oral language difficulties. This pattern is the same as for measures of speech perception. Problems on speech perception and rapid auditory perceptual tasks both seem to be associated with language difficulties rather than reading difficulties, though in the absence of longitudinal data it is difficult to rule out the possibility that they are a distal cause of reading impairments for a subset of children.

There remain other variants of the theory that phonological deficits in dyslexia may arise from a basic auditory perceptual impairment. Witton et al. (1998) suggested that problems in detecting dynamically changing auditory stimuli may be critical. They reported that adults with a history of dyslexia were impaired on both visual and auditory tasks requiring dynamic processing. Similarly, Witton, Stein, Stoodley, Rosner, and Talcott (2002) found that adults with a history of dyslexia had problems in detecting frequency modulation (variations in pitch) but not amplitude modulation (variations in loudness). However, in a study with a large sample of children, some of whom were dyslexic and some of whom had attentional problems, Hulslander et al. (2004) showed that these same tasks did not account for variations in reading ability, once the effects of IQ had been controlled (whereas conventional measures of phonological abilty, including phoneme awareness, RAN, and nonword repetition, did account for substantial amounts of variance in reading ability). This finding raises strong doubt about the theory that reading problems have any specific relationship with problems in perceiving dynamic auditory stimuli. A similar conclusion with even larger samples comes from Heath, Bishop, Hogben, and Roach (2006).

One final variant of the theory is that the phonological impairments seen in children with dyslexia may be caused by a deficit in the perception of rhythm (or amplitude envelope onsets; Goswami et al., 2002). This is measured in tasks requiring children to detect discrete beats in signals that vary in loudness. Goswami et al. (2002) reported data from 24 children with dyslexia, 25 CA controls and 24 younger RA controls. The task involved children detecting beats in stimuli that varied in how suddenly a tone changed in loudness. The stimulus that changed in loudness most suddenly could be perceived easily as containing beats; the question was how much more slowly the change in loudness could be made while still being judged to contain beats (rather than being judged to be slowly varying). The children with dyslexia were significantly worse at detecting the beats than children of the same age ($d = 1.42$, a very large effect) but not significantly different from RA controls ($d = 0.66$, a medium effect). It is reported that beat detection thresholds correlated with reading and spelling ability (and also mathematics ability) but unfortunately these correlations are only reported for the sample of children as a whole, which will tend to inflate their magnitude.

A concern about this study is that the main comparison is actually between children who are markedly superior in reading ability (the CA controls had an average reading standard score of 142) and a group of children who, though described as dyslexic, appear to have average levels of single word reading for their age (an average reading standard score of 101). The theory advocated is that the deficit in rhythm (beat) perception is the origin of a difficulty in syllable segmentation, which in turn leads to the phonological deficit seen in children with dyslexia. It remains to be seen whether further studies will demonstrate the predicted longitudinal relationship between specific problems of rhythm perception and the phonological difficulties seen in children with dyslexia.

Possible alternative causal theories of dyslexia

There is strong evidence that a phonological deficit is one cause of the reading difficulties seen in many children with dyslexia. It remains possible, or even likely,

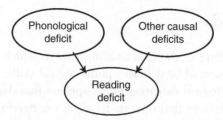

Figure 2.12   Path diagram showing putative causes of dyslexia.

that other factors also may play a causal role in the disorder. It is important to distinguish two ways in which additional causes might operate. An additional cause might operate via its effect on phonological skills (we have already considered two such additional causes of this sort (auditory perceptual or speech perceptual deficits), which some have suggested might be the ultimate cause of a phonological impairment). Other causes might, however, operate separately from the phonological deficit. In a path diagram the arrows from these causes would lead directly to reading, or at least would not lead to reading via the phonological deficit (Figure 2.12).

The most widely studied alternative causal theories of dyslexia have been the Automatization/Cerebellar Deficit Theory (Nicolson & Fawcett, 1990; Nicolson, Fawcett, & Dean, 2001) and the Visual Perceptual (e.g., Lovegrove, Martin, & Slaghuis, 1986) or Visual Attentional Deficit (e.g., Facoetti & Molteni, 2001) theories. Unfortunately, space in this chapter precludes giving a full review of the many studies that have assessed these alternative theories.

While it may seem plausible that problems in visual perceptual or attentional processes could contribute to causing problems in learning to read, attempts to establish this have so far met with very limited success. The two dominant approaches to this idea have produced a complex and sometimes contradictory pattern of findings. A recent methodologically thorough study by Heath, Bishop, Hogben, and Roach (2006) concludes that "deficient perceptual processing in dyslexia may be an associated (and inconsistent) marker of neurological abnormality rather than being causally implicated in reading difficulties" (p. 905). This is essentially the same conclusion that Hulme (1988) and Ramus (2004) reached earlier. While a few individuals with dyslexia have been described who show good phonology coupled with visual processing impairments (Goulandris & Snowling, 1991; Romani, Ward, & Olson, 1999; Valdois, Bosse, & Tainturier, 2004), it seems unlikely that such visual impairments are widespread in dyslexia and their causal status is unknown.

The Automatization/Cerebellar Deficit Theory arose from studies showing that children with dyslexia had difficulties on dual tasks involving motor skills (e.g., balancing and counting at the same time; Nicolson & Fawcett, 1990). However, a study by Raberger and Wimmer (2003) and a meta-analysis by Rochelle and Talcott (2006) suggest that these difficulties may reflect the presence of comorbid ADHD in the children with dyslexia who were included in the research samples. In our view neither this theory nor the visual perceptual/attentional theories are well supported by current evidence.

Etiology of Dyslexia

We have painted a picture of dyslexia as a disorder in which children's progress in learning to read is hampered by deficient phonological skills. We now need to consider why these phonological deficits arise. It appears that dyslexia is heavily influenced by genetic risk factors that operate to affect the development of some of the language systems in the left hemisphere of the brain. However, genes act through environments (Rutter, 2005a) and the environment in which children learn to read also has a marked impact on reading disorders.

The genetics of dyslexia

It has been known for many years that dyslexia runs in families (DeFries Vogler, & LaBuda, 1986) and this suggests that genetic factors play a role. One way of looking at this is in terms of familial risk: 40% of boys and 18% of girls with a dyslexic parent are also dyslexic (Pennington & Smith, 1988). More definite evidence for genetic factors comes from twin studies. Early studies showed that, as expected for a genetically influenced trait, concordance rates for dyslexia were higher in MZ than DZ pairs (e.g., Bakwin, 1973). In the largest twin study of dyslexia to date (The Colorado Twin Study; DeFries, Fulker, & LaBuda, 1987) the concordance rates were 68% for MZ and 38% for DZ twins, which suggests that genetic influences are moderately important (DeFries & Alarcon, 1996).

One drawback to looking at concordance rates is that the method is only really suited to discrete categories that are more typical of physical characteristics such as eye color. However, it is clear that dyslexia is not well described in this way; children have reading problems that vary in degree. To overcome this problem, as described in Chapter 1, DeFries and Fulker (1985) developed a method of genetic analysis for twin data dealing with continuous traits such as reading ability. In these analyses the reading test scores for twins are compared. In the Colorado study a child with dyslexia, who was also a twin, was first selected for the study. These children, selected for having a disorder, are referred to as probands. The DeFries and Fulker method examines the extent to which the MZ and DZ co-twins' reading scores resemble their probands' scores. If genetic similarity influences the extent to which a child has a reading disorder, the MZ co-twins should be more similar to their probands than are the DZ co-twins. This is exactly what was found. In fact, the calculations resulted in an estimated group heritability of around 50% for dyslexia. This can be interpreted as meaning that 50% of the difference in reading scores between the probands and the general population is accounted for by genetic differences. However, heritability appears to be higher (and therefore the role of environmental factors lower) among children with more severe reading disorders (Bishop, 2001) and among those with higher IQs (Olson, Datta, & DeFries, 1999). So, genetic factors may be more important contributory causes of dyslexia in some subgroups of children than others.

An important extension of the behavior-genetic method allows examination of whether two heritable deficits are caused by the same or different genes. Using such an approach, Gayan and Olson (2001) estimated the degree of common genetic influence across literacy and phonological awareness skills in twins selected for poor reading ability. Although phonological decoding (assessed by nonword reading) and orthographic skills (assessed by judging which of two plausible spellings for a word was the correct one) were both significantly heritable, there was only partial overlap between the genetic influences on these variables. Deficits in phonological decoding and poor phonological awareness had shared genetic origins, whereas the genetic influences on orthographic deficits appeared to be somewhat independent of those on phonological awareness. Arguably, this is what might be expected given the role that exposure to print plays in the development of mature orthographic representations.

It is generally accepted that the risk of inheriting dyslexia will depend upon the combined influence of many genes of small effect, as well as environmental influences. In a complex trait such as reading ability there is likely to be a large set of gene loci (quantitative trait loci, QTLs) that are implicated. Various strategies have been used in molecular genetic studies of dyslexia (Fisher & DeFries, 2002). In linkage analysis, DNA from pairs of affected siblings is compared to find regions of the genome that show linkage. Linkage refers to the fact that genes that are close together on a chromosome tend to travel together across generations. Thus, sequences of DNA that are similar across affected relatives can throw light on gene variations that may play a role in determining dyslexia. However, it is important to be aware that finding linkage to a marker only narrows down the search for genes to particular regions of DNA and it is not the same as finding a specific gene.

At the time of writing, the strongest evidence for linkage with dyslexia is a site on the short arm of chromosome 6. The first study to identify this QTL for dyslexia was that of Cardon et al. (1994) using a sample of siblings and fraternal twins. When one sibling had dyslexia, the other sibling was more likely to also have dyslexia if both shared the same form of certain marker genes on the short arm of chromosome 6. Other linkages that have replicated in at least some samples are on the short arms of chromosomes 2, 3 and 18 and the long arm of chromosome 15 (see Fisher et al., 2002; Fisher & Francks, 2006; Parachini, Scerri, & Monaco, 2007, for reviews) and a whole genome scan also identified potential gene loci on chromosomes 13, 21 and the X chromosome.

Most recently, evidence has been presented for a single gene on chromosome 6p (KIAA0319) being a susceptibility locus for developmental dyslexia (Cope et al., 2005). It is known that this gene is expressed in brain tissue though its precise form of action remains unknown. A follow-up study (Harold et al., 2006) has provided a confirmation of this gene locus along with additional evidence pointing specifically to single nucleotide polymorphisms (variations in single base pairs), which it is speculated may be involved in regulating the action of the gene. These results are both complicated and exciting and show that considerable progress is being made towards identifying some of the many specific genes that appear to be implicated in the development of dyslexia.

Environmental influences on dyslexia

In addition to genetic influences, environmental factors, sometimes in combination, also contribute to a child's risk of developing reading problems. It has been known since the epidemiological studies of the 1970s that dyslexia is more common in children from poorer socio-economic circumstances. Direct literacy-related activities in the home are also important and mother's educational level affects the literacy environment they provide for their children (Whitehurst & Lonigan, 1998); however, this may have more of an impact on reading comprehension than on decoding skills (Stevenson & Fredman, 1990).

Importantly, from very early in development, children differ in their interest in books, and where parents themselves have literacy problems there may be limited reading-related experiences on offer in the home (Petrill, Deater-Deckard, Schatsneider, & Davis, 2005). Outside of the home, there is also evidence that schooling can make a substantial difference to reading attainments (Rutter & Maughan, 2002). Over time, the cumulative impact of such processes leads to massive variations in children's exposure to print, a factor known to have an independent effect on reading progress (Cunningham & Stanovich 1990).

Another potent environmental influence that we discussed earlier is the language of learning. Dyslexia is associated with poor decoding and poor phoneme awareness in opaque orthographies such as English, but manifests itself primarily as a problem with reading fluency and spelling in transparent orthographies. In turn, reading instruction practices tend to be different in different languages and these too can be expected to have an effect, though at present this is confounded with language and therefore is not well researched.

Brain processes in dyslexia

Considerable progress has been made over the last decade or so in identifying the brain structures responsible for dyslexia. The evidence reviewed earlier showed that language processes (particularly phonological processes) are impaired in dyslexia. We would therefore expect that the brain regions responsible for language processing will be impaired in dyslexia (see Figure 2.13). In the majority of people, language is lateralized in the left hemisphere of the brain. Clear evidence for this comes from studies of adults who have suffered brain damage. Damage to Broca's area (in the left frontal lobe) typically results in problems in speech production, while damage to Wernicke's area (in the left temporal lobe, behind Broca's area) typically results in problems with understanding speech. We might therefore expect to find abnormalities in the structure and function of these and other left hemisphere language systems in dyslexia.

Evidence from studies of brain structure and function broadly supports these predictions (for a review, see Grigorenko, 2001). At a gross level it appears that the brains of individuals with dyslexia may show less structural asymmetry (in the normal population there is a tendency for the left language-dominant hemisphere to be larger; Leonard et al., 1993). At a more specific level it has been suggested that

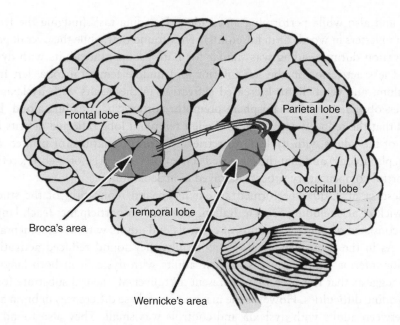

Figure 2.13   Schematic diagram showing the major lobes of the brain and Broca's and Wernicke's areas.

there is less asymmetry in the planum temporale (e.g., Hynd et al., 1990) and the insula (Pennington et al., 2000) of dyslexic brains (both of these are temporal lobe structures implicated in language processing; cf. Eckert, 2004). It should be emphasized that these findings of average group differences conceal great variability among individuals in the relative sizes of these and other brain structures. There is always going to be at best an indirect relationship between assessments of the size of brain regions and how effectively these regions operate. Nevertheless, these findings from studying brain structure are broadly in line with what we would expect: Left hemisphere brain regions appear to show abnormalities of development in dyslexia.

Arguably, more compelling evidence comes from studies of brain activity in children and adults with dyslexia (Demb, Poldrack, & Gabrieli, 1999; Grigorenko, 2001). It is useful to start by considering the brain regions activated in normal adult skilled reading. Thus, when normal adults read words it appears that a circuit of at least three left hemisphere regions is activated: the left mid-fusiform, left anterior fusiform, and left superior temporal cortex (see Plate 2). It appears that the left mid-fusiform is involved in processes associated with uniquely identifying objects and may also be involved in naming. The left anterior fusiform area appears to be involved in retrieving semantic information, while the left superior temporal region appears to be involved in processes related to articulation.

In light of these brain imaging studies of normal reading we can consider results from studies of people with developmental dyslexia. Brunswick, McCrory, Price, Frith, & Frith (1999) compared six adults who had been diagnosed with developmental dyslexia with six control participants while reading words or nonwords aloud, and also while performing an incidental reading task (judging the features present in letters in words or in falsefonts). They found that while the overall pattern of activation during reading was similar for both groups, the adults with dyslexia showed less activation in the left inferior and middle temporal lobe, left frontal operculum, and cerebellum. Increased activation in the adults with dyslexia was, however, observed in left hemisphere premotor cortex when reading aloud. It was argued that the reduced activation in the left temporal lobe reflected deficits in the ability of the adults with dyslexia to retrieve the pronunciations of printed words (lexical phonology) and that the increased activation in the premotor cortex reflected an effortful compensatory process involved in articulation.

Paulesu et al. (2001) performed an extension and replication of the study by Brunswick et al. including French, Italian, and English participants (each language group consisted of matched groups of controls and adults with developmental dyslexia). As in the Brunswick et al. (1999) study, they found reduced activation in posterior inferior temporal areas in their adults with dyslexia in both languages, which suggests that this area may represent a "universal" neural substrate for dyslexic reading difficulties. However the magnitude of these differences in brain activation between adults with dyslexia and controls was small. They also found some subtle differences, such that for English readers areas associated with naming were more strongly activated during reading, while in Italian readers brain areas associated with decoding were more strongly activated. These differences seem to parallel the differences between English and Italian orthography. Reading an irregular script such as English seems to call on areas associated with naming objects, which perhaps suggests a greater involvement of whole word phonology when reading English. Italian is a highly regular script and brain regions concerned with mapping letters onto sounds seem to be more highly activated. These differences though are a matter of degree, and there is extensive overlap in the brain regions involved in both languages. Nevertheless, such results are a tantalizing demonstration of how the learning environment affects the setting up of the neural circuitry of the brain.

Silani et al. (2005) went on to analyze structural MRI scans collected by Paulesu et al. from the same participants with dyslexia who had participated in the cross-language study. The technique used was voxel-by-voxel morphometry, which allows detailed analysis of the density of white matter (nerve fibers) and gray matter (nerve cell bodies) in different brain regions. An important finding of this study was that people with dyslexia showed increases as well as decreases in gray matter density compared to controls in brain regions that showed underactivity during reading (and also in naming). The increases in gray matter density were observed in regions slightly posterior to the left middle temporal gyrus where there was an area of apparent atrophy. Moreover, the increases in gray matter correlated negatively with reading performance such that individuals with more gray matter in these areas had slower reading speed (see Plate 3). A further finding was of less dense white matter in the connecting regions of the speech processing system, including Broca's area (frontal and parietal arcuate fasciculus). In contrast, examination of regions of the cerebellum and visual cortex, implicated by some in the etiology of dyslexia, did not reveal abnormalities. Together these findings point to reduced connectivity in the distributed temporoparietal and frontal networks that are involved in reading and, in particular, phonological and decoding processes. The findings converge with those reported by S. Shaywitz et al. (1998) from an fMRI study of young people with longstanding reading problems since childhood. This study shows that although the persistent poor readers activated posterior reading circuits to the same extent as controls, they did not show normal connectivity between these regions and frontal language areas.

Other brain imaging studies of adults with developmental dyslexia have explored the neural mechanisms underlying the phonological deficit that we have argued is the cognitive basis of dyslexia. In one of the first studies of this sort, Paulesu et al. (1996) compared rhyming and working memory tasks in a PET study with adults with dyslexia. In the rhyming task people had to judge if a pair of consonants rhymed (do P and B rhyme?) and this was compared to a test in which they had to make a judgment about the similarity in shape between a pair of Korean letters. In the memory task people had to detect when one of a pair of letters was presented again in a following sequence. In the rhyme judgment task the adults with dyslexia showed less activation in Wernicke's area and in the left insula amongst other regions, and in the verbal working memory task they showed less activation in several left hemisphere regions, including the insula (see Plate 4). It was suggested that the reduced activation of the insula in both tasks may reflect a "disconnection" between posterior language regions (Wernicke's area) and more frontal language areas (inferior frontal cortex) in dyslexia. S. Shaywitz et al. (1998) used fMRI to study phonological processing in children with dyslexia and found evidence of reduced left hemisphere activation in several left hemisphere regions, including Wernicke's area.

In summary, studies using brain imaging converge on the conclusion that left hemisphere language areas (temporo-parietal cortex) do not function normally in dyslexia (see Price & McCrory, 2005, for a more detailed review). However, the study of brain differences in dyslexia is still at a relatively early stage and although there is some consistency across studies it is difficult to evaluate the causal status of findings. It has to be remembered that reading experience (which may be reduced in people with dyslexia who have found learning to read very difficult) will potentially affect the structure and functional characteristics of brain circuits involved in reading. In this view some of the differences in brain activation patterns seen in people with dyslexia when reading, or performing phonological tasks, may be a consequence rather than a cause of their reading problems. However, evidence for the probable causal role of impairments of brain activation in the development of dyslexia comes from a recent longitudinal study by Hoeft et al. (2007). In this study some 64 children with reading difficulties (who were receiving a variety of reading interventions) were given a range of cognitive measures (including reading, IQ, and phonological processing abilities) as well as a reading task (judging whether pairs of written words rhymed) during which brain activation was measured with fMRI. Patterns of brain activation during the rhyme judgment task (particularly in the right fusiform, middle occipital, and left middle temporal gyri) were longitudinal predictors of increases in decoding ability (nonword reading skills) in these children, and combining these predictors with a range of relevant behavioral measures (including reading, IQ, and phonological skills) gave better predictions of the development of decoding than did the behavioral measures alone. Thus these results suggest that patterns of brain activation seen in a simple reading task can improve predictions of later reading skills better than purely behavioral measures. This in turn is consistent with the idea that such patterns of brain activation may tap into differences in brain function that are causally related to children's ability to learn to read.

With this in mind, another promising way forward is the investigation of the neural correlates of dyslexia in infancy, focusing on children born to families with a history of reading problems. It can be anticipated that some 50% of such children will develop dyslexia. The challenge then is to see if measures of brain response at this early stage in development are predictive of reading status later in childhood. As yet, only preliminary data speak to this issue (e.g., Richardson, Leppänen, Leiwo, & Lyytinen, 2003).

The etiology of dyslexia: A summary

It appears that dyslexia is a disorder strongly influenced by genetic risk factors (at least in many cases). Though the pattern of inheritance for dyslexia is not completely understood, a number of gene markers and one candidate gene have been identified that are associated with the disorder. However, it is likely that many genes in various combinations are involved (polygenic inheritance). These genetic mechanisms must act to influence the development of brain mechanisms that underlie our ability to learn to read. In dyslexia there is evidence for both structural and functional differences in various left hemisphere brain systems that are involved in spoken language and in reading, but the causes of these differences are poorly understood. The language of learning makes a difference to the manifestations of dyslexia and the problem is likely to be exacerbated when combined with social disadvantage.

A Cognitive Theory of Dyslexia

The evidence we have reviewed suggests that the predominant cognitive cause of dyslexia is a deficit in the phonological system (the part of the language system specialized for speech–sound processing). Although other causes have been mooted, the evidence suggests that many of these may reflect comorbidities between dyslexia and other developmental disorders (e.g., ADHD), or if they are causally implicated then this is likely to be to exacerbate the risk of dyslexia rather than as a primary risk factor.

The pervasive phonological deficits seen in dyslexia seem to depend upon problems in the left hemisphere brain systems that subserve speech and language processes (and the development of these systems presumably is under some degree of genetic influence). In this view, the phonological deficits in dyslexia (and presumably the neural correlates of these deficits) will be present during the preschool years and persist after reading develops. However, there are individual differences in dyslexia with respect to the precise pattern and severity of impairments across phonological domains, perhaps suggesting a diffuse pattern of brain difference. It is clear that there are different developmental trajectories that lead to dyslexia (Lyytinen et al., 2006) and it seems that dyslexia can occur in a pure form (as a specific deficit in speech processing mechanisms) or in the context of broader oral language difficulties (Snowling, 2008). In both cases, at the cognitive level this can be conceptualized as a delay or a difficulty in the development of segmental (phonemically structured) phonological representations.

When a child reaches the age of formal reading instruction with nonsegmental or coarse-grained phonological representations, this creates a significant obstacle to reading progress (at least in alphabetic writing systems). Within the triangle model (Plaut et al., 1996), the development of the phonological pathway (the foundation of reading) depends upon the creation of mappings between fine-grained phonological representations and orthographic patterns. In this view, if the normally developing child creates mappings between representations of individual graphemes and phonemes, the child with dyslexia may make connections at a cruder level, perhaps in extreme cases simply mapping between whole printed words and their pronunciations. This idea is illustrated in Box 2.4.

Learning in this way will be slow and inefficient and will not support generalization to new words that are encountered in reading. In prose reading, context provided by meaning and syntax can help the reader to guess the correct pronunciations of words based on partial information (such as the first and last letters in a word) and this may provide an explanation for why children with dyslexia find it easier to read prose than lists of isolated words. Nation and Snowling (1998b) showed that children with dyslexia benefit more from semantic context when reading single words than RA controls. In turn, such findings suggest that the semantic pathway in the triangle model may operate to bootstrap reading in children with dyslexia who have good oral language skills.

Together, research findings suggest that individual differences in the severity of the phonological deficit in dyslexia, together with individual differences in oral language skills, may well explain the wide range of behavioral outcomes that characterize the condition from compensated to persistently poor readers. An attempt to understand individual variation in developmental dyslexia in computational terms was proposed by Harm and Seidenberg (1999). Their formulation was cast with reference to a connectionist model containing a "phonological attractor" network (see Figure 2.14). An important function of this attractor network was to repair noisy phonological inputs using knowledge represented in the network by weights on connections between input and output units. To simulate phonological dyslexia, the network's capacity to represent phonological information was reduced, which can be likened to degrading phonological representations. Harm and Seidenberg's simulations showed that the more severe the impairment that they imposed on the phonological network, the greater the nonword reading deficit. In the case of the most severe impairments, exception word reading was also affected, constituting a severe and pervasive reading disorder.

Harm and Seidenberg's simulations suggest that the severity of a child's phonological deficit will affect their reading profile. It is likely that other cognitive factors

Box 2.4   Illustration of orthography–phonology mappings in normal and atypical reading development

The diagram below tries to represent, very simply, one way of thinking about the effects of learning to read in the absence of phonemically structured representations of speech, as is hypothesized to be the case in dyslexia and perhaps in young normally developing children. For a normally developing child illustrated on the left, their representations of spoken words consist of representations that contain phonemes. In this case when the child learns to read, connections may be established between the individual letters in printed words and the phonemes they correspond to in spoken words. However, for the child with dyslexia the representations of spoken words may be relatively holistic without information about the individual phonemes in the word. In such a case the connections will be at a relatively coarse-grained level. Here we have illustrated the idea that the connections are at the whole word level, which would be an extreme case. The more general point, however, is that in the absence of phonemic representations of speech the mappings created between print and speech will be coarse grained and will not support efficient generalization to unfamiliar words.

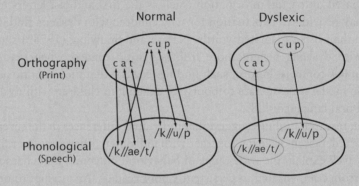

Fine-grained mappings between orthography and phonology in typical readers and coarse-grained mappings in dyslexia.

will also have a role to play in modifying reading (and spelling) performance and this is where, for example, visual difficulties may have a modifying influence. In this regard, Pennington (2006) has argued against the single deficit view of dyslexia as a phonological deficit and proposed that children with dyslexia also show speed of processing deficits. It can be argued that if speed of processing is less than optimal then this is likely to affect learning (Anderson, 1992). Within the Harm and Seidenberg model, a nonoptimal learning parameter affected the model's capacity to read exception words, with a lesser effect on nonword reading. The model predicts, therefore, that children with dyslexia who have speed of processing deficits will have

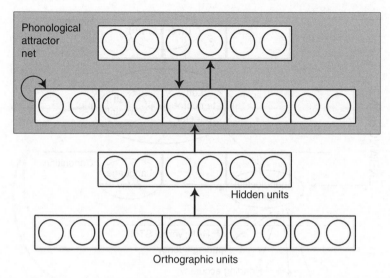

Figure 2.14   Neural network model of reading implemented by Harm and Seidenberg (1999). (Harm, M. W. and Seidenberg, M. S., Phonology, reading acquisition, and dyslexia: Insights from connectionist models, *Psychological Review* 106, p. 499, 1999, published by American Psychological Association and adapted with permission.)

poor exception word reading; to the extent that RAN measures speed of processing, then there is some evidence that this is the case (Manis, Seidenberg, & Doi, 1999).

The conceptualization of dyslexia afforded by connectionist models provides an important bridge between the cognitive and behavioral levels of explanation. Specifically these models allow us to understand how continuous variation in an underlying cognitive skill (phonology) can result in a variety of different behavioral outcomes, such as patterns of reading impairment, perhaps in interaction with other cognitive resources. Importantly, they highlight the fact that satisfactory reading development depends upon the status of phonological representations at the start of reading instruction. They also show explicitly how learning affects development and hence they embody environmental influences.

Figure 2.15 shows a path model of dyslexia, following the conventions used by Morton and Frith (1995). Bold arrows are used to indicate causal links for which there is evidence, and dotted arrows for testable hypotheses.

At the biological level, genes on chromosomes 6, 15, and 18 implicated in dyslexia are hypothesized to affect the development of left hemisphere brain networks and particularly temporoparietal cortex (these influences are depicted in Figure 2.15 as semicircles at the level of Biology). The brain differences are hypothesized to lead to problems with the development of phonological representations (either directly or mediated by delayed language development), which in turn affect reading development and related phonological processes. Within the model, a more severe phonological deficit should lead to more severe decoding problems and feedback to further reduce patterns of brain activity in regions subserving reading and phonology. However, the consequences may be less significant if the language of learning is

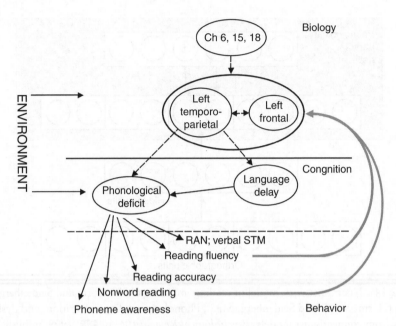

Figure 2.15   A path model of dyslexia showing a phonological deficit as the single proximal cause of a number of behavioral manifestations of dyslexia.

transparent and it is easier to establish grapheme–phoneme correspondences. Figure 2.16 includes a speed of processing impairment as an additional cognitive cause of reading difficulties (Pennington, 2006).

The prediction is that children with only speed of processing impairments will have problems with RAN, short-term memory tasks, and reading fluency, while children with double deficits in phonology and speed of processing will have more severe reading impairments. Potentially these models could be extended to include strengths as well as deficits at the cognitive level. A testable prediction is that the use of intact semantic skills, when present, might ameliorate the effects of poor reading (but not spelling) and lead to altered patterns of brain activity during reading.

Treating Dyslexia

Our understanding of dyslexia has obvious implications for treatment. Children with dyslexia have phonological difficulties that create severe problems in learning to map the letter sequences in printed words (graphemes: letters or letter combinations that stand for phonemes) onto the speech sounds that they represent (phonemes). We should expect, therefore, that teaching methods that help to overcome these phonological problems and that target the mastery of spelling–sound relationships should be particularly effective for children with dyslexia. There is a good deal of evidence that supports this prediction.

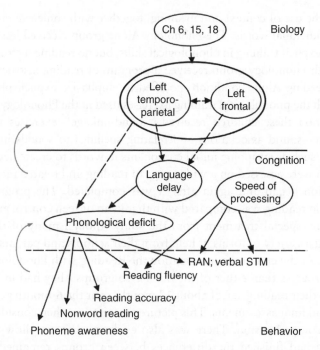

Figure 2.16 A path model of dyslexia showing separate deficits in phonology and speed of processing as causes of the behavioral manifestations of dyslexia.

The best evidence for how to treat dyslexia comes from well-controlled studies of the effectiveness of specific teaching methods. There are really two types of relevant studies: those dealing with older children with diagnosed reading problems, and those that try to prevent reading problems by intervening with young children considered to be at risk of reading problems. We will consider each of these in turn.

Teaching children with dyslexia to read

Hatcher, Hulme, and Ellis (1994) compared the effectiveness of three theoretically motivated interventions for 7-year-old poor readers. The children in this study were selected (based on a screening of all children in the county of Cumbria in the North of England) as being in roughly the bottom 15% for reading ability. Children were not excluded based on IQ, so that many, but certainly not all, of the children would be diagnosed as dyslexic.

The children were allocated to one of four matched groups at the beginning of the study. The method of intervention involved two individual half-hour lessons each week for 20 weeks. The teaching methods were based on the Reading Recovery methods developed by Clay (1985) in New Zealand, and the reading programs involved the children reading books carefully selected to be at an appropriate level of difficulty (the instructional level). There were three forms of intervention. The Reading Alone group received lessons involving reading books at the instructional level with an emphasis on the use of context and meaning, together with some exercises in reading and writing individual words. The Phonology Alone group received lessons involving intensive and explicit training in phonological skills, but no reading instruction. Finally, a Reading with Phonology group received a program of reading instruction based on that in the Reading Alone condition modified to emphasize explicit phonic training combined with the phonological training exercises used in the Phonology Alone condition. In addition these children received "sound-linkage" exercises that included practising letter–sound associations and relating spellings to sounds in words using plastic letters (such as swapping initial consonants in words to create new words).

All children were assessed on a wide range of reading and related measures before the intervention began and again after it was completed. The progress the three groups made in reading was compared with that in an unseen control group who did not receive any special treatment from the study (though many of these children were receiving a variety of forms of help from their schools and parents). The results were striking. At the end of the intervention the Reading with Phonology group had made more progress than either of the other two groups; they had in fact achieved an increase in their reading age of about 12 months over the 6-month period between their initial and final assessments. This picture was similar when considering spelling and reading comprehension. There was also evidence that at follow-up 9 months after teaching had finished the differences between groups remained, though the advantage of the Reading with Phonology group had diminished somewhat.

This study provides clear evidence that children with quite severe reading difficulties can make substantial progress if they are given highly structured individual teaching. The form of teaching that was most effective relates closely to the form of difficulty seen in dyslexia. The Reading with Phonology program directly tackled the children's phonological problems, while at the same time making explicit links between phonology and reading (by the use of sound-linkage exercises). This linkage seems critical to the success of the program because the Phonology Alone group (who actually received roughly twice as much training in phonological skills as the Reading with Phonology group) made substantial improvements in their phonological skills, but this did not translate into reliable improvements in their reading. The effectiveness of the Reading with Phonology teaching program might be related to the ideas presented earlier about how, in order to set up an efficient phonological pathway in the triangle model, the child needs to create links between the letters (or graphemes) in printed words and the phonemes in spoken words that the letters represent. It seems reasonable to suppose that the Reading with Phonology teaching program would be effective in developing the phonological pathway, because the program helps to improve the child's phonological (phonemic) representations of spoken words, while at the same time directly training connections between the phonological and orthographic representations of words through reading practice.

Further analyses of the data from this study (Hatcher & Hulme, 1999) showed that the best predictor of children's responsiveness to teaching (in terms of gains in reading accuracy) was their initial level of skill on a phoneme deletion test. However, children with higher verbal IQ made more progress in developing their reading comprehension skills.

A study by Torgesen and colleagues (Torgesen, 2001; Torgesen et al., 2001) is important in showing the size of gains that can be achieved for children with dyslexia when given sufficiently intensive instruction. In this study 60 8- to 10-year-old children with dyslexia were divided into two groups. One group was taught by the Lindamood Phoneme Sequencing (LIPS) program. In this program a particular emphasis was placed on developing children's awareness of phonemes by articulatory awareness training coupled with phonemic decoding of single words (85% of the time in the program), with just 15% of the time devoted to reading and writing practice with words and texts. The other group was given an Embedded Phonics (EP) program that involved a greater emphasis on reading text coupled with a smaller amount of direct phonic and phonemic awareness instruction. One unusual feature of the study was the intensity of the teaching involved: the children got two individual 50 min lessons each day for 8 weeks (67.5 h of teaching in 8 weeks, compared to 20 h of teaching in 20 weeks in the Hatcher et al. (1994) study).

The results of the study were very impressive. At the end of the intervention there was a small advantage for the LIPS group, but this was not statistically reliable. Both groups, however, had increased their reading accuracy scores to standard scores of around 90 (where the average for the population is 100) in comparison to standard scores in the 70–80 range at the beginning of the study. These figures mean that the children had made large strides in overcoming their reading difficulties, improving their reading scores from the severely impaired range to the lower end of the normal range. These gains were maintained at follow-up 1 and 2 years after the intervention had finished. However, it is worth noting that the children in this study remained very slow readers.

The Torgesen et al. (2001) study, together with some others (Hatcher et al., 1994; Lovett et al., 1994; Wise, Ring & Olson, 1999), indicates that systematic phonic teaching in combination with phonological awareness training is effective in helping to overcome the reading problems in dyslexia. It appears from the Torgesen et al. study that a range of different approaches that embody the basic principles of phonological awareness training and phonic reading instruction may have equivalent effects for many children with dyslexia.

Early interventions to prevent reading failure

An obvious implication of these studies is that early interventions to develop phonemic awareness and an understanding of the links between print and speech should help to prevent the development of reading difficulties in children with dyslexia. There is good evidence to support this idea.

In an early classic study Bradley and Bryant (1983) gave 4-year-old children a sound categorization test (a test assessing sensitivity to rhyme and alliteration). They selected a small subset of children with poor sound categorization skills and divided them into four groups. One group was given sound categorization training, a second group was given sound categorization combined with letter-sound training, while a third group was given semantic categorization training. The hypothesis for children who were poor at sound categorization at age 4 years was that training would improve their phonological skills and prevent the later development of reading difficulties. There was a trend for this to happen, but the greatest gains in reading were made by the children given sound categorization training in combination with letter-sound training.

More recent studies have produced impressive effects in the prevention of reading difficulties for children identified as being at risk of reading failure. Torgesen et al. (1999) gave 88 h of individual teaching to children identified as being the 12% most at risk of reading failure. The intervention started in kindergarten and carried on until second grade. The most effective intervention in this study was a version of the LIPS program described earlier. The children in this study achieved near average levels of reading accuracy and reading rate (standard scores of 99 and 97) that were maintained from second through to fourth grade. Again it is worth emphasizing the long duration and highly intensive nature of the teaching given in this study.

Hindson et al. (2005) provided an intervention involving phoneme awareness training coupled with book reading for children at family risk of dyslexia as well as for children deemed not at risk. A small group of the family at-risk children did not receive the intervention and served as a waiting list control group. The at-risk trained children improved in phoneme awareness and showed better scores on a test of print concepts after the intervention compared to the at-risk waiting list control group. However, the at-risk children were still behind the not-at-risk group in terms of letter-sound knowledge and early reading skills. When followed up 2 years later the at-risk children had weaker reading and spelling skills than the not-at-risk group. Thus the intervention probably helped the at-risk group improve their reading skills but they were not comparable to the not-at-risk group. It was found that a strong predictor of reading skills at the end of the study could be made from kindergarten phoneme awareness skills, and that children with better phoneme awareness responded better to the intervention than children with weaker initial skills.

Hatcher, Hulme, and Snowling (2004) compared four different methods of teaching delivered on a whole-class basis during the first 2 years of formal schooling. The basis of all methods was a highly structured phonically based teaching program (Reading Alone) and this program was supplemented either with rhyme-level phonological awareness training (Reading with Rhyme) or with phoneme awareness training (Reading with Phoneme) or both (Reading with Rhyme and Phoneme). For normally developing children there were no differences in reading skills at the end of the program between the four methods. However, for children deemed to be at risk of reading failure at the beginning of the study, the two conditions involving oral phoneme awareness training showed small but reliable improvements. These interventions, however, were not sufficient to prevent reading difficulties in the at-risk children, though they did result in less severe reading problems than in the other two methods of teaching. Early phoneme awareness skills were a powerful predictor of later reading skills in all of the groups of children (and a much more powerful predictor than rhyme-level skills). This study, like the Hindson et al. study, suggests that phoneme awareness training is a useful component of programs designed to help prevent early reading difficulties. Both studies, however, underline the fact that while interventions may help to ameliorate reading problems they do not eliminate reading problems in samples of at-risk children. It seems likely that to prevent the development of reading problems in such children would require very intensive interventions over extended periods of time.

Treating and preventing reading difficulties in dyslexia: A summary

Theoretically based interventions for dyslexia involving highly structured phonic reading instruction coupled with activities designed to improve phonemic awareness are effective in overcoming reading problems characteristic of dyslexia. Similarly, equivalent approaches applied to younger children deemed to be at risk of developing reading problems are effective in helping to reduce these children's reading problems. None of these approaches represent quick fixes however. Overcoming, or preventing, reading problems in dyslexia requires many hours of highly skilled and intensive teaching. Furthermore, it is likely that many children with dyslexic difficulties will need ongoing specialist teaching to support the development of their reading skills for extended periods of time: The miracle cure so far eludes us.

Chapter Summary

Developmental dyslexia is a common learning difficulty that occurs in around 3–4% of children. The disorder commonly co-occurs with a range of other problems, including attentional, language, and motor difficulties. The problems of children with dyslexia seem to reflect basic problems in the development of brain mechanisms concerned with processing speech sounds (phonological mechanisms). Though a range of other possible causes has been investigated extensively, so far the only well-supported causal hypothesis is that the majority of cases of dyslexia reflect this "phonological core deficit." It appears that genetic risk factors are a powerful causal influence on the development of dyslexia. Studies of the treatment of dyslexia are well advanced and we know a great deal about how to treat or to prevent the development of these children's reading problems. Interventions that involve a combination of highly structured reading instruction coupled with training in phoneme awareness are effective for both treating and helping to prevent the development of the disorder. It is a pity that many children who would benefit greatly from such specialist teaching programs still do not receive them.

3

Reading Disorders II: Reading Comprehension Impairment

Children with reading comprehension impairment (who are sometimes referred to simply as poor comprehenders) have a pattern of reading difficulties that contrasts sharply with that seen in dyslexia. These children recognize words accurately, but have problems understanding the meaning of what they can read aloud with normal accuracy and speed. These children have been much less studied and are less well recognized than children with dyslexia and we will say correspondingly less about this group.

Definition and Prevalence

As we noted in Chapter 2, DSM-IV does not distinguish between difficulties with reading comprehension and difficulties with reading accuracy. As the nature and origins of these two difficulties are quite different, it is crucial to make a clear distinction between them. Reading comprehension impairment is easy to define: In this disorder children show a marked deficit on standardized tests of reading comprehension in contrast to much better scores on tests of reading accuracy. A common criterion for selecting children for research studies has been to require children to have age-appropriate reading accuracy scores but reading comprehension scores at least one year below their expected level. Given the difficulties of interpreting age-equivalent scores (e.g., how much worse is a lag of 1 year's reading age in a child aged 7 years compared to a lag of 1 year's reading age in a child aged 14 years?), a more reasonable diagnostic criterion would simply be to demand that reading comprehension is at least one standard deviation below a child's reading accuracy score on a well-standardized test.

There have been no population-based studies of this disorder but it seemed from early studies that it might be relatively common. Stothard and Hulme (1992) and Nation and Snowling (1997) both identified roughly 10% of unselected samples of primary school children as having significant reading comprehension impairment in the presence of relatively good reading accuracy. However, our own more recent research has suggested that the prevalence of this reading profile varies according to school setting, with fewer poor comprehenders in classrooms in more advantaged catchment areas.

Another factor that may affect the prevalence of poor comprehenders in population samples is the comprehension test used to assess reading. Different tests of reading comprehension place different demands on word-level decoding skills and hence vary in their validity as tests of reading comprehension (as opposed to decoding; Keenan & Betjemann, 2006; Nation & Snowling, 1997). For example, it is sometimes the case that comprehension questions can be answered solely based on general knowledge and without reference to the text.

In the UK, the test that has been most widely used for the assessment of reading comprehension is the Neale Analysis of Reading Ability (Neale, 1989, 1997) in which children read short passages and answer questions about them. Bowyer-Crane and Snowling (2005) analyzed the comprehension questions that make up this test and found that in addition to tapping literal facts they primarily required the use of cohesive inferences. Cohesive inferences are those that are needed to maintain links between different parts of a text (e.g., the processes that are involved in identifying the referents of pronouns) and are therefore critical to understanding. In contrast, the comprehension questions on another test of reading comprehension in use in the UK at the time (The Wechsler Objective Reading Dimensions (WORD); Wechsler, 1993) primarily assessed the ability to make elaborative inferences. Elaborative inferences are made to add information that is not contained in the text. While these undoubtedly lead to a richer or fuller representation of the text, they are not essential for comprehension. Bowyer-Crane and Snowling (2005) went on to show that some children who were considered to have comprehension difficulties according to performance on the Neale test scored within the normal range for comprehension on the WORD test.

The Development of Reading Comprehension: A Theoretical Framework

The role of language skills

To read and understand a text is a complex task drawing on many, if not all, of the processes involved in comprehending spoken language. As we have already said, there is a clear distinction between being able to decode, or read aloud, a passage and being able to comprehend it. Logically, adequate decoding is necessary, but not sufficient, for comprehension. This idea was formalized by Gough and Tunmer (1986) in their Simple View of Reading model. This model is expressed as the formula $R = D \times C$: Reading comprehension (R) is the product of (the result of multiplying together) decoding (D) and linguistic comprehension (C). The model formalizes the idea that an individual's reading comprehension is dependent on their decoding ability: If decoding is zero there can be no reading comprehension and, no matter how good decoding is, if language comprehension is zero there can be no reading comprehension (see Figure 3.1).

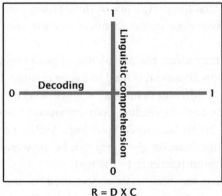

R = D X C

Figure 3.1   The Simple View of Reading model. (Adapted from Decoding, reading, and reading disability, in *Remedial and Special Education* (7) by Gough, P. and Tunmer, W. Copyright (1986) by Sage Publications Inc. Journals. Reprinted by permission of Sage Publications Inc. Journals via the Copyright Clearance Centre.)

Reading comprehension impairment is defined as poor comprehension in the presence of adequate reading accuracy. So for these children the Simple View of Reading model makes a clear prediction that the problem must lie in linguistic comprehension (C). However, in turn, linguistic comprehension depends on the interaction of different subsystems of language, namely grammar (see Box 3.1), semantics (the system of language concerned with word meaning), and pragmatics (concerned with what is relevant in a given context).

A number of studies provide evidence that is consistent with the idea that children's knowledge of word meanings, as well as their ability to deal with the grammatical structure of language, is particularly critical for reading comprehension. Muter, Hulme, Snowling, and Stevenson (2004) conducted a longitudinal study of 90 children in the first 2 years of learning to read (between the ages of roughly 4 years 9 months and 6 years 9 months), described in Chapter 2. At school entry, reading skills, letter-sound knowledge, phonological awareness, and vocabulary knowledge were assessed. A year later these assessments were repeated and in addition tests of syntactic awareness and morphological generation were given to the children.

Syntactic awareness was assessed by a word order correction task (Tunmer, 1989) in which children heard a sequence of words presented in a nonsensical order and were asked to rearrange these words to form a meaningful sentence. For example, the experimenter might say, "Ben throwing was stones," and the child was expected to respond, "Ben was throwing stones."

The morphological generation task assessed children's ability to generate inflected and derived word forms using appropriate word endings to convey a change in meaning. For each item on the test the child was shown a picture and the experimenter then said two sentences, the first sentence included the word-stem and this was followed by a second sentence in which the final word (which was omitted) had to be inflected. Put simply, the child was required to supply the missing word and this always required the child to produce a new morphological form. For example,

Box 3.1   Grammar and morphology

Grammar is the system of language concerned with word order and morphology. Syntax deals with the rules for ordering words in sentences and how these in turn affect meaning. In English, word order is critical to the meaning of sentences. Morphology is the system of language dealing with meaning components of words, and how word meanings can be altered by manipulating these components. To take a very simple example the plural form of a noun in English is usually signaled by adding the plural morpheme (-s) to a word. So we have one cake, or three cakes; in this case we have added a morpheme "s" to the word cake to signal that we are talking about more than one cake. Both morphological and syntactic skills are critical to reading comprehension.

"Here is a tree, here are three ... [trees]," or "The burglar steals the jewels, here are the jewels he ... [stole]."

At the beginning of the study (age 4 years 9 months) and a year later, reading was assessed by measures of single word reading (decoding skill), and at the end of the study (after 2 years in school) all the children completed a prose reading test (Neale Analysis of Reading Ability) in which comprehension was assessed by asking questions about the passages the children had read. For the present purposes, the main question of interest is the extent to which variations in children's syntactic and morphological skills, as well as their vocabulary knowledge, predicted their ability to comprehend what they read at the end of the study. The findings of this are summarized in a path diagram in Figure 3.2.

What this figure shows is that, statistically, children's word reading skills (i.e., decoding skills) at age 5 years 9 months are a powerful predictor of their reading comprehension skills at 6 years 9 months, but after these effects are accounted for children's vocabulary knowledge and their grammatical (syntactic and morphological) skills are additional important predictors of reading comprehension. Together, word recognition skills, vocabulary, and grammatical skills account for 86% of the differences amongst children in reading comprehension skill at the end of the study. The results from this study are exactly as we would expect from the Simple View of Reading model. This pattern provides good support for a causal theory that sees reading comprehension skills depending upon word recognition skills, children's understanding of the meanings of words (vocabulary), and how combinations of words and word elements (syntax and morphology) are used to convey meanings.

The relative importance of decoding and language comprehension skills as predictors of reading comprehension skills appears to change with age. In the very early stages of learning to read, decoding skills are of great importance because at this stage of development there may be relatively large differences in how well children

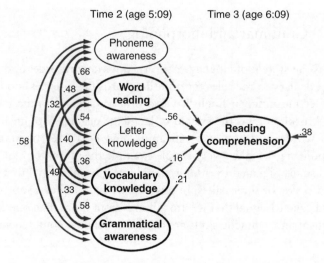

Figure 3.2   Longitudinal predictors of reading comprehension. (Muter, V., Hulme, C., Snowling, M. J., Stevenson, J., Phonemes, rimes, vocabulary and grammatical skills as foundations of early reading development, *Developmental Psychology*, 40, p. 675, 2004, published by American Psychological Association and adapted with permission.)

have mastered basic decoding skills. However, in older children who have had more reading practice, decoding may reach an adequate level for most children and then variations in linguistic comprehension may assume greater importance.

In line with this developmental view, Gough, Hoover, and Petersen (1996) reported a meta-analysis summarizing the patterns of correlations between reading comprehension, listening comprehension, and decoding skills across a wide range of ages. They found that from younger to older ages the correlation between decoding and reading comprehension tended to decrease (i.e., reading comprehension became progressively less dependent on decoding skills) while the correlation between listening comprehension and reading comprehension increased. It follows that some children who make a relatively good start in reading comprehension may succumb to difficulties when decoding skills assume less importance and language comprehension skills come to the fore. Just such a group of "late-emerging" poor readers has been described by Leach, Scarborough, and Rescorla (2003).

Skills involved in developing mental models of text

Psycholinguistic theories of reading comprehension describe the different cognitive processes that are necessary for proficient text processing. Kintsch and Rawson (2005) present a framework for thinking about the types of representations that are involved. The first level of text comprehension is a linguistic level; this refers to basic processes involved in recognizing and understanding words in a text, and assigning these words to their roles in sentences. Next the reader must construct a semantic representation of the intended meaning of a passage, and this requires processes operating at levels higher than the word. Kintsch and Rawson distinguish between a Microstructure and a Macrostructure representation of a text. The Microstructure depends upon creating a set of interrelated idea units (or propositions) in memory. A proposition is an idea unit that will often correspond to a phrase in a text (e.g., *the dog bit the man* is a phrase that maps directly onto a proposition). Deriving the meanings of propositions depends upon knowing the meanings of individual words (in this case *dog*, *man*, and *bit*) and also using grammatical rules to derive the correct meaning from those words, given their form and the way that they are ordered in the sentence (the dog did the biting here, not the man, and this happened in the past). Creating a coherent Microstructure representation of a text is a complex business, and requires at the very least knowledge of vocabulary and grammar (syntax and morphology) and also the ability to use inferences. Inferences are often needed when we are reading. For example, anaphoric reference involves understanding the object that a pronoun stands for, so in a sentence such as *John asked Peter for his ball back*, the pronoun *his* refers to John, and not Peter.

At a still higher level, Kintsch and Rawson (2005) argue that the elements in a Microstructure representation of a text need to be structured into a Macrostructure or higher-level representation involving global topics (each of which might involve a whole set of propositions and their interrelationships). For example, a very simple story might involve a beginning where two characters are introduced, a middle where a surprising event occurs, and an ending where the reasons for the surprising event become clear (story resolution). In the case of such a very simple story the Macrostructure might involve just three global topics with direct connections between them. Children's knowledge of a wider range of story schemas and of different written styles (genre) aids successful comprehension (see Box 3.2).

In the early school years, stories typically relate to familiar themes that children will have heard when read to or in oral stories. In later primary grades, children need to appreciate that authors may portray events in different ways, sometimes re-ordering time sequences and veering from expected endings. Such appreciation must depend upon experience and it is easy to see that fluent readers who read a lot will develop this awareness, while poor readers, or children who are not read to very much, will be at a disadvantage.

Both the Microstructure and Macrostructure representations are part of what Kintsch and Rawson (2005) refer to as the textbase; they are derived directly from the language on the page and they represent the different levels needed by the reader to understand the intended meaning conveyed by the passage. If a reader only had the Microstructure representation of the text they would be lost in the detail of the passage; creating a Macrostructure representation involves abstracting the broad topics in the passage (gist) and representing their interrelationships.

Pragmatic skills: Going beyond the information given

We should note at this point that both listening comprehension and reading comprehension depend upon an area of language we have not yet dealt with:

pragmatics. Pragmatic skills are related to our ability to use language appropriately to convey meanings, and make inferences that go beyond the "information given" to infer a speaker's (or writer's) intended meaning. Adequate comprehension of a passage often involves relating what we have read to our general knowledge. This involves what Kintsch and Rawson call a situation model. If we read about events in a kitchen as a meal time approaches and a mother in this passage says to her child "the table needs setting," a reasonable gloss might be "please help by putting the plates and cutlery on the table so that we can eat" but that is much more than we have read. Clearly many literary devices, such as irony, depend upon multiple layers of possible meanings that need to be processed, held in mind, and reconciled with some broader understanding of a writer's intended meaning. Reading comprehension, like language comprehension on which it is built, is a highly interactive and constructive process that draws on working memory resources. It is therefore not surprising that it is common to find that children who have reading comprehension problems also have problems understanding spoken language.

   In terms of pragmatic language skills, to read with comprehension the reader has to share the same frame of reference as the writer, as well as differentiating what is relevant from what is less so and make inferences that go beyond the literal meaning to extract the writer's intended message. One aspect of pragmatic competence that is particularly important for reading comprehension is the ability to appreciate another person's thoughts and beliefs. This skill is usually referred to as mentalizing or "theory of mind". Theory of mind has its roots in the preschool period when children begin to appreciate the feelings of another person (empathize). However, more advanced understanding is required in order to appreciate linguistic devices such joking, lying, criticism, and irony. Such nonliteral themes are often conveyed in stories. A child who lacks theory of mind will often extract an incomplete understanding of story events. We will return to consider pragmatic aspects of text

Box 3.2   Story schema

Story schemas can be thought of as templates or protocols depicting typical story structures. At a very basic level, a story consists of a beginning (e.g., Once upon a time), a middle (What happened), and an end (e.g., They all lived happily ever after). A more detailed story schema would include the characters and the setting, the event, responses to it, its resolution, and the end of the story setting. Well-known story schemas may depict common experiences, such as a birthday party, a trip to the zoo, or a day at school. Such schemas are a kind of "road map" that can be used to guide comprehension processes.

   Below is an example of a story schema taken from *The Story Maker's Chest* (Carbett, 2005).

Box 3.2 (cont'd)

Suspense story frame

1. Main character sets off to do something/go somewhere.

2. Everything is going well.

3. Suspense builds up – a sound or a glimpse of something out of place and threatening.

4. Main character runs for it or goes to investigate.

5. Main character is caught/sees what it is.

6. It turns out to be harmless.

comprehension in Chapter 8 on autism. Poor reading comprehension is a frequent characteristic of children with autism; indeed many such children conform to the behavioral profile of the "poor comprehender" and are referred to as "hyperlexic" (Nation, 1999).

These ideas about the creation of different forms of representation that underlie our ability to understand text amount in a sense to the reader actively creating a "mental model" that represents the meanings of the passage and relates it to prior knowledge (Johnson-Laird, 1983). Moreover, proficient comprehension depends upon identifying relevant information and keeping this active whilst irrelevant information is rendered less accessible. When considered in this way it is easy to appreciate that reading comprehension will tap into many different cognitive processes, including working memory. Indeed, the allocation of attention to different processes is critical to reading comprehension and depends upon executive processes. The working memory system has limited capacity and therefore it is important to combine the products of comprehension processes on-line. For example, it is not efficient to remember either individual word or sentence meanings once these have been integrated into meaningful chunks. Such detail has to be suppressed (or inhibited) to allow new incoming material to be processed. This process of losing surface detail following successful comprehension is a very general feature of language comprehension (Gernsbacher, 1985).

Comprehension monitoring

There are also a number of metacognitive processes that appear to be related to reading comprehension. One important process is comprehension monitoring, which involves three steps: planning activities prior to reading (considering what the purpose of reading is and what the reader wishes to extract from the text) , self-evaluation, and revision during reading (Ehrlich, Remond, & Tardieu, 1999). When comprehension breaks down it may be important to re-read parts of a passage, or engage in problem solving, to work out the meaning. One notable difference between children with good and poor comprehension skills is in the ability to monitor or actively check their understanding of what they are reading (Baker & Brown, 1984). If a reader fails to monitor their own comprehension, they will fail to detect when comprehension has broken down and so fail to take appropriate compensatory action (e.g., re-reading the passage, or asking someone what an unknown word means).

Summary

Reading comprehension almost certainly involves the full range of processes involved in language comprehension and some other processes that are specific to reading comprehension as well. Figure 3.3 (from Perfetti, Landi, & Oakhill, 2005) summarizes some of the major processes involved. Because reading comprehension is such a complex skill it can break down in a number of ways. As we have seen, one potent cause of reading comprehension failure is poor decoding. However, the children we

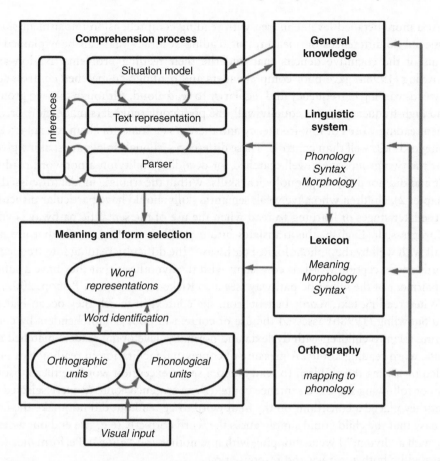

Figure 3.3 Processes involved in text comprehension. (Perfetti, C. A., Landi, N., and Oakhill, J. (2005). The acquisition of reading comprehension skill. In Snowling, M. J. and Hulme, C. (Eds) *The Science of Reading: A Handbook*, p. 229. Oxford, Blackwell.)

are concerned with in this chapter have reading comprehension problems that are not attributable to difficulties in word recognition or decoding. We now turn to consider the profile of reading skills shown by these children.

The Pattern of Reading Impairment in Poor Comprehenders

The diagnosis of reading comprehension impairment depends upon identifying children whose reading comprehension skills are much worse than expected for their level of reading accuracy. It is probably fair to say that many such children go unnoticed at school because they can read aloud accurately and fluently. The basic reading profile of a poor comprehender would be a child who reads a passage accurately but answers questions about the meaning of the passage very poorly.

At a more detailed level, children with reading comprehension impairment show some subtle differences on measures of reading accuracy that can be explained in terms of the cognitive deficits that underlie their reading problems. Nation and Snowling (1998a) gave poor comprehenders and reading-age-matched controls sets of words varying in frequency and regularity to read aloud. Although the two groups read high-frequency words equally well, the poor comprehenders made more errors when reading words of low-frequency and there was a trend for them to read exception words less well than controls. These differences, though small, are striking given that the two groups were well matched for decoding ability on a nonword reading test and did not differ in phonological skills. Within the triangle model (discussed in Chapter 2), children who have weak semantic skills should have particular difficulty in the later stages of learning to read when the use of the semantic pathway is vital to progress. In English, this translates into a problem reading words that are not dealt with well by the "phonological pathway;" the difficulty reading low-frequency words and exception words is consistent with the hypothesis that they have a subtle impairment of the semantic pathway (see also Ricketts, Nation, & Bishop, 2007).

When reading text, words benefit from the context in which they occur. Nation and Snowling (1998b) assessed the use of context in poor comprehenders by comparing them to children with dyslexia and normally developing readers matched for single word reading ability. A measure of contextual facilitation in reading was provided by asking the children to read aloud a set of exception words, either in isolation or following a spoken sentence context. The sentence contexts were selected so that they placed a constraint on the final word to be read but did not make the task so easy that the child could simply guess the word correctly (e.g., we end our assembly with a "hymn;" I went shopping with my mother and "aunt"). Performance was assessed by both accuracy and response time.

The three groups of children (poor comprehenders, children with dyslexia, controls) did not differ in the accuracy with which they read the target words in isolation, confirming that they were adequately matched for single word reading ability. However, there were differences in the effect of context. While, all children benefited from the sentence context, the size of this facilitation was greater in children with dyslexia than the controls matched for reading level; in contrast the poor comprehenders showed a smaller facilitation effect than controls.

In terms of the triangle model, semantic activation from the sentence frame primes the semantic pathway and facilitates the pronunciation of unfamiliar words (see Figure 3.4). Whereas children with dyslexia who have poor decoding skills benefited significantly from the availability of context, poor comprehenders showed little benefit. Interestingly, in the sample as a whole, the size of the contextual facilitation effect correlated with listening comprehension. As expected, the poor comprehenders who showed little effect of context had poor listening comprehension.

In summary, although children with reading comprehension impairment can be described as having intact decoding skills, the experimental studies described above reveal subtle differences in the way that these children's reading skills have developed in comparison to typically developing children.

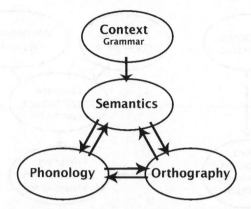

Figure 3.4   The Triangle model of Seidenberg and McClelland (1989). (Seidenberg, M. S. and McClelland, J. A distributed, developmental model of word recognition. *Psychological Review*, 96, p. 526, 2004, published by American Psychological Association and adapted with permission.)

Cognitive Explanations of Reading Comprehension Impairment

Given the pattern of reading difficulties shown by children with reading comprehension impairment (intact decoding and impaired comprehension), there are clear hypotheses about the language profiles we would expect these children to display. Since problems in decoding in dyslexia are so closely associated with phonological difficulties, we would expect phonological abilities to be normal in children with reading comprehension impairment. Conversely, we would expect the semantic and syntactic skills of these children (and possibly their pragmatic skills) to be impaired. Broadly, these expectations are confirmed by research. This leads to a causal model of reading difficulties (see Figure 3.5) in which different classes of oral language skills are causes of different types of reading difficulties. According to this model, impairments of phonological skills will lead to problems in developing word recognition skills in reading, and this in turn may hinder children's reading comprehension skills. Conversely, poor vocabulary and grammatical (morphosyntactic) skills may be a quite separate cause of problems with reading comprehension for some children whose reading accuracy skills are quite adequate (this is the pattern seen in children with reading comprehension impairment).

Phonological skills

The causal model of reading difficulties shown in Figure 3.5 implies that there is no direct relationship between phonological impairments and the profile of reading impairments found in poor comprehenders. In fact, the only way in which poor phonological skills can affect reading comprehension in this model is via word

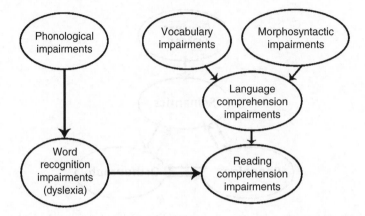

Figure 3.5   Path diagram showing causes of reading comprehension impairment.

recognition difficulties (dyslexia). Stothard and Hulme (1995) compared the phonological skills of a group of children with reading comprehension impairments to
those of a group of age-matched controls. They also included a younger group of
children matched in terms of reading comprehension on the attainment test (a so-
called comprehension-age-matched design). The poor comprehenders' performance
on a Spoonerism task (swapping phonemes between corresponding positions in
spoken words; e.g., after hearing "Shopping List" the child has to say "Lopping
Shist") was equivalent to the performance of the age-controls (and both groups
were better than the comprehension-age-matched controls). The poor comprehenders also read nonwords as well as the age-matched controls, showing that they
were as adept at using phonological information for decoding isolated words.
Similarly, the poor comprehenders spelled words well, and both groups showed
identical levels of phonetic accuracy in their spelling, that is, both groups were quite
accurate in representing the sound structure of words that they failed to spell
correctly. These results show, as expected, that poor comprehenders have intact
phonological skills that underpin the development of their decoding and spelling
skills, a finding that has since been replicated by a number of authors (e.g. Cain,
Oakhill, & Bryant, 2000; Catts, Adlof, & Ellis Weismer, 2006; Nation &
Snowling, 1998a).

As we saw in studies of dyslexia, another way of assessing children's phonological
skills is to use measures of verbal memory. Neither Stothard and Hulme (1992) nor
Cain, Oakhill, and Bryant (2004) found memory differences between poor comprehenders and age or comprehension-age-matched control groups on simple span
tasks, and Nation, Adams, Bowyer-Crane, and Snowling (1999) found that poor
comprehenders recalled lists of short and long words and nonwords as well as age-
matched (CA) controls (following the procedures used by Roodenrys, Hulme &
Brown, 1993, with typically developing children). However, in a second experiment,
the methods used by Walker and Hulme (1999) were used to assess the possible
importance of semantic coding to the recall of word sequences. Here the poor

comprehenders and controls were given lists of concrete (e.g., tooth, plate) and abstract words (e.g., luck, pride) to recall. The typically reading controls showed a large advantage in recalling the concrete words, an effect that demonstrates that access to a semantic representation of the words is important for this memory task (Walker & Hulme, 1999). Although the poor comprehenders recalled the concrete words as well as CA controls, they had significant difficulty recalling the abstract words. These results suggest that poor comprehenders have problems in the representation of abstract words, consistent with a deficit in the semantic system but not with phonological memory processes.

Working memory deficits in poor comprehenders

Phonological short-term memory is just one component of the working memory system (Baddeley, 2003a). Even though poor comprehenders do not differ from normal readers in phonological memory tasks, it remains possible that they will have difficulty when verbal information must be processed and stored simultaneously. Just such processing is required during reading in order for the products of sentence-level comprehension processes, inferences, and general knowledge to be integrated into the situation model of the text. In fact, working memory skills are strong correlates of reading comprehension (Cain, Oakhill, & Bryant, 2004; Leather & Henry, 1994; Seigneuric & Ehrlich, 2005; Seigneuric, Ehrlich, Oakhill, & Yuill, 2000).

Nation et al. (1999) assessed poor comprehenders on a sentence span task (after Daneman & Carpenter, 1980) in which children hear a series of sentences and have to decide whether each is true or false, and finally recall the final words from each of the sentences in order (see Box 3.3). This is clearly a complex task involving language processing (syntax and semantics), memory and attention, as well as executive processes. In this case, the poor comprehenders performed more poorly than the CA controls on the sentence span task, though the two groups performed at identical levels on a spatial working memory span measure. Similar findings were obtained by Cain, Oakhill, and Lemmon (2004), who found that poor comprehenders had significant difficulties on a version of the sentence span task but performed normally on a counting span task (involving counting sets of dots and then recalling the numbers counted).

An important observation made by De Beni, Palladino, Pazzaglia, and Cornoldi (1998) is that poor comprehenders not only recall fewer items correctly in verbal working memory tasks, but they also make more intrusion errors than skilled comprehenders, that is, they included in their responses more items from the memory lists that have been processed but must now be suppressed. In a study to investigate this tendency (De Beni et al., 1998, Experiment 2), two groups of adults differing in reading comprehension skills but similar in logical reasoning ability completed a listening span task in which they had to monitor word strings for the names of animals before recalling the last word in each string at the end of the span task in the usual way. Thus, this task did not require sentence processing as in the typical listening span task but tapped similar executive processes (monitoring for animal names).

Box 3.3　Examples of working memory tasks

Two tasks that are commonly used by experimental psychologists to assess working memory are counting span and sentence span. In counting span the person is shown a sequence of cards with dots on and has to count the number of dots on each card. They then recall the sequence of counts. This is a classic working memory task since it involves combining processing (counting the dots) and storage (holding previous counts in memory in order to recall them). Similarly, in the sentence span task the person hears a sequence of sentences, and has to judge whether each sentence is true before recalling the final word from each sentence.

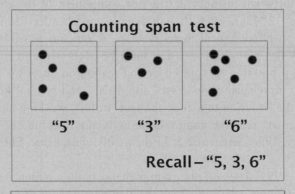

The counting span and sentence span tasks.

Once again, the two groups of participants differed in span and in the total number of words recalled; however they also differed in the intrusion errors they made. While the good comprehenders made similar proportions of intrusion errors consisting of animal and nonanimal names, the poor comprehenders produced a higher number of intrusions from animal names. Thus, poor comprehenders appear to have difficulty with the inhibition of once activated but currently irrelevant information.

Developing this argument further, Palladino, Cornoldi, De Beni, and Pazzaglia (2001) suggested that in order to comprehend text well a reader has to continuously monitor and update the contents of working memory in order to choose relevant information and suppress that which is not relevant. This, they argued, means more than just automatically updating the text representation at a local level and extends to the conscious use of updating strategies. In order to investigate whether good and poor comprehenders differ in their ability to update the contents of working memory, Palladino et al. (2001) carried out a series of five experiments using various updating tasks (see Box 3.4). The basic paradigm used in all five experiments was the same. Lists of words were presented at the rate of one per second and the participant had to monitor the words in the list (e.g., judge the size of each item represented by the words in the list). At the end of each list, the participant (who was an undergraduate student of above or below average comprehension skill) had to respond with, for example, the three or the five smallest items. At the end of the experiment, they were unexpectedly asked to recall all of the items presented.

The experiment yielded a number of different measures. Of most importance here are the number of items correctly recalled from the lists presented for updating and the number of intrusion errors (words presented in the list but not the target ones). In general, poor comprehenders performed more poorly on the updating task and made

---

Box 3.4   The memory updating task

In one version of the memory updating task used by Palladino et al. (2001) (see text), participants were presented with lists of words comprising familiar animals or objects together with abstract words. The task was to monitor the size of the concrete words (animals/objects).

The following is an example of the list containing animals (which was presented in Italian):

Meeting
Sense
Woodpecker
Passion
Law
Cow
Happiness
Amount
Caterpillar
Lamb
Feast
Frog

At the end of the list, the participant had to respond with the three smallest items: *woodpecker, caterpillar, frog.*

more intrusion errors, although at final recall the two groups performed similarly. This pattern of performance suggests that poor comprehenders do not differ from good comprehenders in overall memory capacity but that they have more difficulty suppressing irrelevant information that has been activated in memory.

Taken together, these findings suggest that success in both the working memory task and in reading comprehension may be related not only to the ability to select relevant information but also to suppress irrelevant information in memory. Furthermore, performance worsens as memory updating demands increase. The participants in these studies differ somewhat from those that have been used in the research focusing on children, and no information is available concerning the language skills of the participants who differed in reading comprehension ability. It would be important to explore these tasks in children with reading comprehension impairments and to relate problems on the memory updating tasks to the patterns of oral language difficulties that are common in these children. Problems of establishing the causal status of these memory updating effects remain. It could be that problems in memory updating are a cause of comprehension difficulties; alternatively, it might be that language difficulties are primary and that these in turn underlie the difficulties on the memory updating tasks (which always involve manipulating verbal materials).

Language comprehension problems in poor comprehenders

There is good evidence that poor comprehenders have problems on measures of oral language comprehension, just as they have problems in reading comprehension (Catts et al., 2006). Poor comprehenders typically show poorer knowledge of word meanings on standardized tests of vocabulary (e.g., Nation & Snowling, 1998b) and they often obtain lower scores on tests of verbal IQ (Stothard & Hulme, 1995).

Stothard and Hulme (1992) made a direct assessment of poor comprehenders' oral language comprehension skills at the sentence and passage level. In one test, children listened as passages from the Neale Analysis of Reading Comprehension test were read aloud to them and then answered questions about these passages. The poor comprehenders answered fewer comprehension questions than age-matched controls. The groups were also given the Test for the Reception of Grammar (TROG; Bishop, 1983) in which they heard a sentence and had to choose the picture (from a set of four) that corresponded to the sentence. Once again the poor comprehenders performed less well on this test than age-matched control children and performed only as well as younger comprehension-age-matched controls. Similar findings have been reported on tests of grammatical understanding (Catts et al., 2006) and on tests of grammatical sensitivity (Nation & Snowling, 2000).

One area of language processing that has attracted considerable interest in relation to text comprehension is anaphoric reference. Anaphors are linguistic devices that ensure cohesion within or between sentences. For example, in the following discourse: *James signaled to the waitress at the end of the restaurant. The waitress brought the bill*, the anaphor is the repeated word *waitress*. More usually, *waitress* would be replaced by the pronoun *she* or in some circumstances a general term. In each case, it is necessary to link the anaphor with its antecedent for successful comprehension.

According to Ehrlich and colleagues (Ehrlich, Remond, & Tardieu, 1999; Megherbi & Ehrlich, 2005) poor comprehenders have an impairment of discourse-level processing that affects their processing of anaphora, and in particular pronouns. In French the pronoun system is complex and in addition to signaling syntactic function (subject versus object) it also marks gender (for animate and inanimate objects) and number (singular versus plural). Megherbi and Ehrlich (2005) compared good and poor comprehenders in a cross-modal naming task in which children heard two sentences and had to complete the second sentence by selecting an appropriate pronoun from two displayed on a screen. The pronoun was either consistent with the agent of the sentence (Probe A) or inconsistent (Probe B). For example (adapted from p. 727):

After a long time away, Ellie (A) had dinner with Sebastian (B) in a restaurant.
[Continuation] She chatted cheerfully with:
    [Probe A] him
    [Probe B] her.

Skilled comprehenders showed a significant consistency effect; they could select the pronoun faster if it was consistent with the agent in the sentence than if it was inconsistent. The magnitude of this consistency effect was reduced for poor comprehenders. However in conditions when the protagonist was closer in position in the sentence to the anaphor (when the continuation was *He chatted cheerfully* in the above example), they showed a larger and now significant consistency effect. In two further conditions, the texts had the same structure but they differed in the verb in the second sentence such that it was biased in meaning toward one or other protagonist. In this situation, the poor comprehenders had significant difficulty, particularly when the selection of the pronoun required them to overcome conflicting information primed by the verb. These findings suggest that poor comprehenders have difficulties in activating appropriate pronouns based on prior contextual information; such online language processing difficulties might plausibly contribute to these children's reading comprehension problems.

To investigate discourse-level processes in production rather than comprehension, Cain and Oakhill (1996) investigated narrative skills in poor comprehenders with a specific focus on story organization processes: 12 skilled and 14 less skilled comprehenders aged 7–8 years took part and they were compared with younger controls (aged 6–7 years) matched for reading comprehension skill. The children were asked to tell stories following different kinds of prompts: a topic title (e.g., Animals), a directed title (e.g., The Birthday Party), or a sequence of pictures, (e.g., pictures of a fishing trip). The narratives were then scored according to the child's grasp of story conventions, story event structure, and the use of connectives.

All three groups could use story conventions to produce narratives incorporating an opening, character setting, scene setting, and ending phase. However, the skilled comprehenders produced more coherent stories (see Box 3.5 for examples of complete, intermediate, and nonstory narratives). The difference in coherence was the consequence of the poor comprehenders using fewer connectives joining propositions in

Box 3.5   Examples of narratives varying in event structure. (From Cain, 2003. Reproduced with permission from the British *Journal of Developmental Psychology*, © The British Psychology Society.)

Nonstory
Topic title prompt: "The Farm."

Child's Response: "One day there was a man who had a big farm and there was lots of animals in it. The End."

Intermediate story
Picture sequence prompt: "The Fishing Trip."

Child's Response: "Once upon a time this little girl and her mum and her dad went fishing on a boat and the dad was fishing in the sea and then he saw some birds eating something and then he caught a fish."

Complete story
Picture sequence prompt: "The Fishing Trip."

Child's Response: "One day a family and their little girl decided to go fishing. They went down to the harbor and asked if they could borrow a boat so they could go fishing. Then the dad went fishing, but no fish came and he started to get a bit miserable. Then the little girl threw some bread into the water for some swans and the fish liked the bread and when the fish came up for the bread one of them went near the hook and then the dad caught a big fish and everyone was happy. The End."

the text, particularly in response to topic titles, and even in relation to the younger control group. Cain and Oakhill suggest that a problem with interclausal connectives may be a cause of their comprehension problems. This is an interesting idea; in order to use causal connectives, a child has to have a good command of the semantic relations between clauses and this ultimately depends on language comprehension.

Finally, two comprehensive studies of language skills in poor comprehenders indicate that oral language difficulties are pervasive and quite severe in this group. In the first of these, Nation, Clarke, Marshall, and Durand (2004) compared a group of poor comprehenders to an age-matched control group of children (who also had equivalent text reading accuracy and nonword reading skills to the poor comprehenders). The children were assessed on a wide range of language measures, including measures of vocabulary knowledge (average effect size $d = 1.74$), morphosyntax (average effect size $d = 1.09$), and broader receptive and expressive language skills (average effect size $d = 1.02$). These results show very clearly that the poor comprehenders have quite marked difficulties on a wide range of language measures compared to normally developing children of the same age and level of reading accuracy skills.

In fact, a large proportion of the poor comprehenders (8/23 or 35%), but none of the control children, satisfied a reasonably conservative criterion to qualify for a diagnosis of specific language impairment (SLI).

Second, in one of the largest studies of this group to date, Catts et al. (2006) compared 57 poor comprehenders with 27 poor decoders and 98 typically develop-ing children of the same age, selected from a population-based study of children with language impairments. Each child completed a battery of language and reading tests in kindergarten, second, fourth, and eighth grade and the classification into reader-groups was undertaken using the eighth grade data. Poor comprehenders had reading comprehension skills below the 25th centile as compared with normal range decoding skills. They were matched to the controls in decoding skill. The poor decoders had word recognition skills below the 25th centile and were matched to the normal readers in terms of reading comprehension. Concurrent data were available for performance on tests of receptive vocabulary, grammatical understanding, discourse comprehension, and phonological skills.

As expected, the poor comprehenders but not the poor decoders showed deficits in vocabulary and grammatical skills (in contrast, their phonological skills were normal). The poor comprehenders also showed significant impairments in discourse processing and listening comprehension. Interestingly, poor comprehenders were comparable to poor decoders and typical readers in making an inference when they remembered the premise on which it was based (e.g., if the premise was adjacent to the point where an inference had to be made). However, they were significantly impaired relative to the other groups when the premise and the inference were at a distance from each other in the text (effect size for the difference between poor com-prehenders and controls: $d= 0.64$).

Like Nation et al. (2004), Catts and colleagues reported data regarding the numbers of poor comprehenders who fulfilled diagnostic criteria for language impairment. Since the children were part of a cohort who had been followed because they were considered to be at high risk of language impairment, it was possible to provide accurate figures regarding those who had been given a research diagnosis in kindergarten of specific language impairment (SLI) (see Chapter 4). A relatively low proportion of children from the poor decoder and typical reader groups had a diagnosis of SLI (between 0.3 and 5.8%). However, among poor comprehenders 21.2% were diagnosed as SLI and a further 10.8% had language impairment in the context of low general cognitive ability.

Semantic deficits in poor comprehenders

A number of studies have focused at a detailed level on the nature of the language comprehension difficulties in poor comprehenders and, more specifically, have inves-tigated language processing at the semantic level (e.g., Megherbi & Ehrlich, 2005). It will be recalled from the findings of Nation et al. (1999) described earlier that the poor comprehenders had selective deficits in representing the meaning of abstract words in memory. In addition, Nation and Snowling (1998a) reported that poor comprehenders were slower and more error prone on synonym judgments than control children matched for reading accuracy skill (do these words have similar meanings: *boat* and *ship*?) and produced fewer exemplars in a semantic fluency task (give me as many forms of transport as you can think of).

To investigate poor comprehenders' sensitivity to the semantic relationships between words, Nation and Snowling (1999) used a semantic priming task in which children heard strings of spoken words and nonwords and, on hearing each item, they had to decide if it was a word or not. Target words were primed by spoken words that were related to them in terms of categorical membership (from the same semantic category) and in terms of frequency of association (how often the prime and target co-occur in language). The poor comprehenders, like the controls, showed semantic priming. However, the poor comprehenders showed reduced sensitivity to semantic relations based on category membership. Although they showed category related priming for strongly associated category members (*cat – dog*) they did not do so when the associated category members were not strongly associated (*train – aeroplane*); the controls, in contrast, showed clear priming effects for both types of items. This finding suggests that for poor comprehenders associative relationships between words are less efficiently stored in semantic memory than for normal readers.

Landi and Perfetti (2007) reported further evidence, from an EEG event-related potential (ERP) study, for a basic weakness in semantic processing in poor comprehenders (see Figure 3.6). In this study a group of university students was divided into more and less skilled comprehenders based on a standardized reading test. The more and less skilled comprehenders did not differ in their speed of reading individual words or nonverbal intelligence. Participants performed three tasks while their ERPs were recorded. In the semantic (words) task they saw pairs of words presented sequentially, and had to decide whether they were related in meaning (e.g., *lemon – pear*) or not (e.g. *bear – truck*). The semantic (pictures) task was the same except the items presented were line drawings either from the same category (related) or from different categories (unrelated). Finally, for the phonological (words) task, participants saw pairs of words and had to decide whether the pairs were homophones (related) or not (unrelated).

The more and less skilled comprehenders showed no difference in their ERPs to the phonological task (as expected, given previous demonstrations that good and poor comprehenders perform normally on single word reading and phonological tasks).

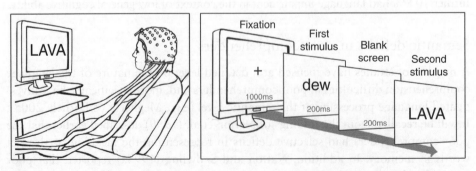

Figure 3.6   Illustration of an ERP experiment conducted by Landi and Perfetti (2007) to investigate semantic processing.

However, on both semantic tasks (pictures and words) the less skilled comprehenders were slower to make their decisions. There were also differences in the strength (amplitude) of ERP components (P200 and N400, occurring roughly 200 ms and 400 ms after stimulus presentation) between the skilled and less skilled comprehenders, particularly in the semantic word task. These differences therefore support the idea that less skilled comprehenders have a basic weakness in accessing information about the meanings of individual words (from either written word forms or pictures).

New word learning in children with comprehension impairment

Given the semantic difficulties observed in poor comprehenders, we would predict that they will have difficulty in establishing new semantic representations, in contrast to children with dyslexia who find it difficult to learn new phonological forms (Aguiar & Brady, 1991).

Nation, Snowling, and Clarke (2007) taught 12 poor comprehenders and 12 normal readers of the same age the names and meanings of four new words. Each new word was a three-syllable nonword with four semantic attributes (three concrete and one abstract attributes in each case): e.g., *a corbealyon is a small, hairy, angry bird*. First, the children were taught the names of the new words and their semantic attributes. After they had learned the associations between the phonological forms and their meanings to criterion, they were asked to define the nonwords and then to retrieve them (the newly acquired phonological forms) in response to the definitions. The following day they again recalled the new phonological forms before completing a task in which they matched the nonwords to pictures of the objects presented with foils.

The poor comprehenders took a similar number of trials to learn the new nonwords as the age-matched controls but they had significantly more difficulty in defining the nonwords whose phonological forms they could retrieve well. There was no group difference in the immediate recall of the nonwords to definitions (arguably a test tapping both phonological and semantic learning) but after the delay of 1 day the poor comprehenders could remember fewer of the semantic attributes of the new words. These findings support the hypothesis that poor comprehenders show normal phonological learning but have difficulty in learning (and consolidating) the semantic attributes of new words.

More generally, poor comprehenders appear to have difficulty in inferring the meanings of new words from context (Cain, Oakhill, & Elbro, 2003; Cain, Oakhill, & Lemmon, 2004), a pattern that also characterizes adults with weak verbal working memory skills (Daneman & Green, 1986). Cain et al. (2003) presented a group of 15 7–8-year-old poor comprehenders with eight short stories, in each of which a novel word was embedded. The children were encouraged to "guess" the meaning of the novel word as soon as it occurred. The word was followed by a defining context either immediately (in the near condition) or after a filler text (in the far condition). After reading the entire text, the children were asked to define the word again and their meanings were scored on a scale of 0–2 (with 2 being recorded when the child had made a full inference regarding the word's meaning).

Children varied in their propensity to provide a correct "guess" for the different words before the defining context and this variation in baseline were taken into account when estimating the ability of the children to define the words in the near and far conditions. The poor comprehenders were worse at giving the meanings of the novel words that had been defined in the passages and they had particular difficulty when the definitions were presented at a distance in the text from the word (resonating with the findings of Catts et al., 2006).

In summary, poor comprehenders have difficulty both in inferring the meanings of new words from context and in remembering the meanings of words they have been directly taught. Such difficulties are likely to contribute to the vocabulary impairments observed in many poor comprehenders and these impairments in vocabulary knowledge are one likely source of the reading comprehension problems seen in these children. Arguably, poor vocabulary knowledge will also affect the ability to make inferences about the relationships between events in a text, particularly when these depend upon an understanding of semantic relations.

Problems in inference skills as a possible cause of reading comprehension impairment

As we have seen, successful reading comprehension requires frequent inferences. The words on a printed page are often not completely explicit and a variety of inferences are used to "go beyond the information given" and fill in the gaps. Different ways of classifying the inferences that are made in reading have been proposed (e.g., Graesser, Singer, & Trabasso, 1994). While there are many different types of inference (see Box 3.6), two types that have been of particular interest in studies of poor comprehenders are cohesive and elaborative inferences. Cohesive inferences are those that are needed to maintain links between different parts of a text (one form of cohesive inference is involved in identifying the referents of pronouns as described earlier). It appears that without adequate use of cohesive inferences comprehension will often fail or be severely limited. Elaborative inferences are those that are made to add information that is not contained in the text. Such inferences may lead to a richer or fuller representation of the text, but often such inferences do not appear to be essential for comprehension. Readers use inferences in reading in complex and flexible ways. It seems that in many contexts readers will not draw all the inferences that they could from a text, but rather they draw the more obvious and more important inferences that are needed to support comprehension. Inferences that are needed to make a text coherent are more likely to be made than inferences that involve elaborations of the information presented. This makes sense in terms of cognitive effort, with readers only making the inferences that are more important for supporting comprehension (Perfetti, Landi, & Oakhill, 2005).

The study by Catts et al. (2006) hinted at the difficulties poor comprehenders have with making inferences. Perhaps not surprisingly, children's ability to make inferences during the process of reading comprehension improves with age. Barnes, Dennis, and Haefele-Kalvaitis (1996) examined developmental differences in inference skills in children between the ages of 6 and 16 years. They controlled for possible

Box 3.6 Examples of different inference types. (Graesser, Singer, & Trabasso, Constructing inferences during narrative text comprehension, *Psychological Review*, 101, pp. 371–395, 1994, published by American Psychological Association and adapted with permission.)

Inference type	Description	Classification (e.g., cohesive)	Source (e.g., knowledge-based)
Anaphora	Forming a link between two terms referring to the same thing: e.g., "The *car* came racing round the corner. Everybody scattered as the *vehicle* crashed into the wall."	Cohesive	Text-based
Pronoun resolution	Linking a pronoun to its previous referent: e.g., "*John* picked up Mary's book. *He* had wanted to read it for ages."	Cohesive	Grammatical knowledge
Case-structure role assignment	Assigning the role of agent, object, recipient, time, or location to a noun phrase: e.g., "The elephant (agent) gave his bananas (object) to the monkey (recipient)."	Cohesive	Grammatical knowledge
Causal antecedent	Provides an explanation for the actions and events in a text: e.g., "The campfire started to burn uncontrollably. Tom grabbed a bucket of water" – inference: Tom grabbed the water to put out the fire.	Local coherence	Knowledge-based
Superordinate goal	The overall goal that motivates the characters in the text. If the following sentence is encountered at the beginning of the story "It was Sam's mum's birthday and Sam wanted to buy her a present," then the superordinate goal, *Sam wanted to buy his mum a present*, would be inferred if the following sentence was encountered at a later point in the story "Sam woke early and went to the shops to find something special."	Global coherence	Knowledge-based

Box 3.6 *(cont'd)*

Inference type	Description	Classification (e.g., cohesive)	Source (e.g., knowledge-based)
Thematic inference	The overall goal or moral of the passage: e.g., never play with fire.	Global coherence	Knowledge-based
Character emotional reaction	The reactions of a character to the actions and events in the text: e.g., "Sam gave his mum a lovely a present" would lead to the inference that his mum was really pleased.	Coherence	Knowledge-based
Causal consequence	The predicted consequences of the actions and events in the text: e.g., "The dragon turned towards the knight and let out a fiery roar" might lead to the inference that the knight was wounded by the dragon.	Elaborative	Knowledge-based
Instantiation of noun category	Elaboration of a specific exemplar from a generic noun, i.e., "fish" becomes "shark" after reading "the fish attacked the swimmer."	Elaborative	Text-based
Instrument inference	Inferring a particular object used by an agent to complete an action, i.e., inferring the knight used a sword from the sentence "the knight lunged at the dragon and pierced his shiny scales."	Elaborative	Knowledge-based
State inference	Static properties of objects, characters, etc., not related to the causal structure of the text: e.g., a dog has a tail.	Elaborative	Knowledge-based
Subordinate goal action	How an agent achieved a goal not relevant to the superordinate goal of the text: e.g., you might infer that Sam took the bus to the shops to buy his mum a present.	Elaborative	Knowledge-based

differences in knowledge between children of different ages by first teaching all the children some novel information that was critical to understanding the passages they were going to read. This "knowledge base" concerned an imaginary planet called Gan and included information such as "Turtles on Gan have ice-skates attached to their feet." After learning the knowledge base to the criterion, the children were given a reading comprehension test about Gan. They found that even the youngest children studied (6–7-year-olds) were able to make inferences required to maintain text cohesion. However, there were clear improvements with age in children's ability to make inferences from the text, even after controlling for possible differences in the children's relevant knowledge. In other words, improvements in inference making with age could not be accounted for by differences in knowledge.

A number of pioneering studies by Oakhill (1982, 1983, 1984) showed that poor comprehenders are poor at making inferences while reading. Oakhill (1983) studied a particular type of inference referred to as instantiation. Instantiation is where a specific meaning for a more general term is inferred from the context. So, for example, having read that *The fish frightened the swimmer* we might infer that this particular fish was a shark. Oakhill found that less skilled comprehenders made fewer instantiations than more skilled comprehenders, suggesting that their determination of the meanings of words was less influenced by the sentence context. Oakhill (1982) also showed that less skilled comprehenders made fewer constructive inferences (inferences that are necessary to integrate two different sources of information) than more skilled comprehenders and that they were less good at drawing inferences that involved integrating what had been read with general knowledge.

Cain and Oakhill (1999) investigated inference generation during reading in poor comprehenders, making a stringent comparison between them and two groups of typical readers, one of the same age (CA controls) and the other comprising younger children who obtained the same comprehension scores on the Neale Analysis of Reading Ability (comprehension-age-matched controls). Two types of inferences were studied: inferences that required the integration of information from two consecutive sentences in a passage (passage based), and inferences that required the integration of information from the passage with general knowledge (general knowledge based). The poor comprehenders were worse at both types of inference than the CA controls, but only worse than the younger comprehension-age-matched controls on the passage-based inferences.

One difficulty with the notion that a deficit in inference making is a cause of reading comprehension impairments is that this is an inherently "high-level" difficulty. It might always be that problems in making inferences are consequences of more basic difficulties (such as poor vocabulary knowledge or limitations of verbal working memory, for example). One possible source of problem in making inferences is knowledge limitation (if you do not know that a common type of dangerous fish is a shark you cannot infer that the fish that frightened a swimmer is likely to be a shark). Cain, Oakhill, Barnes, and Bryant (2001) investigated whether poor comprehenders still show inference problems when background knowledge differences are controlled. The study used the procedure devised by Barnes et al. (1996) (described above) in which, before testing reading comprehension, children were taught a "knowledge base" concerning the imaginary planet Gan. The comparison was between 13 poor comprehenders and 13 good comprehenders who were the same age and matched on reading accuracy level but differing markedly in the number of comprehension questions they could answer correctly on the Neale Analysis of Reading Ability. It was shown that the poor comprehenders were worse than the good comprehenders in answering comprehension questions that involved making inferences from knowledge they had been taught about Gan, even when only counting those questions for which they had correctly answered the corresponding factual question correctly. This parallels the pattern found for younger compared to older children in the Barnes et al. study, that is, younger children (like poor comprehenders) may learn the information relevant to the planet Gan adequately but may then still fail to make an inference from this knowledge when required to do so on a reading comprehension test.

Thus, the problems that poor comprehenders have in answering inference questions are unlikely to be due to limitations in their relevant knowledge, since both groups of children were equally accurate in answering direct questions about this knowledge base. However, equivalent levels of performance on such questions cannot be taken to mean that this knowledge was represented in memory in the same way in both groups of children. It is quite possible that the newly learned information about the planet Gan was less efficiently organized in memory in the poor comprehenders. In line with this possibility, the poor comprehenders in this study were slower to learn the information that they were taught about Gan and they forgot this information more quickly than the control children. The poor comprehenders were also worse at answering literal comprehension questions (questions that did not require inferences). A reasonable conclusion is that problems with inferences are among the problems experienced by poor comprehenders when reading text but that these problems may well reflect more basic processing limitations (such as problems with the organization and storage of information in semantic memory).

Comprehension monitoring deficits in poor comprehenders

Comprehension monitoring refers to the ability to detect when comprehension of a text has broken down and it is an important source of individual differences in reading comprehension even after the effects of verbal skills and working memory are controlled (Cain, Oakhill, & Bryant, 2004). Ehrlich, Remond, and Tardieu (1999) investigated the role of metacognitive monitoring in the processing of anaphora in expository texts by 10-year-old poor comprehenders using a direct self-evaluation task and an inconsistency detection task. The study made use of a self-paced reading procedure in which segments of sentences within paragraphs were displayed on a computer screen and the children advanced the text to the next screen when they were ready to do so; they were also able to review the text if they wished.

In each text, target anaphors were embedded in sentences preceded by one or two introductory sentences. Sentences containing anaphors were segmented into meaning units: Unit 1 contained the target anaphor; Unit 2 and Unit 3 followed and provided further information about the referent. The rationale was that an increase in reading time on critical clauses would reflect implicit evaluation and revision, and the number of times each child "looked back" would reflect explicit evaluation. Finally, for each text, comprehension was assessed using multiple-choice questions.

In the self-evaluation task, each child first read the whole text and then re-read it segment by segment, assessing their own comprehension on a six-point scale. For critical segments, the antecedent of the anaphor was always a subject noun in the preceding sentence. Anaphors were denoted by the repetition of a noun or by a pronoun and they differed in their syntactic function, referring to either the subject or the object of the sentence. To illustrate, in the example below the anaphor functions as the subject of the critical segment in italics (Unit 1) and the following two segments convey further information (Unit 2 and Unit 3):

> Discovering sea animals is a constant source of surprise. Shells brought by the waves are plentiful on most shores. After the tide / *these shells (they) can be picked up* / in the puddles left in the holes on the rocks / or even more easily in the sand covered by sea weeds.

The object versions were identical in structure except for the critical segment:

> *After the tide / people can pick up these shells (them)* / in the puddles left in the holes on the rocks...

The texts were similar for the inconsistency detection task except that target anaphors either repeated the same lexical content or changed this content to a different one with the same gender and number cues but a meaning discontinuity in the text. The children's task was to find the word in each case that did not fit with the text.

In the self-evaluation task, the reading times were longer for the poor comprehenders than for the good comprehenders but processing time was similar in the inconsistency detection task. Importantly, the objective of detecting the inconsistency led to a slowing of some 39% for good comprehenders but only 11% for poor comprehenders, suggesting that skilled comprehenders are better able to modulate their reading when texts lacked coherence. The effect of anaphor consistency was significant but there were group differences. Whereas good comprehenders showed a significant increase in reading time with inconsistency in Unit 1 and extending into Unit 2, poor comprehenders only showed a marginal increase in reading time in Unit 1 and not in Unit 2 or Unit 3. In a similar vein, poor comprehenders made fewer "look backs" and these did not seem to be a function of inconsistency. They also detected fewer inconsistencies and when they did they found it difficult to identify the word at stake. Less skilled comprehenders evaluated their own comprehension as poorer than that of good comprehenders, however there was also an indication from their responses to multiple-choice questions that they tended to overestimate their ability. Overall, the data suggest that poor comprehenders are sensitive to a lack of cohesion but they cannot identify why it occurs. It seems that difficulties in anaphor processing are related to deficiencies in metacognitive monitoring but the causal relationships between these two aspects of comprehension are unclear.

In summary, we still do not have a good understanding of what underpins comprehension monitoring, though a reader's attitude is likely to play a role (Cataldo & Cornoldi, 1998). Indeed, engagement with reading is central to the development of a personal standard of coherence for comprehension (van den Broek, Young, Tzeng, & Linderholm, 1999). Put simply, it is critical for a child to have the objective of understanding what they read and to be motivated enough to "look back" with the purpose of self-correction when something does not make sense. A lack of such motivation may characterize poor comprehenders who do not enjoy reading because they have struggled for many years to understand what they read.

Longitudinal Studies of Children with Reading Comprehension Impairment

It is notable that most of the studies we have described in this chapter are cross-sectional and deal with concurrent relationships. We know of only a handful of longitudinal studies of children with reading comprehension impairment.

An issue that arises when considering the longer term outcome of children with reading comprehension impairment is the stability of the poor comprehender profile. Cain and Oakhill (2006) followed a group of poor comprehenders and a group of normal controls from the ages of 8 years. At follow-up when the children were 11, the majority of poor comprehenders remained poor on a measure of reading comprehension (the Neale Analysis of Reading Ability), and their outcome was predicted by general cognitive ability.

Similar results were obtained from two unpublished studies by K. Nation (personal communication). The first of these was a 6-year follow-up of the poor comprehenders studied by Stothard and Hulme (1992). Of the 28 children in the original sample, 23 were available for reassessment at 13 years of age: 13/14 poor comprehenders and 10/14 CA controls. The level of reading comprehension in the poor comprehender group remained very poor, with the group mean being more than 3 SD below that of the control group. The second study was a follow-up of 18 poor comprehenders originally described by Nation and Snowling (1998a,b) supplemented by a further five children in each group not previously reported. As a group, children identified as poor comprehenders at age 8.5 years continued to show reading comprehension deficits some 4.5 years later. All of the poor comprehenders achieved reading comprehension scores below the mean of the control group at Time 2, and only 4 of the 18 children scored within 1.5 SD of the control mean. Almost half of the sample achieved reading comprehension scores that were in excess of 2 SD below the average level of the control readers.

Catts et al. (2006) investigated the stability of the poor comprehender profile by starting at a later age with a group of poor comprehenders identified in 8th grade and conducting retrospective analyses of their profiles at earlier stages in development. Although it was generally the case that the poor comprehenders had shown oral language difficulties through time, an unexpected finding was that they also showed deficits in phonological awareness in kindergarten when compared with CA controls. There was also a change in their reading status over time, as shown in Box 3.7.

Is it possible that poor comprehenders develop more widespread reading difficulties as they get older? It has already been noted that there is a tendency for poor comprehenders to have difficulty in reading exception words, particularly if they are of low frequency. Furthermore, it would be surprising if comprehension deficits, particularly problems making inferences, did not constrain the growth of a reading vocabulary.

Some evidence that poor comprehenders suffer a decline in reading accuracy over time comes from a study of the reading skills of children with specific language impairment (Bishop & Adams, 1990; Stothard, Snowling, Bishop, Chipchase & Kaplan, 1998). At the age of 8 years, these children (who had experienced preschool language delay) had significantly better reading accuracy than comprehension (the poor comprehender profile). However, a follow-up some 7 years later found them to have more general reading difficulties affecting word recognition, nonword reading, and reading comprehension. It seems likely that these children, who had underlying language weaknesses, had failed to keep pace with their peers because of comprehension difficulties, perhaps coupled with poor motivation to read that resulted in very little reading practice. Moreover the decline was most significant for those with nonverbal IQ below 100.

In summary, there may be more than one developmental pathway to reading comprehension impairments. Furthermore, the nature of cognitive impairments of poor

---

Box 3.7   Growth in reading in poor comprehenders and poor decoders

The four graphs shown below illustrate the pattern of growth on different tests of reading skill for poor comprehenders, poor decoders (equivalent to children with dyslexia), and typical readers in the longitudinal study of Catts, Adlof, and Ellis Weismer (2006). The top two panels show: (a) growth in word recognition (WRMT-R Word ID) and (b) decoding (WRMT-R Word Attack) for the four groups. It is clear that the poor comprehenders and typically developing readers show identical starting points and equivalent growth on these measures between Grades 2 and 8, while the poor decoders show a consistent impairment on these measures across the range of ages studied.

The bottom two panels show growth in reading comprehension as assessed by: (c) the GORT comprehension test and (d) the Woodcock-Reading Mastery Passage comprehension test. On the GORT, the poor comprehenders show severe deficits in reading comprehension that are evident from Grade 4 onwards. In contrast, they actually scored better than the poor decoders on the Woodcock-Reading Mastery Passage comprehension test, which places a heavy emphasis on decoding accuracy (although their performance begins to dip between Grades 4 and 8).

The differing patterns in the top and lower graphs underline the fact that different tests of reading comprehension may pose differing demands.

Box 3.7   *(cont'd)*

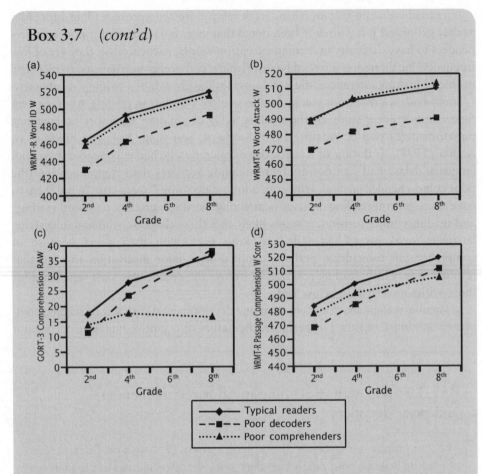

Growth in components of reading from Grade 2 to 8. (Reprinted with permission from Language deficits in poor comprehenders: A case for the simple view, by H. W. Catts, S. M. Adlof, and S. E. Weismer. *Journal of Speech, Language and Hearing Research*, 49(2), 288–289. Copyright 2006 by American Speech-Language-Hearing Association. All rights reserved.)

comprehenders may change with age in complex ways. Longitudinal studies are badly needed to investigate the causes as well as the consequences of reading comprehension impairments.

Summary of Core Cognitive Deficits and Likely Causes of Reading Comprehension Impairment

Children with reading comprehension impairment have difficulties that appear as marked on measures of spoken language comprehension as on measures of reading

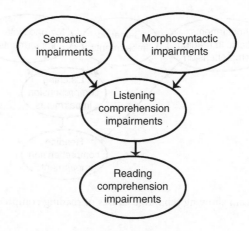

Figure 3.7   Path diagram showing listening comprehension impairments as a mediator of reading comprehension impairments.

comprehension. The studies we have reviewed indicate that these children have basic difficulties in the domains of semantics (understanding word meanings) and grammar (dealing with word formation and understanding how syntactic forms convey meaning). In fact, the language difficulties of a sizable proportion of these children are so severe that they would qualify for a diagnosis of specific language impairment (although the majority of children identified in research studies have never received such a diagnosis). In contrast, these children's phonological skills appear normal in relation to their age. When reading, these children also show problems with higher-level inference skills and have problems linking ideas from different parts of the text and relating what they have read to their general knowledge. It is likely that similar difficulties would be in evidence on tests of spoken language comprehension, though such studies have not been done.

A parsimonious theory of the cognitive bases of reading comprehension impairment in children is shown in Figure 3.7. In this theory there are two partially independent causes of reading comprehension impairment: problems with semantics and problems with morphosyntax. These are impairments of the oral language system, and such problems lead directly to problems with understanding spoken language (listening comprehension impairments). In this theory, the children's problems with reading comprehension are entirely the product of problems with listening comprehension, just as proposed by the Simple View of Reading model.

This theory is certainly a simple and a testable one, but it is probably too simple. The theory shown in Figure 3.8 is a slight elaboration of the theory. Here we postulate an impairment (or set of impairments) in processes specific to reading comprehension. A likely candidate for such an impairment would be a deficit in comprehension monitoring, but there could be others (such as motivational problems to do with a lack of interest in reading, caused by a history of failing to understand what has been read). This alternative theory sees reading comprehension

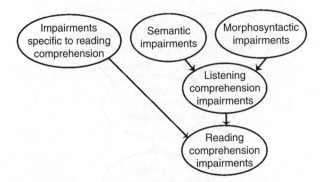

Figure 3.8   Path diagram showing separable causes of reading comprehension impairments.

impairment as being heavily dependent on underlying weaknesses in oral language skills, but with an additional contribution from processes specific to reading.

Speculatively, we would suggest that the first theory might be close to the state of affairs seen in young children with reading comprehension impairment, while the second theory might be closer to the truth for older children with reading comprehension impairment. Given a basic impairment in oral language skills that prevents the development of adequate listening and reading comprehension skills, it is likely that failing to comprehend what is read will have knock-on effects and prevent the child developing strategies (such as comprehension monitoring) that are important for skilled reading comprehension.

Etiology of Reading Comprehension Impairment

Reading comprehension impairment arguably is a less specific or circumscribed disorder than dyslexia and has also been much less studied. For both of these reasons less is known about the possible biological bases of reading comprehension impairment. To our knowledge neither behavioral genetic nor brain imaging studies have been conducted with children selected to show the poor comprehender profile. However, there are some relevant studies that we will outline below.

Genetics of reading comprehension

It seems probable, given its association with language impairment, that genetic influences on reading comprehension impairment will be substantial. One indirect way of assessing this is to consider the role of genetic factors in the development of verbal ability (verbal IQ). We know that reading comprehension impairment is associated with low verbal ability and it is plausible that the deficits in language skills picked up by tests of verbal ability (particularly tests of vocabulary knowledge) are causes of reading comprehension problems. It is well established that verbal ability shows a substantial heritability: in the region of .5 to .6 (for a review, see Plomin, DeFries,

McClearn, & Rutter, 1997). It is likely, therefore, that the verbal deficits that underlie reading comprehension impairment will show significant genetic influence.

A behavior–genetic analysis of reading comprehension was reported by Keenan, Betjemann, Wadsworth, DeFries, and Olson (2006) using a sample of twins from the Colorado study. The sample consisted of 74 MZ, 60 same-sex DZ and 62 opposite-sex DZ twins with a mean age of 11 (ranging from 8 to 17 years) in which at least one member of each pair had reading difficulties. Each child was tested on an extensive test battery. In brief, the measures used for the analysis comprised composite scores of word recognition, listening comprehension, reading comprehension, and IQ. The first aim of this study was to estimate the heritability of individual differences in reading comprehension (see Chapter 1). However, a second aim was to assess the extent to which genetic influences on reading comprehension were shared with genetic influences on word recognition and on listening comprehension.

The analysis used a technique known as Cholesky decomposition, which is a statistical procedure equivalent to hierarchical regression that can be used to estimate how much genetic (or environmental) variance in one trait is shared with genetic (or environmental) variance in another trait. The first analysis was conducted using measures of word recognition, listening comprehension, and reading comprehension. Each of these traits was found to be significantly influenced by genetic factors, with reported heritability estimates of .61 for word recognition, .51 for listening comprehension, and .61 for reading comprehension. Just two independent genetic factors accounted for all of the genetic influence on reading comprehension (see Figure 3.9). The first factor (A1) significantly accounted for individual differences in all three composites: word recognition, listening comprehension, and reading comprehension. After the influence of this factor was taken into account, a second genetic factor (A2) accounted for additional variance in listening and reading comprehension. The third genetic factor tested in the model accounted for no variance

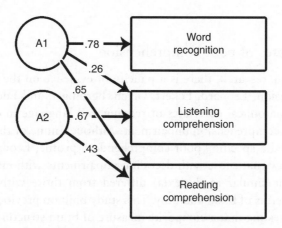

Figure 3.9 Diagram illustrating multiple genetic influences on reading comprehension. (Reprinted with permission of UKLA from Keenan, J., Betjemann, R., Wadsworth, S., de Fries, J., and Olson, R. Genetic and environmental influence on reading and listening comprehension. In *Journal of Research in Reading*, 29(1), 2006.)

in reading comprehension after the influences of the earlier two factors were taken into account. In sum, genetic influences on word recognition and listening comprehension together fully account for individual differences in reading comprehension, a finding that is entirely in keeping with the predictions of the simple view of reading. Moreover, there was one shared environmental influence on all three measures, suggesting that aspects of the home or school environment probably contribute to individual differences in reading and language skills.

As predicted then, there is substantial genetic influence on individual differences in reading comprehension. However, to what extent might this be related to variations in general cognitive ability? To investigate this issue, Keenan and colleagues reported a second analysis of their data, this time first examining genetic influences on IQ and then investigating the extent to which these were shared with other genetic influences on individual differences in reading comprehension. The heritability of IQ in this sample was .68 and the genetic influences on IQ also accounted for variance in word recognition, listening comprehension, and reading comprehension. After the effects of the genetic influences on IQ were taken into account, a second genetic factor accounted for variance in word recognition and reading comprehension but, interestingly, not in listening comprehension. A third genetic factor accounted for variance in both listening and reading comprehension. Together, these findings imply that there is a significant amount of IQ-independent genetic influence on listening comprehension. The authors suggest that this may be due to skills such as comprehension monitoring or inference generation that are not typically tapped by IQ tests but influence reading comprehension.

A limitation of this study was its relatively small sample size for a twin study and the wide age range of children tested. It would be interesting to know if the pattern of genetic and environmental influences on reading comprehension differs with age. It may well do if, as suggested earlier, poor reading comprehension takes its toll on the development of efficient metacognitive strategies, such as comprehension monitoring, over time.

Neural correlates of poor comprehension

Just as for genetic research, there is a paucity of evidence on the neurobiology of poor comprehension. Leonard, Eckert, Given, Berninger, and Eden (2006) examined the neuroanatomical correlates of reading and language in children with or without reading comprehension impairment. Although none of the participants in this study showed a specific "poor comprehender" profile, Leonard et al. (2006) were able to show that those with decoding impairments without comprehension deficits (a profile similar to dyslexia) differed from those with comprehension impairments in terms of brain anatomy. This study built on previous work from the same group suggesting that a composite measure of brain structure in a number of critical regions, the anatomical risk index (ARI), differentiates children with language impairments from typically developing children and children with dyslexia (see Chapter 4). A novel aspect of the study was the attempt to relate this quantitative index of neuroanatomy to behavioral measures of reading and language.

Structural MRI scans were available from 22 children aged 11–16 years who had been tested on a battery of tests comprising measures of phonological skills, rapid automatized naming (RAN), reading and reading comprehension, and receptive and expressive language. The anatomical risk index was calculated for each child from measures of the asymmetry of the planum temporale, combined plana and cerebellar anterior lobe, cerebral volume, and surface area of the first and second Heschl's gyrus (Leonard et al., 2002). Values of the anatomical risk index ranged from negative to positive, with zero representing normal (or low) risk. Two anatomical subtypes were created by splitting the risk distribution at zero.

For present purposes, the important finding was that there was a significant correlation between both reading comprehension and receptive language and the anatomical risk index, with a preponderance of children with negative indices having poor comprehension. Thus, they tended to have smaller cerebral volume and specifically smaller surface area of Heschl's gyri than normal and relatively less leftward asymmetry of the planum temporale, plana, and cerebellar anterior lobe. However, the same children also tended to have multiple deficits in reading and language, so it is not possible to assess the extent to which the risk index was related to comprehension per se. In contrast, children with a more "dyslexic" profile, who had less pervasive difficulties and were free of comprehension problems, tended to have positive risk indices.

A limitation of this study was its small heterogeneous sample and the absence of IQ measures for some of the participants. The findings are therefore badly in need of replication. However, the study suggests that the patterns of brain anatomy associated with reading comprehension deficits probably differ from those associated with dyslexia. This is to be expected, given the growing body of evidence that poor comprehenders have quite widespread language processing difficulties whereas those with dyslexia have more circumscribed difficulties affecting phonological processing. In summary, given its strong relationship with language impairment, it is likely that poor reading comprehension is the product of genetic risk factors associated with differences in the development of brain mechanisms responsible for oral language. However, reading comprehension depends on the use of higher-level comprehension strategies that are fine-tuned over time. The role of environmental influences in producing the poor comprehender profile should not therefore be underplayed. There is, to our knowledge, no research to date that addresses these issues.

Interventions for Reading Comprehension Impairment

Evidence concerning interventions for reading comprehension impairment is limited. A meta-analysis of reading comprehension interventions designed for typically developing children reported that the eight most effective methods for improving text comprehension were: comprehension monitoring, cooperative learning, graphic/semantic organizers for learning new vocabulary, story structure training, question answering, question generation, summarization, and multiple strategy teaching (National Reading Panel, 2000). The "metacognitive" strategies that need to be in place for proficient text comprehension were considered to be the ability to predict, question, clarify, summarize, and imagine. To varying extents, metacognitive strategies draw upon linguistic and cognitive resources and they can be used to help children to build coherent mental models of the texts they read. One method that has been advocated as a way of fostering good comprehension strategies is reciprocal teaching (Brown & Palinscar, 1985). In reciprocal teaching, children are first shown how to apply the strategies by their teacher, who models the process. Children then read a piece of text, paragraph by paragraph, and they learn to practise the strategies of:

- generating questions;
- summarizing;
- attempting to clarify word meanings or confusing text;
- predicting what will happen in the next paragraph.

The teacher supports the student while they practise, giving feedback and additional modeling as necessary. Gradually it is intended that the guided practice becomes a dialogue in which groups of students work together with a text, asking questions of one another, commenting on answers, summarizing, and improving the summary. In a similar vein, activities can include helping one another to infer the meaning of a word or to reason about story events.

Only a few studies so far have specifically investigated the effectiveness of interventions for children selected as poor comprehenders. Yuill and Oakhill (1988) developed an intervention to target inferencing skills. Inference training was compared with comprehension training (based on shared reading and the answering of comprehension questions) and rapid decoding training. Skilled and less skilled comprehenders aged 7 years each received seven sessions of training in one of the three intervention conditions. Reading comprehension ability was measured using the NARA II (Neale, 1997) and it was found that although less skilled comprehenders benefited significantly more from inference training and comprehension training than decoding training, there was no significant difference between the effectiveness of inference training and comprehension training. In the inference training condition gains in individual scores on the NARA were striking, with participants on average showing improvements in comprehension age of 17 months.

Oakhill and Patel (1991) focused on mental imagery training as a potential method for improving the reading comprehension skills of poor comprehenders. Twenty two poor comprehenders and 22 good comprehenders, taught in small groups were instructed using representational and transformational drawings, to picture stories in their minds. They were then encouraged to use their mental images to answer comprehension questions. Oakhill and Patel (1991) found that poor comprehenders benefited more from imagery training than good comprehenders and suggested that "the ability to use imagery strategies may give poor comprehenders a way of helping to circumvent their memory limitations ..."(p. 114). Benefits of mental imagery training for story comprehension were also reported for a small group of children with SLI by Joffe, Cain, and Maric (2007). However, in this study, as in that of

Oakhill and Patel, there was no untreated control group of children with reading or language difficulties, which makes the changes produced by the training difficult to interpret (they may partly be due to simple practice or retesting effects). Nevertheless it seems that the effectiveness of mental imagery strategies as a method of improving reading comprehension skills is worthy of further study.

Johnson-Glenberg (2000) examined whether poor comprehenders would benefit more from a visual training program or a verbal training program. The verbally based reciprocal teaching (RT) program (Brown & Palinscar, 1985) was compared to a visually based visualizing/verbalizing program (Bell, 1986). Fifty-nine poor comprehenders assigned to either one of the training programs or a control group participated in small group teaching over 16 weeks. Both training programs were similarly effective in improving poor comprehenders' reading, language, and memory skills associated with reading comprehension ability. Johnson-Glenberg (2000) suggested that a combination of the two strategies might be particularly powerful.

These studies have taught specific components of reading comprehension and have generated some promising improvements in the reading skills of poor comprehenders. To our knowledge, however, none of these approaches have been evaluated using randomized controlled designs in realistic educational settings.

Summary and Conclusions

Reading comprehension impairment contrasts sharply with the pattern of reading difficulty seen in children with dyslexia. Many children with reading comprehension impairment read with normal speed and accuracy but have great difficulty understanding what they have read; in contrast children with dyslexia struggle to read accurately but may be good at getting the gist from a passage they have great difficulty in decoding. We need to emphasize that these contrasting patterns are extremes, and there are many children with poor reading skills who have both sorts of difficulty (these children have sometimes been termed "garden variety" poor readers; Stanovich, 1994).

The contrasting patterns shown by children with reading comprehension impairment and dyslexia are important practically and theoretically. Theoretically, as we have seen, these two disorders provide evidence that different parts of the language system (phonology, semantics, and grammar) develop somewhat independently. These different language subsystems in turn provide the foundations for different aspects of reading. Word recognition skills in reading depend critically upon phonological skills, while comprehension of text that has been decoded depends upon semantic and morphosyntactic (grammatical) skills.

So far we know less about the cognitive characteristics of children with reading comprehension impairment than we do for children with dyslexia. The best evidence to date indicates that poor comprehenders have difficulties with nonphonological language skills and listening comprehension. At a more detailed level there is evidence that these children have semantic processing difficulties and problems with aspects of grammar, as depicted within the Morton and Frith (1995) framework shown in

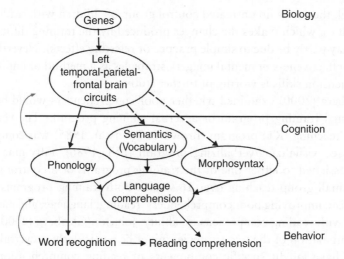

Figure 3.10   Path model showing possible sources of reading comprehension deficits.

Figure 3.10. Together, these basic deficits can be expected to affect the growth of vocabulary knowledge and the ability to make inferences while reading (processes that are essential to text integration) that are part and parcel of the poor comprehender profile. In turn, persistent problems with comprehension may affect the development of metacognitive strategies, such as the "lookback" strategy and compromise comprehension monitoring. Such semantic and grammatical problems may also relate to differences in the way that verbal information is encoded and stored in memory. In this sense we agree with Perfetti, Marron, and Foltz (1996, p. 159) that problems of reading comprehension can be seen as consequences of more basic language comprehension impairments: "the operation of basic processes that identify words, activate their meanings, configure phrases, assemble meanings and so forth." It seems likely that problems with comprehension monitoring may develop as a consequence of reading comprehension difficulties and there is some evidence that intervention programs can effectively foster the development of such strategies.

   In conclusion, we started this chapter with the Simple View of Reading model and within this model poor comprehenders are children with good decoding but poor listening comprehension skills. Such children's difficulties can also be related to the triangle model. When viewed in terms of this model, poor comprehenders have set up the phonological pathway proficiently but have impairments in the semantic pathway, possibly as a consequence of deficient semantic representations. But as we have seen, the problems of poor comprehenders extend well beyond single word reading. As yet, the causal connections between different language skills and the different components of reading comprehension are not well understood and we badly need more longitudinal studies to understand the processes that are operating.

4

Specific Language Impairment

Problems in understanding or producing language are among the most frustrating and isolating handicaps that a child can experience. The term specific language impairment (SLI) is used to refer to children whose oral language skills are much worse than expected given their nonverbal ability (NVIQ) and where other known causes (e.g., deafness) cannot explain the disorder. Recent evidence suggests that SLI is a neurobiological disorder, the development of which depends heavily upon genetic risk factors. However, there is considerable heterogeneity among children with SLI in the pattern of language difficulties that they show; as we shall see, some children with SLI have speech difficulties while others do not, some have difficulties with the social use of language, and others may be effective communicators despite difficulties with expressive language skills.

Definition and Prevalence

The term *Communication Disorders* is used in DSM-IV (American Psychiatric Association, 1994) to describe children who are referred to clinically as SLI whose scores obtained on individually administered measures of language development are below expectation given "nonverbal intellectual capacity." The term can also be applied if a child has suffered an accompanying sensory deficit, learning difficulties, or environmental deprivation, provided that the language difficulties are in excess of those usually associated with these other problems. DSM-IV goes on to distinguish several types of communicative disorder, including expressive disorder (primarily affecting language production), mixed expressive–receptive disorder (affecting language comprehension and production), and phonological disorder (affecting the use of speech sounds to signal meaning). (DSM-IV also has the diagnostic categories of Stuttering and Communication Disorder Not Otherwise Specified. These categories are not relevant to the discussion of SLI as they refer to difficulties with, for example, fluency or voice that impede communication but are not associated with a disorder of language development.)

In a similar vein, ICD-10 (World Health Organization, 1993) lays out criteria for SLI as a child having language skills more than two standard deviations below average for age and at least one standard deviation below nonverbal IQ. It distinguishes receptive from expressive language disorder and excludes children with neurological, sensory, or physical impairments that affect the use of language. Both classification schemes also exclude children who have a pervasive developmental disorder such as autism.

In practice the criteria used to identify children suffering from SLI are quite variable. Typically, to be diagnosed as having SLI a child needs to obtain a low score on a subset of standardized language measures but have no other impairment (such as deafness or a low nonverbal IQ) that might provide an adequate explanation for the language problems (Bishop, 2001). However, in making the diagnosis, different researchers have used different language tests and different levels of impairment as cut-offs. For example, the SLI Consortium (2004) diagnosed children as having SLI if composite scores from the Clinical Evaluation of Language Fundamentals (CELF-R) tests (Semel, Wiig, & Second, 1992) for expressive or receptive language (or both) were at least 1.5 standard deviations (SD) below the average for their age and if their nonverbal IQ was at least 80 (children with lower IQs were excluded).

One of the largest epidemiological studies of SLI is that of Tomblin, Records, and Zhang (1996). In this study tests were used to assess three domains of language function (vocabulary, grammar, and narrative) and two modalities (receptive and expressive). For each of these five areas of language function, composite scores were created to represent a child's performance relative to their age. To qualify for a diagnosis of language impairment children had to perform at least 1.25 SD below average on at least two out of these five language composite scores. In addition, to qualify for the label of specific language impairment (SLI) a child also had to obtain a nonverbal IQ of at least 85 and have typical sensory and socio-emotional development.

Depending on the precise criteria used for diagnosing language impairment, different numbers of children will be identified and the characteristics they show will vary. Prevalence estimates range from 3 to 6% but are complicated by the fact that SLI is not a static condition and some children may resolve their language difficulties as they get older (Bishop & Edmundson, 1987; Tomblin et al., 1997). As with many other developmental disorders, more boys than girls are affected with SLI (3:1–4:1), although the epidemiological study of Tomblin et al. (1997) reported a more even ratio of 1.33:1 boys to girls.

The Persistence of SLI

There are now a number of studies investigating both the short-term (e.g., Aram & Nation, 1980; Conti-Ramsden, Botting, Simkin, & Knox, 2001; Stark et al., 1984) and longer-term outcomes of children with language impairments (e.g. Aram, Ekelman, & Nation, 1984; Botting, 2005; Conti-Ramsden, Simkin, & Botting, 2006; Felsenfeld, Broen, & McGue, 1992; King, Jones, & Lasky, 1982; Stothard, Snowling, Bishop, Chipchase, & Kaplan, 1998). Many children with SLI are recognized in the preschool years, and many cases of language problems in this period resolve as children get older. However, studies suggest that 50–90% of children with SLI continue to exhibit language difficulties through childhood and many go on to have reading difficulties (Bird, Bishop, & Freeman, 1995; Bishop & Adams, 1990; Catts, 1993; Catts, Fey, Tomblin, & Zhand, 2002; Magnusson & Naucler, 1990). However, where the language difficulties are mild or very specific in form the outcomes are generally better.

In an 18-month follow-up of 87 children who, when aged 4 years, exhibited speech–language difficulties, Bishop and Edmundson (1987) identified some of the factors associated with variations in outcome in the short term. On the basis of assessments at age 4 years, the children were classified as having specific language impairment (SLI) or having impaired speech–language skills coupled with impairments of nonverbal IQ (2 SD below the mean – the general delay group). Overall, for some 37% of these children, their language impairment had resolved by age 5½ years. For the SLI children, there was a good outcome for 44% while some 89% of the general delay group continued to show language difficulties. Thus, children with higher IQs had a better chance of overcoming their language difficulties. Bishop and Edmundson went on to show that a subset of three language tests, together with nonverbal IQ, predicted outcome status correctly for 86% of children. The relevant tests were a narrative test requiring the expression of semantic relationships, a test of picture naming, and a test of expressive semantics and syntax. In fact, outcome for 83% of the children could be classified using the narrative task alone.

Bishop and Adams (1990) followed up 83 of the children from the Bishop and Edmundson study when they were 8½ years old. For children whose language impairments had resolved at 5½ years, outcomes at 8½ years were generally good in terms of both their oral language and reading skills. This "resolved" group showed some mild difficulties on two measures of oral language comprehension (*TROG*, a test of receptive grammar, and *WISC* comprehension, a test of social understanding) but otherwise showed average scores on measures of language, reading, and spelling. In contrast the group whose language skills had been impaired at 5½ years continued to show impairments in all aspects of oral language and reading skills, with reading comprehension being on average worse than reading accuracy. Perhaps not surprisingly, the group who showed general delay at 5½ years (poor language and low NVIQ) had the worst outcome, with quite severe impairments on all tests of language and cognitive function at 8½ years.

Stothard et al. (1998) managed to follow up 71 of the children from the original Bishop and Edmundson (1987) study when they were 15–16 years old. In this case the picture had changed slightly in comparison to the pattern reported for these children when they were 8½ years old. For the children with persisting language difficulties and the children with general delay at 5½ years, the pattern remained similar and these children had quite severe impairments in all aspects of language and reading at age 15½ years. In fact there was some evidence that the language skills and nonverbal IQ of the children with persisting language difficulties had shown further declines at this point in time. However, for the children whose language skills were considered to be resolved at 5½ years there was evidence that they were now

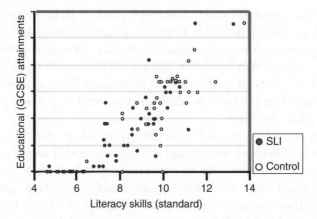

Figure 4.1　Relationship between literacy skills and educational attainments in young people with a history of language impairment. (Data from Stothard et al., 1998.)

performing less well than controls on measures of phonological skills and literacy at age 15 years. These children had shown essentially typical reading skills at age 8½ years, so there is evidence here for late-acting effects that served to impair the development of their phonological and reading skills. It is heartening that for this group of children their oral language skills remained normal at this time point. However, Snowling, Adams, Bishop, and Stothard (2001) found that the grades obtained by these children in school-leaving examinations (GCSE) were lower than for age-matched controls of similar levels of reading skill, and as expected the children whose language problems had persisted at 5½ years had even poorer results. Figure 4.1 based on this same study shows that educational outcomes were quite closely tied to levels of literacy measured at the same point in time.

Overall, this long-term study following children from preschool to adolescence suggests that the prognosis for children whose early language impairments have resolved by the time they go to school is relatively good. However, these children clearly do show a raised risk of developing reading difficulties when they are older, although such problems may only emerge relatively late in development. Equally clearly, the language and cognitive outcomes for children with persisting language difficulties at age 5½ years are relatively poor and this is true for both children with good nonverbal IQ as well as for the children with general delay (whose outcomes, predictably, are worst of all).

Other studies that have assessed the academic skills of adolescents with a history of preschool language impairments confirm that academic difficulties are common (Knox, Botting, Simkin, & Conti-Ramsden, 2002). Aram et al. (1984) reported a 10-year follow-up of 20 children with an initial diagnosis of speech and language difficulties. At age 13–16 years, 40% of the children obtained a verbal IQ score below 80 and these children showed severe impairments on the tests of reading, spelling, and maths. Furthermore, only 25% of these adolescents were in regular classrooms. Aram et al. concluded that the language disorders recognized in these children in the preschool years were only the beginning of longstanding language and academic problems. However, as their study was not restricted to children with normal intelligence, it is difficult to disentangle the specific effects of language disability from the more general consequences of low IQ.

A poor prognosis, even in the face of normal nonverbal intelligence, was also found in a study focusing upon the outcomes of children with receptive language disorders. Mawhood, Howlin, and Rutter (2000) reported a follow-up into adult life of 19 boys, initially diagnosed as having a developmental language disorder affecting comprehension. In this sample, language difficulties were still evident in adulthood; 47% had an oral reading score that fell at or below the 10-year level, 42% were at or below this level in reading comprehension, and 63% were similarly impaired in spelling. Furthermore, none had passed any national examinations at school, although two had later obtained vocational qualifications. A comparison group of children with autistic disorders showed comparatively better prognosis, possibly because they had been educated in specialist settings with educational programs attuned to their needs. Such placement was rare in the SLI group (see Clegg, Hollis, Mawhood & Rutter, 2005, for a report of longer-term outcomes).

Along similar lines, Tomblin, Freese, and Records (1992) identified from clinical records 35 young adults with a history of language difficulty. They were assessed on a large range of language measures when aged 17–25. These adults with a history of SLI differed on all language measures from controls (matched on childhood performance IQ) and also in current performance IQ. One finding of particular interest was that the performance IQ of 20 adults with a history of SLI had declined from 98.5 in childhood to 89.75 in adulthood. This is a similar pattern to that reported by Botting (2005) and Stothard et al. (1998).

To summarize, preschool language difficulties are frequently the precursors of language and academic difficulties that persist into adulthood but there is substantial variation in outcome. For children whose language difficulties do persist into the early school years there is some evidence that these children are likely to show further declines in both language and broader cognitive skills as they get older. Furthermore, even for children whose oral language skills may appear to have resolved in the early school years there is evidence that these children show an increased risk of reading problems, which again may take many years to develop. This pattern supports the claim of Scarborough and Dobrich (1990), who suggest that, even if early language delays appear to resolve, this might be "illusory recovery" with problems emerging once the child is confronted with the task of learning to read and write.

The studies we have considered so far have focused on the language and cognitive outcomes of children with SLI. However, because of the central importance of language skills to social interaction there have been a number of studies that have also assessed the psychosocial outcomes of children with SLI. Evidence from both cross-sectional and prospective longitudinal studies of children with speech–language disorders indicates that there is a heightened risk of psychiatric disorder in these children (Beitchman, Cohen, Konstantareas, & Tannock, 1996). Furthermore more than half of referrals to psychiatric services are children with language difficulties, many of whom were previously undiagnosed (Cohen, 1996).

Baker and Cantwell (1982) were the first to report that the risk of psychiatric problems is lower for children who only have speech disorders than for children with language difficulties. There is also some evidence of an association between lack of improvement in speech–language functioning and the development of a psychiatric disorder (Beitchman et al., 1996; Benasich, Curtiss, & Tallal, 1993). Similar findings were reported by Snowling, Bishop, Stothard, Chipchase, and Kaplan (2006) when they examined the psychosocial outcomes in adolescence of the SLI children recruited by Bishop and Edmundson (1987) at 4 years of age. Overall, the rates of psychopathology were low in this sample, particularly in children whose language difficulties had resolved by the age of 5½ years. The main problems of adolescents with persistent language impairments were difficulties with attention control and social impairments. These problems were somewhat independent of each other, and the language profiles of affected children differed: Attention problems tended to be associated with restricted expressive language difficulties, and social problems with the co-occurrence of receptive and expressive impairments. The comorbid pattern of attention and social problems was associated with globally delayed cognitive development. In line with the view that learning difficulties may mediate between language impairments and behavioral problems, the language-impaired children with the poorest psychosocial outcomes in adolescence also had the poorest poor literacy skills.

Aside from mental health issues, there also appears to be an increased incidence of autism spectrum disorders in follow-up studies of children with language impairments (Conti-Ramsden et al., 2006). However, it would be premature to conclude that such problems are a consequence of language difficulties. On the contrary, Bishop, Whitehouse, Watt, and Line (2008) have argued that contemporary diagnostic criteria for autism spectrum disorder in adulthood are such that many children with a history of language disorder now attract this diagnosis – a case of "diagnostic substitution." Thus in a follow-up study of 38 young adults who as children had been diagnosed with language impairment and not autism, between 8 and 25 (depending on the precise diagnostic criteria) now fulfilled criteria for an autism spectrum disorder and this was particularly common in the case of children who had had problems in the social use of language in childhood (pragmatic language impairment).

Comorbidities between SLI and Other Developmental Disorders

It is clear from the material we have already reviewed that the rates of comorbidity between SLI and other disorders are high and therefore cannot simply be due to chance. The evidence we have on this issue is from studies of clinical rather than epidemiological samples, which makes it impossible to give precise estimates of the true rates of comorbidity in the population. As we have already noted there is substantial comorbidity between SLI and reading disorders, which is a natural consequence of the fact that reading skills develop from a foundation of pre-existing oral language skills (Snowling & Hulme, 2005). There are also very substantial rates of motor coordination disorder among children with SLI, which led Hill (2001) to argue that we should question the use of the term "specific" in the case of children with SLI (because for so many of these children their difficulties are not specific to language). Finally, there is evidence that language problems are often associated with general learning difficulties (low NVIQ). Indeed, even children who satisfy the diagnostic criteria for SLI when they are young (by having an NVIQ in the normal range) may show declines in NVIQ as they get older (Botting, 2005). This pattern suggests that impairments of language in children may often signal quite serious and pervasive problems of development that are likely to have effects on other areas of functioning. In this light, children who really do satisfy the strict criteria for a "specific" language impairment may be quite unusual.

The Typical Development of Language: A Theoretical Framework

Before turning to discuss research investigating the nature and causes of children's speech and language impairments, it is important to outline the typical course of language acquisition as a framework for understanding how this usually robust process breaks down in children with SLI.

The structure of language

As Bishop (1997b) states "language is so readily acquired and so universal that it is easy to forget what a complex phenomenon it is" (p. 1). The language processing system is multicomponental and, as noted in Chapter 3, contains a number of specialized subsystems, namely phonology, grammar, semantics, and pragmatics. Phonology refers to the system of language that uses speech sounds to signal differences in meaning; the phonological difference between *cap* and *gap* signals that the first word means something you wear on your head and the second word means a space between things. Phonology itself contains two subsystems: segmental phonology, concerned with the speech–sound contrasts within words, and suprasegmental phonology, concerned with aspects of the intonation of speech such as tone, duration, and intensity. It is important to distinguish phonology from phonetics, which is concerned with the acoustic and articulatory characteristics of speech sounds. However, phonetic differences between sounds in different word positions do not necessarily signal meaning. For example, the phoneme /d/ is voiced in word-initial position [dog] but devoiced in the word-final position [mad] such that its phonetic realization is more like /t/. This is known as allophonic variation (the same phoneme /d/ is given different realizations in different speech contexts). While speakers of English are sensitive to phoneme differences between words that mark meaning, they are typically unaware of the phonetic differences between allophones (the different realizations of the phoneme /d/ in different contexts).

Most people understand the term "grammar" to mean a system of rules that governs how words can be put together to make coherent sentences. This system is more properly referred to as syntax. Formally, grammar is the system of language that comprises morphology as well as syntax. Morphology refers to the underlying structure of words and the units of meaning (morphemes) they comprise. For example, the word *boy* is a single morpheme but the word *cowboy* can be thought of as containing two morphemes, *cow* and *boy*. In English, there are relatively few words of the *cowboy* type; these are much more common in German or Danish where compounding is frequent. However, English words like *camping* or *camped* also contain two morphemes (camp + *ing*; camp + *ed*) and *decamped* contains three (de + camp + ed). The addition of morphemes to change the meaning of a base form in this way is known as inflectional morphology. Inflections are parts of words (e.g., *-ed, -ing*) that cannot stand alone but which, when combined with a word stem, serve a grammatical function. Inflectional morphemes denote contrasts, such as between past and present tense or between singular and plural forms.

Semantics is the system of language concerned with meaning both at the sentence and the word (lexical) level. It should be clear, therefore, that there is a strong relationship between grammar and semantics. The grammatical structure of a sentence (syntax) is usually closely tied to the meaning it conveys, such that different grammatical forms take particular semantic roles in the sentence (e.g., nouns specify agents or objects whereas verbs specify actions). It should be noted, however, that sentences can be grammatical whilst at the same time semantically implausible in terms of real-world knowledge (e.g., *the fish walked to the bus*). Lexical semantics is more concerned with vocabulary knowledge and might be considered a system in which words are categorized according to their function or meaning relations.

Finally, pragmatics is concerned with how language is used in context. According to Grice (1998), efficient communication depends upon the speaker and listener sharing certain assumptions. These are that communication should be both informative and relevant to the topic under discussion or to the situation: it should be truthful, clear, unambiguous, economical, and delivered in an orderly fashion (Sperber & Wilson, 1995). Violations of these assumptions include talking at length about topics not directly relevant to the present situation or using an inappropriate "register," such as speaking in an overly formal manner for the context. Pragmatic failure commonly occurs when the speaker does not take into account the listener's perspective and either provides too much or too little information to convey communicative intent (see Figure 4.2 for an illustration).

Language acquisition

For many years, theories of language acquisition were dominated by the view that language learning depends upon innate linguistic structures and, in particular, specialized mechanisms for the abstraction of grammatical "rules." Within this theoretical framework, some researchers have hypothesized that problems with grammar seen in SLI may reflect the operation of a single dominant gene (Gopnik & Crago, 1991). An alternative view is that language learning depends critically upon the

Figure 4.2 Cartoon illustrating pragmatic difficulties.

linguistic input to which the child is exposed. In contrast to the view that grammatical categories are innate, this view suggests that the acquisition of language is a gradual process that depends upon abstracting regularities from the language input that the child hears (Chiat, 2001; Tomasello, 2000). Space does not permit a comprehensive review of the very large body of research on typical language acquisition; interested readers are referred to Karmiloff and Karmiloff-Smith (2001) for a useful synthesis. We focus here on the aspects of language development that have been the back-drop to studies of children with SLI, namely the development of auditory and phonological skills, morphosyntax (grammar), and semantics.

The development of auditory and phonological skills
The typical development of language requires the young child to tune in to the acoustic cues that are relevant to the perception of speech (see Box 4.1). It is clear that auditory localization and attention are general prerequisites for this process. More specifically, the perception of speech draws on the capacity to detect word envelope cues signaled by variations in amplitude (loudness), to discriminate pitch changes, and to perceive gaps between different components of the speech signal. However, there are constraints on how learning operates; infants cannot perceive all distinctions in the speech stream and because language learning is social they only become attuned to the distinctions in the language they hear from the people with whom they interact (Kuhl, 2004).

While a number of studies in recent years have investigated the responses of human fetuses to auditory stimuli that might predispose them to attend to ambient speech, there have been relatively few studies of basic auditory processing in neonates and young infants. However, a significant body of research has examined infant speech perception. An influential view for many years has been that neonates are "preprogrammed" to perceive speech categorically, such that they have the potential for learning any one of the world's languages. This sensitivity to phonetic categories is gradually shaped during the first year of life to home in on the contrasts that are relevant in the native language (Mehler & Christophe, 1994) and by about 9 months infants are sensitive to the phonotactic patterns in the language, and prosodic cues enable them to identify potential words (Kuhl, 2004).

The development of speech production skills proceeds alongside that of speech perception and begins with babbling around 6 months of age, which typically involves repetitions of simple syllables. An important tradition in research on phonological development has been to compile inventories of the speech sounds

---

Box 4.1   Speech perception

The complexity of the processes involved in learning to perceive speech may be appreciated by trying to "read" a speech spectrogram of a spoken phrase. Such spectrograms show the frequency of sounds plotted on the vertical axis and time on the horizontal axis; the degree of darkness represents the amplitude (the energy) of the sounds. The figure below shows spectrograms of two very similar spoken phrases. The text at the bottom is spread out to approximate the timing of the sounds in the spoken words. The first thing to note is that it is difficult to identify the sounds represented in the spectrograms (the large amount of energy spread over a wide frequency range for the phoneme /s/ is an exception) or even to identify the boundaries between words. In practice there are no clear boundaries between spoken words in continuous speech where words run into each other and show "coarticulation." Note particularly that the difference in sounds between "walk" and "walked" is not really visible at all; the "-ed" past participle has low salience (low phonetic substance) in continuous speech. It is notable that marking the past tense forms in speech is something that children with SLI find very difficult to learn.

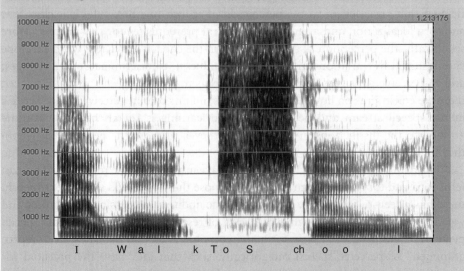

a) I walk to school

Box 4.1 (*cont'd*)

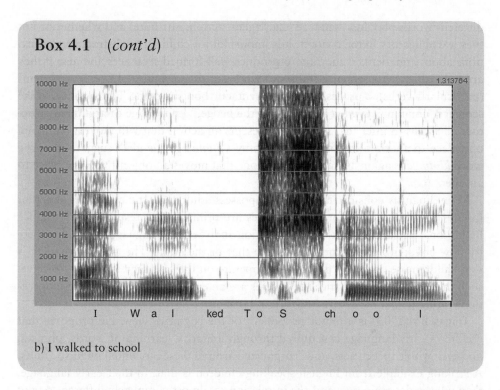

b) I walked to school

used productively by children and to document regularities and consistencies in their use to mark meaning (Ingram, 1981). Often, in the early stages of learning to talk, children use simplification processes to reduce the complexity of the speech they wish to produce. These include dropping word-initial weak (unstressed) syllables (e.g., saying "mato" for *tomato*), reducing consonant clusters (e.g., saying "bick" for *brick* or "wig" for *twig*, and a process called consonant harmony in which different consonants in the word are realized in the same place of articulation (e.g., saying "gog" for *dog* and "wowuway" for *go away*).

The development of grammar

Since the pioneering studies of Roger Brown (Brown & Fraser, 1964) a universal sequence of language development has been acknowledged, with children first communicating using single words, then combining words in two-word utterances before proceeding to use more complex sentence forms. Typically infants between the age of 18 and 24 months will begin to combine words into short phrases. This depends upon them having learned enough words to combine productively and the development of grammar is therefore intricately linked with lexical development (vocabulary knowledge). Lexical development continues into the school years and beyond, however grammatical development proceeds fairly quickly during the preschool period.

A significant hurdle for young children is to learn about the argument structure that underlies the sentences they hear. Argument structure refers to the role that different words play in a sentence (e.g., agent, action, attribute) and whether or not they are obligatory in the context. It is important for children to abstract generalizations about arguments if they are to produce well-formed sentences and also if they are to be able to use sentence frames to work out the meanings of new lexical items (particularly verbs), a process known as syntactic bootstrapping. For instance, in the sentence "mummy *kimmed* the ball into the hedge," knowledge of argument structure allows us to infer that *kimmed* represents an action that will move a ball from one place to another. In contrast, "mummy *kimmed* to the girl" suggests that the word *kimmed* is again an action but not one that moves an object from one place to another.

Many linguists consider that children possess adult syntactic categories and that failures to produce well-formed sentences are primarily the result of performance limitations. Researchers within this tradition analyze child language in order to specify how children's grammar differs from that of the adult. The alternative view is that children use cognitive processes to operate on the language input they receive, such that abstract grammatical categories are an emergent property of these operations rather than a hard-wired feature of language.

Tomasello (2003) is a major proponent of the cognitive view. He proposes that children's early language is acquired through imitative learning of words, phrases, and even whole speech acts, and is organized around these individual linguistic units. A striking example from English-speaking children is that, in their early language, they use the determiners *a* and *the* in relation to almost completely different sets of nouns (Pine & Lieven, 1997). However, from an early stage, children are able to combine various kinds of constructions in creative ways (e.g., *see daddy's car* could be created from *daddy's car* and *see daddy*) but they do not make generalizations until they possess a significant number of exemplars in their repertoire. Using the example of the acquisition of verbs, Tomasello (2000) argues against the view that children have knowledge of the subjects and objects of verbs in general, but rather that children know specific verbs and the relations they can express. For example, a child might know *boy hits*, *thing to hit with*, *hit ball* but not that *boy eats*, *thing to eat with* or *eat cake*.

Similar arguments can be made about knowledge of other grammatical forms, such as inflections. Inflections are the markers that are added to lexical items to signal changes in meaning that are relevant and in agreement with the context in which they are placed. For instance, in English, when there is more than one noun (plurality), -*s* is added to a noun (e.g., books); when the agent of the verb is one person (third person singular), -*s* is added to the verb stem (e.g., he jumps). Tomasello proposes that children only begin to abstract relations across items belonging to the same syntactic category at around their third birthday. An important implication of this view is that early child language may contain a variety of linguistic units together with what appear to be inconsistencies in grammatical ability.

Although it is common to think of language acquisition as following a universal sequence with some uniformity in the ages at which children reach different milestones, there is in fact considerable variation in the rate and style of language development across children. For some children there are also dissociations between

language comprehension and production and between different language components (e.g., lexical versus semantic skills). Bates, Dale, and Thal (1995) draw on data
collected during the standardization of the MacArthur Communicative Development
Inventories (*MCD-I*; Fenson, 1993) to illustrate some of this variability. The *MCD-I*
comprises checklists for parents to complete as a way of documenting their children's language development. The infant version consists of a 396-item checklist of
vocabulary items; parents are asked to indicate the words that the child understands
(comprehension) and those that the child uses (production). The toddler version is
more extensive; it requires parents to mark the words their children produce (from
a possible 680 items) and the range of word combinations they use. Parents of 673
children aged 8–16 months completed the Infant version and parents of 1130 children aged 16–30 months completed the Toddler version of the inventory; in addition, a proportion of the parents completed the inventory again 6 months later to
provide data on the stability of individual differences and the continuities between
different stages of development.

Bates et al. (1995) reported that, for most children, evidence of word comprehension appears between 8 and 12 months, and by 16 months children have a median
receptive vocabulary size of 169 words. Expressive vocabulary emerges somewhat
later, usually around 12 months of age, with a mean of 64 words produced by the
age of 16 months. However, these values mask considerable variation, as indicated
in Figure 4.3.

In a similar vein, there is wide variation in the onset and development of combi-
natorial language from 16 to 18 months onwards. Moreover, measures of mean length
of utterance indicate that typically developing children of the same chronological age

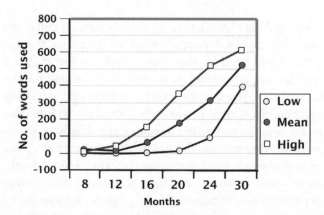

Figure 4.3   Growth in productive vocabulary for children rated as having an average
vocabulary size and for those at the 90th centile (high) and the 10th centile (low). It can be
seen that there is relatively little variation before the end of the first year but after this the
growth trajectories of individual children diverge, with the largest variation being observed
around 24 months, from a low of 89 words to a high of 534 words. (Adapted from Figure
4.7, p. 112, Bates, E., Dale, P. and Thal, D. (Eds – Fletcher, P. and MacWhinney, B.),
Individual differences and their implications for theories of language development. In *The
Handbook of Child Language*, Blackwell, 1995.)

can vary by as much as 6 months to 1 year in the level of grammar they use. One group of children who have attracted attention are so-called "late talkers" (Paul, 2000; Paul, Hernandez, Taylor, & Johnson, 1996). As the term implies, these children are delayed in the development of expressive language at 2 years though their understanding of language is normal; although most of these children catch up with their peers by school age, a substantial minority remain delayed, with problems of grammar and syntax being more common than problems of lexical development (Rescorla, Roberts, & Dahlsgaard, 1997; Rice, Taylor, & Zubrick, 2008).

Another source of variation seen in language development is in the relative rate of development of different language components. Thus, although there are strong correlations between language comprehension and production, some 10% of children show significantly better levels of comprehension than production, and this profile is often seen among late talkers. In contrast, there is little evidence for the dissociation between lexical and grammatical development for children within the normal range, though typically lexical development proceeds somewhat more quickly and is considered the pacemaker of grammatical development. Indeed children do not inflect words until they have used single words for a protracted period of time, and they only begin to combine words when their vocabulary reaches a sufficient size to contain function words, verbs, and adjectives, as well as a stock of common nouns. Together these data suggest that the cognitive underpinnings of receptive and expressive language may differ but there is more commonality to the substrate of grammar and vocabulary.

Language Development in Children with SLI

Arguably, the most striking characteristic of the language of children with SLI is its delayed onset and slow rate of development. As we have seen, the majority of typically developing children produce their first words by the end of the first year. However, the average age at which first words emerge among those with language impairment is around 2 years, with word combinations occurring much later. In addition, most children with SLI have some difficulties with phonology although these difficulties are frequently resolved by school age. The basic pattern in the early stages of language development in children with SLI therefore appears to be protracted development of single word utterances (i.e., slow lexical development) and a delay in learning to combine words into longer utterances. It is common for children with SLI to experience more difficulties with language production than with language comprehension, and there is evidence that children with receptive (comprehension) difficulties may have particularly poor outcomes (Rutter & Mawhood, 1991).

In general, the lexical (word-level) skills of children with SLI are better developed than their grammatical abilities, though they usually possess a restricted range of words for their age. A common manifestation of the lexical problem that children with SLI have is a word-finding difficulty, and their most frequent substitutions are of semantically related words ("goat" for *camel*). The other lexical difficulty that children with SLI typically exhibit is with the acquisition of verbs. It is possible, as suggested by L. Leonard (1998), that this problem is a consequence of their syntactic difficulties because the meaning of verbs is only apparent within a sentence frame.

Children with SLI typically have great difficulty with aspects of receptive and expressive grammar. Their problems encompass syntax and morphology; to some extent these difficulties may be a consequence of slow lexical development but this is not the whole story (Bishop, 2006). A number of theorists have argued that children with SLI have specific difficulties in learning certain rules of syntax (van der Lely, 1994; van der Lely & Stollwerk, 1997; van der Lely, Rosen, & McClelland, 1998) and another difficulty centers on grammatical morphology, particularly verb morphology (Conti-Ramsden, Botting, & Faragher, 2001; Rice, Wexler, & Cleave, 1995). Nonetheless, it is noteworthy that, in most respects, the development of language in children with SLI is along typical lines with relatively few children showing disorder in terms of the type of errors they make. In other words, most of the errors that children with SLI make in their speech are similar to the errors made by younger typically developing children.

The nature and heterogeneity of language problems in SLI

To be classified as having SLI a child typically has to have quite severe problems in a number of domains of language (vocabulary, grammar, and phonology). This contrasts with the language difficulties described in children with dyslexia whose problems are restricted to phonology. Given the complex sets of measures that are used to identify children with SLI, it is not surprising that these children constitute a heterogeneous group with a wide range of language difficulties. There have been a number of attempts to classify children with SLI into subtypes. As we saw for dyslexia, such attempts are fraught with difficulty and most taxonomies leave a substantial number of children unclassified. It has been common to distinguish between problems with receptive language skills (comprehension) and problems with expressive language skills (production). One of the most widely cited classification systems is that proposed by Rapin and Allen (1987), shown in Table 4.1. This classification distinguishes between the domains of language that are affected, rather than according to whether the disorder affects expressive or receptive language function. However, there is inevitable overlap between the two approaches; within the framework proposed by Rapin and Allen (1987), verbal dyspraxia and phonologic programming deficit syndrome primarily affect expressive language skills, whereas receptive and expressive language skills are affected in verbal auditory agnosia, phonologic-syntactic and lexical-syntactic programming deficit syndromes, and more subtly in semantic-pragmatic disorder.

Conti-Ramsden et al. (1997) used a statistical technique known as cluster analysis to identify five profiles of difficulty in a large sample of children attending specialist language units within UK schools. These clusters were as follows:

1 Children with severe expressive and receptive language impairments who performed poorly on all language tests administered as well as in word reading. This was the largest subgroup identified.

Table 4.1 Main subtypes of language impairment according to Rapin and Allen's (1987) taxonomy

Language subtype	Main characteristics
Verbal auditory agnosia	Type of "word deafness" in which the child is unable to understand spoken language
Verbal dyspraxia	A disorder that affects the motor planning of speech but is not associated with a neurological disorder of speech production mechanisms (e.g., dysarthria)
Phonologic programming deficit syndrome	A disorder that affects the production and intelligibility of continuous speech in the absence of problems of comprehension
Lexical-syntactic deficit syndrome	A disorder resembling phonologic programming deficit syndrome in which grammar and sentence production are also affected, and comprehension may be poor
Phonologic-syntactic programming deficit syndrome	A disorder of expressive language, characterized by word-finding problems, limited vocabulary, and errors of sentence production. Speech sounds are normal. Comprehension may also be impaired
Semantic-pragmatic deficit syndrome	A disorder of the use of language for social communication. Utterances are well formed but may be inappropriate, conversation turn-taking is impaired, and language comprehension tends to be overliteral

2   Children with complex multiword deficits who had difficulties with word reading, grammar, and narrative skills but relatively good phonology and expressive vocabulary.

3   Children with expressive-phonological impairments who had adequate expressive vocabulary and comprehension, but poor word reading, phonology, and narrative skills.

4   Children with phonological and single word deficits who had poor expressive vocabulary but were otherwise similar to Profile 3.

5   Children with adequate phonology, expressive vocabulary, comprehension of grammar, and word reading who were considered by their teachers to have difficulties with the social use of language. These children could be considered to have pragmatic language impairments.

Using a similar procedure, van Weerdenburg, Verhoeven, and van Balkom (2006) identified four clusters of Dutch-speaking children with SLI according to their performance on tasks tapping lexical-semantic abilities (including morphology), verbal sequential memory, speech production (phonology), and auditory conceptualization, emphasizing the synergies between the clusters defined by different researchers.

We do not wish to advocate any particular system for classifying children with SLI into distinct groups. However, it is generally accepted that pure speech impairments (sometimes described as speech sound disorder, SSD) are different from the problems seen in children with language impairments (Bird, Bishop, & Freeman, 1995; Nathan, Stackhouse, Goulandris, & Snowling, 2004; Raitano, Pennington, Tunick, Boada, & Shriberg, 2004). It is also generally accepted that impairments affecting the form and structure of language are different in their nature to deficits in the social use of language for communication (Bishop, 1998; Bishop & Norbury, 2002). Such problems in language use for communication and social interaction are now usually referred to as pragmatic language impairment (PLI). Since children with PLI display characteristics usually associated with autism, and the region of overlap between autism and PLI is the subject of an increasing amount of research (Bishop & Norbury, 2002), this is an important group to consider. We focus in this chapter on children with the more classic form of SLI and return to PLI in Chapters 8 and 9.

Linguistic and Cognitive Theories of SLI

Much of the research on SLI has been conducted by psychologists and linguists and these two disciplines offer rather different theoretical explanations of the nature and causes of the disorder. One of the main theoretical accounts of SLI is rooted in the linguistic framework of generative grammar and attributes children's problems to a deficit in linguistic (i.e., grammatical) knowledge. An important assumption of this approach is that the mental representation of language is modular (Fodor, 1983) and operates independently of other cognitive functions. In this "linguistic" view SLI is best understood as a failure to develop (partly innate) grammatical rules. The alternative cognitive approach is grounded in psychology, and sees the problems in SLI as reflecting deficits in processing rather than knowledge of rules. This approach views language as dynamic and distributed in its nature and inherently interactive with many other elements of cognition. On this view, a grammatical deficit is unlikely to occur in isolation, and will be expected to be preceded by, or related to, more basic cognitive deficits. There is little doubt that both of these approaches have contributed to our understanding of SLI.

Linguistic accounts of SLI

Despite the heterogeneity of SLI, it is generally accepted that the use of morphemes and word order to signal meaning (morphosyntax) is an area of marked weakness for many of these children. English-speaking children with SLI use grammatical morphemes (notably inflections) in obligatory contexts much less frequently than do younger typically developing children whose language is at a similar level. A variety of "linguistic" theories of SLI have focused on explaining the grammatical deficits seen in children with SLI. The details of these theories differ considerably but at a fundamental level these theories have the same form: they relate the problems seen in SLI to a deficit in an underlying grammar. In each case the grammar is a formal set of rules that is postulated to underlie the grammatical competence of adult speakers of the language (a generative grammar in the sense first put forward by Chomsky, 1957).

SLI as a problem with grammatical paradigms
Pinker (1979) outlined a formal theory of language acquisition that has been used to investigate the grammatical difficulties seen in children with SLI. He called this theory "the learnability condition." The learnability condition assumes that the child acquires a generative grammar, distinguishable from other formal grammars by its lexical component.

According to Pinker, inflections are stored with the lexical items they relate to as a set of equations:

e.g., [sings] = [sing] + TENSE = present; + NUMBER = singular
[called] = [call] + TENSE = past
[running] = [run] + ASPECT = progressive

To account for how appropriate equations are learned, the theory proposes that children create "paradigms"; a paradigm can be conceived of as a matrix of cells each containing a related affix. At first, the child acquires word-specific paradigms that represent how a particular lexical item is inflected in its different forms. These word-specific paradigms gradually contribute to the development of general paradigms that can be thought of as matrix representations of affixes free of stems (see Box 4.2 for an illustration of how these representations might be conceived). Once general paradigms are in place, the child can use inflections productively to mark new lexical items. Thus, given a new noun, such as *wug*, an inflection is added to signal plurality (two *wugs*) (Berko, 1958) or, in the case of the verb *wug*, to indicate past tense (yesterday they *wugged*).

Using Pinker's theory as a framework, Gopnik (1990) proposed that individuals with SLI are "blind" to syntactic-semantic features, such as the significance of number, gender, animacy, tense, and aspect. This view can then explain why children with SLI will show grammatical impairments that include problems with the selection of correct determiners and the choice of appropriate pronouns. In support of this, Gopnik and Crago (1991) analyzed data from an extended family of children and adults with SLI, focusing on six of the older affected family members (aged 16–74) and making comparisons with data from six unaffected family members (aged 8–17). Although the two groups were not matched for age, the comparison was conservative in that it might be expected that the older group would show more evidence of possessing an adult grammar.

The language tests presented to members of this family included tasks in which the participant had to indicate understanding of a spoken sentence by following a command, to generate plural and derived forms for words and nonsense names and tests of syntactic comprehension tapping active and passive forms, pronouns, and possessives. Participants were also asked to make judgments about the grammaticality of sentences. Table 4.2 presents examples of the linguistic items in each task and summarizes the results.

As can be seen from Table 4.2, the SLI participants appeared to have problems on tests that required the generation of inflectional and derivational morphology and in correcting ungrammatical sentences that required feature marking. However, their performance was unimpaired on syntactic tests that required the comprehension of pronouns, plurals and possessives, and in grammatical judgments about the argument

Box 4.2   Pinker's word-specific and general paradigms for inflections

	Word-specific paradigm			General paradigm		
	Person			Person		
Tense	1st singular	3rd singular	Plural	1st singular	3rd singular	Plural
Present	Walk	Walks	Walk	-	-s	-
Past	Walked	Walked	Walked	-ed	-ed	-ed

In order to explain how paradigms are filled out, Pinker proposes that there is a hierarchy of notions relevant to each type of affixation. For example, inflections that have clear semantic correlates that tend to appear universally across language, such as NUMBER (plurality), will be filled out first, while abstract notions will enter the picture last. An example of an abstract notion would be the ASPECT of a verb, which reflects the way an event is spread out over time. Articles (a, the) are represented in paradigms much as inflections are. In English, there are only two articles; these are differentiated according to DEFINITENESS but in other languages, e.g., French, the article changes to mark GENDER (un/une; le/ la) and NUMBER (les). Importantly, as we shall see later, the phonetic characteristics of an inflection (how acoustically salient it is) also affect its position in the hierarchy.

structure of phrases. The SLI group was also worse on a narrative task in which a cartoon sequence of pictures had to be described. Rather than use a linguistic device such as a pronoun to refer to agents in previous pictures (using *he* to refer to the *man*), which would ensure cohesion across the narrative, the SLI group tended to use full noun phrases, and one participant produced a series of descriptions of the pictures rather than a narrative.

The interpretation of the findings of Gopnik and Crago (1991) is complicated by the small number of participants and the ceiling effects on some of the tasks. In addition, other researchers working with the same family have pointed out that the widespread phonological difficulties experienced by the family members make it difficult to be certain about what causes errors in their spontaneous speech. However, the authors argue that these findings must be understood in terms of the underlying grammar that these people possess. Specifically, they suggest that the level of the grammar that represents abstract morphological features is impaired and that this can explain many of the syntactic errors that they make.

Table 4.2 Examples of Gopnik and Crago's (1991) language tests summarizing the performance of family members with SLI and unaffected members of the same extended family

Task	Examples	Differences between SLI and controls
Pointing to objects (simple)	Please touch the book/s	No difference; however, three SLI individuals responded oddly to singular and plural items
Pointing to objects (complex)	Put the crayon on the balloons	
Generate plural forms for nonsense names in pictures	This is a zoop These are ....(zoops)	SLI impaired
Follow complex commands	Here are three crayons; drop the yellow one on the floor, give me the blue one, and pick up the red one	No difference but trend for SLI to make more errors
Matching reflexive and nonreflexive pronouns to one of four pictures	He washes him He washes himself	No difference
Matching gender pronouns to one of four pictures	He holds him/her He holds them	No difference
Matching to pictures: active and passive negatives	The truck does not pull the car The truck is not pulled by the car	No difference; in 4/7 pairs the SLI case did worse and in 1/7 better
Matching to pictures: contrastive possessives	The girl's baby The baby's mother	Performance of both groups near perfect
Grammaticality judgments and corrections	The boy kiss a pretty girl The little girl is play with her doll	SLI impaired in judging grammaticality and correcting sentences; they were slow to respond
Derivational morphology: complete the sentence	There is a lot of sun It is ----- *(sunny)*	SLI impaired and they were slow to respond
Grammatical Judgments of argument structure (thematic relations)	The girl eats a cookie to the boy	No difference
Tense marking: complete the sentence	Each day he walks 10 miles Yesterday he _____ *(walked)* 10 miles	SLI impaired and they were slow to respond

Source: Reprinted from *Cognition*, 39, Gopnik, M. and Crago, M. B. Familial aggregation of a developmental language disorder, 1–50, copyright (1991), with permission from Elsevier.)

One apparent problem for the idea that an impairment in abstract morphosyntactic rules is the explanation for the speech errors made by the SLI cases in this family is that, within individual affected family members, correct grammatical forms (e.g., "I like books") co-existed with incorrect forms (e.g., "I like python") in the same person. Similarly, although they could comprehend pronouns accurately, they tended not to produce them in narrative where pronominal reference would have been appropriate. There was also a tendency in the written work of two of the younger family members to produce correct forms of irregular words more often than of regular ones. These inconsistencies between different examples that apparently require a common underlying rule seem to pose problems for the idea that the individuals with SLI do not possess a given rule. However, Gopnik and Crago argue that these observations suggest that the SLI family members depend upon lexical learning to acquire new words as unanalyzed wholes rather than lexical items that are marked according to the parameters specified by general paradigms. While this might be true, such an explanation becomes very difficult to test. Whenever a given rule appears to operate this can be attributed to learning an item as an "unanalyzed" whole, and when a rule appears to fail it can be attributed to failure of the rule. Returning to Pinker's framework, Gopnik and Crago (1991) proceeded on the basis of these results to make the bold conclusion that "a single dominant gene controls for those mechanisms that result in a child's ability to construct the paradigms that constitute morphology" (p. 47).

Rather than positing a difficulty in acquiring morphological paradigms, van der Lely and colleagues (van der Lely, 1994; van der Lely & Stollwerck, 1997) propose a higher-level deficit in relating such paradigms correctly. The Representational Deficit for Dependent Relations (RDDR) theory predicts difficulties with agreement and tense marking. It also makes predictions regarding the use and comprehension of passive sentences (e.g., *The boy is chased by the girl*) and pronominal reference (e.g., *Baloo Bear says Mowgli is tickling him*), both of which rely on long-distance syntactic relationships (van der Lely & Harris, 1990). Children with SLI have striking difficulties with these types of sentence and with other aspects of language that are structurally complex and hierarchically organized. According to the Computational Grammatical Complexity hypothesis (van der Lely, 2005), the heterogeneity seen in SLI is due to deficits in complex computation in at least one of three rule-governed systems in the grammar: syntax, morphology, or phonology.

SLI and the extended optional infinitive
Rice and Wexler and their colleagues (Rice, 2000; Rice & Wexler, 1996) have proposed a slightly different account of the grammatical difficulties observed among children with SLI. We will focus here on tense and agreement marking for verbs; in English, the marker *-ed* is typically used to indicate past tense, and *-s* to mark third person singular. As Figure 4.4 shows, whereas typically developing children have mastered the use of such grammatical markers by 5 years of age, children with SLI have not and do not appear to be on track toward the adult grammar.

The linguistic theory behind this account is complicated, though understanding its details is not necessary to understand the basic findings in relation to SLI. In order to describe the theory, it is necessary first to define "finiteness" in relation to verbs.

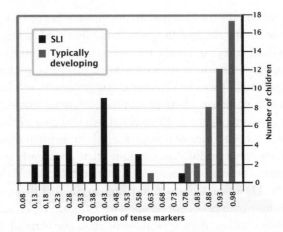

Figure 4.4   Number of 5-year-old children producing different proportions of tense markers correctly: (○) typically developing; (●) SLI. (After Rice, 2000, with permission.)

In English, verbs may take a finite or nonfinite form. Finite verbs can function on their own as the main verb of a phrase (e.g., he *sings*), whereas nonfinite verbs (e.g., *to go*) usually need to combine with another grammatical form in a phrase (e.g., *he wants to go* to school). The marking of finite verbs for agreement and tense is obligatory (he walk*s*, she walk*ed*; see Box 4.3). In contrast, nonfinite verbs are not marked but take the bare stem (e.g., they liked to *walk*, she made him *walk*; in these two cases the bare stem of the verb is combined with the infinitival particle *to* or with an auxillary verb *made*). To complicate matters further, in English this distinction is not always clear because a finite verb is not always marked by a surface form. For example, the singular present tense form *I walk* is finite and there is no grammatical marker on *walk*, but there would be if we changed this to *She walks*.

According to Wexler (1994), there is a phase in typical development in which children do not mark tense in main clauses yet they understand that finiteness has grammatical properties. Thus, at the same time as they omit tense and agreement markers, they will not use agreement where the adult grammar does not allow it. Wexler described this as the Optional Infinitive (OI) Stage. Since many errors in the speech of children with SLI appear to conform to this description well after the age at which such errors have been overcome in typically developing children, Rice, Wexler, and Cleave (1995) proposed that the grammatical development of SLI might be characterized as within an Extended Optional Infinitive (EOI) Stage.

To test the predictions of this theory for English children with SLI, Rice et al. (1995) compared the performance of a group of 21 children with SLI aged 55–68 months with that of two groups of typically developing children. The first was a group of age-matched 5-year-olds, and the second a group of 3-year-old children matched for mean length of utterance (MLU) to the children with SLI. The children in these groups were given a number of tasks to assess whether they were still showing signs of using OI constructions. The children's language was assessed by collecting spontaneous language samples and also in structured play settings that attempted to elicit particular grammatical structures. The simplest example to explain is the use of markings for past tense (adding *-ed* to the verb stem, as in "he walk*ed*"). To elicit

Box 4.3   Grammatical marking of finite verbs

Agreement of subject and verb
In the verb phrase "she walks," *-s* marks the agreement of the verb *walk* with the subject *she* (first person singular). If instead we said "she walk" that would be ungrammatical.

Tense marking
In the phrase "yesterday they walk*ed*," *-ed* conveys that walking occurred in the past. If instead we said "yesterday they walk" that would be ungrammatical.

A complication
In English, a finite verb is not always marked by a surface form. For example, the singular present tense form *I walk* is finite but there is no grammatical marker on *walk*; there would be if we changed this to *She walks*.

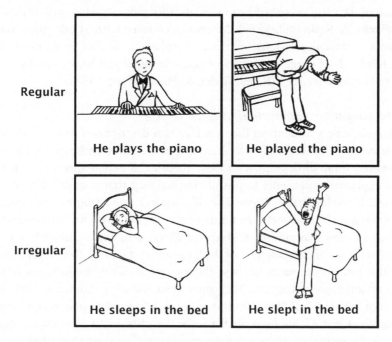

Regular

He plays the piano   He played the piano

Irregular

He sleeps in the bed   He slept in the bed

Figure 4.5   Illustration of past tense generation task.

the children's use of the past tense marker they were shown pictures. For example, they were shown a picture of a boy climbing up a ladder and were told "the boy is climbing the ladder." The child was then shown another picture where the boy had finished climbing the ladder, and asked "What did the boy do?" In this case an appropriate and grammatically correct response would include the phrase "he climb*ed* the ladder …" or "the boy climb*ed* the ladder…" in which the past tense marked (*-ed*) form of the verb "climb" is used (see Figure 4.5 for an illustrative example).

The results were quite striking. In this setting the typical 5-year-old children used the marked past tense form of the verb (climb*ed*) correctly in 92% of their utterances, whereas the corresponding figures for the 3-year-olds was 50%, and for the SLI children it was only 27%. Thus the children with SLI were less likely than younger 3-year-old children to produce the correct -*ed* past tense form of verbs. (Similar patterns of results were obtained for marking the first person singular -*s* form of verbs, and for using the correct forms of the auxiliary verbs *be* and *do*.)

In summary, the SLI children showed specific difficulties in mastering an aspect of morphosyntax (marking verb forms for tense and agreement). In this respect their mastery of a grammatical rule was even less advanced than younger typical children who were matched for mean length of utterance (a commonly used measure of level of language development). This pattern suggests that this is more than simple delay in development and suggests they have specific difficulties in representing the finiteness of verbs. The deficit within the EOI theory is considered one of knowledge; the children do not know that tense marking is obligatory in the main clause. According to Rice and Wexler (1996), children with SLI use this immature grammar for much longer than unaffected children. Problems with tense-marking morphemes are present in comprehension (as tested by grammaticality judgments) as well as production (Rice, Wexler, & Redmond, 1999). Moreover, children with SLI do not catch up to their peers in their use of tense-marking morphemes, so that while most children reach adult levels of usage by 5 years of age, one might still hear a child with SLI at age 8 say "Granny see me" (Rice, Wexler, & Hershberger, 1998).

Evaluating linguistic (grammatical) theories of SLI

These linguistic or grammatical theories give rich descriptions of some of the more pronounced language difficulties that are common among children with SLI. There are, however, some difficulties with these theories as explanations of SLI. In each case the explanation amounts to postulating a deficit that is essentially an internal component of the language system: The children lack one or more components of an adult grammatical rule system. In terms of the approach we are advocating in this book such an explanation is unsatisfactory: We need an explanation for why such a component (or set of components) of the language system fails to develop. One reaction to this from proponents of these theories would likely be in terms of nativist theories of language acquisition. According to such theories language might be seen as a kind of "instinct" (Pinker, 1994) that depends critically upon innate knowledge for its development. Going even further some theorists might even see aspects of the grammatical system depending upon innate prespecified rules that allow the system to develop when given only certain rudimentary inputs. In this view then, children with SLI "lack a gene" for grammar (Gopnik & Crago, 1991). We do not find such nativist arguments convincing, though they continue to be debated widely (Crain & Pietroski, 2001; Sampson, 2005). Ultimately however, such explanations are always open to being reduced to more basic levels of explanation of the sort that have been pursued in the cognitive theories of SLI that we will consider below. At a more specific level, there are a number of forms of evidence that pose problems for grammatical theories of SLI.

To begin with, it is worth emphasizing that the deficits in using morphology seen in children with SLI are not absolute. It is not that these children never use certain morphological markers such as *-ed* to signify the past tense or that they show an absolute absence in understanding a given grammatical rule, but they produce such constructions or appear to follow certain rules less often and less consistently than typically developing children. In fact the types of morphological errors seen in children with SLI are usually the same as those seen in younger typically developing children learning the same language. It is also the case that children with SLI appear to use morphology productively, as shown by overgeneralization errors such as "he throw*ed* it." Such errors show that children with SLI appear to be learning the morphological system of the language in much the same way as younger typically developing children; it is just that they find such learning harder (as they do learning the lexical system of the language). Such graded patterns of performance seem hard to capture in terms of a rule deficit.

Further problems come from observations in children with SLI learning different languages. English is a language in which the morphological system is relatively simple. However, there are many other languages that have much richer morphological systems. Naively, if children with SLI cannot "learn the rules of morphology" we might expect this to pose greater problems in languages with richer morphological systems. In fact the opposite seems to be the case (see L. Leonard, 2000), with children with SLI who are learning languages with rich inflectional morphologies having less trouble with inflections than their counterparts learning English. For example, Italian-speaking children with SLI are similar to younger language-matched children in their comprehension and use of verb inflections, as well as adjective agreement and noun plural inflections, although this level is lower than that of age-matched controls (Bortolini & Leonard, 1996; Leonard, Bortolini, Caselli, McGregor, & Sabbadini, 1992). In a similar vein, the use of verb inflections is relatively robust for Spanish-speaking children with SLI (Bedore & Leonard 2001) and for those who speak Hebrew, which is an inflectionally rich language (Dromi, Leonard, Adam, & Zadunaisky-Ehrlich, 1999). These cross-linguistic observations create a challenge for linguistic accounts of SLI that place the deficit at the level of universal grammatical structures or rules. Rather, the problem may be in the identification and/or interpretation of the evidence in the input. Leonard (2000) speculates that there may be a number of aspects of the nature of the language input heard by English-speaking children that contribute to their difficulties in mastering inflectional morphology. In essence, this view aligns with cognitive theories of language acquisition (Tomasello, 2000).

Finally, we should note that the necessity of postulating formal grammatical rules to explain the patterns of verb morphology development in typically developing children has been questioned. For example, Freudenthal, Pine, and Gobet (2006) investigated the patterns of OI development in Dutch- and English-speaking children. They present a simple computational model that shows a bias to encoding the end of utterances. They argue that such a bias coupled with information about the pattern of utterances actually heard by children (from analyses of large databases of child-directed speech) can explain the key features of children's acquisition of verb morphology. The model also does a good job in accounting for differences in the pattern of learning between Dutch and English, which relates to differences in the pattern of input (child-directed speech) in the two languages. Once again, such evidence and theorizing aligns well with cognitive theories of language acquisition (Tomasello, 2000).

Cognitive theories of SLI

Cognitive theories of SLI seek to find problems in basic mechanisms that might account for the language learning difficulties shown by these children. Broadly speaking, the cognitive deficits underlying SLI have been conceptualized as either general or specific. One general factor is speed of processing. Language learning is a complex task that requires the use of general processing resources and it is therefore precisely the kind of task that might suffer in the face of limited cognitive processing capacity. Within this view, a general resource limitation may underlie SLI (Kail & Salthouse, 1994) and consistent with this idea is the finding that there is considerable shared variance between language skills and nonverbal abilities (Colledge et al., 2002). In contrast, the "specific processing deficit" view suggests a deficit in specific processes (e.g., certain auditory perceptual processes) that may be necessary for learning and using language effectively.

Speed and capacity limitations in SLI

Much of the evidence used to argue for a general capacity limitation in SLI comes from trade-offs between performance and task complexity observed during language processing tasks. In spoken language production, errors such as word omissions increase with sentence complexity, and this effect is more marked in children with SLI than in younger children with similar language levels. In experimental tasks, children with SLI show difficulties with fast mapping and novel word learning, and these difficulties are exacerbated at faster rates of presentation (Ellis Weismer & Hesketh, 1996). Children with SLI are also slower at word recognition in lexical decision and word monitoring tasks, and demonstrate inefficient sentence comprehension (Montgomery, 2000).

If a general capacity limitation rather than a language-specific impairment is involved in SLI, then deficits should also be apparent on a wide range of tasks, both verbal and nonverbal. Nonverbal examples include mental rotation and peg moving (Bishop, 1990; Johnston & Ellis Weismer, 1983), while verbal tasks include picture naming (Lahey & Edwards, 1996; Leonard, Nippold, Kail, & Hale, 1983) and grammaticality judgments (Wulfeck & Bates, 1995). Findings such as these have led to the proposal of a generalized slowing hypothesis (Kail, 1994). In the largest study to date to examine the issue of generalized slowing, Miller, Kail, Leonard, and Tomblin (2001) directly compared the response times (RT) across a range of linguistic and nonlinguistic tasks for children with SLI and IQ-matched controls, as well as for a group of children with nonspecific language impairment (NLI). Both language-impaired groups were slower than the control group, with the NLI group (who were of lower IQ) showing the greatest slowing.

If reduced speed of processing is causally involved in SLI, rate of stimulus presentation should affect language performance. Hayiou-Thomas, Bishop, and Plunkett (2004) used a novel experimental approach to simulate SLI in children with typically developing language. In this study, 6-year-old children were required to decide if sentences were grammatical or not when they were presented in compressed speech at 50% of the normal speech rate. Performance in this grammaticality judgment task resulted in a similar pattern of errors to that reported in SLI: good performance on noun morphology (plural -s) and very poor performance on verb morphology (past tense -ed and 3rd person singular -s). Similar results were obtained in a condition with increased memory load. The finding that an SLI-like pattern of performance can be induced in children with intact language by increasing processing demands provides some support for the hypothesis that a processing deficit may underlie language performance in SLI. However, the children also had difficulty in a control condition involving judgments about phrases containing prepositions (in, on, at), a difficulty not typically reported in SLI, reducing the strength of this evidence.

Auditory processing deficits in SLI

Another influential hypothesis of SLI proposes that it is caused by a low-level auditory processing deficit, which negatively affects language development by compromising speech perception. Much of the work in this area was originally motivated by the research of Tallal and colleagues, who used a procedure now known as the Auditory Repetition Task (ART); (discussed in Chapter 2). In this task the children first learn to associate two different sounds with two buttons, so that they can reliably press Button 1 for Sound 1 and Button 2 for Sound 2. After this pretraining the children go on to hear two-tone sequences and have to copy the sequence they hear by pressing the correct buttons in the correct order (1-1, 1-2, 2-1, or 2-2). Children with SLI had difficulty with this task when the tones were brief (75 ms) and the inter-stimulus interval between the tones was short (150 ms or less; Tallal & Piercy, 1973). This was interpreted as evidence for a temporal processing deficit in SLI that specifically affected the processing of rapidly changing auditory information. Speech, which by its nature comprises rapidly changing sequences of auditory information, is thus very vulnerable. Consistent with this idea, Tallal and Piercy (1974) went on to show that SLI children had difficulty "repeating" (by means of button presses) sequences of stop consonants (e.g., /ba/ and /da/) in which the critical contrast occurs in the first few milliseconds, but performed better on the same task with sequences of vowels in which the critical differences between the stimuli were of longer duration. However, a number of replications of Tallal's early studies have found that while SLI children may on average perform poorly on the ART task this difficulty is not restricted to the rapidly presented stimuli (e.g., Bishop, Bishop, et al., 1999).

A different task that has been used in this area is auditory backward recognition masking (ABRM). In this task a masking sound interrupts the processing of features of the test tones that have preceded it. This effect is particularly strong when the interval between test tone and masker is short. Wright et al. (1997) compared 8-year-old children with SLI and age-matched controls using the ABRM paradigm and reported a dramatic group difference in the thresholds at which the tone could be identified. In fact, there was no overlap in performance between the language-impaired and the control groups in this condition (compared with conditions when the masker was presented simultaneously with the tone or before it in a forward masking position). Performance was better for both language-impaired (LI) children and controls when the tone was presented in "spectrally notched" noise in which frequencies near to the frequency of the tone were excluded rather than in filtered (bandpassed) noise. However children with LI particularly benefited in the backward masking condition and derived less benefit in forward and simultaneous masking conditions. A further important finding was that subsequent testing of four individuals from the LI group showed that, when the spectral notch in the masker was increased, performance could be improved to control levels. Together these findings suggest that children with SLI experience severe auditory processing impairments in certain temporal and spectral contexts.

Following on from this finding, a growing body of evidence suggests that frequency discrimination may be problematic for at least a subgroup of children with SLI (Hill, Hogben, & Bishop, 2005; McArthur & Bishop, 2004a; Mengler, Hogben, Michie, & Bishop, 2005). It appears that across a number of studies perhaps 30–40% of children with SLI have problems on frequency discrimination tasks (G. McArthur, personal communication). Moreover, amongst children with SLI, those with poor frequency discrimination tend to show poor nonword reading in relation to those with normal thresholds (who have more specific difficulty reading irregular words; McArthur & Bishop, 2004a,b).

One of the first studies to look at several indices of central auditory processing in the same individuals was reported by Bishop, Carlyon, Deeks, and Bishop (1999), who estimated thresholds for detecting backward masked tones, frequency modulation, and frequency discrimination using temporal cues, and compared these with performance on the ART measured 2 years earlier. There were marked individual differences on the backward masking and frequency modulation tasks and performance on these tasks correlated with each other and with the ART measure taken 2 years earlier, suggesting that these different auditory tasks were tapping into a common process that remained stable over time. However, none of the auditory tasks showed reliable differences between the SLI and control children, and performance on the auditory tasks tended to correlate better with measures of nonverbal ability than measures of language skill. Overall, the small differences in performance between the SLI and control children, coupled with high degrees of variability within groups, led these authors to conclude that auditory deficits were neither necessary nor sufficient as causes of language impairments.

To date, relatively few studies have investigated the acoustic cues that signal prosodic features of language in SLI, such as duration and amplitude. Sensitivity to such cues may be an important precursor to the extraction of segmental information required for word learning. To explore this issue, Corriveau, Pasquini, and Goswami (2007) assembled a group of 21 children with SLI aged 7–11 years and compared them with two comparison groups on a series of auditory and phonological processing tasks. The first was a group of age-matched controls (CA controls) and the second a younger comparison group of children matched for receptive and expressive

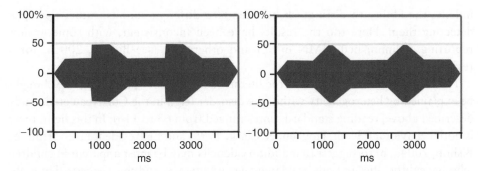

Figure 4.6 Schematic illustration of the stimuli used to assess amplitude envelope onset rise time. (Reprinted with permission from Basic auditory processing skills and specific language impairment: A new look at an old hypothesis by K. Corriveau, E. Pasquini, and U. Goswami. *Journal of Speech, Language and Hearing Research*, 50(3), 652. Copyright 2007 by American Speech-Language-Hearing Association. All rights reserved.)

vocabulary knowledge (LA controls). The key auditory tasks were tests of amplitude envelope onset rise time and duration discrimination, assumed to be important for the perception of stressed and unstressed syllables in words. There were two tasks assessing amplitude envelope rise time, each requiring the child to judge between a standard and a target tone. In each case, the child was told to indicate the "sharper" stimulus in terms of its onset (see Figure 4.6). In two tasks assessing duration discrimination, pairs of tones were presented and the child had to indicate the longer tone. In addition, each child completed a temporal order judgment task, an intensity discrimination task, and tests of phoneme deletion and rime oddity.

The authors report that between 70 and 80% of the children with SLI performed below the 5th centile for their age on one of the tests of amplitude envelope onset rise time and in the duration discrimination tasks, despite showing normal performance on the temporal order judgment and intensity discrimination tasks. However, the effect sizes for the difference between the children with SLI and the CA controls are much lower in terms of Cohen's *d* on the critical amplitude rise time tasks (one-ramp threshold: 0.49; two-ramp threshold: 0.18) than are group differences in phoneme deletion (2.58) and rime oddity (2.12), and they are similar in magnitude to the effect size for group differences in nonverbal IQ (0.47). Moreover, the SLI group scored more poorly than controls on tests of working memory and nonword repetition tasks. Thus the interesting conclusion of this study, that sensitivity to duration and amplitude envelope cues is impaired in SLI and predictive of language and literacy outcomes, must remain tentative pending further studies in which groups are better equated for general cognitive resources.

In a similar vein, the literature using electrophysiological measures to examine the neural correlates of auditory processing in SLI is mixed. Here some groups have reported group differences in components of the ERP (event-related potential) that correspond to detection of an auditory stimulus (e.g., Tonnquist-Uhlen, 1996), while others have failed to find reliable differences (e.g., Marler, Champlin, & Gillan, 2002). A different component of the ERP, the mismatch negativity (MMN), indexes the ability to distinguish between two different sounds, rather than just detecting them. Here too the results have been inconsistent, with some groups reporting a diminished MMN in SLI and others not (see Bishop, 2007a, for a review).

The inconsistencies observed in the literature on auditory processing in SLI might be explained by heterogeneity within the disorder (e.g., in the Corriveau et al. study described above, reading standard scores ranged from 63 to 116). In this light, there is both behavioral (Heath, Hogben, & Clark, 1999) and ERP evidence (McArthur & Bishop, 2004a, b) to suggest that auditory deficits may be most apparent in children who have difficulties in both oral language and literacy, and this suggests that auditory processing deficits may be particularly associated with language difficulties that include phonological problems. Second, the profile of auditory deficit may depend on the age at which children are tested and, following findings that the brain wave-forms of many children with SLI resemble those of younger children, Bishop and McArthur (2005) have suggested that there may be a maturational delay in cortical processing of auditory stimuli. A third possibility is that the problems seen in some children with SLI on auditory perceptual tasks reflect more general problems of sustaining attention in difficult and often lengthy tasks. In relation to this hypothesis it would be interesting for more studies to combine measures of auditory processing in children with SLI with a broader range of measures tapping nonauditory speed of processing. Finally, it clearly remains possible that auditory processing deficits may be a "synergistic risk factor" for language impairment (Bishop, Carlyon, Deeks, & Bishop, 1999) that, in the context of other risk factors, contributes to language learning problems.

Phonological memory deficits in SLI
Another causal hypothesis of SLI places the proximal deficit in the phonological memory system. This theory was first proposed by Gathercole and Baddeley (1990), who examined verbal working memory processes in a group of six children with SLI, comparing them to age- and verbal-age-matched controls. Although the children with SLI performed typically on tests of speech discrimination and articulation rate, and showed the normal effect of word length in memory, they had significant difficulty on a test of nonword repetition relative to CA (but not verbal-age) control children. The authors argued from this finding that SLI could be traced to a deficit in the ability to represent material in phonological form in working memory. In subsequent work, Gathercole and colleagues have argued that children need the capacity to store phonological material in short-term memory in order to learn new words (Baddeley, Gathercole, & Papagno, 1998). Thus, individual differences in phonological memory are predictors of the ability to learn new vocabulary in the native language and in foreign language learning (Service, 1992).

In the last decade, other studies have confirmed the presence of nonword repetition deficits in many children with SLI (Dollaghan & Campbell, 1998) and, along with past tense elicitation, nonword repetition has been found to be an excellent behavioral marker of SLI, discriminating children diagnosed with SLI from control children with a high degree of accuracy (Conti-Ramsden, Botting, & Farragher, 2001) even when their language difficulties have resolved (Bishop, North, & Donlan, 1996). Nonword repetition also appears to be a more effective marker of language impairments than standardized language tests in ethnic minority populations and those who speak nonstandard dialects (Dollaghan & Campbell, 1998). Finally, nonword repetition ability has been shown to be highly heritable in twin studies (Bishop et al., 1996; Kovas, Hayiou-Thomas et al., 2005). In an important study investigating the heritability of temporal order processing and phonological memory, Bishop, Bishop et al. (1999) tested 37 same-sex twins aged 7–13 years, one of whom in each pair had a language impairment, and 104 same-sex twin pairs of the same age from the normal population on Tallal's auditory repetition task (see above) and on Gathercole and Baddeley's nonword repetition test. In line with previous research, this study showed that children with SLI were impaired on both the ART and the nonword repetition test. Moreover, nonword repetition was a more robust predictor of language performance on tests of receptive grammar, comprehension, memory for sentences, and word finding than was ART, which only predicted receptive grammar when nonword repetition, age, and IQ were controlled. Importantly, whereas nonword repetition was highly heritable in this sample, ART was not.

The evidence that children with SLI show impaired performance on tests of nonword repetition is strong, though perhaps this is not surprising given that this is a measure of one aspect of language function (phonology). The best interpretation of the nonword repetition problems seen in children with SLI is far from clear. In one view nonword repetition is a complex phonological task that involves segmenting an unfamiliar spoken form, generating an appropriate speech output representation, and articulating the response (Snowling, Chiat, & Hulme, 1991). In this view problems of nonword repetition may simply be a relatively pure measure of the phonological processing difficulties that are one symptom of SLI. An alternative view is that nonword repetition indexes a deficit in holding temporary phonological representations in memory, which in turn are causally related to the impairments of vocabulary development observed in this population (Gathercole, Tiffany, Briscoe, Thorn, & ALSPAC team, 2005). Evidence refuting the strong version of this hypothesis comes from dissociations between nonword repetition and vocabulary knowledge in language impaired samples (Snowling, 2006) and from the finding that nonword repetition deficits are not universal in children with SLI (Catts, Adlof, Hogan, & Ellis Weismer, 2005). In short, although phonological memory resources are one component of new word learning, semantic factors and factors influencing the mapping of phonological onto semantic representations must also play a role. Whether nonword repetition deficits are best seen as a symptom or a cause of SLI remains open to debate.

Word learning deficits in SLI
Young children show a remarkable facility for learning new words, with estimates of vocabulary growth of around 10 words per day in the preschool years. In contrast, as we have seen, children with SLI show slow acquisition of the lexical and grammatical components of language. It is possible that, although these difficulties affect

different domains of language, they may be related. To the extent that children use sentence frames to infer the meanings of new words (syntactic bootstrapping), their word learning will be limited. The corollary is that these children will have limited resources for using the meaning of words to infer their grammatical relations (semantic bootstrapping). Notwithstanding this, the language learning difficulties of children with SLI could be attributable to a deficit in verbal association learning or in the storage of new word forms in memory.

Rice and her colleagues have conducted a series of elegant experiments examining a process described as Quick Incidental Learning (QUIL) in children with SLI. QUIL refers to a child's ability to discover the meanings of new words in naturalistic settings. The paradigm that this group has developed to assess QUIL is one in which children are exposed to new words, embedded in narrative, voiced over a short video film. Children are assigned randomly to experimental or control groups. The children in the experimental groups hear novel words in the place of familiar words during the video (e.g., viola for violin; aviate for fly), whereas the children in the control groups hear the familiar items. Before the film starts, children's knowledge of the control and novel words is assessed (pretest). At the end of the film, the children are tested for their understanding of the novel words that have been introduced using a four-choice vocabulary test in which the child has to point to the correct picture depicting the new word they have heard (post-test). Distracter items typically include another picture depicting a new word from the film and two other pictures from the film depicting items that were not named.

Rice, Oetting, Marquis, Bode, and Pae (1994) used this paradigm to investigate the effect of the frequency with which novel nouns and verbs were included in the film on children's ability to learn their meanings. In one condition they heard the novel words 10 times each (F10), in another 3 times (F3), and in the control condition not at all. Thirty children with SLI, aged 4–6 years, took part in the experiment, randomly assigned to frequency-10, frequency-3, and control conditions. Their performance was compared to that of individually age-matched controls as well as to younger children matched for mean length of utterance (MLU). As well as examining the performance of the children at pre- and post-test, this experiment included a test to see how well the children remembered the words 3 days later (retention test).

The results of study were complex, with different groups performing differently at the three different test points. However, the main findings are shown in Figure 4.7. Basically in the 10 condition both the SLI and CA control groups made significant gains in their word knowledge between pre- and post-test, while the younger controls did not. Strikingly however, whereas the control group knew even more words at a delayed retention test, the SLI group did not improve any further. In the 3 condition, the SLI and the younger MLU group made similar gains and losses, both of which were minimal, whereas again the CA controls gained in word knowledge throughout and after the experiment. The SLI group learned more verbs than nouns at post-test but made correspondingly greater losses from this word category.

Overall the results indicated that children with SLI learned on average 2.5 new words between pre-and post-test, a gain that was comparable to that seen among

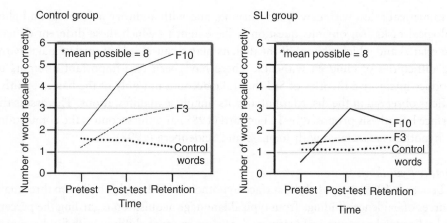

Figure 4.7 New word learning by children with SLI and controls: F10 (bold line) shows learning after 10 exposures; F3 (dashed line) shows learning after 3 exposures; control words (dotted) were untaught. (Reprinted with permission from Frequency of input effects on word comprehension of children with specific language impairment, by M. L. Rice, J. B. Oetting, J. Marquiz, J. Bode, and S. Pae. *Journal of Speech and Hearing Research*, 37(10), 106–122. Copyright 1994 by American Speech-Language-Hearing Association. All rights reserved.)

controls of the same age, although their absolute scores were lower. Thus, children with SLI seem to be able to form new associations between words and their referents, given a few instances of the new words. However this new word learning is not stable, such that 3 days later they suffer losses particularly of words from the verb category.

Oetting, Rice, and Swank (1995) extended this work to investigate the ability of older children with SLI, aged 6–8 years, to learn words from four categories: objects, actions, attributes, and affective states. There were five words in each category and each appeared five times. Once again, the SLI group showed specific difficulty in learning new action words (verbs) although they showed gains in their knowledge of the words from the object and affective state categories. The investigators did not test retention in this experiment, nor did they include a younger control group. Nonetheless, the findings add to the evidence that children with SLI have particular difficulty acquiring verbs. This difficulty may be because verb learning requires the abstraction of grammatical relations, whereas the semantic knowledge that underlies object names is relatively transparent. The data show that the view that vocabulary learning in SLI is constrained by phonological memory is too narrow since word learning depends upon the grammatical as well as the phonological attributes of the words to be learned.

Hybrid cognitive–linguistic accounts of SLI

The pattern of findings associated with the linguistic and cognitive theories of SLI that we have considered is quite disparate: children with SLI have difficulty with

grammatical rules, with new word learning, and with auditory perceptual and phonological tasks. An obvious question is the extent to which these different deficits
are related and which (if any) of the deficits play a causal role in the language learning difficulties of children with SLI. There have been two important attempts to
produce integrative theories of SLI that take account not only of the basic cognitive
deficits observed in the disorder but also its linguistic manifestations. The first is the
surface hypothesis proposed by L. Leonard (1989) and the second is the connectionist hypothesis associated with Joanisse and Seidenberg (1998).

Surface hypothesis
L. Leonard (1989) proposed the surface hypothesis of SLI, which builds on three main
sources of evidence: findings from typical language acquisition regarding the perceptual salience of grammatical features; data showing that children with SLI have processing limitations; and evidence from cross-linguistic research suggesting that
factors such as perceptual salience, redundancy, relative frequency, pronounceabil-
ity, and regularity are important in determining which aspects of a particular language
will be hardest for children with SLI to learn.

To take one example, in English many grammatical morphemes that appear late in
the speech of typically-developing children are low in phonetic substance and the same
grammatical distinctions are acquired earlier in some other languages where the
phonetic substance of the markers of these distinctions is higher. It seems plausible
therefore that these morphemes will be vulnerable in English because of their surface
properties (rather than their grammatical identity), particularly when there are resource
limitations. Even within grammatical morphology some morphemes are more vulnerable than others; English-speaking children with SLI have particular problems with the
past tense -*ed* and third person singular -*s* inflections, with the possessives, the infinitival *to*, as well as articles (Leonard, 1989). These are all morphemes with short
duration relative to the words surrounding them. In contrast, the progressive inflection
-*ing* does not seem to pose particular difficulty because this is of much longer duration
than the morphemes noted above, especially when it is in final position in a sentence.

The characteristics of the language and the consequent predictions of which elements
are likely to be most vulnerable are only half of the equation; the other half is the
presumed processing limitation in the child with SLI (be it processing speed or poor
sensitivity to auditory cues). The surface hypothesis suggests that limitations of processing will compromise the processing of morphemes, particularly those of brief duration.

Support for the surface hypothesis has come from a range of studies in English and
other languages (Leonard, 1998). The illustration from English given above contrasts
the relative difficulty posed by morphemes of low phonetic substance (past tense -*ed*
and third person singular -*s*) and the relative ease of processing those of high phonetic
substance (present progressive -*ing*). The comparison of SLI in English and in Italian
is also of note. In English, production of the articles *the* and *a* poses difficulty for
children with SLI, with about 55% of these retained in language samples. In Italian,
difficulties with articles depend highly upon their phonological form. Hence, articles
are retained 74% of the time in feminine form when they end with vowels (*la, una, I*)
but only 7% of the time when they end in consonants (*il, un*). Thus the surface

hypothesis demonstrates how cognitive impairments in SLI, coupled with details of the surface form of the language, could in principle account for the manifestations of SLI and how these vary according to the language that is being learned.

Connectionism

A second attempt to integrate cognitive and linguistic accounts of SLI comes from connectionist computational modeling. The connectionist perspective of SLI explains the high-level syntactic deficits seen in children with SLI in terms of lower-level deficits in phonological encoding and representation, which in turn are attributable to auditory perceptual deficits. In some ways this approach could be seen as an attempt to produce a computationally explicit version of the surface hypothesis (Leonard, 1989) and is also compatible with the phonological hypothesis of SLI (Chiat, 2001). In a computational model, one can directly manipulate the quality of the phonological representation and quantify the effect on the learning of particular syntactic structures, thereby allowing a rigorous test of the hypothesized causal relationship.

Joanisse and colleagues have applied this approach to examine two structures of particular interest in SLI: pronouns, which have been central to the RDDR hypothesis (Joanisse & Seidenberg, 2003); and the English past tense, which has formed the focus of the influential Extended Optional Infinitive hypothesis (Joanisse & Seidenberg, 1998). In the pronoun study, a sentence processing model learned to associate a pronoun or reflexive to the correct antecedent (in *Baloo Bear says Mowgli is tickling him*, the *him* refers to Baloo Bear; in *Baloo Bear says Mowgli is tickling himself*, the *himself* refers to Mowgli). When a perceptual deficit was simulated by distorting the phonological input to the model, correct performance on pronouns and reflexives decreased significantly. Importantly, the model could still resolve pronouns when additional semantic information (such as gender) was available, thus simulating the pattern of performance in SLI. In the past tense study, the model learned to associate the phonological and semantic representations of verbs; a perceptual deficit was simulated by adding random noise to the phonological representations during the training phase. The result again corresponded to the pattern of performance in SLI: Regular, irregular, and nonword past tense generation were all impaired, but – critically for demonstrating that rule-like behavior can emerge in the absence of explicit rules – the decrement was most marked for nonwords (Joanisse, 2004).

One of the advantages of the connectionist perspective, not yet fully exploited, is that it may be able account for how variations in different resource pools (say in the perceptual and cognitive domains) might be reflected in heterogeneity of language profiles. Increasingly it is becoming clear that there is no single cause of SLI. Rather, as we shall see, it may be the behavioral outcome of a number of different risk factors (Bishop, 2006).

Summary of linguistic and cognitive theories of SLI

It will be clear by now that understanding the cognitive basis of SLI is much more complex than understanding reading disorders. A number of the proposed explanations for SLI are explanations that are "internal" to the language system; this would include theories that see SLI depending upon deficits in one or more components of an adult grammar. It would also include theories positing that SLI represents a deficit in word learning either as a result of problems relating phonological and semantic representations or as a result of problems in maintaining a phonological code in memory for long enough to support longer-term learning. Accepting explanations for SLI in terms of deficits in language processing modules aligns with accepting nativist explanations of typical language development. As we noted earlier such explanations seem less than totally satisfactory but clearly, given evidence for the heritability of language skills that we will discuss below, it remains possible that there will prove to be deficits in the development of language-specific mechanisms in children with SLI.

There have been two attempts to identify more basic cognitive impairments that might explain the language learning problems of SLI. The first sees the problem in SLI as a speed of processing deficit. The evidence for speed of processing deficits in children with SLI is good, but the problem with this as an explanation of SLI is that it is too general a deficit. Speed of processing tends to increase in the course of typical development (Kail, 1993) and shows deficits in children with general learning difficulties (low IQ; Kail 1992). Therefore, it is not at all clear why the speed of information processing deficit in SLI does not just result in general learning difficulties rather than problems that are specific to language learning. One response to this criticism would be to point out that many children who satisfy current diagnostic criteria for SLI show a pattern of deficits that is far from "specific" (e.g., Hill, 2001). In this view speed of processing impairments may be one cause of SLI (that may quite possibly interact with other causes). The second basic deficit that has attracted a lot of attention as a possible cause of SLI is a deficit in auditory information processing. This seems in many ways an eminently plausible theory of SLI since learning spoken language clearly must depend upon adequate auditory input. The evidence we have reviewed suggests that this deficit is at most a weak contributor to the language learning problems seen in children in SLI, though the possibility that an early deficit in auditory processing has downstream effects on language development (e.g., Benasich & Tallal, 2002) has not been well tested. Overall, it seems we so far lack a clear and well-supported cognitive level of explanation for the language learning problems seen in children with SLI. Given the complexity of language, and the heterogeneity of language difficulties seen in children with SLI, it seems likely that explanations of SLI may require multiple deficits that may have differing effects on the development of partially separable language subsystems (Bishop, 2006).

The Etiology of SLI

Genetic risk factors and SLI

Quantitative genetics

A growing number of twin studies now show that SLI is a highly heritable disorder. Considering SLI categorically, more MZ twin pairs are concordant for the disorder than DZ twins, consistent with genetic influence on SLI (Tomblin & Buckwalter, 1998). Interestingly, concordance rates are increased for MZ pairs and decreased for DZ pairs if definitional criteria are broadened to include children with nonspecific language impairment (i.e., they may have low nonverbal skills in addition to the language deficit; Bishop, 1994; Hayiou-Thomas, Oliver, & Plomin, 2005) or children who may have had speech and language therapy but do not fulfill formal diagnostic criteria (Bishop, North, & Donlan, 1996). There is also recent evidence that the heritability of SLI is greater for children with speech difficulties (who are primarily those ascertained in referred samples) than for those with language difficulties of the same level of severity in the absence of speech problems (Bishop & Hayiou-Thomas, 2008). Interestingly, this latter group is also less likely to be referred for speech and language therapy.

Twin studies have also shown significant genetic influence on quantitatively assessed language skills, both in the normal range and at the low extreme (Bishop, Kovas et al., 2005, Spinath, Price, Dale, & Plomin, 2004; Stromswold, 2001; North, & Donlan, 1995). In two recent studies that included a wide range of language measures in large samples of preschool children, there was consistent evidence of moderate genetic effects on diverse areas of language skill, from syntax to phonology (Byrne et al., 2002; Kovas, Hayiou-Thomas, et al., 2005). However, these studies also provide some evidence that genetic effects may be weaker, and environmental effects stronger, for vocabulary, and that some of the strongest genetic effects are apparent for deficits in expressive rather than receptive language skills.

Molecular genetics

Quantitative genetics has confirmed a genetic influence on SLI, and pointed to the components of language that are most likely to be influenced by this genetic effect. Molecular genetic studies in this area were fueled by the discovery of the FOXP2 mutation in a UK family with many of its members affected by speech and language impairment (the KE family; Lai, Fisher, Hurst, Vargha-Khadem, & Monaco, 2001). The FOXP2 mutation on chromosome 7 was present in all 15 family members with the speech and language impairment, and not present in the unaffected family members, thus making it both a necessary and sufficient cause of the language impairment in the KE family. However, the KE family, although initially described in terms of specific grammatical deficits, has an unusual type of speech and language impairment that includes deficits in orofacial motor control. Such orofacial dyspraxia is not typical in SLI, and indeed the FOXP2 mutation was not found in samples of more typical children with SLI (SLI Consortium, 2002).

Genome screens in linkage studies of SLI have so far identified four potential QTLs (chromosomal regions linked to a disorder): SLI1 on chromosome 16q, SLI2 on chromosome 19q, SLI3 on chromosome 13q, and SSD on chromosome 3p (SLI Consortium, 2002, 2004; Stein et al., 2004). Although it is still early days, this work supports the idea that SLI is a multifactorial disorder, and that some of the heterogeneity seen at the behavioral level may be reflected in the genetic etiology. It also suggests that at least one of the component processes likely to be involved in SLI, phonological short-term memory, may be a promising place to begin unpicking the complex pathways from genotype to phenotype (Newbury, Bishop, & Monaco, 2005).

Environmental factors

It is likely that, as with most common disorders, SLI will be associated with interactions between multiple genes and multiple environmental factors (Rutter, 2005a). Much of the research on the environmental factors that influence language development has focused on the normal range of variation, rather than addressing SLI directly. Nonetheless, it is likely that at least some of the same variables will contribute to risk status for SLI. One plausible candidate is the quality of the linguistic environment provided in the home: Speaking directly to children, encouraging them to talk, and parents' use of decontextualized language and a diverse and complex vocabulary are all linked to larger vocabularies in children.

Another frequently cited environmental variable that may affect language development is otitis media with effusion (OME), an infection of the middle ear that is very prevalent among young children (commonly referred to as glue ear). Recurrent bouts of OME could plausibly affect speech perception and thereby general language acquisition; however, there is no evidence that it is an important risk factor for SLI, particularly when it occurs in isolation (see Bishop, 1997b).

Neurobiology of SLI

Children with SLI do not typically show any detectable brain abnormality but findings suggest that subtle neurodevelopmental abnormalities appear to be implicated. Unfortunately, progress in this field has been hampered by a lack of agreement surrounding diagnostic criteria and the inclusion of individuals with comorbid disorders in study samples. In addition, it needs to be borne in mind that few studies have conducted comprehensive analyses: frontal and temporal regions have attracted the most scrutiny and the majority of studies have relied on single methods of investigation (C. Leonard, Eckert, & Bishop, 2005).

A small number of studies have used brain imaging or electrophysiological techniques to reveal converging evidence of abnormalities in brain structure and function in individuals with SLI. Abnormalities of structure have primarily been reported in frontal and perisylvian language regions of the cortex, most often on the left but sometimes bilaterally distributed. Studies that have investigated the basal ganglia have also found damage or reduction in volume, as well as changes bilaterally in the structure of the cerebellum. The small number of functional imaging studies confirm patterns of under- or overactivation of these same areas during language processing tasks (Ullman & Pierpont, 2006).

Two sets of recent investigations deserve discussion because they have used more comprehensive methods of analysis. Studies of the KE family in which many members are affected by severe speech and language difficulties have compared affected and nonaffected family members. In initial studies, Vargha-Khadem and colleagues (Belton, Salmond Watkins, Vargha-Khadem, & Gadian, 2002; Vargha-Khadem et al., 1998; Watkins et al., 2002) revealed reduced gray matter in Broca's area with increased gray matter in left anterior insular and right sensorimotor cortex, changes in volume in regions of the basal ganglia and thalamus, and bilaterally increased gray matter in posterior temporal cortex and angular gyrus. Subsequent studies have broadly replicated this pattern of abnormalities although detailed analyses reveal variability in the quantities of gray matter in different regions. One problem in generalising from studies of the KE family, as noted above, is that it may not be representative of the SLI population.

C. Leonard et al. (2002) examined brain structure in children with SLI, contrasting them with children with dyslexia. This research strategy is useful because it controls for the comorbidity of language and reading impairments. Leonard et al. (2002) reported that the two groups were differentiated in that those with SLI had a smaller surface area of Heschl's gyrus on the left than those with dyslexia, and the planum temporale tended to be symmetric. Drawing together this and previous work, Leonard and colleagues proposed an anatomical risk index ranging from a positive risk associated with phonological difficulties (larger cerebral and auditory cortex and more marked asymmetries than the population norm) to a negative risk associated with comprehension deficits (for brains showing smaller cerebral and auditory cortex and less marked asymmetries).

To assess the validity of this risk index, C. Leonard et al. (2006) obtained structural MRI scans from 22 children with language learning impairments aged 11–16 years who were also assessed across three domains: phonological processing, literacy skills, and receptive and expressive language. The MRI scans were evaluated by raters blind to subject identity and hemisphere of origin. Overall, measurements of cerebral volume were smaller than expected for age for the group and there was an expected trend for cerebral volume to be greater in boys. For all children, better language performance was associated with slightly positive risk indices (indicative of normal anatomy). Importantly, children with negative risk indices had more severe deficits and deficits in more domains than children with positive risk indices who had fewer deficits (primarily affecting phonology) with relative sparing of receptive language and reading comprehension. The findings of this study are intriguing but they are in need of replicating on larger samples of children with specific and more general language processing impairments.

The neuroscientific study of language impairment is still in its infancy but together findings suggest that brain development is atypical in SLI (though it should be noted that anatomical risk is sometimes seen in the brains of those who do not show language impairments). Ullman and Pierpont (2005) propose a conceptual framework, "the procedural deficit hypothesis" (PDH), that holds promise for integrating research on the neural, cognitive, and linguistic bases of SLI and also explains heterogeneity in the linguistic and nonlinguistic deficits found in the disorder. According to the PDH, a substantial number of individuals with SLI have abnormalities of brain structures that constitute the procedural memory system, and these individuals may compensate to varying degrees by relying on the declarative memory system.

The PDH draws on dual-route views of language processing (e.g., Pinker, 1994). According to Ullman and Pierpont (2005), rule-governed components of language fall under the remit of the procedural memory system, while associative lexical learning is handled by the declarative memory system. In SLI, the PDH proposes that a disordered procedural memory system should impair the development of grammar across domains (syntax, morphology, and phonology) whilst allowing specific instances of rule-like behavior to be acquired by rote learning, enabled by the intact declarative memory system. Examples would include the ability of some children to rote-learn past tense forms (e.g., *walked*) without being able to generate novel forms, or the ability to repeat words but not nonwords that require the abstraction of phonological structure. Such compensation would be more likely for high-frequency or particularly salient forms.

Part of the appeal of the PDH as an explanatory framework, however, is that it also addresses the nonlinguistic deficits often observed in SLI. Procedural and declarative memory are not language specific, but rather two domain-general systems that are appropriate for different types of information processing. Therefore, nonlinguistic processes that are mediated by the procedural system – such as the learning and execution of complex sequences and hierarchies across cognitive and motor domains – should also be impaired in SLI. Conversely, functions that rely on declarative memory, such as the acquisition and representation of semantic and declarative knowledge, should be spared. The neural corollary of this approach is that the frequently observed comorbidity between SLI and other developmental disorders, such as ADHD and dyspraxia, may be accounted for by the overlapping brain structures and cognitive processes involved.

In its present form, the PDH is highly productive but it has limitations. In particular, as pointed out by Thomas (2005), the ability of the language system to compensate (for a procedural learning deficit) must be constrained in some way in the light of the relatively poor outcome for many children with SLI. Furthermore, more specific predictions are needed with regard to *which* children with SLI have a deficit of the procedural memory system, and what the theory predicts their comorbid conditions should be. The PDH is an intriguing hypothesis; it remains to be seen how well it can account for the complex etiology of SLI and its manifestations across development.

Treatment of SLI

There is a sizeable literature on interventions for children with speech and language impairments. However many studies are informal and a recent systematic review identified only 25 studies with adequate methodology to examine the progress of children and adolescents with primary language impairments in response to interventions (Law, Garret, & Nye, 2004). The interventions varied in duration and included focused therapies to promote specific linguistic skills as well as approaches that aimed to foster language skills in natural environments. Interventions that focused on expressive phonology and vocabulary development were found effective, with less evidence of effectiveness for interventions tackling expressive syntax or receptive language skills. There was little evidence that therapist-delivered interventions were any more effective than those delivered by parents, or of group therapy being more effective than individual approaches, although one study suggested that the involvement of peers was helpful. When interpreting these findings it needs to be borne in mind that the evidence base is limited, and within each study there was considerable variation in response to the intervention.

One specific form of intervention that has generated considerable research interest as an intervention for SLI because of its theoretical underpinnings is training in rapid auditory processing. According to Tallal and her colleagues (Merzenich et al., 1996; Tallal et al., 1996), the causal connection between auditory processing and language comprehension skills provides a clear rationale for capitalizing on the brain's plasticity for change and training children with SLI in rapid auditory processing skills. In two companion papers, Merzenich et al. (1996) and Tallal et al. (1996) reported positive results from a training program for children with language learning impairments that incorporated computerized games and activities to promote rapid auditory processing skills (*Fast ForWord*; Scientific Learning Corporation, 1997). However, this program is intensive and multifaceted, making it very hard to be sure which components produce such training effects. Furthermore, subsequent studies have not found the program to be more effective than intervention programs that do not manipulate the input processing rate (e.g., Cohen et al., 2005; Gillam, Loeb and Friel-Patti, 2001; Gillam et al., 2008). Finally, Bishop, Adams, and Rosen (2006) reported a training study that compared a computerized grammatical training program where in one condition the speech was acoustically modified to lengthen and amplify dynamic (changing) portions of the signal. The participants were children with SLI who had significant receptive language difficulties and were attending specialist schools. There were no reliable effects of training overall and no evidence that the acoustically modified speech was more effective.

Perhaps even more problematic for the approach advocated by Tallal et al. (1996) are findings that although it is possible to train auditory processing skills to within normal limits, transfer to language tasks is often minimal (McArthur, Ellis, Atkinson, & Coltheart, 2008), and receptive language skills may be particularly resistant to treatment. These findings also clearly pose serious problems for the theory discussed above, that deficits in rapid auditory temporal processing are a cause of the problems seen in children with SLI. Bishop et al. (2006) make the important point that children with SLI can comprehend grammatical constructions, often to about 90% accuracy, but they persist in making occasional errors – these findings imply that it is not grammatical competence per se that should be targeted by interventions. Arguably, the use of language in natural settings may be a more effective approach than the use of computer-based training regimes for children with such difficulties (Fey, Long, & Finestack, 2003). Furthermore, the accepted clinical view that interventions play an important role in improving aspects of socio-emotional and behavioral adjustment, and may also reduce parental stress, should not be underestimated.

Summary and Conclusions

The causal chain from the putative genetic risk factors for SLI to its educational and psychosocial outcomes is complex and varied. There appear to be several different developmental trajectories and, at the present time, the causal mechanisms are only

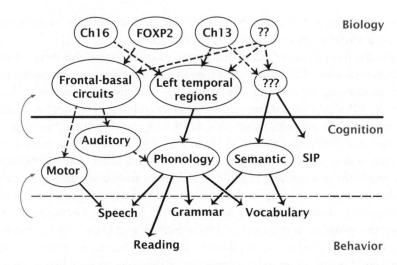

Figure 4.8   A path model for specific language impairment. (SIP = speed of information processing.)

partly understood. Importantly, genes have their action on brain structures through environments (Rutter, 2005b), and these aspects of the etiology of SLI are under-researched. However, advances in knowledge of the cognitive and behavioral pheno-type of SLI are beginning to bear fruit, both in terms of refining neurobiological research questions and in providing a framework for clinical practice.

Figure 4.8 shows a path diagram with separate biological, cognitive, and behav-ioral levels of explanation (Morton & Frith, 1995) that summarizes some of the research we have reviewed in this chapter. At the biological level, a number of genetic markers have been associated with SLI and these, in interaction with environmental influences, presumably result in atypical patterns of brain development in SLI. Although the links between neurobiological correlates and cognitive-level deficits are not fully understood, associations with multiple deficits in phonology and seman-tics are hypothesized, moderated by speed of processing deficits. Sensory impair-ments are also shown at this level but the causal association between these and the cognitive deficits remain highly controversial.

The mappings between cognitive deficits and behavioral outcomes are predicted based on what is known from studies of typical development. The heterogeneity within SLI is captured by the complex array of causal arrows that are shown. However, single deficits are also permitted within this model and single deficits will likely lead to different developmental trajectories than those associated with multi-ple deficits. For example, a child with a single deficit in phonology may present with speech sound disorder and, depending on severity, with concomitant literacy prob-lems. More typically, in children diagnosed with SLI, multiple deficits are observed leading to complex patterns of language delay and disorder.

Importantly within this putative model there are interactions with environmental input and experience at the biological and behavioral levels, and in turn behaviour may affect cognition through feedback loops. There is as yet limited evidence on how environmental experience can modify the behavioral manifestations of SLI, but key factors such as linguistic environment and the possible effects of intervention are represented in this model. We would emphasize that the model presented here is both complex and tenuous, and this we believe presents a realistic view of our current understanding of SLI. The reality is that SLI is a highly complex and probably heterogeneous disorder (or set of disorders) and at the moment we are far from having a complete or unifying theory of how best to explain the disorder. It is striking that the model shown here is considerably more complicated than the models of causal influences we considered in Chapters 2 and 3 for reading disorders.

5
Mathematics Disorder

In comparison to some of the disorders dealt with so far, particularly disorders of reading and language, there has been less research into the nature and causes of mathematical difficulties in children. Interest in these disorders seems to be expanding rapidly now. In many ways there are clear parallels between work on children's mathematical difficulties and research on children's reading difficulties. In both cases, we have an example of a specific difficulty in acquiring a critical educational skill. It seems likely that one of the reasons why less research has been devoted to children's mathematical difficulties than children's reading difficulties is that the typical developmental pattern for mathematical skills is more complex, and harder to understand, than in the case of reading. This in turn makes attempts to understand mathematical difficulties all the harder.

We will refer to problems in this area as mathematics disorder (MD). Alternative terms from adult neurology, particularly dyscalculia (literally an impairment of calculation) and acalculia (literally an inability to perform calculation), are still sometimes used to refer to mathematics disorder in children.

Definitions and Prevalence

The Diagnostic and Statistical Manual of Mental Disorders (DSM-IV; American Psychiatric Association, 1994) defines mathematics disorder as follows "mathematical ability, as measured by individually administered standardized tests is substantially below that expected given the person's chronological age, measured intelligence and age-appropriate education." This definition is essentially identical to the equivalent definition of reading disorder quoted in Chapter 2. This is an explicitly developmental definition, since mathematical skills need to be below the level expected for a person's age, intelligence, and educational experience. In contrast to studies of reading disorders, there has not been a great controversy about the use of a discrepancy definition of mathematics disorder (a definition that requires mathematical abilities to be out of line with intelligence). Some of the same issues raised in relation to a discrepancy definition of reading disorder apply to mathematics disorder as well (see Chapter 2). While there is no doubt that on average children of higher IQ tend to be better at arithmetic than children of lower IQ, this does not demonstrate that IQ is a cause of arithmetic problems, and there are rare cases of individuals of very low IQ who have superior calculation abilities (e.g., Hermelin & O'Connor, 1991).

The prevalence of mathematics disorder is less well documented than for reading disorders. In the UK, Lewis, Hitch, and Walker (1994) assessed reading, maths (arithmetic), and nonverbal ability using group tests in all 9- and 10-year-old children in a single school district. There were some problems with ceiling effects on the tests (which may lead to underestimates of the number of children with difficulties). They used a simple cut-off approach to defining difficulties (rather than a regression-based approach). A child was regarded as showing a specific difficulty if their standard score on the maths achievement test was less than 85 (roughly the bottom 15% of the population) in the presence of normal nonverbal ability and reading (at or above a standard score of 90 on both). Using this criterion, they reported that only 1.3% of children showed a specific impairment in maths but another 2.3% had both maths and reading problems defined in an analogous way. Thus, 3.6% of these children would be classified as having a mathematics disorder. Another large-scale study using laxer criteria (a standard score of 92, the bottom 30% of the population) found combined rates of mathematics disorder (with and without reading problems) of 11.2% (Share, Moffitt, & Silva, 1988). A large US study reported a figure of around 6% (Baker & Cantwell 1985) and in Israel Gross-Tsur, Manor, & Shalev (1996) reported a prevalence of 6.5%. Both Lewis et al. and Gross-Tsur et al. showed that it is common for mathematics disorder to co-occur with reading disorders. Given the different populations studied and the different criteria for classification adopted it is difficult to compare the prevalence rates from these different studies. It is clear, however, that mathematics disorder occurs quite frequently and that these problems are often associated with reading disorders.

As in studies of dyslexia, studies of mathematics disorder have usually used children selected according to an IQ discrepancy definition. The aim of using such a definition is to identify children with mathematical difficulties that cannot be explained in terms of more general learning difficulties. In some studies to be considered below, a direct comparison has been made between children with mathematics disorder and children with a mathematics disorder combined with a reading disorder (mathematics disorder/reading disorder).

The Typical Development of Number Skills: A Theoretical Framework

In order to consider the problems some children experience in mastering mathematical skills we first need to consider how such skills typically develop. Laying out the typical course for the development of numerical and mathematical skills is difficult, because the skills involved are complex and quite diverse. How, for example, are counting, arithmetical calculations such as addition and multiplication, and higher

$$\begin{array}{r} 2 \\ +4 \\ \hline \end{array} \qquad \begin{array}{r} 18 \\ -6 \\ \hline \end{array} \qquad \begin{array}{r} 54.01 \\ +48.89 \\ \hline \end{array} \qquad \begin{array}{r} 45 \\ \times 5 \\ \hline \end{array}$$

$$\frac{3}{4}-\frac{1}{4}= \qquad \frac{2}{5}=\underline{\quad}\% \qquad 13\overline{)403} \qquad \frac{1}{6}+\frac{1}{3}=$$

What is 15% of 180?

A car's fuel consumption is 10 **miles** per liter.

How many liters will it use over a 94 **kilometer** journey?

_____ liters.

Figure 5.1   Examples of the types of questions used in a standardized arithmetic test. (Adapted from the British Ability Scales II; Elliott, 1996.)

mathematical skills such as geometry and algebra related to each other? In what follows we only consider the development of basic number skills (understanding what numbers represent, and in turn the ability to count) and the development of basic arithmetic operations (particularly addition and subtraction). Most of the research on mathematics disorder has focused on children identified as having problems in learning basic arithmetical skills as measured by standardized tests. For example, the Wechsler Objective Number Dimensions test (Rust, 1996), the British Ability Scales (Elliott, Smith, & McCullouch, 1978) and British Ability Scales II (Elliott 1996) include tests of written arithmetic that begin with simple addition and subtraction problems suitable for young children and progress to more complex sums including multidigit multiplication and long division (see Figure 5.1).

Number concepts and the development of counting

Preverbal numerical abilities
In the last decade or so great excitement has been generated by the discovery that some primitive numerical abilities are possessed by animals and preverbal human infants (for a review see Dehaene, 1997). For example, rats can be trained to press one lever when two light flashes or two tones occur and another lever when four light flashes or four tones occur. When subsequently the animals are presented with mixtures of events that are synchronized (a flash and a tone at the same time) they respond in line with the number of events (the number of lights and tones; Church & Meck, 1984). This suggests some basic appreciation of numerical quantity in these animals. Perhaps more impressively, Woodruff and Premack (1981) trained a chimpanzee to select a physically matching stimulus – to choose a half-full glass of liquid that matched another rather than to choose a glass that was three-quarters full. What would the chimp now do if they were shown a half-full glass, and had to choose whether to match it with half an apple or three-quarters of an apple?

Figure 5.2   A chimpanzee in the study by Rumbaugh et al. (1987) selects a tray containing the larger number of food items. (Rumbaugh, D., Savage-Rumbaugh, S., and Hegel, M., Summation in the chimpanzee (Pan troglodytes), *Journal of Experimental Psychology: Animal Behavior Processes*, 13(2), 109, 1987, published by the American Psychological Association and reprinted with permission.)

The chimp chose the half apple, but clearly this cannot be based on any simple perceptual attribute.

Chimps will also select a tray with the larger number of food objects on it, without training, even when the food objects are arranged in a way that is misleading if they could not perform something akin to basic addition (Rumbaugh, Savage-Rumbaugh, & Hegel, 1987; see Figure 5.2). For example, a chimp might be offered a tray with a pile of five chocolate pieces and a pile with just one piece (six in total), versus a tray with a pile of four and a pile of three pieces (seven in total). The chimp will choose the tray with seven pieces, but this shows they must appreciate that the two small piles are greater than a large pile and a pile with just one chocolate in it. Such abilities at first seem very surprising, but arguably there has been considerable evolutionary pressure for animals to deal with numerical quantities and relationships when foraging for food.

Similar evidence suggests that human infants have some basic preverbal understanding of number. In a striking demonstration of this, Wynn (1992) showed 5-month-old infants a toy, which was then covered by a screen, then another identical toy was shown being placed behind the screen. When the screen was removed there were either one or two toys present; infants showed surprise (looked longer) when only one toy was present when the screen was removed. It seems the babies were expecting two objects because they had seen an object added to the place where there was already one object. With larger numbers of objects, when care is taken to control for cues such as surface area and density, it seems that 6-month-old infants

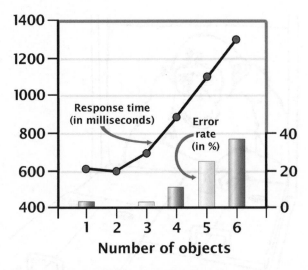

Figure 5.3   Subitizing: Reaction time is fast in identifying between one and three items but increases steeply thereafter. (Mandler, G. and Shebo, B. J., Subitizing: An analysis of its component processes, *Journal of Experimental Psychology: General*, 111 (1), 1–22, 1982, published by the American Psychological Association and adapted with permission.)

can discriminate between groups of 8 and 16, or 16 and 32 dots, but not between 16 and 24 dots (Xu & Spelke, 2000; Xu, Spelke, & Goddard, 2005).

Evidence such as this from studies of animals and preverbal human infants suggests that some basic numerical skills exist in the absence of language. This numerical system is probably somewhat imprecise and can only deal with small numbers of objects. Nevertheless, it has been suggested that such a preverbal "number sense" may form a foundation for more complex verbally elaborated number skills in humans (Dehaene, 1997). Evidence from older children and adults for such a rapid, if approximate, number processing mechanism comes from "subitizing" (Mandler & Shebo, 1982; see Figure 5.3). If people are shown displays of randomly arranged dots they can say how many are present equally rapidly for displays of between one and three; however for displays of four or more there is a clear increase in the time taken to respond as the number increases. This suggests that people can directly apprehend (grasp) differences in the number of objects present up to three but that after this a slower and more effortful mechanism akin to counting must be employed.

Finally there is evidence from a variety of sources that our understanding of numbers depends upon continuing access to some form of preverbal magnitude-based system. One sort of evidence comes from studies involving judging the relative magnitude of different numbers. In this task (Moyer & Landauer, 1967) people are simply presented with pairs of digits (e.g. 3 vs. 4 or 2 vs. 8) and asked to decide as quickly as possible which digit represents the large magnitude by pressing a key. The finding is that people are quicker to make such judgments when the difference between the digits is larger (people are quicker to choose 8 as the larger digit when it is paired with 2 than when it is paired with 7). This finding is referred to as the symbolic distance effect (SDE; see Figure 5.4); such an effect is the opposite to what

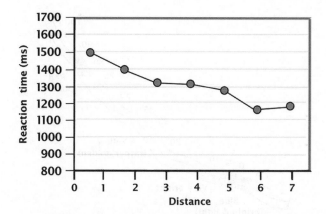

Figure 5.4   The time taken by 6-year-old typically developing children to judge which of two simultaneously presented digits represents the larger quantity (for digits 2–9). Digit pairs that are similar in numerical magnitude (a symbolic distance of 1: e.g., 2 vs. 3; 3 vs. 4; 4 vs. 5; etc.) are hard to make judgments about (slow reaction time); as the symbolic distance between pairs of digits increases, the task becomes progressively easier (faster reaction times).

we would expect if comparing the numbers involved counting. Instead the pattern parallels a pattern found when we compare the physical size of objects and provides evidence that even in adulthood our understanding of the magnitudes represented by numbers depends on accessing some form of analogue representation.

Such findings have been related to the idea that the magnitudes represented by numbers may depend upon access to a mental number line, where numbers are arranged in positions from left (small) to right (large; see Figure 5.5). This is an idea put forward a long time ago by Galton (1880). A further characteristic of the mental number line is that it seems to involve some sort of unequal spacing (or compression) as we go from small to large numbers, that is, the distance on the number line between 1 and 2 is larger than the distance between say 8 and 9. Evidence for this idea of a nonlinear number line comes from the finding that in the Moyer and Landauer task people are quicker to judge that 2 is larger than 1 than they are to judge that 9 is larger than 8 (the problem size effect). Note, once again, that if such comparisons were based on counting these two problems should be equally easy. As we shall see later there is now some evidence that children with mathematics disorder suffer problems in the nonverbal representation of numerical magnitudes.

The development of counting
Gelman and Gallistel (1978) studied children from around 2 years upwards and proposed that learning to count depended on a number of "how to count" principles:

1   The one-to-one principle: Each object to be counted gets one and only one count word.
2   The stable order principle: The count words (one, two, three, four ...) must be used in a fixed order.

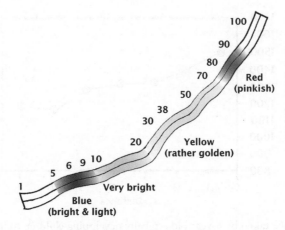

Figure 5.5   A diagram of the mental number line. After Galton, 1880, who suggested that people imagined colors at different points on the number line. (Galton, F., Statistics of mental imagery, *Mind*, *19*, 1880, pp. 301–318, by permission of Oxford University Press.)

3   The cardinality principle: The last count word used represents the cardinal value, or number of things in the set, that has been counted.

Gelman and Gallistel also proposed a further two principles that they considered less fundamental:

4   The abstraction principle: Any collection of objects can be counted (how many pieces of fruit are here?).
5   The order irrelevance principle: The order in which objects are counted has no effect on the outcome.

In Gelman and Gallistel's view these early "how to count" principles depend upon basic innate constraints on development that guide the development of effective counting skills. In this view, the principles outlined above are somehow known before children have learned to count. Such a claim is controversial and more recent evidence suggests that understanding the "how to count" principles may emerge from prolonged practice of using counting procedures (Rittle-Johnson & Siegler, 1998; Sophian, 1998). By whatever means children master counting, it is clear that it provides a critical foundation for the more advanced arithmetic operations such as addition and subtraction that are taught in school. Counting is fundamentally a form of measurement and one that is more flexible and precise than the form of measurement revealed in subitizing or in studies of animals' and infants' preverbal numerical abilities. Just how (or even if) preverbal number skills feed in to the development of verbal counting skills in older children remains an important, if unresolved, issue. Recent evidence (Gilmore, McCarthy, & Spelke, 2007) suggests that some approximation skills come quite naturally to young children when presented with simple addition and number comparison tasks. However, such ease with approximation tasks contrasts with the marked difficulty many children have in mastering basic computation skills, perhaps suggesting a disjunction between primitive estimation skills and exact computation skills.

The Typical Development of Early Arithmetic Skills

By the time children go to school they are generally proficient at counting, at least for numbers up to 10, and these counting skills form a foundation for the development of arithmetic skills. To become numerate demands more; children need to learn conventional systems and to use their mathematical thinking meaningfully and in logical situations (Nunes & Bryant, 1996).

We will concentrate on the developmental pattern found in studies of pre-school and primary-school-age children (mostly in the USA and the UK). Children are expected to master a range of arithmetical skills during the primary school years. These skills will involve (roughly in the following order) single digit addition, subtraction, multiplication, and division, and the extension of these skills to multidigit numbers. Children in the later primary school years are also required to master fractions and deal with proportions and percentages.

Single digit addition

One of the complexities in studying arithmetical development is that often a given problem can be solved in different ways (using different procedures or strategies). There is a great deal of evidence showing that the strategies children use develop in sophistication with age and practice. This is well illustrated by studies of simple addition.

Understanding how to add a pair of single digits (e.g., 2 + 2) is the first type of arithmetic operation to be formally taught in school. Even single digit addition is a complex skill. Young children, before they have entered school, may first learn to perform addition using the sum procedure. So, given the sum 2 + 3, a young child might count aloud or on fingers "one, two … three, four, five" – the last count word used here corresponds to the sum, just as in counting a set of objects. However a more effective counting strategy for solving such a sum is a count on strategy whereby the child states the number represented by the first digit and then counts up from there "two – three, four, five." Finally, the most sophisticated strategy involves the realization that identifying the larger of the two digits and then counting up from that involves less counting (such a strategy should therefore be easier and less error prone). This is referred to as the min strategy and involves the child understanding the commutativity principle: changing the order of the numbers in the sum does not alter the result (2 + 3 is the same as 3 + 2).

There is evidence that understanding commutativity is related to children using the min procedure for addition. For example, Baroody and Gannon (1984) assessed commutativity by showing kindergarten children pairs of sums (e.g., 2 + 4 and 4 + 2) and asking them to judge whether the answer to both sums would be the same. Evidence for commutativity involved children answering such questions quickly and without counting. Children who did this were more likely to solve simple addition sums (e.g., 2 + 6) using the min strategy. However, it was not uncommon for children to show understanding of commutativity but not to use the min strategy, which suggests that children may first need to understand commutativity before they can go on to apply this to selecting the min strategy when faced with an addition problem (Baroody & Gannon, 1984; Cowan & Renton, 1996).

This discussion of the very early stages of learning addition brings out a fundamental distinction that is central to understanding the development of arithmetic. This is the distinction between conceptual and procedural knowledge (essentially the distinction between knowing and doing). When a child is given a problem to solve, they may select a count all or a count on procedure (with or without consistently applying a min strategy). These two procedures are both "correct" in that they will give the right answer. However, even in this very simple case the child may "know" something (commutativity) that does not necessarily translate directly into what they "do" (using a min strategy to solve the problem).

Thus, addition, which is the earliest arithmetical skill to be taught in school, can be seen as a natural extension of counting. Later, as children learn the number bonds, they can begin to retrieve these automatically. Development involves change in the mix of strategies that are used. Importantly, the development in long-term memory of an association between the problem integers (e.g., 3 + 4) and the answer that is generated (7) requires practice in the execution of basic computations. With each execution, the probability of direct retrieval of that number fact or bond increases. This direct retrieval strategy is rapid and highly efficient and is the culmination of many less automatic computations of the relevant sums. (An analogy might be drawn with basic reading skills where after some limited number of effortful decodings of a word the child learns to retrieve the correct pronunciation and associated meaning of a printed word relatively rapidly and effortlessly.) It follows that children who have difficulty with the more basic count-based strategies for addition will take a long time to acquire a database of number facts, and they may therefore fail to achieve automaticity in arithmetic skills (Geary, 1993). Furthermore if count-based addition procedures are inaccurate and error prone this may lead to considerable problems if incorrect problem solutions are stored in permanent (long-term) memory.

How are number bonds stored in memory?

A number of formal models have been proposed for how the knowledge underlying the direct retrieval of answers to addition problems is stored in long-term memory. Ashcraft (1982, 1987, 1992) proposed a model in which arithmetic facts are stored in an associative network with retrieval occurring via a process of spreading activation. In this model there is a two-dimensional table, with addends (the digits to be added) along each side of the table, and the answer is obtained from combining the two addends at the intersection (activating the row for "2" and the column for "3" activates a cell corresponding to 5). The more frequently the input nodes corresponding to two addends are simultaneously activated along with the correct answer (activating the input nodes 3 and 2 along with the output node 5), the more accurately and quickly the correct answer will be retrieved. Activation in this network spreads more quickly for smaller valued problems (Ashcraft & Battaglia, 1978). This assumption of the model provides an explanation for a fundamental aspect of arithmetic performance, referred to as the problem size effect: People, even adults, are typically faster and more accurate when adding smaller (3 + 2) than larger pairs of digits (8 + 9).

Campbell (1995) proposed a more complex model of both addition and multiplication fact retrieval in which there are physical codes for digits (the symbols 1–9) that are associated with magnitude representations (an analogue magnitude representation of the sort proposed by Dehaene, 1997). The magnitude representations are less precisely specified for larger magnitudes and this accounts for the greater difficulty in distinguishing between pairs of large magnitude numbers than small magnitude numbers (Dehaene, 1997; Moyer & Landauer, 1967). In terms of this model, retrieving the answer to a given addition problem (2 + 3) depends upon associations between representations in the physical code (associations between the symbols 2 and 3) as in Ashcraft's model, as well as associations between these codes and the magnitude representations they represent. The lesser precision of the magnitude representation for larger problems in this model provides an explanation for the problem size effect (slower and more error-prone performance for large problems). Furthermore, it is postulated that the number of potentially interfering associations between physical codes tends to increase as digit pairs get larger. Thus in this model as problem size increases the number of competing associations in the physical code representations increases and the precision of the associated magnitude code decreases, and these influences both tend towards slower and more error-prone responses to larger problems.

Siegler's model (Siegler, 1988; Siegler & Shrager 1984) is simpler in that associations between digit pairs and both correct and incorrect answers are stored in memory according to the frequency with which the digit pair has been associated with the different answers. The stronger and more numerous the associations between a sum and incorrect solutions in memory, the slower and more error prone will be retrieval of the correct answer. In this view the problem size effect should be strong in children (where many inaccurate solutions may be stored with appreciable frequency) but this effect should disappear with extensive practice (the associations between 3 + 2 → 5 and 8 + 9 → 17 should eventually be equally easy to retrieve if each problem has been encountered and answered correctly enough times). In this model, the problem size effect is essentially a form of frequency effect, such that problems that are encountered often yield faster and more accurate responses.

The details of these different models are not crucial for present purposes. All the models agree that associations between number representations are formed in memory, and these associations are influenced by the frequency with which they occur. All of the models considered would anticipate that errors in counting during problem solving by children will tend to make their retrieval of the correct answers to addition problems slower and more error prone, and that is the basic pattern found in children with mathematics disorder. Much more research would be needed to identify whether detailed patterns of addition performance in children with mathematics disorder can be used to constrain or test these different models.

Summary of the typical development of arithmetic

We have concentrated on the development of addition skills for pairs of single digit numbers because these have been so thoroughly studied and some of the principles revealed probably apply generally to other aspects of arithmetic (subtraction, multiplication, and division). Even in what is the simplest example of arithmetic (adding two digits) there are multiple procedures (strategies) that a child might use. The evidence is that children typically move through these strategies in the order described (count all, count on, count on from min) initially using fingers as an aid to counting. It is important to note that all three strategies are correct in the sense of yielding the correct answer, but the developmental sequence is one of moving from a less efficient, more effortful, procedure to a more efficient one. Finally such computational strategies gradually generate knowledge in long-term memory with practice and repeated use so that when given a sum (e.g., 3 + 5) the child can rapidly retrieve from long-term memory the correct answer (8). This is an example of the cumulative nature of mathematical development. If a child has problems in counting, these will lead to problems in executing basic procedures for addition, which in turn will lead to problems in creating an effective knowledge base of number facts in long-term memory. This raises the possibility that mathematical difficulties observed in older children (say addition problems in a 9-year-old child) may depend upon difficulties with basic procedures at an earlier stage (problems in learning to count accurately when the child was much younger).

The Nature of Arithmetic Difficulties in Children with Mathematics Disorder

Before considering the possible cognitive causes of mathematics disorder, it is useful to describe the pattern of difficulties shown by these children on basic arithmetic tasks. Geary (1990) studied a group of 29 children with "learning disabilities" (LD) who had weak reading and arithmetic skills with an average age of 8 years 4 months. These children were reassessed on standardized tests 10 months after their initial tests and 16 children with continuing problems in arithmetic were identified. Each child completed a set of single digit addition problems presented on a computer screen, which allowed the speed of the child's spoken response to be recorded. Observations made on each trial noted whether the child counted aloud or on their fingers, or used their fingers in another way. The 16 children with continuing maths difficulties were more likely to make errors in counting when solving these simple addition problems, and though they were less likely to retrieve answers from memory for the problems, on the trials when they did so they were more likely to make an error. Thus these children's addition was inaccurate compared to that of children of their own age when using either a counting or a direct retrieval strategy. The LD children when using counting strategies did not count more slowly than the typically developing children, though their speed of counting was more variable. Overall, the pattern reported by Geary is compatible with the idea that the children with LD (who had both mathematics disorder and reading disorder) have problems in counting accurately. Such problems with counting might account for difficulties in solving addition problems with a counting strategy. In addition the frequent counting errors made by these children may also contribute to the difficulties they have in using a direct retrieval strategy (because the counting errors they make when solving addition problems tend to lead them to store faulty representations of number bonds in long-term memory). However, one problem in interpreting the difficulties shown by this group of children is that the majority appeared to have impairments of both reading and arithmetic.

Jordan, Hanich, and Kaplan (2003) conducted a 16-month longitudinal study of four groups of children: mathematics disorder (MD), reading disorder (RD), mathematics disorder/reading disorder (MD/RD), and typically achieving children matched for age. There were just over 40 children in each group who were selected by giving group tests of reading and arithmetic to over 600 7- to 9-year-old children. The MD and MD/RD children did not have particularly severe arithmetic difficulties, with an average arithmetic percentile score of 22 (MD) or 21 (MD/RD) (i.e., on average these children were in the bottom 22% of children in terms of their achievements on the standardized arithmetic test used).

The children were given a battery of arithmetic measures on four occasions: place value, requiring the child to identify which digit in a two- or three-digit written number corresponded to the number of units, tens, or hundreds; calculation principles, in which the child had to respond quickly to the second of two sums, where the second sum could be solved easily on the basis of having given the answer to the first (e.g., 47 + 86 = 133; so 86 + 47 = ?); number fact retrieval, involving a speeded measure of simple addition; exact calculation, involving a set of eight written addition and subtraction problems; story problems, where the child was presented orally with an arithmetic word problem to solve; and approximate arithmetic, where children had to select the answer to a sum that was closest to the correct value (e.g., 4 + 5 = 10 or 20?). The results of this study were clear in showing that the MD/RD children tended to have more severe difficulties on all of the arithmetic tasks than the MD, group (and significantly more severe problems on exact calculation, story problems, and calculation principles) even though they had not differed significantly in terms of the standardized test on which they had been identified at screening. Perhaps surprisingly, both the MD and MD/RD children showed the same rates of improvement on arithmetic measures as the control group. The MD/RD group tended to use an immature addition strategy (finger counting) more than did the RD and control groups.

This study shows that the problems with arithmetic identified in the 7–9-year-old range tend to be stable, and surprisingly there were no differences in the rate of development of arithmetic skills in the MD group compared to control children (however, arguably these children did not have severe difficulties to begin with). The MD children tended to use immature, slow, and error-prone calculation strategies and to have problems in retrieving correct solutions from long-term memory. One further important finding is that the MD/RD children clearly had more severe problems than the MD children. Finally, the RD children in this study showed a tendency to have weaker arithmetic skills than controls on most measures (except approximate arithmetic). This finding suggests that the phonological deficits found in the RD children may have some small effects on arithmetic, but these problems are different to those causing difficulties for the MD children. In this view the MD/RD children may suffer from two relatively independent deficits: a phonological deficit (perhaps giving rise to problems learning and executing the count sequence) and a more basic arithmetical deficit (which is not phonologically based but is present also in the MD children).

Cognitive Bases of Difficulties in Children with Mathematics Disorder

Studies of children with mathematics disorder (with or without a reading disorder) have investigated a number of the components of arithmetic development outlined above. Likely potential causes of arithmetical difficulties include:

1 Number (magnitude) representation problems: basic difficulties in representing numbers (learning number symbols (5) and number words (five) and mapping these onto the underlying magnitudes they represent).
2 Counting problems.
3 Number fact storage problems: difficulties in learning and storing the solutions to problems (e.g., 3 + 5 = 8) that form the basis of the direct retrieval strategy for mental arithmetic problems.
4 Attentional control and working memory problems: problems in executing the processes (strategies) required to solve a problem because of problems in storing and manipulating information in working memory or problems of attentional control involved in selecting and monitoring the execution of these strategies.

We have listed these potential problems in order of their complexity and we will consider each of them in turn. This is not an exhaustive list of possible cognitive deficits and nor are the deficits mutually exclusive (different children might have some, all, or none of these deficits). It is also worth noting that these potential cognitive deficits might, developmentally, be causally related to each other. For example, initial problems in representing numbers might in turn lead to problems in counting, which in turn may lead to problems in learning problem solutions that are to be stored in memory. Such problems with counting and/or retrieval processes will in turn place extra demands on attentional resources and might lead to apparent working memory/attentional control difficulties. We are arguing here that there may be a developmental "cascade" of difficulties, with problems with elementary processes early in development (e.g., counting problems) leading to other problems later in development (e.g., problems with direct number fact retrieval). However, depending upon the age at which children are studied, the original problems may have largely resolved in groups of older children (an 11-year-old child with mathematics disorder may appear to count competently, but that does not mean that problems with counting when they were 5 years old may not have contributed to the problems now observed). These possible interrelationships between difficulties makes identifying the basic, or primary, cognitive causes of mathematics disorder particularly challenging.

Problems of number representation

There is a limited amount of evidence that children with mathematics disorder have basic problems with number representation. Geary, Hoard, and Hamson (1999) found that a minority of children with mathematics disorder/reading disorder could not name "12" when it was presented visually, and that some of these children could not write "13" when it was dictated to them. These children were accurate, however, when given equivalent tasks with single digit numbers. Furthermore they report that for a group of MD children (who were of higher IQ than the MD/RD group) there were no equivalent problems in reading or writing these numbers. Unfortunately only a small array of numbers was assessed in this study, there were no measures of speed taken, and accuracy levels were essentially at ceiling. A small number of the MD and MD/RD children in this study were also reported to make errors on an untimed digit comparison task where they were required to choose the digit representing the larger number from a pair (e.g., 5–7) while age-matched typically developing children were essentially perfect on this task. Landerl, Bevan, and Butterworth (2004) studied 10 RD, 10 MD and 10 MD/RD children who were around 8–9 years old. Unfortunately, standard scores for these groups' reading and arithmetic skills are not given, and nor was any information presented on their verbal IQ (groups were matched on nonverbal IQ), making their cognitive profiles difficult to discern. It appears that the RD group had age-appropriate arithmetic skills and severely deficient reading skills, the MD group had weak reading skills and moderately impaired arithmetic skills, and the MD/RD group had severe reading problems and similar arithmetic skills to the MD group. The children were asked to name single and double digit numbers and color patches presented on a computer screen. The results suggested that only the MD group were slower than controls to name single digit numbers, while all three groups (MD, MD/RD, and RD) were slower than controls to name double digit numbers. The RD group were slowest to name the colors but the MD and MD/RD groups also appeared somewhat slow on this task.

These children were also asked to make speeded comparisons of the magnitude of single digit numbers (which is the larger number: 4 vs. 6?) or the physical size of two numbers (which is bigger: 4 vs. 6?, when the physical size of the digit varied independently of its numerical magnitude). There were no differences between the four groups of children on the physical size judgment task, which rules out any general differences in perceptual or motor speed between the groups that could affect their judgments of numerical magnitude. However, the MD and MD/RD groups were slower than both the control and RD group in judging numerical magnitudes. This is an important result and provides support for the idea that children with mathematics disorder (with or without accompanying reading disorder) have a basic deficit in representing numerical information. Similar effects were obtained by Passolunghi and Siegel (2004), who compared a group of 22 10-year-old children with mathematics disorder to a group of 27 control children matched for age and vocabulary knowledge. (It should be noted that although the MD and control children did not differ on a standardized measure of reading comprehension, there was a moderate difference between the groups on this measure ($d = 0.38$) and no assessment of reading accuracy or speed was taken – hence these children may not be a totally pure MD group). The MD children were slower and less accurate in making odd/even judgments about single and multidigit numbers, and slower in making magnitude judgments about 16 single and multidigit numbers.

Finally, in a larger-scale study, Rousselle and Noël (2007) examined the speed of digit magnitude judgments (which is the larger number, 2 or 4?) in 42 children with mathematics disorder (16 of whom had mathematics disorder/reading disorder) and 42 age-matched control children (the children were 7 years old, and those with mathematics disorder were in the lowest 15% of the population for mathematical skills). The MD and MD/RD children showed equivalent levels of performance on this task, and were much slower than controls (effect size $d = 1.2$). Strikingly, these same groups did not differ in their ability to make speeded judgments about the number of lines presented in two sets side by side on the computer screen (which group of lines contains more?). Hence the difficulty in children with mathematics disorder appeared specific to accessing numerical magnitudes, and did not extend to judging numerosity. The evidence from these group studies is paralleled by an earlier case study of an adult university student with dyscalculia. Butterworth (1999) described the case of "Charles" who showed severe deficits on a number comparison task.

In summary, the studies of Landerl et al. (2004), Passolunghi and Siegel (2004), and Rouselle and Noël (2007) provide support for the claim that MD children may have a very basic deficit in representing the meaning of numbers (the magnitude signified by a digit). This is a deficit not shared with RD children. The finding of these low-level problems in representing numerical magnitudes in MD children suggests that some aspect of a preverbal "number module" or "number sense" (as proposed by Dehaene, 1992; Butterworth, 1995) may be a core feature of children with mathematics disorder. It seems possible, but far from certain, that this problem may in turn contribute to problems in learning to count.

Counting problems in children with mathematics disorder

Application and understanding of count principles
Children with mathematics disorder have problems in learning to count. Geary, Bow-Thomas, and Yao (1992) studied counting in a group of 13 7-year-old children with mathematics disorder/reading disorder. These children scored between the 2nd and 42nd percentile on an arithmetic test (meaning there was a wide range from severe to mild arithmetical difficulties in the group). It is mentioned that many of these children had associated reading problems, though no information on the children's reading skills, or IQs, is presented. In this study the children watched a puppet count an array of objects and had to indicate whether the puppet had counted correctly or not. Sometimes the puppet counted correctly but on other trials made an error by violating one of Gelman and Gallistel's principles of counting (such as

counting either the first or last item in the array twice – a violation of the one-to-one correspondence principle). These MD/RD children, compared to control children of the same age, often incorrectly accepted trials when the first object was counted twice as correct. It was suggested that this might have reflected a difficulty holding the information about the initial count in memory until the children were allowed to respond to say whether the count was correct or incorrect. The MD/RD children were also more prone than control children to wrongly indicate that trials on which the puppet did not count adjacent items consecutively were wrong. This suggests a limited understanding of the essential features of counting, though one might argue that the children here were sensitive to the fact that counting things in a nonadjacent order is a nonoptimal strategy that might easily lead to errors in counting.

In an extension to this study (Geary et al., 1999) children in Grades 1 and 2 of at least low-average IQ with either mathematics disorder, reading disorder or both (mathematics disorder/reading disorder) were selected. The results essentially replicated those of Geary et al. (1992) in showing that both groups with mathematics disorder (MD and MD/RD) differed from children with reading disorder and controls on the nonadjacent count trials (wrongly claiming that these were incorrect) and on the first item double-count trials (for the younger children only). The MD children performed just like the MD/RD children, indicating that the earlier results of Geary et al. (1992) were unlikely to be due to including children with both mathematics disorder and reading disorder.

It appears that many young children with mathematics disorder have some limitations in their understanding of the conceptual basis of counting, though the problems they have in this domain do not appear to be severe. Geary et al. (1992) argued that the MD children in their study largely understood Gelman and Gallistel's three fundamental principles of how to count (one-to-one invariance, stable order, and cardinality), though they tended to see some irrelevant aspects of counting (adjacency) as important, just as younger typically developing children often do (Briars & Siegler, 1984).

Problems with counting speed
Passolunghi and Siegel (2004) found that their group of 10-year-old children with mathematics disorder were slower to count arrays of 7–10 dots on cards than were controls. Landerl et al. (2004) asked their children with mathematics disorder, mathematics disorder/reading disorder and reading disorder to count as quickly as possible from 1 to 20, from 45 to 65, and from 1 to 20 in twos. Both the MD and MD/RD groups were slower at counting, particularly in the higher range of numbers tested, and when counting in twos. The RD group were also somewhat slower but not as slow as the MD and MD/RD groups. These findings must be treated as tentative given the small sample sizes involved, but they suggest that children with mathematics disorder may be slower to learn to count, and that when they are older they remain slow at counting.

It appears from these studies that children with mathematics disorder may have a basic deficit in number representation (as assessed by their difficulties on the number magnitude judgment task described earlier). In contrast, children with reading disorder do not have such a deficit, but do share with MD children some difficulty in counting (less severe than the problems encountered by MD children). Tentatively, we suggest that both of these problems (number representation and counting diffi-culties) might contribute to the problems of learning arithmetic experienced by MD children.

Problems in storing numerical information in long-term memory

Children with mathematics disorder seem to have great difficulty retrieving number facts from memory. There are at least two ways of thinking about this problem. First, it might simply reflect the fact that these children have not had the typical opportunities to learn and store this information in long-term memory. Given that these children make frequent counting errors when trying to solve addition prob-lems, it is possible that they have limited opportunities to learn the correct answer to a problem because they generate so many incorrect solutions (which may also be stored in memory and so contribute to slow and error-prone performance). This idea probably provides a partial reason for the problems these children have in retrieving number facts from memory but it seems unlikely that it provides a sufficient expla-nation for most of the problems observed.

A second possibility is that there are problems in either encoding information into memory or in storing it adequately once it is encoded. In this view even when a child with mathematics disorder correctly generates the answer to a problem by counting (3 + 5 = 8; correct!), this information either does not get encoded into the long–term memory system or it is not stored efficiently (some models of how such number fact storage may operate were discussed earlier). The notion of an encoding or storage deficit of this sort is hard to test and there does not appear to be any direct evidence to support it.

This idea relates to questions of how such number facts are stored. Are the number fact storage mechanisms based on a common verbally based memory mechanism or are they dependent upon a separate system (a separable number fact memory system)? Brain damage in adults can produce highly selective deficits in arithmetic in the absence of deficits in spoken and written language processing. Such evidence cer-tainly suggests that, at least in the adult system, the retrieval of number facts depends on a relatively independent memory system. Many patients have been described who show selective impairments of different aspects of number fact knowledge (addition, subtraction, multiplication; van Harskamp & Cipolotti, 2005), which further sug-gests separable storage systems for different aspects of number fact knowledge. Furthermore, aphasic patients have been described (Whalen, McCloskey, Lindemann, & Bouton, 2002) who are unable to generate a phonological representation of a number problem (they cannot read aloud the numbers correctly, nor perform judg-ments about phonological forms of the number words: Do 4 and *sour* rhyme? Do 4 and *pour* rhyme?) but nevertheless can retrieve number facts reasonably accu-rately. This suggests that storage of number facts in memory depends at least in part on a nonphonological code. This might mean that number facts are stored in an abstract meaning-based code (McCloskey & Macaruso, 1995), in some very abstract speech-based code (Dehaene & Cohen, 1995), or in multiple (phonological and semantic) codes, as in Campbell's multicode model described earlier.

It seems possible that children with mathematics disorder do suffer from a specific deficit in the long-term storage of number facts in memory (though convincing evidence for this idea still needs to be found). The evidence from neuropsychology certainly indicates that in adults the storage of number facts depends upon one or more relatively abstract codes that are independent of other phonological or semantic memory representations. It is plausible, therefore, that children with mathematics disorder might experience a specific problem in establishing such memory representations, perhaps wholly or partially, as a consequence of the more basic problems in representing numerical magnitudes described earlier. In Campbell's (1995) model of addition for example, number fact retrieval depends upon the activation of a magnitude representation, and such representations appear to be impaired in children with mathematics disorder.

Working memory problems

The term working memory (WM) refers to the ability to store and process information at the same time (Daneman & Carpenter, 1980; Just & Carpenter, 1992). Arithmetic is one of the clearest examples of a "real life" working memory task. Consider being presented with the problem "14 plus 17" in spoken form. To answer this problem you have to remember the two numbers (addends), retrieve and execute the appropriate procedures, and finally articulate the answer. This involves holding information in memory while at the same time retrieving and operating on other information.

Hitch (1978) provided a classic demonstration of the role of working memory in arithmetic. Hitch asked adults to solve orally presented multidigit addition sums (e.g., 423 + 63). The most frequent calculation procedure used by adults here would be to add the units first, then the tens, and finally the hundreds. Hitch varied a number of aspects of the task to manipulate the load imposed on working memory. On some trials people could write down the answer in right-to-left order (starting with the units and so lessening the load on memory) while on other trials they had to write the answer in left-to-right order (so the entire sum had to be solved before any of the answer could be written down). Errors increased when the answer had to be written in the order imposing the higher memory load (left-to-right). Errors decreased when part of the sum (the first, second, or both addends) was presented in written form to reduce memory load and errors increased when the number of "carry" operations increased. All these results are consistent with the idea that working memory storage demands are one source of difficulty in performing mental arithmetic.

Working memory, as used so far, is a theoretically neutral term in relation to the specific mental processes involved. Working memory storage depends upon multiple interacting systems with different coding and storage processing limitations. According to one influential model (Baddeley, 1986; Baddeley & Hitch, 1974) it is necessary to distinguish mechanisms specialized for the retention of visual information (the visuospatial sketch pad) from mechanisms specialized for the retention of

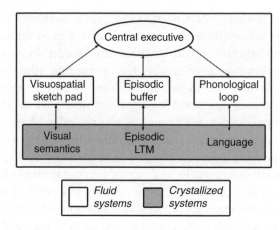

Figure 5.6   Diagram of Baddeley's working memory model. LTM = long-term memory. (Reprinted by permission from Macmillan Publishers Ltd, *Nature Reviews Neuroscience* (vol. 4, p. 835, Baddeley, A. D., Working memory: Looking back and looking forward), copyright 2003.)

phonological information (the phonological loop), and both of these systems interact with an attentional control system (the central executive). More recent versions of this model have postulated further components, including an episodic buffer (Baddeley, 2003b; see Figure 5.6).

For present purposes we simply need to stress that multiple systems will be involved in the storage and processing of arithmetic problems. At a minimum we need to postulate a role for phonological coding, visual spatial coding, and central attentional processes. Given a spoken word problem ("seventeen plus twenty-three") people will likely generate a phonological representation in an obligatory fashion, but may also often elect to generate a visuospatial representation of the problem (an image of the corresponding problem written down). Executive or attentional resources are likely to be involved in creating and maintaining such representations, and also in retrieving the information and procedures (from long-term memory) that are required to solve the problem. Even for solving a simple problem, the array of information that may need to be retrieved from permanent memory can be considerable, including deciding on the correct procedure to use, knowledge of count sequences (more important in younger, less skilled children), knowledge of rote-learned number facts (more important in older, more skilled children), and perhaps higher-level strategies such as checking on whether the answer generated is plausible and, if it is, checking on whether it is correct or not (perhaps by recalculating, in the same or a different way).

This discussion makes it clear that inefficiencies in certain component processes are likely to contribute to increases in memory load during calculation. So, for example, if number fact retrieval is inefficient this could mimic a working memory limitation. Developmentally, increases in the efficiency of working memory skills appear to be associated with changes in a number of other processes. In particular developmental increases in working memory performance with age appear to be highly correlated with increases in the speed with which elementary cognitive processes can be performed (Kail, 1991).

We can see that to propose that mathematics disorder arises from a "working memory" problem is no more than to propose a set of quite diverse possible deficits. It is useful to distinguish three different ideas about possible working memory limitations as potential causes of mathematics disorder.

Problems in phonological memory?
Arithmetic clearly depends in part on the use of information held in a phonological code, as in the use of verbal counting strategies. Problems in holding and manipulating information in a phonological code might contribute to problems in arithmetic. To assess this possibility we need to focus on studies that have selected children with mathematics disorder without reading disorder because it is very well established that children with reading disorder show problems on phonological memory tasks.

The results from studies of children with mathematics disorder compared to age-matched control children suggest that problems in phonological memory tasks (recalling, in order, lists of spoken words) are either small or absent. McLean and Hitch (1999) compared a small group of 12 9-year-old children with mathematics disorder (whose arithmetic scores fell in the bottom 25% of a large group of children who had been tested) with an age-matched group of children with normal arithmetic scores who were closely matched for reading ability. No measures of general ability (IQ) were obtained. There was a difference in digit span scores between the two groups (an effect size of $d = 0.95$) that certainly would have been significant on a larger sample. However, such a difference might well reflect uncontrolled differences in general ability (IQ) between the groups.

Passolunghi and Siegel (2001) studied a group of 9-year-old children with mathematics disorder and compared them with a group of children matched for age, vocabulary, and reading comprehension skills. There were no differences between these groups on a measure of memory span for words. Similarly, Passolunghi and Siegel (2004) studied a group of 10-year-old children with mathematics disorder and a group of children matched for age and vocabulary skills. The two groups did not differ on memory span for words or digits (the children with mathematics disorder were actually slightly better at recalling the lists of words). Similar results to this were also reported by Temple and Sherwood (2002), who compared a group of children with mathematics disorder (an arithmetic age 12 months below chronological age; 6/10 of these children had a chromosomal disorder called Turner's syndrome) with an age-matched control group matched for verbal IQ. There was no sign of any difference between groups on measures of memory span for digits, or for lists of one-, two-, or three-syllable words. Geary, Hoard, and Hamson (1999) also found no difference in digit span between 15 children with mathematics disorder (without reading problems) and a group of control children with typical arithmetic skills matched for age and IQ.

Overall it is clear that deficits in phonological memory are not typically found in children with mathematics disorder when care is taken to exclude possible effects of poor reading or differences in general ability (IQ).

Problems in visuospatial memory processes

McLean and Hitch (1999) found large differences on the Corsi blocks test (imitating the order in which a number of blocks are tapped; Box 5.1) between children with mathematics disorder and age-matched controls, though such differences might reflect differences in general ability (IQ) that were not assessed. Temple and Sherwood (2002) reported no differences on this task between children with mathematics disorder and age-matched controls, however the difference between the two groups (a medium effect size, Cohen's d = 0.53) would have been significant on a larger sample. This effect, however, is in turn almost certainly associated with the lower spatial ability that is typically reported for children with Turner's syndrome. Finally, Bull, Johnston, and Roy (1999) found that 7-year-old children selected for high or low arithmetic ability did not differ (Cohen's d = 0.16) on Corsi blocks.

In summary, the few studies to date fail to find clear evidence of visuospatial memory problems in children with mathematics disorder, though the methodological limitations of the studies do not allow strong conclusions to be drawn. Since tests of spatial and nonverbal IQ typically correlate moderately with measures of arithmetic skill (Fennema & Sherman, 1977; McGee, 1979) it would actually be surprising

Box 5.1   Corsi blocks

The Corsi blocks task is a classic test of spatial memory. In this test, the examiner taps a series of blocks, starting with two blocks. The participant is required to reproduce the sequence by tapping blocks in the same order as in the demonstration. The examiner gradually increases the difficulty of the task by increasing the length of the sequence to be copied until a ceiling level (or spatial span) is reached. The task taps spatial memory and also places significant demands on executive skills.

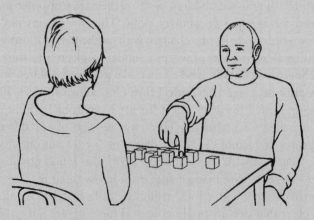

Person taking the Corsi blocks test.

if children with mathematics disorder showed completely age-appropriate visuospatial memory skills.

Problems in attentional/executive processes

Typical measures of working memory (WM) involve the simultaneous processing and storage of information. For example in reading span (Daneman & Carpenter, 1980) people have to read a sequence of sentences aloud, answer a question about whether each sentence is true or not, and, after a sequence of sentences have been read, recall the final word from each sentence in the correct order (see Figure 3.6). In counting span (Case, Kurland, & Goldberg, 1982) the person is required to count the number of dots on a sequence of cards, and then recall the count totals in the correct order (see Figure 3.6).

One characteristic of these WM tasks is that they are very demanding of attention. Engle, Tuholski, Laughlin, and Conway (1999) gave a number of WM tasks, together with a number of conventional short-term memory (STM) tasks (digit span and word span) and tests of general fluid intelligence (GF) to a large group of adults. They showed that measures of WM were separate from (though correlated with) measures of STM. They argued that what was shared between the WM and STM measures reflected memory storage, and the "extra" thing measured by WM tasks was executive attention. When the variance common to WM and STM was statistically removed from the WM measures, these measures still correlated well with GF, but when the variance common to WM and STM was removed from the STM measures these measures no longer correlated with GF. Engle (2002) has argued persuasively that the WM construct is "related to, maybe isomorphic to, general fluid intelligence and executive attention" (p. 22).

There are now several studies of children with mathematics disorder showing deficits on complex WM tasks (such as listening span and counting span). For example, Passolunghi and Siegel (2001, 2004), in the studies described earlier, found that the children with mathematics disorder were worse on two WM tasks involving sentences as well as on a counting span task. As noted before, these same children did not differ on simple STM measures. On more classic "executive" tasks, Bull et al. (1999) found that their samples of 7-year-old children of high- or low-arithmetic ability differed on several aspects of the Wisconsin Card Sorting Test, notably perseveration (see also Bull & Scerif, 2001), and McLean and Hitch (1999) found that their mathematics disorder group did much worse than age-matched controls on a timed "Trail-Making" task. In this task, the children had to use a pencil to connect alternating sequences of numbers and letters (e.g., 1-A, 2-B) or numbers and colors (e.g., 1-yellow, 1-pink, 2-yellow, 2-pink). As noted before these groups were not equated for IQ, but the large differences between groups (Cohen's d = 1.5 on the colors trail-making task) coupled with the absence of appreciable differences on some other non-executive tasks suggest that these measures of executive function are probably not simply the product of uncontrolled differences in general ability between groups.

In summary, it is clear that there are large and consistent differences in executive function between children with mathematics disorder and typically developing children of the same age.

Summary of working memory in mathematics disorder

Children with mathematics disorder show deficits on complex working memory tasks, whether these tasks involve numbers (counting span) or not (listening span). In contrast, the same children in a number of studies do not show consistent differences on simple measures of verbal or visual short-term memory (recalling lists of words, or remembering the order in which a set of Corsi blocks is tapped). As outlined earlier, performing arithmetic clearly places heavy demands on working memory executive processes, and deficits revealed on such tasks are therefore likely potential causes of problems in learning arithmetic. However a number of caveats need to be considered.

First it might be argued that the working memory executive deficits found in children with Mathematics Disorder are so complex that they might always be reducible to some simpler underlying process. For example, Kail (1991) suggested that speed of processing may underlie increases in working memory capacity with age. It is at least plausible that the executive deficits found in children with mathematics disorder might be reduced to a processing speed deficit. Bull and Johnston (1997) found that processing speed accounted for unique variance in arithmetic ability among 7-year-old children after controlling for differences in reading ability; children with lower arithmetic ability were slower than controls at number naming and sequencing, number matching, pegboard speed, one-syllable speech rate, and reciting the alphabet. In contrast, the groups did not differ on short-term memory tasks. However, no IQ data were provided, and therefore processing speed may have been a proxy for general ability. Durand, Hulme, Larkin, and Snowling (2005) found that speed of information processing (as assessed by speed of visual search) was not a unique predictor of arithmetic skill after the effects of IQ and the speed of number comparison had been accounted for. This suggests that the speed of processing numerical information (rather than general information processing speed) may be critical for the development of arithmetic skills.

A second caveat concerns cause and effect relationships. A working memory executive impairment appears to be a highly general "nonmodular" deficit. As discussed earlier, Engle goes as far as to suggest that executive function "maybe isomorphic to general fluid intelligence." We need to be concerned therefore as to whether such a general deficit can really explain the highly selective deficits in arithmetic displayed by many children with mathematics disorder who, by definition, given the way in which they are selected, are often of normal IQ.

Variability among children with mathematics disorder

It may be that different children with mathematics disorder suffer from different underlying cognitive deficits (and, given the complexities involved in learning to do arithmetic outlined above, this seems quite likely). For example, some children might suffer from a deficit in counting, while others have a more fundamental problem with the representation of numerical magnitudes. In-depth single case studies of children with mathematics disorder have described different patterns of difficulty in different children. Macaruso and Buchman (1996) described a woman who had experienced problems in learning arithmetic throughout her life. She had great problems in number fact retrieval that did not appear to be associated with problems with counting, nor with any general difficulty in retrieving (non-numerical) information from long-term memory. This pattern suggests she had a specific problem in storing number facts in memory. In line with this, Badian (1983) suggested that some children with mathematics disorder have problems in learning and retrieving number facts while others have problems in dealing with the spatial layout of written arithmetic problems. O'Hare, Brown, and Aitken (1991) described the case of a child who had difficulty naming numbers or writing them to dictation, combined with other difficulties including problems in distinguishing left from right, in identifying their fingers, and in writing (a cluster of symptoms often referred to as developmental Gerstmann syndrome; Kinsbourne & Warrington, 1963; see Box 5.2). However, such difficulties in reading and writing numbers are rare among children with mathematics disorder, according to Badian (1983).

Geary (2004) has suggested that there may be three subtypes of mathematics disorder:

1. A procedural subtype in which children show problems learning to use simple arithmetical strategies that may be linked to verbal memory problems.
2. A semantic memory subtype associated with difficulties in retrieving number facts from long-term memory.
3. A visuospatial subtype involving problems with the spatial representation of number.

Box 5.2   Gerstmann syndrome (from *http://www.ninds. nih.gov/disorders/gerstmanns/gerstmanns.htm*)

Gerstmann syndrome is a neurological disorder characterized by four primary symptoms: a writing disability (agraphia or dysgraphia), a lack of understanding of the rules for calculation or arithmetic (acalculia or dyscalculia), an inability to distinguish right from left, and an inability to identify fingers (finger agnosia). In adults, the syndrome may occur after a stroke or in association with damage to the parietal lobe (see figure below).

There are reports of the syndrome, sometimes called developmental Gerstmann syndrome, in children. The cause is not known. Most cases are identified when children reach school age, a time when they are challenged with writing and math exercises. Generally, children with the disorder exhibit poor handwriting and spelling skills, and difficulty with arithmetic skills, including addition, subtraction, multiplication, and division. An inability to differentiate right from left and to discriminate among individual fingers may also be apparent. In addition to the four primary symptoms, many children also have reading

Box 5.2   *(cont'd)*

problems and difficulty copying simple drawings. Children with a high level of intellectual functioning as well as those with brain damage may be affected with the disorder.

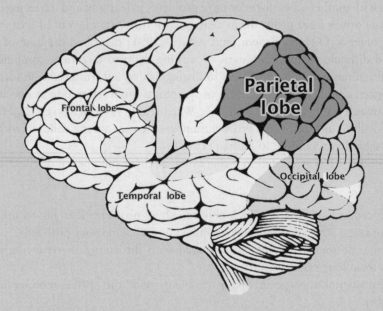

Principal fissures and lobes of the cerebrum viewed laterally, highlighting the parietal lobe (adapted from the 20th US edition of *Grey's Anatomy of the Human Body*, originally published in 1918).

Related proposals were also made by Temple (1989, 1991), who described children with mathematics disorder who had problems with arithmetic procedures and those who had problems with number fact retrieval. Based on the review of earlier cognitive deficits we might add a "number sense" subtype with basic problems in understanding numerical magnitudes (Butterworth, 1999). These suggestions and the variations in the profile of difficulties shown by case studies of children with mathematics disorder are potentially important, and it would be useful for future studies to try to characterize the differences among children with mathematics disorder more carefully. One difficulty is that typically attempts to subtype children with mathematics disorder use descriptions that are closely related to details of their performance on simple arithmetic tasks. It will be more satisfactory, ultimately, if such subtypes could be based more clearly on underlying cognitive deficits that give rise to the differences in arithmetic performance that are observed. For the time being, however, there is too little evidence to say that there are clearly distinguishable "subtypes" of mathematics disorder with different causes.

Summary of the cognitive bases of mathematics disorder

The nature of mathematics disorder is much less well understood than reading disorders, and this reflects the fact that we understand much less about the mechanisms of mathematical skills and their development than we do for reading skills and their development. For the most part in this chapter we have concentrated on the difficulties some children encounter when learning simple arithmetic skills (particularly learning addition). There is certainly much more to learning mathematics, or even to learning arithmetic, than learning about addition. However, the typical development of addition skills has been studied in more detail than other aspects of arithmetic, and children with mathematics disorder show very clear problems on this simple aspect of arithmetic.

Mathematical skills depend upon a complex interplay between nonverbal and verbal cognitive systems, and mathematical skills are arguably more diverse and more complex than reading skills. It seems likely from a cognitive perspective that mathematics disorder may result from a number of underlying deficits, including deficits in a nonverbal "number sense" system located in parietal brain areas, as well as verbal processes (such as counting) and executive processes that interact with this system.

It appears that further progress in this area is likely to depend upon longitudinal studies that attempt to focus on more well-defined arithmetical skills (such as counting, addition, subtraction, and multiplication). These studies should also seek to identify whether clear differences in the patterns of problems exist across children. At the moment, the paucity of longitudinal studies in this area is quite striking. Longitudinal studies are essential in order to describe how the profile of arithmetic problems changes with age. Such studies would allow us to assess whether particular cognitive deficits can be identified early in life that would reliably predict later problems in learning arithmetic. Such longitudinal predictive evidence will be critical for helping us to identify the cognitive causes of mathematics disorder.

The Etiology of Mathematics Disorder

Genetic influences on mathematics disorder

There is evidence for substantial genetic and environmental influences on the development of mathematical skills generally, and more specifically on the development of mathematics disorder. Conceptually, it is important to distinguish between genetic effects that operate to influence the development of normal variations in an ability (assessed by the heritability estimate for the ability) from genetic effects that operate to determine a disability (assessed by the heritability of group differences between people with a disability and people without it). It might be, for example, that particular genes influence whether individuals inherit a vulnerability to developing mathematics disorder. However, if these genes were uncommon in the population they might play no role in accounting for individual differences among people in the normal range of mathematics ability. In fact, the evidence suggests that the same genes that influence normal variations in mathematical skills in the population are also involved in influencing the development of mathematics disorder (Plomin & Kovas, 2005). We will consider briefly the evidence for genetic influences on both normal variations in mathematical skills and mathematics disorder. According to the arguments put forward by Plomin and Kovas (2005) these genetic influences are largely the same, which, if confirmed, would indicate that mathematics disorder is simply the lower end of the continuum of mathematical skill and not a discrete clinical entity.

There is good evidence that mathematics disorder tends to run in families (Shalev et al., 2001) but this may reflect either shared environment or genetic effects. Twin studies give one way of separating genetic from environmental effects. In the large-scale UK Twins Early Development Study (TEDS), Kovas, Harlaar, Petrill, and Plomin (2005) found evidence for substantial heritability for normal variations in mathematical skills in a sample of almost 3000 twin pairs. There were substantial overlaps between the genes responsible for arithmetic and general intelligence, and arithmetic and reading, though the degree of overlap was far from perfect, suggesting that there are specific genetic effects on the development of arithmetic skills.

There are very few studies that have directly assessed possible genetic influences on mathematics disorder (i.e., that have assessed the heritability of the group deficit in mathematical skills found in children with mathematics disorder compared to control children). Alarcon, DeFries, Light, and Pennington (1997) reported a study of the heritability of mathematics disorder in a small-scale study of 40 identical (MZ) and 23 nonidentical (DZ) twin pairs. At least one member of each twin pair had mathematics disorder (defined as a score on the standardized WRAT arithmetic subtest of 1.5 standard deviations below average, which corresponds to roughly the bottom 10% of the population). There were higher degrees of similarity in diagnostic category (mathematics disorder/control) for the MZ twin pairs (.73) than the DZ twin pairs (.56), which suggests a role for genetic effects that was not significant given the small sample size in this study. However, a more powerful analysis (DF extremes analysis; DeFries & Fulker, 1985), which treats mathematical skills as a continuous variable rather than as a dichotomy (mathematics disorder/control), yielded a group heritability estimate of .38. This estimate suggests that 38% of the average difference between the twins with mathematics disorder and the unselected population was due to genetic factors.

In a recent study with a much larger sample size (Oliver et al., 2004) the heritability of mathematics disorder was assessed by selecting children in the bottom 15% of the population on teacher ratings of children's mathematical abilities. A strength of this study is the very large sample size (2178 twin pairs), though arguably a weakness is that the teacher ratings of mathematical skills are a less than ideal measure. This study yielded quite a high group heritability estimate for mathematics disorder of .65 (compared to the estimate of .38 reported by Alarcon et al., 1997). This same study also yielded a similarly sized individual differences heritability estimate of .66 for a composite teacher rating of mathematical skill.

A further study, based on the same Twins Early Development Study (TEDS) sample, used objective Web-based measures of different aspects of mathematical skill: mathematical application, understanding number, computation and knowledge, mathematical interpretation, and non-numerical processes (Kovas, Petrill, & Plomin, 2007). In this study some 2052 children (470 pairs of MZ twins and 781 pairs of DZ twins) were tested when they were 10 years old. This study yielded moderate estimates of heritability for the different aspects of mathematical ability assessed (ranging from .30 to .45). These heritability estimates are lower than the estimate reported by Oliver et al. (.66) and it seems plausible that the lower estimates of genetic influence here may reflect the use of objective measures (rather than teacher ratings, which may be biased because teachers tend to overestimate the degree of similarity in MZ twin pairs). The results from this study might be seen as supporting the importance of generalist genes as influences on diverse aspects of mathematical ability (as advocated by Plomin & Kovas, 2005).

In summary, current evidence suggests that there are substantial genetic influences on mathematics disorder and it has been argued that the same genetic influences may also operate to influence individual differences among people in the normal range of mathematical ability (Plomin & Kovas, 2005). However, even accepting such heritability estimates, there remains room for substantial environmental influences on mathematical skills. Furthermore, the heritability for the mathematics disorder group deficit should not be taken to imply that remedial teaching or other interventions cannot be effective in helping to improve those children's mathematical skills.

There are no "genes" for mathematics or for mathematics disorder. However, genes do affect processes controlling protein synthesis, which, via the processes operating in epigenesis, affect the development of the brain structures that allow us to learn mathematics. For these reasons it is important not to see genetic effects as deterministic and immutable. Instead, genes operate in the context of a wide range of biological and experiential factors to influence the development of our ability to learn and to perform mathematics.

Brain bases of mathematics disorder

Until recently the vast majority of work on the brain bases of arithmetic and its disorders has been with adults, though recently work has begun to examine brain mechanisms in children with mathematics disorder. We will begin by considering work on adults as a foundation for the smaller amount of work with children.

Based on a review of brain imaging and the effects of brain lesions in adults Dehaene, Piazza, Pinel, and Cohen (2003) proposed three separable, though interconnected, brain systems in the parietal lobe that play a role in number processing (see Plate 5). The neural substrate of a "number sense" system that is activated when comparing numerical magnitudes or estimating appears to depend critically upon bilateral areas of the horizontal intraparietal sulcus (HIPS). Bilaterally areas of the posterior superior parietal lobe (PSPL) also appear to be activated in tasks that require the shifting of spatial attention, such as approximating and number comparison tasks, and it was suggested that this system supports a process of orienting attention to particular regions of a mental "number line." Finally, the left angular gyrus (the area that when lesioned gives rise to Gerstmann's syndrome) appears to be more active in verbal calculation tasks such as exact addition. In addition to these three "core" number areas, areas in the prefrontal and cingulate cortex are systematically activated when adults are asked to perform calculations, and these other areas may (speculatively) be involved in attentional processes required in calculation.

It seems reasonable to suppose that problems in the development of the brain systems identified as critical to arithmetic in adults may be fundamental to the problems observed in children with mathematics disorder, though as yet direct evidence for this is lacking (Wilson & Dehaene, 2007). Consistent with the idea of arithmetic difficulties being associated with parietal dysfunction, several studies have shown parietal deficits in Turner's syndrome, a syndrome associated with arithmetic deficits (e.g., Reiss, Mazzocco, Greenlaw, Freund, & Ross, 1995). Perhaps most strikingly, Isaacs, Edmonds, Lucas, and Gadian (2001) reported a specific reduction in gray matter in the left HIPS in a group of adolescents with mathematics disorder (without reading disorder) who had been born prematurely, compared to a control group without mathematics disorder who had been born equally prematurely. This difference in the left HIPS was only found for children with problems with calculation, and not for another group of children who had problems with mathematical reasoning.

Further evidence for the role of the HIPS in number processing comes from recent brain imaging studies. Cantlon, Brannon, Carter, and Pelphrey (2006) used a numerosity adaptation paradigm (see Figure 5.7) in which subjects view a series of displays of the same number of items that differ in other respects (size and shape). They found that changes in numerosity (but not changes in irrelevant attributes such as shape) resulted in increased activation (measured by fMRI) in the HIPS in 4-year-old children as well as adults. This study suggests that the approximate numerical system of preschool children has structural and functional similarities with the numerical system used by adults. The finding that the HIPS is active during this task as well as during number comparison judgment tasks (deciding which digit represents the larger magnitude – 3 vs. 7) suggests that symbolic number representation in adults may build upon an approximate number sense system, with both depending upon neural systems in the HIPS. Temple and Posner (1998) investigated brain potentials during symbolic and nonsymbolic number comparison in adults and 5-year-old children and found that ERP localization in children was similar to adults. This again is consistent with the idea that comparisons of numerical and physical magnitudes depend upon common neural mechanisms in both adults and children.

As far as we are aware only one study has compared patterns of brain activation in children with mathematics disorder and in matched typically developing children (Kucian et al., 2006). In this study children completed three tasks: approximate calculation, exact calculation, and nonsymbolic magnitude comparison (see Box 5.3).

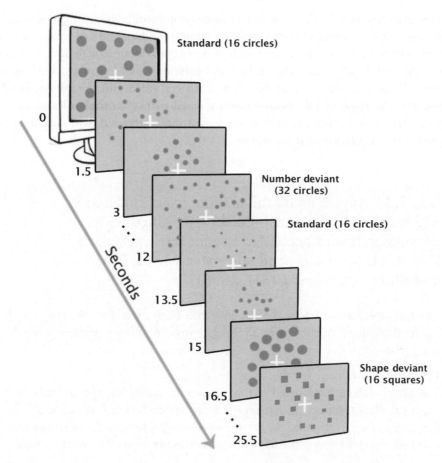

Figure 5.7 The numerosity adaptation task used by Cantlon et al. (2006). Here the participants (adults and 4-year-old children) passively view a stream of displays on a computer screen. The majority of displays contain the same number and same type of elements (16 circles of differing size). Occasionally a display is presented that deviates from the standard *either* in the number of elements present (Number deviants) *or* the shape of the elements (Shape deviants). (Adapted from Cantlon, Brannon, Carter, & Pelphrey, 2006.)

There were no significant behavioral differences in performance in these tasks between children with and without mathematics disorder. During the exact calculation and magnitude comparison tasks children with mathematics disorder also activated similar parietal and prefrontal regions to children in the control group. However, during approximate calculation, children with mathematics disorder showed less parietal activation than control children. This could be interpreted as evidence for a missing or less developed link between the approximate numerical system and symbolic number representation system in children with mathematics disorder (described in this study as dyscalculia). Caution is needed here, as this is the first study of its kind and activations in those areas were positively correlated with accuracy.

The brain activation patterns of children with mathematics disorder ($N = 18$) and control children ($N = 20$) during each condition are shown in Plate 6. Children with mathematics disorder (children with DD or developmental dyscalculia in Kucian et al.'s terminology) showed greater variability among children and had weaker activation in most of the neuronal network involved in approximate calculation, including the intraparietal sulcus and the middle and inferior frontal gyrus of both hemispheres. There was evidence that the left intraparietal sulcus, the left inferior frontal gyrus, and the right middle frontal gyrus seemed to play crucial roles in correct approximate calculation because brain activation correlated with accuracy in approximate calculation in these regions.

Box 5.3   Approximate calculation, exact calculation, and magnitude comparison tasks (Reprinted with permission from Kucian, K., Loenneker, T., Dietrich, T., Dosch, M, Martin E., and von Aster, M. G., *Behavioral and Brain Functions*, 2 (31), 2006)

The tasks performed under fMRI consisted of approximate calculation and exact calculation, approximate and exact control conditions, and a magnitude comparison task.

Calculation task
The calculation task consisted of three cycles of alternating approximate and exact calculation blocks. In the approximate calculation task the child selects the number that is closest to the correct answer to the sum. In the exact calculation task the child selects the number that corresponds to the correct answer.

Calculation

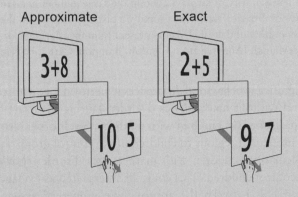

Control task: Luminosity
The control condition for the calculation trials was a discrimination task involving gray light patches, again presented during three cycles of approximate and exact discrimination blocks. In the exact control task, subjects had to

Box 5.3 *(cont'd)*

match sequentially presented gray-scale patterns. In the approximate control task, they were asked to pick the gray-scale pattern with the most similar luminosity (brightness) to the standard. Alternative solutions were more alike in the exact control condition than those in the approximate control condition.

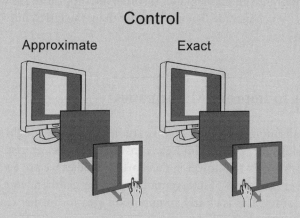

Control

Magnitude comparison

In the magnitude comparison task participants had to compare two sets of different objects (pictures of fruit or vegetables) and select the set with the larger number of objects. The maximum number of objects displayed on one side was 18. The differences between the two sets were: 1, 2, 3, or 4 in the first block; 9, 10, 11, or 12 in the second block; and 5, 6, 7, or 8 in the third block. Fixation during rest served as the control condition for magnitude comparison.

Summary of brain bases of mathematics disorder
There is evidence for neural circuits involved in the understanding of physical and numerical magnitudes and calculation that include the horizontal intraparietal sulcus (HIPS), the posterior superior parietal lobe (PSPL), the left angular gyrus, and areas in the prefrontal and cingulate cortex. Current evidence suggests that underdevelopment of the HIPS may result in a deficient "number sense" system, and that such problems are associated with mathematics disorder at least in some cases (Isaacs et al., 2001). Children with mathematics disorder also appear to show less activation in parietal areas (which include, but are broader than, the HIPS) during approximate calculation tasks.

Interventions to Improve Mathematics

There are a small number of good quality studies that have sought to improve the mathematical skills of young children considered to be at risk of developing mathematics disorder. So far, however, there are no studies we are aware of that have investigated the effectiveness of interventions for older children who have developed mathematics disorder. This is clearly an important area for further research (Dowker, 2005).

Prevention

Griffin and colleagues (Griffin & Case, 1996; Griffin, Case, & Siegler, 1994) conducted a whole-class intervention study using "Number Worlds": a package of teacher-led whole-class instruction, interactive games, and other activities designed to improve the number skills of disadvantaged kindergarten children. This was a theoretically based intervention designed to facilitate the development of a "number line representation" in these children. At the end of the kindergarten year the intervention group performed better than an untreated control group and their attainments in conceptual and procedural tests of arithmetic approached those of a normative comparison group. This is an encouraging result, though it does not mean that such a program will prevent the development of mathematics disorder in the small minority of children at risk of the disorder.

   Ramani and Siegler (2008) reported encouraging results from a short-term intervention study conducted with 5-year-old disadvantaged children attending a headstart program in the USA. The intervention was based on children playing a board game with an adult. The "number" board game had 10 consecutively numbered squares on the board, and the child span a spinner that showed a 1 or a 2. The child and the adult took turns in the game and moved their place holder on the board in accordance with the number shown on the spinner. Children were required to count on from the number on the square where they were. So, for example, if the child was on square 3 and the spinner indicated a 2 they would say "4, 5" as they moved their place holder on the board to square 5 (the numbers were also marked on the squares of the board). An analogous form of the board game involved only colored squares without numbers and a spinner that had colors on it corresponding to the colors of the squares on the board. Children were assigned randomly to the number or color version of the game, and played it in individual sessions with an adult for five sessions lasting roughly 20 min each. Before and after the intervention, numerical skills were assessed with four tasks: counting from 1 to 10; number line estimation (marking a line marked with 0 and 10 at the ends to indicate the position of an intermediate number); numerical magnitude comparison (choosing the numerically large number from two numbers presented side by side); and numeral identification (naming a series of numerals between 1 and 10 presented in random order). The children in the number version of the game showed substantial improvements in numeral identification ($d = .69$), numerical magnitude comparison ($d = .79$), counting ($d = .74$), number line estimation accuracy ($d = .76$), and the linearity of number line judgments ($d = 1.00$). In a sense, improvements in numeral identification and counting measures are unsurprising since they were practised during the game. However, it is encouraging that there were also gains in numerical magnitude comparison and number line estimation, two tasks that arguably are less directly targeted in the game and might be seen as tapping children's understanding of numerical quantities. The effects obtained in this study (with young typically developing children) are encouraging, given the brief time spent on the "game-based" intervention.

Fuchs et al. (2005) conducted a large-scale intervention study with 1st grade children identified as being at risk of developing mathematics disorder. Based on screening 564 children from 41 1st grade classes, 127 children were identified as being at risk of developing mathematics disorder based on a group test of mathematics, followed by individual testing of over 300 children with the Woodcock-Johnson III (Woodcock, McGrew, & Mather, 2001) Calculation and Applied Problems mathematics test. These at-risk children represented roughly the bottom 21% of the sample in terms of their mathematical skills and they were randomly assigned to an intervention (70) or a nonintervention (69) group. The maths outcomes for these two groups were compared to those of a not-at-risk group of 180 children. The at-risk groups had full-scale IQ scores of 85, compared to 95 for the not-at-risk group.

The intervention was delivered by 12 trained tutors to 37 small groups of two or three children in 30-min sessions. Each group teaching session was followed by 10-min individual sessions with a computer program that gave simple addition and subtraction problems for the child to solve, coupled with feedback on correct responses. A total of 48 teaching sessions were given. The intervention sessions followed a highly structured, scripted format and the groups only moved on to harder activities when all children showed mastery of the concepts taught in a session (based on an individually administered test at the end of each session). Hence the program, though taught to groups of two or three children at a time, was sensitive to variations in children's rate of learning. The trained at-risk children showed significantly greater improvements than the untreated at-risk group (with medium effect sizes ranging from $d = 0.57$ to 0.70) on three measures: Woodcock-Johnson

Calculation (a written test of basic arithmetic), Grade 1 Concepts Applications (a standardized spoken test with written responses tapping a variety of mathematical concepts), and Story Problems (a set of arithmetic problems presented orally in story format). However there were no significant improvements between these two groups on the other four outcome measures tapping mathematical skills.

Estimates of how many children would satisfy a conventional discrepancy-based criterion for mathematics disorder (a discrepancy of 1 SD between IQ and math) using a variety of outcome measures showed average rates of around 3.2% for the at-risk untreated group compared to around 2.5% for the at-risk treated group. It was found that teachers' ratings of children's attention, their working memory scores (on a listening span measure), and phonological awareness scores were all unique predictors of some of the math outcome measures after the effects of group, intervention, and a range of other possible predictors had been controlled.

Wilson, Revkin, Cohen, Cohen, and Dehaene (2006) reported the results of a small-scale intervention study with nine 7–9-year-old children with mathematics disorder. The children were given a short-term intensive intervention involving a computer-based game designed to improve their "number sense." The results showed improvements after the intervention on some measures (subitizing speed and numerical magnitude comparison speed) but not on other measures, some of which are arguably closer to everyday arithmetic skills (e.g., addition speed). In addition the absence of a control group makes it difficult to draw any strong conclusions from this study since we do not know how much improvement the children may have made on the speeded number judgment measures simply as a result of repeated testing.

Summary of interventions for mathematics

The evidence from these prevention and intervention studies is encouraging insofar as they show positive effects on children's arithmetic skills, and in one case a reduction in the rates of children who would qualify for a diagnosis of mathematics disorder. The effects obtained by Fuchs et al. (2005) were, however, quite variable across the measures used (with null effects on a number of measures). It appears that we are in need of further large-scale studies of this sort that preferably follow children for longer periods of time. So far we really do not have any evidence concerning how well older children with severe mathematics disorder can be helped to overcome their problems and this is an area where research is badly needed.

It is worth noting here that problems of anxiety specifically related to math are common in adults, and furthermore it appears that such math anxiety operates specifically to interfere with the working memory operations needed to solve more complex math problems (Ashcraft, Kirk, & Hopko, 1998). In this view math anxiety can have clear adverse effects on performing, and presumably on learning to perform, arithmetic. As far as we know comparable studies have not been conducted with children and in particular no studies of math anxiety in children with mathematics disorder have been reported. However, the developmental implications of this research are clear. It seems likely that early difficulties in learning math may contribute to the development of math anxiety, which in turn will impede the processes involved in performing and learning math. This suggests that early interventions to help circumvent math problems, and the anxiety associated with them, may be particularly valuable.

Summary and Conclusions

Mathematics disorder (problems in mastering number skills and arithmetic) is relatively common in children. There are some clear analogies between mathematics disorder and dyslexia insofar as both of these conditions affect relatively circumscribed areas of cognition that have very direct educational implications. Compared to studies of dyslexia, however, our understanding of mathematics disorder remains quite limited. This reflects a less advanced understanding of typical arithmetic development, compared to typical reading development, and also the fact that much less research has directly focused on children with mathematics disorder than on children with dyslexia. Research on arithmetic development and mathematics disorder now appears to be increasing rapidly.

A number of clear conclusions can be drawn from the work we have considered in this chapter. Though pure cases of Mathematics Disorder occur, it is important to emphasize that many more children have mathematics disorder and reading disorder. These MD/RD children typically have more severe arithmetic problems than children with mathematics disorder alone. It seems likely that this is because the pure MD children have a more limited cognitive deficit than children with MD/RD. One hypothesis is that pure mathematics disorder might commonly arise from a deficit in a nonverbal "number sense" system, and that MD/RD children have additional difficulties with the verbal aspects of learning arithmetic. Understanding the similarities and differences between children with mathematics disorder and mathematics disorder/reading disorder is a key issue for future research.

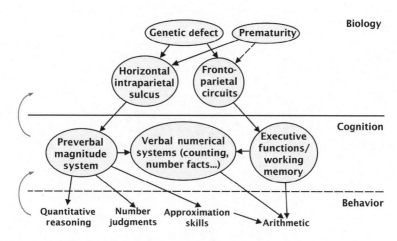

Figure 5.8   A path model of mathematics disorder.

A better understanding of the cognitive bases of mathematics disorder will require longitudinal studies to identify the likely causes of the disorder, and it will be important to try to use relatively pure measures of arithmetic rather than standardized tests that typically conflate many different skills (such as addition, subtraction, and multiplication) into a single score. As in the case of reading disorders, impressive advances have been made in understanding the genetic and brain mechanisms of mathematics disorder. Multiple overlapping sets of genes seem to be responsible for influencing normal variations in arithmetic and the arithmetic deficits seen in mathematics disorder. It seems likely that these genes will influence the development of brain structures in the parietal lobe that underlie our ability to understand numerical magnitudes and perform calculations. However, it is also likely that genetic influences will operate by influencing the development of other brain regions that have also been identified as being involved in learning and performing arithmetic. Figure 5.8 shows a causal path model of mathematics disorder that is consistent with the major findings we have considered in this chapter.

6

Developmental Coordination Disorder

Problems with the development of motor skills in children are relatively common and may be associated with a number of conditions that affect the brain and nervous system (such as cerebral palsy). Here we will focus on children who experience problems in developing motor skills although they do not suffer from any diagnosed disease. Such problems are referred to in DSM-IV as developmental coordination disorder (DCD). Older terms that have been used to refer to this group of children include clumsy child syndrome and developmental dyspraxia and agnosia (agnosia literally means a difficulty in recognizing objects; and this terminology stresses that these children typically have difficulties affecting both motor control and perception).

Definitions and Prevalence

In DSM-IV the criteria for diagnosing DCD are significant problems in motor coordination that are out of line with those expected for a child's age and IQ. It is specified that such problems should significantly interfere with a child's academic achievements (problems with handwriting and drawing are common) or with activities in daily life (problems in learning to dress, and in sports and games, are common). This is a discrepancy definition, analogous to the definitions of other forms of specific learning difficulty, because problems with motor skills need to be out of line with IQ (taking account of the fact that severe learning difficulties may be associated with motor coordination problems). The definition is also a developmental one because the assessment of motor coordination difficulties needs to be related to a child's age. The usefulness of using IQ as a means of excluding children from getting a diagnosis of DCD has been questioned (Geuze, Jongmans, Schoemaker, & Smits-Englesman, 2001; Henderson & Barnett, 1998). There is a lack of good evidence for a correlation between IQ and motor skills (at least in the normal range) and it is clear that some children with severe learning difficulties (IQ below 70) perform adequately on motor tasks. It has been suggested, therefore, that it may be more useful to consider cases of children with low IQ and poor motor skills as showing DCD with comorbid learning problems (Geuze et al., 2001).

In practice a diagnosis of DCD should preferably be made using a standardized test of motor skill (Sugden, Chambers, & Utley, 2006; *www.dcd-uk.org*). However, rating scales for use by parents and teachers have been developed that are likely to be useful for screening purposes: The Early Years Movement Skills Checklist (Chambers & Sugden, 2006) and the Developmental Coordination Disorder Questionnaire (DCDQ; Wilson, Kaplan, Crawford, Campbell, & Dewey, 2000). There are fewer tests of motor skills (and they tend to be less well standardized) than tests of language and intelligence, which probably reflects the fact that the assessment of motor skills has been given a lower priority in research and clinical practice than the assessment of IQ and language skills.

The two most widely used tests of motor skill are the Movement Assessment Battery for Children (Movement ABC; Henderson & Sugden, 1992; this was recently revised as the Movement ABC 2; Henderson, Sugden, & Barnett, 2007) and the Bruininks-Oseretsky Test of Motor Proficiency (BOTMP; Bruininks, 1978). The Movement ABC (see Figure 6.1) is an individually administered test that is standardized for children from 4 to 12 years of age. The test assesses three areas of motor function (manipulative skills, ball skills, and balance skills) and yields a total impairment score that can be used to derive a percentile score for each age group. The BOTMP is also an individually administered test that is standardized on children aged 4½ to 14½ years and also contains measures of both fine and gross motor skills. Both of these tests have quite good reliability and there is moderate agreement (around 80%) between them when used to diagnose DCD (Crawford, Wilson, & Dewy, 2001). There is little doubt that the availability of more tests of motor function (and tests that included assessments of handwriting and drawing ability that are excluded from the Movement ABC) will be useful for studies of children with motor impairments, and Barnett, Henderson, and Scheib (2007) have recently published a standardized test of handwriting speed.

The children identified as having DCD in different research studies have varied widely in the severity of their motor problems: ranging from the 5th centile (e.g., Mon-Williams, Pascal, & Wann, 1994) to the 15th centile (e.g., Dwyer & McKenzie, 1994). The majority of studies reviewed by Geuze et al. (2001) used the 15th centile or below as a selection criterion for DCD (one standard deviation below normal), which does not represent a severe problem and it has been suggested that setting a cut-off of the 5th centile is more appropriate for identifying children with clinically significant difficulties (Sugden, 2007). In any developmental disorder the cut-off point used to distinguish typical from impaired performance will always be arbitrary to some extent. However, it is important to bear in mind that children with less severe forms of a disorder may well show different characteristics to more severely affected children. It is often argued that, given the dependence of motor skills on maturational changes, it is hard to reliably diagnose DCD in preschool children. The majority of studies have focused on children 6–12 years where a diagnosis can probably be made much more reliably (Geuze et al., 2001).

Population estimates of the prevalence of DCD vary widely (5–18%) and these estimates depend both on the tests and the cut-offs used for diagnosis (Geuze, et al., 2001). In a large-scale Swedish study Kadesjo and Gillberg (1999) studied a

Figure 6.1 A child completing some of the tasks from the Movement ABC.

representative sample of roughly 400 children aged 6 years 8 months to 7 years 8 months in mainstream schools. Parents and teachers completed questionnaires and interviews about each child's development, including a version of the Connors' rating scale to identify ADHD. Physical education teachers and a researcher each conducted independent observations of children performing two different series of motor tasks to assess gross and fine motor skills. The reliabilities of the tests used were generally good. It is reported that 5% of the children could be considered to have severe DCD, and another 8.6% moderate DCD. In both cases there was a preponderance of boys (male:female ratio 4:1 and 7.3:1, respectively). This study, using a small but representative epidemiological sample, demonstrates that children with DCD are quite common and that the disorder is much more common in boys than girls. This study also reported that there are significant rates of comorbidity between DCD and other cognitive and emotional disorders (see below). Similar results to this were obtained by Wright and Sugden (1996) using a randomly selected sample of 427 children in Singapore. In this study they first identified the bottom 15% of the sample as having weak motor skills based on a screening test and then gave more intensive assessments to these children. On the basis of the more detailed assessments some 4% of the total sample were identified as having DCD.

The Persistence of DCD

A widespread, if mistaken, view is that children with DCD grow out of their difficulties. There are now several studies that have followed-up children diagnosed with DCD into adolescence (Cantell, Smyth, & Ahonen 2003, Cousins & Smyth, 2003; Dunn et al., 1986, Geuze & Borger, 1993; Helgren, Gillberg, Gillberg, & Ennerskog, 1993; Knuckey & Gubbay, 1983; Losse et al., 1991; Shager, Demetriou, & Pervez, 1986). A reasonable conclusion from these studies is that although a minority of children with DCD may grow out of their motor difficulties, most are likely to remain less well coordinated than their peers into late adolescence. The difficulties they have at secondary school include problems with handwriting and the presentation of work, and difficulties in science, art, design, and technology (Losse et al., 1991). It has been reported that children with comorbid ADHD and DCD appear to have particularly severe problems in adulthood (compared to children with ADHD but without DCD; Rasmussen & Gillberg, 2000).

Comorbidities between DCD and Other Developmental Disorders

Comorbidities between DCD and other developmental disorders appear to be very common indeed. Many children with autism spectrum disorders or with ADHD (with or without hyperactivity) show significant problems with motor coordination (Gillberg, 1999), as do many deaf children (Wiegersma & van der Velde, 1983). Kadesjo and Gillberg (1999) in their epidemiological study found that, of children with DCD, 47% displayed five or more symptoms of ADHD and 19% met criteria for a diagnosis of ADHD. The corresponding rates in the non-DCD children in the sample were 9% and 2%, respectively. There were also associations between DCD and ADHD and both oppositional defiant disorder and reading and language problems in this study. High rates (roughly 50%) of DCD in samples of children diagnosed with ADHD were reported by Pitcher, Piek, and Hay (2003). Hill, Bishop, and Nimmo-Smith (1998) showed that children diagnosed with SLI had problems imitating manual gestures that were almost as severe as the problems shown by a small group of children diagnosed as having DCD. Hill (2001), based on a review of other studies of children diagnosed with SLI, went on to argue that the substantial comorbidity between DCD and SLI was enough to question the use of the term "specific" in the case of children with SLI. Kaplan, Wilson, Dewey, and Crawford (1998) studied a large group of 224 children referred because of learning and attention

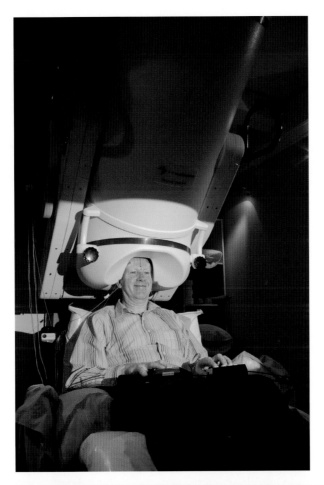

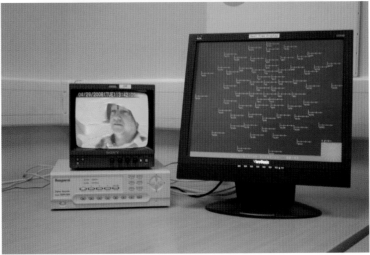

Plate 1 A magnetoencephalography (MEG) scanner in use. Top panel shows the participant in the scanner; bottom panel shows patterns of brain activity recorded from a set of "virtual electrodes" identified from MEG activity.

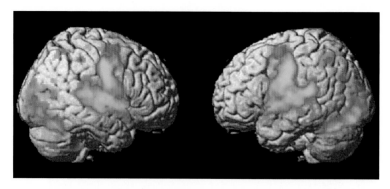

Plate 2   Images from fMRI scans showing the major areas that are activated during reading aloud. Price, C. J. and McCrory, E. (2005) Functional brain imaging studies of skilled reading and developmental dyslexia. In Snowling, M. J. and Hulme, C. (Eds) *The Science of Reading: A Handbook* (pp. 135–154). Oxford, Blackwell.)

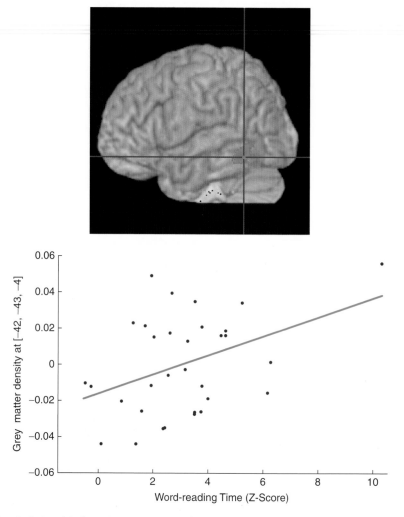

Plate 3   Relationship between gray matter density increases and reading performance in people with dyslexia. (Silani, G., Frith, U., Demonet, J-F., Fazio, F., Perani, D., Price, C., et al. Brain abnormalities underlying altered activation in dyslexia: A voxel-based morphometry study. *Brain* (2005), 128, 2453–2461, by permisssion of Oxford University Press.)

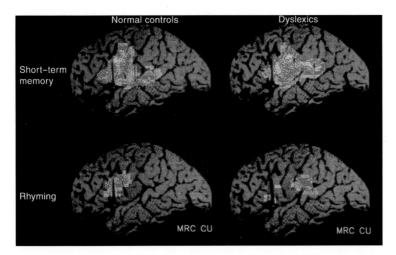

Plate 4 Patterns of brain activity revealed by positron emission tomography (PET) in typical readers and adults with dyslexia during a verbal short-term memory task and a rhyme judgment task. Note that there are reduced levels of brain activation during the performance of these verbal tasks in people with dyslexia. (Paulesu, E., Frith, U., Snowling, M., Gallagher, A., Morton, J., Frackowiak, F. S. J., et al. Is developmental dyslexia a disconnection syndrome? Evidence from PET scanning. *Brain* (1996), 119, 143–157.)

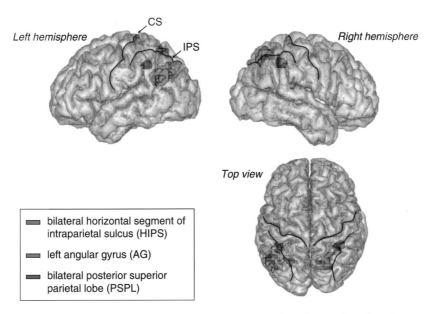

Plate 5 Brain regions implicated in number processing and arithmetic based on brain imaging data. (Three parietal circuits for number processing, Dehaene, S., Piazza, M., Pinel, P., and Cohen, L., *Cognitive Neuropsychology*, 2003, Psychology Press, reprinted by permission of the publisher (Taylor and Francis Ltd, *http://www.tandf.co.uk/journals.*)

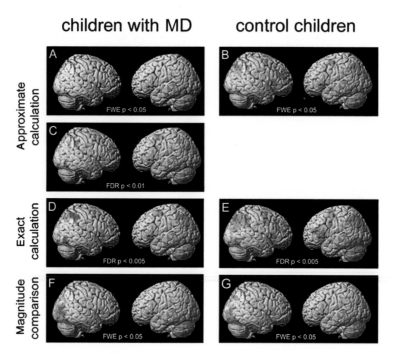

Plate 6 Patterns of brain activation during approximate calculation, exact calculation, and magnitude comparison tasks in children with mathematics disorder (labeled MD) and normally developing children. Brain activation patterns of children with MD ($N = 18$) and control children ($N = 20$) during each condition are depicted on the SPM standard brain template. The activated brain regions were subjected to FWE or FDR correction with a minimum number of 10 parietal voxels, except (C) where the cluster comprises only five voxels. (A, B, C) Approximate calculation vs. approximate control condition. (D, E) Exact calculation vs. exact control condition. (F, G) Magnitude comparison vs. rest. (Reprinted with permission from Kucian, K., Loenneker, T., Dietrich, T., Dosch, M., Martin, E., and von Aster, M. G., *Behavioral and Brain functions*, 2(31), 2006.)

problems (but not because of motor problems). They found that a high proportion of these children satisfied the criteria for being diagnosed as DCD and that comorbidity between DCD, and either ADHD or RD was very common in this group. They suggested that DCD is better thought of not as a discrete disorder, but rather a manifestation of "atypical brain development" that often results in the development of other disorders as well; we return to this issue in Chapter 9 when we consider the relationship between DCD and nonverbal learning difficulties.

It is worth noting that the studies of comorbidity considered here, with the exception of Kadesjo and Gillberg (1999), have all used clinical samples rather than representative epidemiological samples of children. This makes it hard to estimate the "true" rates of comorbidity between DCD and some other disorders in the general population (because children with combined disorders may be more likely to be referred for examination). Nevertheless, the rates of co-occurrence between DCD and other disorders in clinical samples are so high in all these studies that there seems little doubt that these are genuine effects (a child having DCD means they are significantly more likely to have other problems such as language or attentional problems as well). This impression is confirmed by the Kadesjo and Gillberg (1999) study described above, which provides evidence for high rates of comorbidity between DCD and ADHD and reading and language problems. One likely interpretation of such comorbidities is that a variety of genetic and environmental factors that adversely affect brain development may have diverse effects. Such observations also underline the fact that it may be difficult to categorize a child as having a single disorder: Many of the children studied by Hill (2001) might qualify to be diagnosed as having DCD or SLI. The fact that these children were given a diagnosis of SLI probably reflects the judgment that the educational consequences of these children's language learning difficulties were much more serious than their motor learning difficulties.

The Typical Development of Motor Skills: A Theoretical Framework

As in the case of any disorder, to understand the problems some children experience in developing adequate motor skills we need first to consider how such skills typically develop.

Maturational processes in motor development

A newborn infant has very limited skills of movement. Muscle tone or strength is low and movements are limited with a predominance of what appear to be reflex actions. Reflexes are simple motor functions that may be important for survival and appear to depend upon relatively "hard-wired" circuits in the nervous system; examples of simple reflexes present in the newborn baby are sucking, blinking, and swallowing. A number of more complex reflex actions may be present at birth, such as the grasping reflex (closure of the infant's hand when a finger is placed on the palm)

Figure 6.2 The stepping reflex in an infant. When the infant is held with his weight supported and his feet touching a surface, movements akin to walking can often be elicited.

or the rooting reflex (when the infant's cheek is touched they will turn their head and open their mouth to find and suck the object that touched them). It is easy to see the evolutionary advantage of responses such as the rooting and sucking reflex, while other reflexes such as the stepping reflex (see Figure 6.2) appear to be primitive precursors of motor circuits that will develop fully later. Some early reflexes gradually drop out of the infant's repertoire of movements in the first few months of life.

It is generally accepted that the development of many motor skills such as reaching and walking depends upon maturational changes. Maturation refers to a gradual unfolding of behaviors that are under strong genetic influence. Maturational theorists argue that the regularities in the form and timing of motor development reflect regularities in genetically driven processes of physical and brain development. Walking is a good example of a motor skill that has been seen as reflecting gradual maturational changes. The ability to walk independently develops gradually and usually emerges somewhere around 12–14 months of age. The development of walking depends upon a number of developmental processes, including increasing muscular strength and the development of the neural systems responsible for motor control.

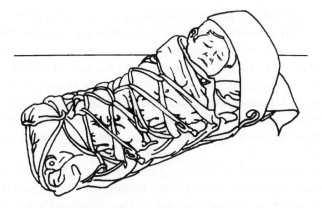

Figure 6.3 Picture of Hopi infant bound to a cradle board.

It is generally believed that central pattern generators (neural circuits in the spinal cord) are important for the development and control of walking (Duysens & Van de Crommert, 1998). Such neural circuits appear to be part of our human genetic endowment, though the early development of walking shows quite marked and rapid changes in the timing and form of movements, which presumably reflect the effects of learning.

Evidence for maturation comes from the fact that walking develops in a more or less universal form in humans. An early study compared Hopi native American infants who were reared either in a traditional or nontraditional way. The traditionally reared infants spent most of the first year of their lives bound to cradle boards that severely restricted their movements (see Figure 6.3), while the other group were left free to move (Dennis & Dennis, 1940). The finding that the two groups walked at the same time on average has been widely cited as evidence for the power of maturational processes in determining the development of walking. However, environmental inputs clearly have an effect, particularly on the timing of the development of walking (e.g., Zelazo, Zelazo, & Kolb, 1972).

Perceptual processes and motor control

Perceptual processes play a vital role in adult motor control and in the development of motor skills in childhood. Perceptual inputs from the inner ear concerning body orientation and movement are critical to balance (see The Vestibular System: A Primer. http://vestibular.wustl.edu/science.html). The semicircular canals of the inner ear are fluid-filled cavities containing hair cells, much like the hair cells in the cochlea that are responsible for hearing. When the head moves, the movement of fluid in the semicircular canals moves the hair cells, which in turn generate neural signals coding the direction and speed of movement. Menière's disease involves a swelling of these structures in the inner ear and results in disturbances of balance.

Other perceptual systems involved in motor performance and motor development are proprioception and kinesthesis. These two terms are similar in meaning and are sometimes used interchangeably. Proprioception was originally used to refer to awareness of the positions of different parts of the body in a static posture (Sherrington, 1906) whereas kinesthesis (movement sense) more strictly refers to our awareness of bodily movements. For the present purposes we will often use the term kinesthesis to refer to both our sense of the position of parts of the body and our sense of their movements. Kinesthesis is a complex sensory system that we are unaware of most of the time, and it depends upon receptors in the joints and muscles and probably upon efference copy information (information from motor command systems in the brain that is used to monitor the movements that have been initiated).

Finally, and crucially, many motor actions depend upon visual information to initiate and guide movements. Most actions we take have to be guided in relation to the position of objects in the environment and not surprisingly visual impairments cause immense problems for motor control. In the case of vision, information about spatial relationships (where things are in relation to parts of the body) is likely to be particularly important. Studies of reaching to grasp seen objects have been used extensively to study the role of vision in motor control. Here the position and size of the object are specified by visual information. Skilled reaching involves bringing the hand to contact the object, with the hand being opened to the correct size in anticipation of grasping the object.

The importance of sensory and perceptual information for the control of movement is such that we should be aware that whenever we refer to motor skills this is really an abbreviation for what more accurately we would refer to as perceptuomotor skills. There is evidence that vision is the dominant sensory modality for guiding and controlling our movements. Vision appears to operate to "calibrate" the perceptuomotor system. Some of this evidence comes from ingenious experiments examining adaptation to displaced vision caused by prisms.

Held and Hein (1963; Held, 1965) gave adults prismatic goggles to wear that displaced vision laterally. When wearing the prisms, things which appeared to be directly in front of the person were, in reality, some distance to one side of center (see Figure 6.4). In these circumstances people would reach to grasp objects and miss them. However, seeing their hand at the same time as the object that they had failed to grasp enabled them to then grasp the object. Quite quickly, after a number of inaccurate reaches, people were able to "recalibrate" their motor system and reach accurately for things seen through the prismatic goggles. This is a form of rapid perceptual-motor learning. Critically, after the prisms were removed these people would at first misreach for things (they "saw" things in the wrong place) but again they soon recalibrated the system to its original state.

It appears that such recalibration depends upon participants making active movements and then detecting the mismatch between their intended and actual hand positions. Held and Hein (1963) argued that such prismatic adaptation effects provide a model for the usual role of vision in specifying object locations for the motor system, and they interpreted such effects as evidence for a "sensorimotor map" or "space coordinate" system. Having the system operate in this way makes it flexible and stable, and able to cope with changes during development, such as the changes in the size of the limbs produced by growth.

Figure 6.4   The effects of prismatic distortions on the control of pointing (Adapted from Held, 1965.)

It has been argued that vision is the dominant sense for calibrating the sensorimotor map. Evidence for the dominance of vision comes from two sources. First, if both visual and proprioceptive information is present, visual information dominates. For example, when wearing prisms that displace vision, vision dominates so that movements are made to the seen location of an object even though this conflicts with the proprioceptively "felt" position (Harris, 1965). Second, vision appears to be the sense modality with the greatest acuity or accuracy as a means of locating places in space and it has been argued that it is adaptive for the greatest weight to be given to vision in calibrating the sensorimotor map because proprioceptive information is inherently less accurate in specifying spatial positions (Lee, 1978; von Hofsten & Rosblad, 1988).

Physiologically, it appears that such a sensorimotor map depends upon topographically (spatially) organized overlapping maps coding visual, auditory, and motor space, and neural systems with these properties have been identified in several areas of the brain. First, in the superior colliculus there are neurons that integrate converging inputs from the different sensory modalities into a body-centered map of space and they appear to direct orienting movements of the eyes, head, body, or pinnae of the ears toward the source of a target (for a review see Patton, Belkacem-Boussaid, & Anastasio, 2002). In addition to these topographically organized multimodal maps in the superior colliculus, there are large areas of the cortex in the macaque monkey brain that code spatial information and movements in a multimodal fashion. In particular areas of the frontal lobe (the dorsal and ventral premotor cortex) appear to code movement patterns and areas in the parietal lobe (around and inside the intraparietal sulcus) contain cells coding the multimodal sensory information needed for guiding movements (see Figure 6.5). It appears that neural

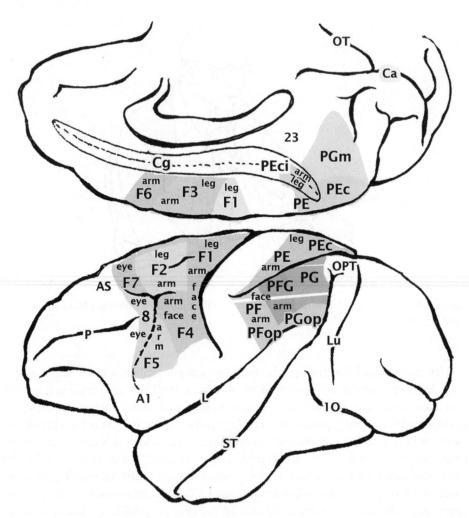

Figure 6.5   Diagram showing key areas of frontal and parietal cortex in the macaque monkey brain concerned with motor control. (Reprinted from *Electroencephalography and Clinical Neurophysiology*, 106, Rizzolatti, G., Luppino, G., and Matelli, M., The organization of the cortical motor system: New concepts, p. 285, copyright (1998), with permission from Elsevier.)

circuits involving communication between these frontal and parietal areas of the brain are heavily involved in the control of movements (Rizzolatti, Luppino, & Matelli, 1998).

Visually guided reaching

A great deal of what we know about motor control has come from studies of visually guided reaching and grasping (for a review, see Jeannerod, 1997). The precision grip of the human hand (holding an object with the opposed thumb and index finger) is considered a recent evolutionary development, though one that other apes come close to possessing (Christel, 1993). Studies of patients with lesions of the parietal lobe indicate that the mechanisms responsible for reaching and grasping are separable and depend upon different visual subsystems. Patients AT (Jeannerod, Decety, Michel, & 1994) and RV (Goodale, Miller, Jakobson, & Carey, 1994) both showed relatively normal ability to reach for an object (i.e., bring their hand to the position of a seen object) but had severe problems in getting their hand configured in the correct size to grip the object. They appeared to have a deficit in using visual information to configure the opening of their hand to the correct size to grip an object. Very surprisingly, however, both patients showed normal performance in making comparisons between the sizes of objects they were shown. They seemed to perceive the size of objects correctly but did not have access to this information to control the opening of their hand in order to grip an object. It is argued that conscious judgments of size depend upon a ventral (cortical) visual system while problems in grasping are related to a dorsal (midbrain) visual system that is damaged in these patients. This dorsal portion of the visual system seems to be critical for guiding action.

Conversely, patients with visual agnosia (impaired ability to recognize objects) following damage to the ventral visual stream appear to have impaired perception of object properties but intact reaching and grasping. Goodale et al. (1991; see also Milner et al., 1991) described a patient DF who had a lesion to her occipital lobe. DF had severely impaired recognition of simple shapes and poor size discrimination, but she could reach for objects and adjusted the size of her hand accurately in order to grasp the objects she was reaching for. Hence, there seems to be a double dissociation between ventral systems responsible for object recognition and dorsal systems responsible for the visual guidance of action (see Box 6.1). At the risk of oversimplification, the information provided by the ventral (cortical) systems seems available to conscious awareness and forms the basis for judgments about the size and shape of objects, while information provided by the dorsal (subcortical) visual systems appears to be largely unconscious and closely coupled to the systems' guiding movement.

Imitation and the mirror neuron system

It is likely that learning by imitation (copying actions that we see others perform) plays an important part in motor development. Children may imitate actions they see others perform and the direct teaching of motor skills (such as sporting skills) often depends upon demonstrations of what to do that the pupil then tries to imitate. It appears that some very basic imitative abilities are present in human infants from birth (Meltzoff & Moore, 1976).

In the early 1990s imitative abilities were given a new prominence by the discovery of a mirror neuron system (MNS) in the brain of monkeys (DiPelligrino, Klatchy, & McCluskey, 1992; Rizzolatti, Fadiga, Gallese, & Fogassi, 1996; for a recent review of the MNS see Iacobani & Dapretto, 2006). In these studies Rizzolatti and colleagues were recording activity from single neurons in areas of cortex in the frontal and parietal lobes of macaque monkeys while they were reaching for and grasping objects. Mirror neurons are neurons that fire both when the monkey

Box 6.1   The human visual cortex (from *http://en. wikipedia.org/wiki/Visual_cortex*)

The primate visual system consists of about 30 areas of the cerebral cortex called the visual cortex. The visual cortex is divided into the ventral stream and the dorsal stream. The ventral stream is associated with object recognition and form perception. It has strong connections to the medial temporal lobe (which stores long-term memories), the limbic system (which controls emotions), and the dorsal stream (which deals with object locations and motion). From caudal to rostral, the ventral stream consists of visual areas V1 (primary visual cortex), V2, V4, and the areas of the inferior temporal lobe: PIT (posterior inferotemporal), CIT (central inferotemporal), and AIT (anterior inferotemporal). Each visual area contains a full representation of visual space, that is, it contains neurons whose receptive fields together represent the entire visual field. Visual information enters the ventral stream through the primary visual cortex and travels through the rest of the areas in sequence.

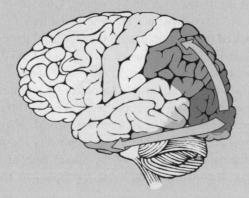

Illustration of the dorsal (upper) and ventral stream (lower) systems originating in the human visual cortex.

performs a particular movement and also when the monkey sees the experimenter or another monkey perform the same movement. These neurons appear to code object-oriented actions whether they are performed by the monkey or another actor performing the same action, and they therefore appear to be part of neural circuits representing, at a quite abstract level, particular motor actions. When we see another person perform an action, it appears that the circuits that would control the same movement if we were to perform it are automatically activated. The same is also true when people are asked to imagine making movements. For example, Decety et al. (1994) found increases in neural activity in several cortical motor areas (measured in a PET scan) when participants were asked to imagine grasping objects that were shown to them. These studies, showing a close correspondence between the

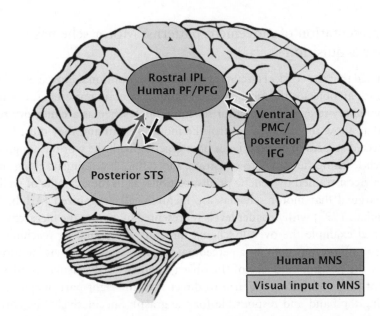

Figure 6.6 Diagram of human mirror neuron system. (Reprinted by permission from Macmillan Publishers Ltd, *Nature Reviews Neuroscience* (Vol 7(12), p. 943, Iacoboni, M. and Dapretto, M., The mirror neuron system and the consequences of its dysfunction), copyright 2006.)

neural activity underlying motor actions and imagined actions, may help to explain the finding that engaging in mental practice of a skill helps to improve that skill (e.g., Feltz & Landers 1983).

Studies using brain imaging techniques (Rizzolatti & Craighero, 2004) suggest that a human MNS (equivalent to the one identified by recording from single neurons in the macaque monkey brain) is located in parts of the frontal and parietal lobe (the inferior parietal lobule and inferior frontal gyrus) and these two areas appear to receive visual inputs from neurons in the superior temporal sulcus (STS) (see Figure 6.6). The frontal and parietal MNS circuits respond strongly when actions are performed, imagined, observed, planned, or imitated and it is inferred that these areas of the human brain contain mirror neurons that are equivalent to those that have been recorded directly in equivalent areas of the macaque brain (see Hamilton, 2008). There are also other regions stretching from the lateral occipital cortex through the middle temporal gyrus to the STS that appear to be activated when we observe an action being performed. The MNS is part of the motor system and appears central to how actions are represented. It is critical to both the performance of motor actions and our ability to interpret and imitate the actions of others. Damage to the MNS in patients results in a form of motor impairment (apraxia) characterized by an inability to perform hand actions in daily life or to imitate such actions or perform them when told to do so (Buxbaum, Kyle, & Menon, 2005).

The representation of movement patterns: Motor schemas and their acquisition

It is assumed that the cortical circuits controlling our volitional movements (of which reaching for an object is the most studied example) contain representations of action plans commonly referred to as motor schemas. Such schemas are memory representations that allow the brain to control the motor system and they must be learned and perfected as a result of experience of interacting with the world (though in many cases such learning functions to constrain and refine development along lines that are heavily constrained by genetic predispositions, as in the example of walking). It is often argued that motor schemas are hierarchically organized (Arbib, Erdi, & Szentagothai, 1997) with broader levels represented higher up the hierarchy. To take a simplified example the overall schema directing the action of reaching for and grasping an object may contain a perceptual schema (which uses visual information to specify the position and size of the object), and two subschemas controlling the movement (one controlling the arm to direct it to the right part of space, another controlling the hand and responsible for the grasp). Speculatively, the cortical circuits that include mirror neurons may effectively be the neural instantiation of motor schemas. Many of the details about how motor schemas are represented and learned remain to be understood.

Recently, studies of motor control and motor development, have been highly influenced by ideas from an "ecological" or "dynamic systems" perspective (Thelen, 1995). Bernstein (1967) argued that the complexity of movements was such that it would be terribly inefficient (and perhaps impossible) for the organism to program each movement in detail. Bernstein argued that a solution to this problem was for movements to be planned centrally at a highly abstract level, and that many details of the movement will result directly from the biomechanical constraints that are present in the systems of joints and muscles in the limbs. Arguably, the representations of movement patterns coded by the MNS are highly abstract and provide evidence in line with Bernstein's ideas. Such ideas have led to the development of mathematical theories of the control of rhythmic movements (Kelso, Holt, Rubin, & Kugler 1981) in which the dynamic systems controlling movement may show abrupt changes between different "stable" states of operation. Such views, when applied to motor learning and development, suggest that much of what is learned involves the gradual adjustment of parameters in the motor control system that are operating at a highly abstract level.

Summary of the typical development of motor skills

Motor skills in children develop gradually over many years, and this development seems to be constrained by maturational processes that govern the development of the nervous system. Virtually all movements are heavily dependent on perceptual inputs, particularly information from vision, the vestibular (balance) system, and proprioception (sense of body movement). For this reason we should think of these skills as "perceptual-motor" skills rather than simply motor skills. Many movements that we make depend upon extensive practice and learning, and the representations of movement patterns stored in the brain are often referred to as motor schemas. Such schemas are represented in cortical circuits that extend across the frontal, temporal, and parietal lobes of the brain.

The Nature of Movement Difficulties in Children with DCD

Before considering the possible cognitive causes of the difficulties experienced by children with DCD it is useful to describe their pattern of difficulties. Clinically, the symptoms of DCD can vary considerably and may include gross motor difficulties, such as problems running, hopping, jumping, catching a ball, and balancing, and fine motor difficulties in activities such as dressing (doing up buttons and laces), drawing and writing, and using eating utensils. Because tests such as the Movement ABC assess diverse motor skills, poor performance on a small subset of tasks may be sufficient to result in a diagnosis of DCD. Speech-motor skills can be affected and problems of pencil control affecting writing and drawing are widespread. Given the diagnostic criteria used for DCD it is very probable that there will be heterogeneity, with different children showing different patterns of motor difficulties.

A number of studies have now examined the speed and accuracy of simple movements in children with DCD. These studies give us a more detailed description of the form of motor difficulties found in this group. Invariably, in the studies considered here, children are matched to typically developing children for age and sometimes also for verbal ability (e.g., Smyth & Mason, 1997).

Smyth and Mason (1997) studied a large group of DCD and control children on a task involving grasping a bar in order to turn it either clockwise or anticlockwise. This task requires the person to choose either an overhand or underhand grip depending upon the direction that the bar is to be rotated in order to keep the rotation of the forearm that is needed within the comfort zone. There were no differences between the DCD and control children in their ability to select the appropriate grip posture (a simple motor planning task that involves spatial information). However, on another spatially based movement task (von Hofsten & Rosblad, 1988; see Figure 6.7) that involved sticking a pin into the underside of a table in a position matching the position of a target on top of the table, the DCD children were less accurate than controls. (Similar problems on this task were reported for smaller groups of DCD children by Mon-Williams, Wann, and Pascal (1999) and by Schoemaker et al. (2001).) The children performed this task in three different conditions:

1 Vision – the child looked at the dot on the table top while positioning the pin under the table.
2 Proprioception – the child placed their finger on the target dot on the table top and then closed their eyes while trying to place the pin in the corresponding position on the underside of the table.
3 Vision and proprioception – the child touched the dot and looked at it while positioning the pin under the table.

Figure 6.7   Diagram of the task developed by von Hofsten and Rosblad (1988): (*left*) visual condition; (*middle*) visual and proprioceptive condition; (*right*) proprioception condition (eyes closed).

The proprioception condition was much harder than the other two conditions for all children, confirming the importance of visual information for guiding movements even when the hand cannot be seen, as von Hofsten and Rosblad (1988) had shown in typically developing children. Finally, the children with DCD were also less accurate in an arm posture matching task (the experimenter put one of the child's arms into a particular position and the child, with their eyes closed, had to move the other arm into the corresponding position).

A number of studies have examined the speed with which movements are made in children with DCD, using measures of reaction time (the time from a signal to begin a movement) and movement time (the time taken to complete a movement). The movements of children with DCD tend to be slower and more variable in their timing than those of typically developing children. Henderson, Rose, and Henderson (1992) studied an aiming task, in which children had to move their finger from a start key to a response key. They found that the children with DCD were slower to begin to move and moved more slowly and with greater variability than control children. The children with DCD also had difficulties with timing when trying to synchronize their movements with an external cue (move when you hear the fifth beep in a regular series). Van Dellen and Geuze (1990) and Huh, Williams, and Burke (1998) also found that movements in children with DCD were slower and more variable than those of control children. The same pattern, with slower movement times and longer movement trajectories, was found by Ameratunga, Johnston, and Burns (2004) when children with DCD were required to point to targets with their preferred hand. As in the study by Smyth and Mason, the aiming of both groups suffered to similar extents when visual information was not available. However, in one study (Smits-Engelsman, Wilson, Westenberg, & Duysens, 2003) children with DCD were asked to draw a line to connect two circles either once or repeatedly, and it was reported that although the DCD children performed less accurately they were actually faster than controls. This pattern suggests problems in monitoring the speed of movement needed that is compatible with an acceptable level of accuracy.

Another task in which the timing of movements is critical is rotary pursuit tracking. Here the child sees a light source moving in an irregular circular motion and attempts to track the light using a stylus. Lord and Hulme (1988) compared the performance of DCD and control children on this task. They found that the DCD children were poorer at tracking the light source on early trials, which they argued reflected problems in using visual feedback to control movements. However, both groups showed increased tracking accuracy across trials suggesting that all children were learning to develop motor programs to anticipate the trajectory of the light (which followed the same pattern across trials). This suggests that many of the DCD children were able to develop new motor programs in this task (though a minority of them failed to do this). Finally, children with DCD have also been shown to have difficulties with timing in the very simple task of repeatedly tapping their finger (Piek & Skinner, 1999).

Hill and Wing (1998, 1999) reported a detailed analysis of the timing of grip forces when lifting and lowering an object held in a precision grip (between the opposed thumb and index finger) in two children with DCD, compared to two control children of the same age. They found evidence for small differences in timing the coordination of different forces when lifting objects in these two children with DCD. In the absence of control data from a larger group of control children it is hard to judge how unusual these differences in the timing of grip forces are.

Different profiles of motor difficulties in children with DCD?

A critical question is the extent to which different children with DCD show meaningful differences in the form of motor difficulties they experience. Do some of these children only have problems with fine motor control, and others only problems with gross motor skills for example? Ideally to investigate the heterogeneity of difficulties seen in children with DCD we would start with data on large samples of typically developing children tested on a wide range of different motor tasks. Based on such normative data meaningfully different aspects of motor skill could be identified before seeing if different children with DCD show problems with different aspects of motor skill (and perhaps on different tasks tapping the putative causes of the disorder as well). This is really analogous to identifying the different aspects of ability that are measured in standardized IQ tests, before going on to assess variations in ability among special populations of children. Unfortunately this has not been done, and the commonly used measures of motor skill (such as the Movement ABC) are designed only to assess clinical impairments rather than being sensitive enough to assess the continuous variations amongst typically developing children.

Nevertheless a number of studies have examined the possible heterogeneity of motor difficulties among children with DCD. Three studies (Dewey & Kaplan, 1994; Hoare, 1994; McNab, Miller, & Polatajko, 2001)) have attempted to identify subgroups of children with different forms of motor difficulties using a statistical technique called cluster analysis. This depends upon finding correlated deficits amongst subgroups of children. In all of these studies the scores on different tests are expressed in relation to the average levels of performance of the group of children (often just a clinical DCD group, but sometimes a combined group of DCD and control children). The characteristics of the subgroups identified are therefore effectively profiles of relative strengths and weaknesses (compared to other children who have motor difficulties). It is also important to note that different studies of this sort have often used somewhat different measures, which makes comparing the findings from the different studies difficult. Dewey and Kaplan (1994) studied a group of 51 DCD children who scored at least 1 SD below average on a screening test of motor skills and 51 age- and sex-matched controls. Based on scores from measures of motor functioning and balance they proposed that the DCD group could be divided into three groups:

1   Severe deficits in all areas.
2   Deficits in balance and transitive movements.
3   Deficits in motor sequencing.

Hoare (1994) studied a group of children with DCD and borderline DCD using measures of kinesthetic acuity, visual perception, copying drawings, manual dexterity, balance, and running speed. This study identified five subtypes of DCD children:

1   Good balance.
2   Good visual-motor performance.
3   Generalized perceptual dysfunction.
4   Good kinesthetic ability (better described as poor fine motor skills; see McNab et al., 2001).
5   Motor execution problems.

McNab et al. (2001) attempted to replicate the study of Hoare (1994) using data from a sample of 62 children with DCD whose motor abilities were at least 1 SD below average for their age. The measures used were very similar to those used by Hoare and included measures of kinesthetic acuity, visual perception, copying drawings, manual dexterity, balance, and running speed. This study identified very similar subgroups to Hoare:

1   Good balance (13% sample; children with poor gross and fine motor skills, but relatively normal balance and visual-perceptual skills).
2   Good visual-motor performance (17% sample; poor balance and kinesthetic skills, with fine motor skills being better than gross motor skills).
3   Generalized perceptual-motor dysfunction (23% sample; problems in all areas including poor fine and gross motor skills and both visual and kinesthetic problems).
4   Poor fine motor skills (32% sample; poor fine motor skills and drawing abilities coupled with visual-perceptual deficits).
5   Poor gross motor skills (15% sample; problems with gross motor skills including running speed, with relatively better fine motor skills and copying ability).

Thus both the Hoare (1994) and McNab et al. (2001) studies agree in identifying a subgroup of children with DCD with good static balance skills and another with generalized motor problems (these subgroups are also supported by the findings of Dewey & Kaplan, 1994). There is also some support for a distinction between fine and gross motor problems, with problems in fine motor skills appearing to be linked to problems of visual perception. Differences between studies in the measures used and the samples studied make definite conclusions about subtypes difficult. It is notable that the two studies using the most similar measures generated similar sub-types (Hoare, 1994; McNab et al., 2001). It is also probably worth stressing that differences among children with DCD may well reflect variations in underlying dimensional abilities (perhaps balance and visual-perceptual skills would be two such dimensions) and if this is accepted it may be that attempts to force different cases into different categories may be misplaced, or at least limited in their likely success.

Summary: Clinical description, diagnosis, and subtypes in DCD

Children with DCD are diagnosed based on inadequate performance on standard-ized tests of motor skills compared with typically developing children of the same age. Many of these children have quite general problems with diverse forms of motor tasks. There is some evidence that the pattern of motor difficulties differs between children with DCD, with some children showing particular difficulties with fine motor skills (skills involving hand movements and manipulation of objects) and others showing more marked problems with gross motor skills (skills involving movements of the whole body) that may be related to problems of balance. However, it is probably fair to say that evidence for clearly defined subtypes is lacking and it seems likely that further progress in trying to identify subtypes (or different dimen-sions of impairment) will depend upon clearer hypotheses about the underlying pro-cessing impairments that may lead to specific forms of movement difficulties. This is the issue to which we now turn.

Cognitive Explanations of DCD

Perceptual deficits as a cause of motor difficulties in DCD

A dominant approach to explaining the motor learning difficulties found in children with DCD has been in terms of perceptual impairments. (An earlier term used to refer to this group of children was developmental apraxia and agnosia, agnosia is a term used to refer to disorders of perception and this captures the central role of perceptual disorders seen in the clinical profile of these children by early investiga-tors in this field.) From the review of perceptual processes and their role in motor control and motor learning presented earlier in the chapter, there are four areas of sensory/perceptual processing that might seem likely explanations for the motor dif-ficulties seen in children with DCD. First, given the dominance of vision in the con-trol of action, a visual-perceptual deficit seems a likely possibility. A second possibility is that there is a problem with proprioception/kinesthesis. Third, there might be particular problems in translating between visual and kinesthetic or motoric information, which would represent a specific deficit in the integration of perceptual information from the two modalities most closely associated with movement (a cross-modal integration deficit). Finally, there might be a problem with balance in children with DCD, and this might lead to problems particularly in the area of gross motor skills (movements of the whole body in which balance is critical). The majority of studies have concentrated on studies of visual and kinesthetic perception and we will consider these areas first. A useful meta-analysis of studies in this area was conducted by Wilson and McKenzie (1998).

Visual-perceptual deficits

A very early study of visual, kinesthetic, and cross-modal perception in children with DCD was reported by Hulme, Biggerstaff, Moran, and McKinlay (1982). Here a group of children with DCD and age-matched typically developing children were compared on four closely matched tasks. Each task involved children making judgments about the relative length of straight lines (see Figure 6.8). In the visual task (the V-V task) the child looked at two Perspex boxes one on top of the other. They were shown a "standard" line in the aperture of the lower box. This line was then removed from view and the child directed the experimenter to extend a line in a corresponding window in the aperture of the upper box until the line was the same length as the first presented "standard" line.

The kinesthetic task (K-K task) was analogous. Here the child grasped a rod that was screened from view and moved it along a slot to a stop (the lengths of the movements made were the same as the lengths of the standard lines presented in the V-V task). After making this movement the rod was moved back to the start of the slot, and the child attempted to replicate the length of the movement just made (with the stop removed). The two cross-modal conditions involved combinations of these two within-modal tasks. In the visual-kinesthetic task (V-K task) the child saw a line presented visually as in the V-V task, and then tried to replicate the length of the line seen by moving the rod along the slot the same distance. In the kinesthetic-visual (K-V) task the child made a movement of the rod to the stop (just as in the K-K task) and then directed the experimenter to extend a visual line so that it matched the length of the movement they had just produced.

It may be worth noting that the hypothesis guiding this study was that children with DCD would have particular difficulties with either the cross-modal or kinesthetic judgment tasks (all of which involved motor output), while the V-V condition would function as a kind of control condition and not show group differences. The results of the study were clear but unexpected. The DCD children showed the largest difference in performance on the V-V task (Cohen's $d = 1.2$) and smaller differences in the K-K task and the two cross-modal tasks (Cohen's d ranging from 0.7 to 0.5).

Correlations were computed between performance on the four perceptual judgment tasks and measures of the children's motor skills. The strongest correlations (the only ones to be significant) were between performance on the V-V task and a composite measure of motor ability in each group (0.34 and 0.40 for the DCD and control group). It was argued that problems on this simple visual task (judging the

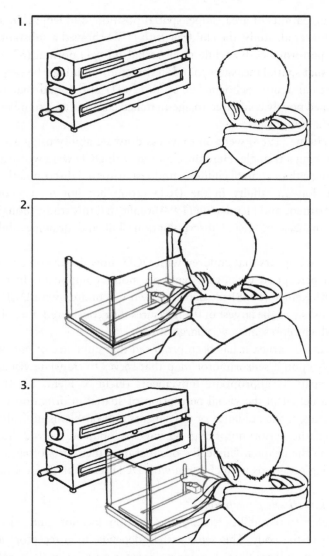

Figure 6.8 An illustration of the experimental set-up used for the assessment of visual, kinesthetic, and cross-modal perception by Hulme et al. (1982).

length of successive visually presented straight lines) may tap a very basic deficit in visual-spatial processing in the DCD group, and that such a deficit might in turn explain these children's difficulties in learning and performing motor tasks. A subsequent study (Hulme, Smart, & Moran, 1982) established that the problem the children with DCD had in judging the length of visually presented lines did not reflect problems of memory, and were not a secondary consequence of problems in controlling eye movements when inspecting the lines.

These deficits were explored further by Lord and Hulme (1987 a,b), who found wide ranging problems on visual-spatial tasks in children with DCD. Here the children with DCD performed more poorly than controls on measures of size constancy, and on discriminations of area, slope, spatial position, and length. In addition, just as in the Hulme et al. study, the children with DCD showed a substantial deficit on measures of performance IQ while their verbal IQ was normal (82 vs. 106). The deficits on visual-spatial measures found in this study could not be explained by differences in visual acuity. Schoemaker et al. (2001) also found that children with DCD performed poorly compared to age-matched controls on a number of measures of visual-spatial judgments.

Lord and Hulme (1988) went on to assess drawing ability using a simple task of copying or tracing a triangle. Here the children with DCD were worse at drawing or tracing a triangle than control children, and visual-spatial discrimination ability correlated with drawing ability in the DCD group but not in the control group. Henderson, Barnett, and Henderson (1994) replicated this study, though in this case the correlation between visual discrimination skill and drawing ability was not significant.

In summary it appears that children with DCD show deficits on a range of simple visual-spatial perceptual tasks that have no motor component. In the review by Wilson and McKenzie (1998) the deficit shown by children with DCD on complex visuospatial tasks was the largest of the measures they considered ($r = .548$, equivalent to $d = 1.3$, which represents a very large effect).

As we discussed earlier, it has been proposed that guidance of our movements in space depends upon a sensorimotor map that serves to translate visually perceived locations to spatially appropriate movements (Held & Hein, 1963). It could be argued that a deficit in the visual perception of spatial information will inevitably lead to problems in the guidance of movements and problems in "calibrating" and "recalibrating" the sensorimotor map during development. We will discuss this idea further later in the chapter. Clinically, occupational therapists often use visual perceptual training programs with children with DCD (Cermak & Larkin, 2002).

Problems of kinesthetic perception

Kinesthesis refers to our ability to sense the position, location, and velocity of movement of parts of the body. This sense system depends upon receptors in the muscle spindles and skin, and possibly also copies of motor output signals (corollary outflow or efference copy information). By definition, trying to isolate kinesthesis as a perceptual system from motor control processes is difficult, if not impossible. Typically in studies of children with DCD, kinesthetic perception has been assessed by measures of sensitivity to passive movements of the limbs or judgments by the child of their own active movements. Given that children with DCD suffer from movement difficulties, there is a degree of circularity to finding they have problems in judging their own movement patterns and possibly judgments of passive movements will give a "purer" measure of kinesthetic perception uncontaminated by movement execution problems. Perhaps the first attempt to relate kinesthetic perceptual problems in children to motor difficulties was the work of Laszlo and Bairstow (1981a). These studies used a measure referred to as the kinesthetic sensitivity test (KST; Laszlo & Bairstow, 1985a). This test contains two subtests: a kinesthetic acuity test, and a kinesthetic perception and memory test.

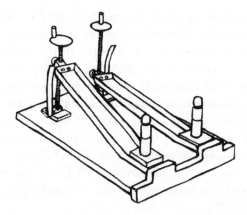

Figure 6.9 The kinesthetic acuity apparatus used by Laszlo and Bairstow (1985a).

The kinesthetic acuity test measures arm and hand position and involves an apparatus with two runways that face away from the child (see Figure 6.9). The angle of the two runways is adjustable and each has a wooden block with a handle that can slide up the runway. The child reaches under a screen and grasps the two handles and the examiner then pulls the child's hands up to the top of the two runways and then back to the bottom again (a passive movement). The two runways are set to different angles and on each trial the child simply has to indicate which hand went higher.

The kinesthetic perception and memory test involves a series of curved closed patterns that are cut into Perspex disks. The child again reaches under a screen and holds a peg while the examiner moves their hand holding the peg around the pattern on the disk twice. The child removes their hand and the examiner then rotates the disk. The child is then shown the disk and asked to move it back to the orientation it was in when their hand was moved around the pattern. This is a highly complex measure with many components, including memory requirements and the ability to translate a kinesthetic memory trace into a visual code to support judgments about the orientation of the disk.

Bairstow and Laszlo (1981) claimed that 8 out of 14 children with DCD could be considered "kinesthetically blind" though no data were reported to support this assertion. Subsequently Laszlo and Bairstow (1985b) in a poorly controlled study claimed that practice on the KST led to improvements in kinesthesis and that this transferred into improvements in motor skill, as assessed by a drawing task.

Laszlo and Bairstow's studies reported no data from children with a diagnosis of DCD. Lord and Hulme (1987b) compared a group of children with DCD and age-matched controls (the same children as studied by Lord and Hulme, 1987a) on the KST. There were no reliable differences in performance between the groups on either subtest of the KST ($d = 0.58$ and 0.08 for the acuity test and perception and memory test, respectively) and it appears this result may, in part, simply be a consequence of the poor reliability of the KST. Doyle, Elliott, and Connolly (1986) had made this point earlier and Elliott, Connolly, and Doyle (1988) used a modified test procedure with the kinesthetic acuity test from the KST to improve its reliability. In a group of 100 typically developing children between the ages of 3 years 10 months and 11 years 10 months they found that their modified KST acuity measure correlated with a range of motor skill measures (r ranging from .24 to .47). However the kinesthetic measure and motor measures all correlated strongly with age (r ranging from .41 to .85) and once the effects of age on motor performance were accounted for there was no additional relationship between kinesthetic skill and motor skill. Perhaps the strongest evidence that the kinesthetic acuity test from the KST does not distinguish between children with DCD and controls comes from a study of a large group (96) of children with DCD and age-matched controls by Smyth and Mason (1997), who found no trace of a difference between the groups on this measure ($d = 0.07$).

The evidence reviewed so far indicates that kinesthesis, at least as measured by the KST, does not discriminate children with DCD from controls. Nevertheless, Laszlo Bairstow, Bartrip, and Rolfe (1988) went on to claim that there was a causal relationship between kinesthesis and poor motor skills in children. This claim was based on a training study but unfortunately there are a number of problems in interpreting this study, most prominently that tests of kinesthetic ability were included as part of both the pretest and outcome measures (the results may therefore simply demonstrate that training on kinesthetic measures improves subsequent scores on the KST). Other studies (Polatajko et al., 1995; Sims, Henderson, Hulme, & Morton, 1996) have failed to find any selective improvement in motor skills following kinesthetic training.

The evidence reviewed shows that the KST is not a measure that is sensitive to differences between children with DCD and controls. Nevertheless there is evidence from somewhat more complex tasks that kinesthetic ability is poor in children with DCD. Piek and Coleman-Carman (1995) reported that an active version of Laszlo and Bairstow's KST test did differentiate between DCD and control children. Also, as noted earlier, Hulme et al. (1982) found that children with DCD were worse than controls on a task requiring them to reproduce the length of a linear movement they had just made. Similarly, Smyth and Mason (1997) found that children with DCD had problems in moving their arm into a position that matched the position that their other arm had been placed in by the examiner. All of these tasks involve spatial judgments and active movements to make a response. The difficulties that DCD children show on these tasks may therefore simply be an inevitable consequence of their motor difficulties (Wilson & McKenzie, 1998).

Balance and postural control

Most tests of motor impairment (such as the Movement ABC; Henderson and Sugden, 1992) include tests of balance, and these measures often pose problems for children with DCD. Poor balance skills have been reported to be common in groups of children with DCD in a number of studies (van Dellen & Geuze, 1990; Visser, Geuze, & Kalverboer, 1998; Wann, Mon-Williams, & Rushton, 1998) and the studies of subtypes of children with DCD described earlier suggest that a substantial proportion of children with DCD have problems with balance.

The sense of balance and its relationship to the maintenance of postural control is complex. It appears that postural control depends upon a combination of vestibular, visual, and proprioceptive sensory inputs and our relative reliance on these different sensory inputs may be adjusted in different conditions (Oie, Kiemel, & Jeka, 2002). The role of vision in the control of posture is demonstrated simply by the observations that the degree of body sway when standing increases when the eyes are closed and people who are blind will sway more when standing than controls with normal vision (Edwards, 1946).

The effects of visual information on balance were investigated experimentally by Lee and colleagues (Lee & Aronson, 1974; Lee & Lishman, 1975; Lishman & Lee 1973) using a "swinging room" (see Figure 6.10). In this case the participant is standing surrounded by a large mock-up room suspended from the ceiling. In this situation when the room swings adults are induced to sway and may fall over if they are standing on a narrow support. Young children are more sensitive to sway than adults and are often bowled over by the sway even when standing on the floor. The postural sway induced by the swinging room shows the power of vision in influencing postural control in both adults and children. The greater susceptibility of young children to the swinging room suggests that they are either more dependent on vision

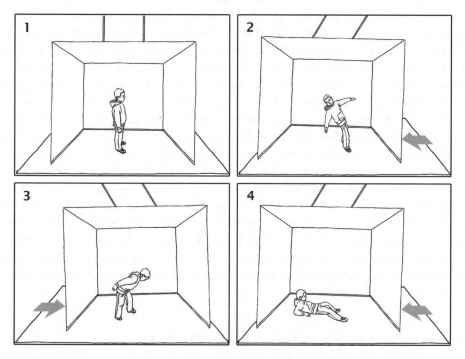

Figure 6.10   A swinging room apparatus. The false room fills the child's field of view. When the room is stationary (1) balance is normal. If the room sways (2, 3) toward and away from the child, balance is disturbed and the child may sway to compensate for the seen movement. In extreme cases the disturbance of balance caused by the swaying room may cause the child to fall over (4).

for postural control or less able to compensate when visual information conflicts with other cues (vestibular and proprioceptive cues).

Wann, Mon-Williams, and Rushton (1998) studied the effects of a swinging room on posture in a small group of six children with DCD and a larger group of children and adults. The swinging room induced sway in the adults but to a smaller extent than in the typically developing control children, as expected. Two of the children with DCD who had scored normally on a test of balance showed equivalent degrees of sway to control children of the same age. However, the other four children with DCD showed abnormally large degrees of sway for their age (equivalent to that seen in much younger children), suggesting they were unusually reliant on visual information for postural control. In line with this, the DCD group overall showed a greater degree of sway when standing with their eyes closed than control children. Geuze (2003) also reported that children with DCD and poor balance had particular difficulty maintaining their balance when their eyes were closed.

Balance is important when we walk. The fact that walking in complete darkness is perfectly possible shows that adequate balance while walking can be maintained by the vestibular and kinesthetic systems in the absence of vision. However, as just described, vision normally contributes to postural stability and may be more important for stability in some children with DCD than for typically developing children. Deconick et al. (2006) reported a study in which they compared walking in the light with walking in the dark in a group of children with DCD and typically developing age-matched control children. The pattern of walking in typically developing children was essentially unaffected by darkness (the children walked along a straight walkway toward a small LED light at one end). However, the children with DCD chose to walk more slowly in the dark and showed greater swaying of their upper body, indicating that their balance and postural stability were impaired by the absence of visual input. This study extends the findings of Wann et al. (1998) and Geuze (2003), which showed that children with DCD may place more reliance on vision for static balance, to show equivalent effects on the control of balance during walking.

Overall, it seems that a significant proportion of children with DCD experience problems with balance that will contribute to problems with gross motor skills (movements of the whole body). These problems of balance are not yet well understood but they may in some cases reflect an abnormally high degree of dependence on visual input in the control of postural stability. However, this pattern of excessive reliance on visual information might arise as a form of compensation for problems with the vestibular and proprioceptive systems that are normally important for maintaining a stable posture.

A Cognitive-Perceptual Theory of DCD: DCD as a Noisy Sensorimotor Map

It remains to pull together the work considered on cognitive deficits found in children with DCD. Our proposal is that many of the deficits in motor control seen in children with DCD can be explained by a deficit in developing a sensorimotor map.

The sensorimotor map is a system that relates positions of objects in visual space to positions in motor space (a system relating "seen" positions to "felt" positions). We will outline this theory briefly below.

The clearest cognitive deficit identified in children with DCD is a visual-perceptual deficit: more specifically, the deficit appears to be one in processing spatial information in the visual modality. So, for example, children with DCD have difficulties in dealing with size, length, and shape information in visual tasks, but there is no evidence that they suffer problems in nonspatial-visual tasks (they may, for example, be good at discriminating the color and brightness of stimuli, rather than their size and orientation). We have also considered evidence that vision is the dominant sense in determining our awareness of spatial relationships, and that vision is used to "calibrate" the sensorimotor map that relates movements of the body to where things are seen to be in visual space.

The functions of the sensorimotor map might best be illustrated in relation to reaching for an object we see in front of us. The position of the object is specified visually but the sensorimotor map enables us to relate the position of a seen object to a "felt" position in motor space. (As we discussed earlier, there is evidence of multimodal representations of sensory and motor space in the superior colliculus and areas of the parietal and frontal lobes of the brain.) The operation of a sensorimotor map can easily be demonstrated. Look at an object that is within reach and then close your eyes and reach for the object. You will find that it is easy to move your hand quite accurately to the object when your eyes are closed. This must depend upon relating information about where the object was seen to the movements needed to bring your hand to the object. This means that the position specified for an object visually – say 30° to the left and 30 cm from the head at waist level – is represented directly in an overlapping map specifying the same position in motor space. There is a direct correspondence between where things are "seen" to be and where they are "felt" to be. Such superimposed maps of visual and motor space allow visual information to be translated effortlessly into spatial coordinates of the movement needed to bring the hand to the position of the object.

These ideas lead directly to a cognitive theory of the movement problems seen in children with DCD. Let us suppose that from early in life visual information about spatial location is degraded in the sense of being highly variable or prone to error. Such a deficit in encoding spatial position in the visual modality will lead to problems in creating a sensorimotor map (the brain's map of where things are will be "blurred" or smeared so that positions are only represented in an approximate way). A deficit in the sensorimotor map will lead directly to problems in producing movements that are guided accurately in space.

It should be noted that such a problem would not only affect movements controlled by vision. Suppose you are seated in front of a table and the task is to look at a cross marked on the table top and touch the middle of the cross with your index finger. Touching the cross in this task is easy. Now suppose you are asked to reach underneath the table and touch the position corresponding to the cross on the underside of the table. This is more difficult, but can be done with reasonable accuracy by most children and adults (von Hofsten & Rosblad, 1988). Our ability to perform this task when our hand is hidden from view under the table depends critically upon the sensorimotor map. The point is encoded on the map when it is seen, and the movement is organized to bring the hand to the correct position using correspondences encoded in the map between "seen" and "felt" positions. In fact, touching the cross on the table top with your hand in view arguably depends less upon the sensorimotor map than making the corresponding movement when your hand is hidden from view under the table. This is because when we can see the cross and also our hand moving toward it on the top of the table any errors of movement (discrepancies between where the hand is and the center of the cross) can be seen and corrected using visual feedback.

Different versions of this task were studied by von Hofsten and Rosblad (1988). In the visual condition the child looks at the cross and reaches under the table to indicate the position with their eyes open. In the visual and proprioceptive condition the child puts one hand on top of the table and touches the cross with their finger; they then reach under the table to touch the same position with their other hand. Finally, in the proprioceptive condition the child touches the point on top of the table and then closes their eyes while they reach under the table to touch the same position with their other hand (see Figure 6.7).

Accuracy in this task is equivalent in the visual and in the visual and proprioceptive conditions when the position on top of the table can be seen, but accuracy is much lower in the proprioceptive condition when visual information is absent. This is another demonstration of the critical role of vision in controlling spatially guided actions. It should be noted that in the proprioceptive condition the position of the cross on the top of the table is initially registered visually, before the child then has to close their eyes. The fact that this condition is much harder than the corresponding visual and proprioceptive condition (when the child can keep looking at the cross) shows that there must be a memory component to the task such that the accuracy of visual information encoded in the sensorimotor map degrades over time. This was confirmed experimentally by von Hofsten and Rosblad (1988) by imposing a 30 s delay in both the proprioceptive condition and in a visual "memory" condition where the child saw the position of the dot and then had to close their eyes before placing the pin in the corresponding position under the table. In the visual memory condition, accuracy declined substantially with the introduction of a 30 s delay, whereas accuracy remained more or less the same in the proprioceptive condition. They also reported that in the proprioceptive condition children positioned the pin on the underside of the table quite slowly, whereas when visual information was removed in the visual memory condition the preferred strategy was to move quickly and place the pin in position before memory of the dot's seen position faded. Thus it seems that positions registered visually on the sensorimotor map are subject to a loss of accuracy with time.

As described earlier, Smyth and Mason (1997) studied this task in children with DCD, who were less accurate in all modalities and, like the control children, were least accurate in the proprioceptive condition when vision was not available. These problems are well explained in terms of a deficient sensorimotor map in children with DCD. A deficient sensorimotor map would be a necessary consequence of a noisy or degraded visuospatial perceptual system, which we have extensive evidence for in these children.

The extent to which the idea of DCD as arising from a noisy sensorimotor map can explain all of the problems of motor control seen in these children is not clear. More specifically, it might seem that this is unlikely to explain the problems of balance that are commonly reported in these children. However, balance does depend on visual input and to this extent balance problems might arise in some children as a secondary consequence of impairments of visuospatial processing. While this is possible, it also seems quite likely that some children with DCD may experience problems of balance because of problems in the vestibular and proprioceptive systems, which also contribute to balance and postural stability. It seems important to explore these issues in future studies that assess all of these sensory systems in children with DCD and relate possible visual, vestibular, and proprioceptive perceptual deficits to different motor tasks selected so that they do, or do not, require balance and postural stability.

Finally, the approach adopted in this chapter has been to seek explanations for DCD in systems "external" to the motor system. In such an approach, the natural place to begin is with perceptual processes. There is no doubt that motor skills are heavily dependent upon perceptual systems. There is also clear evidence for impairments in perceptual processes in children with DCD. It remains quite possible, that some (or all) of the causes of DCD will reside in systems intrinsic to motor control. If this is the case the sensorimotor account of DCD advanced here will be found wanting. At the moment, however, it seems important to explore how far perceptual deficits can take us in accounting for the patterns of motor difficulties seen in children with DCD.

Etiology

It has been suggested that the problems faced by children with DCD reflect basic problems with brain development that may in turn be associated with other cognitive problems (Kaplan et al., 1998). It is fair to say that the mechanisms responsible for the abnormalities of brain development leading to DCD are not well understood but there is evidence that both environmental and genetic risk factors are operating.

A recent behavior–genetic study using questionnaire-based measures of DCD and ADHD with a large sample of twins (Martin, Piek, & Hay 2006) indicates a substantial heritable influence on each disorder, as well as a substantial shared genetic influence. In this study parents (mostly mothers) of 1285 pairs of Australian twin pairs aged 5–16 years completed questionnaire-used measures of ADHD (the Australian Twin Behavior Rating Scale (ATBRS), which contains questions based on DSM-IV criteria for ADHD, and the Strengths and Weaknesses of ADHD Symptoms and Normal Behaviour scale (SWAN)). Symptoms of DCD were assessed with the Developmental Coordination Disorder Questionnaire (DCDQ), which asks the parent to rate their child in relation to other children of the same age on a number of specific questions about motor coordination, such as "throws a ball in a controlled and accurate fashion compared to other children of the same age." This study yielded estimated heritabilities (additive genetic effects) of .69 for DCD and .74–.76 for ADHD, indicating very substantial heritability for both disorders. Looking for common genetic effects on the two disorders revealed that there was substantial shared heritability between ratings of inattention and ratings of movement control on the DCDQ (72%). There was also substantial shared heritability between ratings of inattention and quality of handwriting (66%). This study therefore supports the view that both DCD and ADHD are highly heritable and that the frequent co-occurence of the two disorders may reflect common genetic risk factors. It is worth pointing out that because the same parent rated both twins on all measures, this might be expected to lead to overestimates of the degree of similarity between identical (MZ) twin pairs. If parents consistently overestimate the degree of similarity in MZ twin pairs (compared to DZ twins) this would tend to inflate the estimates of heritability obtained. Nevertheless, the data presented suggest a substantial role for genetic influences on the development of DCD.

There is also evidence that being born prematurely is a risk factor for developing DCD. Jongmans, Mercuri, Dubowitz, and Henderson (1998) studied a group of children born prematurely and admitted to a neonatal intensive care unit. To qualify for inclusion in the study the children had to be born at 35 weeks or less gestational age, have had a minimum of three cranial ultrasound scans at daily intervals, have no congenital abnormalities, and have been followed up in clinic before the age of 2 years. Out of 397 children, 219 in the study satisfied these criteria. Of these, 26 had cerebral palsy and were excluded from further study. In the sample included in the study some 48% of the premature children had perceptuomotor difficulties that "might affect day-to-day living."

Holsti, Grunau, and Whitfield (2002) reported longitudinal follow-up data from 73 children born prematurely with extremely low birthweight compared to a sample of 18 nonpremature infants matched for social class. The 73 children in the low birthweight group were selected after excluding children with major impairments (including cerebral palsy, sensory handicaps, and children with VIQ or PIQ less than 85). At age 8 years, 37/73 (51%) of the low birthweight group satisfied the criteria for a diagnosis of DCD (defined as being more than 1 SD below the mean on a composite score on the Bruininks-Oseretsky Test of Motor Proficiency) compared to a rate of 1/18 (5%) in the control group. The DCD group showed lower PIQ but normal VIQ, as in many other studies.

A Biological/Cognitive Model of DCD

Much of the evidence we have reviewed so far is brought together in Figure 6.11. The human motor system depends upon extensive cortical and subcortical systems that are responsible for planning and executing movements, using perceptual (particularly visual) inputs for guidance. In terms of the deficits seen in children with DCD there is good evidence for genetic risk factors operating, and prematurity is also an independent risk factor. These effects are likely to operate to influence the

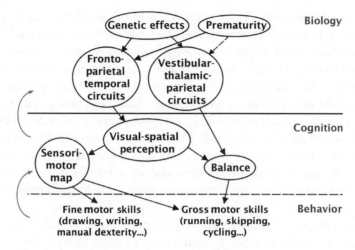

Figure 6.11 A path model for developmental coordination disorder.

development of brain structures responsible for perceptuomotor systems and also the vestibular-thalamic balance system. At a cognitive level, we suggest that visual-spatial deficits impair the development of a sensorimotor map that relates seen and felt positions in space. This system is separate from the system responsible for balance. Deficits in the sensorimotor map are likely to cause widespread problems for both fine motor skills and gross motor skills (gross motor skills involve movements of the body or body parts through space) while problems of balance are likely to be particularly important for learning and executing gross motor skills.

The Treatment of DCD

The treatment of DCD has generally been dealt with by physiotherapists and occupational therapists. It is fair to say that to date there is a dearth of well-controlled studies of the effects of treatment and in particular there is an absence of experimental studies that try to compare different approaches to each other or to untreated control groups. Two recent reviews of interventions for children with DCD are Sugden (2007) and Wilson (2005).

Sugden (2007) draws a distinction between two different approaches to intervention that he refers to as process approaches and functional skill approaches. Process approaches are essentially concerned with identifying deficits in children with DCD and then targeting interventions to remedy these deficits. The effect of kinesthetic training on children with DCD mentioned earlier (e.g., Laszlo & Bairstow, 1985a) is an example of this approach. Theoretically, if a deficit that was a plausible cause of the movement difficulties of children with DCD could be identified then a training program that successfully ameliorated such a deficit should in turn improve these children's motor skills.

In contrast, the functional skills approach is less theoretically based. The aim of this approach is to identify important skills the child needs and wants to learn (riding a bike or catching a ball might be two examples). A program of guided practice is then devised to help the child master the skills identified as important. This might begin with the child practising pedalling on a fixed training bike, move on to practising riding a bike with stabilizing wheels on the back, and then to practising riding with support from an adult that could be gradually withdrawn as the child's balance and confidence on the bike increased. The functional approach does not start from any particular "theory" about why the child with DCD has problems in learning a particular skill, but rather simply seeks to identify particular motor tasks that need to be mastered and puts in place a structured program to help the child master each of the skills identified.

One attraction of the process approach to intervention is that if an underlying causal deficit could be rectified it should lead to quite general improvements in diverse motor skills. For example, if problems with balance lead to problems with walking, skipping, hopping, and riding a bike, all these skills should benefit if balance skills can be improved. While this is certainly true theoretically, evidence for such effects so far is lacking. As already described above, attempts to train kinesthetic skills in children with DCD (e.g., Laszlo & Bairstow, 1985a; Laszo et al., 1988) suffered from numerous problems of design and measurement and later studies argued that kinesthetic training was not effective (e.g., Sims & Morton, 1999). As Wilson (2005) noted in his review, when describing kinesthetic training programs, "This approach no longer appears in the research literature and finds little support in clinical practice" (p. 818).

Another older example of a process approach was the work of Ayres (1979), who developed sensory integration therapy. The aim of this approach was to provide proprioceptive, kinesthetic, and vestibular stimulation to improve the sensory and sensory integration deficits that were thought to underlie the children's movement problems. However, a review of earlier studies by Hoehn and Baumeister (1994) concluded that the current research findings may well be sufficient to declare sensory integration therapy demonstrably ineffective. Similarly Wilson (2005) concluded from a review of sensory integration therapy studies that training studies reveal poor treatment effects, calling into question the conceptual underpinnings of the approach. It is clear that the disappointing results from kinesthetic training and sensory integration therapy, amongst others, have rather dampened enthusiasm for process-oriented approaches to the treatment of DCD (see Wilson, 2005). Such negative results do not demonstrate that process-oriented approaches cannot be successful but to date the evidence for this class of therapies is extremely weak.

In contrast, functional skill approaches to the treatment of DCD appear to have gained wide popularity. One example of such an approach is the Cognitive Orientation to daily Occupational Performance program (CO-OP; Missiuna, 2001; Polatajko & Mandich, 2004). In this program the therapist concentrates on developing the child's use of executive problem-solving skills. The child is involved in choosing the tasks they wish to master and in each task selected a problem-solving approach to mastering the task is used. This involves the following method: Goal (identify a goal for action), Plan (develop a plan to achieve it), Do (carry out the plan), Check (evaluate the outcome). Children are typically given 12 sessions with a trained "mediator" who uses verbal prompts to guide the child in using the strategies taught. It is common to also train parents in the approach so that it can be applied outside the therapy sessions. This then is a task-focused approach to remediation and does not attempt to remediate the putative underlying causes of a child's movement difficulties. As Wilson (2005) argued, the effects of CO-OP, as assessed by case studies showing improvements in the specific functional skills taught, are promising (Wilcox & Polatajko, 1993) and the effects seem to be maintained over time (Polatajko, Law, Miller, Schaffer, & McNab, 1997). However, it also appears that the effects are task specific (only the things that are taught improve).

A similar "metacognitive" approach to training is Neuromotor Task Training (NTT; Schoemaker, Niemeier, Reynders, & Smits-Engelman, 2003). In this approach the therapist starts with an assessment of a child's strengths and weaknesses, and analyzes the cognitive and motor processes that appear to be deficient in the child. For example, it might be judged that a child has particular problems in setting the parameters for executing a task (judging the force and timing required to throw a ball). In such a case the child might be given practice throwing balls of different sizes and weights over different distances. The aim here (just as in CO-OP) is to break down tasks into their component skills and practice easier components of a task before moving on to the harder ones. Schoemaker et al. (2003) report the results of a small-scale study of NTT in which 10 children with DCD were given the treatment once a week over 18 weeks. The children were assessed on the Movement ABC and a measure of handwriting before the treatment, in the middle of treatment (9 weeks), and at the end of treatment (18 weeks). Just five children with DCD served as a control group but they were only assessed twice (once at the beginning of the study and again after 9 weeks) and these children appeared to have better movement skills at the beginning of the study than the treated children. Nevertheless, the results reported in this study seem encouraging. The untreated control group's scores on the Movement ABC did not change in the 9-week period (they tended to get worse) while the treated group showed quite large improvements in their ABC scores over the same period and showed further improvements in the last 9 weeks of therapy. Clearly, a larger study, with random assignment of children to treatment or a waiting-list control group, is needed to assess this pattern of results more rigorously. There seems little doubt that functional skill approaches such as CO-OP and NTT are likely to be useful, not least because the successes they engender will be reinforcing and motivating for the child. It is also likely that the metacognitive or analytical aspects of these programs (training the child to reflect on the nature of their problems and how best to tackle them) are likely to show transfer if the child can be taught to apply them successfully in new situations. However, reports that generalization from such training programs tends to be poor are also potentially problematic, and this leaves room for further studies to explore process-oriented approaches in the hope of finding interventions whose effects will generalize better. This mixed-model approach to intervention is advocated by Wilson (2006). It is clear that so far work on treatments for DCD is in its infancy, and a great deal more work needs to be done in this area. Progress seems likely to depend in turn on a better theoretical understanding of the causes of the disorder and its possible heterogeneity.

Summary and Conclusions

Developmental coordination disorder (DCD) is a common form of learning difficulty that occurs in quite a severe form in around 5% of children. DCD also commonly co-occurs with a range of other disorders such as ADHD, dyslexia, language impairment, and autism. The problems of children with DCD seem to reflect basic problems in the development of brain mechanisms that control movement. It appears that risk factors operating to cause DCD include genetic susceptibility as well as environmental insults that may compromise brain development (being born prematurely is a powerful risk factor). At a cognitive level, we have argued that a likely cause of this disorder is a visuospatial perceptual deficit that in turn compromises the development of a sensorimotor map that relates "seen" positions to "felt" positions in space. In addition, it is likely that problems with systems responsible for balance may play an additional role in causing motor difficulties in some children with DCD. Studies of the treatment of DCD are in their infancy, but recent functional skill approaches suggest that these children can be helped to master key motor skills by appropriate training.

7

Attention Deficit Hyperactivity Disorder

Attention deficit hyperactivity disorder (ADHD) is a chronic, debilitating condition that, as its name implies, affects an individual's ability to control attention and behavior in an optimal and adaptive manner. The disorder often occurs together with the tendency to be overactive and impulsive and is frequently associated with educational underachievement, antisocial behavior, underperformance at work, and poor psychosocial adjustment.

ADHD has often been portrayed negatively by the media and there are many misconceptions surrounding its nature and etiology; while some have asserted that ADHD is "on the increase," others doubt its very existence. So unhelpful has this confusion been that a consortium of scientists signed an International Consensus Statement in 2001. According to this statement, "ADHD involves a serious deficiency in a set of psychological abilities and ... these deficiencies pose serious harm to most individuals possessing the disorder" (Barkley, Edwards, Laneri, Fletcher, & Metevia, 2001, p. 89). Indeed, as children with ADHD grow up, they are more likely than their peers to experience teenage pregnancy, have multiple car accidents, and to suffer depression and personality disorders. Moreover, although psychological and pharmacological interventions are known to help the condition, less than half of those affected receive any form of treatment.

We begin this chapter with a discussion of the nature and prevalence of ADHD and how it is usually assessed. We then outline what is known about how children learn to regulate their behavior and, within this framework, we consider theories of the possible causes of ADHD in which self-regulation appears to be lacking. In contrast to the other disorders considered in this book, progress in understanding ADHD has been heavily influenced by pharmacological studies, which have demonstrated the effectiveness of certain drugs for its treatment. This evidence in turn relates to ideas about the neurobiology of ADHD and, in particular, the roles of the frontal and prefrontal cortex and frontobasal circuits in the regulation of behavior.

ADHD: Definition and Prevalence

DSM-IV defines ADHD on the basis of elevated symptoms on two dimensions: inattention and hyperactivity/impulsivity. According to DSM-IV, children meet criteria for the disorder by having six or more symptoms of inattention, hyperactivity/impulsivity, or both. Thus, there are three main subtypes of ADHD: the primarily "hyperactive–impulsive" (HI) type, the primarily "inattentive" (IA) type, and the combined type (see Box 7.1). The most thoroughly researched is the combined subtype, and less is known about the primarily hyperactive–impulsive and primarily inattentive subtypes. It is important to note that each of these subtypes may show subclinical symptoms relating to the other impairment (inattention or hyperactivity/impulsivity). Gomez, Harvey, Quick, Scharer, and Harris (1999) studied the relationships between the different symptoms used to diagnose ADHD using the DSM-IV criteria in a large (1275) representative sample of children ranging in age from 5 to 11 years. They found that a two-factor model that separated hyperactivity/impulsivity from inattention was much better than a one-factor model that combined all items. However the two factors correlated quite strongly (around .7). This study found quite low rates for the different subtypes: IA (1.6%), HI (0.2%), and combined (0.6%), giving an overall rate of 2.4% when the subtypes were combined.

Other terms that may be seen in the literature referring to ADHD include ADD (now an outdated term) and "hyperactive" and hyperkinetic disorder (ICD-10; World Health Organization, 1992). The ICD-10 category of hyperkinetic disorder requires both hyperactivity and inattention (i.e., symptoms of the combined type of ADHD) and it also requires that such symptoms are displayed at a rate that is sufficiently high to reach a diagnosis in more than one setting (i.e., typically at both home and school). Thus the diagnostic criteria for hyperkinetic disorder (ICD-10) are more stringent than those for ADHD using the DSM-IV criteria.

Formally the diagnostic criteria for ADHD in DSM-IV require that symptoms of inattention or hyperactivity should be displayed (to some degree) in at least two settings (e.g., home and school), and have persisted for at least 6 months to a degree that is maladaptive and out of line with age expectation. Signs of inattention include difficulty in focusing or maintaining attention, failing to listen carefully or to follow instructions, distractibility, organizational difficulty, and forgetfulness. Signs of hyperactivity or impulsivity relate more to overt behavioral tendencies such as fidgeting, being "on the go" all the time, talking excessively, blurting-out answers, and interrupting other people when speaking to them. Normally, some of the signs should have been recognized before the age of 7 years and there must be clear evidence of significant impairment in social, academic, or occupational functioning. The definition of hyperkinetic disorder requires the presence, simultaneously, of attention deficit, hyperactivity, and impulsivity in more than one situation and therefore this diagnosis is closest to that of the combined type of ADHD.

Box 7.1   ADHD: Diagnosis and Symptomatology (adapted from *http://www.nimh.nih.gov/health/ publications/adhd/symptoms.shtml*)

There are three subtypes of ADHD: the predominantly hyperactive–impulsive type; the predominantly inattentive type; and the combined type (both inattentive and hyperactive–impulsive symptoms).

Hyperactivity–impulsivity

Hyperactive children always seem to be "on the go" or constantly in motion. They dash around touching or playing with whatever is in sight, or talk incessantly. Sitting still at dinner or during a school lesson or story can be a difficult task. They may squirm and fidget in their seats or roam around the room. Or they may wiggle their feet, touch everything, or noisily tap their pencil. Hyperactive teenagers or adults may feel internally restless. They often report needing to stay busy and may try to do several things at once.

Impulsive children seem unable to curb their immediate reactions or think before they act. They will often blurt out inappropriate comments, display their emotions without restraint, and act without regard for the later consequences of their actions. Their impulsivity may make it hard for them to wait for things they want or to take their turn in games. They may grab a toy from another child or hit out when they are upset. Even as teenagers or adults, they may impulsively choose to do things that have an immediate but small payoff rather than engage in activities that may take more effort yet provide much greater but delayed rewards.

Some signs of hyperactivity–impulsivity are:

- feeling restless, often fidgeting with hands or feet, or squirming while seated;
- running, climbing, or leaving a seat in situations where sitting or quiet behavior is expected;
- blurting out answers before hearing the whole question;
- having difficulty waiting in line or taking turns.

Inattention

Children who are inattentive have a hard time keeping their minds on any one thing and may get bored with a task after only a few minutes. If they are doing something they really enjoy, they have no trouble paying attention. But focusing deliberate, conscious attention to organizing and completing a task or learning something new is difficult.

Box 7.1   (cont'd)

Homework is particularly hard for these children. They will forget to write down an assignment, or leave it at school. They will forget to bring a book home, or bring the wrong one. The homework, if finally finished, is often full of errors and erasures. Homework is often accompanied by frustration for both parent and child.

The DSM-IV gives these signs of inattention:

- often becoming easily distracted by irrelevant sights and sounds;
- often failing to pay attention to details and making careless mistakes;
- rarely following instructions carefully and completely losing or forgetting things like toys, pencils, books, or tools needed for a task;
- often skipping from one uncompleted activity to another.

Children diagnosed with the predominantly inattentive type of ADHD are seldom impulsive or hyperactive, yet they have significant problems paying attention. They may appear to be daydreaming, "spaced-out," easily confused, slow-moving, and lethargic. They may have difficulty processing information as quickly and accurately as other children. When the teacher gives oral or even written instructions, these children may have a hard time understanding what they are supposed to do and make frequent mistakes. Yet these children may sit quietly, unobtrusively, and even appear to be working but not fully attending to or understanding the task and the instructions.

These children do not show significant problems with impulsivity and over-activity in the classroom, in the playground, or at home. They may get along better with other children than the more impulsive and hyperactive types of ADHD, and they may not have the same sorts of social problems so common with the combined type of ADHD. Often their problems with inattention may be overlooked, but they need help just as much as children with other types of ADHD who cause more obvious problems in the classroom.

According to DSM-IV the prevalence rate for ADHD is around 3–5% of children of primary school age. A recent study involving a representative sample of more than 10,000 children in the UK (Meltzer & Gatward, 2000) indentified children at risk of hyperkinetic disorder based on rating scales and structured interviews, and arrived at a population estimate of 1.4%. As noted earlier, the criteria for hyperkinetic disorder are more stringent than the DSM-IV criteria for ADHD, and as such hyperkinetic disorder can be considered a more severe, and so less common, form of ADHD.

It is generally accepted that ADHD is more common in boys. Boys outnumber girls by approximately 3:1 in community samples, and in clinically referred samples the ratio may be as high as 9:1. Consistent with the referral of fewer girls than boys, many research studies have used exclusively male samples and therefore less is known about ADHD in girls. Although it used to be thought that ADHD resolved with age, with its effects diminishing from adolescence onwards, this is no longer considered to be the case. An important issue is the extent to which the same symptoms are valid markers of the disorder at different ages, and for boys versus girls. Some adults who refer themselves because of ADHD symptomatology do not have a childhood diagnosis and this is particularly likely to be the case when women (who are at low risk of disruptive disorders) are affected (Willoughby, 2005). It should be noted that many studies of the prevalence of ADHD exclude children with the purely inattentive (IA) form of the disorder (which by definition is hard to detect) and it is estimated that this occurs in around another 1% of the school-age population (Gomez et al., 1999; Taylor & Sonuga-Barke, 2008).

Comorbidities between ADHD and Other Developmental Disorders

ADHD tends to co-occur with other developmental and psychiatric disorders at high rates. Most of the negative outcomes for ADHD are exacerbated by the presence of comorbid conditions, especially aggression and conduct problems. Estimates for comorbidities in childhood are approximately 60% for oppositional defiant disorder, 20% for conduct disorder, 25% for mood disorders, 25% for anxiety disorders, 30% for learning disorders such as dyslexia, and somewhat higher for developmental coordination disorder (Taylor, 2006). In adulthood, documented comorbidities also include mood and anxiety disorders, and alcohol or drug abuse (Biederman, 2005; Tannock, 1998). These are possibly secondary consequences of the primary disorder. Much of the research on ADHD has not controlled carefully enough for comorbid conditions and must therefore be interpreted cautiously. An important challenge for research is to unravel the causes and consequences of the core problems of ADHD, and to understand the nature of its association with different comorbid conditions (Oosterlaan, Logan, & Sergeant, 1998).

The Assessment of ADHD

The clinical assessment of ADHD in childhood normally comprises a multidisciplinary assessment that includes school observations, semistructured interviews with parents, clinical observations, and parent and teacher ratings of a child's behavior. Evidence from teacher and parent ratings, even though these may be discrepant, are weighted heavily when deciding whether a diagnosis of ADHD is appropriate. This might at first appear somewhat subjective. However, one of the trademarks of ADHD is the marked fluctuation in performance observed across time, settings, and tasks. So the key to diagnosis is not whether a child can pass a given test in a structured situation but how well they can regulate their behavior during everyday activities over extended periods of time. Viewed in this way parent and teacher observations are essential as they are based on large samples of a child's behavior.

Generally, two basic techniques are used to assess a child's behavioral status. The first involves a semistructured interview, either with the child or with the child's parents (e.g., The Parental Account of Children's Symptoms (PACS); Taylor, Schachar, Thorley & Wieselberg, 1986). The second and most frequently used method is a behavior rating scale. Such scales take the form of questionnaires, which ideally are completed by both a parent and a teacher in order to reduce bias and allow an assessment of any cross–situational variability in behavior. Scales that are used widely include the Conners' Rating Scales (Conners, 1996), the Child Behavior Checklist (CBCL: Achenbach & Edelbrook, 1983), and the Strength and Difficulties Questionnaire (SDQ: Goodman, 1997). Items on the latter ask parents or teachers to indicate whether each of a number of statements applies to a child's behavior recently, for example whether the child can sit still and to what extent they think before they act. For more information, see *http://www.sdqinfo.com/*.

In addition, the use of standardized tests of attention can be very useful in helping to make a diagnosis and a vigilance task will often be administered. In one such task, the Continuous Performance Test (Conners, 1996), the participant has to monitor a display of signals for an extended amount of time, pressing a button whenever a nontarget stimulus appears. When a target appears, the participant has to withhold responding. In the classic version of this test monitoring is required for 14 min, during which time participants view a sequence of letters on a computer screen. The task is to press a button whenever a given letter occurs (say X) but *only if* it is followed by an O – not when it is followed by another letter of the alphabet. Performance on vigilance tasks is typically measured by the frequency of errors of omission (missing a target letter) and commission (responding to an X when it is not followed by an O.

In addition there are a number of standardized attention tests for the assessment of adults (Test of Everyday Attention (TEA): Robertson, Ward, Ridgeway, & Nimmo-Smith, 1994; Behavioral Assessment of Dysexecutive Syndrome (BADS): Wilson, Alderman, Burgess, Emslie, & Evans, 1996) and children (Behavioural Assessment of Dysexecutive Syndrome in Children (BADS-C): Emslie, Wilson, Burden, Nimmo-Smith, & Wilson, 2003; Test of Everyday Attention for Children (TEA-Ch): Manly, Robertson, Anderson, & Nimmo-Smith, 1998; NEPSY II: Korkman, Kirk, & Kemp, 2007). Some of these tests are widely used in the diagnosis of ADHD as well as in assessments of children with dyslexia to assess attention control (e.g., Snowling, Muter, & Carroll, 2007).

To increase the reliability of the diagnostic information from parent and teacher rating scales, direct behavioral observations are sometimes used. However, because they are time consuming, they have rarely been included in research studies. A limitation inherent in using direct observations is that observers are most likely to detect externalizing behaviors – so the child whose behavior is characterized by hyperactivity or disruptiveness is more likely to be identified than the child whose inattention goes unnoticed, perhaps because of a quieter temperament. The corollary of this is that children with attention disorders who internalize their difficulties (and may experience emotional problems) may not give cause for concern. For this reason it can be argued that there is pressing need to identify objective markers of ADHD that are not subject to observer bias.

There are three core symptoms of ADHD (of the combined type): inattention, hyperactivity, and impulsiveness. Arguably, given the fractionation of ADHD into the inattentive (ADHD-IA) and hyperactive–impulsive (ADHD-HI) subtypes, these three symptoms need to be considered as somewhat independent. In particular, hyperactivity (being restless, fidgety, and "on the go") and impulsiveness (acting out of turn, interrupting people, being reckless) seem to separate from pure inattention (failing to persist with activities, failing to focus on details of a task, being "in a dream"). In practice, virtually all of the research on ADHD has focused on children who show the more noticeable symptoms of hyperactivity and impulsiveness (since it is these symptoms that get the children noticed and diagnosed as having ADHD).

In relation to explaining the problems of hyperactivity and impulsiveness seen in children with ADHD, there has been a strong consensus that this reflects a problem of behavioral inhibition/executive control. However, there is a degree of circularity in this view since ADHD is diagnosed when there are signs that an individual has difficulty with self-regulation in a variety of settings and so behaves in an uninhibited way. Therefore, in order to understand the causes of ADHD it is important to operationalize the term "behavioral inhibition" and to consider the development of executive control in the typically developing child.

Before we go further, it should be stated that ADHD as a disorder is clearly quite different to those we have considered so far in this book. The disorders considered so far (dyslexia, reading comprehension impairment, specific language impairment, developmental coordination disorder, mathematics disorder) might all be seen as "modular" disorders, in which a fairly specific brain system (or small set of modules) fails to develop adequately. In contrast, in ADHD it is much less clear that we would want to consider common explanations for the disorder, such as "behavioral inhibition" or "executive function," as modules. Instead, such systems appear to reflect higher-level "supervisory" systems (Pennington & Ozonoff, 1996; Shallice, 1988) that could be characterized as "horizontal" faculties (Fodor, 1983) that are involved in the planning, execution, and monitoring of diverse forms of behavior. In this respect, ADHD is clearly going to be a difficult disorder to characterize at a cognitive level (due to the broad range of factors affected) and we have sympathy for Morton's (2004) concerns about the usefulness of broad concepts such as executive dysfunction as explanations for the disorder. Nevertheless, a dominant theory of ADHD has been that it reflects a deficit in one or more aspects of executive function (Barkley, 1997; Pennington & Ozonoff, 1996). Before considering this and other theories we will first consider ideas about the nature of executive functions and their typical development.

The Nature of Executive Control/Behavioral Inhibition and their Typical Development

Executive function (or functions) is a term that is widely used in psychology but it is a broad term that different theorists use in somewhat different ways. At a broad level, executive functions are considered to be processes that operate in a "top-down"

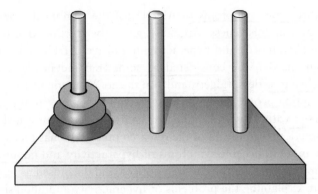

Figure 7.1 The Tower of Hanoi. In this neuropsychological test, the aim is to move the three rings on the left peg to the far right peg in as few moves as possible. A ring can only be placed either on an empty peg or on top of a larger one. To try out the test for yourself go to *http://www.mazeworks.com/hanoi/*.

fashion to control and organize cognitive processes during the performance of complex cognitive tasks. It is important to point out that much of the original impetus for studies of executive functioning came from studies of neuropsychological patients who had suffered damage to the frontal lobes of the brain. A very famous example was Phineas Gage, who showed great changes in his behavior and personality following massive damage to the frontal lobes of his brain. Although some patients with damage to the frontal lobes may show quite well-preserved performance on a variety of well-defined cognitive tasks, many of them show severe difficulties on complex tasks that appear to involve (among other things) the ability to plan and monitor one's performance (Shallice, 1988). One example of such a task is the classic Tower of Hanoi (Figure 7.1), which involves moving rings in the correct order from one peg to another. Another frequently used task is the Wisconsin Card Sorting Task (described below).

The difficulty surrounding the use of the term "executive function" is real because it is used to explain aspects of behavior that can be difficult to characterize rigorously or define clearly. To improve our understanding of what constitutes executive functions, research has used broad sets of possible measures and subjected the results to factor analysis (a statistical technique that assesses the extent to which different measures tend to correlate together to define separable constructs). Based on such studies (see Miyake et al., 2000) it appears that executive functions depend upon at least four separable (but correlated) factors: (1) response inhibition and execution; (2) working memory and updating; (3) set shifting and task switching; (4) interference control. In addition it seems that planning or organization might be seen as an additional (and perhaps higher-level) executive function. As will be clear from this brief discussion, executive functions appear to be diverse, and nonmodular in the sense that they cut across different tasks; indeed it is a defining characteristic of executive functions that they may be involved in managing and coordinating the performance of different tasks.

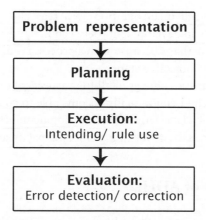

Figure 7.2   A problem-solving framework for understanding executive functions. (Zelazo, P. D., Carter, A., Reznick, J. S., and Frye, D., Early development of the executive function: A problem-solving framework, *Review of General Psychology*, 1(2), p. 200, 1997, published by the American Psychological Association and adapted with permission.)

Zelazo, Carter, Reznick, and Frye (1997) considered how best to conceptualize the development of executive functions and developmental difficulties in self-regulation. Focusing on preschool development, they outlined a framework for the study of executive functions that lays out a sequence of steps required for problem-solving. This framework consists of four stages: problem representation, planning, execution, and evaluation (see Figure 7.2). Children's plans are literally rules formulated in silent self-directed speech. An increase in the complexity of children's rules and levels of embedding in these systems allows increased control over thought.

Considerable research involving typically developing preschool children has focused on the processes of planning, execution, and evaluation. Planning has been tested using tasks such as mazes and the Tower of Hanoi as well as social planning tasks, for example trying to deceive another person. Importantly, none of these tasks can be considered pure in the sense of tapping planning alone; they inevitably draw upon other skills as well, including verbal and spatial abilities.

Converging evidence (reviewed by Zelazo et al., 1997) suggests that there are marked changes between 3 and 5 years of age in children's inclination to plan, although planning skills continue to develop into the school years. Plan execution has been explored in tasks tapping rule-use, for example the use of conditionals to guide behavior as in the children's game "Simon says," where children are instructed to perform different acts but only when the instruction is preceded by the signal "Simon says." Here there are changes between 40 months when children do whatever is instructed regardless of what "Simon says" to around 49 months when they can accomplish the task. Success on more difficult tasks, such as one in which two rules have to be obeyed simultaneously (squeeze the ball when you see the red light and refrain from squeezing when you see the green light), does not occur until around 5 years. Finally, problem evaluation (which comprises knowing when a goal has been reached, and error detection and correction) can be considered fundamental to development, learning, and metacognition. Whereas children can detect another person's errors very early in development (between 2.5 and 3 years), they take much longer to correct errors, perhaps because such a process requires flexibility of thought and the ability to take an objective stance.

Overall, there are dramatic changes in all four aspects of executive function during the preschool period as children gradually become able to control their problem-solving behavior. Zelazo et al. (1997) argue that developmental changes in executive control are limited by the growth of working memory capacity and the ability to reflect.

Cognitive Theories of ADHD

Children with ADHD have marked problems in regulating their behavior and inhibiting their responses (hyperactivity and impulsivity are two core features of the ADHD profile). In this respect the disorder clearly relates to ideas about the executive control of behavior. The idea that ADHD reflects a core deficit in "behavioral inhibition" was first proposed by Barkley (1997). This cognitive theory is closely related to earlier views that the problems of behavioral regulation observed in children with ADHD are similar to those seen in patients with damage to the frontal lobes of the brain (which is sometimes referred to as the frontal metaphor of ADHD; Pennington & Ozonoff, 1996).

Barkley's model of behavioral inhibition

Building on earlier work by Douglas (1972) and Quay (1988), Barkley (1997) proposed a conceptual model of ADHD in which the proximal cause of the disorder was a deficit of behavioral inhibition. In so doing, Barkley drew heavily on two complementary theories – one of the evolution of language (Bronowski, 1977) and one of the role of frontal and prefrontal cortex in primates and man (Fuster, 1989). Both theoretical accounts ascribed to the frontal lobes the capacity for hindsight, forethought, and linking events over time, and for the self-regulation of emotion. In addition, the internalization of language was considered to provide a means of reflection and exploration, analysis, and synthesis (reconstitution), while functioning of the premotor cortex was essential for the execution of novel sequences of behavior. From this perspective, Barkley argued that the development of adaptive and flexible behavior depends on the child's capacity to delay responding to external stimuli in order to bring responses under self-directed control. In turn, this depends on the development of neural networks in the prefrontal lobes, the socialization of the child, the success of these actions in the past for maximizing the net consequences of behavior, and the ongoing reinforcement of self-regulatory behaviors.

In Barkley's model, behavioral inhibition was the core deficit in ADHD, and a degree of behavioral inhibition was necessary for the development of other aspects of executive function. Barkley distinguished four components of executive function that depended on behavioral inhibition for their development and operation: working memory (holding information in mind), self-regulation of affect, motivation, and arousal (emotional self-control), internalization of speech (describing and reflecting on one's behavior), and reconstitution (abstracting rules to govern behavior and generating contextually appropriate behaviors). All of these executive abilities are involved separately and together in the control and organization of motor responses.

Barkley's theory emphasized the possible importance of executive functions in accounting for the symptoms seen in ADHD. In practice, however, many of the studies in this area have not been guided strongly by theories of executive function. Often diverse executive tasks have been selected based on the "the frontal metaphor" view of ADHD (e.g., Pennington & Ozonoff, 1996), which notes that such tasks are often impaired in adults with damage to the frontal lobes who sometimes appear to show similar behavioral deficits to children with ADHD. We will begin by describing some of the tasks typically used for assessing executive skills before turning to consider evidence for deficits on a range of executive tasks in children with ADHD.

Executive function tasks

A wide range of tasks has been used to assess executive function in children and adults. Amongst the most common of these are planning tasks, such as the Tower of Hanoi (shown above in Figure 7.1), and tasks tapping working memory and memory updating as described in Chapter 3 (see Boxes 3.3 and 3.4). Other tasks tap the ability to attend selectively to a given set of cues, whilst ignoring or suppressing extraneous information. The most widely used task tapping such interference control is the Stroop task (Stroop, 1935). Here participants have to name the color of the ink of a set of color-words (e.g., the word *red* printed in "blue") and, to do so, have to suppress the automatic tendency to respond with the name of the printed word. The speed with which a participant can do this is compared with the speed at which they can name neutral stimuli in the same colors (e.g., color-patches or strings of symbols devoid of meaning – XXXX). A measure of interference control is derived by subtracting the naming speed in the neutral condition from the naming speed in the Stroop condition and the size of this effect depends on the relative speed of the reading and the color-naming responses, as well as on the individual's ability to resist interference. Finally, a classic task that requires the participant to inhibit habitual responses and to shift set in order to solve a problem is the Wisconsin Card Sorting Task (see Box 7.2).

Response inhibition

According to Barkley's model (1997), ADHD can be traced to a fundamental disorder of behavioral inhibition: an inability to inhibit a prepotent response (the default) to stop responding and to control interference. The task that has been used most widely to test this idea is the Stop-Signal Task (Schachter & Logan, 1990). In this task, the child performs a primary "go task," whilst monitoring for a "stop signal" that indicates the response to the primary task should be inhibited. For a child, such ability may be required when they are engaged in a game of chase and the school bell rings, indicating that the child needs to stand still. In the stop-signal paradigm, the

Box 7.2   The Wisconsin Card Sorting Task

The Wisconsin Card Sorting Task (WCST) is a classic test of set-shifting. The figure below shows four stimulus cards, each bearing symbols differing in number, color, and shape. The participant is given a set of response cards each showing symbols comprising a different combination of number, color, and shape (as in the card in the second row). At the start of the test, the examiner places the four stimulus cards on the table, and tells the person to sort the response cards onto each pile. Feedback is provided to allow the examinee to abstract the sorting rule (which for the card shown could be either its color or the number of symbols on it). The examinee is also warned that the sorting rule will change as the test progresses (e.g., reinforcement might first be for color and then shift to number).

There are a number of ways of scoring the test, including the number of shifts accomplished and the number of perseverative responses following a shift in the rule, but basically the difficulty here is for the participant to realize the rule has changed and search for a new rule.

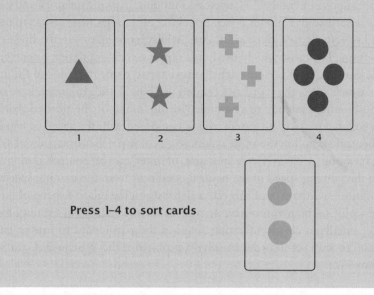

Press 1–4 to sort cards

primary task is usually a visual choice reaction time task (e.g., pressing the "x" button on a keyboard when an X is presented and the "o" button when an O is presented). On a randomly occurring proportion of trials (usually about 25%), the primary task stimulus is followed by a stop signal (e.g., a tone/beep). This stop signal is the cue to inhibit the planned response to the primary task or "go signal". In one version of the stop-signal paradigm, the interval between the stop signal and the individual's own mean reaction time (RT) is varied across trials. This involves first calculating the participant's expected RT on the "go task" from their performance across a block of trials, and then in the next block presenting the stop signal at different time intervals before this RT – say 100, 250, 350, and 500 ms (in the extreme, for children with a low hit rate, the stop signal may be presented simultaneously with the onset of the go stimulus; see Box 7.3). Importantly, children are instructed to respond as quickly as possible on the task and not to slow their responding to wait for the stop signal.

It should be clear that the probability of inhibiting the go response will be related to the delay between the go and stop signals: the Stop-Signal Delay (SSD). It will also depend on an individual's ability to inhibit their motor response. More formally, the probability of response inhibition depends on the outcome of a "race" between the go process and the stop process (Logan, Cowan, & Davis, 1984). If the go process is faster than the stop process, then the individual executes the response; if the stop process is faster than the go process, then the response is inhibited. The speed of the stopping process is referred to as the Stop-Signal Reaction Time (SSRT) and this is calculated

---

Box 7.3   The Stop-Signal Task (adapted from Solanto, Arnsten, & Castellanos, 2001)

The Stop-Signal Task (SST) provides an index of the ability to inhibit a prepared motor response.

The primary task is a speeded visual choice reaction time task. The child presses a key as quickly as possible to indicate which of two possible letters has been presented on the screen. Performance on the primary task provides an estimate of an individual child's overall speed (mean RT).

The stop signal is a tone presented randomly on a proportion of trials after the go signal; the stop signal indicates that the child is to inhibit the response to the go signal (not press the key). The interval between the stop signal and the individual's mean RT is varied over trials.

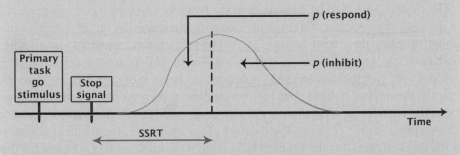

The measure derived from this task is the Stop-Signal Reaction Time (SSRT). This measure can be interpreted as a measure of the speed of a stopping process. SSRT is not measured directly but rather is inferred on the basis of the distribution of RTs when there is no stop signal and on the probability of inhibition to signals presented at different times.

from the proportion of successful stop trials across blocks of trials where the delay between the go and stop signals is varied. Children with ADHD typically show longer SSRTs than typically developing children. However, they also differ from controls on other measures derived from the task. In particular, the slope of the inhibition function relating the probability of inhibition to the stop interval is flatter in children with ADHD, the mean RT for the go trials has sometimes been found to be longer, the standard deviation of the RTs is greater, and often children with ADHD make a lower proportion of successfully inhibited responses (e.g., Solanto et al., 2001).

Rubia et al. (2001) compared a clinical sample of 56 children with ADHD aged 7–15 years with both a psychiatric control group of 16 children and a group of 23 typically developing children on a range of tasks designed to assess impulsivity in the broadest sense (monitoring of responses and inhibition). The three groups were matched for age and IQ. The test battery consisted of the Stop-Signal Task, a simpler Go/No-Go Task and a Reversal Task. In the Go/No-Go Task, a motor response had to be executed or inhibited depending on whether an image of an aeroplane appeared on the screen (which it did on 70% of trials); the response had to be inhibited if a bomb was presented (on 30% trials). In the SST, a plane appeared for 1000 ms followed 30% of the time by a bomb, either after 150 ms (10%) or 250 ms (20%). The task was to press a button with the right finger if the plane appeared alone. The Reversal Task was a test of cognitive flexibility; in this task, the previously learned stimulus–response association had to be inhibited in order to learn a new association. Thus, in the Go/No-Go Task, the instruction switched from "respond to planes not bombs" to "respond to bombs not planes."

Three additional tasks were included to assess response output and timing processes in more detail. The first required finger tapping in synchrony with a sensory input at the rate designated by the stimulus onset. The second required the child to finger-tap continuously when a plane appeared on the screen, to periodically interrupt the tapping when a stop signal appeared, and to resume tapping when the plane reappeared (after 2500 ms). The third task required tapping to be synchronized with the appearance of a plane that appeared every 5 s for 200 s (the Delay Task).

The children with ADHD differed from the typically developing controls primarily on the tasks that required inhibition of discrete motor responses rather than in motor timing or when they were required to interrupt automatic activities. In all three inhibition tasks, group differences in the probability of inhibition were significant, with children with ADHD showing less inhibition and being more error prone than the typically developing controls (but not the children in the psychiatric control group). It was also notable that on all of these tasks the group with ADHD showed more variable performance than the controls. The measure of variability was the standard deviation of the reaction times for the primary task; there were substantial effect sizes for this group difference, ranging from 0.52 for the Reversal Task to 2.45 for the SST. Moreover, although group differences in SSRT were not statistically significant, the ADHD group was three times more variable in terms of this measure than the controls.

Variability in the performance of children with ADHD is underlined by the findings of a comprehensive study by Kuntsi, Oosterlaan, and Stevenson (2001). This study failed to find robust differences between children with ADHD and controls in inhibition in the SST. However, there were group differences in both the mean RT for the primary task and the standard deviation (variability) of the RTs. Indeed the effect size was highest for the standard deviation of RTs (0.83) and this was the strongest predictor differentiating children with ADHD from controls in a discriminant function analysis. Together these findings are in keeping with those of a meta-review by Oosterlaan, Logan, and Sergeant (1998), which concluded that children with ADHD are not less likely to inhibit their responses than typically developing children but, rather, they show both slow RTs on the primary task and variable inhibitory responses. Such variability is not captured well by statistics that assume the underlying distribution of RTs is normal when in fact, particularly for children with ADHD, it shows a significant positive skew with many long reaction times (Leth Steenson, King-Elbaz, & Douglas, 2000; see Figure 7.3 for an example).

In summary, while there is some evidence for a deficit in response inhibition in children with ADHD, the pattern from these studies is not overwhelmingly clear. The SST is a complex one involving a primary task (a choice reaction time task) coupled with the requirement to inhibit responding on some trials in response to an auditory stop signal. On the primary reaction time task children with ADHD tend to be slower and more variable in their response times and to commit more errors. It has been suggested that the overall pattern of data from the SST is compatible with a generally slow, and variable, speed of information processing in children with ADHD (Kuntsi et al., 2001; Sergeant, Oosterlaan, & van der Meere, 1999). This, however, does not amount to a specific deficit in "response inhibition" and as such provides only weak support for Barkley's claim that this is a primary cognitive deficit in children with ADHD.

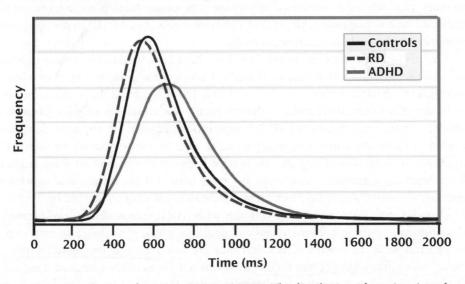

Figure 7.3   Distribution of reaction times in ADHD. The distribution of reaction times for children with ADHD (positively skewed) and for controls and children with dyslexia (who both have less skewed distributions). The greater positive skew (higher rates of very slow reaction times) in the distribution for children with ADHD is highly diagnostic. (Data from an unpublished study conducted by Gooch: Gooch, Hulme, & Snowling, 2008.)

Working memory and temporal processing

As well as controlling impulses and inhibiting prepotent responses, the frontal lobes are involved in planning, shifting, and maintaining strategy sets and organizing and implementing strategies. Arguably, many of these processes depend upon working memory and a number of studies have investigated working memory skills in children with ADHD. In addition to tasks such as sentence span and counting span, many studies have used spatial span tasks such as Corsi blocks (see Figure 5.6), or the CANTAB test in which the participant searches spatial locations to find tokens while remembering not to return to any locations where tokens were previously found.

Martinussen, Hayden, Hogg-Johnson, and Tannock, (2005) report a meta-analysis of studies of working memory deficits in children with ADHD. They report that children with ADHD show deficits on spatial memory storage tasks (average $d = 0.85$) and spatial central executive tasks (average $d = 1.06$) that are greater than the deficits found on comparable verbal storage tasks (average $d = 0.47$) or verbal central executive tasks (average $d = 0.43$). These deficits in working memory could not be accounted for by differences in measures of language skill or general IQ between the children with ADHD and controls. These results suggest that deficits on working memory tasks (particularly spatial working memory) are an area of difficulty for children with ADHD. Approaching this association from the opposite angle, Gathercole et al. (in press) have reported that problems of inattention are widespread among children who are screened and selected as having low working memory.

In recent years, there has been growing interest in the possibility that some of the behavioral symptoms of ADHD are due to temporal processing deficits. An ability to judge and keep track of the passage of time is fundamental to planning, organization, and time management, all areas of behavioral deficit in ADHD that in turn are associated with working memory problems.

A number of different experimental methods have been used to investigate temporal processing. The most widely used method involves the comparison of two brief intervals of similar duration (e.g., 500–600 ms). However, tasks requiring durations to be reproduced are also common; these typically use visual stimuli with durations of up to 1 min. Since these kinds of temporal processing task are attention demanding and require the control of interference as well as the temporary storage and updating of visual or auditory stimuli, it is perhaps not surprising that some studies have reported a positive association between temporal processing and working memory measures. According to a meta-review of six studies conducted by Toplak, Dockstader, and Tannock (2006), children with ADHD show deficits on duration discrimination tasks in both the visual and auditory modalities. They also tend to be more variable in their performance and they are prone to underestimate temporal durations in time reproduction tasks. Questions remain as to the causes of these difficulties and further research is needed to elucidate these.

Summary: Deficits in executive functions as a cause of ADHD

As we made clear earlier, an executive impairment seems worryingly broad as a potential explanation for the deficits observed in children with ADHD (cf. Morton,

2004). However, the studies we have reviewed here have made some progress in making the idea of an executive deficit in children with ADHD more specific.

There are now a number of meta-analyses examining the usefulness of executive function tasks for differentiating ADHD from other disorders (Pennington & Ozonoff, 1996; Willcutt, Doyle, Nigg, Faraone, & Pennington 2005). Willcutt, Doyle et al. (2005) considered 13 executive function tasks tapping four domains of functioning: response inhibition and execution, working memory and updating, set shifting and task switching, and interference control. From this analysis it would appear that differences have been reported between children with ADHD and controls on all of the 13 executive tasks considered, with a mean effect size of $d = 0.54$. The largest effect sizes were associated with studies of response inhibition, vigilance, planning, and working memory. Children with ADHD have also been consistently reported to be slower on measures of perceptual speed, such as Coding and Digit Symbol tasks from the Wechsler scales (Pennington & Ozonoff, 1996). In contrast, small effects and inconsistent results have been reported for set shifting, Stroop interference, and visuospatial orienting.

However, as Willcutt, Doyle et al., (2005) noted in their meta-analysis, the magnitude of group differences in executive function measures ($d=0.4$–0.6) is much smaller than the group differences in ADHD symptoms ($d=2.5$–4.0). One might object to this comparison: Given that children with ADHD are selected on the basis of parental and teacher reports of symptoms, it would be difficult to find equally large differences between ADHD and control children on more purely cognitive measures such as executive function tasks. Nevertheless, the effect sizes for the deficits on executive function tasks do seem smaller than would be expected if these executive tasks tap a major cause of the disorder. In addition it has been reported that fewer than half of the children studied with ADHD typically show reliable deficits on executive function tasks (Nigg, Willcutt, Doyle, & Sonuga-Barke, 2005) and the correlations between measures of executive function and the severity of ADHD symptoms are typically quite small ($r=0.15$–0.35). These observations therefore raise problems for the idea that deficits in executive function are either a sufficient or necessary cause of ADHD.

It remains possible that executive function deficits are one contributory cause of ADHD, but this is at best a tentative claim and one that will require large-scale longitudinal studies with diverse measures to test it.

ADHD as a problem of fluctuating performance

The ideas we have considered so far try to explain ADHD in terms of a deficit in certain cognitive processes. So, for example, ADHD might reflect a difficulty in inhibiting responses or a deficit in working memory. In each case, however, the explanation is in terms of a consistent deficit in a given cognitive process (in this respect such explanations are like many we have dealt with earlier in this book in relation to other disorders).

There is, however, a very different way of thinking about the cognitive problems in children with ADHD, which is in terms of variability of performance. In this view children with ADHD can perform cognitive functions normally; it is just that their performance is highly variable. Some of the evidence we have already considered is consistent with this view, for example, Kuntsi et al. (2001) found that the variability of RTs in children with ADHD was larger (with more very slow responses) than for control children.

One paper has recently suggested that ADHD might be conceived of as reflecting variable performance (Castellanos et al., 2005). Such a view requires a different approach to data analysis; specifically, it requires analyses that look at variations in performance within an individual across time (time series analyses). Castellanos et al. (2005) present analyses of RT data from ADHD and control children. Both groups of children showed variations in RT across time with the same periodicity; such a pattern is consistent with some basic oscillatory process that affects the efficiency of the nervous system in all children (Castellanos et al. review data from a number of animal studies that reveal similar oscillations in several physiological processes, including heart rate). Most interestingly, however, the analyses presented showed much greater increases in RT as a function of these oscillations in the children with ADHD, that is, both groups showed slowed RTs at similar time intervals but these slowings were much larger in the children with ADHD.

It is too early to judge the likely generality or importance of intrachild variations in performance as a potential explanation for the cognitive deficits seen in children with ADHD, but this appears to be a potentially important avenue for future studies.

Motivational Theories of ADHD

In contrast to cognitive accounts of ADHD, other theories have emphasized possible abnormalities in systems responsible for motivation or arousal as explanations for ADHD. According to such theories, an altered state of arousal or motivation leads to a different response pattern in children with ADHD.

ADHD as a problem of signaling delayed rewards

According to the most prominent theory of this type, children with ADHD may show an aversion to the delay of rewards (Sonuga-Barke, Taylor & Heptinsall, 1992; Sonuga-Barke, Taylor, Sembi, & Smith, 1992). Such "delay aversion" can be thought of as a motivational style; the child could wait if necessary but strongly prefers not to. One possible consequence of delay aversion is that children may show different preferences for rewards that vary in their timing. This idea is embodied in theories that make use of terminology taken from animal learning theory that stress the role of reinforcers (rewards) in regulating behavior. Rewards tend to be more effective in strengthening a response if they occur soon after the response. A hypothetical gradient showing this "delay of reinforcement" is shown in Figure 7.4 for children with ADHD and controls.

The delay gradient is assumed to be steeper and shorter in children with ADHD (Aase & Sagvolden, 2006). Thus, children with ADHD experience a faster decline in the effectiveness of reinforcement as the delay between behavior and reward increases.

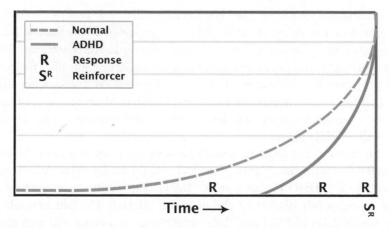

Figure 7.4   Theoretical delay-of-reinforcement gradients for ADHD (solid line) and controls (dotted line). (Redrawn from Aase & Sagvolden, 2006, with permission.) Infrequent, but not frequent, reinforcers produce more variable responding in young children with attention deficit/hyperactivity disorder (ADHD). *Journal of Child Psychology and Psychiatry, 47,* 457–447.

It follows that they do not like to wait and they cannot defer gratification; hence they present as impulsive in cognitive style and cannot work effectively over extended periods when sustained attention is required. Sonuga-Barke and colleagues (Sonuga-Barke, Taylor, & Heptinsall, 1992; Sonuga-Barke, Taylor, Sembi, & Smith, 1992) have argued that ADHD is the outcome of a neurobiological impairment in the power and efficiency with which the contingency between present action and future rewards is signaled. As a consequence, children with ADHD become delay-averse and, unlike typically developing children, do not learn to control their impulses; instead they avoid delays by choosing immediate rewards or they fill delays with hyperactive and distracting behaviors.

In the laboratory, delay aversion has been demonstrated using a task in which the child has to make a choice between a small reward associated with a shorter delay and a large reward associated with a longer delay. The rewards are usually given as tokens as the task proceeds and the tokens are exchanged at the end of the session for money or for small gifts. Using this technique, Sonuga-Barke, Taylor, Sembi, and Smith (1992) found that children with ADHD preferred to choose a one-point reward associated with a delay of 2s rather than a two-point reward following a delay of 30s. In contrast, there were no group differences when delays were not followed by a reward, or when the session length was fixed, such that the optimal strategy for everyone was to choose small rewards.

Kuntsi et al. (2001) tested delay aversion using a computer-presented Space game. In the game the child had to make a choice between an immediate reward (one point, involving a 2s prereward delay) and a larger delayed reward (two points, involving a 30s prereward delay). The experimenter also rated the child's apparent delay aversion during the task on a scale of 1–3. Consistent with earlier findings, the children with ADHD chose the larger reward significantly less often than controls and this difference remained significant after IQ was controlled. The groups also differed on ratings of aversion to delay. However, when symptoms of comorbid conduct disorder were controlled, the main effect of group was no longer significant for either measure. Since few studies examining delay aversion have controlled for comorbid conduct problems, it is difficult to say how specific the delay aversion impairment is to ADHD. Moreover, it is important to be explicit that different causes of impulsivity are not mutually exclusive and delay aversion and inhibition may tap different aspects of the ADHD phenotype.

With this in mind, a collaborative study between the proponents of different theories of ADHD assessed the validity of the SST and the choice delay task as measures of impulsivity in ADHD (Solanto et al., 2001). This study drew children from a database of rigorously diagnosed children with ADHD; 45 children took part in both the choice delay and SST and their performance was compared with that of 29 age-matched controls. In addition, parents and teachers completed the Conners' scale as well as a checklist for symptoms of ADHD and oppositional defiant disorder (ODD). A novel aspect of this study was the inclusion of structured observations of the classroom behaviors of the children (such as annoying others, clowning, interference to teacher, gross-motor movements, and acts of physical aggression). These observations were completed using a modified time-sampling technique yielding 16 min of data. Each observer recorded the behaviors of one child with ADHD and one "control" from the same classroom, blind to diagnostic status.

As expected, there were robust differences between groups in mean SSRT ($d = 0.68$) and in the probability of inhibition ($d = 0.89$). In the delay aversion task (choice delay), the children with ADHD chose the larger reward 34% of the time compared with 58% for the control group ($d = 0.90$). Performance on the choice delay task was moderately correlated with teacher ratings of impulsivity, hyperactivity, and conduct problems, and with classroom observations of interference, gross-motor movements, and physical aggression, while SSRT correlated with classroom observations of interference and physical aggression.

A limitation of this study was that the data from the SST for 14 children had to be excluded either because of a high number of omission errors on "go" trials or a low probability of inhibition. It is also unfortunate that no data on IQ for the control group were available. Notwithstanding this, the measures that best discriminated the ADHD from the control group were the probability of inhibition in the SST and the percentage of large reward (long delay) choices in the delay aversion task. When considered separately in a discriminant function analysis the probability of inhibition classified 68% of children correctly and the percentage of long delay choices classified 71% of children correctly; when entered simultaneously these two measures gave an overall correct classification rate of 87.5%, suggesting that the two measures may indeed tap partially independent aspects of the ADHD condition.

The cognitive energetic model of ADHD

One of the issues that we have alluded to is that performance in children with ADHD is variable; coupled with this, they display slow speeds of processing. This kind of behavioral profile – sometimes described as "sluggish" – could potentially be explained either in terms of cognitive deficiencies in executive control, or by recourse to suboptimal levels of arousal and a lack of consistent effort. Sergeant and his colleagues (Oosterlann, Logan & Sergeant, 1998; Sergeant, 2005; Sergeant & van der Meere, 1988) have proposed that the overall efficiency of information processing is determined by the interaction of computational resources (e.g., processing and storage capacity), state factors such as motivation and arousal, and executive functions. From this perspective, "single-deficit" models of ADHD are not sufficient because they fail to take into account the role of task parameters in the determination of performance (Sergeant, 2005). For example, the rate of stimulus presentation alters the energetic state of an individual and thereby affects performance (through a change in speed–accuracy trade-off). In this way, fast rates of stimulus presentation can lead to overarousal, with fast inaccurate responding as a consequence. On the other hand, slow rates of stimulus presentation may lead to underarousal and slow, inaccurate responding. Children with ADHD appear to have difficulty in modulating their energetic state such that they generally perform more poorly at slow rates of presentation but more normally with a fast rate of stimulus presentation. Generally, they may have difficulty in maintaining an optimal arousal state with consequent difficulties for the organization of motor responses.

Sergeant uses what he describes as the "cognitive energetic" model to explain the variable profile of arousal and responding in ADHD. The model has three interacting levels. At the highest level is the executive or management system, which ultimately controls four general stages of processing at the lowest level: encoding, search, decision, and motor organization. The executive control in this system is mediated by three distinct energetic pools: effort, arousal, and activation. Effort refers to the energy necessary to meet task demands and encompasses motivation and response to contingencies. Arousal refers to phasic responding that is time-locked to stimulus presentation and typically influenced by novelty and signal intensity. Activation refers to physiological readiness to respond and is affected by preparation, alertness, time of day, and time on task. The cognitive energetic model is appealing in that it provides an account of both cognitive and motivational differences in ADHD; however it is, as yet, not well specified and, as acknowledged by its proponents, the model is complicated and testing it will depend upon finding satisfactory measures of arousal, activation, and effort.

ADHD Subtypes: Different Etiologies for Inattention and Hyperactivity?

As we said earlier, DSM-IV distinguishes between two dimensions of impairment that occur in children with ADHD: inattention and hyperactivity/impulsivity. This gives rise to the three subtypes of ADHD: the primarily "hyperactive–impulsive" (HI) type, the primarily "inattentive" (IA) type, and the combined type. Inattention and hyperactivity/impulsivity seem like quite different symptoms (though they correlate quite well, around .7) and we need to consider carefully the extent to which these symptoms may depend upon different underlying impairments at the biological (genetic and brain mechanisms) and cognitive levels of explanation.

An early study by Barkley, Dupaul, and McMurray (1990) suggested that subtypes of ADHD may differ in etiology. This study involved 90 clinically referred 6–12-year-old children with attention disorders: 42 classified as showing ADD with hyperactivity (ADD+H) and 48 with ADD but without hyperactivity (ADD–H) (as defined by DSM-III; American Psychiatric Association, 1980). They were compared to a group of 16 children with learning disabilities and 34 control children.

There were no differences between the groups in prenatal, perinatal, or early development but both ADHD groups were reported to have poorer motor control than the learning disabled or the control groups. Similarly, there were no significant group differences in family background factors, such as marital satisfaction, life stress, or depression, but all clinical groups reported more psychological distress than controls. Comparisons between the two subtypes revealed some important differences. Those with hyperactivity were noisier and more disruptive, had problems with peer relationships, and were more likely to be in classes for children with emotional and behavioral disorders. Moreover, they had more relatives with ADHD, aggressiveness, and substance abuse. Those without hyperactivity tended to appear more confused, to daydream, and to present as lethargic; they showed fewer off-task behaviors but more problems on vigilance tasks. Although they did not differ in attainments from the hyperactive subgroup, they were more likely to be in special education classes for learning disabled children and were less likely to have pervasive conduct problems but were more likely to be depressed (though rates of depression were generally low). In addition, more of their relatives had learning difficulties and suffered anxiety disorders. This study provides a description of the different clinical manifestations of the ADHD-HI and ADHD-IA subtypes, but does not clarify the extent to which these subtypes may reflect different underlying causal mechanisms.

Chhabildas, Pennington, and Willcutt (2001) compared the neuropsychological profiles of children with ADHD diagnosed according to DSM-IV criteria as predominantly HI ($n=14$), predominantly IA ($n=67$), or of the combined subtype ($n=33$) who were recruited from the Colorado twin study. In addition to completing tests of reading, spelling, and IQ, each child was assessed on two tests of inhibition (the continuous performance task and the SST), two tests of processing speed (the Trail-Making Test and WISC coding), and a measure of sustained attention (vigilance).

The HI subgroup did not differ from a control group of nonaffected twins in IQ but the other two subgroups gained lower IQ scores (IA and combined); in addition, these latter two subtypes also had poorer reading skills. It is important to bear these differences in mind when assessing the performance of the different ADHD subgroups. The profiles of impairment differed somewhat across tasks. However, a reasonable summary is that the IA and combined subtypes performed similarly to one another and less well than controls whereas the HI subgroup (of whom there were only 14) had less difficulty overall on the cognitive tasks. In dimensional analyses in which symptoms of IA or symptoms of HI were used to predict variations in the cognitive tasks (measures of inhibition, processing speed, and vigilance), every cognitive measure was best predicted by measures of inattention whereas hyperactivity was not a predictor of these impairments.

Thus, children who showed symptoms of inattention (whether in isolation or in combination with hyperactivity) showed a range of cognitive impairments that are typical of children with ADHD, while children from the predominantly HI subgroup generally performed normally on these cognitive processing tasks. This study suggests that a number of the cognitive symptoms (impairments of inhibition, processing speed, and vigilance) that are said to characterize children with ADHD are actually associated with inattention but not with symptoms of hyperactivity. This seems to be a finding of great importance, and it suggests that future studies should measure symptoms of inattention and hyperactivity separately, and look for separable causes for these different symptoms. However, as the authors note, the sample of children in the predominantly HI group was small and the samples studied here were relatively old (10–12 years old on average), which means that the pattern reported really needs to be replicated.

The Role of Comorbidities in Accounting for some Symptoms of ADHD

ADHD shows high rates of comorbidity with a range of other disorders, particularly general learning difficulties, anxiety, conduct disorder, and oppositional defiant disorder. An important issue, therefore, is the extent to which some characteristics found in samples of children with ADHD may reflect such comorbid conditions. It could be that some of these characteristics are a product of comorbid impairments that are not central to understanding the nature and causes of ADHD.

This question has been pursued most with respect to the relationship between ADHD and reading disorders (Adams & Snowling, 2001; August & Garfinkel, 1989, 1990). An important design feature of such studies is exemplified by an early study by Pennington, Grossier, and Welsh (1993), which revealed some striking findings. This study involved three groups of children: a group of children with ADHD, a group of children with reading disorders (RD) who did not have attentional problems, and a comorbid group of children who had ADHD and RD. The children were given two sets of tasks to complete, one set to tap executive function (the putative core deficit in ADHD) and the other to tap phonological skills (the core deficit in dyslexia; see Chapter 2). As expected, the pure ADHD group showed executive deficits while their phonological processing was normal. In contrast, the pure RD group performed poorly on tests of phonological processing but they had no difficulty with the executive function tasks. Of particular interest was how the comorbid group would perform. In fact, the comorbid group in this study resembled the RD group in showing phonological deficits. They were not impaired on the executive tasks, suggesting that their attentional problems may be a secondary consequence of their learning difficulties rather than the primary outcome of an underlying attentional deficit. Pennington and colleagues referred to this interpretation as the "phenocopy" hypothesis, by which they meant that the comorbid group displayed behaviors mimicking those of ADHD, but without sharing the same underlying cognitive profile. Interestingly, children in this group also appeared to be subject to more social and family adversity than children in the pure RD group, suggesting that environmental factors may be important in determining their behavioral symptoms.

Despite the intuitive appeal of the phenocopy hypothesis, subsequent studies, including some by the same group, have not supported its predictions (Willcutt et al., 2001; Willcutt, Pennington, Chhabildas, Olson, & Huslander, 2005). Willcutt et al. (2001) used the same factorial design to investigate two cognitive phenotypes (executive function and phonological awareness) in children with ADHD, RD, or both disorders. The children who took part were all twins aged between 8 and 16 years and were diagnosed on the basis of parent ratings of behavior; all had IQ above 70; 93 of them had RD alone, 28 had ADHD alone, and 48 had comorbid RD + AD, and their performance was compared with that of 102 typically developing children. The test battery was comprehensive and included several measures of phonological awareness and executive function. A phonological awareness composite measure was derived from performance on three tasks: Pig Latin, in which the task is to strip away the first phoneme from a word and place it at the end of the word followed by "ay" (e.g., mat – "atmay"), phoneme deletion (say "plift" without the /p/), and the Lindamood auditory conceptualization test in which blocks represent phonemes and the task is to add, remove, or transpose blocks to reflect changes in nonwords spoken by the examiner. The executive function measures tapped the ability to maintain and shift set, behavioral inhibition, and working memory. Once again composite scores were derived. The working memory composite comprised performance in sentence span, counting span, and the Trail-Making Test, the inhibition composite comprised performance on the Stop-Signal Task (SSRT) and errors of commission on the continuous performance task, and the set-shifting composite comprised perseveration on the Wisconsin Card Sorting Task and errors on a continuous naming task.

Before reporting the results of Willcutt et al.'s (2001) study it is important to point out that the "pure" RD and ADHD subgroups were not completely free of symptoms of the other disorder. Thus, the RD group had significantly more symptoms of ADHD than did the controls, and the ADHD group scored more poorly than the controls on the reading tests. Both of these findings remained significant when IQ was controlled, highlighting the fact that children with categorical diagnoses may still show subclinical versions of other disorders. Notwithstanding this, there was a significant effect of RD for all the reading and executive function measures, whereas the main effect of ADHD was only significant for inhibition and phonological awareness. When IQ was controlled the group effects on the inhibition composite remained significant and the RD effect remained significant for phonological awareness and working memory, whereas none of the group differences were significant for set-shifting. Importantly, the profile shown by the comorbid RD+ADHD group was not like that of the RD group, as predicted by the phenocopy hypothesis. Rather, the children in this group were more impaired than the other groups on the working memory and inhibition composites, suggesting that they may have a more severe form of disorder involving deficits associated both with ADHD and with dyslexia.

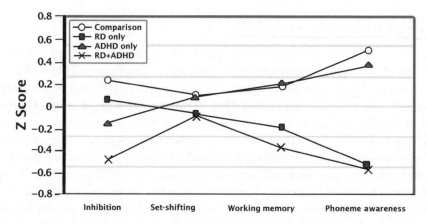

Figure 7.5 Profiles of groups with RD (dyslexia), ADHD, and comorbid RD+ADHD on tests of inhibition, set-shifting, working memory, and phoneme awareness. (Willcutt, E. G., Pennington, B. F., Tunick, R. A., Boada, R. J., Chhabildas, N. A., et al., A comparison of the cognitive deficits in reading disability and attention-deficit/hyperactivity disorder, *Journal of Abnormal Psychology*, 110, p. 166, 2001, published by the American Psychological Association and adapted with permission.)

In line with previous research, the findings of Willcutt et al.'s (2001) study support a double dissociation between executive function and phonological awareness phenotypes. This is shown clearly in Figure 7.5, which depicts the performance of the three clinical groups alongside that of controls on tests of inhibition and phonological awareness. However, there is reason to believe that this double dissociation may not be complete – a subsequent study by the same group, using a very similar sample of children, found that RD groups were impaired on several measures of executive function, including inhibition, with deficits most pronounced on tests of processing speed and working memory (Willcutt, Pennington, et al., 2005). The reason for the discrepancy between these sets of findings is not clear; they highlight that there is a pressing need to examine more carefully the relationships between reading and attention disorders and to explore the possibility that they may have a shared etiology.

Etiology of ADHD

Research on the biological bases of ADHD has arguably been more influential in helping to understand the disorder than for the other disorders considered so far in this book. Research in this area has involved psychopharmacology (drug treatments and their mode of action on psychological and brain processes), genetics, and studies of brain structure and function. We will begin with studies of psychopharmacology because these studies have, in turn, been highly influential in guiding studies of genetic risk factors for ADHD.

Psychopharmacology of ADHD

Research on ADHD has attracted the interest of psychopharmacologists far more than any of the other disorders we have considered. This interest follows from the idea that ADHD reflects impairments in the regulation of the brain's neurotransmitter systems and evidence that certain drug treatments can help to reduce the symptoms of ADHD. Before we go on to discuss what is known about the etiology of ADHD, it is therefore important to outline the mechanisms of neural transmission.

Nerve cells transmit information by electrical signals called action potentials. However, the transmission of information from one nerve cell to another depends upon chemicals called neurotransmitters. Nerve cells communicate with each other at structures called synapses. In simple terms, neurotransmitters can be found in nerve cells, packaged into "vesicles," and they are released into the synaptic cleft (the gap between nerve cells) when an action potential arrives and causes depolarization of the presynaptic neuron. The effect of a neurotransmitter depends on the receptors to which it binds, leading either to excitation or inhibition of the postsynaptic cell. In other words, the neurotransmitter can encourage the next neuron to fire or inhibit its action. Many of the neurotransmitters that are released into the synapse are removed by a process called reuptake, which is regulated by neurotransmitter transporters.

Among the neurotransmitters, catecholamines play a critical role in the functioning of the brain's prefrontal cortex (PFC). The PFC appears to play a critical role in guiding attention and inhibiting distracting stimuli. Two important catecholamines are dopamine, generally considered to be involved in voluntary movement and motivation, and norepinephrine, which is involved in the mechanisms regulating arousal. In fact, it has been demonstrated that depletion of both dopamine (DA) and norepinephrine (NE) can be as detrimental to performance on tasks tapping PFC as removing the cortex itself (Arnsten & Li, 2005). Either too little or too much stimulation of the DA receptors impairs working memory function in rats and monkeys, with performance following a U-shaped curve in response to dosage of dopamine agonists (drugs that block the operation of dopamine as a neurotransmitter). In a similar vein, low to moderate levels of NE have beneficial effects on the functioning of prefrontal cortex, whereas high concentrations (such as those released during stress) impair performance.

The role of the basal ganglia in relation to neurotransmitters also deserves mention. The basal ganglia are subcortical structures (two in each hemisphere) that are involved in the biosynthesis of neurotransmitters. The basal ganglia comprise the caudate nucleus, putamen, and globus pallidus (see Figure 7.6); they have interconnections with the cortex and thalamus, and receive inputs from frontal and motor areas via the striatum. Arguably, knowledge of the mechanisms of action of neurotransmitters both in animals and in man has set the stage for investigations of the etiology of ADHD, which is characterized by difficulties in the voluntary control of movement and arousal.

Interest in the possible role of the catecholamines in ADHD was stimulated by observations that treatment with drugs that affect catecholamine transmission

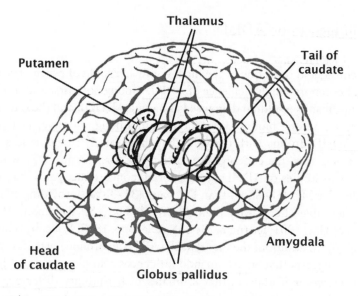

Figure 7.6 Schematic diagram showing basal ganglia.

improved the symptoms of children with ADHD, for example, methylphenidate (Ritalin), which blocks both dopamine and norepinephrine transporters and improves the symptoms of ADHD (Arnsten & Li, 2005). The blocking of these transporters (that reabsorb dopamine and norepinephrine and so reduce their action as neurotransmitters) equates to increasing the effective availability of both these neurotransmitters in the brain. (Other drugs such as amphetamines have similar effects on these neurotransmitters, but are used only occasionally now in the treatment of ADHD because of their potentially harmful side effects.) More direct evidence for abnormalities in dopamine transport (reabsorption) in ADHD comes from brain imaging studies that have measured levels of dopamine transporter in different brain regions using drugs containing radioactive isotopes that bind selectively to the dopamine transporter. These studies show increased activity of the dopamine transporter in various brain regions of interest (particularly the striatum) in adults and children with ADHD (for a review, see Spencer et al., 2005). Furthermore three studies using the same methods have shown reduced levels of dopamine transporter activity after treatment with methylphenidate (Ritalin). Finally treatment with methylphenidate has been shown to improve measures of neuropsychological functioning in people with ADHD, including measures of inhibition (Boonstra, Kooij, Oosterlaan, Sergeant, & Buitelaar, 2005; Turner, Blackwell, Dowson, McLean, & Sahakian, 2005) sustained attention (Boonstra et al., 2005), and working memory (Turner et al., 2005).

In summary, the evidence for a disorder of dopamine transmission (and to a lesser degree norepinephrine) in ADHD seems strong. The best interpretation of this finding, and whether abnormalities of dopamine reuptake are a fundamental biological cause of ADHD or a downstream consequence of other more fundamental disturbances in brain function, remains open to debate.

Genetic influences on ADHD

Quantitative genetics

ADHD is considered to be one of the most highly heritable of psychiatric disorders. Family studies report a high incidence of ADHD among both first and second degree relatives of probands (children diagnosed as having ADHD), and the rates of ADHD are also greater among biological relations than among adoptive relatives of children with ADHD. In line with the view that these family resemblances in ADHD reflect genetic effects, the concordance rates differ for MZ and DZ twins. A large number of twin studies of ADHD have reported concordance rates that are significantly higher for MZ (58–82%) than DZ pairs (31–38%), providing evidence that ADHD is heritable (Levy, McLaughlin, Wood, Hay, & Waldman, 1996; Levy, McStephen, & Hay, 2001; Sherman, McGue, & Iacono, 1997; Willcutt, Pennington, & DeFries, 2000). In addition, the fact that the MZ concordance was less than 100% in all studies suggests that environmental influences also play a role in the etiology of ADHD. However it appears that estimates of heritability differ depending on who is the informant regarding behavioral symptoms and what instruments are used. For example, Levy et al. (1996) used data from a questionnaire based on DSM-III and completed by mothers of an Australian sample of probands with ADHD and found concordance rates of .82 for MZ and .38 for DZ twins. In contrast, Goodman and Stevenson (1989) reported wide ranging concordance rates from .48 to .79 for MZ and .08 to .44 for DZ twins in a UK sample, depending on the informant and instrument used. Notwithstanding the issue of bias raised by these figures, a recent meta-review reports a mean heritability estimate of .75 for individual differences in attention, which is very substantial and there is evidence of considerable stability by age (Reitveld, Hudziak, Bartels, van Beijsterveldt & Boomsma, 2004).

Molecular genetic approaches

Most molecular genetic studies of ADHD have focused on genes that operate to influence the functioning of dopamine systems in the brain. These genes are of specific interest because drugs such as methylphenidate (Ritalin) that reduce the reuptake of dopamine are known to be effective treatments for ADHD. So far, two gene variants of the dopamine receptor (DRD4) and the dopamine transporter (DAT) have been found to be associated with ADHD. In addition a further five gene variants that aid neurotransmitter release have also been identified. However, the effects of each of these genes are small, with odds ratios ranging from 1.18 to 1.46 (Faraone et al., 2005). This means that the effects of such genes are not going to explain the occurrence of the disorder in most individuals (and suggests they may only contribute to the risk of ADHD in combination with other genes). Moreover, because of comorbidities, ADHD is likely to be genetically heterogeneous. In fact, there appears to be some overlap on chromosome 6 between linkage regions reported for ADHD and for reading disorder (RD), which might be explained by pleitropy, a term used to refer to the process whereby the same set of genes is linked to a number of different phenotypes (Willcutt et al., 2002).

To investigate genetic overlap between ADHD and RD, Gayan et al. (2005) assessed 505 individuals from 119 nuclear families on tests of reading and language and recorded ADHD symptoms via an interview. Each individual also contributed DNA, which was analysed to identify genetic markers across 22 chromosomes. The rationale behind the method was to ask whether higher levels of genetic resemblance between siblings at a certain locus correlated with greater similarity for a behavioral trait (e.g., a component of reading or of ADHD). As expected, there were large correlations between reading and language variables in this sample, with the correlation between reading and inattention being moderate (and low with hyperactivity). The criterion for affectation status (for RD and ADHD) was set at 1.5 or more SD below/above the population mean in either phenotype. On this basis, 36% of the RD individuals also met the criteria for ADHD. The investigators proceeded to conduct linkage analysis to identify markers associated with ADHD and bivariate analyses to identify markers associated with both ADHD and RD.

There were two informative behavioral phenotypes: one was a composite ADHD score and the other ADHD symptoms in combination with poor orthographic coding (OC) as measured by a test requiring the participants to say which of two spellings was correct (e.g., salmon/sammon). The main linkage peaks were on chromosomes 14 (for ADHD and for ADHD-OC) and 20 (for ADHD-OC). Thus, there was suggestive evidence of pleitropic loci in the regions of chromosomes 14q32 and 20q11. In addition, the univariate analysis suggested three areas of linkage to ADHD, depending on how the phenotype was defined: for hyperactive symptoms, these were 7q21; for symptoms of inattention, 9p24; and for the composite ADHD score, 16p13. The region on chromosome 7 overlaps with a previously identified region of linkage and contains one of the genes implicated in the dopaminergic pathway. More research is required to clarify the genes and gene pathways that carry the risk of ADHD; this poses a serious challenge, given the heterogeneity of the disorder and its overlap with other disorders.

Endophenotypes

Arguably, symptom-based classifications (i.e., categorical diagnoses) have been slow to bear fruit in unraveling the mappings between susceptibility genes and behavioral outcomes in ADHD. As a consequence, there is increasing interest in an alternative approach, namely the identification of "endophenotypes" (Skuse, 2001). Endophenotypes can be defined as heritable traits that index an individual's liability to develop or manifest a given disease (Castellanos & Tannock, 2002). It is hoped that endophenotypes will relate more directly to the biological etiology of a disorder than many of the symptoms that currently are studied – though it is important to note that endophenotypes are just as likely to be modified by environmental influences as any other brain process or behavior trait.

Doyle et al. (2005) suggested that in order for a process to be a useful endophenotype it should be possible to measure it reliably, it should show evidence of heritability, and it should appear in unaffected relatives, although it need not be universal in the condition. Possible endophenotypes of ADHD include working memory (especially visuospatial memory), inhibition, temporal processing, state regulation, and a shortened delay gradient, all of which show some genetic influence and partial familial overlap, especially inhibition and processing speed (Doyle et al., 2005). The investigation of endophenotypes is likely to grow rapidly in the coming years, and holds the potential for identifying both risk and protective factors in the etiology of ADHD.

Social and environmental risk factors

The majority of research suggests that the effects of individual gene products on ADHD are small and that genes involved in the transmission of ADHD are probably also involved in the transmission of other disorders (e.g., autism). This means it is important to also consider the contribution of environmental risk factors to ADHD. Environmental factors that have been associated with ADHD include prenatal factors such as maternal smoking and exposure to maternal alcohol drinking during pregnancy, lead exposure both in utero and in childhood, birth complications and low birthweight, severe early deprivation such as major disruptions of attachment, ongoing family and psychosocial adversity, and, in some cases, dietary effects (Biederman, 2005; Taylor, 2006).

One particularly clear form of evidence concerning diet comes from a double-blind trial of the effects of artificial food color and additives (McCann et al., 2007). In this well-controlled study it was found that artificial colors and a preservative added to fruit drink led to increased hyperactivity in 3- and 8/9-year-old children in the general population. The effect sizes here were around 0.2, suggesting that this is a small effect, but this study shows very clearly that these food additives are one potential cause of hyperactivity in children.

Of course some other associations between environmental risks and ADHD may be the consequence of ADHD in parents rather than direct causes of the disorder. Indeed, both the active and passive correlation of genetic and environmental factors can influence behavioral outcomes in ADHD. Parents of children with ADHD will often themselves exhibit continuing patterns of hyperactivity and impulsivity that provide poor models for the development of organization and self-management skills. Children's own ADHD behaviors may also evoke negative or critical responses from parents and these may in turn increase oppositional behaviors or compound feelings of low self-esteem leading to a downward spiraling of behavior. More specifically, a delay-averse motivational style may elicit punitive reactions from parents and perpetuate the failure to engage with delay-rich environments. These within-family processes may serve to reinforce patterns of persistent pathology. For this reason, parent training programs may provide an important component of the management of ADHD.

Neurobiology of ADHD

The majority of the early studies of the brain bases of ADHD focused on the structure of the prefrontal lobes and its reciprocal connections with the ventromedial region of the striatum. More recent investigations have included the basal ganglia.

Research samples have ranged widely in age, which may mean that some results are artefactual, although in an important study Castellanos et al. (2002) showed that developmental changes in brain structure were parallel in ADHD and control samples, suggesting that brain differences appear to be consistent across age.

A number of studies of brain structure now indicate that total cerebral volume is smaller in ADHD, and localized abnormalities of several brain regions, notably the prefrontal cortex, basal ganglia, and corpus callosum, have been reported (Castellanos, et al., 1996; Tannock, 1998). In contrast, no differences have been found in the region of the putamen (shown on Figure 7.6). In light of this, it is interesting to note that Casey et al. (1997) found that behavioral measures of response inhibition in ADHD correlated with anatomical measures of frontal-striatal circuitry but not the putamen.

Neuroimaging studies have built on structural studies to test hypotheses regarding the neurobiological bases of ADHD. Following a review of 12 studies using a variety of experimental paradigms, including those tapping inhibition, working memory, and vigilance, Bush, Valera, and Seidman (2005) reported that individuals with ADHD show a consistent pattern of frontal dysfunction with altered patterns of activity in anterior cingulate, dorsolateral prefrontal, and ventrolateral prefrontal cortices, as well as associated parietal, striatal, and cerebellar regions. Taking a narrower focus, Aron and Poldrack (2005) examined studies investigating inhibition and found deficits in right inferior prefrontal cortex, basal ganglia, and related neurotransmitter systems.

Building on these reviews, Dickenstein, Bannon, Castellanos, and Milham (2006) used a meta-analytic technique to provide an overview of the findings from all of the studies of ADHD to that time. The technique used is called activation likelihood estimation, a quantitative analysis that examines, voxel by voxel, the likelihood of activation across neuroimaging studies. This voxel-wise approach gives good spatial resolution, which is important in the case of ADHD considering that spatial distinctions are substantial in the frontal lobes.

Dickenstein et al. (2006) identified 16 studies yielding 134 foci of activation in ADHD and 180 in controls. Separate analyses were conducted for each group and the two activation maps were then compared to investigate differences in patterns of activation. Moreover, because various different paradigms were used in these studies, the authors also report a subanalysis restricted to studies of inhibition (e.g., Go/No-Go and Stop-Signal tasks). Taken together, the findings of the meta-analysis confirmed previous studies in highlighting widely distributed regions of underactivity in individuals with ADHD affecting anterior cingulate, dorsolateral prefrontal, inferior prefrontal, and orbitofrontal cortices, as well as regions in the basal ganglia and parietal cortices. These differences may reflect decreases in the spatial extent of activations, more spatial dispersion, or decreased functional connectivity. The authors also caution that they may be the result of statistical noise (e.g., more movement in ADHD group).

Finally, a small number of studies employing electrophysiological measurements have found significant differences in EEG measured at several sites between children with ADHD and controls. However, it is unclear whether to interpret these as indices of under- and overarousal, or of delayed brain maturation. In a similar vein, ERP studies have investigated the P300, which is generated when participants attend and discriminate events. Together these studies suggest that in ADHD the P300 is smaller in amplitude in response to targets, and its latency is longer. Perhaps most interestingly, Lazzaro et al. (1997) reported greater variability in P300 responses in children with ADHD and also found that such variability was reduced by stimulant medication. This variability is consistent with evidence of greater variability in reaction time (RT) measures found in ADHD described earlier. Such findings are also broadly consistent with the predictions of the cognitive–energetic model that views difficulty in the maintenance and control of arousal and activation to be a significant factor in ADHD.

In sum, although there are still relatively few studies of the neural correlates of ADHD, findings converge well with those of behavioral studies. A limitation of these studies has been the focus on brain regions of interest and therefore other areas of abnormality may have been missed. More generally, the effects of age and stage of development on patterns of activation have not been investigated. Hence it is difficult to ascertain what the primary impairments are and whether other impairments may be secondary consequences of these. Indeed, there is still a long way to go before it will be possible to trace causal pathways from biology through cognition to the social and behavioral outcomes of this complex disorder.

Interventions for ADHD

The complexities of ADHD are such that intervention demands a multiprofessional approach and ideally there should be a management plan that addresses behavioral, educational, and social issues (Taylor, 2006). From a theoretical perspective it is important to distinguish between treatments that address core problems (and may therefore help to demonstrate causes) and those that aim to ameliorate symptoms.

The main treatment for ADHD, unlike the other disorders in this book, is pharmacological. Drug treatments are used to improve neural transmission, with the aim of reducing hyperactivity, impulsivity, and inattentiveness. Most effective treatments for ADHD target catecholamine transmission, for example methylphenidate (Ritalin), which blocks dopamine and norepeniphrine transporters (Arnsten & Li, 2005). However, behavior therapy programs are also useful, particularly if parents are involved (Tannock, 1998). Cognitive behavior therapy (CBT) may help older children and young adults with ADHD to manage their difficulties, but it is generally a less effective therapy for individuals with ADHD.

In 1992, a major multicentre study evaluating different interventions for ADHD was funded by the US National Institute of Mental Health and Department of Education. "The Multimodal Treatment Study of Children with ADHD" (MTA) was a randomized trial (Box 7.4) that compared the efficacy of three forms of treatment: medication, behavioral management, or a combination of the two, relative to regular community care (which acted as a control condition). The participants in the trial were 579 children aged 7 years to 9 years 9 months, all of whom met DSM-IV criteria for ADHD (combined type). On entering the trial, the children were randomly assigned to one of three treatment arms or to community care for 14 months, during which time the researchers monitored behavioral symptoms, social skills and relationships, and educational achievements.

The behavioral treatment program incorporated parent training, child-focused treatment, and a school-based intervention integrated in the school year. By most standards, the treatment was extremely comprehensive; the parent program involved 27 group sessions and 8 individual sessions per family. The same therapist also conducted teacher consultations biweekly. The child-focused therapy involved attendance at an 8-week summer camp (for 5 days per week and 9 hours per day) where assistants worked with the children in recreational settings using a points reward system, time out, social reinforcement, and other well-established techniques for shaping desirable behavior. In addition to the teacher consultations regarding the management of behavioral difficulties, the school-based work also involved a teaching assistant working alongside the child for 60 school days. Throughout the school year, a daily report card was used to communicate between school and home.

The medication treatment was also carefully supervised. It started with a 28-day double-blind trial of different doses of methylphenidate. During this phase, the child's response was monitored by taking parent ratings of attention and behavior. These data were then used in reaching agreement on the correct dose (or to the administration of an alternative drug treatment if the best dose was placebo). Following this phase, children were seen monthly by pharmacotherapists to monitor side effects and for

---

Box 7.4   Randomized controlled trials

A randomized controlled trial (RCT) is now considered the "gold standard" method for evaluating the efficacy of a medical or health treatment, and increasingly RCTs are being used to evaluate educational interventions. An RCT involves the random allocation of participants to different forms of treatment. Such random allocation should minimize any differences between treatment groups (such as severity of symptoms at the beginning of the study) that might bias the outcome of the study.

To provide validation of a treatment's efficacy, it is crucial that an RCT is reported in a standard and transparent way that allows critical appraisal. To safeguard this process, a group known as the Consolidated Standards of Reporting Trials (CONSORT) has devised a minimum set of recommendations for reporting RCTs, known as the CONSORT Statement (Altman et al., 2001). The CONSORT Statement gives a checklist detailing how a trial should be reported in a journal article under conventional headings such as Title, Abstract, Introduction, Methods, Results, and Discussion. It encourages the reporting of participant flow through the trial as a flow diagram (see below).

Box 7.4   *(cont'd)*

When trials are reported in this way, they are easy to interpret and their findings can be used to make clinical recommendations with confidence.

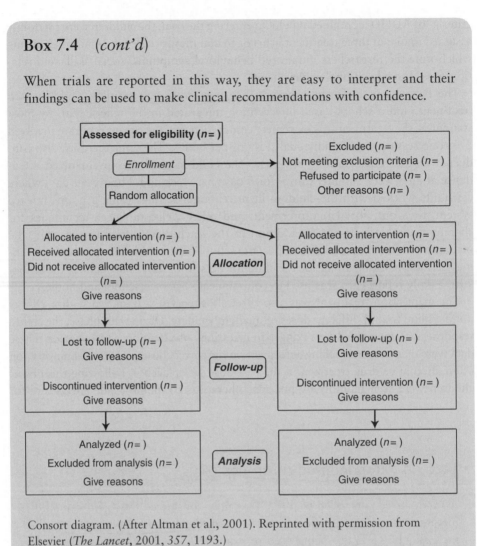

Consort diagram. (After Altman et al., 2001). Reprinted with permission from Elsevier (*The Lancet*, 2001, *357*, 1193.)

support and encouragement. The combined treatment integrated the two management strategies and involved regular liaison between teacher-consultant and pharmacotherapist. A management plan (based on a manual) provided guidelines as to when adjustments should be made to the behavioral or the pharmacological treatment.

The treatment ran for 14 months. At the end of the treatment period, all four groups showed a significant reduction in ADHD symptoms but the combined treatment and medication treatments were more effective than the behavioral intervention and community care programs. The combined and medication treatments showed effect sizes (greater reductions in rated hyperactivity and rated inattention compared to the control group) in the region of $d = 0.5$–0.7, which indicates that being on the medication has quite a substantial effect on the symptoms of ADHD.

The combined treatment was not significantly better than medication alone in reducing the core symptoms of ADHD (in fact the reductions were slightly greater in the medication only group) but it is noteworthy that combined treatment outcomes were achieved with lower levels of medication. There were few treatment arm differences in outcomes as measured by aggressive/oppositional symptoms, social skills, anxiety and depression, parent–child relations, and academic achievement, though the combined treatment proved better than the behavioral treatment for internalizing problems, aggressive/oppositional signs, and for reading achievement.

The findings of the MTA study suggest that the physiological changes brought about by methylphenidate operate to reduce the core symptoms of ADHD. This supports the idea that deficits in dopaminergic systems are one of the proximal causes of the condition. Importantly, however, treatment outcomes for the different arms depended on whether or not the children experienced a comorbid anxiety disorder. In children with anxiety, the behavioral treatment was as good as medical management and combined treatment, whereas in those without anxiety the behavioral treatment was not as effective as the other two active treatments. These findings suggest that some of the behavioral symptoms of children with ADHD who are also anxious may be related to their anxiety. It seems possible that the behavioral treatment was effective in reducing anxiety and as a consequence reduced the symptoms of ADHD. Conversely these results suggest that for children with a "purer" form of ADHD who are not anxious the behavioral treatment given was not particularly helpful in treating the core symptoms of ADHD.

One conclusion from the MTA study is that methylphenidate is an effective treatment for children with ADHD. However, the drug does not cure the condition and needs to be taken continuously in order to reduce the symptoms of inattention and hyperactivity. There is also evidence that long-term use of the drug tends to slow children's rates of growth. Furthermore the follow-up of children from the MTA study suggests that differences in the relative effectiveness of the interventions diminish over time. Swanson et al. (MTA Cooperative Group, 2004) reported that 10 months after the end of the trial the differences in ADHD symptoms between the two groups of children on methylphenidate and the two nonmedicated groups had roughly halved. These changes in the effectiveness of the intervention were accounted for by changes in which children were continuing to take the medication (many of the children who took the drug while in the trial stopped after the trial ended, while other children not given the drug during the trial then started taking it). Interestingly, parallel effects were also noted for differences in children's growth (children who continued taking the drug showed reduced growth compared to children who stopped taking the drug or never took it).

At this same point in time (10 months after the end of the trial) it was reported that phenylphenidate appeared to improve objective measures of inhibition and reaction time in those children taking it. Epstein et al. (2006) studied 316 children from the MTA sample using a continuous performance task in which they had to press a space bar whenever they saw a letter but not when they saw the letter X, which appeared 10% of the time. Children receiving medication had lower errors of omission and commission on this task and showed faster and less variable RTs.

There was also less positive skew in the RT distribution for those on medication, suggesting that they experienced fewer and less severe lapses in attention. Together these findings are consistent with the idea that medication, while it continues to be taken, improves measures of attention and information processing efficiency.

Finally, at a further follow-up 2 years after the trial ended (Jenkins et al., 2007) there were no remaining differences in treatment effectiveness between the groups (though overall all groups showed reduced levels of ADHD symptoms compared to baseline at this time). It is not yet established whether the absence of treatment effects at this long-term follow-up reflects changes in the medication regime adopted by different children from the different intervention groups; in light of the earlier follow-up study (MTA Cooperative Group, 2004) this seems a likely explanation for the pattern found.

In summary, the MTA study is a very large and methodologically rigorous evaluation of the effectiveness of methylphenidate, with and without behavioral intervention as a treatment for ADHD. In the short to medium term it is clear that methylphenidate is effective in reducing the symptoms of ADHD (at least while children continue to take the drug). However, the long-term follow-up of the children in this trial suggests that many children stop taking the drug, while others not initially prescribed the drug may start to take it. It seems important, we believe, to conduct further studies of the effectiveness of purely behavioral interventions for children with ADHD. It seems likely that such interventions, if started early in a child's development and continued over extended periods of time, may prove effective, particularly for children with less severe problems. It seems important that the evidence for the effectiveness of methylphenidate in the MTA study is not overinterpreted and used to dismiss the possible usefulness of behavioral interventions in the treatment and management of ADHD (Westen, Novotny, & Thompson-Brenner, 2004).

Towards a Neurocognitive Theory of ADHD

ADHD is a complex disorder with diverse symptoms. There has been a great deal of work trying to understand the psychological impairments seen in children with ADHD and their genetic, environmental, and neural bases. In our view, there are quite fundamental problems in how best to conceptualize ADHD. Arguably, these problems reflect both the complexity of the disorder and the research strategies that have dominated this area so far.

It is worth taking stock of the "facts" that any adequate theory of ADHD will have to account for. ADHD is a severe neurodevelopmental disorder that is relatively common (it affects around 3% of children to at least some degree). It is a disorder that is strongly influenced by genetic risk factors. ADHD is very different to the other disorders we have considered so far in terms of the complexity of its behavioral manifestations. There is no simple test or set of tests that can be used to diagnose ADHD (unlike in the case of reading or mathematics disorders); instead its diagnosis relies principally on parent and teacher rating scales, though direct observations of children and clinical interviews also play a role. The reason why rating scales are so widely used is because they tap into large samples of a child's behavior in a range of settings. The symptoms used to diagnose ADHD consist of two partially independent but correlated dimensions: inattention and hyperactivity/impulsivity.

How then should ADHD be conceptualized? A variety of cognitive or motivational deficits have been proposed as possible explanations of ADHD. The most prominent cognitive theory of ADHD has seen it as a deficit in "executive function." In terms of Fodor's (1983) terminology, executive processes are a "horizontal faculty" with the potential to affect the operation and development of a wide range of different cognitive domains. Hence, the executive deficits observed in ADHD will have wide-ranging effects. There are a number of problems with the executive impairment account of ADHD. One problem is that it is too vague and general an explanation: There is evidence for impairments on some executive tasks in children with ADHD, but not others. However, even on executive tasks where impairments are found, these are typically quite small effects (Willcutt, Doyle, et al., 2005), and such deficits are typically only found in a small proportion of children with ADHD (Nigg et al., 2005). These observations mean that an executive deficit in ADHD is very unlikely to provide a complete explanation for the disorder (executive deficits might be one cause of ADHD but it is unlikely that they are the sole, or most important, cause of the disorder).

Limitations to the executive theory of ADHD have led to other types of explanation being sought. A major alternative class of explanation is to see ADHD as a form of motivational deficit. We would term these motivational theories as "noncognitive" insofar as they postulate differences in arousal or emotional processes. The dominant motivational theory has been framed in terms of "delay aversion" in children with ADHD (Sonuga-Barke, Taylor, & Heptinsall, 1992; Sonuga-Barke, Taylor, Sembi, & Smith, 1992). Delay aversion might be seen as a type of motivational style (preferring immediate gratification to a larger reward after a delay). Alternative motivational theories postulate more wide-ranging deficits in the modulation of arousal and motivational processes in children with ADHD (Sergeant, 2005). In a direct comparison between the executive and delay aversion accounts of ADHD it was found that these two deficits were at least partially independent in that the two deficits together did a better job of discriminating between ADHD and control children than did either deficit alone (Solanto et al., 2001).

A reasonable starting point therefore might be to postulate a dual-deficit theory of ADHD. Perhaps the simplest form such a theory might take is represented in Figure 7.7.

In this view there are two broad, relatively independent, cognitive risk factors (executive deficits and motivational deficits) that cause the development of the behavioral symptoms of ADHD. For the moment we have left the details of this theory deliberately vague (both the executive deficits and motivational deficits would need to be more clearly specified). The important point is that the theory postulates two separate areas of impairment in children with ADHD. The two-headed arrows here represent the correlations between the different factors in the population. Current evidence suggests that the correlation between executive and motivational

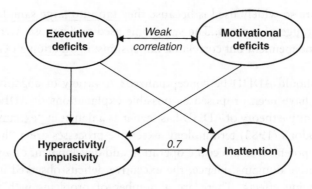

Figure 7.7   Dual-deficit theory of ADHD.

deficits is not strong (Solanto et al., 2001). In contrast there is a substantial correlation between the ratings of hyperactivity/impulsivity and inattention in the population (we have shown this as a correlation of .7, see Gomez et al., 1999). In this model, the executive and motivational deficits both contribute to the observed symptoms of hyperactivity/impulsiveness. In contrast, the symptoms of inattention depend upon the executive deficits alone. The correlation between hyperactivity/impulsivity and inattention reflects the common effect of executive deficits coupled with the unique effect of delay aversion on hyperactivity/impulsivity. This model is essentially a more general and simplified version of the "dual pathway" model proposed by Sonuga-Barke (2002).

According to this model, the development of ADHD is the developmental outcome of two distinct processes. The first deficit is in executive processes, which may be associated with dysfunction in the prefrontal cortex and mesocortical circuits. The second deficit involves differences in motivational mechanisms, which may involve mesolimbic reward circuits. We should emphasize that this is neither a complete nor adequate theory of ADHD. Nevertheless, it seems quite plausible that executive deficits and motivational deficits are two contributory causes to the symptoms seen in many children with ADHD. As discussed earlier, however, the notion of an executive deficit is almost certainly too broad (children with ADHD do not show problems in set switching and susceptibility to interference, though they do show difficulties on speeded tasks, including the Stop-Signal Task, and on a number of working memory tasks), as is the proposal of a general arousal/motivational deficit. One final problem for such a theory is that executive deficits appear to be quite general problems that are also displayed by other groups of children, including those with autism spectrum disorders and broader learning difficulties, so that the extent to which they can be considered a specific cause of ADHD would require careful consideration.

Building on this model, Castellanos, Sonuga-Barke, Millham, and Tannock (2006) draw upon the distinction proposed by Zelazo and Muller (2000) between "cool" executive function, reflecting cognitive aspects associated with the dorsolateral prefrontal cortex, and "hot" executive function, reflecting mechanisms of motivation and emotion and associated with orbital and medial prefrontal cortex. Within this elaborated model, abnormalities either in maintaining instructional set (cool executive function) or motivational state (hot executive function), or both, may account for the variability seen in responding. However, nonreciprocal connections between these two systems suggest a hierarchy whereby emotion and/or motivation affects cognitive processing, which in turn can regulate motor outputs. Interestingly, there are synergies between this model and the conceptual model of ADHD proposed by Barkley (1997), which distinguished executive skills such as working memory, goal-directed behavior, and creativity from aspects of self-regulation such as motivation, affect, and arousal.

The highly simplified model shown in Figure 7.7 is a purely psychological model of ADHD. However, the evidence we have considered shows that ADHD is a disorder that is under strong genetic influences. Genetic risk factors appear to have clear effects on neurotransmitters in the brain (particularly dopamine and norepinephrine). The details of these genetic mechanisms are not yet understood and it seems likely that many diverse genes of small effect will be causally related to the development of ADHD. There is evidence for genetic effects on dopamine transporter mechanisms that may be related to the development of ADHD, though once again the magnitude of such effects appears to be too small to provide anything close to a complete account of the origins of the disorder (so genetic effects on the dopamine transporter mechanism will not be sufficient to account for ADHD, though such effects may be one contributory cause of the disorder).

It may be, however, that if we take a more biological view of the disorder we should not expect a coherent cognitive or psychological account of the disorder. Figure 7.8 shows a tentative "biological" view of ADHD; the empty ovals at the top of the diagram represent the likely involvement of multiple genes.

According to this model there are numerous genetic influences on dopaminergic and noradrenergic pathways in the brain. It is also assumed that patterns of activity in these two systems interact, so that activity in each system has some effect on the other. These neural systems in turn are postulated to affect the development and operation of diverse psychological processes, including executive functions, motivational processes related to reward, and potentially other unspecified motivational/cognitive systems. These processes in turn ultimately explain the symptoms whose ratings lead to a diagnosis of ADHD. Once again we would stress that this diagram is in no way intended to be a complete model of ADHD and its development. The model is incomplete and underspecified in many ways. However, we believe this model gives a different way of thinking about a disorder such as ADHD. In this model the unifying constructs are biological (abnormalities in dopaminergic and noradrenergic pathways) and such abnormalities in neurotransmitter systems may have diverse psychological functions. However, in this view there may not be any unifying psychological account for the disorder. This is a slightly disturbing prospect (at least for cognitive psychologists like us) and we have deliberately phrased this alternative in a fairly stark way. In reality, the structure of the psychological mechanisms underlying the development of ADHD may yield a clearer picture if given continued scrutiny.

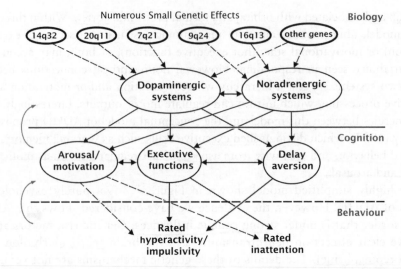

Figure 7.8   Path diagram showing a possible biological model of the origins of ADHD.

We believe, however, that in this field it may be particularly important to relate underlying biological mechanisms (gene effects on neurotransmitter systems) to psychological impairments. This is a case where the study of endophenotypes may be particularly important.

Summary and Conclusions

It is clear that our understanding of ADHD reflects an unusual and uneven state of knowledge. ADHD is a highly heritable disorder that appears related to problems in neurotransmitter function. From a practical point of view, methods for the diagnosis of ADHD have shown major advances and we have good evidence from the MTA randomized controlled trial that stimulant drugs can be an effective treatment. In contrast, our understanding of the psychological mechanisms involved in the development of ADHD remains quite limited. This reflects in part the complexity of the disorder and in part the research strategies that have dominated this area. It may be useful to contrast psychological research on ADHD with research on another disorder where our understanding is more advanced (developmental dyslexia).

In the case of dyslexia the nature of the phenotype we are trying to understand is clearly specified: it is a difficulty in mastering visual word recognition skills in reading. In this sense the deficit in dyslexia is modular (a deficit in the visual word recognition system). There are many longitudinal studies examining the typical development of word recognition skills in reading. There are also well-developed formal models of word recognition processes and their development that allow us to evaluate quite specific hypotheses about the nature of the problems that children with dyslexia experience in learning to read. Case–control studies and longitudinal studies of children at familial risk of dyslexia have converged on the conclusion that problems in the phonological component of oral language are the proximal cause of problems in learning to read in most cases of dyslexia.

In contrast, in ADHD, the "phenotype" is hard to characterize and the behaviors shown by children with ADHD can vary markedly over time and in relation to the environment they are tested in. In fact one view of the disorder is that variability of performance is one of its defining characteristics (Castellanos et al., 2005). The defining characteristics of the disorder are nonmodular and involve broad constructs such as hyperactivity, impulsivity, inattention, delay aversion, and problems of executive function and arousal (these diverse terms might be brought together under the umbrella term of behavioral regulation). There is a dearth of normative longitudinal studies on how these aspects of behavioral regulation develop, and the theories we have in this area are limited. This is also paralleled by a dearth of longitudinal studies of children with ADHD and theories of limited specificity. In summary, better specified theories of the development of behavioral regulation, coupled with more detailed characterizations of development in this area, may in turn lead to clearer hypotheses about the core deficits in ADHD. It remains likely, however, that the deficits found in children with ADHD may well be heterogeneous and will likely involve diverse aspects of cognitive and motivational functioning.

8

Autism

Autism is a severe and persistent social impairment that occurs in combination with problems of verbal and nonverbal communication, together with restricted patterns of behavior. People with autism also experience perceptual abnormalities, including both over- and undersensitivity to sensory stimuli. It was Kanner, an Austrian psychiatrist, who in 1943 first used the term autism to describe the extreme "aloneness" of children with this devastating developmental disorder. Subsequently Wing (1980) defined a triad of impairments that characterizes the classic syndrome, namely impairments of reciprocal social interaction, communication, and imagination. Together these impairments strike at the heart of sociability and it is therefore not surprising that autism is sometimes described as a pervasive developmental disorder (PDD; Gillberg, 2006). We begin this chapter with a review of findings concerning the nature and characteristics of autism before discussing methods of assessment and diagnosis. We then turn to a consideration of the typical development of sociability as a framework within which to discuss the abnormalities of reciprocal social interaction that are observed in autism. The focus of the chapter is on cognitive theories of the causes of autism and we will discuss how these may relate to its neurobiological basis and treatment.

Definition and Prevalence

Although the classic picture of autism is of a child who is aloof and passive, there is much variation within the disorder and some individuals appear "odd," intrusive, or socially inappropriate rather than withdrawn. In severe cases, a child may be mute or echolalic (i.e., echo back what is said to them). In milder cases, incessant talking can be observed, frequently dominated by the autistic person's "own agenda" and with little attention to the conventional rules of conversation. With regard to repetitive behaviors, symptoms range from rocking to and fro and a persistent preoccupation with small parts of objects (e.g., spinning wheels), through lining up toys, to special interests such as train-spotting and other obsessive behaviors. In addition, the sensory abnormalities that are experienced by children with autism can be extremely distressing and are often associated with high levels of anxiety.

Formally, according to DSM-IV (American Psychiatric Association, 1994), there are three main diagnostic criteria for autistic disorder: (1) a qualitative impairment in social interaction, which might be shown, for example, by a difficulty in developing peer relationships or a lack of social or emotional reciprocity; (2) a qualitative impairment in communication, for example difficulty in initiating and sustaining conversation or a lack of age-appropriate imaginative play; and (3) restricted, repetitive, and stereotyped behavior such as adherence to rigid rules, stereotyped and repetitive mannerisms, or a persistent preoccupation with object parts.

However, it is now widely accepted that there are a group of related conditions that have at their core an impairment of socialization and the term "autism spectrum disorders" has come into common usage to describe these difficulties (Wing & Gould, 1979). In addition to classic autism, autism spectrum disorders (ASD) include Asperger syndrome, high-functioning autism, and atypical autism. There is as yet no consensus as to the precise criteria for differentiating between these different disorders. Much research has recently tried to clarify the distinction between Asperger syndrome and high-functioning autism (Frith, 2004). Debate continues about the validity of this distinction (Prior, 2004) but many consider that Asperger syndrome is best distinguished from classic autism by the relatively well-developed language skills shown by these individuals. Nonetheless, like other developmental disorders, autism is not a static condition; the precise symptoms of autism not only change with age and education but also may vary according to the temperament of the affected person and the other skills they possess. Importantly, however, the core social impairments persist beyond these variations. In this chapter we will use the term "autism" to describe findings reported from children with the classic syndrome and "high functioning autism" when the focus has been on people with autism who have IQ within the normal range. The term autism spectrum disorder (ASD) will be used when investigators have used a broader definition when assembling their study sample. The use of the term ASD is important because it draws attention to how autism, like other disorders we have dealt with, is a dimensional disorder and how severe symptoms need to be in order for an individual to be diagnosed as having autism will sometimes be open to debate.

Based on a review of 23 epidemiological surveys conducted between 1966 and 1998, Fombonne (1999) reported that the prevalence of autism has increased in recent years from 4.3 cases per 10 000 prior to 1988 to 7.2 per 10 000 in the ensuing years. These figures suggest that, even allowing for increased rates of diagnosis, classic autism is quite a rare disorder. However, a recent UK survey estimated that 1 in every 100 children would qualify for diagnosis with some form of autism spectrum disorder (Baird et al., 2006). The reasons for this raised prevalence are not fully understood but at least in part it reflects improved recognition and detection of autism together with a broadening of the diagnostic concept and definitions (Bishop, Whitehouse, Watt, & Lione, 2008; Wing & Potter, 2002). On average, there are more boys than girls affected by autism, with a reported gender ratio of 3.8 boys to every girl. Differences in gender ratios are more pronounced among individuals of normal IQ where the ratio of boys to girls is 6:1.

Comorbidities with Other Developmental Disorders

The autistic spectrum contains children and adults with a wide range of intellectual ability and comorbid impairments and is unrelated to social class or ethnicity. Fombonne (1999) reported that some 19% of people with autism are free of intellectual impairments whereas some 42% have severe learning difficulties and 8–35% live in residential schools or homes. The high proportion of people with autism who also have severe learning difficulties (defined as an IQ below 70) is a striking aspect of the disorder. Six percent of affected individuals also have a medical condition, most commonly epilepsy (17%) but a raised incidence of Fragile X and tuberous sclerosis has also been reported. On the other hand as many as 50% of people with autism exhibit a special talent or "savant skill." Arguably, repetitive and obsessive behaviors may contribute to the development of such skills, which are highly dependent on practice (Pring, 2007).

Assessment and Diagnosis

The complexity of autism and the diversity of its behavioral manifestations mean that assessment and diagnosis are by no means straightforward. Once the domain of psychiatrists, autism assessment is now undertaken by a wide range of professionals and this has necessitated the development of standardized interview and assessment schedules (Lord & Risi, 1998). In turn, the availability of such methods has begun to have an impact on research studies, which are now more easily compared than in the past when the criteria used to recruit participants varied considerably.

The gold standard diagnostic tools for the assessment of autism are the Autism Diagnostic Observation Schedule (ADOS; Lord, Rutter, DiLavore, & Risi, 1999) and the Autism Diagnostic Interview (ADI-R; Rutter, LeCouteur, & Lord, 2003). The ADOS comprises a set of props and activities designed to elicit behaviors diagnostic of the syndrome. These behaviors are rated, yielding continuous scores that can be used to evaluate performance against diagnostic criteria for autism and autism spectrum disorders. Since the ADOS is restricted to the context of the observation environment it should ideally be used in combination with the ADI, which is a semi-structured interview for parents or caretakers covering the developmental history and the current functioning of the person being evaluated. Like the ADOS, the ADI-R provides scoring algorithms for differentiating autism from other pervasive developmental disorders. However, agreement between the two instruments is only moderate (Risi et al., 2006). In the UK, two other interview schedules are in use, the DISCO (Wing, Leekam, & Gould, 2002) and the 3Di (Skuse et al., 2004) (see Box 8.1), the latter providing agreement with the ADOS and designed to assess the current behavior of high-functioning individuals. Notably, the focus of these diagnostic tools has been on reliability and validity rather than efficiency. Briefer assessments that are useful for screening purposes and in research are provided by a number of rating scales, namely the Social Communication Questionnaire (SCQ; Rutter, Bailey, & Lord, 2003),

Box 8.1 Examples of interview questions from the 3Di (Skuse et al., 2004) relating to each part of the triad (by kind permission of the authors)

Reciprocal social interaction
When meeting someone [child] knows well outside the home, does [child] smile in greeting?
Does [child] usually share without you needing to suggest it?
Does [child] ever laugh or smile in situations that most people would find anything but funny?

Communication
Does [child] ever point spontaneously to nearby objects to express interest?
Does [child] ask questions although [child] already knows the answers?
Has [child] ever played a game in which there are several figures or animals and they are talking to one another?

Repetitive behaviors and stereotyped patterns
Was there ever a time when [child] had an absorbing interest in letters or numbers?
Has [child] ever shown any finger or hand mannerisms (e.g., hand flapping before the eyes) when excited or distressed?
Was there ever a time when [child] became absorbed in studying objects from unusual angles..?

the Childhood Autism Rating Scale (CARS; Schopler, Reichler, & Rochen-Renner, 1998), and the Social Responsiveness Scale (SRS; Constantino, 2002).

In recent years, there has been considerable interest in developing screening tools for the early identification of autism. These measures have been applied to the general population and to at-risk samples. They typically include aspects of giving, showing, and following eye gaze (Baird et al., 2000; Baron-Cohen et al., 1996). Although such screening devices can predict later autism, they also fail to detect a significant number of cases. Fombonne (1999) reported that, on average, two non-autistic children screen positive but are not found to be autistic for every child identified with autism. Notwithstanding this, more recent studies have suggested that the predictive value of screening instruments can be improved by follow-up telephone interviews and hence hold promise for the early detection of the disorder (Kleinman et al., 2008).

Theories of Autism

Early psychodynamic theories concerning the causes of autism focused on the role of poor parenting skills and Kanner (1943) had described the mothers of autistic children as being unusually cold "refrigerator mothers." However, through the pioneering work of researchers such as Hermelin and O'Connor (1967), who were among the first to apply the methods of experimental psychology to the study of developmental disorders, these theories were gradually replaced by cognitive explanations of autistic behavior. We will focus on a number of prominent theories of autism from the perspective of cognitive psychology, namely the theory of mind, executive function, weak central coherence, and the enhanced perception theories. There are other hypotheses that cut across these, for example the praxis/imitation theory (Pennington, 2002), the mirror neuron hypothesis (Hamilton, 2008; Oberman & Ramachandran, 2007; Williams, Whiten, Suddendorf, & Perrett, 2001), and the extreme male-brain theory (Baron-Cohen, 2002; Baron-Cohen & Hammer, 1997), but we do not have space to cover those here. We begin by outlining what is known about the typical development of sociability as a framework within which to consider the abnormalities of reciprocal social interaction that are observed in autism.

The Typical Development of Social Interaction

During the first year of life, infant sociability is characterized by a range of nonverbal behaviors that underpin language, communication, and social interaction. From soon after birth, infants are attracted to the human face and they look longer when faces elicit mutual gaze. By 4 months, infants can discriminate the gaze direction of another person and they can disengage attention from a central stimulus when a peripheral stimulus appears, though they cannot yet follow gaze reliably (Hood, Willen, & Driver, 1998). From 4–6 months, infants begin to show the ability to direct attention to cued spatial locations and they start to use another's head turn to locate a target if it is visible in the visual field. It is only older infants who can follow gaze alone and use it to learn about objects and faces. Thus, prior to 9 months, communication between infants and caregivers mostly consists of face-to-face turn-taking episodes that involve sharing of emotion. The term dyadic interaction (two people forming a unit) is used to describe such behaviors. Later, infants begin to coordinate the focus of their attention with that of others (joint attention) such that they enter a triadic relationship between self, other, and object and begin to use gesture to request help in obtaining things (e.g., protodeclarative pointing) (see Figure 8.1).

Joint attention has been the focus of research in relation to autism because the ability to engage in a triadic relationship is thought to be a precursor of the ability to understand the perspective and intentions of another person (referred to as theory of mind) as well as to language and other cognitive skills. In turn, theory of mind is considered a prerequisite for the development of shared and pretend play (from about 18 months; Leslie, 1987) and for more sophisticated understanding of other minds (mentalizing) around 3 years. Together these early emerging social behaviors set the stage for sibling and peer interactions and, later, social and adaptive functioning. However, although the core impairment in autism is social, it would be incorrect to assume that such difficulties reflect completely aberrant social development in infancy. For example, children with autism typically recognize familiar persons and

Figure 8.1 Picture of mother and child in triadic interaction.

respond differentially toward them. Thus, as we shall show, their impairments are selective and include problems of social orientation, joint attention, imitation, empathy, and emotional expression (Klinger & Dawson, 1996).

Joint attention in autism

Although the face is a potent stimulus for typically developing children, it has been thought for many years that infants with autism show less interest in the face than typically developing children and they tend to look less at the eye region; they also engage in less mutual gaze and some actually find direct gaze aversive. Leekham, Baron-Cohen, Perrett, and Milders (1997) showed that, on average, children with autism can detect where other people are looking but their ability to spontaneously follow a change in another person's gaze direction is developmentally delayed, sometimes by several years (and the tendency to do so depends on mental age; Leekham, Hunnisett, & Moore, 1998).

A number of different theories have been proposed to account for the delay in eye-gaze monitoring observed in autism. These include a lack of motivation to follow another person's attention, an inability to monitor and control attention, or an inherent social impairment that renders them slower to learn the associations between attention cues and affective rewards (Nation & Penny, 2008). Leekham, Lopez, and Moore (2000) used a joint attention paradigm to study the ability of preschool children with autism to orient to people and objects with and without rewards, and to shift attention from one location to another. The comparison was between 20 children with autism of higher and lower ability and 20 developmentally delayed (DD) controls matched on nonverbal IQ and aged between 2 years 10 months and 5 years 7 months. The child sat opposite the experimenter in a cubicle that also contained two black boxes, one on either side of the experimenter about one meter away. There was a "Thomas the Tank Engine" with flashing lights under the lid of each box, which could be revealed by the action of a second experimenter as a reward.

First, in a pretrial session, the experimenter tried to gain eye contact by looking at the child. If this did not succeed, she called the child by name and then, if need be, followed this with an encouraging "look at me" command. When the experimenter felt she had established contact with the child, she shifted her gaze to one of the boxes on the left or the right (which were at this stage not visible to the child). The experimenter's head-turn signaled the beginning of a trial that lasted 6 s and ended with the experimenter turning back to center her attention on the child. After four trials there was a training phase in which the second experimenter activated the train 2 s after the start of the head-turn and then a test phase in which activation of the train was contingent on the child's head-turn matching the direction of the experimenter's.

The children's gaze-following was assessed by classifying behaviors on each trial as spontaneous, learning, perseverating, or other. For children with developmental delays (DD) there was more evidence of spontaneous gaze-following than learning, whereas the opposite was the case for the autistic group. In addition, whereas 53% of the DD group consistently responded to the experimenter's bids and gaze direction, only 11% of the children with autism did so. Together, these findings are suggestive of an autism-specific delay in both dyadic and triadic interaction. Moreover, gaze-following behaviour was related to developmental level for the group with autism, with those with lower IQ faring worse than very low functioning developmentally delayed children without autism.

Evidence consistent with the view that joint attention is one of the key precursors of autism comes from a longitudinal study of 18 children with autism identified in the CHAT screening study between the ages of 20 and 43 months (Charman, 2003). At 20 months, in addition to administering tests of receptive and expressive language and nonverbal IQ, the investigators carried out observations of the children's spontaneous play, imitation, and joint attention. A number of different activities were used as settings in which to measure joint attention. In one such task, the child was shown a series of mechanical toys that provoked uncertain responses and their eye gaze was monitored. The key behavior was a gaze switch between the toy and the adult. In another task, the experimenter teased the child by offering him or her a toy and then withholding it. The key behavior was a look toward the experimenter's eyes.

When nonverbal IQ was controlled, gaze switching at 20 months correlated with receptive language at the same point in time, and it was also predictive of receptive and expressive language at 42 months. There were associations between symptom severity on the ADI-R and joint attention behaviors but these were stronger concurrently than longitudinally. Moreover, when nonverbal IQ was controlled, it was only the domain score for nonverbal communication that showed the association. Overall, the findings suggest that children who perform better on measures of joint attention show less severe social and communication difficulties at 42 months, and that early social communicative behaviors relate to language ability.

Although the findings of this study must be interpreted cautiously given the small sample size, it is interesting to note that, much later on in development, brain regions involved in gaze processing (notably superior temporal sulcus) show less sensitivity to observed shifts in gaze processing in people with ASD compared to controls. Pelphrey, Morris, and McCarthy (2005) used event-related functional MRI to show that activation in superior temporal sulcus was increased in typical adults when a manikin they viewed shifted their gaze in a direction that was inconsistent with their presumed intention (compared to consistent trials when gaze direction matched intention). In contrast, individuals with ASD showed no significant increase. Furthermore, a measure of the percentage change in activation in this brain region between congruent and incongruent trials was correlated significantly with measures of social interaction and nonverbal communication derived from the ADI-R.

Cognitive Theories of Autism

For many years, different theories of autism were regarded as competing explanations for the social difficulties that are observed. Increasingly, however, it is accepted that autism is a complex disorder that is unlikely to have a single cause (Bowler, 2007; Happé, Ronald, & Plomin, 2006; Pennington, 2006). We will begin by considering the major theories and then turn to consider these theories related to each other.

Theory of mind (mentalizing)

Parents of children with autism often report that their children seem oblivious to the feelings of others and that they can be "egocentric" in their behavior. Later in life, adults with high-functioning autism will sometimes talk about the difficulty they have in understanding what other people are thinking, or interpreting why people act in specific ways. In order to understand that another person has beliefs and desires that are different from one's own, it is necessary to have a specific kind of cognitive ability, often referred to as "theory of mind" (TOM) – the ability to impute mental states to other people (Premack & Woodruff, 1978). Within the model of Morton and Frith (1995), 'TOM' is a specific module that develops independently of general cognitive ability, and can be specifically impaired in autism. More recently, the skill has been referred to as "mentalizing" (Frith, 2003) to make clear that this is an automatic, unconscious ability and not an explicit ability to theorize as the term TOM implies.

The classic task used to assess TOM is Wimmer and Perner's (1983) false-belief task. In their original study, these authors demonstrated that 4-year-old children were able to understand that a person depicted in a scenario held a false belief about reality, and that this belief (rather than the real state of affairs) would predict their behavior. In Baron-Cohen, Leslie, and Frith's (1985) adaptation of this task, the child watches a short scenario in which two dolls appear, Sally and Anne. Sally has a basket and Anne has a box. Sally has a marble, which she puts into her basket and then she goes out for a walk. While Sally is away, Anne takes the marble from the basket and places it in her box. Then Sally returns and the child is told that she wants to play with her marble. The experimenter then asks the critical question: "Where will Sally look for her marble?" The correct answer to the question is that she will look in her basket where she thinks she has put it, and not in the box where it really is.

In this influential study, Baron-Cohen et al. tested a group of 20 children with autism using the Sally Anne task (Figure 8.2). In order to rule out the possibility that any difficulty they encountered might be due to the general cognitive demands of the task, they included two comparison groups: a group of 27 much younger typically developing children of similar mental age to the children with autism (with a mental age above 3 years), and a group of 14 children with Down syndrome (also of similar mental age). The results were striking. Whereas the majority of the typically developing children (85%) and those with Down syndrome (86%) answered correctly by pointing to the basket, only a minority of the children in the autistic group (20%) answered correctly (instead of indicating where Sally believed the marble was, they pointed to where they knew that the marble really was). The effect size for the difference between the autistic and control children was very large ($h = 1.448$) (the statistic h here is a nonparametric equivalent of Cohen's d). The authors argued from these findings that children with autism have difficulty inferring the beliefs of others and in using this information to predict their behavior. In short, they showed a deficit in TOM or an "inability to represent mental states."

A series of ingenious experiments from Uta Frith's lab went on to provide converging evidence for the TOM deficit in autism (Frith, 2003), and an important experimental control was provided by the "false-photo" task first used by Leekam and Perner (1991) to provide a parallel to the standard "false-belief" task. In the false-photo task, a cat is sitting on a chair where it is photographed. Next the cat is moved to another location (analogous to Sally's marble being moved while she is out of the room) and the child is asked "where is the cat in the photograph?" This question requires similar logic to the false-belief question. However, the physical photo still shows the old state of affairs and the child does not have to make an inference about (false) beliefs. When children with autism were compared with typically developing children of similar mental age on the false-belief and false-photo tasks the typical 4-year-olds found the false-photo task more difficult than the false-belief task, whereas the children with autism showed the opposite pattern – they understood the false-photo task perfectly but failed the Sally Anne task.

In spite of these compelling results, it could be argued that the false-belief task is actually harder than the false-photo task; this is because it requires the child both to infer a mental state and to suppress knowledge of the real state of affairs, which are in conflict with their false belief (Bowler, 2007; Perner & Leekam, 2008). A paradigm that does not suffer from this confound was used by Sodian and Frith (1992) to investigate the ability of children with autism to infer mental states in a situation

This is Sally.   This is Anne.

Sally has a basket.   Anne has a box.

Sally has a marble. She puts the marble into her basket.

Sally goes out for a walk.

Anne takes the marble out of the basket.

and puts it into the box.

Now Sally   She wants to play
comes back.   with her marble.

Where will Sally look for her Marble?

Figure 8.2 Illustration of the Sally Anne task. (Adapted from Frith, U., 2003, Chapter 10: Thinking about minds, *Autism: Explaining the Enigma*, Blackwell.)

that was demonstrably understood. This experiment involved a contrast between sabotage (preventing someone achieving their goal by physical means) and deception (preventing the same action by mental means). In the basic game, a child interacted with two puppets, a friend who was a rabbit and an enemy who was a wolf. The child had to keep a piece of candy in a box. The child was told that every time the rabbit got the candy, they would get two pieces and therefore it was in their interest to help the rabbit. On the other hand, when the wolf got the candy, the child got none so they should not help the wolf. The children engaged with the game well and had no difficulty in learning its rules. The critical contrast then was between the "sabotage" and "deception" conditions.

In the sabotage condition, the child was given a padlock and key and told they could lock the box to prevent the wolf getting the candy and open it for the rabbit. In the deception condition, the padlock was removed and the child had to use mental tactics; essentially they had to tell lies to prevent the wolf getting the candy. So, whenever the wolf asked from afar "is the box open," the skill was to say "it is locked," whereas when the rabbit asked the same question they should say "it is open." Although the children with autism could prevent the wolf stealing the candy in the sabotage condition by locking the box, they found it extremely difficult to tell the lie in the deception condition. The authors argue that these findings underline the specific problem in mentalizing that is characteristic of autism. However, their interpretation is not absolutely water-tight because the deception task (lying) requires verbal ability whereas locking a box does not. In addition, to succeed on this task requires considerable flexibility of thought, not least the ability to suppress the natural way of responding. Hence uncontrolled group differences in linguistic ability or executive skill may weaken the conclusion that the difficulty of the children with autism was specifically attributable to a TOM deficit.

A more significant issue for the TOM theory of autism is how to explain the fact that a substantial number of people with ASD pass TOM tasks, arguably at a later than normal mental age of around 10 years (Happé, 1995). It is clear that some individuals may succeed on TOM tasks through the application of logic to the understanding of mental states yet do not necessarily possess normal social competence. Arguably, more basic socioperceptual deficits may underlie their social difficulties. For example, Bowler and Thommen (2000) reported that children with ASD were less likely to notice patterns of movement involving the coordinated action of animate shapes, a skill important for the development of understanding of personal relationships. In a similar vein, Castelli, Frith, Happé, and Frith (2002) found that even high functioning adults with Asperger syndrome found it more difficult than controls of similar mental age to attribute mental states to animated shapes moving as though they were intentional agents (e.g., a blob with a down-turned head-like shape that looks sad when a "mother-like" blob ignores it).

Thus, Tager-Flusberg (2001) has suggested that it is important to distinguish two different components of TOM, a social-perceptive and a social-cognitive component. In an important study directed toward this end, Klin, Jones, Schultz, Volkmar, and Cohen (2002) used eye-tracking to study the viewing patterns of an individual with ASD and a matched control as they watched social and nonsocial scenes from a classic film. While the control participant looked to the eyes to extract meaning in the social scene, the person with ASD looked more at the mouth area. The control participant also scanned the scene more than the person with ASD. In contrast, in physical scenes, the person with ASD shifted visual attention more quickly than the control participant. The investigators went on to extend this experiment in a group study. The people with ASD focused on the mouth area of the protagonist in the film twice as often as controls and two and a half times less on their eyes. The best predictor of group membership was in fact the time spent looking at the eyes and the more participants viewed the objects rather than the people in the scenes the less socially competent they were. Although these results are striking it needs to be borne in mind that this was a small-scale study and is in need of replication. Moreover, a recent study by Back, Mitchell, and Ropar (2007) suggests that children with autism are as able to use the eye region of the face to infer mental states as controls matched on age and IQ; how they interpret information gleaned from where they are looking remains an open question.

Taking a slightly different perspective on TOM, Hobson and Meyer (2005) argued that children with autism have a lesser propensity to identify with the psychological stance of someone else and this is why they are limited in their ability to shift perspective as well as in their social competence. To test this idea, they developed the "Sticker" test in which a child sits opposite an experimenter who communicates with them about where to place a series of stickers. The basic idea is for the child to indicate, by reference to his or her own body, where the experimenter should place a sticker on their (the experimenter's) body. This is something that most 3- and 4-year-olds can do. In contrast, instead of using their own body as a point of reference, Hobson and Meyer (2005) reported that children with autism rarely used self-reference to convey an instruction to their partner – rather they tended to point to the tester. In a similar vein, Meyer and Hobson (2004) examined imitation in an assessment of self- and other-orientation in children with autism and control children with general learning difficulties. In this study, the experimenter and the child sat on a testing mat 20 inches from each other. A blue tape across the mat 5 inches from the experimenter and one 5 inches from the child demarcated their own personal areas. The experimenter placed objects for four different tests at specific locations in relation to herself, the child, and the center of the mat. She then told the child to watch while she demonstrated an action followed by, "Now you." Each action was produced in one of two orientations, close to the experimenter or close to the child. The variable of interest was the location in which the child would imitate the action (experimenter, child, center of the mat). As predicted by the theory, children with autism were less likely to imitate the action by reference to themselves when the experimenter had performed the action in relation to herself. Moreover, they showed a greater tendency than control children with general learning difficulties to do exactly what the experimenter had done in the identical location.

Taking stock of these findings, Hobson and his colleagues propose that children with autism have a biologically based deficit in the ability to relate to others as "selves" and this may underlie cognitive deficits in TOM, as well as altering other aspects of the developmental trajectory they follow. Although the difficulties highlighted by these studies are inextricably bound up with problems of communication that confound interpretation, the methods used represent an interesting avenue for future research exploring the causes of TOM deficits in autism (Bowler, 2007).

Summary: TOM in autism

There is evidence of a significant delay in the acquisition of TOM in children with autism (Happé, 1995) and even after succeeding on TOM tasks most people with autism continue to lack intuitive mentalizing skills and hence have difficulty reading others' minds. As a "theory of autism" TOM focuses on the core features of autistic people's difficulties with social relationships and interactions and assumes that these difficulties reflect a basic difficulty in representing the mental states of other people. This then is an example of a "modular" deficit that explains the social impairments seen in autism in terms of a highly specific but high-level cognitive deficit. However, contrary to an ultracognitive view, it seems likely that the TOM deficit in autism may have its origins in more primitive social behaviors that originate earlier in life than the stage at which children typically pass false-belief tasks. One problem for the theory is that a sizable proportion (at least 20%) of children with autism do pass TOM tests. Among higher functioning groups of people with Asperger syndrome who may show clear autistic-like social impairments most (73% in a study by Bowler, 1992) pass even complex TOM tests. In sum, while there is little doubt that many children with autism show clear problems on TOM tasks, the fact that many people with ASD succeed on such tasks questions the extent to which such a deficit is adequate as a causal explanation for the social impairments that are observed. It remains possible, but far from certain, that impaired development in TOM (or mentalizing) is one cause of the social impairments seen in ASD.

Executive function

Deficits in executive function have been prominent as a possible explanation for some of the deficits seen in children with ADHD (see Chapter 7) and have also been used to explain some of the deficits seen in people with autism. As we noted in Chapter 7 the breadth of processes encompassed by the term executive function makes this a potentially problematic form of explanation. The executive function theory was originally proposed as an alternative explanation for the failure of children with autism on false-belief tasks. In a nutshell, the demands of false-belief tasks include the disengagement of attention from the "here and now" to allow the suppression of reality. If children with autism suffer "executive dysfunction" this would preclude such thought. This hypothesis gained momentum because many of the behaviors observed in autism are suggestive of poor executive control, for example rigidity and perseveration, the strong liking for repetitive behaviors and rituals, and insistence on sameness (Pennington & Ozonoff, 1996). In fact, Ozonoff, Pennington, and Rogers (1991) compared individuals with high functioning autism with controls on executive function and TOM tasks and found executive deficits to be a more robust correlate of autism than TOM deficits.

Executive deficits may also provide an explanation for the deficits in imagination that are often seen as an area of impairment in autism. Turner (1999) reported widespread deficits in the ability to generate novel behavior in autism. In two sets of verbal fluency tasks, participants had to generate as many words as they could beginning with the letter F, A, or S or as many exemplars of the category Food, Animals, or Countries. Participants with autism produced fewer examples than children with general learning difficulties of the same mental age, and they failed to use self-cueing by way of phonemic or semantic clustering to aid performance. In a similar vein, they had difficulty in providing possible uses for conventional and nonconventional objects in tests of ideational fluency, and they showed less creativity in their responses. In design fluency, although they drew as many designs as controls, they made more errors that violated the rules they had been given and when these were taken into account they generated fewer novel responses. Overall the pattern of performance shown by the autistic group was consistent with an impaired ability to generate novel responses and to regulate responses, with many of the most able of the autistic children being the most impaired. Arguably, a difficulty in thinking of novel solutions may affect behavior in a wide range of situations, perhaps including social situations when behaviors can be unpredictable (Turner, 1999).

Russell and his colleagues used an ingenious range of experimental tasks to test the hypothesis that children with autism have impairments in the regulation of thought and action. In one of their first studies, Russell, Mauthner, Sharpe, and Tidswell (1991) used the nonverbal "windows task" to assess whether individuals with autism could infer the utility of a deceptive act (see Figure 8.3). In the windows task, the participant sits opposite an opponent facing two opaque boxes. Unknown to either player, one box contains a treat (a chocolate). The participant's task is to point to one of the boxes to indicate to the opponent that he or she should open it. If the opponent opens the baited box, they win the treat. If the opponent opens the empty box, the child wins. Hence, the child learns that it is best if possible to point to the empty box (so that they themselves will get the treat).

In the next phase of the experiment, there are windows in the boxes so that the child can see which one holds the treat and which is empty. The aim is to use this knowledge to tell the opponent to open the empty box, which requires an inference about the utility of deceiving the opponent. Russell et al. (1991) found that typically developing children around the mental age of 4 years could accomplish this task successfully but children with autism of similar mental age could not. Furthermore, success on the windows task related to performance on a false-belief task.

Hughes and Russell (1993) went on to suggest that children with autism might be failing deception tasks because of an inability to perform the behavioral strategy necessary for deception: that is, they could not disengage attention from the focal object (the desired chocolate in the box) in order to refer (typically by pointing) to a place where there was no object. Within this view, the windows task was difficult for the children with autism because, in addition to it requiring an appreciation of competition or deception, it involved both inhibiting a prepotent response (obtaining the chocolate) and holding an arbitrary rule in working memory ("point to the empty box to get the chocolate"). In order to differentiate failure due to a difficulty in

Figure 8.3 Experimental set-up for the windows task. (Reprinted from *Cognitive Development*, 18, Russell, J., Hala, S., and Hill, E., The automated windows task: The performance of preschool children, children with autism and children with moderate learning difficulties, p. 114, copyright (2003), with permission from Elsevier.)

disengaging attention from failure due to a difficulty in understanding deception, Hughes and Russell (1993) compared the performance of children when an opponent was present with performance when there was no opponent. In the no-opponent conditions, the experimenter sat next to the child and, like them, was able to see which box contained the chocolate treat. The experimenter had a pile of treats and on each trial placed one of these into one of the boxes while the child had their eyes closed. When the child opened their eyes, they had to indicate to the experimenter which box to open.

In the windows task, the initial experimental trial is critical because this is when the participant must first make an inference about how to "deceive" their opponent (or in no-opponent trials they must first disengage from the desired object). Seventy percent of the children with autism were not able to do this and instead of indicating the empty box they indicated the baited box containing the chocolate (compared to 37% of the mental-age-matched controls with general learning difficulties). Moreover a striking 50% of the children with autism continued to make this mistake for the subsequent 20 trials, irrespective of whether or not there was an opponent in the game. This was not true for the children with general learning difficulties who were often wrong on the first trial but then improved.

Hughes and Russell (1993) designed a second executive task with similar components to the windows task but which removed any need for competition. The task was basically to retrieve a marble from a platform in a box, but there was a complication:

a direct reach into the box broke an infrared light beam, which then caused the marble to drop through a trapdoor out of sight. To avoid this happening there were two ways to retrieve the marble (defined as "detours"). First, when a yellow light came on, the child could turn a knob on the right side of the box, which caused the marble to flip out of the box toward the child. Second, when a green light appeared, this "knob route" was not available but the child could use a switch on the left side of the box to extinguish the light beam and thereby allow a direct reach. The task was easy to understand and, unlike the windows task, it did not require a referential act.

Forty autistic participants aged 6–19 years took part in this study, along with 25 learning disabled (LD) participants of the same age and 20 typically developing preschoolers. Although the task was extremely easy for the typically developing children, and more than 90% of the LD group successfully retrieved the marble using the "switch" (detour) route, only 55% of the group with autism did so. The group with autism made a number of different errors, including persevering in their use of the direct route, repeating a previously successful strategy (touching the knob), and failing to follow up one successful strategy (the switch route) with another one.

Together these data suggest that participants with autism have difficulties disengaging from a salient object even when no interpersonal competition is involved. However it is noteworthy that they had no trouble using the "knob route" to retrieve the marble. The feature that sets this detour route apart from the "switch route" is the direct causal connection between the knob turn and the marble retrieval. In contrast, the "switch route" required the planning of two sequential strategies. Thus, the problem that children with autism have does not appear to be simply one of disengaging; rather, it might be better characterized as a difficulty in inferring and/or using arbitrary means-ends combinations of rules.

Hughes, Russell, and Robbins (1994) followed up these observations by assessing children with autism on two executive tasks: the intradimensional/extradimensional (ID/ED) shift task (which taps some of the same processes as the Wisconsin Card Sorting Task but is easier; see Box 8.2) and an analogue of the Tower of Hanoi task (see Figure 7.1) assessing planning ability.

As expected, the autistic group were significantly more impaired than the group with learning difficulties in the ID/ED shift task. Although they performed like mental-age-matched controls on the pretransfer trials (stages 1–5) and on the intradimensional shift and reversal (stages 6 and 7), they had difficulty with the extradimensional shift (stages 8 and 9), behaving as if they were "stuck-in-set". Thus, they had difficulty in disengaging from the patterns that had been reinforced over the earlier trials.

The planning task involved two sets of three colored balls shown in three "stockings" in the lower half of the computer screen. The child's task was to copy the three stockings in the upper display, moving one ball at a time (by touching it and touching an empty stocking). For each test, a yoked problem required the child to follow a series of moves executed by the computer, which provided baseline information on motor initiation and execution times. Problems that required four or five moves to completion proved difficult, especially for the autistic group. Only 13% of the children with autism could solve half of these problems, compared with 49% of the

LD and 65% of the typically developing group. Moreover, data from the yoked problems indicated that the difficulty of the children with autism could not be attributed to motor impulsivity, initial latencies, or execution times. Rather their problems seemed to reflect a difficulty in following arbitrary rules.

Box 8.2   The ID/ED task (Reprinted from *Neuropsychologia*, 32, Hughes, C., Russell, J., Robbins, T., Evidence for executive dysfunction in autism, 481, copyright (1994), with permission from Elsevier.)

The ID/ED shift task is a nonverbal task that requires some of the same processes as the Wisconsin Card Sorting Task. It involves nine stages, with the child progressing to the next stage when they reach a predetermined criterion. The task can therefore be used to determine exactly at what point the child encounters difficulty.

In the ID/ED shift task the participant is shown a display of four boxes on a computer screen, two at the top and two at the bottom. In each trial, two different patterns are displayed in two of these boxes (the location is varied but this is not relevant); the task is to decide which is correct (and feedback is given).

The child is given the following instructions:
One of the patterns is correct, and one is wrong. Have a guess at which is correct. If you have made the correct choice, the computer will show the word *correct* in green. If you get it wrong the computer will show the word *wrong* in red. After the child learns the correct pattern to point to (stage 1), the contingencies change (stage 2) and the task proceeds:

- At stage 3, white lines are introduced into the boxes with the figures; the contingencies remain the same.
- At stage 4, the white lines are superimposed on the figures; the contingencies remain the same.
- At stage 5 the contingencies are reversed.
- At stage 6 there is a critical "intradimensional shift" in which it is now necessary to choose one of two new shapes.
- At stage 7 the contingencies are reversed.
- At stage 8 there is an extradimensional shift. At this point, the child has to respond to a further new set of exemplars for which the contingencies are related to the white lines that were only randomly reinforced in the earlier stages.
- At stage 9 there is a final reversal.

Box 8.2 *(cont'd)*

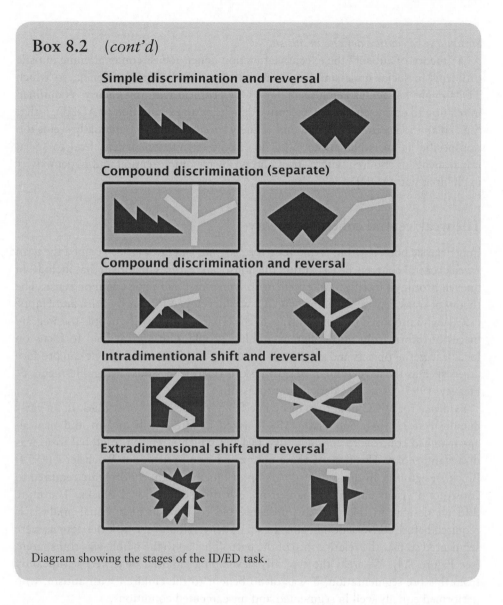

Diagram showing the stages of the ID/ED task.

These findings underline the problems that children with autism have on executive function tasks. Indeed, it is striking that no subject with autism passed both the ID/ED and the Tower of London tests and 67% failed both tests. What is less clear is how to interpret the findings in relation to the behavioral symptoms of autism. Going beyond failure on TOM tasks and the demonstration of executive function deficits, Russell and his colleagues have suggested that there is a primary deficit in intentionality in autism and, as a consequence of this, their mental lives lack the necessary control to develop a concept of themselves as agents. This in turn could be the basis of a deficit in theory of mind. Although intriguing, this hypothesis is difficult to test and must remain speculative in the absence of longitudinal, prospective data.

Summary: Executive deficits in autism

As a "theory of autism" the executive function deficit focuses on explaining autistic problems in social understanding in terms of a broad cognitive deficit, to which TOM might be seen as being secondary. One problem with this theory, as outlined in relation to our discussion of executive deficits as an explanation of ADHD, is that the explanation seems too broad and vaguely specified. It also potentially seems too nonspecific as an explanation: Why do executive function deficits lead to social impairments in children with autism and problems of inattention and hyperactivity in children with ADHD?

The weak central coherence theory

In her classic book *Autism: Explaining the Enigma*, Uta Frith (1989) coined the term "weak central coherence" to capture the nonsocial features of autism that include an uneven profile of intelligence, excellent rote memory, and poor common sense. The theory of weak central coherence (WCC) was developed further by Frith and Happé (1994) who proposed that, in contrast to the typical tendency for people to integrate pieces of information into coherent wholes, people with autism tend to focus on local features of objects and situations. Importantly, this processing style can produce assets such as the development of savant skills (Hermelin, 2001; Pring, Hermelin, & Heavey, 1995), as well as deficits in processing.

Evidence for WCC in autism has come from a wide range of studies. In an early demonstration, Shah and Frith (1983) asked children with autism and mental-age-matched controls to complete two tasks in which attention to global form was disadvantageous. The first of these comprised two versions of Wechsler's (1974) Block Design test. In the standard version of Block Design, children are required to construct a visual pattern (design) from 2–9 three-dimensional blocks. The more difficult designs in this task are unsegmented so that detailed visual analysis is required before construction begins. In a parallel version of the task the designs were segmented so that the relationship of the parts (blocks) to the whole was transparent (see Figure 8.4). Whereas the typically developing children benefited significantly from this pre-segmentation, it was of no benefit to the children with autism, who performed equally well in segmented and unsegmented conditions.

The second task was the Children's Embedded Figures test (Witkin, Oltman, Raskin, & Karp, 1971). Here the child has to locate a small detail (e.g., a triangle) embedded in a larger form (e.g., a child's pram). To complete the task, which is timed, the child has to ignore the global form during the search for the target object. The children with autism outperformed the typically developing children on the embedded figures task, underlining their superior attention to detail and/or ability to inhibit the global context.

An important feature of the WCC theory is that it is not modality specific. Evidence of the failure to integrate information in context has also been drawn from demonstrations in the auditory and verbal domains. Heaton, Pring, and Hermelin (2001) reported that children with autism show an unusually good ability to detect the

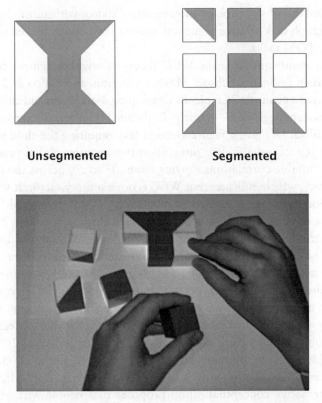

Unsegmented **Segmented**

Figure 8.4 Illustration of Block Design in segmented and unsegmented form.

individual tones in musical chords. Foxton et al. (2003) went on to ask individuals with ASD and typically developing controls to judge the similarity between sequences of pure tones requiring matching of pitch direction changes. When features of the melody (such as the actual pitches and time points of pitch direction) were altered, controls found this task harder whereas the performance of the ASD group was unaffected by changes in the coherence of the auditory whole.

In the verbal domain, excellent rote memory and, in particular, the ability of people with autism to recall unstructured word lists (Hermelin & O'Connor, 1967; Tager-Flusberg, 1991), is consistent with the notion of WCC but this finding has not always been replicated (Lopez & Leekam, 2003). In a similar vein the frequent occurrence of "hyperlexia" (Nation, 1999) among individuals with ASD reflects a tendency to focus on lower-level reading skills without paying attention to context. A popular task for investigating this tendency is the homograph task (Frith & Snowling, 1983), in which the participant reads a sentence containing an ambiguous word (e.g., the actor came on stage and made a big *bow*). The position of the ambiguous word in the sentence is varied (early versus late), as is the frequency of the different pronunciations of the homograph (high–low). Snowling and Frith (1986) reported that the children with autism of low but not high verbal mental age found it difficult to take context into account when reading homographs, and Happé

(1997) extended this observation by showing that children with autism have difficulties on the homograph task relative to mental-age-matched controls even if they succeed on first-order TOM tasks.

However, a significant issue for WCC theory is whether central coherence is a unitary construct. Pellicano, Gibson, Maybery, Durkin, and Badcock (2005) assessed the correlation in a group of 76 typically developing 4- to 5-year-old children between different tests tapping WCC, namely Embedded Figures, Pattern Construction (a version of Block Design), a Figure-Ground task requiring the child to find hidden shapes, and a test of visual-motor integration that requires global processing. They found highly variable correlations ranging from .03 to .70 across the different pairings of measures, which indicates that WCC is not a unitary factor. It was also found that correlations between measures of WCC and TOM were weak. A follow-up study using the same measures (Pellicano, Maybery, Durkin, & Maley, 2006) assessed 40 5- to 7-year-old children with ASD and typically developing children who acted as controls. The children with ASD performed better than controls on the embedded figures, pattern construction, and figure-ground tasks, and worse on the visual-motor integration task; however, performance on the four different tasks did not intercorrelate in either group, once again arguing against the notion of a domain-general factor of weak central coherence. Futhermore, a number of negative findings now cast doubt on the strong version of WCC theory (Clarke, 2005; Lopez & Leekam, 2003; Mottron, Burack, Iarocci, Belleville, & Enns, 2003; O'Riordan, Plaisted, Driver, & Baron-Cohen, 2001; Ropar & Mitchell, 1999). In this light, an important alternative conceptualization proposes that people with autism possess enhanced perceptual function (e.g., Mottron & Belleville, 1993).

A clear demonstration of enhanced perception in autism comes from a study by O'Riordan et al. (2001), who found that individuals with autism show superior performance in visual search tasks. Visual search tasks are used widely in experimental psychology to investigate attentional processing and they have also been adapted for clinical use. Search tasks are of two types: Feature search requires the detection of a target that is uniquely defined by one feature (e.g., a blue X in an array of red Ts and green Xs), and conjunctive search involves searching for a target that shares each of its features with the distractors (e.g., a red cross in an array of red Ts and green Xs). The basic findings are that feature search is a parallel process for which search time is relatively independent of the number of distractors, whereas conjunctive search shows a more linear increase in time with the number of distractors, indicative of a serial search process. In their first experiment, O'Riordan et al. (2001) asked 6- to 9-year-old children with autism to search displays of 5, 15, or 25 elements arranged in a square array and measured the reaction time (RT) to indicate whether or not a target was present. Stimuli varied in color (red or green) and shape (S, T, or X). In the feature search conditions the target was defined uniquely by form, and in conjunctive search conditions the target was unique in its combination of form and color.

The pattern of results from the control group (who were matched to the clinical group in age and IQ) was as expected: feature search was a relatively easy parallel process and conjunctive search was harder with longer RTs that increased with the

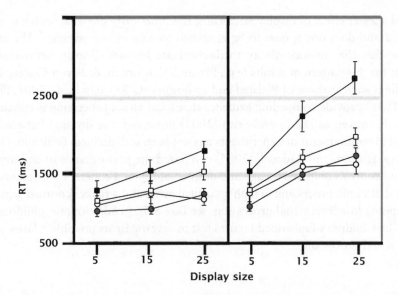

Figure 8.5 Response times for visual search for target present (left panel) and target absent (right panel) trials for group with autism (open symbols) and a control group (filled symbols). The groups did not differ in the feature search task (circles) but the group with autism was faster in the conjunctive search task (squares). (O'Riordan, Plaisted, K., Driver, J., and Baron-Cohen, S., Superior visual search in autism. *Journal of Experimental Psychology: Human Perception and Performance*, 27, p. 722, 2001, published by the American Psychological Association and or adapted with permission.)

size of display (see Figure 8.5). The children with autism showed a similar pattern in the feature search condition but for them the increase in mean RT for conjunctive search was less marked and the increase in RT with display size was not as dramatic. There were also significant differences between the groups in the target absent trials – the increased time taken to complete these trials over target-present ones was less for those in the group with autism. This finding can be taken as indicative of a less exhaustive search process.

A possible limitation of this experiment is that the feature search task may not be sensitive enough to demonstrate group differences, perhaps because of a ceiling effect on performance. To counter this possible criticism, the authors designed a second experiment that included a harder feature search task. In this task, stimuli were distinguished from one another by a featural difference along a single stimulus dimension. In the easy version the task was to detect an oblique line in an array of vertical lines; in the hard task the stimulus features were reversed and the task was to detect a vertical line among oblique lines. The relative difficulty of the latter task is referred to as the "search asymmetry effect."

For the control group, the overall RT and the increase in RT with larger display sizes were greater when detecting a vertical line among oblique lines than in the reverse case. Once again, the children with autism performed like controls in the easy task but in the asymmetric version they were not slowed down to the same extent and they showed a lesser effect of display size. Thus, the superiority of visual search in autism is robust and does not appear to be restricted to conjunctive searches. The authors propose that the superior ability to discriminate between display items may well account for this pattern of results (e.g., Plaisted, O'Riordan, & Baron-Cohen, 1998).

Findings such as those of Plaisted and colleagues (O'Riordan et al., 2001; Plaisted et al., 1998) provide compelling evidence that local visual processing is enhanced in autism. However, as Dakin and Frith (2005) point out, the division between local and global requirements of experiments has not been well defined. Pellicano, Gibson, Maybery, Durkin, and Badcock (2005) compared the performance of children with ASD and controls matched on age and nonverbal IQ on a coherent motion task tapping global visual processing in higher cortical areas and a flicker contrast sensitivity task tapping low-level visual processing (see Box 8.3). In addition, the children completed the Children's Embedded Figures test to investigate its possible relationship to global visual processing.

Box 8.3   Coherent motion and contrast sensitivity tasks

Tests of coherent motion involve assessing a person's sensitivity to patterns of movement. This is typically assessed using computer-controlled displays of small dots or squares (see below). If each dot moves in a different, randomly selected direction, no "direction" of movement can be seen. If, however, all the dots move in the same direction (say, horizontally from left to right) we can see clearly that the dots are moving in one direction. To measure people's sensitivity to coherent motion, displays are presented that vary in the proportion of dots moving in the same direction. In this way a threshold measure can be obtained: How many dots need to move in the same direction for the person to be able to accurately report the direction of movement? Typically people can detect the direction of movement when somewhere between 10 and 20% of the dots move in the same direction. This measure has been interpreted as a measure of the sensitivity of the magnocellular visual system. Examples of such random dot coherent motion displays can be viewed online at *http://viperlib.york.ac.uk/*. See, for example:

> *http://viperlib.york.ac.uk/scripts/Portweb.dll?field=filename&op=matc hes&value=seq1.mov&template=main_record&catalog=proto1*

Contrast sensitivity is a measure of the limit of visibility for low contrast patterns – how faded or washed-out images can be before looking just a gray blur. Contrast sensitivity is usually measured using black and white stripes. More precisely the stripes vary continuously in the form of a sine wave grating from dark to light. This is illustrated in the figure below, which shows a sine wave

Box 8.3 *(cont'd)*

grating that varies from high spatial frequency at the right (narrow stripes) to low spatial frequency at the left (broad stripes). The contrast of the stripes (difference in relative luminance) varies from top to bottom; so the top of the figure looks uniformly gray to most people while the stripes appear quite clear at the bottom of the figure. Notice also that the stripes appear to remain clearer higher up in the middle spatial frequencies. This reveals that the visual system is more sensitive to variations in contrast in the middle range than at very high (fine stripes) or very low (broad stripes) spatial frequencies

Image supplied by kind permission of Izumi Ohzawa at the Visual Neuroscience Laboratory, Osaka University, Japan (*http://ohzawa-lab.bpe.es.osaka-u.ac.jp/*).

The global motion task consisted of 100 bright dots randomly distributed on a dark background. On each trial, a variable proportion of the dots moved coherently up or down amongst the randomly moving dots and the child simply had to indicate whether the movement was up or down. The contrast sensitivity task required the child to detect the flicker in one of two 1 s stimulus intervals. Both tasks used an adaptive procedure with feedback to vary the difficulty of the perceptual task; an individual's threshold was determined to be that at which performance was 75% correct. The majority of the ASD group showed elevated thresholds on the global dot motion task although there was a wide variation of thresholds within the group, whereas their performance was indistinguishable from that of controls in the flicker task. Overall, the ASD group were quicker to find the figures in the embedded figures, replicating previous findings. Intriguingly, there was a significant negative relationship between global motion thresholds and mean time taken on the embedded figures test for children with ASD but not for those in the control group (perhaps because of the restricted range of scores in the motion detection task for the typically developing children).

One limitation of this study is that the two groups were not matched for verbal ability. Nonetheless it is noteworthy, as the authors point out, that any uncontrolled differences in IQ did not translate into differences on the flicker task. They go on to suggest that the children with autism may have difficulty recruiting additional cooperative processes in higher cortical areas that are necessary to perceive global coherent motion.

The accumulation of evidence pointing to perceptual abnormalities in autism has led to a growing interest in whether these may contribute to the social impairments that are observed. In relation to this, one promising line of enquiry concerns the perception of what is known as "biological motion," the kinds of movements associated with human behavior.

Blake, Turner, Smoski, Pozdol, and Stone (2003) assessed the ability of 8- to 10-year-old children with autism to perceive biological motion. As a control task, they included a difficult perceptual grouping task. The biological motion sequences were animations based on video recordings of a person engaged in a range of activities such as kicking, jumping, and climbing, compiled by placing markers on the joints of the person in each frame. Sequences of normal biological motion were presented, each for 1 s, along with an equal number of phase-scrambled sequences consisting of identical individual dots in which it was not possible to discern biological motion. The child's task was to report which display was moving like a person.

For the global form task, the screen was split into four quadrants filled with short lines at random orientations. In one quadrant at random there was a small group of eight lines forming a quasi-circle. The clarity of this target was varied by introducing "jitter" into the orientation of the elements of the circle. Over trials, the degree of jitter varied adaptively and the jitter threshold at which a participant could perform at the 71% correct level was determined. Since this was a difficult task, it started with very easy trials for practice and participants only proceeded to the main experiment when they were performing accurately in the practice phase – in fact only 12 out of 25 children with autism recruited could complete the task. The mental age of these children was equivalent to the chronological age of the typically developing control group.

Although there was no difference in jitter threshold between the clinical and control groups, the children with autism found it more difficult to detect biological motion. Interestingly, there was a correlation between the severity of autism, as indicated by the ADOS-G ($r = .66$) and CARS ($r = .66$) total scores, and performance on the biological motion task. However, there was also a strong correlation between mental age and performance on the biological motion task ($r = .75$), which may account for this relationship. The authors suggest that the neural mechanisms for integrating local motion signals into global coherent biological activity are compromised in autism, consonant with the findings of Pellicano et al. (2005) discussed above. More speculatively, the findings may go some way toward explaining the deficits in recognition of facial expressions and in following gaze direction in autism.

Summary: Weak central coherence as a theory of autism
Children with autism show a variety of abnormalities on measures of perceptual functioning. Originally, it was suggested that these perceptual abnormalities could be captured by the notion of WCC. Unfortunately, further research has suggested that different tasks designed to measure this construct do not really hang together. We are therefore left with a set of findings that are a little difficult to summarize, but the striking thing is that children with autism do perform very well on a number of low-level perceptual tasks, which suggests an unusual ability to process detailed information. Clinically, people with autism quite often show unusual responses to sensory stimuli (particularly sounds) and these responses may reflect abnormalities in low-level sensory processes. It remains difficult, however, to assess the possible role of these perceptual differences in autism as causes of other symptoms in the disorder. With few exceptions (e.g., Blake et al., 2003), correlations between measures of perceptual functioning and measures of autistic symptoms have not often been reported; if perceptual differences in autism cause other symptoms, they should correlate with them.

Is there a single theory of autism?

A case can be made that each of the three theories of autism we have discussed may play some role in explaining the symptoms of the disorder. However, a growing number of both published and unpublished studies have failed to replicate classic findings (see Bowler, 2007, for a comprehensive analysis of some of the inconsistencies between studies of the cognitive impairments found in children with autism). The reasons for conflicting findings are varied and to some extent null results may reflect broadening of the criteria for ASD (resulting in samples with less severe impairments being studied). However, another possibility is that different aspects of the autistic triad each require different causal theories and it is not going to be possible to develop a single, unitary theory of autism. Indeed, it may be the case that there is fractionation of the triad, particularly as development brings about improvements, for example, in language skills. In short, there is a pressing need for studies to consider how well different theories of autism account for the behavioral symptoms that characterize the disorder and to quantify the overlap of different deficits at the level of individual cases.

Individual differences in autism spectrum disorders

Our previous discussion has focused on three of the main cognitive theories of autism but we have alluded to the possibility that a comprehensive theory of autism is likely to be multifactorial. It is also important to try to understand how autism relates to other developmental disorders and to identify deficits that are specific and universal to autism in contrast to those that cut across disorders (Morton & Frith, 1995).

Relationships between cognitive deficits and autistic behaviors

In order to investigate the relationship between TOM, executive function (EF) deficits, and autistic symptomatology, Joseph and Tager-Flusberg (2004) assessed 31 verbally able children with autism or pervasive developmental disorder not otherwise specified (PDD-NOS), aged between 5 and 14 years. In addition to assessments of language skill and nonverbal ability, the children participated in a series of tasks tapping TOM and EF skill. Overall, performance on TOM tasks was correlated with performance on EF tasks, but when language skill and nonverbal ability were controlled the only correlation that remained significant was between TOM and one of the EF tasks, the "Knock-Tap" task (see Box 8.4). Since this task requires inhibition and working memory, as does success on a false-belief task, this finding is in line with the hypothesis proposed by the Russell group that EF deficits may explain performance on TOM tasks.

The authors went on to examine the relationship between TOM and EF performance and symptom severity as assessed by ADOS-scores in three domains: communication, social interaction, and repetitive behaviors. Both TOM and EF abilities were inversely related to ADOS communication symptoms but neither construct related to reciprocal social interaction or repetitive behaviors once language was controlled. Using a different measure of symptom severity derived from the 3Di (Skuse et al., 2004), White (2006) provided converging evidence of a relationship between TOM and communication ability. However, in the sample as a whole, performance on cognitive tasks predicted only a small amount of variance in behavior, with TOM being a stronger predictor than EF skills.

Pellicano et al. (2006) extended this approach to investigate the relationships between WCC, TOM, and EF and to examine how well these measures predicted symptom severity in the autistic group. Once again, this study incorporated several

Box 8.4   The "Knock-Tap" task

The Knock-Tap task is a test of executive function suitable for preschool children. It is based on Luria's work and requires the child to knock on the table (with their fist) when the experimenter taps the table (with the palm of his or her hand) and to tap when the experimenter knocks. In order to complete this task successfully, the child has to inhibit the natural (or prepotent) response (copying the examiner exactly) in order to execute the new action according to the specified rule. The child is first asked to tap when the experimenter taps and then, in the conflict condition, to make the opposite response (knock).

measures of each construct and symptom severity was assessed using the ADI. In addition to showing group differences in all three cognitive domains, Pellicano et al. reported that group membership could be predicted for 99% of cases from six tasks, namely embedded figures, visual-motor integration, the figure-ground task, TOM, pattern construction, and Tower of London. Thus, measures tapping each construct were needed in order to differentiate children with autism from controls.

To assess the prevalence of different deficits, the number of children with ASD who fell more than 1 SD below that of the control mean was calculated for each variable (above the mean in the case of WCC tasks). For WCC tasks, fast performance on embedded figures was found in 92% of children with ASD and superior performance on pattern construction and figure-ground task in 78 and 92%. On TOM tasks, 68% of the ASD group showed deficits and between 28–55% showed EF deficits, depending on the measure used. Thus, this study provided validation for each of the three main cognitive theories of autism. However, it provided no evidence of an association between cognitive deficits in any of the three domains and the severity of autism symptoms.

Taken together, these findings suggest that cognitive deficits are not strong predictors of autistic symptoms at the behavioral level. However, it is important to bear in mind that autistic behaviors might be considered complex outcomes of a developmental process that begins in infancy and is modified through environmental experience. Reciprocal interactions between language and sociability as well as compensatory processes may complicate the behavioral picture. A further possibility is that the domains of impairment that characterize the triad may not reflect the optimal way of classifying different behaviors to relate back to cognitive deficits. The kind of multivariate study that we have described above represents an important approach that needs to be extended to longitudinal studies that explore the developmental trajectories of autistic behaviors and underlying cognitive skills.

Autism and language impairment

In the early days of its investigation, autism was considered to be a language impairment. However, although communication deficits are a key feature of the autistic triad, a wide range of communicative behaviors are observed: Some individuals with autism have little speech or are mute, while others speak fluently but use language pedantically. Furthermore, idiosyncratic use of vocabulary as well as unusual prosody is common. In general, it is believed that the development of grammar and syntax is in line with mental age in autism, though some specifically abnormal linguistic features have been documented, for example difficulty with the use of pronouns (especially I and me).

Tager-Flusberg and Joseph (2003) assessed the language skills of 89 children with autism aged between 4 and 14 years and presented data bearing on the language profiles of 44 of these children whose nonverbal IQ fell within the typical range. The assessment battery consisted of tasks tapping speech articulation, nonword repetition, morpheme generation, receptive and expressive vocabulary, and tests of receptive and expressive language. The children were divided into three subgroups based on their language skills: those with typical language (total language score >85 on a standardized test), borderline language (70–84), or impaired language (language score <70). The children with impaired language had normal speech-articulation but they showed impairments of grammar and vocabulary. Furthermore, their performance was impaired on two tests considered to be markers of language impairment, nonword repetition, and morpheme generation. This group profile was borne out well at the level of the individuals in the group, suggesting there is validity in postulating an SLI subtype of autism.

In contrast to children with structural language impairments characteristic of SLI, children with high-functioning autism (especially Asperger syndrome) do not exhibit appreciable language delay or disorder. However, they can be very literal in their understanding. To provide an example, a child with autism commented that there would be "no point choosing a rock cake to eat because it would be too hard." More generally, people with autism have difficulty using language for the purpose of communication (pragmatics). Pragmatic difficulties affect the form and use of language and encompass difficulties in communicating what is relevant in a given situation, speaking in an inappropriate register for the context, and failing to respect the turn-taking rules of conversation. Children with "pragmatic language impairment" (Bishop, 1998), sometimes referred to as semantic pragmatic disorder, are also prone to misunderstand what is being said because they are overliteral or dominated by their own agenda.

For many years there has been debate about the degree of overlap between autism, pragmatic language impairment, and Asperger syndrome. According to Bishop (1989), the interrelationship between these three disorders can be described according to two continua: meaningful verbal communication and interests, and social relationships (see Figure 9.1). Within this view, individuals with pragmatic language impairment lie in between people with autism and people with Asperger syndrome in terms of meaningful verbal communication but they show more typical interests and social relationships. More recent research has suggested that it is very difficult to differentiate these subtypes of communication impairment, and there may be limited utility in doing so. A more productive way forward is to focus on dimensions of language skill, such as grammatical ability or pragmatic skills, and to consider how these relate to individual differences among children with autism.

One aspect of language skill that has been investigated in detail in children with ASD is inferencing ability. Poor inferencing might be considered an aspect of the difficulty people with autism have in integrating information in context (WCC) and this difficulty may be at the root of difficulties in reading (Snowling & Frith, 1986) as well as spoken language comprehension (Joliffe & Baron-Cohen, 1999). Norbury and Bishop (2002) compared children with high functioning autism, children with pragmatic language impairment (PLI), and children with SLI with typically developing children matched for age and nonverbal ability on a story comprehension task. To comprehend well, it was necessary for the children to remember literal information from the stories and to make text-connecting and gap-filling inferences. Their comprehension was assessed by asking them to answer questions after they had heard the stories.

Overall, there was a group difference in comprehension, and for all children the questions requiring gap-filling inferences were significantly more difficult than the questions requiring literal information or text-connecting inferences. However, the group difference masked considerable variability within each of the groups and an analysis of individuals found that the "poor comprehender" profile applied to 25% of the children with SLI, 33% of the PLI group, and 50% of the children with autism. Furthermore, 70% of the children with autism had specific difficulty in answering questions that required inferences as compared to questions requiring them to provide literal information. These findings are in line with the predictions of the WCC theory of autism; however it is worth noting that such problems were not only seen in the group with autism, and not all of the children with autism showed them.

Norbury (2005) went on to conduct an experimental investigation of another important aspect of spoken and written language comprehension, namely the ability to suppress irrelevant information. This study used a novel design feature, which was to compare children with ASD who also fulfilled criteria for language impairment (ASD-L) with children with autism whose verbal skills were within the normal range (ASD-O). It also included two comparison groups: children with language impairment (LI) and typically developing controls (TD). The groups were matched for age and their nonverbal IQs were all within the normal range (though the LI group had lower nonverbal scores). The LI and ASD-L groups were impaired on all language measures but did not differ from each other, and nor did the ASD-O and TD groups.

Norbury (2005) used a modification of a paradigm devised by Gernsbacher and Faust (1991) to assess contextual facilitation and suppression processes in language comprehension. The paradigm makes use of the fact that ambiguous words (e.g., *bank*) have a dominant (*money*) and a subordinate (*river*) meaning; it is thought that, during language comprehension, both meanings of ambiguous words are initially activated but inappropriate meanings are subsequently suppressed to ensure the development of a coherent memory representation that does not include irrelevant details.

Having first established that the children in this study knew both dominant and subordinate meanings of a set of 22 ambiguous words, these words were placed in sentence frames that primed either the dominant or the subordinate meaning of the ambiguous word. The child's task was to listen to the sentence and then they were shown a picture and they had to decide if it "fitted" the sentence. The first condition assessed contextual facilitation, which was done by comparing the accuracy and RT for the picture verification task in two contexts: when the picture followed a neutral sentence (e.g., "he ran from the bank"), and when it followed a biased sentence context that primed the ambiguous word (e.g., "he stole from the bank"). The second condition investigated suppression by comparing accuracy and RT to reject the picture of an ambiguous word (e.g., *river*) following an ambiguous sentence (e.g., "he stole from the bank") and accuracy and RT for picture rejection following a nonambiguous sentence (e.g. "he stole from the shop"). Processing of both dominant and subordinate meanings was tested in both conditions.

All groups were faster and more accurate when judging pictures following biased as opposed to neutral sentences and dominant meanings were processed faster than subordinate meanings. The LI and ASD-L groups showed less contextual facilitation in terms of accuracy than the groups with typical language, perhaps because they had difficulty in using the semantics of the verbs in the sentence to generate contextual expectancies. Turning to suppression, all groups were slower to reject irrelevant picture meanings following ambiguous sentences, suggesting that the subordinate meaning of the ambiguous word remained active over the 1000-ms interval and interfered with processing. The results of this study suggest that neither a difficulty in contextual processing nor a difficulty with suppression is a specific or universal feature of autism. With regard to both the contextual facilitation and suppression effects, there was some evidence of impairment in the groups with poor language but the group with ASD who had verbal skills within the normal range were unimpaired.

Taken together, the findings from work that compares children with ASD and children with language impairment underlines the fact that it is essential to control for language level when assessing the performance of individuals with autism. There would appear to be good evidence of overlap between ASD and LI in some individuals (suggestive of an SLI subtype of autism), while problems of pragmatics are not exclusive to this subtype. In turn, not all children with pragmatic problems have problems with integrative processes such as making inferences, but these two difficulties commonly co-occur in ASD (Norbury & Bishop, 2007).

Autism and ADHD

Although it is not conventional to diagnose ADHD in a child with autism (Reiersen, Constantino, Volk, & Todd, 2007), comorbidities between ASD and ADHD may account for some of the reported research findings, particularly in relation to executive deficits (see Chapter 7). In addition, many children with ADHD are rated by their parents as showing pragmatic language impairments (Bishop & Baird, 2001), suggesting an overlap in language profiles.

In one of the most comprehensive studies to date, Geurts, Verte, Oosterlaan, Roeyers, and Sergeant (2004) compared children with high functioning autism with children with ADHD and typically developing controls across five major domains of executive functioning: inhibition, visual working memory, planning, cognitive flexibility, and verbal fluency. The group with autism were indistinguishable from the ADHD group (who were tested off medication) on tests of inhibition, switching attention, and fluency but they had more difficulty with tasks requiring planning and cognitive flexibility. These findings suggest that the executive profiles of the two disorders may be different, a point also made by Pennington and Ozonoff (1996) in their seminal review. For present purposes the important point is that future studies should take account of symptoms of inattention and hyperactivity (as well as language) when theorizing about the core deficits in autism. More generally, the overlap between autism and other developmental disorders is a complicating factor that requires further research if we are to refine theoretical understanding of this complex developmental disorder.

Etiology of Autism

Despite the complexities of autism at the level of cognition and behavior, a considerable research effort has been directed toward understanding its biological bases. Given heterogeneity in behavior across the autism spectrum and possible comorbid conditions, it is perhaps not surprising that research evidence is in a state of flux. We briefly discuss what is known, with the proviso that this will be subject to change as theories of autism are refined.

Genetics of autism

Family and twin studies show evidence for a powerful role of genetic risk factors in the development of autism. Folstein and Rutter (1977) were the first to show that there was a higher concordance rate for autism in monozygotic than in dizygotic twins, suggestive of a genetic etiology. More recently, LeCouteur et al. (1996) extended these findings to show that nonconcordant twins often experience cognitive or social deficits constituting a broader phenotype of autism.

Although heritability estimates for autism are as high as 90%, progress in finding susceptibility genes has been disappointing. To some extent this might be because of variability in the phenotype of autism as well as genetic heterogeneity, with up to 15 genetic regions thought to be contributing to the risk (Gupta & State, 2006). In short, it is clear that multiple gene loci will be involved, each of small effect (Maestrini, Paul, Monaco, & Bailey, 2000).

In the absence of strong leads as to the loci of genes implicated in autism, a number of groups have conducted whole genome scans using DNA from pairs of relations that share the disorder. Using this technique, gene markers were identified on chromosomes 2, 7, 16, 17, and 19 by the International Molecular Genetic Study of Autism Consortium (IMGSAC, 1998), with the most consistent results across studies being for regions on chromosome 7q. However, a meta-analysis also suggests linkage for a locus on 17q, the evidence being particularly strong when the focus was on families with male-only transmission or when analysis was restricted to male-only sibling pairs (Gupta & State, 2006).

A further area of interest to molecular geneticists has been a region of chromosome 15q11-13 because of its relationship to other developmental disorders. Two related disorders, Angelman's syndrome and Prader-Willi syndrome, both involve deletions on this chromosome and share some of the behavioral features of autism. Indeed, there may be considerable mileage in studying disorders with a known genetic basis that are commonly associated with autism. Tuberous sclerosis is one such genetic disorder; this causes benign tumorous growths in the brain and leads to autism in 50% of cases (with epilepsy being a feature in some 80% of these). An intriguing hypothesis following from this is that a tumor in the "social brain" network may lead to epilepsy during the critical phases of social development (Bolton, Park, Higgins, Griffiths, & Pickles, 2002).

At the present time, the search for autism susceptibility genes is active but faces a number of difficult challenges. Factors that may complicate the interpretation of genetic studies include differences in the ascertainment of cases as well as differences in the age, gender, and IQ range of samples. Furthermore, it seems likely that different genes will be involved in specifying different features of the triad of symptoms that define autism. A recent population-based twin study of over 3000 twin pairs aged 7–9 years reported only modest correlations between measures of autistic traits in the three core areas of the triad (social impairments, communication difficulties, and repetitive behaviors) and, even more surprisingly, only a low correlation was found between social and communication impairments (Happé, Ronald, & Plomin, 2006). This was equally true for the general population as when only children with extreme scores were considered. Moreover, although genetic analyses indicated each of the different aspects of the triad was highly heritable, most of the genetic effects were specific to one aspect of the triad and there was little genetic overlap. Although a degree of caution is required as these findings in part reflect the ways in which the constructs were measured, together they suggest that the genes that contribute to the risk of developing autism may have distinct influences on different aspects of the phenotype, and they segregate among relatives explaining the broader autistic phenotype.

To meet the challenges that lie ahead in understanding the genetic basis of autism, an international collaboration of scientists (Autism Genome Project; AGP) is analyzing DNA from large numbers of affected families worldwide. Many of the genetic differences between humans that contribute to the susceptibility to developmental disorders are due to duplications or deletions of genes. A specific focus has therefore been to look for copy number variations (CNVs: the differences in the number of copies of a particular gene present in the genome of an individual) using new gene technologies (Buckley, Mantripragada, Piotrowski, Diaz de Ståhl, & Dumanski, 2005; Sebat et al., 2004). The approach has led to the discovery of a new putative locus on chromosome 11, and a gene called "neurexin" that is believed to be involved in the contact and communication of neurons (Autism Genome Project Consortium, 2007).

Children at family risk of autism

Given the significant heritability of autism, a number of studies have begun to investigate its developmental precursors by studying the infant siblings of children with an autism diagnosis. In one of the largest of these studies, Zwaigenbaum et al. (2005) followed 65 infant siblings (from a total sample of 150) up until 24 months of age, assessing them at 6 and 12 months using an autism observational scale and a behavioral task tapping visual orienting. The observation scale (AOSI; Bryson, Zwaigenbaum, McDermott, Rombargh, & Brian, 2008) comprised structured procedures for the detection of risk markers for autism, such as poor eye contact, a lack of social smiling, and atypical reactivity. In addition, parents provided ratings of infant temperament.

At 24 months, behavioral outcomes were assessed by administration of the Autism Diagnostic Observational Schedule (ADOS), mindful that any "diagnosis" would be preliminary and the possibility that some children might develop further autistic symptoms by 36 months. Nevertheless, 7 siblings fulfilled criteria for autism and a further 12 for ASD. In general, there were very few differences between these children and the remainder of the "at risk" group at 6 months, however there was greater differentiation at 12 months. At this stage of development, the presence of seven or more risk markers on the observation scale identified 6/7 children later classified as having autism compared to 2/58 nonautistic infant siblings and 0/23 controls. The significant risk markers included atypical eye contact, visual tracking, disengagement of visual attention, orienting to name, social smiling, reactivity, social interest, and sensory-oriented behaviors. In addition, those later diagnosed with autism showed a decrease in the ability to disengage attention (from a central fixation point to a peripheral stimulus) between 6 and 12 months, and their ability to disengage attention at 12 months predicted ADOS scores for social communication at 24 months.

Studies of children at high risk of autism, like those that have followed the progress of children at family risk of dyslexia, are important theoretically because they allow the testing of causal hypotheses. Moreover, from the clinical perspective, the findings lead naturally to better procedures for early identification and intervention before the behavioral consequences of autism (and its neural correlates) are compounded.

Environmental risk factors

Given the strong role of genetic risk factors in autism, the role of environmental risk factors has received relatively little attention. However there is reason to believe that autistic-like behaviors may on rare occasions follow severe privation in early childhood, principally the almost total absence of social interaction associated with extremely poor care or sensory deprivation.

Rutter et al. (1999) investigated the development of 111 Romanian children who were adopted into the UK after the fall of the Ceaucescu regime. At the time of adoption these children were severely deprived: half had a weight below the 3rd centile and half displayed severe learning difficulties (IQ below 70), with many suffering medical complaints. Their poor condition was the result in most cases of having been raised in an institution in which there was no personal caregiving, little social interaction, and poor nutrition. Despite these terrible beginnings, the majority of these children made remarkable progress following their arrival in the UK and many were functioning normally, both cognitively and socially, within 2 years of adoption. However there was an unusually high prevalence of autistic behaviors at the age of 4 years in this cohort in comparison with a sample of adoptees from within the UK.

Thus, 6% of the Romanian adoptees (11 children) fulfilled diagnostic criteria for autism. In all 11 cases, parent interviews and observational data indicated that these children had significant difficulties with communication and social relationships, and circumscribed interests and preoccupations with sensory stimuli were common. One child had shown language and social regression at the age of 20 months and three had severe cognitive impairments, likely associated with organic factors. However, all three had learned Makaton sign language and used it flexibly, and two made frequent social approaches. The remaining seven children were higher functioning and, although they were comparable to a longitudinal comparison group of children with typical autism at 4 years, by the age of 6 years their symptoms were much milder. In addition they showed a rise of some 20 points in IQ during this 2-year period. A further 6% of the sample showed milder, usually isolated autistic features, principally repetitive behaviors and sensory preoccupations rather than marked sociocognitive deficits. They had entered the UK at a younger age than the children in the group with autism.

There are some similarities between the characteristics of the children with autistic behaviors in the Romanian sample and those of a group of children born blind studied by Brown, Hobson, and Lee (1997). Although autism is not typically found among congenitally blind children, it does seem to occur more often than in typical children, particularly where there are additional cognitive impairments (Pring, 2007). For these children, the autistic behaviors are somewhat atypical and there is some evidence that they diminish over time. Brown et al. (1997) proposed that they may be the result of reduced perspective-taking following from the lack of visual experience. The fact that fewer congenitally blind children of normal IQ showed the quasi-autistic pattern suggests that such children might be able to compensate for their sensory deprivation, perhaps by utilizing auditory and tactile information to engage in dyadic and triadic interactions.

In summary, the incidence of autistic features among the Romanian adoptees studied by Rutter and his colleagues is sufficiently elevated for this pattern of behavior to be linked to severe privation in early childhood and atypical development of attachment relationships. The conditions of care among congenitally blind children who succumb to autism are much better by comparison. Nonetheless, they may also be considered to be deprived of the early experiences afforded by social interaction for sharing the perspectives of another person. Such sharing of experience through joint attention, as we have seen, may be a critical precursor of TOM and subsequent social relationships, as well as language development. Privation of such experiences will have even more significant consequences when children also have additional handicaps, such as those associated with low IQ. Importantly, however, in both the Romanian adoptees and the blind children, the autistic behaviors were short lived and the progress of these children was better than normally predicted in autism. Together these findings suggest that the behavioral profile of these children might be considered a "phenocopy" of autism but with a different etiology to ordinary "autism."

Neural correlates of autism

The search for neural correlates of autism, like that for susceptibility genes, has uncovered a range of different findings. Furthermore, it is difficult to disentangle brain mechanisms that are causes of autism from those that are consequences, because individuals not only fail to acquire important skills, but they may also develop a distinctive cognitive style and, to varying degrees, they may utilize compensatory processes (Volkmar, Lord, Bailey, Schultz, & Kiln, 2004).

In line with the wide range of neuropsychological assets and deficits seen in children with autism, functionally diverse brain systems appear to be affected

(McAlonan et al., 2005) and an important hypothesis is that the autistic brain shows underconnectivity between regions, plausibly associated with white matter abnormalities (Just, Cherkassky, Keller, Kana & Minshew, 2007; Just, Cherkassky, Keller, & Minshew, 2004). Structural brain abnormalities include findings of increased neuronal cell size and increased cell packing density in regions of the limbic system that subserve emotional and social behavior, and in the cerebellum (Bailey, Phillips, & Rutter, 1996). More generally, a widespread view is that autism is associated with large brain size. Such increase in brain volume is not evident from birth but emerges between the ages of 2 and 4 years, suggesting it may be due to a failure of normal pruning that eliminates faulty connections and optimizes neural functioning (Courchesne et al., 2001).

Although the "big brain" theory of autism is appealing and may go some way toward accounting for the lack of top-down modulation observed as WCC, findings are mixed and again suggestive of heterogeneity. In a study of 47 children with ASD conducted by Tager-Flusberg and Joseph (2003) only 14% of the sample showed evidence of large brain size. However, there was a relationship between head circumference (an indirect measure of brain size) and IQ profile. Specifically, head circumference was significantly larger in children with higher performance IQ than verbal IQ, than in those with higher performance than verbal IQ or those with balanced profiles.

Aside from differences in gross brain structure, functional brain imaging studies of autism have made progress in identifying a network of brain regions that are active during mentalizing and underactive in children with ASD (Baron-Cohen et al., 1999; Happé et al., 1996). This network, termed the "social brain", involves medial prefrontal cortex, temporoparietal junction, and temporal poles (see Figure 8.6). Castelli et al. (2002) found that individuals with ASD showed less activation than controls in these three critical regions when viewing animations of geometric figures moving with intention. Importantly, patterns of occipital activation indicated that all participants devoted more visual attention to these displays than to those involving fighting or chasing, but the brains of the people with autism showed less connectivity to temporal regions.

An important hypothesis proposed by Mundy (2003) is that TOM deficits might be traced to impairments in dorsal medial-frontal cortex (DMFC: Brodmann's areas 8 and 9) and anterior cingulate (AC), regions involved in the development of joint attention in infancy and specifically the tendency to initiate joint attention. In a similar vein individual differences in the activity of this system appear to predict the severity of the social and communicative symptoms associated with autism (Pelphrey, Morris, & McCarthy, 2005). It should be noted that the DMFC/AC complex also contributes more broadly to executive control skills such as planning and self-monitoring of goal-directed behaviors. Thus, this hypothesis has the potential to integrate a number of different features of autism beyond the social ones, notably the repetitive behaviors as well as impairments of eye and motor movements that are often observed.

Finally it is important not to overlook the possibly significant role of subcortical mechanisms in the etiology of autism. Johnson (2005) reviews evidence from studies

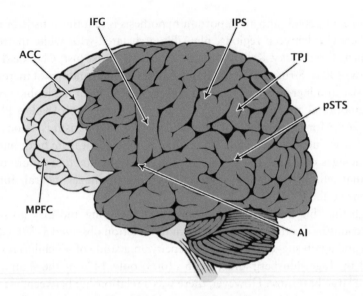

Figure 8.6   Location of key brain regions that show activation during social cognition. From left to right: MPFC, medial prefrontal cortex; ACC, anterior cingulate cortex; IFG, inferior frontal gyrus; IPS, interparietal sulcus; TPJ, temporoparietal junction; pSTS, posterior superior sulcus; AI, anterior insula. Reprinted from *Current Biology*, 17(16), Frith, C. D. and Frith, U., Social cognition in humans, 726, copyright (2007), with permission from Elsevier.)

of adults for the role of a subcortical system comprising amygdala, superior colliculus, and pulvinar in face recognition. This system is thought to be responsible for the rapid detection of low spatial frequency information involved in face detection and possibly in the modulation of activation in the cortical systems responsible for face identification. The crucial point for the present argument is that subcortical activation in infancy has the potential to determine the regions of the cortex that become incorporated into the social brain network. It follows that early disruption of this system, for example when there is amygdala dysfunction, would constrain the processing of socially salient stimuli. Another developmental consequence would be that visual cortical processes would be less tuned to low spatial frequencies, which behaviorally could manifest as WCC or a bias to perceptual features rather than configural processing.

In summary, there are currently a number of different hypotheses regarding the neural correlates of autism. It is clear that there could be no single locus for such a complex disorder and a hypothesis that is generating considerable research interest is that there is less anatomical and functional connectivity between brain regions in autism. Such underconnectivity, associated with poor synchronization across activated brain regions, may explain the major disruption of higher cognitive functions observed in ASD and the apparent lack of integration of different aspects of information processing noted by several authors.

Autism Outcomes and Treatments

Outcome in adulthood

Like all of the disorders considered in this book, autism persists into adulthood and outcomes are varied. In order to understand the developmental course of autism it is important to conduct longitudinal studies and, so far, such studies are rare.

Mawhood, Howlin, and Rutter (2000) examined the cognitive and psychosocial outcomes in their early 20s of 19 young people with autism and a comparison sample of 20 young people with a history of receptive language impairment (LI). Both groups had been studied from the age of 7–8 years following initial diagnosis and were the subject of a number of published studies. In young adulthood, both groups had similar IQ scores and there was some evidence that the group with autism had increased significantly in verbal IQ over time (by 16 points on average). Strikingly in the face of these gains, the communicative competence of these individuals was now less good than that of the language-impaired group and they showed higher levels of stereotyped language. Literacy outcomes were poor in both groups (between the 9- and 12-year levels of attainment) but perhaps not unexpectedly poor given the general difficulties experienced by these individuals in many aspects of their behavior.

In terms of psychosocial outcomes, the group with autism showed a wider range of difficulties despite the fact that they had had more consistent educational provision than the LI group. A similarly poor prognosis for autism was reported by Howlin, Goode, Hutton, and Rutter (2004) from a larger-scale study of people with autism who had been diagnosed at the age of 7–8 years and followed up between the ages of 21 and 48 (mean age of 24 years). The majority of people in this cohort had left school without formal qualifications although there was some variability, with three obtaining degrees and two with postgraduate qualifications. A third of the group were in employment and the others were either involved in work-based schemes or programs of training.

Ratings from the ADI conducted with parents indicated that stereotyped behaviors and unusual preoccupations persisted into adulthood. Over a third of the group still lived at home, about half were in residential settings, and only a minority lived independently. In addition, the majority of the group were rated as having no friends or acquaintances and very few had had a close sexual relationship. Overall, outcome was best predicted by childhood IQ; just over 20% of the group were considered to have a good outcome and this was most common among those with IQ above 70.

Interventions for Autism

Over the years since its first description a wide range of treatments have been proposed for autism spectrum disorders and there have even been reports of "miracle cures." However there is no "cure" for autism and the favored approaches focus on managing the symptoms of the disorder. According to the U.S. National Academy of Science, no single approach is best for all individuals with ASD or for the same person across time (National Research Council, 2001). Hence treatment approaches need to consider the current needs of the individual, their cognitive strengths and difficulties, and the environments in which they are interacting.

In general terms, psychological and educational treatments for autism take a dual perspective, aiming to reduce challenging behaviors (such as self-harm or temper tantrums) and to increase social and communicative behaviors, and there is an emphasis on supporting parents (Howlin, 1998). Pharmacological interventions have their place but generally the specific impact of different treatments has not been evaluated. Applied behavior analysis (ABA) is the most commonly studied treatment to date. ABA is an umbrella term for a type of highly structured intervention program that is individualized according to the needs of the child through detailed behavioral assessment and the design of reinforcement strategies to encourage new behaviors. Although there is encouraging evidence of benefit (Smith, Groen, & Wynn, 2000), the evidence base is again sparse and problems of generalization are paramount. In the absence of controlled trials, most clinicians believe that the most effective interventions are delivered early before secondary behavioral consequences take hold, and that children with autism do best in structured educational settings. Indeed, there is modest evidence for the efficacy of early intervention (Rogers & Vismara, 2008). However, the crux of the treatment problem is that what children with autism need most is improved ability to take part in social interaction, but social behavior is unpredictable and therefore social skills are difficult to teach.

One promising intervention for social communication was evaluated by Aldred, Green, and Adams (2004) in a pilot randomized controlled trial. The rationale for the treatment was that children with autism benefit from a high degree of sensitive parental input to encourage communicative interaction and language development. Accordingly, 28 children with autism aged 2 years to 5 years 11 months were randomly allocated to receive either routine care or routine care plus a social communication intervention. The broad aim of the social communication program was to adapt parental responses in interactions to facilitate the child's active communication exchanges and to signal pragmatic intentions. The initial focus was on shared attention, followed by parental sensitivity and responsiveness. The training consisted of an initial series of parental workshops, followed by six, monthly therapy sessions and further sessions to review video-recorded sessions between child and parent.

The findings of this study were encouraging; the treatment group made significantly greater improvements in reciprocal social interaction and in parent-rated expressive language as a result of the intervention. Moreover these improvements were associated with an increase in parental communication and a decrease in asynchronous interactions.

Towards a Theory of Autism

Autism (like ADHD, which we considered in the last chapter) is a complex disorder with diverse behavioral manifestations. Although there is heterogeneity in autism at the biological, cognitive, and behavioral levels, it is fair to say that up until very recently the literature has been dominated by unitary theories of the disorder and (again as with ADHD) the role of noncognitive factors has been down played. It would seem unlikely that a single underlying cognitive cause could ever explain the diversity of symptoms that are observed in autism. Against this, the diagnosis of autism, with a social impairment at the core, is valid and the co-occurrence of the different symptoms of the triad together with perceptual abnormalities sets it aside from related disorders. For a theory of autism to be viable it must be able to explain the diversity of symptoms that are observed yet have a common pathway through which the development of social relationships is affected. We begin by outlining a theory that emphasizes the social–affective underpinnings of autism and predicts some of the "downstream" effects. We then proceed to discuss a radically different alternative: that it is time to fractionate the autistic triad and to consider autism as representing the comorbidity of a number of different disorders.

Social referencing theory

Hobson and colleagues (Hobson, 1993; Hobson & Meyer, 2005) have developed a theory of social referencing (or identification) that provides an interesting framework within which to integrate some of the evidence we have considered. According to Hobson and colleagues, social referencing in triadic interaction – the relationship between the child, the other, and the object of their joint attention – plays a vital role in the development of self-awareness, creativity (imagination), and investigation. According to the theory, becoming emotionally engaged with others leads to the structuring of subsequent development and is critical to the development of an understanding of other people as intentional beings. In the absence of this process, development is atypical. Within this framework, there can be many different reasons why children may fail to develop social referencing. These would include impairments in basic mechanisms such as perception, imitation, and learning as well as a different motivational system in which social–affective relations are of low importance. Social referencing would also fail to develop, typically in conditions of environmental deprivation, leading to "phenocopies" of autism. A lack of social referencing affects the development of a sense of self and self-control that is associated with the executive function account of autism, and would have both direct and indirect effects on the development of language and communication. This tentative hypothesis is depicted in Figure 8.7. As can be seen, the model keeps partially separate the cognitive and emotional aspects of autism and aims to show how impairments of social reference and triadic interaction may mediate the behavioral symptoms that characterize the autistic triad.

Fractionating the autistic triad

Recently, a very different approach to understanding autism has come to the fore (Happé, Ronald, & Plomin, 2006; Whitehouse, Barry, & Bishop, 2007); in this view we should abandon attempts to understand autism as a single entity, and instead view it as a disorder in which the triad of impairments (impairments of social

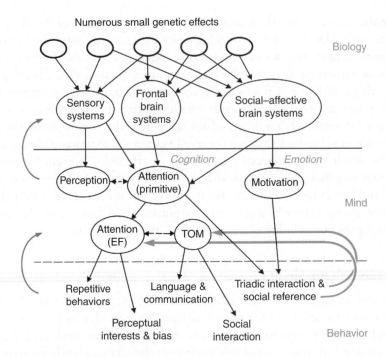

Figure 8.7   A path model of autism.

interaction, communication, and restricted and repetitive behaviors) co-occur but with each having a separate basis. The arguments for doing this are varied (Happé et al., 2006). First, the correlation between different parts of the triad in the general population is quite low (roughly $r = .1–.4$); a corollary of this is that different children may have impairments in just one component of the triad. Second, it appears that the three parts of the triad have separable genetic bases, which fits in with findings from studies showing that relatives of people with autism may show only parts of the triad of impairments (the broader phenotype of autism). It remains the case that different aspects of the triad do occur together at rates that are greater than would be expected by chance and why this is so remains to be explained. Such co-occurrences might reflect some common (perhaps somewhat nonspecific) genetic effects. Alternatively, it may reflect patterns of interaction between different parts of the triad. For example, it seems plausible that a severe social impairment might have knock-on effects on the development of language skills.

Whitehouse et al. studied language and communication skills in parents of children with ASD, parents of children with SLI, and parents of typically developing children. The parents of children with ASD performed typically on measures of language ability but showed some signs of pragmatic language difficulties similar to those seen in autism. Conversely the parents of children with SLI had some weaknesses in nonpragmatic aspects of oral language, but performed typically on measures of pragmatic language use. This suggests that the language difficulties seen in SLI and ASD populations are different, with different patterns of inheritance.

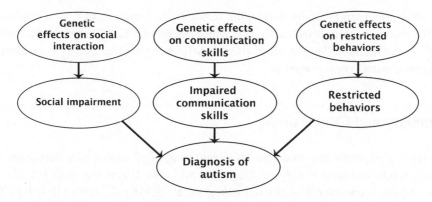

Figure 8.8 Path model illustrating the fractionation of the autism triad.

Whitehouse et al. propose that SLI and ASD reflect different heritable disorders, and that for ASD it is necessary to postulate that the three parts of the triad are inherited separately. They also speculate that in some cases the triad of impairments seen in autism may operate to impair the development of nonpragmatic aspects of language, to mimic the patterns of language difficulty seen in children with SLI. This proposal is illustrated in the diagram in Figure 8.8.

We would emphasize that this is not in any way a complete theory of autism, but it makes an explicit claim that the impairments used to define autism are separable forms of impairment that can occur independently of each other. This view, if it is accepted, will push us to more complex theories of autism that seek explanations of the separate aspects of the triad, and it is likely to be informed by the findings of prospective longitudinal studies that follow children at high risk of autism by virtue of having an affected sibling (e.g., Landa & Garret-Meyer, 2006).

Autism and Emotion: A Role for Noncognitive Factors

We would also speculate that theories in this area (like theories of ADHD) are likely in the near future to become less "cognitive" and accommodate emotional and motivational aspects of development. While our experience of emotion undoubtedly involves cognitive processes (particularly the appraisal of social signals that appear to be impaired in autism) there are processes in emotional and motivational systems that do not seem reducible to cognitive processes (Oatley & Jenkins 1996) and impairments in such systems require more scrutiny in research on autism. It is striking that most of the work we have described in this chapter focuses on highly abstract cognitive accounts of autism. In contrast to this, very little attention has been paid to affect or emotion in children with autism. We would speculate that understanding the social impairments seen in children with autism may depend on some basic motivational disorder in these children (as, for example, suggested by social referencing theory); in short, children with autism seem to find social interaction intrinsically less rewarding than typically developing children. To some extent this may account for the inconsistencies between studies, which, as Bowler (2007) argues, are data in need of explanation. Such a motivational difference, if valid, seems very hard to capture in purely cognitive terms.

Summary and Conclusions

Autism is a relatively rare and severely debilitating life-long disorder that, even following recent increases in rates of diagnosis, probably affects less than 1% of children. Autism is commonly associated with general learning difficulties (low IQ). The core features of autism are a triad of symptoms involving impairments of social interaction, communication, and restricted interests and repetitive behaviors. Autism is very strongly influenced by genetic risk factors, though it is possible that in rare cases extremely severe deprivation/maltreatment early in life may give an increased risk of autism. Because of the complexity of the symptom complex used to define it, autism is almost certainly a biologically and phenotypically heterogeneous disorder. The growing recognition that the behaviors used to diagnose autism may reflect the extremes of normal variation has led to the use of autism spectrum disorders (ASD) as an increasingly common diagnostic label. The dominant theories of this disorder have emphasized the importance of deficits in theory of mind (mentalizing ability), executive function, and perceptual abnormalities, though the extent to which any of these deficits can explain the triad of impairments seen in autism remains contested. More recent theories have suggested that different aspects of the triad of deficits seen in autism will require separate forms of explanation. Studies of the treatment of autism are in their infancy, but recent evidence suggests that programs designed to improve communication and language skills can have modest beneficial effects. In practice treatments focus on how best to support children and their families to cope with the diverse difficulties encountered in this disorder.

Understanding Developmental Cognitive Disorders: Progress and Prospects

We have considered a wide range of developmental disorders, including those of language, reading, arithmetic, motor skills, attention, and social interaction. We hope readers who have made it this far will have got a sense of the excitement and real progress that research in this field has generated. In this chapter we draw together some of the important lessons that have been learned. We also want to consider some of the complex issues that remain to be understood. We will highlight issues that cut across the different disorders we have considered.

Understanding Disorders Depends on Understanding Development

Development involves change. To understand abnormalities of development is to understand why the patterns of change seen in some children follow an atypical course. This is a purely conceptual point: Given that all children begin life without certain sets of skills (including language, reading, and arithmetic skills for example), the task of understanding why a minority of children fail to develop such skills adequately must be framed in terms of the processes that allow the majority of children to master such skills. Thus, as we argued in Chapter 1, if we are ever to understand developmental disorders we will have to relate the patterns seen in such disorders to patterns of typical development and their variations. We hope the evidence and theories discussed in previous chapters have served to flesh out this argument. We think it is notable that disorders where understanding seems most developed (e.g., developmental dyslexia) are ones where patterns of typical development are best described and understood. Conversely, disorders that seem less well understood are ones where the patterns of typical development are also less clear (e.g., attention deficit hyperactivity disorder, ADHD). A skeptic might point out that understanding reading (or at least understanding how we learn to decode print, which is the area of difficulty in dyslexia) is a simpler task than understanding the development of attention. We agree, but would nevertheless claim that a better understanding of the typical development of attention and behavioral regulation will be critical for advancing knowledge of ADHD. The corollary of our view about understanding developmental disorders in terms of patterns of typical development is that these two endeavors are inextricably linked; studies of disorders place powerful constraints on theories of typical development.

It may be that a few readers are still not convinced of the need for a developmental approach to studying developmental disorders. Considering specific examples may be persuasive in this regard. One example, already cited, of how a specific deficit has very different effects in childhood compared to adulthood is the case of deafness. Deafness in early childhood typically has profound effects on the development of speech skills in children, while becoming deaf in adulthood leaves speech skills relatively intact. Another very clear example comes from the effects of brain injury on language functions. In adults, damage to areas of the left hemisphere of the brain often results in highly selective impairments in language skills (for most people, language functions are lateralized in the left hemisphere). For example, damage to parts of the left frontal lobe (Broca's area) in adults typically results in a form of expressive language difficulty (expressive aphasia) in which speech is labored and ungrammatical, while speech comprehension is relatively well preserved. Conversely, damage to areas of the left superior temporal gyrus (Wernicke's area) typically results in severe problems of language comprehension but relatively preserved language production. A large variety of other language disorders, including disorders of reading and spelling, are also commonly associated with damage to specific areas of the left hemisphere in adults.

In contrast to the pattern found in adults, lateralized brain lesions in early childhood are not usually associated with language difficulties. For example, Muter, Taylor, and Vargha-Khadem (1997) studied a group of children with unilateral brain lesions that had occurred just before, or just after, birth. There were essentially no differences between the language skills of children with left or right hemisphere lesions. The IQs of these children were also generally well preserved, although there was some evidence for modest reductions in nonverbal, but not verbal, IQ. This pattern was interpreted in terms of both hemispheres of the brain being capable of subserving the development of language skills early in life, coupled with a tendency for language functions to be "spared" at the expense of nonverbal skills. In other words, early brain damage may result in certain "nonlanguage brain areas" being recruited to support the learning of language, even at the expense of the development of nonverbal skills. It appears that the developing brain has the potential for reorganization to compensate for damage and that this potential for reorganization is gradually lost as development proceeds (the adage about the difficulty of teaching old dogs new tricks comes to mind!).

A final example, from a very different domain that has not been covered in this book, concerns the use of psychoactive drugs and their effects on mental health. There is some evidence that heavy cannabis use may predispose people to develop schizophrenia; however the evidence suggests that this only applies when cannabis use occurs before adulthood (Arseneault, Cannon, Witton, & Murray, 2004; Moore et al., 2007; Zammit, Allebeck, Andreasson, Burgess, Lundberg & Lewis, 2002).

Overall, these diverse forms of evidence show very clearly the need to consider developmental disorders from a developmental perspective. It is clear that the effects of particular causes of development disorders will have different effects at different ages or stages of development. Arguably, impairments will have their greatest impact when development is progressing rapidly. Moreover, because different cognitive domains develop in parallel, a delay in one domain may have an impact on development in another system. An illustration of this phenomenon of downstream effects comes from language acquisition. It has been argued that there is a sensitive period for the development of grammar and that this in turn depends on vocabulary size. Thus, Locke (1993) hypothesized that children whose vocabulary development is delayed may succumb to persisting grammatical impairments if, at the stage in development when a grammatical acquisition device is in operation, vocabulary size constrains its efficacy.

Development Depends upon Genes and Environments

In broad terms, as outlined in Chapter 1, we can think of development as depending upon three classes of influence: genes (G), environments (E), and interactions between them (G × E). Genetic factors have a strong role to play in most, if not all, of the disorders we have discussed. Conversely, genetic effects are not fixed or immutable and there is growing evidence for feedback loops from the environment to the mechanisms controlling gene expression. Put crudely, the genes we carry may be switched on or off by environmental influences. This idea gives a biological mechanism to which we can relate the ample evidence for the importance of gene/environment interaction (G × E). A classic example of this is the interaction between a specific genetic predisposition and maltreatment in the genesis of conduct disorder (see Chapter 1).

Genetic and environmental factors represent the "ultimate" causes of development and disorders of development. However, another important lesson is that these causes need to be thought of probabilistically. We are not born with genes that make us dyslexic, nor are we born into an environment that makes us dyslexic. We may, however, be born with genes that give an increased risk of developing dyslexia, but this risk will in turn be moderated by environmental factors. So, broadly, we can think of the causes of any disorder probabilistically in terms of genetic and environmental risk factors and their interaction (G, E, and G × E). However, a satisfying explanation for developmental disorders needs to go beyond specifying the genetic and environmental risk factors that are important for its development. In addition we need to understand how such risk factors affect the development of brain mechanisms, which in turn underlie the psychological mechanisms that control behavior.

Risks are Continuous and Disorders are Dimensional

These ideas about genetic and environmental risk factors make it clear that virtually all risk factors are continuous (weaker or stronger), not absolute (present/absent).

Some risk factors may act relatively independently (additively) but other sets of risk factors may interact so that they may not simply add together but instead have multiplicative (synergistic) effects (a small genetic risk and a small environmental risk may together produce a large risk). Arguably, an important exception to this generalization are certain genetic disorders that depend upon single gene effects, such as tuberous sclerosis or Huntington's disease. Such diseases do represent distinct categories, and a person either has or has not got the gene that causes the disease. However, even in such apparently simple single-gene disorders there may be wide variations in how the disease expresses itself that are not yet well understood (e.g., variations in the age of onset of the degenerative neural changes that characterize Huntington's disease). However, the disorders we have considered in this book do not represent single gene effects, but rather the effects of many genes (most of which are still not identified) operating in interaction with a range of (typically still to be identified) environmental causes. Such disorders therefore depend upon continuously varying genetic and environmental risk factors. By continuous we mean that there may be a wide range of degrees and types of genetic and environmental risk factors operating in the population to cause the development of these disorders.

If risks are continuous, this leads us to expect the differences we observe in the phenotype (behavioral characteristics of the disorders) to be dimensional. Theoretically, all the disorders considered in this book are best thought of in dimensional terms (i.e., as the low end of normal variations in skill/ability). Where we place the cut-off between normality and abnormality will always be, to some extent, arbitrary and one attempt to deal with this issue is embodied in several definitions in the *Diagnostic and Statistical Manual of Mental Disorders* (DSM-IV; American Psychiatric Association, 1994), which specify that for diagnosis a disorder should for example "significantly interfere with academic achievement or activities of daily living..." (an extract from the definition for reading disorder). Nevertheless, a dimensional approach does not necessitate that we abandon categorical names for disorders. Categorical terms can be useful in aiding communication; we just need to be aware that they are a shorthand for an extreme position on a dimension (or possibly on more than one dimension in complex disorders such as autism).

Multiple Risks: Resilience and Compensation

If risk factors are multiple and interactive, some individuals who experience one or more of the risk factors for a disorder may not succumb to it. An individual may carry a gene conferring a risk for a disorder, but other genes or environmental influences may prevent the disorder developing. Conversely, an individual may not carry any genetic risk factors for a disorder but might, due to extreme environmental effects, develop a disorder. Environmental risk factors include pre- and postnatal biological risks (such as maternal rubella during pregnancy or brain injury at birth) as well as purely psychological risks (such as maltreatment or neglect). Resilience and compensation are two related but different concepts that have been discussed in relation to these effects.

Resilience refers to the interaction between an individual's makeup and the way they respond to environmental adversity. The term has been used to describe individuals who show "a relative resistance to environmental risk experiences" (Rutter, 2006). The concept of resilience has been invoked most often in relation to psychosocial or emotional disorders. For example, some people may succumb to depression as a result of adverse life events such as bereavement or losing a job, while others may manage to cope better with such adversities (showing relatively short-lived negative moods but not developing depression). Resilience is probably an important concept in relation to the development of cognitive disorders as well. For example, it appears that a minority of children who experienced severe deprivation in Romanian orphanages developed autistic symptoms (Rutter et al., 1999); a reasonable assumption is that some of those children who did not develop autism, despite equivalently severe maltreatment, displayed resilience conferred by genetic differences.

Resilience conveys the idea that some individuals may not succumb to a disorder despite being exposed to risks associated with developing the disorder. In contrast, compensation is a term used to refer to processes that allow individuals to cope well with a disorder when it has developed. A variety of environmental and genetic differences may contribute to compensation. For example, good teaching might help a child with dyslexia to compensate for their difficulties and so achieve reading and spelling skills within the normal range. Perhaps more speculatively, a range of other cognitive strengths may allow a child to compensate for a weakness in another domain. For example, a child with speech difficulties (which affect their phonological system) but good language (semantic and grammatical) skills may learn to read better than a child with both speech and language difficulties.

A pervasive idea is that IQ may function as a compensatory resource, so that children with cognitive difficulties of higher IQ will be better able to cope with those difficulties than children of lower IQ. As we discussed in Chapter 3, this view has been severely challenged in relation to dyslexia, and there is little evidence that (across quite a broad range) children with dyslexia of higher IQ learn to decode better than children of lower IQ. However, because children with dyslexia of higher IQ may be able to benefit more from context in reading, this may enable them to develop a larger "sight vocabulary" in reading and thus further in development such individuals may have the cognitive resources to seek out better jobs despite their low levels of literacy. There is also some evidence that children with SLI of higher IQ have a better prognosis, suggesting that IQ can help to compensate for an underlying language-learning weakness. It seems that the role of IQ as a compensatory factor is worthy of further study in other disorders (such as mathematics disorder and developmental coordination disorder). However, it is also probably worth emphasizing that IQ is not a particularly satisfying explanatory construct. Differences in IQ may be a proxy for the efficiency of a number of quite general cognitive processes (such as learning, attention, and speed of processing). Similarly, IQ may also be a proxy for a variety of quite nonspecific genetic, environmental, and brain-based differences between individuals. Claims that IQ acts as a compensatory resource need to be developed to explain how compensation comes about.

Are Risks and Disorders Specific?

The disorders we have dealt with so far represent relatively clear diagnostic categories, however a number of proposed developmental disorders do not fit quite so neatly into traditional diagnostic categories. Bishop (1989) was one of the first to discuss a disorder falling at the intersection of two categorical diagnoses: language impairment and Asperger syndrome. This disorder, described at the time as semantic/pragmatic disorder (now called pragmatic language impairment, PLI), is a subtype of SLI characterized by semantic deficits and communication impairments (Rapin & Allen, 1987). Bishop (1989) observed continuities between the communication difficulties observed in semantic pragmatic disorder and those experienced by people with Asperger syndrome who, despite their relatively good levels of structural language, tend to use language in an odd or overly formal way and display subtle comprehension difficulties.

Pragmatic language impairment

To explain the continuities between semantic pragmatic disorder and Asperger syndrome, Bishop (1989) suggested that both disorders lie on a continuum of meaningful verbal communication at an intermediate point between abnormal communication (as seen in classic autism) and normal communication (see Figure 9.1). However, the two disorders were considered to differ in terms of the social relationships and interests of affected persons. Thus, whereas children with PLI enjoy relatively typical social relationships and have a wide range of interests, those with Asperger syndrome typically have social difficulties and fairly circumscribed interests.

This view of pragmatic language impairment embodies a dimensional view of the relationship between different disorders. Although there is evidence that PLI may be a useful diagnostic category for some children who would not qualify for a diagnosis of autism spectrum disorder (Norbury & Bishop, 2002), attempts to agree about the "borders" of this condition are fraught with difficulties, particularly as children develop and may change their interests as well as their communicative abilities. The idea that children collect different diagnoses as they develop is not an attractive one and it can be a cause of significant confusion and distress to parents. Thus, conditions like PLI that fall at the intersection of different disorders pose a pertinent issue for both theory and practice.

Nonverbal learning difficulty

"Nonverbal learning difficulty" (NLD) is a form of learning difficulty that is defined in terms of the co-occurrence of two or more different disorders. NLD is not classified as a disorder in DSM-IV but clinically such children are often referred for educational assessment because of poor attainments associated with perceptual disorders and impairments of mathematical cognition.

The strongest proponent of a syndrome of NLD is Rourke (1989; Rourke, 1995), who described its principal clinical features in terms of neuropsychological assets

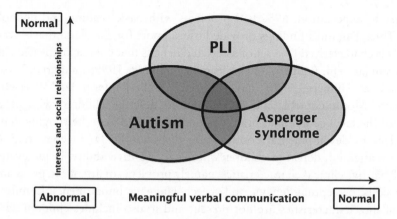

Figure 9.1   Diagram showing the overlap between autism, pragmatic language impairment, and Asperger syndrome. (Reprinted with permission from Bishop, D. V. M., *British Journal of Disorders of Communication*, 24, 1989.)

and deficits. Academically, typical strengths are in single-word reading and spelling, with difficulties affecting handwriting, reading comprehension, mathematics, and arithmetic. The principal neuropsychological asset in NLD is said to be the capacity to deal with information derived through the auditory modality, whereas the primary deficit is in visual-perceptual-organizational abilities, complex psychomotor skills, tactile perception, and nonverbal problem solving. According to Rourke (1989) socio-emotional and adaptive deficits also characterize the syndrome and encompass extreme difficulties in adapting to novel situations and significant deficits in social competence and social interaction.

Outside of Rourke's research group there have been few systematic studies of children with NLD, not least because the diagnostic criteria have been poorly specified. However, the profile has been validated by its possible association with particular disorders, such as Asperger syndrome (Klin, Volkmar, Sparrow, Cicchetti, & Rourke, 1995; McKelvey, Lambert, Mottron, & Shevell, 1995), Turner syndrome (Temple & Carney, 1993), and Williams syndrome (Atkinson et al., 2001). This evidence suggests that NLD should not be thought of as a disorder with specific and universal features (Morton & Frith, 1995), or even as an overarching syndrome. Rather, it is a set of symptoms that are not domain specific but often occur together.

Consistent with this view, Durand (2004) described a case-series of 43 children who were operationally defined as showing an NLD profile. These children had been referred to an educational psychologist for an assessment of learning difficulties and had a performance IQ at least 10 points lower than their verbal IQ (mostly the IQ discrepancies were of at least 20 points). Durand assessed these children on tests tapping a range of constructs highlighted by Rourke as domains of impairment in NLD. These included arithmetic skills, listening comprehension, visuospatial skills, and motor abilities. Within this group, only 6/43 children showed impairments in all five domains, about 65% showed impairments in visuospatial or motor skills, and a smaller proportion, some 40%, had poor listening comprehension. Moreover, contrary to expectation, 69% had problems with basic reading and phonological skills. Thus, Durand's findings provide little support for the claim that a syndrome of NLD is characterized by a set of assets and deficits that cohere in affected children.

In a similar vein, Gillberg and colleagues (Gillberg, 1999; Landgren, Pettersson, Kjellman, & Gillberg, 1996) have used the umbrella term DAMP (Deficits in Attention, Motor control, and Perception) to describe children who previously attracted the label of minimal brain dysfunction. DAMP can be roughly defined as equivalent to developmental coordination disorder (DCD) in combination with pervasive attention deficit in children of typical cognitive ability. In its severe form, DAMP has five clinical characteristics, namely problems of attention, gross and fine-motor skills, perceptual deficits, and speech–language impairments. In mild forms, some of the characteristics are not present and it also includes children with pure DCD and pure ADHD.

According to population studies conducted by Gillberg's group, DAMP occurs in severe form in 1–2% of 7-year-old children and its milder variants in 3–6%; generally more boys than girls are affected. While children with DAMP come from all social classes and some have high IQ, mean social class and IQ are typically a little lower than in the general population. Longitudinal studies suggest that in the pre-school years children with DAMP are considered hyperactive or inattentive and they show motor coordination problems and speech–language delays, although these are typically not serious enough to warrant clinical referral. By the end of the preschool period a reluctance to draw or paint is often noted, as are accidents in games with peers. In the early school years these children have difficulties in concentrating or sitting still and in acquiring reading and writing skills, and they are unable to interact with their peers in an age-appropriate fashion. By the age of 10, the clinical picture can be quite different with fewer motor difficulties and attention problems but an increase in behavioral problems and dyslexia, problems that persist into adolescence.

It should be clear from this discussion that both nonverbal learning difficulty (NLD) and DAMP describe patterns of impairment in which sets of deficits co-occur with varying severity. Terms such as DAMP or NLD may be useful in drawing attention to the fact that many children seem to have complex patterns of difficulties that span more than a single diagnostic category (i.e., these terms really refer to commonly occurring patterns of comorbidity). However, we would argue that it is probably better to define the skills that are implicated in these disorders in terms of underlying dimensions, with an individual's position free to vary on each dimension. This of course leaves the issue of the frequency of the co-occurrence between the different dimensional symptoms to be established and in turn such comorbidities need to be explained.

In the absence of rigorous research on NLD it is difficult to identify the relevant dimensions that would underpin a model of its relationship to other disorders. There is, however, agreement that visuospatial deficits are involved (indeed it is possible that these underlie the commonly co-occurring motor difficulties) and clinical accounts suggest that disorders of mathematical cognition are central to the reasons for educational referral (and it is possible that these also, at least in part, reflect visuospatial deficits).

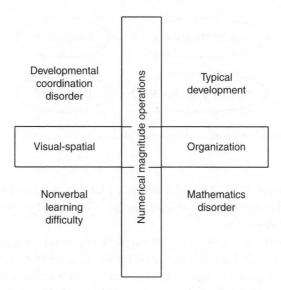

Figure 9.2   Two-dimensional model of nonverbal learning difficulties.

Figure 9.2 shows a two-dimensional model of two distinct but probably correlated dimensions, both of which are likely to be highly dependent on systems in the
parietal lobe: visualspatial organization skills and access to a numerical magnitude
system. In the upper left quadrant of the model are children with poor perceptual
skills but who do not experience deficits of the numerical magnitude system; such
children would show a relatively pure form of DCD. In the lower right quadrant are
children with deficits in the numerical magnitude system but normal perceptual
functioning. These children would show relatively pure forms of mathematics disorder.
NLD, in the lower left quadrant, represents a dual deficit with impairments on both
dimensions. The framework can therefore accommodate the notion that disorders of
motor skills and arithmetic are common but not universal features of NLD. However,
it only partially accommodates the overlap between NLD and disorders such as
Asperger syndrome (in terms of deficits in perceptual organization) and does not
account for the shared deficits in social adaptation, which hint at the involvement of
a further underlying dimension, namely that of social cognition. Longitudinal data
are badly needed to clarify the role of development in determining a child's position
in this spectrum of disorders and to investigate the role of genetic and environmental
factors in the etiology of NLD.

   This discussion of PLI, NLD, and DAMP brings out the fact that some common
clinical profiles suggest that children with developmental disorders often show rather
complex and nonspecific sets of difficulties. The degree of specificity shown in developmental disorders is perhaps one of the key areas of theoretical development at the
moment. There can be no doubt that there is some degree of specificity to the disorders
that occur, and this in turn provides support for the idea of modularity in cognitive
functions. For example, cases of children with specific problems in learning to read
(dyslexia) exist, as do children with specific problems in learning arithmetic

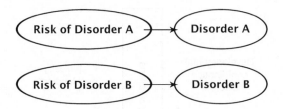

Figure 9.3   Path model showing uncorrelated risk factors for separate disorders.

(mathematics disorder). This provides evidence that the cognitive mechanisms under-lying reading and arithmetic are (at least partly) independent or modular in the way in which they develop.

The starting point for most research on developmental cognitive disorders has embodied the view that disorders are modular and that separate risk factors operate to cause separate disorders (such as dyslexia and mathematics disorder). We might express this in a simple path model as shown in Figure 9.3.

In this model we have completely independent risks leading to completely inde-pendent disorders. Unfortunately for most, if not all, of the disorders we have con-sidered this simple picture is inadequate; there is good evidence that disorders tend to co-occur, which is referred to as comorbidity.

Comorbidity

Comorbidity is defined as the co-occurence of two different disorders or diseases in the same individual. Estimating rates of "true" comorbidity can be difficult simply because it requires representative samples of children. Suppose for simplicity that 10% of children have dyslexia, and 10% of children have mathematics disorder. If the disorders are independent, the number of children expected to have both disor-ders is given by the product of the proportion of children with each disorder (0.1 × 0.1 = 0.01, or 1%). We say that true comorbidity exists when the rates of co-occurrence of the two disorders are higher than such a chance rate (1%) (Caron & Rutter, 1991). However, if we study clinical samples it is always possible that chil-dren with more than one disorder will be more likely to be referred for treatment, which is why we need to use representative samples of children. Although the evi-dence from representative samples is more limited than we would like, there is no doubt that comorbidity between seemingly unrelated disorders is rife. For example, children with mathematics disorder are likely to also have reading disorders, chil-dren with SLI are likely to also have developmental coordination disorders, and children with ADHD are likely to have a range of other disorders including reading disorders. It is probably fair to say that for a long time comorbidities were regarded as something of a nuisance in the field of developmental cognitive disorders. More recently, it has been realized that understanding the origins of comorbidities will have profound implications for understanding the causes of disorders.

It is common to distinguish between homotypic and heterotypic comorbidity (Angold et al., 1999). Homotypic comorbidity refers to the co-occurrence of disorders from the same diagnostic group (i.e., disorders that appear similar); an example would be the comorbidity between language impairments and dyslexia, which are both language disorders. Heterotypic comorbidity refers to the co-occurrence of disorders from different diagnostic groups (i.e., disorders that appear dissimilar); an example would be the comorbidity between ADHD and dyslexia. If we accept that both of these forms of comorbidity between different developmental disorders reflect true comorbidities (i.e., they are not artefacts of biases in sampling), how are we to explain them? Clearly the existence of comorbidity appears at odds with the specific risk/specific disorder model outlined above. Instead, comorbidity prompts us to consider the extent to which different disorders may arise from shared risk factors (i.e., whether the same cause can give rise to different disorders).

Neale and Kendler (1995) outlined a number of possible explanations for comorbidity and developed a statistical framework that allows different models of comorbidity to be tested. The first possible model for true comorbidity that they considered is referred to as alternate forms. In this model two disorders are seen as arising from the same underlying risk factor (liability); the disorder that is expressed is the product of other random factors. It has been suggested that the comorbidity between preschool speech and language disorders and dyslexia may represent an example of this form of comorbidity (see Catts, Adlof, Hogan, & Ellis Weismer, 2005; Pennington 2006) in which the two disorders differ in terms of the severity of the underlying liability.

Pennington (2006) discusses at length the possibility that one form of preschool speech and language disorder (speech sound disorder (SSD), sometimes also referred to as articulation disorder or phonological disorder) and dyslexia represent alternate forms of the same disorder. In this view, a severe liability to the disorder might show up as a frank speech difficulty in a preschool child and if that deficit persists it would then lead to difficulties when the child came to learn to read (so the child might then be diagnosed with dyslexia). A milder impairment might not lead to a frank speech disorder in the preschool years (it might lead to the child being somewhat delayed in their speech development, which is commonly reported for children with dyslexia) but might nevertheless lead to phonological problems that were sufficient to cause difficulties in learning to read. There is good evidence that many children with early speech–language difficulties go on to experience later reading problems (e.g., Snowling, Bishop, & Stothard, 2000) and conversely many children diagnosed with reading difficulties appear from retrospective reports to have experienced delays in early speech and language skills (e.g., Rutter & Yule, 1975). Finally, in samples of children selected to be at genetic risk of dyslexia, many show signs of speech–language delay in the preschool period (e.g., Gallagher, Frith & Snowling, 2000; Scarborough 2000).

All of these observations are broadly in line with a severity model that sees early speech difficulties and dyslexia arising from a single liability (severely affected children show speech difficulties early in development, followed by dyslexia when they enter school; less severely affected children show only mild speech difficulties that

	Dyslexia present	Dyslexia absent
Speech–language problems present	Speech problems/ dyslexia	Speech problems/ no dyslexia
Speech–language problems absent	No speech problems/ dyslexia	No speech problems/ no dyslexia

Figure 9.4   Classification showing four possible combinations of dyslexia and speech–language impairment.

may not be recognized but they may nevertheless go on to develop dyslexia). Pennington (2006) argues that to explain why many children with early speech and language difficulties appear not to develop reading problems we would have to postulate that these children have a different underlying cognitive deficit to those children who do go on to develop reading problems (perhaps both of these subgroups of children with speech difficulties have phonological problems, but they might be phonological problems of different sorts). This argument seems correct. We can think of this in terms of a 2×2 classification as shown in Figure 9.4.

In terms of a severity model the speech problems/dyslexia (both disorders present) and no speech problems/no dyslexia (neither disorder present) categories are both expected. The speech problems/dyslexia group can be seen as the product of a severe liability. The no speech problems/no dyslexia group can be seen as the absence of the liability. The speech problems/no dyslexia group requires explanation but follows naturally if we simply assume that a mild liability leads children to have mild speech–language difficulties that resolve by the time they come to learn to read.

However, the speech problems/no dyslexia category does not appear to be explicable in terms of a simple (one factor) dimension of severity (if these children have a severe liability this explains why they show early speech–language difficulties; but why then do they not go on to develop reading difficulties?). If this is the case we need to postulate one or more other factors (such as a supportive environment or protective effects from other genes) that allow these children to compensate for their speech difficulties sufficiently to escape developing reading difficulties.

In order to evaluate these ideas we need to consider data from longitudinal studies of the relationship between preschool speech impairments and school-age reading difficulties. As we described in Chapter 4, children's speech disorders can occur in pure form or together with impairments of receptive and expressive language. Catts (1993) was the first to highlight a difference between impairments of phonological awareness and impairments of speech production as risk factors for reading impairments, with pure speech impairments carrying a low risk. In a replication and extension of this work, Nathan, Stackhouse, Goulandris, and Snowling (2004) followed the progress of 47 children with speech disorders from the age of 4 years to 6 years 7 months. An important finding was that preschool language ability (rather than speech skills) was a unique predictor of phoneme awareness at 5 years 8 months, and that children with speech and language difficulties (but not those with pure speech problems) showed delayed development of phoneme awareness. Phoneme awareness, together with early word recognition, went on to predict literacy outcome just before the children were 7 years of age, and children with a history of pure speech problems were indistinguishable from controls in reading and spelling at this stage in their development. Stothard, Snowling, Bishop, Chipchase, and Kaplan, (1998) followed children classified as having isolated speech problems at the age of 4 to school leaving age and also found that pure speech disorder was not a risk factor.

However not all studies have reported such a good outcome for those with speech impairments. Raitano, Pennington, Tunick, Boada, and Shriberg (2004) reported phonological awareness deficits in children with a history of speech sound disorder but no significant language impairment whose speech problems had resolved before the age of 6 years. In this light it is important to note a proposal made by Leitão, Hogben, and Fletcher (1997) that children with deviant speech processes are likely to succumb to deficits in phonological awareness whereas those with normal but delayed speech development will not. Few studies have analysed the quality of children's speech production and hence the hypothesis proposed by Pennington, that children in the speech problems/no dyslexia category may have phonological problems of a different sort to those in the speech problems/dyslexia category, remains untested (cf. Pascoe, Stackhouse, & Wells, 2006).

In our view a reasonable summary of the findings on children with speech impairments supports a critical age hypothesis proposed by Bishop and colleagues (Bird, Bishop, & Freeman, 1995; Bishop & Adams, 1990). According to this hypothesis children who have speech difficulties that persist to the point at which they need to use phonological skills for learning to read are at high risk of reading problems. There is a proviso: It appears to be critical that these children's speech difficulties are accompanied by poor phoneme awareness. Persisting speech difficulties in the absence of deficits in phoneme awareness do not appear to impact on the development of word-level reading skills. Aside from speech impairments, children who have impairments in oral language skills beyond phonology are highly vulnerable to reading disorders (Catts, Fey, Tomblin & Zhang, 2002); these encompass both word-level decoding deficits and deficits in reading comprehension (Bishop & Adams, 1990; Stothard et al., 1998).

The developmental nature of reading and language impairments makes understanding their interrelationships complex. Indeed it is clear from prospective studies of children at family risk of dyslexia that children follow a number of different developmental pathways to literacy acquisition (Lyytinen et al., 2006; Snowling et al., 2003) and it is difficult to predict which individuals will become poor readers from their preschool status. Together these findings highlight the fact that learning to read is an interactive process involving a range of oral language skills. Within this view, a critical factor determining how well a child learns to read is not a history of speech or language impairment but rather the precise balance of oral language skills possessed by the child at the time when they are learning to read. This point was emphasized by Bishop and Snowling (2004), who argued that the relationship between SLI and dyslexia can be best conceptualized in terms of a two-dimensional space: a phonological dimension and a broader oral language dimension. The two groups share phonological deficits (the primary risk for decoding difficulties) but differ in terms of the broader language skills that are required for reading comprehension.

A different way of viewing comorbidity that might be well suited to understanding developmental cognitive disorders is within a framework in which selective impairments have cascading effects on emergent cognitive processes downstream of the impairment itself. Within this view, such downstream effects can be within the same domain of cognitive function or a different one, depending upon timing and the influence of other genetic and environmental risk and protective factors. To return again to the example of language acquisition, for children whose language development is delayed the timing of formal reading instruction may be particularly crucial in determining whether or not they develop a reading problem. If the notion of both dimensional abilities and the timing of development is taken seriously, then we would expect developmental cognitive disorders to be heterogeneous, which we would argue at a fine-grained level they are.

Separate Risks or Overlapping Interacting Risks?

The recognition of comorbidities has moved us away from a strictly modular view with separate risks for separate disorders, to a more complex view in which we need to think about multiple overlapping risks that may have interactive effects. This argument has recently been advanced by a number of people, including Pennington (2006) and Bishop (2007). For example Bishop has suggested a model for the causation of SLI as depending upon separate environmental and genetic risk factors affecting different cognitive mechanisms. This theory is illustrated in Figure 9.5. In this

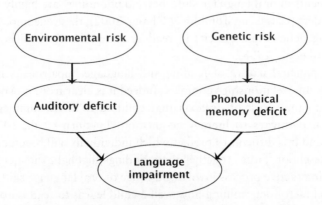

Figure 9.5   Model of the causes of SLI. (Developmental cognitive genetics: How psychology can inform genetics and vice versa, Bishop, D. V. M., *Quarterly Journal of Experimental Psychology*, 2006, Psychology Press, reprinted by permission of the publisher (Taylor and Francis Ltd, *http://www.tandf.co.uk/journals*).)

view neither an inherited phonological memory deficit nor an environmentally acquired auditory perceptual impairment will be sufficient to give rise to SLI, but both together might do so.

Somewhat similar arguments have been made in relation to dyslexia. These views do not dispute the central role that appears to be played by phonological deficits in the causation of dyslexia, but do argue that the effects of such deficits may be exacerbated by other problems or mitigated by compensatory resources (Pennington, 2006). Some evidence relevant to this comes from Snowling (2008), who reported a case-series describing the cognitive profiles of 20 "literacy-impaired" adolescents from a prospective study of children at familial risk of dyslexia, comparing them with 24 individuals from the same high-risk sample who had normal literacy. Data from these children were used to describe their performance on four composite measures: phonological processing, visuospatial skills, attention, and oral language. Deficits in each of these domains was defined as performance at least one standard deviation below the control mean.

As might be expected given the argument we have made so far, there was a strong correlation between literacy skill and the number of cognitive deficits observed in the at-risk group as a whole (the more deficits a child had, the worse their literacy skills were). Thus, it was more common for the literacy-impaired group to have multiple impairments than the group with normal literacy. Among the literacy-impaired group, the most common deficits were in phonology and attention but visual deficits and language impairments were also observed and it was notable that in only one case was there a single deficit in phonology. Among those defined as having normal literacy in the at-risk group, the most prevalent deficits were in attention control whereas neither visual nor language impairments were common. In two cases there was evidence of a phonological deficit but literacy skills were normal.

Together these findings provide support for the view that a child is more likely to reach the diagnostic threshold for dyslexia if they have a phonological deficit. However, this is only part of the story; it appears to be more common for a literacy problem to reach a diagnostic threshold if an individual has deficits in more than one cognitive domain. Moreover, a phonological deficit does not always lead to dyslexia; some 30% of the at-risk group with phonological deficits had impaired spelling but their reading was apparently normal. Together these findings suggest that among children at family risk of dyslexia those with better literacy outcomes show more selectivity in impairments and hence may be more able to compensate for a genetic liability.

These results present a complex picture but one that likely reflects the varied trajectories of development observed in any developmental disorder. Although it is possible at the group level to identify risk factors pertaining to developmental disorders, such an approach does not do justice to the epigenetic landscape within which development unfolds. In the case of dyslexia, there is strong evidence that the primary risk factor is poor phonology, but it is becoming clear that a range of cognitive factors within the individual can work to modify its behavioral expression.

The mechanisms of comorbidity

There is no doubt that the issue of comorbidity poses some real challenges to current ways of thinking about the nature and causes of developmental disorders. There are two issues considered earlier that are relevant to thinking about comorbidity. The first is the idea that disorders need to be seen in dimensional terms. To date, most discussions of comorbidity have tended to be framed in terms of categorical diagnoses. Indeed the definition of comorbidity as "the co-occurrence of two diseases or disorders within an individual" depends upon the use of categorical labels. However, if we view disorders as dimensional, comorbidity translates into the idea that different dimensions of impairment correlate with each other. This view in turn might be seen simply as the corollary of the idea that skills in the general population tend to correlate: People who are good in one cognitive domain (say language) are likely to be better than average in other domains (say mathematics or music).

Genetic mechanisms of comorbidity.
The idea of correlated dimensions of ability/disability needs to be explained. Such correlations are likely to reflect both environmental and genetic influences, and there is no doubt that a better understanding of comorbidities will depend upon the use of genetically sensitive research designs (i.e., designs such as twin and adoption studies that can identify the operation of genetic influences). It is also relevant to emphasize that, for all the disorders we have considered, genetic influences appear to depend upon multiple genes, each of which have small effects (polygenic inheritance). Recent studies of genetic influences on developmental disorders (e.g., Plomin & Kovas, 2005; Happé, Ronald, & Plomin, 2006) have emphasized the idea of "generalist genes." There is evidence of three sorts showing that genes may have general (i.e., nonspecific) effects on cognitive development and cognitive disorders (Plomin & Kovas, 2005). First, genes that are responsible for disabilities seem largely the same as the genes responsible for normal variations in abilities (this provides support for the argument that disorders or disabilities should be seen as the lower end of a dimension of normal skills). Second, genes that affect one aspect of a disability also tend to influence other aspects (e.g., there are common genetic effects on grammatical and vocabulary skills). Third, and perhaps most surprisingly, genes that affect one disability (e.g., reading disorder) seem also to affect others (e.g., mathematics disorder). This last effect suggests a genetic basis for comorbidities. To put this point crudely, there may be genes that code for problems with brain development that operate in somewhat nonspecific ways. Of course, the degree to which genetic effects are general is not complete and there is some degree of genetic specificity underlying different disorders. However, the current evidence suggests that the extent of shared genetic influences on different disorders is much larger than might have been expected.

One example of shared genetic influences on seemingly disparate aspects of development comes from a study by Bishop (2002). Bishop studied a sample of monozygotic and dizygotic twins where one or both twins had received a diagnosis of SLI. Analyses indicated evidence for shared genetic influences on measures of speech production accuracy and tapping speed, and nonword repetition and tapping speed. Thus common genes appeared to be influencing the development of both speech and manual motor skills. In Chapter 4 we described evidence that children with SLI commonly have comorbid problems with motor development, and this study suggests that both forms of difficulty may depend in part upon shared genetic influences.

Brain mechanisms of comorbidity

Irrespective of how genetic mechanisms contribute to the comorbidities observed between disorders, we need to consider how such genetic effects operate to influence brain development and behavior. A plausible cause of comorbidity is that there is anatomical proximity between brain regions that subserve different cognitive functions, and in particular shared neural networks.

In Chapter 4 we discussed such an argument, proposed by Ullman and Pierpont (2005), to account for the frequent co-occurrence of specific language impairment with developmental coordination disorder. In a similar vein, Castellanos, Sonuga-Barke, Milham, and Tannock (2006) hypothesized that the variability seen within ADHD might be accounted for by the involvement of a network of distributed cortical loops. Specifically, they proposed that pathways consisting of striatal-nigral-striatal and thalamocorticothalamic networks provide the neuroanatomical basis through which motivational factors (related to medial prefrontal cortex) influence executive control (subserved by dorsal prefrontal cortex), which in turn influence motor pathways. Possibly for this reason, developmental coordination disorders occur in up to half of children with ADHD.

We are at a very early stage in understanding how both genetic differences and environmental experiences shape the development of neural networks. The knowledge that we have accumulated from investigating the endpoint of developmental disorders needs to be re-examined in the light of data emerging from prospective studies of high-risk groups. Such data will bring us closer to an understanding of the primary causes and consequences of disorders and their comorbidities in terms of differing patterns of brain development.

Environmental influences on comorbidity

The role of environmental factors in the etiology of developmental cognitive disorders, and particularly in understanding comorbidity, remains little studied. As yet we only have sketchy answers to basic questions such as how the outcomes of reading and language impairments depend on social class variables or how children with ADHD fare in response to different forms of parenting. In this light, our discussion must be considered speculative. It certainly seems reasonable to assume that a child who possesses susceptibility genes for a developmental disorder will fare less well if they experience adverse environmental conditions. For example, it has been suggested that maternal smoking and drug abuse may be risk factors for ADHD (Taylor, 2006).

It may also be important to differentiate between environmental factors operating at different levels. In cases of social deprivation, it seems likely that different children within the same family will suffer similar adversity (though individual differences in resilience will have an influence). It is also important to consider the effects of the specific environment experienced by individual children. Educational interventions may be important here. For example, if the teacher of a child with dyslexia understands that this same child is at risk of problems with arithmetic, the use of specialist teaching strategies to support the development of arithmetic may prevent difficulties in this area developing. In contrast, when no specific strategies are put in place, the likelihood of mathematical difficulties as a comorbid disorder will be increased. The environment that a child with a developmental disorder chooses for him or herself may also play a role in the development of a secondary disorder. For example, a child with specific language impairment may avoid social interaction and hence reduce their opportunity to enjoy the range of play and games activities that encourages the development of fine and gross motor skills. Such a child may increasingly resemble one with developmental coordination disorder as they develop, whereas a more gregarious child might overcome a delay in motor development by virtue of extended practice during play.

In summary it is important to acknowledge the interplay of genetic and environmental factors. A child's active choice of their environment, as witnessed for example by the child with dyslexia who chooses nonliterary pursuits, is a case of active gene–environment correlation. At the same time, if the child is born into a family with reading difficulties, it may be that there are fewer books in the home and that less value is placed on literacy: a case of passive gene–environment correlation. If the same child is never picked at school to take part in class reading activities, this is an example of reactive gene–environment correlation; the teacher is reacting to his or her difficulties and thereby altering the environment they experience. In short, the child is an active participant in the environment and the experiences that shape their development and is not just a passive recipient of the genes they inherit.

Finally, there is currently a great deal of research interest in the process of gene–environment interaction, an enterprise that has borne fruit in understanding why some individuals develop depression in response to stressful life events and others do not (Caspi et al., 2002). The study of gene–environment interaction in the field of developmental cognitive disorders is only just beginning (see McGrath et al., 2007). However as candidate genes for disorders are identified, this opens up the possibility of investigating such effects, for example the differential response to intervention in children with different combinations of risk alleles.

Environmental Influences on Developmental Cognitive Disorders

The cognitive approach espoused in this book, by design, focuses on the mental processes that are operating within an individual child. However, genes act through environments, which together shape brain functions and cognitive processes. As we have stressed repeatedly, development is a highly interactive process and understanding developmental disorders will need to encompass multiple influences on development. It may seem to some readers that we have stressed the role of genetic influences on the disorders covered at the expense of considering environmental influences. We hope here to do something to redress that balance.

It might be argued that while identifying the susceptibility genes for different disorders has proved challenging so far, it may prove to be a relatively easy part in understanding most disorders (Rutter, 2002). Because different genes with small effects potentially interact, both with other genes and with a range of environmental influences, once such interactions are taken seriously the challenges of tracing causal pathways from genes operating in environments to variations in brain function become truly daunting. For all the disorders we have considered there is little doubt that environmental influences on their development are important. At the most basic level we have often quoted heritability estimates for different disorders. Heritability estimates assess the proportion of variance in a population attributable to genetic differences. So, for example, the heritability of dyslexia has been estimated to be around .5, meaning that 50% of the differences in reading skills between children with dyslexia and the general population are attributable to genetic differences. (There are technical issues to do with the fact that such estimates of broad heritability may tend to overstate the importance of genetic effects – because gene–environment interactions are counted as part of the genetic variance – that we will not dwell on here.) The important point, however, is that the range of heritabilities considered in this book always leaves a substantial proportion of the variance unaccounted for, and this variance is likely to reflect environmental influences. Thus, in quantitative terms, environmental influences on development are generally substantial and cannot be ignored.

One other important point to make is that heritability is not a fixed immutable quantity. Changes in the environment may change the heritability of a characteristic. Leaving that aside, estimates of significant heritability do not mean that environmental changes cannot produce important changes in a characteristic. Human height is highly heritable, but in the recent past in affluent societies there have been substantial increases in average height that are attributable to improved nutrition. A similar example comes from the study of intelligence. Although intelligence is highly heritable it has been shown that if children from disadvantaged backgrounds are adopted into good environments then substantial increases in IQ may follow (Duyme, Dumaret, & Tomkiewicz, 1999). By analogy, while reading skills may be highly heritable, that does not mean that improvements in educational provision cannot enable the vast majority of children to attain "adequate" reading skills. This does not imply that we can eliminate individual differences in reading skills by teaching. On the contrary, it is likely that even when reading is well taught there will remain substantial variations in reading skills in the population. However, if improved teaching can bring about overall increases in reading levels for all children, this may mean that those children with the weakest reading skills end up with "adequate" reading skills that enable them to access a range of other opportunities. (The analogy of increasing height given better nutrition should be clear here.) This idea of changing the level of a characteristic while leaving the distribution of skills unchanged is illustrated graphically in Figure 9.6. The important point is that, given current knowledge and technologies, environmental influences on development are easier to alter than genetic effects. Recognizing the importance of genetic effects should not deter us from attempts to improve the developmental outcomes of children at risk of a variety of developmental cognitive disorders.

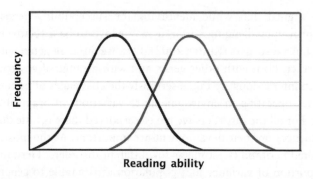

Reading ability

Figure 9.6   Graph showing two normal distributions of reading ability. Hypothetically, increases in the intensity and quality of teaching might shift the distribution of reading skills in the population to the right (everyone becomes a better reader) while leaving the variations among children in their levels of reading skill unaltered.

To some extent our lesser coverage of environmental influences on developmental disorders reflects the fact that understanding the environmental causes of disorders is conceptually and practically very difficult. The range of potential environmental influences on the development of cognitive processes is very broad (ranging from diseases, birth complications, and nutrition to more purely psychosocial factors such as parenting practices and school experiences) and the methods needed to demonstrate environmental influences on development are complex and demanding (see Rutter, 2005a, for a review). There are nevertheless some clear effects of environmental influences on both the typical development of skills and disorders of those skills. Language development shows clear evidence of influences from patterns of communication that the child experiences. For example, it is known that twins typically lag behind singleton children in terms of their language development (Rutter & Redshaw, 1991). Since twins should not differ systematically in their genetic makeup from their singleton siblings, this provides evidence that environmental circumstances influence language development. It appears that these differences in language development in twins reflect differences in patterns of parent–child communication and interaction (Rutter, Bailey, & Lord, 2003; Thorpe, Rutter, & Greenwood, 2003). To make things more complicated, it appears that the relative importance of genetic influence (i.e., heritability) on the development of verbal skills varies as a function of family environment. The heritability of verbal skills is higher in twins reared in families who score high on a measure of family "chaos" (Asbury, Wachs, & Plomin, 2005).

There is also evidence for a range of environmental risk factors of a more biological nature on the development of cognitive disorders. So, for example, being born prematurely (which at least in some cases probably reflects environmental factors) is a risk factor for developing mathematics disorder and developmental coordination disorder. There is also evidence that maternal smoking during pregnancy is a risk factor for the development of ADHD (e.g., Thapar, Langley, Asharson, & Till, 2007).

So far, however, we must accept that we understand little about the wide range of environmental influences (parents, home, schools, and neighborhoods, let alone educational policies) that may contribute to the causation and amelioration of developmental cognitive disorders. Not only does this constitute a major omission but it also highlights an unwitting bias in our current understanding. After some 30 years of very active research on children's disorders of language and cognition, it is still the case that the majority of study samples are small and highly selected. Furthermore, the samples mostly consist of children whose parents have sought referrals because of concerns about their child's development. When such samples are the basis for quantitative genetic research, a restricted range of environments will be represented and estimates of heritability will be inflated, thus again demoting the role of environment. There is an urgent need for the field to move toward working with representative samples. More longitudinal studies of representative samples of children would be particularly valuable in helping to provide answers to questions of causality, as exemplified by the highly influential Isle of Wight studies (Rutter & Maughan 2005).

In a similar vein, Hobcraft (2006) calls for closer collaboration with demographers in order to understand the interplay between genetic factors, family endowments, and previous experiences in shaping individual behavior, whilst stressing the importance of pathways rather than single causes. Such an approach would be fruitful for understanding the causes and consequences of developmental disorders.

Whither (or Wither?) a Cognitive Perspective on Developmental Cognitive Disorders?

To some people, the rapid advances in genetic and neuroimaging techniques might hold the promise of replacing cognitive psychological studies of developmental disorders. As cognitive psychologists this is a view we would reject. Cognition is the level of explanation that mediates between brain processes and behavior. Understanding the cognitive processes underlying behavior offers the most direct approach to diagnosis and treatment. Moreover, clarification of the cognitive phenotypes of behavioral disorders is essential for understanding their genetic and neural bases.

However, the view that developmental disorders are dimensional and frequently comorbid has some profound methodological implications for studies of their cognitive, neural, and genetic bases. The vast majority of studies that we have considered in this book consist of case–control studies. In such studies children are selected because they fulfill certain diagnostic criteria: in the case of SLI for example, usually poor performance on a range of language tests coupled with a nonverbal IQ above 80. Such a group of children is then compared to a group of typically developing children of the same age (or sometimes the same language ability). In some studies (but by no means all) attempts are made to select "pure" clinical cases that do not show signs of comorbid disorders. In practice, however, even when this is attempted it is only ever likely to be partly successful. Furthermore, if comorbidities between different disorders are as pervasive as recent evidence suggests, the selection of "pure" cases may be practically impossible (too many tests would need to be given to each child), perhaps theoretically impossible (excluding all possible comorbidities will result in no "pure" cases to study!), and if it can be done at all such an approach will result in the selection of children who are unrepresentative of the group of children (say children with SLI) we set out to study.

This might seem like a counsel of despair. It is not, but it does hold some implications for future studies. First, in case–control studies it seems that more time and trouble needs to be taken to allow a broader assessment of a child's pattern of strengths and weaknesses. It is likely that this will reveal that many cases are "impure" but with data about levels of other difficulties in a sample we can at least try to exclude such associated difficulties as possible explanations for the candidate causal deficits that are identified. Second, this perspective makes the use of multivariate studies more attractive. Such studies would involve the assessment of broad ranges of abilities in large representative samples of children. This in turn allows us to identify the correlates of certain abilities/deficits to be identified. Once again, making assessments as broad as possible allows other potential confounding differences to be excluded as possible explanations for the correlations that are found. In both case–control and multivariate studies we badly need more data from longitudinal studies that track the changes in deficits over time, and the predictors of such changes. It is likely that the use of individual growth curve modeling will become much more widespread in this area in the coming years, though such methods will require frequent reassessments of children's skills (to chart growth trajectories) and preferably fairly large samples.

A final and highly promising approach (that is a variant of multivariate longitudinal studies) is given by prospective longitudinal studies of children at family risk of disorders. Comparing the development of such children to that of children at low risk of the disorder is a powerful technique. Such studies offer the opportunity of tracking the development of brain–behavior relationships, monitoring progress across different cognitive domains and examining the influence of environmental factors. In turn, by comparing the cognitive profiles of affected and nonaffected members of at-risk families, it will be possible to gain a better understanding of the dimensional nature of disorders and of the factors that lead some individuals to reach a threshold for "diagnosis."

Family "at-risk" studies will also help in the search for endophenotypes. As Gottesman and Gould (2003) argue, for diseases with complex genetics (like cognitive disorders), genotypes are not strongly indicative of phenotypes. Hence the search for candidate genes has had only limited success. The concept of an endophenotype captures a process intermediate between the genotype and phenotype. To take an example from reading disorders, poor phonological skill is an endophenotype of dyslexia (Snowling, 2008). Endophenotypes are less complex than disorders and frequently are observed among nonaffected, as well as affected, family members. Endophenotypes may therefore help in finding the genetic vulnerabilities that, together with other liabilities (genetic or environmental), are the source of the disorder itself.

An excellent example of the utility of this approach comes from research on the causes of SLI (Chapter 7). Having discounted the possibility that a heterogeneous disorder like SLI could have a single cause, Bishop (2006) describes how the investigation of putative endophenotypes has elucidated its etiology. The starting point for these investigations was the finding that poor nonword repetition does not only characterize affected twins with SLI but also frequently their co-twins who do not fulfill diagnostic criteria for the condition. Behavior–genetic analyses using nonword repetition as a measure of an endophenotype of SLI revealed substantial genetic influence. Subsequently, a gene marker was identified on chromosome 16 showing strong associations with poor nonword repetition (Newbury, Bishop, & Monaco, 2005). It will be recalled that SLI is also typically associated with deficits in inflectional morphology (particularly with marking the regular past tense and third person singular forms of verbs). Bishop, Adams, and Norbury (2006) asked 6-year-old twins to repeat nonwords and to complete a task requiring them to add past tense endings to verbs (yesterday he jump(ed) into the pool). Once again, they found a substantial genetic influence on nonword repetition and this was also the case for inflectional morphology. However, bivariate analyses produced no strong evidence for a genetic association between performance on the two tasks, suggesting that different genes are associated with each of the endophenotypes. Moreover, scrutiny of the data indicated that children with a single deficit were less likely to be identified clinically as cases of SLI than were those with both deficits. These findings dovetail with those of Snowling (2008), who found that children with literacy difficulties were more likely to be diagnosed as dyslexic if they had impairments in both phonological and broader language skills. Together these findings point to an important conclusion: A child is more likely to reach a conventional threshold for diagnosis if more than one cognitive process is impaired. Arguably, this in turn reflects the fact that development follows multiple pathways and, as Waddington (1966) originally proposed, it shows a remarkable self-righting tendency.

Dimensional Comorbid Disorders: Implications for Assessment and Treatment

Seeing disorders as dimensional with frequent comorbidities also has important (and constructive) implications for educational and clinical practice. This view moves us away from "putting kids in boxes" and leads us to phrase diagnoses in more subtle and nuanced ways. To say "John has dyslexia and dyspraxia" is to take a snapshot of his current performance on some standardized tests of reading and motor skills. Worryingly such labels are sometimes endowed with unwarranted explanatory force: saying that "John cannot read because he is dyslexic" simply restates the problem but does nothing to explain the cause of the reading problem. Dimensional statements lead naturally to descriptions of strengths and weaknesses that may carry direct implications for educational management. For example, to say that John "has severe phonological and reading difficulties coupled with some difficulties with fine motor skills including handwriting" is arguably more useful than saying he has dyslexia and dyspraxia, and leads directly to educational recommendations (John needs help learning to read, and help in improving his handwriting).

A recurrent issue in this book has been the relationship between understanding disorders and developing treatments for them. We believe that there is a close, but indirect, relationship between theory (understanding a disorder) and practice (treating a disorder). At the most basic level, understanding the nature of the cognitive processes that are deficient is fundamental to planning effective treatments for different disorders. However, the links between understanding a disorder and devising treatments to ameliorate it are somewhat indirect. Suppose we decide that we have identified a major cognitive cause of a particular disorder (e.g., that a phonological deficit is a cause of developmental dyslexia, or that visuospatial deficits are a cause of developmental coordination disorder). The most obvious approach to treatment is to devise programs to train out the cognitive deficit and observe if the training improves symptoms of the disorder (train phonological skills and see if reading improves; train visuospatial skills and see if motor skills improve). The first issue here is to identify whether the deficit is amenable to training (phonological skills are; we do not yet know how easily visuospatial skills can be trained). If a deficit cannot be trained effectively it may be that we need to accept the deficit and teach the child ways to minimize its effects. These two alternatives "teaching to a deficit" or "teaching round a deficit" have long been recognized in special education.

Assuming a putative causal deficit can be improved by training, it is essential to assess the effects of such training on the disorder itself. It is always possible that a deficit can be reduced by training but that such improvements will not transfer to the critical behavioral problems seen in the disorder. For example, Hatcher, Hulme, and Ellis (1994) showed that phonological training produced large improvements in the phonological skills of children with reading difficulties, but these improvements did not result in significant improvements in these children's reading skills. However, giving these children phonological training combined with reading instruction was highly effective in helping them learn to read (more effective than spending the same amount of time on either reading or phonological training alone). This makes the important point that newly acquired skills may not directly generalize and that it is always essential to evaluate rigorously the effects of interventions that appear to be theoretically well founded. The methods for evaluating such interventions are now well understood and several examples of randomized controlled trials have already been described in earlier chapters. We should note in passing that it is depressing to see how many theoretically ill-founded recommendations for intervention are nevertheless still applied in the field of developmental disorders, and how poor sometimes the evaluation of such interventions are methodologically (Bishop, 2007b; Rack, Snowling, Hulme, & Gibbs, 2007).

Finally, as we argued in Chapter 1, treatment studies can be powerful ways of assessing causal theories of disorders. In fact, arguably, randomized controlled trials are the best way for trying to test causal theories about the origins of cognitive disorders (or other forms of disorder). A strong test of a causal theory is provided by a training study that can bring about improvements in the proposed cause of the disorder, and by using random assignment of children to groups we can reduce the likelihood that any effects of the treatment are attributable to uncontrolled and unmeasured differences between the treated and untreated groups.

We should note, however, that the process of working from an RCT to test and develop causal theories is far from straightforward. In practice RCTs are expensive and difficult to conduct and there is often a temptation to add in many components to a treatment to maximize the chances that it will "work." There is, however, one statistical approach to analyzing RCTs that seems to hold great promise for increasing their theoretical power. This involves the assessment of mediators. The idea is that it should be possible to assess the extent to which improvements in an outcome measure are attributable to (statistically mediated by) improvements in a deficient skill that has been trained (see Kraemer, Wilson, Fairburn, & Argas, 2002, for a discussion of mediators and moderators of outcomes in treatment trials). We will explain this approach briefly.

The idea of a mediator was first introduced in a classic paper by Baron and Kenny (1986). A mediator is an intervening variable (or process) that can explain the effects of a "cause" on an "outcome." It may be useful to go back to the example of lung cancer and its relationship to smoking considered in Chapter 1. As we noted in Chapter 1, the idea that smoking causes lung cancer can be represented in the form of a path diagram (Figure 9.7).

To provide support for such a theory, we could collect longitudinal data relating variations in smoking earlier in life to later rates of lung cancer. Statistically, if smoking causes lung cancer, we would expect that variations in how heavily people smoke and for how long would predict the likelihood of them getting lung cancer (assessed in an appropriate regression analysis).

As we argued in Chapter 1, such a theory could be expanded and strengthened by measuring some intervening variables that provide a plausible biological mechanism for causing lung cancer. It appears that components of cigarette smoke cause damage to the DNA in cells in the lung, and this DNA damage causes these cells to grow into tumors. To look for effects of this statistically we would therefore measure rates of mutations in lung cell tissue in smokers. We could then draw and evaluate a more complex path diagram.

In this diagram (Figure 9.8) the presence of lung cell mutations mediates the effects of smoking on cancer. Baron and Kenny developed statistical methods for assessing whether mediators were operating. Basically, in a regression analysis, to support a mediation model, we would want to show four things: (1) that smoking is associated with lung cancer (Path A); (2) that smoking is associated with lung cell mutations (Path B); (3) that lung cell mutations are associated with lung cancer (Path C); and (4) if points 1–3 are true the effects of smoking as a predictor of lung cancer (Path A) should be weakened (or eliminated) if we account for the effects of lung cell mutations (Path B/C). In such a model, if the effects of smoking on lung cancer are completely mediated by lung cell mutations then there should be no direct effect of

Figure 9.7   Path diagram showing that smoking causes cancer.

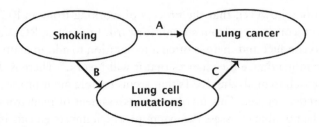

Figure 9.8   Path diagram showing that lung cell mutations mediate the effects of smoking.

smoking on rates of lung cancer (Path A should be of negligible importance) once the effect of mutations is accounted for. This idea is represented in the diagram by a dotted arrow (i.e., a statistically nonsignificant regression weight). The details of the statistics need not detain us; the point is simply that methods have been developed and subsequently refined (Shrout & Bolger, 2002; Stone & Sobel, 1990), which allow us to assess the extent to which intervening variables "mediate" or explain the effects of a putative cause (smoking) on an outcome (lung cancer).

The application of these ideas to RCTs is, we hope, obvious. In an RCT we assign children randomly to receive a treatment (the treatment, if it works, is then established as a cause of the improvement). By measuring intervening processes we can try to explain how the treatment works. One example of such an analysis is that cited in Chapter 7 (MTA Cooperative Group, 2004, from the MTA trial for children with ADHD). In that analysis it was reported that variations in the effectiveness of methylphenidate (Ritalin) as a treatment for ADHD were mediated by treatment compliance; the drug worked if children took it, but the fact that children tended to stop taking the drug after the trial accounted for the lessening of the treatment's effectiveness over time. Arguably treatment compliance is a practically important, but not a theoretically interesting, intervening variable.

A more theoretically interesting example of such an analysis comes from an intervention study designed to prevent early alcohol/drug use and early sexual activity in African-American children (Brody et al., 2004). The intervention aimed to foster a regulated and communicative parenting style. The authors were able to show that the parental intervention produced the desired changes in children's attitudes to a variety of issues, including attitudes to alcohol/drug use and early sexual behavior. Most critically, a path analysis of the sort described above showed that the intervention's effects on children's attitudes were mediated by changes in parenting style.

A similar example, in the domain of cognitive disorders, comes from our own work on reading difficulties. Returning to the evidence and theories discussed in Chapter 2 there is evidence that problems in learning to read depend critically upon children's knowledge of letter sounds and their ability to identify phonemes within spoken words (these are the foundations of the alphabetic principle; Byrne, 1998). Bowyer-Crane et al. (2008) reported the results of an RCT in which children identified as having weak oral language skills at school entry were randomly assigned to a phonology with reading intervention or an oral language (vocabulary and narrative) intervention. The phonology with reading intervention produced modest but reliable increases in children's reading skills at the end of the intervention compared to the oral language intervention. Subsequent analyses have shown that the effects of the phonology with reading intervention were mediated by increases in children's letter knowledge and their ability to manipulate phonemes in spoken words. This pattern provides support for the theory that guided the development of the intervention: The phonology with reading program was effective precisely because it increased children's letter knowledge and phoneme manipulation abilities. Such a result provides support for the causal theory that guided the development of the intervention.

Achievements and Aspirations for Understanding Developmental Cognitive Disorders

Research on developmental disorders is in a healthy and vigorous condition. Although this is a young scientific discipline, no one, we hope, would doubt that we have learned a great deal about all the disorders we have discussed in the last decade or two. For each disorder we have a quite extensive understanding of its characteristics and the likely risk factors that lead to its development. Such understanding, in turn, helps to inform diagnosis and treatment. However it is also probably fair to say that current theories and methods are in a state of flux.

One of the guiding principles of studies in this field, as in the rest of cognitive psychology, has been the idea of modularity: that the mind consists of separable systems or modules that presumably are instantiated in separable neural circuits in the brain. We have no doubt that a degree of modularity of mind exists and this is shown in part by evidence of the very different profiles shown by the different disorders discussed in this book. However, it is clear that in developmental disorders highly modular deficits are relatively rare and often children show complex patterns of co-occurring impairments. The field is currently wrestling with how best to conceptualize such comorbidities. It is probably important that our precious theoretical baby (modularity) does not get thrown out with the slightly murky bath water. If there were no modularity in the developing mind this book would look very different. However, developmental cognitive disorders are certainly less independent than we or many others had hoped or expected them to be.

In our view, the next decade is likely to see exciting advances in understanding developmental disorders. There are real signs that genetic, brain imaging, computational modeling, and experimental cognitive techniques are coming together to improve our understanding. The power of these different approaches will come from combining them effectively. The ultimate aim, to trace developmental causal pathways from genes and environments via brains to cognition and behavior, will only be realized by the more complete integration of these different perspectives or levels of analysis. Tracing pathways is not a call for reductionism: Each level of analysis is important and ultimately understanding the relationships between the different levels in causal theories will enrich our understanding at all levels. Cognitive psychologists should not feel worried about being made redundant by geneticists or neuroscientists! Finally, as well as seeing theories that more effectively unite different levels of explanation, we expect the next generation of theories to become more truly interactive; there is not a one-way street running from genes to brains to behavior. Our own behaviour depends upon, but produces feedback to, our brain. Changes in the brain and our other bodily organs, in turn, may affect patterns of gene expression. Understanding how mechanisms at these different levels affect each other to control development represents a remarkable challenge, but one that we have already made a useful start on.

Glossary

American Psychiatric Association (APA): The main professional organization of psychiatrists in the USA. Publishes the DSM (see below).

Amygdalae (singular amygdala): Groups of neurons located within the medial temporal lobes of the brain that perform a role in processing emotional reactions (part of the limbic system).

Anaphora: A linguistic device for maintaining coherence both within and across sentences. Anaphoric reference is often signaled by the use of a pronoun such as *he, she,* or *they* (in subject position) and *him, her,* and *them* (in object position).

Angular gyrus: A region of the brain involved in processes related to language and cognition. Located in the inferior parietal lobe near the superior edge of the temporal lobe.

Anxiety disorder: A blanket term covering several different forms of pathological anxiety, fears, and phobias.

Applied behavior analysis (ABA): Functional analysis of the role of environmental factors in determining behavior, undertaken in order to design and implement a management plan to produce a significant improvement in behavior (often used in the management of autism).

Apraxia: An inability to make purposeful motor movements.

Asperger syndrome (AS): A neurobiological disorder named after a Viennese physician, Hans Asperger. People with AS show marked deficiencies in social skills, have restricted interests, and often have obsessive routines. A disorder on the autism spectrum in which language development is normal (see also *Autism spectrum disorder*).

Atypical autism: Term used to describe a condition similar to autism in which the specific behavioral criteria required for the diagnosis of autism are not fulfilled.

Autism Diagnostic Interview (ADI): A semistructured parent interview covering the developmental history of the referred person used in the diagnosis of autism.

Autism Diagnostic Observation Schedule (ADOS): A standardized protocol for assessing the social and communicative behaviors associated with autism. The examiner elicits a designated set of behaviors from the participant and assigns these to predetermined categories.

Autism spectrum disorder (ASD): A group of psychological conditions characterized by pervasive abnormalities of social interaction and communication, as well as restricted interests and repetitive behavior. The three main forms of ASD are autism, Asperger syndrome, and pervasive developmental disorder not otherwise specified (PDD-NOS).

Basal ganglia: A group of nuclei in the brain interconnected with the cerebral cortex, thalamus, and brainstem; associated with a variety of functions, including motor control, cognition, emotion, and learning.

Behavioral theories: Theories that aim to explain behavior in terms of environmental contingencies.

Block Design: A subtest of some IQ tests that assesses visuospatial skills. The examinee is required to arrange blocks to reproduce a pattern within a time limit (also referred to as pattern construction on some scales).

BOLD response: Blood Oxygen Level Dependent hemodynamic response – the basis of fMRI. The BOLD response measures changes in blood oxygen levels, which reflect changes in metabolic activity in groups of neurons, and is used to infer which regions of the brain are active in a particular task.

Catecholamines: Chemical compounds used in neuronal transmission.

Cerebellum: A structure at the bottom and back of the brain involved in coordination of movements and for learning skilled behaviors.

Chromosomes: Structures of DNA and protein that are found in the nucleus of cells. Chromosomes carry the genetic material of the individual.

Chronological age (CA) match: A research strategy in which a group of clinical cases are compared with a group of typically developing children of the same chronological age.

Cochlear: The auditory portion of the inner ear. The cochlear is a coiled structure filled with a liquid that moves hair cells in response to the vibrations coming from the middle ear and converts this motion into electrical signals, which travel along the auditory nerve to structures in the brainstem.

Coherent motion: A measure of the sensitivity of the magnocellular visual system to movement; assessed by tasks in which large collections of stimuli (usually dots) move with different degrees of "coherence" of direction.

Cohesive inference: An inference that requires the integration of textual information. For example in "Sally went to the supermarket. She bought some milk" the reader must be able to link *she* with *Sally* in order to understand the text.

Communication disorders: A diagnostic category in DSM-IV (American Psychiatric Association, 1994) used to describe children whose scores obtained on individually administered measures of language development are below expectation given "nonverbal intellectual capacity."

Comorbidity: The presence of one or more disorders (or diseases) in addition to a primary disease or disorder.

Comprehension monitoring: The ability to recognize when your own comprehension of a text has broken down.

Concordance rate: The rate of co-occurrence of a categorical measure in twin pairs (i.e., the proportion of twins in a sample who both fall into the same category).

If concordance rates are higher for identical (MZ) than nonidentical (DZ) twins, this is consistent with the characteristic being heritable.

Conduct disorder: A behavioral disorder that is characterized by an inability to follow rules and to behave in a socially acceptable way (see also *Oppositional defiant disorder*).

Congenital: A disorder or disease that is present from birth.

Connectionist model: A theory implemented as a computer program that simulates a basic cognitive process through the learning of simple associations.

Constructive inference: An inference that is required in order to integrate different sources of information, such as information from a text with general knowledge.

Contrast sensitivity: A measure of the limit of visibility for low contrast patterns.

Cortex (cerebral cortex): The outermost layer of the brain, which is the site of cognitive functions.

Declarative memory: The aspect of human memory that stores specific facts. It refers to memories that can be consciously retrieved, or declared.

Decoding: The ability to decipher printed words and translate them into pronunciations.

Derivational morphology: The part of grammar that deals with the derivations of words. For example, the syntactic change brought about by the addition of a suffix to a word stem: *glory* (noun) + *fy* → *glorify* (verb).

Diagnostic and Statistical Manual of Mental Disorders (DSM): The American handbook for mental health professionals that lists different categories of mental disorders and the criteria for diagnosing them, according to the American Psychiatric Association. The acronym DSM is usually followed by a Roman numeral that indicates the edition number (e.g., DSM-IV).

Dizygotic (DZ) or fraternal twins: Twins who develop from two fertilized ova and share 50% of their segregating (varying) genes on average.

Dopamine: A neurotransmitter critical to brain activity and arousal.

Dopamine transporter: A protein that binds the neurotransmitter dopamine and performs reuptake of it from the synapse into a neuron.

Dorsolateral prefrontal cortex (DL-PFC): Part of the frontal lobes of the brain that is connected to a variety of areas that allow it to play a role in the integration of sensory and mnemonic information and the regulation of intellectual function and action.

Dyspraxia: A disorder characterized by the partial loss of the ability to coordinate and perform certain purposeful movements and gestures in the absence of motor or sensory impairments.

EEG (electroencephalogram): A recording of the brain's changes in electrical activity over time, taken from electrodes placed on the surface of the head.

Effect size: A measure of the magnitude of an observed effect, often expressed in standard deviation units.

Elaborative inference: An inference that requires the integration of textual information with knowledge external to the text. Elaborative inferences are not vital to comprehension but are thought to lead to a richer representation of a text.

Endophenotype: A hereditary characteristic associated with a condition that may be shared by affected and unaffected relatives.

Epidemiology: The study of representative samples of a population, usually with a focus on factors that may explain health and illness.

Epigenesis: A process of "unfolding" during development that depends on the interaction of genetic and environmental influences.

ERP (event-related potential): Patterns of time-locked electrical (EEG) brain activity evoked by a stimulus.

Exception words: Words for which the written form does not follow the normal grapheme–phoneme mappings of the language (e.g., yacht). Also sometimes referred to as irregular words.

Executive functions (EF): Mental operations that enable an individual to disengage from the immediate context in order to guide behavior by reference to mental models or future goals. These interacting but potentially dissociable operations include working memory, response inhibition, planning, and cognitive flexibility.

Expressive language disorder: A communication disorder affecting language production that is characterized by limited use of vocabulary and poor grasp of grammar, resulting in a difficulty in communication.

Fine motor skills: Motor skills that involve the coordination of small movements, usually of the hands (e.g., threading beads, holding a knife and fork to eat, and pencil control).

Frontal lobe: An area of the cortex at the front of each cerebral hemisphere, in front of (anterior to) the parietal lobes. The frontal lobes are involved in a variety of functions, including "executive" or regulatory functions.

Functional magnetic resonance imaging (fMRI): A process that measures functionally induced changes in brain activity using the BOLD response, which assessed changes in blood oxygen levels associated with neural activity.

Grapheme: The minimal unit of an alphabetic writing system. Graphemes include single letters (e.g., *t*) and small groups of letters (e.g., *th*) corresponding to a phoneme.

Graphemic parsing skills: Sensitivity to graphic features of letters and the ability to segment letter strings into the graphemes that map to phonemes (sounds).

Gross motor skills: Large coordinated movements, such as those involved in walking, jumping, and riding a bike.

Heritability: Heritability is an estimate of the extent to which differences among individuals in a population reflect genetic differences. A heritability estimate of zero would mean that genetic differences played no role in explaining the differences among people in a characteristic, whereas a heritability estimate of 1.0 would mean that genetic differences accounted entirely for the differences observed.

Heterotypic comorbidity: The co-occurrence in an individual of two disorders of different types (e.g., dyslexia and developmental coordination disorder).

High-functioning autism (HFA): Persons with many or all the symptoms of autism who have an IQ in the normal or superior range.

Homotypic comorbidity: The co-occurrence in an individual of two disorders from the same group (e.g., dyslexia and language impairment – both language learning difficulties).

Hyperactivity: A state in which a person is abnormally physically active or restless.

Hyperlexia: A disorder in which children with delayed language and cognitive development show surprisingly advanced word recognition skills but poor text comprehension. Often associated with autism.

Inattention: Difficulty in focusing or maintaining attention, often coupled with a failure to listen carefully or to follow instructions.

Inflected word form: A base word with an added morpheme that may indicate grammatical information (e.g., tense or gender). An example would be *dog* + *s* → *dogs*.

Inflectional morphology: The system concerned with adding an inflection to change the form (prefix, suffix, or vowel change) of a word to reflect grammatical status.

Instantiation: A specific meaning that can be inferred from context, even though only a general term may be present.

Interference control: The ability to attend selectively to a given set of cues, whilst ignoring or suppressing extraneous information (inhibition).

Intraparietal sulcus: Region of the parietal lobe thought to be involved in arithmetic function and visual spatial processing.

Kinesthesis: Sense of position and movement of parts of the body.

Learning disability (LD): Term used (especially in the USA) to refer to a group of disorders that affect academic and functional skills, including the ability to read, write, spell, calculate, reason, and organize information.

Lexical reading: The use of reading strategies that involve direct retrieval of knowledge of words, as contrasted with decoding words by the use of rules to relate letters to their pronunciations.

Limbic system: A set of brain structures, including the hippocampus and amygdala, that support a variety of functions, particularly emotion.

Linkage: A set of genes or alleles that are inherited together.

Longitudinal study: The study of a group of individuals that involves repeated assessments over time. Such studies are uniquely informative about patterns of developmental change.

Magnetic resonance imaging (MRI): A noninvasive technique used to visualize brain structure and function.

Magnocellular system: Part of the visual system that is specialized for the detection of motion and contrast at low levels of luminance.

Mean length of utterance (MLU): The average number of morphemes in a child's spoken language; a higher MLU is taken to indicate a higher level of language proficiency.

MEG (magnetoencephalography): An imaging technique used to measure the changes in the magnetic field produced by the brain's activity.

Mental model: An internal representation of a particular aspect of the external world.

Meta-analysis: A statistical technique that can be used to summarize the results from several studies.

Metacognition: Knowledge of one's own cognitive processes.

Methylphenidate: A stimulant drug commonly used to treat ADHD.

Mirror neuron system: A system in the frontal and parietal lobes that is postulated to be activated when an animal sees another animal perform an action. The mirror neuron system appears to be an integral part of the motor system and plays a key role in imitation (and, more controversially, in understanding others' intentions).

Molecular genetics: The field of biology concerned with the structure and function of genes at a molecular level.

Monozygotic (MZ) or identical twins: Twins who develop from a single fertilized ovum (zygote) and therefore share 100% of their segregating (varying) genes.

Morpheme: A morpheme is the smallest meaningful unit in a language.

Morphology: The system of language concerned with the meaning units (morphemes) in words.

Muscle spindles: Receptors that measure changes in muscle length and muscle tension.

Neale Analysis of Reading Ability (NARA): A test commonly used in the UK to measure reading accuracy, comprehension, and rate. Children read short passages aloud and answer questions about them.

Neural network: A network or circuit of neurons in the brain. Artificial neural networks are computational models of brain processes.

Neurobiology: Studies of structure and function of the nervous system.

Neuroimaging: Techniques to image the structure, function, or neurochemistry of the functioning brain. Major techniques include magnetic resonance imaging (MRI), functional magnetic resonance imaging (fMRI), and magnetoencephalography (MEG).

Nonwords: Letter or phoneme strings that can be pronounced according to the phonological system of a language but do not exist in the language.

OME: Otitis media with effusion, which refers to fluid in the middle ear without symptoms of an acute ear infection (commonly referred to as "glue ear").

Onset: The part of the syllable containing the consonant or consonants that precedes the vowel (e.g., *st* in start).

Opaque orthography: A writing system with irregular sound–spelling correspondences (also known as deep orthography).

Oppositional defiant disorder: A psychiatric category characterized by disobedient, hostile, and defiant behavior toward authority figures.

Paired-associate learning: A task that involves learning the association between a set of stimuli and a set of responses (e.g., learning that a particular object has a specific name).

Path diagram: A diagram that represents the hypothesized causal relationships between two or more constructs.

Percentile: A term that expresses an individual's score in relation to others in the population. A score at the 35th percentile (or centile) means that 35% of the population would be expected to obtain a lower score.

Pervasive developmental disorder (PDD): A group of disorders characterized by delays in the development of multiple basic functions, including socialization and communication.

Phenocopy: A pattern of behavior that resembles a recognized behavioral pattern (phenotype) that develops in the absence of the genetic risk factors typically associated with the phenotype.

Phenotype: An observed characteristic of an organism, for example eye color, height, or reading ability.

Phoneme: The smallest unit of speech that distinguishes meaning.

Phonemic awareness: The ability to identify phonemes in spoken words, assessed by tasks such as phoneme segmentation and blending.

Phonological awareness: The ability to identify and manipulate the sound structure of language (e.g., to segment words into syllables, onsets, rimes, and phonemes).

Phonological dyslexia: A "subtype" of dyslexia characterized by the ability to read familiar words better than nonwords.

Pleitropy: The idea that a given gene can be expressed in different ways (depending on a range of other genetic and environmental influences).

Positron emission tomography (PET): An imaging technique that involves the injection of radioactive isotopes, which produces a three-dimensional image or map of functional processes in the brain (this technique is now rarely used and has effectively been replaced by fMRI and MEG).

Pragmatics: The system concerned with the relevant and appropriate use of language.

Prefrontal cortex: The anterior part of the frontal lobes of the brain, lying in front of the motor and premotor areas.

Premotor cortex: An area of cortex in the frontal lobe of the brain, responsible for sensory guidance sequencing and planning of movement.

Proband: In genetics, an individual in a twin pair or family study identified as having a disorder or characteristic.

Procedural memory: Memory for actions or routines that may not be available for conscious recollection.

Prognosis: A term denoting the likely outcome of a disease or disorder.

Proprioception: Awareness of the positions of different parts of the body in a static posture.

Quantitative genetics: Studies that identify the hereditary basis of traits based on relating similarities among individuals to their degree of genetic relatedness.

Quantitative trait locus (QTL): A region of a chromosome that is associated with continuous variation in a trait or dimension, such as reading skill.

Rapid automatized naming (RAN): A task in which a matrix of symbols (such as color patches, digits, or letters) is presented for a person to name as quickly as possible.

Reading-age-matched (RA) design: A case–control research design used to compare children with dyslexia with younger children reading at the same level of competence.

Regression: A statistical technique, related to correlation, that examines the relationship of a dependent variable (outcome) to one or more independent variables (explanatory or predictor variables).

Response inhibition and execution: The ability to produce a motor response to a target stimulus (execution) and to stop this process on demand.

Rime: The part of the syllable containing the vowel and the coda (e.g., *at* in bat).

Segmental phonology: The part of phonology that refers to the speech–sound contrasts within words.

Semantic bootstrapping: Children's use of conceptual knowledge to create grammatical categories when acquiring their first language.

Semantic pragmatic disorder (SPD): A developmental disorder that affects the semantic aspect of language (the meaning of what is being said) and the pragmatics of language (using language appropriately in social situations). It is now more commonly referred to as pragmatic language impairment.

Semantics: The aspect of language that deals with meaning.

Sensorimotor map: An internal representation of space that relates positions of parts of the body to external space; used to guide movements.

Simple view of reading: The hypothesis that both language comprehension and decoding are necessary for reading comprehension, and that neither alone is sufficient.

Situation model: A mental model representing the meaning of a text and its relationship to pre-existing knowledge.

Spatial memory: The memory systems responsible for representing information about the positions of objects in the environment.

Specific language impairment (SLI): Term used for children who have difficulties with language acquisition that are unexpected, given their nonverbal ability (NVIQ), and cannot be explained by other causes (e.g., deafness).

Speech disorders or speech sound disorders: Disorders in which some speech sounds in a child's native language are either not produced, not produced correctly, or are not used correctly.

Standard deviation: A measure of the variability (spread) in a set of data.

Story schema: A general framework or template for typical story structures.

Strengths and Difficulties Questionnaire (SDQ): A widely used behavior rating scale, normally completed by parents and teachers, used to screen for hyperactivity, emotional difficulties, conduct, and peer problems; it also contains a "prosocial" scale.

Striatum: A subcortical brain structure that consists of the caudate nucleus and the putamen.

Superior colliculus: Midbrain structure that receives both motor and sensory inputs that is involved in the orientation of the eyes and head to sensory stimuli.

Suprasegmental phonology: System of phonology concerned with aspects of speech such as stress and intonation.

Surface dyslexia: A "subtype" of dyslexia characterized by the ability to read non-words accurately and to read regular words (like *cat*) better than exception words (like *yacht*).

Susceptibility gene: A gene that confers an increased risk of developing a disorder.

Syntactic bootstrapping: Children's use of syntactic knowledge to help them learn the meanings of words.

Syntax: Part of the grammar of a language that deals with word order and agreement.

Theory of mind (TOM): A person's ability to attribute mental states (e.g., thoughts and beliefs) to themselves and others, and the appreciation that other people's mental states may be different to their own. Sometimes now referred to as "mentalizing."

Transparent orthography: A writing system in which there is close to a one-to-one correspondence between spellings and sounds (also known as a shallow orthography).

Validity: In test theory, the extent to which a test measures what it proposes to measure.

Verbal dyspraxia: A disorder of the motor planning of speech that is not attributable to peripheral impairments of speech motor control.

Verbal short-term memory: The memory systems that allow us to retain an ordered sequence of verbal material for a limited period of time.

Vestibular system: The sensory system, depending upon inputs from the inner ear, involved in maintaining balance.

Voxel: A term used to refer to the volume of a three-dimensional space or grid; often used in the visualization and analysis of data from brain scans.

Waiting list control group: A comparison group from whom treatment is withheld in a controlled trial. After the evaluation is complete, the waiting list group receives the treatment.

Weak central coherence (WCC) theory: The theory that people with autism tend to focus on local features of objects and situations, whereas normal people integrate pieces of information into coherent wholes.

Working memory: Memory processes used for the temporary storage and manipulation of information during the course of performing other cognitive tasks. For example, performing mental arithmetic depends upon the ability to hold information in memory while performing other operations (such as retrieving numerical information from memory, and storing intermediate products in a calculation).

References

Aase, H., & Sagvolden, T. (2006). Infrequent, but not frequent, reinforcers produce more variable responding in young children with attention deficit/hyperactivity disorder (ADHD). *Journal of Child Psychology and Psychiatry, 47*, 457–447.

Achenbach, T. M., & Edelbrook, C. S. (1983). *Manual for the Child Behavior Checklist and Revised Child Behavior Profile*. Burlington, VT: University of Vermont, Department of Psychiatry.

Adams, J. W., & Snowling, M. J. (2001). Executive function and reading impairments in children reported by their teachers as 'hyperactive'. *British Journal of Developmental Psychology, 19*, 293–306.

Adlard, A., & Hazan, V. (1998). Speech perception in children with specific reading difficulties (dyslexia). *Quarterly Journal of Experimental Psychology A, 51A*, 153–177.

Aguiar, L., & Brady, S. (1991). Vocabulary acquisition and reading ability. *Reading and Writing, 3*, 413–425.

Alarcon, M., DeFries, J., Light, J., & Pennington, B. (1997). A twin study of mathematics disability. *Journal of Learning Disabilities, 30*(6), 617–623.

Aldred, C., Green, J., & Adams, C. (2004). A new social communication intervention for children with autism: Pilot randomized controlled treatment study suggesting effectiveness. *Journal of Child Psychology and Psychiatry, 45*, 1420–1430.

Altman, D. G., Schulz, K. F., Moher, D., Egger, M., Davidoff, F., Elbourne, D., et al. (2001). The revised CONSORT statement for reporting randomized trials: Explanation and elaboration. *Annals of Internal Medicine, 134*, 663–694.

Ameratunga, D, Johnston, L. M., & Burns Y. R. (2004). Goal directed upper limb movements in children with and without DCD: A window into perceptual-motor dysfunction? *Physiotherapy Research International, 9*, 1–12.

American Psychiatric Association (1980). *Diagnostic and statistical manual of mental disorders (DSM-III)* (3rd ed.). Washington, DC: American Psychiatric Association.

American Psychiatric Association (1994). *Diagnostic and statistical manual of mental disorder (DSM IV)* (4th ed.). Washington, DC: American Psychiatric Association.

Anderson, M. (1992). *Intelligence and development: A cognitive theory*. Oxford: Blackwell.

Angold, A., Costello, E. J., & Erkanli, A. (1999). Comorbidity. *Journal of Child Psychology and Psychiatric, 40*(1), 57–87.

Aram, D. M., & Nation, J. E. (1980). Preschool language disorders and subsequent language and academic difficulties. *Journal of Communication Disorders, 13*, 159–170.

Aram, D. M., Ekelman, B. L., & Nation, J. E. (1984). Preschoolers with language disorders: 10 years later. *Journal of Speech and Hearing Research, 27*, 232–244.

Arbib, M. A., Caplan, D., & Marshall, J. C. (1982). *Neural models of language processes.* New York: Academic Press.

Arbib, M. A., Erdi, P., & Szentagothai, J. (1997). *Neural organization: Structure, function, and dynamics.* Cambridge, MA: MIT Press.

Arnsten, A. F., & Li, B.-M. (2005). Neurobiology of executive functions: Catecholamine influences on prefrontal cortical functions. *Biological Psychiatry, 57*, 1377–1384.

Aron, A. R., & Poldrack, R. A. (2005). The cognitive neuroscience of response inhibition: Relevance for genetic research in ADHD. *Biological Psychiatry, 57*, 1285–1292.

Arseneault, L., Cannon, M., Witton, J., & Murray, R. M. (2004). Causal association between cannabis and psychosis: Examination of the evidence. *British Journal of Psychiatry, 184*(2), 110–117.

Asbury, K., Wachs, T., & Plomin, R. (2005). Environmental moderators of genetic influence on verbal and nonverbal abilities in early childhood. *Intelligence, 33*, 643–661.

Ashcraft, M. H. (1982). The development of mental arithmetic: A chronometric approach. *Developmental Review, 2*(3), 213–236.

Ashcraft, M. H. (1987). Children's knowledge of simple arithmetic. A developmental model of simulation. In J. Bisanz, C. J. Brainerd, & R. Kail (Eds.), *Formal methods in developmental psychology. Progress in cognitive development research* (pp. 302–338). New York: Springer Verlag.

Ashcraft, M. H. (1992). Cognitive arithmetic: A review of data and theory. *Cognition, 44*(11-2), 75–106.

Ashcraft, M. H., & Battaglia, J. (1978). Cognitive arithmetic: Evidence for retrieval and decision processes in mental addition. *Journal of Experimental Psychology: Human Learning and Memory, 5*(4), 527–538.

Ashcraft, M. H., Kirk, E. P., & Hopko, D. (1998). On the cognitive consequences of mathematics anxiety. In C. Donlan (Ed.), *The development of mathematical skills* (pp. 175–196). Hove, UK: Psychology Press.

Atkinson, J., Anker, S., Braddick, O., Nokes, L., Mason, A., & Braddick, F. (2001). Visual and visuo-spatial development in young Williams Syndrome children. *Developmental Medicine and Child Neurology, 43*, 330–337.

August, G. J., & Garfinkel, B. D. (1989). Behavioural and cognitive subtypes of ADHD. *Journal of the American Academy of Child and Adolescent Psychiatry, 28*, 739–748.

August, G. J., & Garfinkel, B. D. (1990). Comorbidity of ADHD among clinic-referred children. *Journal of Abnormal Child Psychology, 18*, 28–45.

Autism Genome Project Consortium (2007). Mapping autism risk loci using genetic linkage and chromosomal rearrangements. *Nature Genetics, 39*, 319–328.

Ayres, A. J. (1979). *Sensory integration and the child.* Los Angeles: Western Psychological Services.

Back, E., Mitchell, P., & Ropar, D. (2007). Do the eyes have it? Inferring mental states from animated faces in autism. *Child Development, 78*, 397–411.

Baddeley, A. D. (1986). *Working memory.* Oxford: Oxford University Press.

Baddeley, A. D. (2003a). Working memory and language: An overview. *Journal of Communication Disorders, 36*, 189–208.

Baddeley, A. D. (2003b). Working memory: Looking back and looking forward. *Nature Reviews Neuroscience, 4*, 829–839.

Baddeley, A. D., & Hitch, G. J. (1974). Working memory. In G. Bower (Ed.), *The psychology of learning and motivation: Advances in research and theory* (pp. 47–90). New York: Academic Press.

Baddeley, A. D., Gathercole, S., & Papagno, C. (1998). The phonological loop as a language learning device. *Psychological Review, 105*, 158–173.

Baddeley, A. D., Thomson, N., & Buchanan, M. (1975). Word length and the structure of short-term memory. *Journal of Verbal Learning and Verbal Behavior, 14*, 575–589.

Badian, N. A. (1983). Arithmetic and nonverbal learning. In H. R. Myklebust (Ed.), *Progress in learning disabilities* (Vol. 5, pp 235–264). New York: Grunt & Stratton.

Bailey, A., Phillips, W., & Rutter, M. (1996). Autism: Towards an integration of clinical, genetic, neuropsychological, and neurobiological perspectives. *Journal of Child Psychology and Psychiatry, 37*, 89–125.

Baird, G., Charman, T., Baron-Cohen, S., Cox, A., Swettenham, J., Wheelwright, S., et al. (2000). A screening instrument for autism at 18 months of age. A 6-year follow-up study. *Journal of the American Academy of Child and Adolescent Psychiatry, 39*, 694–702.

Baird, G., Simonoff, E., Pickles, A., Chandler, S., Loucas, T., Meldrum, D., et al. (2006). Prevalence of disorders of the autism spectrum in a population cohort of children in South Thames: The Special Needs and Autism Project (SNAP). *Lancet, 368*, 210–215.

Bairstow, P. J., & Laszlo, J. I. (1981). Kinaesthetic sensitivity to passive movements in children and adults, and its relationship to motor development and motor control. *Developmental Medicine and Child Neurology, 23*, 606–616.

Baker, L., & Brown, A. L. (1984). Metacognitive skills and reading. In P. D. Pearson, M. L. Kamil, & P. Mosenthal (Eds.), *Handbook of reading research* (pp. 353–394). White Plains, NY: Longman.

Baker, L., & Cantwell, D. P. (1982). Psychiatric disorder in children with different types of communication disorder. *Journal of Communication Disorders, 15*, 113–126.

Baker, L., & Cantwell, D. P. (1985). Developmental arithmetic disorder. In H. I. Kaplan & B. J. Sadock (Eds.), *Comprehensive textbook of psychiatry* (4th ed., pp. 1697–1700). Baltimore: Williams & Wilkins.

Bakwin, H. (1973). Reading disability in twins. *Developmental Medicine and Child Neurology, 15*, 184–187.

Barkley, R. A. (1997). Behavioral inhibition, sustained attention, and executive functions: constructing a unifying theory of ADHD. *Psychological Bulletin, 121*, 65–94.

Barkley, R. A., DuPaul, G. J., & McMurray, B. (1990). Comprehensive evaluation of attention deficit disorder with and without hyperactivity as defined by research criteria. *Journal of Consulting and Clinical Psychology, 58*, 775–789.

Barkley, R. A., Edwards, G., Laneri, M., Fletcher, K., & Metevia, L. (2001). Executive functioning, temporal discounting, and sense of time in adolescents with attention deficit hyperactivity disorder (ADHD) and oppositional defiant disorder (ODD). *Journal of Abnormal Child Psychology, 29*, 541–556.

Barnes, M. A., Dennis, M., & Haefele-Kalvaitis, J. (1996). The effects of knowledge availability and knowledge accessibility on coherence and elaborative inferencing in children from six to fifteen years of age. *Journal of Experimental Child Psychology, 61*, 216–241.

Barnett, A. E., Henderson, S. E., & Scheib, B. (2007). *Detailed assessment of speed of handwriting*. London: Harcourt Assessment.

Baron, R., & Kenny, D. (1986). The moderator–mediator variable distinction in social psychological research. *Journal of Personality and Social Psychology, 51*, 1173–1182.

Baron-Cohen, S. (2002). The extreme male brain theory of autism. *Trends in Cognitive Sciences,* 6, 248–254.

Baron-Cohen, S., & Hammer, J. (1997). Parents of children with Asperger syndrome: What is the cognitive phenotype? *Journal of Cognitive Neuroscience, 9,* 548–554.

Baron-Cohen, S., Cox, A., Baird, G., Drew, A., Nightingale, N., Morgan, K., et al. (1996). Psychological markers in the detection of autism in infancy in a large population. *British Journal of Psychiatry, 168,* 158–163.

Baron-Cohen, S., Leslie, A., & Frith, U. (1985). Does the autistic child have a "theory of mind"? *Cognition, 21,* 37–46.

Baron-Cohen, S., Ring, H. A., Wheelwright, S., Bullmore, E. T., Brammer, M., & Simmons, A. (1999). Social intelligence in normal and autistic brain: An fMRI study. *European Journal of Neuroscience, 11,* 1891–1898.

Baroody, A. J., & Gannon, K. (1984). The development of the commutativity principle and economical addition strategies. *Cognition and Instruction, 1,* 321–339.

Bates, E., Dale, P., & Thal, D. (1995). Individual differences and their implications for theories of language development. In P. Fletcher & B. MacWhinney (Eds.), *The handbook of child language* (pp. 96–151). Oxford: Basil Blackwell.

Bedore, L., & Leonard, L. (2001). Grammatical morphology deficits in Spanish-speaking children with specific language impairment. *Journal of Speech, Language and Hearing Research, 44,* 905–924.

Beitchman, J. H., Cohen, N., Korstantareas, M., & Tannock, R. (1996). *Language, learning and behavior disorders.* New York: Cambridge University Press.

Bell, N. (1986). *Visualizing and verbalizing for language comprehension and thinking.* Paso Robles, CA: Academy of Reading Publications.

Belton, E., Salmond, C., Watkins, K., Vargha-Khadem, F., & Gadian, D. (2002). Bilateral grey matter abnormalities in a family with mutation in FOXP2. *NeuroImage, 16,* 101–44.

Benasich, A. A., & Tallal, P. (2002). Infant discrimination of rapid auditory cues predicts later language impairment. *Behavioural Brain Research, 136,* 31–49.

Benasich, A. A., Curtiss, S., & Tallal, P. (1993). Language, learning and behavioural disturbances in childhood: a longitudinal perspective. *Journal of the American Academy of Child and Adolescent Psychiatry, 32*(3), 585–594.

Berko, J. (1958). The child's learning of English morphology. *Word, 14,* 150–177.

Bernstein, N. (1967). *The co-ordination and regulation of movements.* London: Pergamon.

Besner, D., Twilley, L., McCann, R. S., & Seergobin, K. (1990). On the association between connectionism and data: Are a few words necessary? *Psychological Review, 97*(3), 432–446.

Biederman, J. (2005). Attention-deficit/hyperactivity disorder: a selective overview. *Biological Psychiatry, 57,* 1215–1220.

Bird, J., Bishop, D. V. M., & Freeman, N. H. (1995). Phonological awareness and literacy development in children with expressive phonological impairments. *Journal of Speech and Hearing Research, 38,* 446–462.

Bishop, D. V. M. (1983). *Test for the reception of grammar.* Manchester: Department of Psychology, University of Manchester.

Bishop, D. V. M. (1989). Autism, Asperger's syndrome and semantic-pragmatic disorder: Where are the boundaries? *British Journal of Disorders of Communication, 24,* 107–121.

Bishop, D. V. M. (1990). Handedness, clumsiness and developmental language disorders. *Neuropsychologia, 28,* 681–690.

Bishop, D. V. M. (1994). Is specific language impairment a valid diagnostic category? Genetic and psycholinguistic evidence. *Philosophical Transactions of the Royal Society, Series B, 34,* 105–111.

Bishop, D. V. M. (1997a). Cognitive neuropsychology and developmental disorders: uncomfortable bedfellows. *Quarterly Journal of Experimental Psychology, 50A*, 899–923.

Bishop, D. V. M. (1997b). *Uncommon understanding*. Hove: Psychology Press.

Bishop, D. V. M. (1998). Development of the children's communication checklist (CCC): A method for assessing qualitative aspects of communication impairment in children. *Journal of Child Psychology and Psychiatry, 39*, 879–892.

Bishop, D. V. M. (2001). Genetic influences on language impairment and literacy problems in children: Same or different? *Journal of Child Psychology and Psychiatry, 42*, 189–198.

Bishop, D. V. M. (2002). The role of genes in the etiology of specific language impairment. *Journal of Communication Disorders, 35*, 311–328.

Bishop, D. V. M. (2006). Developmental cognitive genetics: How psychology can inform genetics and vice versa. *Quarterly Journal of Experimental Psychology, 59*(7), 1153–1168.

Bishop, D. V. M. (2007a). Using mismatch negativity to study central auditory processing in developmental language and literacy impairments: Where are we, and where should we be going? *Psychological Bulletin, 133*, 651–672.

Bishop, D. V. M. (2007b). Curing dyslexia and ADHD by training motor co-ordination: Miracle or myth? *Journal of Paediatrics and Child Health, 43*, 653–655.

Bishop, D. V. M., & Adams, C. (1990). A prospective study of the relationship between specific language impairment, phonological disorders and reading retardation. *Journal of Child Psychology and Psychiatry, 31*, 1027–1050.

Bishop, D. V. M., Adams, C. V., & Norbury, C. F. (2006). Distinct genetic influences on grammar and phonological short-term memory deficits: Evidence from 6-year-old twins. *Genes, Brain and Behavior, 5*(2), 158–169.

Bishop, D. V. M., & Baird, G. (2001). Parent and teacher report of pragmatic aspects of communication: Use of the Children's Communication Checklist in a clinical setting. *Developmental Medicine and Child Neurology, 43*, 809–818.

Bishop, D. V. M., & Edmundson, A. (1987). Language-impaired 4-year-olds: Distinguishing transient from persistent impairment. *Journal of Speech and Hearing Disorders, 52*, 156–173.

Bishop, D. V. M., & Hayiou-Thomas, E. (2008). Heritability of specific language impairment depends on diagnostic criteria. *Genes, Brain and Behavior, 7*, 365–372.

Bishop, D. V. M., & McArthur, G. A. (2005). Individual differences in auditory processing in specific language impairment: A follow-up study using event-related potentials and behavioural thresholds. *Cortex, 41*, 327–341.

Bishop, D. V. M., & Norbury, C. F. (2002). Exploring the borderlands of autistic disorder and specific language impairment: A study using standardised diagnostic instruments. *Journal of Child Psychology and Psychiatry, 43*(7), 917–929.

Bishop, D. V. M., & Snowling, M. J. (2004). Developmental dyslexia and specific language impairment: Same or different? *Psychological Bulletin, 130*, 858–888.

Bishop, D. V. M., Adams, C., & Rosen, S. (2006). Resistance of grammatical impairment to computerised comprehension training in children with specific and non-specific language impairments. *International Journal of Language and Communication Disorders, 41*, 19–40.

Bishop, D. V. M., Bishop, S. J., Bright, P., James, C., Delaney, T., & Tallal, P. (1999). Different origin of auditory and phonological processing problems in children with language impairment: evidence from a twin study. *Journal of Speech, Language and Hearing Research, 42*, 155–168.

Bishop, D. V. M., Carlyon, R. P., Deeks, J. M., & Bishop, S. J. (1999). Auditory temporal processing impairment: Neither necessary nor sufficient for causing language impairment in children. *Journal of Speech, Language and Hearing Research, 42*(6), 1295–1310.

Bishop, D. V. M., North, T., & Donlan, C. (1995). Genetic basis of specific language impairment: Evidence from a twin study. *Developmental Medicine and Child Neurology, 37,* 56–71.

Bishop, D. V. M., North, T., & Donlan, C. (1996). Nonword repetition as a behavioural marker for inherited language impairment: Evidence from a twin study. *Journal of Child Psychology and Psychiatry, 37,* 391–403.

Bishop, D. V. M., Whitehouse, A. J. O., Watt, H., & Line, H. (2008). Autism and diagnostic substitution: Evidence from a study of adults with developmental language disorder. *Developmental Medicine and Child Neurology, 50.* 341–345.

Blake, R., Turner, L., Smoski, M., Pozdol, S., & Stone, W. (2003). Visual recognition of biological motion is impaired in children with autism. *Psychological Science, 14,* 151–157.

Blonigen, D. M., Hicks, B. M., Krueger, R. F., Patrick, C. J., & Iacono, W. G. (2005). Psychopathic personality traits: Heritability and genetic overlap with internalizing and externalizing psychopathology. *Psychological Medicine, 35,* 637–648.

Boada, R., & Pennington, B. (2006). Deficient implicit phonological representations in children with dyslexia. *Journal of Experimental Child Psychology, 95,* 153–193.

Bolton, P. F., Park, R. J., Higgins, J. N. P., Griffiths, P. D., & Pickles, A. (2002). Neuro-epileptic determinants of autism spectrum disorders in tuberous sclerosis complex. *Brain, 125*(6), 1247–1255.

Boonstra, A., Kooij, J. J., Oosterlaan, J., Sergeant, J., & Buitelaar, J. (2005). Does methylphenidate improve inhibition and other cognitive abilities in adults with childhood-onset ADHD? *Journal of Clinical and Experimental Neuropsychology (Neuropsychology, Development), 27,* 278–298.

Bortolini, U., & Leonard, L. B. (1996). Phonology and grammatical morphology in specific language impairment: Accounting for individual variation in English and Italian. *Applied Psycholinguistics, 17,* 85–104.

Botting, N. (2005). Non-verbal cognitive development and language impairment. *Journal of Child Psychology and Psychiatry, 46,* 317–326.

Bowey, J. A. (2005). Predicting individual differences in learning to read. In M. J. Snowling & C. Hulme (Eds.), *The science of reading: A handbook* (pp. 155–172). Oxford: Blackwell.

Bowler, D. M. (1992). "Theory of mind" in Asperger's syndrome. *Journal of Child Psychology and Psychiatry, 33,* 877–893.

Bowler, D. M. (2007). *Autism spectrum disorders: Psychological theory and research.* Chichester: Wiley.

Bowler, D. M., & Thommen, E. (2000). Attribution of mechanical and social causality to animated displays by children with autism. *Autism, 4,* 147–171.

Bowyer-Crane, C. A., & Snowling, M. J. (2005). The relationship between inference generation and reading comprehension. *British Journal of Educational Psychology, 75,* 189–201.

Bowyer-Crane, C., Snowling, M. J., Duff, F., Fieldsend, E., Carroll, J., Miles, J., et al. (2008). Improving early language and literacy skills: Differential effects of an oral language versus a phonology with reading intervention. *Journal of Child Psychology and Psychiatry, 49,* 422–432.

Bradley, L., & Bryant, P. E. (1978). Difficulties in auditory organisation as a possible cause of reading backwardness. *Nature, 271,* 746–747.

Bradley, L., & Bryant, P. E. (1983). Categorising sounds and learning to read – a causal connection. *Nature, 301,* 419–521.

Brainerd, M. S., & Doupe, A. (2002). What songbirds teach us about learning. *Nature, 417,* 351–358.

Bretherton, L., & Holmes, V. M. (2003). The relationship between auditory temporal processing, phonemic awareness, and reading disability. *Journal of Experimental Child Psychology, 84*, 218–243.

Briars, D., & Siegler, R. S. (1984). A featural analysis of children's counting. *Developmental Psychology, 20*, 607–618.

Brody, G., Murry, V., Gerrard, M., Gibbons, F., Molgaard, V., McNair, L., et al. (2004). The strong African American Families Program: Translating research into prevention programming. *Child Development, 75*, 900–917.

Bronowski, J. (1977). *A sense of the future*. Cambridge, MA: MIT Press.

Brown, A., & Palinscar, A. (1985). *Reciprocal teaching of comprehension strategies: A natural program for enhancing learning*. Urbana-Champaign: University of Illinois.

Brown, R., & Fraser, C. (1964). The acquisition of syntax. *Monographs of the Society for Research in Child Development, 29*, 43–79.

Brown, R., Hobson, R. P., & Lee, A. (1997). Are there autistic-like features in congenitally blind children? *Journal of Child Psychology and Psychiatry, 38*, 693–703.

Bruck, M. (1990). Word recognition skills of adults with childhood diagnoses of dyslexia. *Developmental Psychology, 26*, 439–454.

Bruininks, R. (1978). *The Bruininks-Oseretsky test of motor proficiency*. New York: Haworth Press.

Bruno, J., Manis, F., Keating, P., Sperling, A., Nakamoto, J., & Seidenberg, M. (2007). Auditory word identification in dyslexic and normally achieving readers. *Journal of Experimental Child Psychology, 97*, 183–204.

Brunswick, N., McCrory, E., Price, C., Frith, C., & Frith, U. (1999). Explicit and implicit processing of words and pseudowords by adult developmental dyslexics: A search for Wernicke's Wortschatz. *Brain, 122*, 1901–1917.

Bryson, S., Zwaigenbaum, L., McDermott, C., Rombough, V., & Brian, J. (2008). The Autism Observation Scale for Infants: Scale development and reliability data. *Journal of Autism and Developmental Disorders, 38*(4), 731–738.

Buckley, P., Mantripragada, K., Piotrowski, A., Diaz de Ståhl, T., & Dumanski, J. (2005). Copy-number polymorphisms: Mining the tip of an iceberg. *Trends in Genetics, 21*, 315–317.

Bull, R., & Johnston, R. S. (1997). Children's arithmetical difficulties: Contributions from processing speed, item identification and short-term memory. *Journal of Experimental Child Psychology, 65*, 1–24.

Bull, R., & Scerif, G. (2001). Executive functioning as a predictor of children's mathematical ability: Inhibition, switching, and working memory. *Developmental Neuropsychology, 19*, 273–293.

Bull, R., Johnston, R., & Roy, J. (1999). Exploring the roles of the visual-spatial sketch pad and central executive in children's arithmetic skills: views from cognition and developmental neuropsychology. *Developmental Neuropsychology, 15*, 421–442.

Bush, G., Valera, E., & Seidman, L. (2005). Functional neuroimaging of attention deficit/ hyperactivity disorder: A review and suggested future directions. *Biological Psychiatry, 57*, 1273–1284.

Butterworth, B. (1995). Editorial. *Mathematical Cognition, 1*, 1–2.

Butterworth, B. (1999). *The mathematical brain*. London: Macmillan.

Buxbaum, L. J., Kyle, K. M., & Menon, R. (2005). On beyond mirror neurons: Internal representations subserving imitation and recognition of skilled object-related actions in humans. *Cognitive Brain Research, 25*(1), 226–239.

Byrne, B. (1998). *The foundation of literacy: The child's acquisition of the alphabetic principle.* Hove, UK: Psychology Press.

Byrne, B., Delaland, C., Fielding-Barnsley, R., Quain, P., Samuelsson, S., Hoien, T., et al. (2002). Longitudinal study of early reading development in three countries: Preliminary results. *Annals of Dyslexia, 52,* 49–73.

Cain, K. (2003). Text comprehension and its relation to coherence and cohesion in children's fictional narratives. *British Journal of Developmental Psychology, 21,* 335–351.

Cain, K., & Oakhill, J. V (1996). The nature of the relationship between comprehension skill and the ability to tell a story *British Journal of Developmental Psychology, 14,* 187–201.

Cain, K., & Oakhill, J. V. (1999). Inference making ability and its relation to comprehension failure in young children. *Reading and Writing, 11*(5/6), 489–507.

Cain, K., & Oakhill, J. V. (2006). Profiles of children with specific reading comprehension difficulties. *British Journal of Educational Psychology, 76,* 683–696.

Cain, K., Oakhill, J. V., Barnes, M. A., & Bryant, P. E. (2001). Comprehension skill, inference-making ability, and their relation to knowledge. *Memory and Cognition, 29,* 850–859.

Cain, K., Oakhill, J. V., & Bryant, P. E. (2000). Phonological skills and comprehension failure: A test of the phonological processing deficit hypothesis. *Reading and Writing, 13,* 31–56.

Cain, K., Oakhill, J., & Bryant, P. E. (2004). Children's reading comprehension ability: Concurrent prediction by working memory, verbal ability, and component skills. *Journal of Educational Psychology, 96,* 31–42.

Cain, K., Oakhill, J., & Elbro, C. (2003). The ability to learn new word meanings from context by school-age children with and without language comprehension difficulties. *Journal of Child Language, 30,* 681–694.

Cain, K., Oakhill, J., & Lemmon, K. (2004). Individual differences in the inference of word meanings from context: The influence of reading comprehension, vocabulary knowledge, and memory capacity. *Journal of Educational Psychology, 96,* 671–681.

Campbell, J. (1995). Mechanisms of simple addition and multiplication; a modified network-interference theory and simulation. *Mathematical Cognition, 1,* 121–164.

Campbell, S. C. (1995). Behavior problems in preschool children: A review of recent research. *Journal of Child Psychology and Psychiatry, 36*(1), 113–149.

Cantell, M. H., Smyth, M. M., & Ahonen, T. P. (2003). Two distinct pathways for developmental coordination disorder: Persistence and resolution. *Human Movement Science, 22*(4/5), 413–431.

Cantlon, J., Brannon, E., Carter, E., & Pelphrey, K. (2006). Functional imaging of numerical processing in adults and 4-y-old children. *PLoS Biology, 4*(5), e125 doi:110.1371/journal. pbio.0040125.

Caramazza, A. (1986). On drawing inferences about the structure of normal cognitive systems from the analysis of patterns of impaired performance: A case for single-case studies. *Brain and Cognition, 5,* 41–66.

Caravolas, M. (2005). The nature and causes of dyslexia in different languages. In M. J. Snowling & C. Hulme (Eds.), *The science of reading: A handbook* (pp. 336–356). Oxford: Blackwell.

Caravolas, M., Volín, J., & Hulme, C. (2005). Phoneme awareness is a key component of alphabetic literacy skills in consistent and inconsistent orthographies: Evidence from Czech and English children. *Journal of Experimental Child Psychology, 92,* 107–139.

Cardon, L. R., Smith, S. D., Fulker, D. W., Kimberling, W. J., Pennington, B. F., & DeFries, J. C. (1994). Quantitative trait locus for reading disability on chromosome 6. *Science, 266,* 276–279.

Caron, C., & Rutter, M. (1991). Comorbidity in child psychopathology: concepts, issues and research strategies. *Journal of Child Psychology and Psychiatry, 32*(7), 1063–1080.

Case, R., Kurland, M., & Goldberg, J. (1982). Operational efficiency and the growth of short-term memory span. *Journal of Experimental Child Psychology, 33,* 386–404.

Casey, B. J., Castellanos, F. X., Giedd, J. N., Marsh, W. L., Hamburger, S. D., Schubert, A. B., et al. (1997). Implication of right fronto-striatal circuitry in response inhibition and attention-deficit/hyperactivity disorder. *Journal of the American Academy of Child and Adolescent Psychiatry, 36,* 374–383.

Caspi, A., McClay, J., Moffitt, T., Mill, J., Martin, J., Craig, I. W., et al. (2002). Role of genotype in the cycle of violence in maltreated children. *Science, 297,* 851–854.

Castellanos, F. X., & Tannock, R. (2002). Neuroscience of ADHD disorder: the search for endophenotypes. *Nature Reviews Neuroscience, 3,* 617–628.

Castellanos, F. X., Giedd, J. M., Marsh, W. L., Hamburger, S. D., Vaituzis, A. C., Dickstei, D. P., et al. (1996). Quantitative brain magnetic resonance imaging in ADHD. *Archives of General Psychiatry, 53,* 607–616.

Castellanos, F. X., Lee, P. P., Sharp, W., Jeffries, N. O., Greenstein, D. K., & Clasen, L. S. (2002). Developmental trajectories of brain volume abnormalities in children and adolescents with attention-deficit hyperactivity disorder. *Journal of the American Medical Association, 288,* 1740–1748.

Castellanos, F.X., Sonuga-Barke, E. J. S., Milham, M., & Tannock, R. (2006). Characterizing cognition in ADHD: Beyond executive dysfunction. *Trends in Cognitive Sciences, 10,* 117–123.

Castellanos, F.X., Sonuga-Barke, E., Scheres, A., DiMartino, A., Hyde, C., & Walters, J. (2005). Varieties of attention-deficit/hyperactivity disorder-related intra-individual variability. *Biological Psychiatry, 57,* 1416–1423.

Castelli, F., Frith, C., Happé, F., & Frith, U. (2002). Autism, Asperger syndrome and brain mechanisms for the attribution of mental states to animated shapes. *Brain, 125*(8), 1839–1849.

Castles, A., & Coltheart, M. (1993). Varieties of developmental dyslexia. *Cognition, 47,* 149–180.

Cataldo, M. G., & Cornoldi, C. (1998). Self-monitoring in poor and good reading comprehenders and their use of strategy. *British Journal of Developmental Psychology, 16,* 155–165.

Catts, H. W. (1993). The relationship between speech–language and reading disabilities. *Journal of Speech and Hearing Research, 36,* 948–958.

Catts, H. W., Adlof, S., & Ellis Weismer, S. (2006). Language deficits in poor comprehenders: A case of for the simple view. *Journal of Speech, Language and Hearing Research, 49,* 278–293.

Catts, H. W., Adlof, S. M., Hogan, T. P., & Ellis Weismer, S. (2005). Are specific language impairment and dyslexia distinct disorders? *Journal of Speech, Language and Hearing Research, 48,* 1378–1396.

Catts, H. W., Fey, M. E., Tomblin, J. B., & Zhand, X. (2002). A longitudinal investigation of reading outcomes in children with language impairments. *Journal of Speech, Language and Hearing Research, 45,* 1142–1157.

Cermak, S. A., & Larkin, D. (2002). *Developmental Coordination Disorder.* Florence, KY: Thomson Delmar Learning.

Chambers, M., & Sugden, J. (2006). *Early years movement skills: Description, diagnosis and intervention.* Chichester, UK: Wiley.

Chapman, L. J., & Chapman, J. P. (1973). *Disordered thought in schizophrenia.* Englewood Cliffs, NJ: Prentice Hall.

Charman, T. (2003). Why is joint attention a pivotal skill in autism? *Philosophical Transactions of the Royal Society B, 358*, 315–324.

Chhabildas, N. A., Pennington, B. F., & Willcutt, E. G. (2001). A comparison of the cognitive deficits in the DSM-IV subtypes of ADHD. *Journal of Abnormal Child Psychology, 29*, 529–540.

Chiappe, P., Chiappe, D., & Siegel, L. (2001). Speech perception, lexicality, and reading disability. *Journal of Experimental Child Psychology, 80*, 58–74.

Chiat, S. (2001). Mapping theories of developmental language impairment: premises, predictions and evidence. *Language and Cognitive Processes, 16*, 113–142.

Chomsky, N. (1957). *Syntactic structures.* Den Haag: Mouton.

Christel, M. I. (1993). Grasping techniques and hand preferences in apes and humans. In H. Preuschoft & D. Chiveis (Eds.), *Hands of primates* (pp. 91–108). New York: Springer-Verlag.

Church, R. M., & Meck, W. H. (1984). The numerical attribute of stimuli. In H. L. Roitblat, T. G. Bever, & H. S. Terrace (Eds.), *Animal cognition* (pp. 445–464). Hillsdale, NJ: Lawrence Erlbaum Associates.

Clarke, P. J. (2005). *Patterns of memory asset and deficit in children with autism spectrum disorders.* PhD Thesis, University of York, UK.

Clay, M. (1985). *The early detection of reading difficulties* (3rd ed.). Tadworth, UK: Heinemann.

Clegg, J., Hollis, C., Mawhood, L., & Rutter, M. (2005). Developmental language disorder – a follow up in later adult life. Cognitive, language and psychosocial outcomes. *Journal of Child Psychology and Psychiatry, 46*, 128–149.

Cohen, J. (1988). *Statistical power analysis for the behavioral sciences* (2nd ed., Vol. 2). Hillsdale, NJ: Lawrence Erlbaum Associates.

Cohen, N. J. (1996). Unsuspected learning impairments in psychiatrically disturbed children: Developmental issues and associated conditions. In J. H. Beitchman, M. M. Konstantareas, & R. Tannock (Eds.), *Language, learning, and behavior disorders: Developmental, biological, and clinical perspectives* (pp. 105–127). New York: Cambridge University Press.

Cohen, W., Hodson, A., O'Hare, A., Boyle, J., Durrani, T., McCartney, E., et al. (2005). Effects of computer-based intervention using acoustically modified speech (FastForward-Language) in receptive language impairment: Outcomes from a randomized controlled trial. *Journal of Speech, Language and Hearing Research, 48*, 715–729.

Colledge, E., Bishop, D. V. M., Koeppen-Schomerus, G., Price, T., Happe, F., Eley, T., et al. (2002). The structure of language abilities at 4 years: A twin study. *Developmental Psychology, 38*, 749–757.

Coltheart, M., & Davies, M. (2003). Inference and explanation in cognitive neuropsychology. *Cortex, 39*, 188–191.

Coltheart, M., Masterson, J., Byng, S., Prior, M.; & Riddoch, J. (1983). Surface dyslexia. *Quarterly Journal of Experimental Psychology, 35*, 469–495.

Conners, C. (1996). *Conners' Rating Scales™ – Revised (CRS-R).* London: Psychological Corporation.

Conrad, R. (1964). Acoustic confusions in immediate memory. *British Journal of Psychology, 55*, 75–84.

Constantino, J. N. (2002). *Social Responsiveness Scale.* Los Angeles, CA: Western Psychological Services

Conti-Ramsden, G., Botting, N., & Faragher, B. (2001). Psycholinguistic markers for specific language impairment (SLI). *Journal of Child Psychology and Psychiatry, 42*, 741–748.

Conti-Ramsden, G., Botting, N., Simkin, Z., & Knox, E. (2001). Follow-up of children attending infant language units: Outcomes at 11 years of age. *International Journal of Language and Communication Disorders, 36*, 207–219.

Conti-Ramsden, G., Crutchley, A., & Botting, N. (1997). The extent to which psychometric tests differentiate subgroups of children with SLI. *Journal of Speech, Language and Hearing Research, 40*, 765–777.

Conti-Ramsden, G., Simkin, Z., & Botting, N. (2006). The prevalence of autistic spectrum disorders in adolescents with a history of specific language impairment (SLI). *Journal of Child Psychology and Psychiatry, 47*, 621–628.

Cope, N., Harold, D., Hill, G., Moskvina, V., Stevenson, J., Holmans, P., et al. (2005). Strong evidence that KIAA0319 on chromosome 6p is a susceptibility gene for developmental dyslexia. *American Journal of Human Genetics, 76*, 581–591.

Corbett, P. (2005). *The story makers' chest. Teaching creative writing.* Andover, UK: Philip & Tacey.

Corriveau, K., Pasquini, E., & Goswami, U. (2007). Basic auditory processing skills and specific language impairment: A new look at an old hypothesis. *Journal of Speech, Language and Hearing Research, 50*(3), 647–666.

Courchesne, E., Karns, C. M., Davis, H. R., Ziccardi, R., Carper, R. A., Tigue, Z. D., et al. (2001). Unusual brain growth patterns in early life in patients with autistic disorder: An MRI study. *Neurology, 57*(2), 245–254.

Cousins, M., & Smyth, M. M. (2003). Developmental coordination impairments in adulthood. *Human Movement Science, 22*, 433–459.

Cowan, R., & Renton, M. (1996). Do they know what they are doing? Children's use of economic addition strategies and knowledge of commutativity. *Educational Psychology, 16*, 407–420.

Crain, S., & Pietroski, P. (2001). Nature, nurture and universal grammar. *Linguistics and Philosophy, 24*, 139–186.

Crawford, S. G., Wilson, B. N., & Dewey, D. (2001). Identifying developmental coordination: Consistency between tests. *Physical and Occupational Therapy Pediatrics, 20*, 29–50.

Crowder, R. G. (1978). Memory for phonologically uniform lists. *Journal of Verbal Learning and Verbal Behavior, 17*(1), 73–89.

Cunningham, A., & Stanovich, K. (1990). Assessing print exposure and orthographic processing skill in children: A quick measure of reading experience. *Journal of Educational Psychology, 82*, 733–740.

Dakin, S. C., & Frith, U. (2005). Vagaries of visual perception in autism. *Neuron, 48*, 497–507.

Daneman, M., & Carpenter, P. A. (1980). Individual differences in working memory and reading. *Journal of Verbal Learning and Verbal Behavior, 19*, 450–466.

Daneman, M., & Green, I. (1986). Individual differences in comprehending and producing words in context. *Journal of Memory and Language, 25*, 1–18.

Davis, J. (1985). *The logic of causal order.* Beverly Hills, CA: Sage Publications.

De Beni, R., Palladino, P., Pazzaglia, F., & Cornoldi, C. (1998). Increases in intrusion errors and working memory deficit of poor comprehenders. *Quarterly Journal of Experimental Psychology, 51A*, 305–320.

Daecety, J., Perani, D., Jeannerod, M., Bettinardi, V., Tadary, B., Mazziotta, J., et al. (1994). Mapping motor representations with position emission tomography. *Nature, 371*, 600–602.

de Weirdt, W. (1988). Speech perception and frequency discrimination in good and poor readers. *Applied Psycholinguistics, 9*, 163–183.

Deconick, F. J. A., De Clercq, D., Savelsbergh, G. J. P., Van Coster, R., Oostra, A., Dewitte, G., et al. (2006). Visual contribution to walking in children with Developmental Coordination Disorder. *Child: Care, Health and Development, 32*(6), 711–722.

DeFries, J. C., & Alarcon, M. (1996). Genetics of specific reading disability. *Mental Retardation and Developmental Disabilities Research Reviews, 2,* 39–47.

DeFries, J. C., & Fulker, D. W. (1985). Multiple regression analysis of twin data. *Behavior Genetics, 15,* 467–473.

DeFries, J. C., Fulker, D. W., & LaBuda, M. C. (1987). Reading disability in twins: Evidence for a genetic etiology. *Nature, 329,* 537–539.

DeFries, J., Vogler, G. P., & LaBuda, M. C. (1986). Colorado family reading study: An overview. In J. Fuller & E. Simmel (Eds.), *Perspective in behaviour genetics.* Hillsdale, NJ: Lawrence Erlbaum Associates.

Dehaene, S. (1992). Varieties of numerical abilities. *Cognition, 44,* 1–42.

Dehaene, S. (1997). *The number sense: How the mind creates mathematics.* New York: Oxford University Press.

Dehaene, S., & Cohen, L. (1995). Towards an anatomical and functional model of number processing. *Mathematical Cognition, 1,* 83–120.

Dehaene, S., Piazza, M., Pinel, P., & Cohen, L. (2003). Three parietal circuits for number processing. *Cognitive Neuropsychology, 20,* 487–506.

Demb, J. B., Poldrack, R. A., & Gabrieli, J. D. E. (1999). Functional neuroimaging of word processing. In R. Klein & P. McMullen (Eds.), *Converging methods for understanding reading and dyslexia* (pp. 243–304). Cambridge, MA: MIT Press.

Denckla, M. B., & Rudel, R. G. (1976). Rapid automatised naming: Dyslexia differentiated from other learning disabilities. *Neuropsychologia, 14,* 471–479.

Dennis, W., & Dennis, M. (1940). The effect of cradling practices upon the onset of walking in Hopi children. *Journal of Genetic Psychology, 56,* 77–86.

Dewey, D., & Kaplan, B. J. (1994). Subtyping of developmental neuropsychology. *Developmental Medical Child Neurology, 10,* 205–284.

Dickenstein, S., Bannon, K., Castellanos, F., & Milham, M. (2006). The neural correlates of attention deficit hyperactivity disorder: An ALE meta-analysis. *Journal of Child Psychology and Child Psychiatry, 47,* 1051–1062.

DiPelligrino, A. Klatchy, R., & McCluskey, B. (1992). Time course of reshaping for functional responses to objects. *Journal of Motor Behavior, 21,* 307–316.

Doll, R., & Hill, A. B. (1950). Smoking and carcinoma of the lung. Preliminary report. *British Medical Journal, 2,* 739–748.

Doll, R., & Hill, A. B. (1954). The mortality of doctors in relation to their smoking habits. A preliminary report. *British Medical Journal, 2,* 1451–1455.

Dollaghan, C., & Campbell, T. (1998). Nonword repetition and child language impairment. *Journal of Speech, Language and Hearing Research, 41,* 1136–1146.

Douglas, V. I. (1972). Stop look and listen: The problem of sustained attention and impulse control in hyperactive and normal children. *Canadian Journal of Behavioral Science, 4,* 259–282.

Dowker, A. (2005). *Individual differences in arithmetic: Implications for psychology, neuroscience and education.* Hove, UK: Psychology Press.

Doyle, A. E., Willcutt, E., Seidman, L., Biederman, J., Chouinard, V.-A., Silva, J., et al. (2005). Attention-deficit/hyperactivity disorder endophenotypes. *Biological Psychiatry, 57,* 1324–1335.

Doyle, A. J. R., Elliott, J. M., & Connolly, K. J. (1986). Measurement of kinaesthetic sensitivity. *Developmental Medicine and Child Neurology, 28*, 188–193.

Dromi, E., Leonard, L. B., Adam, G., & Zadunaisky-Ehrlich, S. (1999). Verb agreement morphology in Hebrew-speaking children with specific language impairment. *Journal of Speech, Language and Hearing Research, 42*, 1414–1431.

Dunn, H., Ho, H., Crichton, J., Robertson, A., McBurney, A., Grunaur, V., et al. (1986). Evolution of minimal brain dysfunctions to the age of 12–15 years. In H. Dunn (Ed.), *Sequelae of low birth-weight: the Vancouver study. Clinics in Developmental Medicine 95/96* (pp. 249–272). London: McKeith Press.

Dunn, J. C., & Kirsner, K. (1988). Discovering functionally independent mental processes: The principle of reversed association. *Psychological Review, 95*, 91–101.

Durand, M. (2004). *Nonverbal learning difficulties: Mathematical and cognitive deficits.* Unpublished PhD thesis, University of York.

Durand, M., Hulme, C., Larkin, R., & Snowling, M. J. (2005). The cognitive foundation of reading and arithmetic skills. *Journal of Experimental Child Psychology, 91*, 113–136.

Duyme, M., Dumaret, A.-C., & Tomkiewicz, S. (1999). How can we boost IQs of 'dull children'?: A late adoption study. *Proceedings of the National Academy of Sciences of the USA, 96*(15), 8790–8794.

Duysens, J., & Van de Crommert, H. W. A. A. (1998). Neural control of locomotion; Part 1: The central pattern generator from cats to humans. *Gait and Posture, 7*, 121–141.

Dwyer, C., & McKenzie, B. E. (1994). Impairment of visual memory in children who are clumsy. *Adapted Physical Activity Quarterly, 11*, 179–189.

Eckert, M. A. (2004). Neuroanatomical markers for dyslexia: A review of dyslexia structural imaging studies. *The Neuroscientist, 10*, 362–371.

Edwards, A. S. (1946). Bodysway and vision. *Journal of Experimental Psychology, 36*, 526–535.

Ehri, L. C. (1992). Reconceptualising the development of sight word reading and its relationship to recoding. In P. B. Gough, L. C. Ehri, & R. Treiman (Eds.), *Reading acquisition* (pp. 107–143). Hillsdale, NJ: Lawrence Erlbaum Associates.

Ehri, L. C. (2005). Development of sight word reading: Phases and findings. In M. J. Snowling & C. Hulme (Eds.), *The science of reading: A handbook* (pp. 135–154). Oxford: Blackwell.

Ehrlich, M. F., Remond, M., & Tardieu, H. (1999). Processing of anaphoric devices in young skilled and less skilled comprehenders: Differences in metacognitive monitoring. *Reading and Writing: An Interdisciplinary Journal, 11*, 29–63.

Elliot, L. L., Scholl, M. E., Grant, J. O., & Hammer, M. A. (1990). Perception of gated, highly familiar spoken monosyllabic nouns by children with and without learning disabilities. *Journal of Learning Disabilities, 23*, 248–253.

Elliott, C. (1996). *British Ability Scales II.* Windsor, UK: NFER-Nelson.

Elliott, C., Smith, P., & McCullouch, K. (1978). *British Ability Scales.* Windsor: NFER-Nelson.

Elliott, J. M., Connolly, K. J., & Doyle, A. J. R. (1988). Development of kinaesthetic sensitivity and motor performance in children. *Developmental Medicine and Child Neurology, 30*, 80–92.

Ellis, A., & Young, A. (1988). *Human cognitive neuropsychology.* Hove, UK: Lawrence Erlbaum Associates.

Ellis Weismer, S., & Hesketh, L. (1996) Lexical learning by children with specific language impairment: Effects of linguistic input presented at varying speaking rates, *Journal of Speech and Hearing Research, 39*, 177–190.

Emslie, H., Wilson, F. C., Burden, V., Nimmo-Smith, I., & Wilson, B. A. (2003). *Behavioural Assessment of the Dysexecutive Syndrome for Children (BADS-C).* Suffolk, UK: Thames Valley Test Company.

Engle, R. W. (2002). Working memory capacity as executive attention. *Current Directions in Psychological Science, 11*(1), 19–23.

Engle, R. W., Tuholski, S. W., Laughlin, J. E., & Conway, A. R. A. (1999). Working memory, short-term memory, and general fluid intelligence: A latent-variable approach. *Journal of Experimental Psychology: General, 128*, 309–331.

Epstein, J., Conners, C., Hervey, A., Tonev, S., Arnold, L., Abikoff, H., et al. (2006). Assessing medication effects in the MTA study using neuropsychological outcomes. *Journal of Child Psychology and Psychiatry, 47*, 446–456.

Facoetti, A., & Molteni, M. (2001). The gradient of visual attention in developmental dyslexia. *Neuropsychologia, 39*, 352–357.

Faraone, S., Perlis, R., Doyle, A., Smoller, J., Goralnick, J., Holmgren, M., et al. (2005). Molecular genetics of attention deficit/hyperactivity disorder. *Biological Psychiatry, 57*, 1313–1323.

Felsenfeld, S., Broen, P. A., & McGue, M. (1992). A 28-year follow-up of adults with a history of moderate phonological disorder: Linguistic and personality results. *Journal of Speech and Hearing Research, 35*, 1114–1125.

Feltz, D., & Landers, D. (1983). The effects of mental practice on motor skill learning and performance: A meta-analysis. *Journal of Sport and Exercise Psychology, 5*, 25–57.

Fennema, E., & Sherman, J. (1977). Sex-related differences in mathematics achievement, spatial visualisation and affective factors. *American Educational Research Journal, 14*(1), 51–71.

Fenson, L. (1993). *MacArthur Communicative Development Inventories*. San Diego, CA: Singular Publishing Group.

Fey, M. E., Long, S. H., & Finestack, L. H. (2003). Ten principles of grammar facilitation for children with specific language impairments. *American Journal of Speech-Language Pathology, 12*, 3–15.

Fisher, R. A. (1926). On the capillary forces in an ideal soil: Correction of the formulae given by W.B. Haines. *Journal of Agricultural Science, 16*, 492–503.

Fisher, S. E., & DeFries, J. C. (2002). Developmental dyslexia: Genetic dissociation of a complex trait. *Nature Neuroscience, 3*, 767–780.

Fisher, S. E., & Francks, C. (2006). Genes, cognition and dyslexia: Learning to read the genome. *Trends in Cognitive Sciences, 10*, 250–257.

Fisher, S. E., Francks, C., Marlow, A. J., MacPhie, I. L., Newbury, D. F., Cardon, L. R., et al. (2002). Independent genome-wide scans identify a chromosome 18 quantitative-trait locus influencing dyslexia. *Nature Genetics, 30*, 86–91.

Fodor, J. (1983). *The modularity of mind*. Cambridge, MA: MIT Press.

Fodor, J. (2000). *The mind doesn't work that way: The scope and limits of computational psychology*. Cambridge, MA: MIT Press.

Fodor, J. (2005). Reply to Steven Pinker 'So How Does The Mind Work?' *Mind and Language, 20*, 25–32.

Folstein, S., & Rutter, M. (1977). Infantile autism: a genetic study of 21 twin pairs. *Journal of Child Psychology and Psychiatry, 18*, 297–331.

Fombonne, E. (1999). The epidemiology of autism: A review. *Psychological Medicine, 29*, 769–786.

Fowler, A. (1991). How early phonological development might set the stage for phoneme awareness. In S. A. Brady & D. P. Shankweiler (Eds.), *Phonological processes in literacy: A tribute to Isabelle Liberman* (pp. 97–117). Hillsdale, NJ: Lawrence Erlbaum Associates.

Foxton, J., Stewart, M., Barnard, L., Rodgers, J., Young, A., O'Brien, G., et al. (2003). Absence of auditory 'global interference' in autism. *Brain, 126*, 2703–2709.

Fraga, M. F., Ballestar, E., Paz, M. F., Ropero, S., Setien, F., Ballestar, M. L., et al. (2005). Epigenetic differences arise during the lifetime of monozygotic twins. *Proceedings of the National Academy of Sciences of the USA, 102*(30), 10604–10609.

Frank, H. (1936). "Word blindness" in school children. *Transactions of the Opthamological Society of the UK, 56,* 231–238.

Freudenthal, D., Pine, J. M., & Gobet, F. (2006). Modelling the development of children's use of optional infinitives in Dutch and English using MOSAIC. *Cognitive Science, 30,* 277–310.

Frith, C. D., & Frith, U. (2007). Social cognition in humans. *Current Biology, 17*(16), R724–R732.

Frith, U. (1985). Beneath the surface of developmental dyslexia. In K. Patterson, M. Coltheart, & J. Marshall (Eds.), *Surface dyslexia: Neuropsychological and cognitive studies of phonological reading* (pp. 301–330). London: Lawrence Erlbaum Associates.

Frith, U. (1989). *Autism: Explaining the enigma.* Oxford: Blackwell.

Frith, U. (2003). *Autism: Explaining the enigma.* (2nd ed.). Oxford: Blackwell.

Frith, U. (2004). Confusions and controversies about Asperger syndrome. *Journal of Child Psychology and Psychiatry, 45,* 672–686.

Frith, U., & Happé, F. (1994). Autism: beyond 'theory of mind'. *Cognition, 50,* 115–132.

Frith, U., & Snowling, M. J. (1983). Reading for meaning and reading for sound in autistic and dyslexic children. *British Journal of Developmental Psychology, 1,* 329–342.

Frith, U., Wimmer, H., & Landerl, K. (1998). Differences in phonological recoding in German and English speaking children. *Scientific Studies of Reading, 2*(1), 31–54.

Fuchs, L. S., Compton, D. L., Fuchs, D., Paulsen, K., Bryant, J. D., & Hamlett, C. L. (2005). The prevention, identification, and cognitive determinants of math difficulty. *Journal of Educational Psychology, 97,* 493–513.

Fuster, J. M. (1989). *The prefrontal cortex.* New York: Raven Press.

Gallagher, A., Frith, U., & Snowling, M. J. (2000). Precursors of literacy-delay among children at genetic risk of dyslexia. *Journal of Child Psychology and Psychiatry, 41,* 203–213.

Galton, F. (1880). Statistics of mental imagery. *Mind, 5,* 301–318.

Gathercole, S. E., & Baddeley, A. D. (1990). Phonological memory deficits in language disordered children: Is there a causal connection? *Journal of Memory and Language, 29,* 336–360.

Gathercole, S. E., Alloway, T., Kirkwood, H., Elliott, J., Holmes, J., & Hilton, K. (in press). Attentional and executive function behaviours in children with poor working memory. *Learning and Individual Differences.*

Gathercole, S. E., Tiffany, C., Briscoe, J., Thorn, A. S. C., & ALSPAC team (2005). Developmental consequences of poor phonological short-term memory function in childhood: a longitudinal study. *Journal of Child Psychology and Psychiatry, 46,* 598–611.

Gayan, J., & Olson, R. K. (2001). Genetic and environmental influences on orthographic and phonological skills in children with reading disabilities. *Developmental Neuropsychology, 20*(2), 483–507.

Gayan, J., Willcutt, E., Fisher, S. E., Francks, C., Cardon, L. R., Olson, R., et al. (2005). Bivariate linkage scan for reading disability and attention-deficit/hyperactivity disorder localizes pleitropic loci. *Journal of Child Psychology and Psychiatry, 46,* 1045–1056.

Geary, D. C. (1990). A componential analysis of an early learning deficit in mathematics. *Journal of Experimental Child Psychology, 49,* 363–383.

Geary, D. C. (1993). Mathematical disabilities: Cognitive, neuropsychological and genetic components. *Psychological Bulletin, 114,* 345–362.

Geary, D. C. (2004). Mathematics and learning disabilities. *Journal of Learning Disabilities, 37*, 4–15.

Geary, D. C., Bow-Thomas, C. C., & Yao, Y. (1992). Counting knowledge and skill in cognitive addition: A comparision of normal and mathematically disabled children. *Journal of Experimental Child Psychology, 54*, 372–391.

Geary, D. C., Hoard, M. K., & Hamson, C. O. (1999). Numerical and arithmetical cognition: Patterns of functions and deficits in children at risk for a mathematical disability. *Journal of Experimental Child Psychology, 74*, 213–239.

Gelman, R., & Gallistel, C. R. (1978). *The child's understanding of number*. Cambridge, MA: Harvard University Press.

Gernsbacher, M. A. (1985). Surface information loss in comprehension. *Cognitive Psychology, 17*, 324–363.

Gernsbacher, M. A., & Faust, M. E. (1991). The mechanism of suppression: a component of general comprehension skill. *Journal of Experimental Psychology: Learning, Memory, and Cognition, 17*, 245–262.

Geurts, H., Verte, S., Oosterlaan, J., Roeyers, H., & Sergeant, J. A. (2004). How specific are executive functioning deficits in attention deficit hyperactivity disorder and autism? *Journal of Child Psychology and Psychiatry, 45*, 836–854.

Geuze, R. H. (2003). Static balance and developmental coordination disorder. *Human Movement Science, 22*, 527–548.

Geuze, R. H., & Borger, H. (1993). Children who are clumsy: Five years later. *Adapted Physical Activity Quarterly, 10*, 10–21.

Geuze, R. H., Jongmans, M., Schoemaker, M., & Smits-Englesman, B. (2001). Clinical and research diagnostic criteria for developmental coordination disorder: A review and discussion. *Human Movement Science, 20*, 7–47.

Gillam, R. B., Loeb, D. F., & Friel-Patti, S. (2001). Looking back: A summary of five exploratory studies of Fast ForWord. *American Journal of Speech-Language Pathology, 10*, 269–273.

Gillam, R. B., Loeb, D. F., Hoffman, L. M., Bohman, T., Champlin, C. A., Thibodeau, L., et al. (2008). The efficacy of Fast ForWord language intervention in school-age children with language impairment: A randomized controlled trial. *Journal of Speech, Language and Hearing Research, 51*(1), 97–119.

Gillberg, C. (1999). *Clinical child neuropsychiatry* (2nd ed.). Cambridge, UK: Cambridge University Press.

Gillberg, C. (2006). Autism spectrum disorders. In C. Gillberg, R. Harrington, & H.-C. Steinhausen (Eds.), *A clinician's handbook of child and adolescent psychiatry* (pp. 447–488). Cambridge, UK: Cambridge University Press.

Gilmore, C. K., McCarthy, S. E., & Spelke, E. (2007). Symbolic arithmetic knowledge without instruction. *Nature, 447*, 589–591.

Gomez, R., Harvey, J., Quick, C., Scharer, I., & Harris, G. (1999). DSM-IV AD/HD: Confirmatory factor models, prevalence, and gender and age differences based on parent and teacher ratings of Australian primary school children. *Journal of Child Psychology and Psychiatry, 40*(2), 265–274.

Gooch, D., Hulme, C., & Snowling, M. (2008). Profiles of impairment in children with co-morbid RD and ADHD. *Seventh International Conference of the British Dyslexia Association*, Harrogate, UK.

Goodacre, R. (2005). Metabolomics – the way forward. *Metabolomics, 1*, 1–2.

Goodale, M. A., Miller, A. D., Jakobson, L. S., & Carey, D. P. (1994). A neurological dissociation between perceiving objects and grasping them. *Nature, 349*, 154–156.

Goodman, R. (1997). The Strengths and Difficulties Questionnaire. *Journal of Child Psychology and Psychiatry, 38*, 581–586.

Goodman, R., & Stevenson, J. (1989). A twin study of hyperactivity – 2. The aetiological role of genes, family relationships and perinatal adversity. *Journal of Child Psychology and Psychiatry, 30*, 691–709.

Gopnik, M. (1990). Feature-blind grammar and dysphasia. *Nature, 344*, 715.

Gopnik, M., & Crago, M. (1991). Familial aggregation of a developmental language disorder. *Cognition, 39*, 1–50.

Goswami, U., & Bryant, P. E. (1990). *Phonological skills and learning to read*. London: Lawrence Erlbaum Associates.

Goswami, U., Thomson, J., Richardson, U., Stainthorp, R., Hughes, D., Rosen, S., et al. (2002). Amplitude envelope onsets and developmental dyslexia: A new hypothesis. *Proceedings of the National Academy of Sciences of the USA, 99*(16), 10911–10916.

Gottesman, I., & Gould, T. (2003). The endophenotype concept in psychiatry:etymology and strategic intentions. *American Journal of Psychiatry, 160*, 636–645.

Gottlieb, G. (1992). *Individual development and evolution: The genesis of novel behavior*. New York: Oxford University Press.

Gough, P. B., & Tunmer, W. E. (1986). Decoding, reading and reading disability. *Remedial and Special Education, 7*, 6–10.

Gough, P. B., Hoover, W. A., & Petersen, C. L. (1996). Some observations on a simple view of reading. In C. Cornoldi & J. Oakhill (Eds.), *Reading comprehension difficulties* (pp. 1–13). Mahwah, NJ: Lawrence Erlbaum Associates.

Goulandris, N., & Snowling, M. J. (1991). Visual memory deficits: A plausible cause of developmental dyslexia? Evidence from a single case study. *Cognitive Neuropsychology, 8*, 127–154.

Graesser, A. C., Singer, M., & Trabasso, T. (1994). Constructing inferences during narrative text comprehension. *Psychological Review, 101*, 371–395.

Grice, P. (1998). Logic and conversation. In A. Kasher (Ed.), *Pragmatics: Critical concepts* (Vol. IV, pp. 145–161). London: Routledge.

Griffin, S., & Case, R. (1996). Evaluating the breadth and depth of training effects when central conceptual structures are taught. *Society for Research in Child Development Monographs, 59*, 90–113.

Griffin, S., Case, R., & Siegler, R. (1994). Rightstart: Providing the central conceptual prerequisites for first formal learning of arithmetic to students at-risk for school failure. In K. McGilly (Ed.), *Classroom lessons: Integrating cognitive theory and classroom practice* (pp. 24–49). Cambridge, MA: Bradford Books, MIT Press.

Griffiths, Y. M., & Snowling, M. J. (2001). Auditory word identification and phonological skills in dyslexic and average readers. *Applied Psycholinguistics, 22*, 419–439.

Griffiths, Y. M., & Snowling, M. J. (2002). Predictors of exception word and nonword reading in dyslexic children: The severity hypothesis. *Journal of Educational Psychology, 94*(1), 34–43.

Grigorenko, E. L. (2001). Developmental dyslexia: An update on genes, brains, and environments. *Journal of Child Psychology and Psychiatry and Allied Disciplines, 42*, 91–125.

Grosjean, F. (1980). Spoken word recognition processes and the gating paradigm. *Perception and Psychophysics, 28*, 267–283.

Gross-Tsur, V., Manor, O., & Shalev, R. S. (1996). Developmental dyscalculia: Prevalence and demographic features. *Developmental Medicine and Child Neurology, 1*(38), 25–33.

Gupta, A. R., & State, M. W. (2006). Genetics of autism. *Brazilian Journal of Psychiatry, 28,* 30–39.

Gurd, J. M., & Marshall, J. C. (2003). Dissociations: Double or quits? *Cortex, 39,* 192–195.

Hall, J. W., Ewing, A., Tinzmann, M. B., & Wilson, K. P. (1981). Phonetic coding in dyslexic and normal readers. *Bulletin of the Psychonomic Society, 17,* 177–178.

Hamilton, A. F. (2008). Emulation and mimicry for social interaction: A theoretical approach to imitation in autism. *Quarterly Journal of Experimental Psychology, 61,* 101–115.

Happé, F. (1995). The role of age and verbal ability in the theory of mind task performance of subjects with autism. *Child Development, 66,* 843–855.

Happé, F. (1997). Studying weak central coherence at low levels: Children with autism do not succumb to visual illusions. A research note. *Journal of Child Psychology and Psychiatry, 37*(7), 873–877.

Happé, F. (1999). Autism: Cognitive deficit or cognitive style? *Trends in Cognitive Sciences, 3*(6), 216–222.

Happé, F., Ehlers, S., Fletcher, P., Frith, U., Johansson, M., Gillberg, C., et al. (1996). 'Theory of mind' in the brain. Evidence from a PET scan study of Asperger syndrome. *Neuroreport, 8,* 197–201.

Happé, F., Ronald, A., & Plomin, R. (2006). Time to give up on a single explanation for autism. *Nature Neuroscience, 9,* 1218–1220.

Harm, M. W., & Seidenberg, M. S. (1999). Phonology, reading acquisition and dyslexia: Insights from connectionist models. *Psychological Review, 106,* 491–528.

Harold, D., Paracchini, S., Scerri, T., Dennis, M., Cope, N., Hill, G., et al. (2006). Further evidence that the KIAA0319 gene confers susceptibility to developmental dyslexia. *Molecular Psychiatry, 11,* 1085–1091.

Harris, C. S. (1965). Perceptual adaptation to inverted, reversed, and displaced vision. *Psychological Review, 72,* 419–444.

Hatcher, P. J., & Hulme, C. (1999). Phonemes, rhymes and intelligence as predictors of children's responsiveness to remedial reading instruction: Evidence from a longitudinal intervention study. *Journal of Experimental Child Psychology, 72*(2), 130–153.

Hatcher, P. J., Hulme, C., & Ellis, A. W. (1994). Ameliorating early reading failure by integrating the teaching of reading and phonological skills: The phonological linkage hypothesis. *Child Development, 65,* 41–57.

Hatcher, P. J., Hulme, C., & Snowling, M. J. (2004). Explicit phoneme training combined with phonic reading instruction helps young children at risk of reading failure. *Journal of Child Psychology and Psychiatry, 45*(2), 338–358.

Hayiou-Thomas, M. E., Oliver, B., & Plomin, R. (2005). Genetic influences on specific versus non-specific language impairment in 4-year-old twins. *Journal of Learning Disabilities, 38,* 222–232.

Hayiou-Thomas, M. E., Bishop, D. V. M., & Plunkett, K. (2004). Simulating SLI: General cognitive processing stessors can produce a specific linguistic profile. *Journal of Speech, Language and Hearing Research, 47*(6), 1347–1362.

Heath, S. M., Bishop, D. V. M., Hogben, J. H., & Roach, N. W. (2006). Psychophysical indices of perceptual functioning in dyslexia: A psychometric analysis. *Cognitive Neuropsychology, 23,* 905–929.

Heath, S. M., Hogben, J. H., & Clark, C. D. (1999). Auditory temporary processing in disabled readers with and without oral language delay. *Journal of Child Psychology and Psychiatry, 40*(4), 637–647.

Heaton, P., Pring, L., & Hermelin, B. (2001). Musical processing in high functioning children with autism. In R. J. Zatorre & I. Peretz (Eds.), *The biological foundations of music.* (Vol. 930, pp. 443–444). New York: New York Academy of Science.

Hecht, S. S. (1999). Tobacco smoke carcinogens and lung cancer. *Journal of the National Cancer Institute, 91,* 1194–1209.

Held, R. (1965). Plasticity in sensory-motor systems. *Scientific American, 213,* 84–94.

Held, R., & Hein, A. (1963). Movement-produced stimulation in the development of visually guided behavior. *Comparative Physiology and Psychology, 56,* 872–876.

Helgren, L., Gillberg, C., Gillberg, C. I., & Ennerskog, I. (1993). Children with deficits in attention, motor control and perception (DAMP) almost grown up: General health at sixteen years. *Developmental Medical Child Neurology, 35,* 881–893.

Henderson, L., Rose, P., & Henderson, S. (1992). Reaction time and movement time in children with a developmental disorder. *Journal of Child Psychology and Psychiatry, 33,* 895–905.

Henderson, S.E., & Barnett, A. (1998). The classification of specific motor coordination disorders in children: Some problems to be solved. *Human Movement Science, 17,* 449–470.

Henderson, S.E., & Sugden, D. (1992). *Movement Assessment Battery for Children.* London: Psychological Corporation.

Henderson, S. E., Barnett, A., & Henderson, L. (1994). Visuospatial difficulties and clumsiness on the interpretation of conjoined deficits. *Journal of Child Psychology and Psychiatry, 35,* 961–969.

Henderson, S. E., Sugden, D. A., & Barnett, A.E. (2007). *Movement Assessment Battery for Children – second edition (Movement ABC-2).* London: Pearson Education.

Hermelin, B. (2001). *Bright splinters of the mind: A personal story of research with autistic savants.* London: Jessica Kingsley.

Hermelin, B., & O'Connor, N. (1967). Remembering of words by psychotic and subnormal children. *British Journal of Psychology, 58,* 213–218.

Hermelin, B., & O'Connor, N. (1991). Talents and preoccupations in idiots-savants. *Psychological Medicine, 21,* 959–964.

Hill, E. (2001). Non-specific nature of specific language impairment: A review of the literature with regard to concomitant motor impairments. *International Journal of Language and Communication Disorders, 36,* 149–171.

Hill, E. L., & Wing, A. M. (1998). The use of grip force to compensate for inertial forces during voluntary movement. In K. J. Connolly (Ed.), *The psychobiology of the hand* (pp. 199–212). London: MacKeith Press.

Hill, E. L., & Wing, A. (1999). Coordination of grip force and load force in developmental coordination disorder: A case study. *Neurocase, 5,* 101–107.

Hill, E. L., Bishop, D. V. M., & Nimmo-Smith, I. (1998). Representational gestures in Developmental Coordination Disorder and specific language impairment: Error-types and the reliability of ratings. *Human Movement Science, 17(4/5),* 655–678.

Hill, P., Hogben, J., & Bishop, D. (2005). Auditory frequency discrimination in children with specific language impairment: A longitudinal study. *Journal of Speech, Language and Hearing Research, 48(5),* 1136–1146.

Hindson, B., Byrne, B., Fielding-Barnsley, R., Newman, C., Hine, D. W., & Shankweiler, D. (2005). Assessment and early instruction of pre-school children at risk for reading disability. *Journal of Educational Psychology, 97,* 687–704.

Hitch, G. J. (1978). Mental arithmetic: Short-term storage and information processing in a cognitive skill. In A. M. Lesgold, J. W. Pellegrino, S. D. Fokkema, & R. Glaser (Eds.),

Cognitive psychology and instruction: Proceedings of the NATO International Conference (pp. 331–338). Amsterdam: Plenum Press.

Hoare, D. (1994). Subtypes of developmental coordination disorder. *Adapted Physical Activity Quarterly, 11,* 158–169.

Hobcraft, J. (2006). The ABC of demographic behaviour: How the interplays of alleles, brains, and contexts over the life course should shape research aimed at understanding population processes. *Population Studies, 60*(2), 153–187.

Hobson, R. P. (1993). The intersubjective domain: Approaches from developmental psycho-pathology. *Journal of the American Psychoanalytic Association, 41S,* 167–192.

Hobson, R. P., & Meyer, J. A. (2005). Foundations for self and other: A study in autism. *Developmental Science, 8*(6), 481–491.

Hoeft, F., Ueno, T., Reiss, A. L., Meyler, A., Whitfield-Gabrieli, S., Glover, G. H., et al. (2007). Prediction of children's reading skills using behavioral, functional, and and structural neuroimaging measures. *Behavioral Neuroscience, 121,* 602–613.

Hoehn, T. P., & Baumeister, A. A. (1994). A critique of the application of sensory integration therapy to children with learning disabilities. *Journal of Learning Disabilities, 27,* 338–350.

Holsti, L., Grunau, R. V., & Whitfield, M. F. (2002). Developmental coordination disorder in extremely low birth weight children at nine years. *Journal of Development, Behavior and Pediatrics, 23*(1), 9–15.

Hood, B. M., Willen, J. D., & Driver, J. (1998). Adult's eyes trigger shifts of visual attention in human infants. *Psychological Science, 9*(2), 131–134.

Howlin, P. (1998). Practitioner review: Psychological and educational treatments for autism. *Journal of Child Psychology and Psychiatry, 39,* 307–322.

Howlin, P., Goode, S., Hutton, J., & Rutter, M. (2004). Adult outcomes for children with autism. *Journal of Child Psychology and Psychiatry, 45,* 212–229.

Hughes, C., & Russell, J. (1993). Autistic children's difficulty with mental disengagement from an object: Its impications for theories of autism. *Developmental Psychology, 29,* 498–510.

Hughes, C., Russell, J., & Robbins, T. (1994). Evidence for executive dysfunction in autism. *Neuropsychologia, 32,* 477–492.

Huh, J., Williams, H. G., & Burke, J. R. (1998). Development of bilateral motor control in children with developmental coordination disorders. *Developmental Medicince and Child Neurology, 40,* 474–484.

Hulme, C. (1981). *Reading retardation and multi-sensory teaching.* London: Routledge and Kegan Paul.

Hulme, C. (1988). The implausibility of low-level visual deficits as a cause of children's reading difficulties. *Cognitive Neuropsychology, 5*(3), 369–374.

Hulme, C., & Snowling, M. J. (1992). Deficits in output phonology: An explanation of reading failure? *Cognitive Neuropsychology, 9,* 47–72.

Hulme, C., Biggerstaff, A., Moran, G., & McKinlay, I. (1982). Visual, kinaesthetic and cross-modal judgements of length by normal and clumsy children. *Developmental Medicine and Child Neurology, 24,* 461–471.

Hulme, C., Goetz, K., Gooch, D., Adams, J., & Snowling, M. J. (2007). Paired-associate learning, phoneme awareness and learning ro read. *Journal of Experimental Child Psychology, 96,* 150–166.

Hulme, C., Hatcher, P., Nation, K., Brown, A., Adams, J., & Stuart, G. (2002). Phoneme awareness is a better predictor of early reading skill than onset-rime awareness. *Journal of Experimental Child Psychology, 82*(1), 2–28.

Hulme, C., Quinlan, P., Bolt, G., & Snowling, M. J. (1995). Building phonological knowledge into a connectionist model of the development of word naming. *Language and Cognitive Processes, 10*, 387–391.

Hulme, C., Smart, A., & Moran, G. (1982). Visual perceptual deficits in clumsy children. *Neuropsychologia, 20*(4), 475–481.

Hulme, C., Thomson, N., Muir, C., & Lawrence, A. (1984). Speech rate and the development of short-term memory. *Journal of Experimental Child Psychology, 38*, 241–253.

Hulslander, J., Talcott, J., Witton, C., DeFries, J., Pennington, B., Wadsworth, S., et al. (2004). Sensory processing, reading, IQ and attention. *Journal of Experimental Child Psychology, 88*, 274–295.

Hynd, G., Semrud-Clikeman, M., Lorys, A., Novey, E. S., & Eliopulas, D. (1990). Brain morphology in developmental dyslexia and attention deficit disorder. *Archives of Neurology, 47*, 919–926.

Iacoboni, M., & Dapretto, M. (2006). The mirror neuron system and the consequences of its dysfunction. *Nature Neuroscience Reviews, 7*, 942–951.

IMGSAC (1998). A full genome screen for autism with evidence for linkage to a region on chromosome. *Human Molecular Genetics, 7*, 571–578.

Ingram, D. (1981). *Procedures for the phonological analysis of children's language.* Baltimore: University Park Press.

Isaacs, E., Edmonds, C., Lucas, A., & Gadian, D. (2001). Calculation difficulties in children of very low birth weight: A neural correlate. *Brain, 124*, 1701–1707.

Jeannerod, M. (1997). *The cognitive neuroscience of action.* Oxford: Blackwell.

Jeannerod, M., Decety, J., & Michel, F. (1994). Impairment of grasping movements following bilateral posterior parietal lesions. *Neuropsychologia, 32*, 369–380.

Joanisse, M. F. (2004). Specific language impairments in children: Phonology, semantics and the English past tense. *Current Directions in Psychological Science, 13*(4), 156–160.

Joanisse, M. F., & Seidenberg, M. S. (1998). Specific language impairment: A deficit in grammar or processing? *Trends in Cognitive Sciences, 2*(7), 240–247.

Joanisse, M. F., & Seidenberg, M. S. (2003). Phonology and syntax in Specific Language Impairments: Evidence from a connectionist model. *Brain and Language, 86*, 40–56.

Joanisse, M. F., Manis, F. R., Keating, P., & Seidenberg, M. S. (2000). Language deficits in dyslexic children: Speech perception, phonology and morphology. *Journal of Experimental Child Psychology, 77*, 30–60.

Joffe, V. L., Cain, K., & Maric, N. (2007). Comprehension problems in children with specific language impairment: Does mental imagery training help? *International Journal of Language and Communication Disorders, 42*, 648–664.

Johnson, M. H. (1997). The neural basis of cognitive development. In W. Damon, D. Kuhn, & R. Siegler (Eds.), *Handbook of child psychology, cognition, perception and language.* (Vol. 2, pp. 1–49). New York: Wiley.

Johnson, M. (2005). Subcortical face processing. *Nature Reviews Neuroscience, 6*, 765–774.

Johnson-Glenberg, M. C. (2000). Training reading comprehension in adequate decoders/poor comprehenders: Verbal versus visual strategies. *Journal of Educational Psychology, 92*(4), 772–782.

Johnson-Laird, P. N. (1983). *Mental models.* Cambridge, MA: Harvard University Press.

Johnston, J., & Ellis Weismer, S. (1983). Mental rotation abilities in language-disordered children. *Journal of Speech and Hearing Research, 26*, 397–403.

Johnston, R., Rugg, M., & Scott, T. (1987). Phonological similarity effects, memory span and developmental reading disorders: The nature of the relationship. *British Journal of Psychology, 78*, 205–211.

Joliffe, T., & Baron-Cohen, S. (1999). A test of central coherence theory: Linguistic processing in high-functioning adults with autism or Asperger syndrome – is local coherence impaired? *Cognition, 71*, 149–185.

Jones, G. V. (1983). Note on double dissociation of function. *Neuropsychologia, 21*(4), 397–400.

Jongmans, M. J., Mercuri, E., Dubowitz, L. M. S., & Henderson, S. E. (1998). Perceptual-motor difficulties and their concomitants in six-year-old children born prematurely. *Human Movement Science, 17*(415), 629–653.

Jordan, N. C., Hanich, L. B., & Kaplan, D. (2003). A longitudinal study of mathematical competencies in children with specific mathematics difficulties versus children with comorbid mathematics and reading difficulties. *Child Development, 74*(3), 834–850.

Joseph, R., & Tager-Flusberg, H. (2004). The relationship of theory of mind and executive function to symptom type and severity in children with autism. *Development and Psychopathology, 16*, 137–155.

Just, M. A., & Carpenter, P. A. (1992). A capacity theory of comprehension: Individual differences in working memory. *Psychological Review, 99*, 122–149.

Just, M. A., Cherkassky, V. L., Keller, T. A., Kana, R. K., & Minshew, N. J. (2007). Functional and anatomical cortical underconnectivity in autism: evidence from an fMRI study of an executive function task and corpus callosum morphometry. *Cerebral. Cortex, 17*(4), 951–961.

Just, M. A., Cherkassky, V. L., Keller, T. A., & Minshew, N. J. (2004). Cortical activation and synchronization during sentence comprehension in high-functioning autism: Evidence of underconnectivity. *Brain, 127*(8), 1811–1821.

Kadesjo, B., & Gillberg, C. (1999). Developmental coordination disorder in Swedish 7-year-old children. *Journal of the American Academy of Child and Adolescent Psychiatry, 38*(7), 820–828.

Kadesjo, B., & Gillberg, C. (2001). The comorbidity of ADHD in the general population of Swedish school-age children. *Journal of Child Psychology and Psychiatry, 42*, 487–492.

Kail, R. (1991). Developmental change in speed of processing during childhood and adolescence. *Psychological Bulletin, 109*, 490–501.

Kail, R. (1992). General slowing of information processing by persons with mental retardation. *American Journal of Mental Retardation, 97*, 333–341.

Kail, R. (1993). Processing time decreases globally at an exponential rate during childhood and adolescence. *Journal of Experimental Child Psychology, 56*, 254–265.

Kail, R. (1994). A method for studying the generalized slowing hypothesis in children with specific language impairment. *Journal of Speech and Hearing Research, 37*, 418–421.

Kail, R., & Salthouse, T. A. (1994). Processing speed as a mental capacity. *Acta Psychologica, 86*, 199–225.

Kanner, L. (1943). "Autistic disturbances of affective contact". *Nervous Child, 2*, 217–250.

Kaplan, B. J., N. Wilson, B., Dewey, D., & Crawford, S. G. (1998). DCD may not be a discrete disorder. *Human Movement Science, 17*(415), 471–490.

Karmiloff, K., & Karmiloff-Smith, A. (2001). *Pathways to language: From fetus to adolescent.* Cambridge, MA: Harvard University Press.

Karmiloff-Smith, A. (1992). *Beyond modularity: A development perspective on cognitive science.* Cambridge, MA: MIT Press.

Keenan, J. M., & Betjemann, R. (2006). Comprehending the Gray Oral Reading Test without reading it: Why comprehension tests should not include passage-independent items. *Scientific Studies of Reading, 10*, 363–380.

Keenan, J., Betjemann, R., Wadsworth, S., DeFries, J., & Olson, R. (2006). Genetic and environmental influences on reading and listening comprehension. *Journal of Research in Reading, 29*(1), 75–91.

Kelso, J. A. S., Holt, K. G., Rubin, P., & Kugler, P. N. (1981). Patterns of human interlimb coordination emerge from the properties of non-linear, limit-cycle oscillatory processes: theory and data. *Journal of Motor Behavior, 13*, 226–261.

King, R. R., Jones, C., & Lasky, E. (1982). In retrospect: A fifteen year follow-up report of speech-language disordered children. *Language, Speech and Hearing Services in Schools, 13*, 24–32.

Kinsbourne, M., & Warrington, E. K. (1963). The developmental Gerstmann syndrome. *Archives of Neurology, 8*, 490–501.

Kintsch, W., & Rawson, K. (2005). Comprehension. In M. J. Snowling & C. Hulme (Eds.), *The science of reading: A handbook* (pp. 209–226). Oxford: Blackwell.

Kleinman, J., Robins, D., Ventola, P., Pandey, J., Boorstein, H., Esser, E., et al. (2008). The modified checklist for autism in toddlers: A follow-up study investigating the early detection of autism spectrum disorders. *Journal of Autism and Developmental Disorders, 38*, 827–839.

Klin, A., Jones, W., Schultz, R., Volkmar, F., & Cohen, D. (2002). Defining and quantifying the social phenotype in autism. *American Journal of Psychiatry, 159*, 895–908.

Klin, A., Volkmar, F. R., Sparrow, S. S., Cicchetti, D. V., & Rourke, B. P. (1995). Validity and neuropsychological characterization of Asperger Syndrome: Convergence with Nonverbal Learning Disabilities Syndrome. *Journal of Child Psychology and Psychiatry, 36*(7), 1127–1140.

Klinger, L. G., & Dawson, G. (1996). Autistic disorder. In E. Mash & R. A. Barkley (Eds.), *Child psychopathology* (pp. 311–339). New York: Guilford Press.

Knox, E., Botting, N., Simkin, Z., & Conti-Ramsden, G. (2002). Educational placements and National Curriculum Key Stage 2 test outcomes of children with a history of SLI. *British Journal of Special Education, 29*, 76–82.

Knuckey, N. W., & Gubbay, S. S. (1983). A prognastic study. *Australian Paediatric Journal, 19*, 9–13.

Korkman, M., Kirk, U., & Kemp, S. L. (2007). *NEPSY II.* San Antonio, TX: PsychCorp-Harcourt Assessments.

Kovas, Y., Harlaar, N., Petrill, S. A., & Plomin, R. (2005). 'Generalist genes' and mathematics in 7-year-old twins. *Intelligence, 33*(5), 473–489.

Kovas, Y., Hayiou-Thomas, M. E., Oliver, B., Dale, P. S., Bishop, D. V. M., & Plomin, R. (2005). Genetic influences in different aspects of language development: The etiology of language skills in 4.5-year-old twins. *Child Development, 76*, 632–651.

Kovas, Y., Petrill, S. A., & Plomin, R. (2007). The origins of devise domains of mathematics: Generalist genes but specialist environments. *Journal of Educational Psychology, 99*, 128–139.

Kraemer, H., Wilson, T., Fairburn, C., & Agras, W. (2002). Mediators and moderators of treatment efects in randomized clinical trials. *Archives of General Psychiatry, 59*, 877–883.

Krashen, S. (1973). Lateralization, language learning and the critical period: Some new evidence. *Language Learning, 23*, 63–71.

Kucian, K., Loenneker, T., Dietrich, T., Dosch, M., Martin, E., & von Aster, M. G. (2006). Evidence for impaired neural networks for number processing in children with developmental dyscalculia. *Behavioral and Brain Functions, 2*, 31, (doi: 10.1186/1744–9081–2–31).

Kuhl, P. (2004). Early language acquisition: Cracking the speech code. *Nature Reviews Neuroscience, 5*, 831–843.

Kuntsi, J., Oosterlaan, J., & Stevenson, J. (2001). Psychological mechanisms in hyperactivity: I Response inhibition deficit, working memory impairment, delay aversion, or something else? *Journal of Child Psychology and Psychiatry, 42*, 199–210.

Lahey, M., & Edwards, J. (1996). Why do children with specific language impairment name pictures more slowly than their peers? *Journal of Speech and Hearing Research, 39*, 1081–1098.

Lai, C. S., Fisher, S. E., Hurst, J. A., Vargha-Khadem, F., & Monaco, A. P. (2001). A forkhead-domain gene is mutated in severe speech and language disorder. *Nature, 413*, 519–523.

Landa, R., & Garret-Mayer, E. (2006). Development of infants with autism spectrum disorders: A prospective study. *Journal of Child Psychology and Psychiatry, 47*, 629–638.

Landerl, K., & Wimmer, H. (2000). Deficits in phoneme segmentation are not the core problem of dyslexia: Evidence from German and English children. *Applied Psycholinguistics, 21*, 243–262.

Landerl, K., Bevan, A., & Butterworth, B. (2004). Developmental dyscalculia and basic numerical capacities: A study of 8–9-year-old students. *Cognition, 93*, 99–125.

Landgren, M., Pettersson, R., Kjellman, B., & Gillberg, C. (1996). ADHD, DAMP and other neurodevelopmental/psychiatric disorders in 6-year old children: epidemiology and co-morbidity. *Developmental Medicine and Child Neurology, 38*, 891–906.

Landi, N., & Perfetti, C. (2007). An electrophysiological investigation of semantic and phonological processing in skilled and less-skilled comprehenders. *Brain and Language, 102*, 30–45.

Laszlo, J. I., & Bairstow, P. J. (1985a). *Perceptual-motor behaviour: Developmental assessment and therapy*. London: Holt, Rinehart & Wilson.

Laszlo, J. I., & Bairstow, P. J. (1985b). Kinaesthesis: Its measurement training and relationship to motor control. *Quarterly Journal of Experimental Psychology, 35*, 411–421.

Laszlo, J. I., Bairstow, P. J., Bartrip, J., & Rolfe, U. T. (1988). Clumsiness or perceptuo-motor dysfunction? In A. M. Colley & J. R. Beech (Eds.), *Cognition and action in skilled behaviour* (pp. 293–309). Amsterdam: Elsevier Science Publishers.

Law, J., Garret, Z., & Nye, C. (2004). The efficacy of treatment for children with develop-mental speech and language delay/disorder: A meta-analysis. *Journal of Speech, Language, and Hearing Research, 47*, 924–943.

Lazzaroa, I., Andersona, J., Gordon, E., Clarkeb, S., Leongb, J., & Mearesa, R. (1997). Single trial variability within the P300 (250–500 ms) processing window in adolescents with attention deficit hyperactivity disorder. *Psychiatry Research, 73*, 91–101.

Le Couteur, A., Bailey, A., Goode, S., Pickles, A., Gottesman, I., Robertson, S., et al. (1996). A broader phenotype of autism: The clinical spectrum in twins. *Journal of Child Psychology and Psychiatry, 37*(7), 785–801.

Leach, J. M., Scarborough, H. S., & Rescorla, L. (2003). Late-emerging reading disabilities. *Jounal of Educational Psychology, 95*, 211–224.

Leather, C. V., & Henry, L. A. (1994). Working memory span and phonological awareness tasks as predictors of early reading ability. *Journal of Experimental Child Psychology, 94*, 88–111.

Lee, D. N. (1978). On the functions of vision. In H. Pick & E. Saltzman (Eds.), *Modes of perceiving*. Hillsdale, NJ: Lawrence Erlbaum Associates.

Lee, D. N., & Aronson, E. (1974). Visual proprioceptive control of standing in human infants. *Perception and Psychophysics, 15*, 529–532.

Lee, D. N., & Lishman, J. R. (1975). Visual proprioceptive control of stance. *Journal of Human Movement Studies, 1*, 87–95.

Leekam, S. R., & Perner, J. (1991). Does the autistic child have a metarepresentational deficit? *Cognition, 40*, 203–218.

Leekam, S.R., Baron-Cohen, S., Perrett, D., & Milders, M. (1997). Eye-direction detection: A dissociation between geometric and joint attention skills in autism. *British Journal of Developmental Psychology, 15*(1), 77–95.

Leekam, S. R., Hunnisett, E., & Moore, C. (1998). Targets and cues: Gaze-following in children with autism. *Journal of Child Psychology and Psychiatry, 39,* 951–962.

Leekam, S. R., Lopez, B., & Moore, C. (2000). Attention and joint attention in preschool children with autism. *Developmental Psychology, 36,* 261–273.

Leitão, S., Hogben, J., & Fletcher, J. (1997). Phonological processing skills in speech and language impaired children. *European Journal of Disorders of Communication, 32,* 73–93.

Lenneberg, E. (1967). *Biological foundations of language.* New York: Wiley.

Leonard, C. M., Eckert, M., & Bishop, D. (2005). The neurobiology of developmental disorders. *Cortex, 41,* 277–281.

Leonard, C. M., Eckert, M., Given, B., Berninger, V., & Eden, G. (2006). Individual differences in anatomy predict reading and oral language impairments in children. *Brain, 129,* 3329–3342.

Leonard, C. M., Lombardino, L. J., Walsh, K., Eckert, M. A., Mockler, J. L., & Rowe, L. A., et al. (2002). Anatomical risk factors that distinguish dyslexia from SLI predict reading skill in normal children. *Journal of Communication Disorders, 35,* 501–531.

Leonard, C. M., Voeller, K. K., Lombardino, L. J., Morris, M. K., Hynd, G. W., Alexander, A. W., et al. (1993). Anomalous cerebral structure in dyslexia revealed with magnetic resonance imaging. *Archives of Neurology, 50*(5), 461–469.

Leonard, L. B. (1989). Language learnability and specific language impairment in children. *Applied Psycholinguistics, 10,* 179–202.

Leonard, L. B. (1998). *Children with specific language impairment.* Cambridge, MA: MIT Press.

Leonard, L. B. (2000). Specific language impairment across languages. In D. Bishop & L. Leonard (Eds.), *Speech and language impairments in children: Causes, characteristics, intervention and outcome* (pp. 115–130). Hove, UK: Psychology Press.

Leonard, L. B., Bortolini, U., Caselli, M. C., McGregor, K., & Sabbadini, L. (1992). Morphological deficits in children with specific language impairment: The status of features in the underlying grammar. *Language Acquisition, 2,* 151–179.

Leonard, L. B., Nippold, M. A., Kail, R., & Hale, C. (1983). Picture naming in language-impaired children. *Journal of Speech and Hearing Research, 26,* 609–615.

Leslie, A. M. (1987). Pretence and representation: The origins of a 'theory of mind'. *Psychological Review, 94,* 412–426.

Leth-Steenson, C., King-Elbaz, Z., & Douglas, V. (2000). Mean response times of ADHD children: A response distributional approach. *Acta Psychologica, 104,* 167–190.

Levy, F., McLaughlin, M., Wood, C., Hay, D., & Waldman, I. (1996). Twin–sibling differences in parental reports of ADHD, speech, reading and behaviour problems. *Journal of Child Psychology and Psychiatry, 37,* 569–578.

Levy, F., McStephen, M., & Hay, D. A. (2001). The diagnostic genetics of ADHD and subtypes. In F. Levy & D. A. Hay (Eds.), *Attention, genes and ADHD* (pp. 35–57). Hove, UK: Psychology Press.

Lewis, C., Hitch, G. J., & Walker, P. (1994). The prevalence of specific arithmetic difficulties and specific reading difficulties in 9- to 10-year old boys and girls. *Journal of Child Psychology and Psychiatry, 35,* 283–292.

Lishman, J. R., & Lee, D. N. (1973). The autonomy of visual kinaesthesis. *Perception and Psychophysics, 2,* 287–294.

Locke, J. L. (1993). *The child's path to spoken language.* Cambridge, MA: Harvard University Press.

Logan, G. D., Cowan, W. B., & Davis, K. A. (1984). On the ability to inhibit simple and choice reaction time responses: A model and a method. *Journal of Experimental Psychology: Human Perception and Performance, 10,* 276–291.

Lopez, B., & Leekham, S. R. (2003). Do children with autism fail to process information in context? *Journal of Child Psychology and Psychiatry, 44*, 285–300.

Lord, C., & Risi, S. (1998). Frameworks and methods in diagnosing autism spectrum disorders. *Mental Retardation and Developmental Disabilities Research Reviews, 4*, 90–96.

Lord, C., Rutter, M., DiLavore, P., & Risi, S. (1999). *Autism Diagnostic Observation Schedule*. Los Angeles, CA: Western Psychological Services.

Lord, R., & Hulme, C. (1987a). Perceptual judgements of normal and clumsy children. *Developmental Medicine and Child Neurology, 29*, 250–257.

Lord, R., & Hulme, C. (1987b). Kinaesthetic sensitivity of normal and clumsy children. *Developmental Medicine and Child Neurology, 29*, 720–725.

Lord, R., & Hulme, C. (1988). Visual perception and drawing ability in clumsy and normal children. *British Journal of Developmental Psychology, 6*, 1–9.

Losse, A., Henderson, S., Elliman, D., Hall, D., Knight, E., & Jongmans, M. (1991). Clumsiness in children – do they grow out of it? A 10-year follow up study. *Developmental Medicine and Child Neurology, 33*, 55–68.

Lovegrove, W., Martin, F., & Slaghuis, W. (1986). The theoretical and experimental case for a visual deficit in specific reading disability. *Cognitive Neuropsychology, 3*(2), 225–267.

Lovett, M. W., Borden, S. L., DeLuca, T., Lacrerenza, L., Benson, N. J., & Brackstone, D. (1994). Treating the core deficits of development dyslexia: Evidence of transfer of learning after phonologically and strategy based reading training programs. *Developmental Psychology, 30*, 805–822.

Lundberg, I., Olofsson, A., & Wall, S. (1980). Reading and spelling skills in the first school years predicted from phonemic awareness skills in kindergarten. *Scandinavian Journal of Psychology, 121*, 159–173.

Lyon, R., Shaywitz, S. E., & Shaywitz, B. A. (2003). A definition of dyslexia. *Annals of Dyslexia, 53*, 1–14.

Lyytinen, H., Erskine, J. M., Tolvanen, A., Torppa, M., Poikkeus, A.-M., & Lyytinen, P. (2006). Trajectories of reading development: A follow-up from birth to school age of children with and without risk for dyslexia. *Merril-Palmer Quarterly, 52*(3), 514–546.

Macaruso, P., & Buchman, A. (1996). *Mathematical fact retrieval in a case of acquired dyscalculia*. Paper presented at the Eastern Psychological Association Meeting, Philadelphia, PA.

Mack, K. J., & Mack, P. A. (1992). Induction of transcription factors in somatosensory cortex after tactile stimulation. *Molecular Brain Research, 12*(1–3), 141–147.

Maestrini, E., Paul, A., Monaco, A. P., & Bailey, A. (2000). Identifying autism susceptibility genes. *Neuron, 28*, 19–24.

Magnusson, E., & Naucler, K. (1990). Reading and spelling in language disordered children – linguistic and metalinguistic pre-requisites: A report on a longitudinal study. *Clinical Linguistics and Phonetics, 4*, 49–61.

Mandler, G., & Shebo, B. J. (1982). Subitizing: An analysis of its component processes. *Journal of Experimental Psychology, 111*, 1–22.

Manis, F. R., & Bailey, C. E. (2001). *Longitudinal study of dyslexic subgroups*. Paper presented at the 4th International conference of the British Dyslexia Association, York, UK.

Manis, F. R., Custodio, R., & Szeszulski, P. A. (1993). Development of phonological and orthographic skill: A 2-year longitudinal study of dyslexic children. *Journal of Experimental Child Psychology, 56*, 64–86.

Manis, F. R., McBride-Chang, C., Seidenberg, M. S., Keating, P., Doi, L. M., Munson, B., et al. (1997). Are speech perception deficits associated with developmental dyslexia? *Journal of Experimental Child Psychology, 66*(2), 211–235.

Manis, F. R., Seidenberg, M., & Doi, L. M. (1999). See Dick RAN: Rapid naming and the longitudinal prediction of reading subskills in first and second graders. *Scientific Studies of Reading, 3*(2), 129–157.

Manis, F. R., Seidenberg, M. S., Doi, L. M., McBride-Chang, C., & Petersen, A. (1996). On the bases of two subtypes of developmental dyslexia. *Cognition, 58*(2), 157–195.

Manly, T., Robertson, I. H., Anderson, V., & Nimmo-Smith, I. (1998). *Test of Everyday Attention for Children (TEA-Ch)*. London: Harcourt Assessment.

Marler, J. A., Champlin, C. A., & Gillam, R. B. (2002). Auditory memory for backward masking signals in children with language impairment. *Psychophysiology, 29*, 767–780.

Marler, P. (1970). A comparative approach to vocal learning: song development in white-crowned sparrows. *Journal of Comparative Physiology and Psychology, 71*, 1–25.

Marr, D. (1983). *Vision: A computational investigation into the human representation and processing of visual information*. San Francisco., CH: W. H. Freeman.

Marshall, C. M., Snowling, M. J., & Bailey, P. J. (2001). Rapid auditory processing and phonological ability in normal readers and readers with dyslexia. *Journal of Speech, Language and Hearing Research, 44*(4), 925–940.

Martin, N. C., Piek, J. P., & Hay, D. (2006). DCD and ADHD: A genetic study of their shared aetiology. *Human Movement Science, 25*(1), 110–124.

Martinussen, R., Hayden, J. D. C., Hogg-Johnson, S., & Tannock, R. (2005). A Meta-analysis of working memory impairments in children with attention-deficit/hyperactivity disorder. *Journal of the American Academy of Child and Adolescent Psychiatry, 44*, 377–384.

Masterson, J., Hazan, V., & Wijayatilake, L. (1995). Phonemic processing problems in developmental phonological dyslexia. *Cognitive Neuropsychology, 12*(3), 233–259.

Maughan, B., & Hagell, A. (1996). Poor readers in adulthood: psychosocial functioning. *Development and Psychopathology, 8*, 457–476.

Mawhood, L., Howlin, P., & Rutter, M. (2000). Autism and developmental receptive language disorder – a comparative follow-up in early adult life. I: Cognitive and language outcomes. *Journal of Child Psychology and Psychiatry, 41*, 547–559.

McAlonan, G. M., Cheung, V., Cheung, C., Suckling, J., Lam, G. Y., Tai, K. S., et al. (2005). Mapping the brain in autism. A voxel-based MRI study of volumetric differences and intercorrelations in autism. *Brain, 128*(2), 268–276.

McArthur, G. M., & Bishop, D. V. M. (2004a). Frequency discrimination deficits in people with specific language impairment: Reliability, validity, and linguistic correlates. *Journal of Speech, Language and Hearing Research, 47*, 527–541.

McArthur, G. M., & Bishop, D.V. M. (2004b). Which people with specific language impairment have auditory deficits. *Cognitive Neuropsychology, 21*, 79–94.

McArthur, G. M., Ellis, D., Atkinson, C., & Coltheart, M. (2008). Auditory processing deficits in children with reading and language impairments: Can they (and should they) be treated? *Cognition, 107*, 946–977.

McCann, D., Barrett, A., Cooper, A., Crumpler, D., Dalen, L., Grimshaw, K., et al. (2007). Food additives and hyperactive behaviour in 3-year-old and 8/9-year-old children in the community: A randomised, double-blinded, placebo-controlled trial. *Lancet, 370*, 1560–1567.

McCloskey, M., & Macaruso, P. (1995). Representing and using numerical information. *American Psychologist, 50*, 351–363.

McDougall, S., Hulme, C., Ellis, A. W., & Monk, A. (1994). Learning to read: The role of short-term memory and phonological skills. *Journal of Experimental Child Psychology, 58*, 112–123.

McGee, M. G. (1979). Human spatial abilities: Psychometric studies of environmental, genetic, hormonal, and neurological influences. *Psychological Bulletin, 86*, 889–918.

McGrath, L., Pennington, B. F., Willcutt, E. G., Boada, R., Lawrence, D., Shriberg, L., et al. (2007). Gene environment interactions in speech sound disorder predict language and preliteracy outcomes. *Development and Psychopathology, 19*, 1047–1072.

McKelvey, J. R., Lambert, R., Mottron, L., & Shevell, M. I. (1995). Right-hemisphere dysfunction in Asperger's Syndrome. *Journal of Child Neurology, 10*, 310–314.

McLean, J. F., & Hitch, G. J. (1999). Working memory impairments in children with specific arithmetic learning difficulties. *Journal of Experimental Child Psychology, 74*, 240–260.

McNab, J. J., Miller, L. T., & Polatajko, H. J. (2001). The search for subtypes of DCD: Is cluster analysis the answer? *Human Movement Science, 20*(1/2), 49–72.

Megherbi, H., & Ehrlich, M.-F. (2005). Language impairment in less skilled comprehdners: The on-line processing of anaphoric pronouns in a listening situation. *Reading and Writing, 18*, 715–753.

Mehler, J., & Christophe, A. (1994). Language in the infant's mind. *Philosophical Transactions: Biological Sciences, 346*, 13–20.

Mello, C. V., Vicario, D. S., & Clayton, D. F. (1992). Song presentation induces gene expression in the songbird forebrain. *Proceedings of the National Academy of Sciences of the USA, 89*, 6818–6822.

Meltzer, H., & Gatward, R. (2000). *The mental health of children and adolescents in Great Britain: Summary report*. London: Office for National Statistics.

Meltzoff, A. N., & Moore, M. K. (1976). Imitation of facial and manual gestures by human neonates. *Science, 198*, 75–78.

Mengler, E. D., Hogben, J. H., Michie, P., & Bishop, D. V. M. (2005). Poor frequency discrimination is related to oral language disorder in children: A psychoacoustic study. *Dyslexia, 11*(3), 155–173.

Merzenich, M. M., Jenkins, W. M., Johnston, P., Schreiner, C., Miller, S. L., & Tallal, P. (1996). Temporal processing deficits of language-learning impaired children ameliorated by training. *Science, 271*, 77–80.

Meyer, J. A., & Hobson, R. P. (2004). Orientation in relation to self and other: The case of autism. *Interaction Studies, 5*, 221–244.

Miller, C. A., Kail, R., Leonard, L. B., & Tomblin, J. B. (2001). Speed of processing in children with specific language impairment. *Journal of Speech, Language and Hearing Research, 44*(2), 416–433.

Milner, A. D., Perrett, D. I., Johnston, R. S., Benson, P. J., Jordan, T. R., Heeley, D. W., et al. (1991). Perception and action in "visual form agnosia". *Brain, 114*, 405–428.

Missiuna, C. (2001). *Children with developmental coordination disorder. Strategies for success*. New York: Haworth Press.

Miyake, A., Friedman, N. P., Emerson, M. J., Witzki, A. H., Howerter, A., & Wager, T. D. (2000). The unity and diversity of executive functions and their contributions to complex "frontal lobe" tasks: A latent variable analysis. *Cognitive Psychology, 41*, 49–100.

Montgomery, J. (2000). Relation of working memory to off-line and real-time sentence processing in children with specific language impairment. *Applied Psycholinguistics, 21*, 117–148.

Mon-Williams, M., Pascal, A. E., & Wann, J. P. (1994). Ophthalmic factors in developmental co-ordination disorder. *Adapted Physical Activity Quarterly, 11*, 170–178.

Mon-Williams, M., Wann, J. P., & Pascal, A.E. (1999). The integrity of visual-proprioceptive mapping in developmental coordination disorder. *Developmental Medicine and Child Neurology, 41*, 247–254.

Moore, T., Zammit, S., Lingford-Hughes, A., Barnes, T., Jones, P., Burke, M., et al. (2007). Cannabis use and risk of psychotic or affective mental health outcomes: A systematic review. *Lancet, 370*, 319–328.

Morais, J., Cary, L., Alegria, J., & Bertelson, P. (1979). Does awareness of speech as a sequence of phones arise spontaneously? *Cognition, 7,* 323–331.

Morton, J. (2004). *Understanding developmental disorders: A cognitive modelling approach.* Oxford: Blackwell.

Morton, J., & Frith, U. (1995). Causal modelling: A structural approach to developmental psychopathology. In D. Cicchetti & D. J. Cohen (Eds.), *Manual of developmental psychopathology* (pp. 357–390). New York: Wiley.

Mottron, L., & Belleville, S. (1993). A study of perceptual analysis in a high-level autistic subject with exceptional graphic abilities. *Brain and Cognition, 2,* 279–309.

Mottron, L., Burack, J., Iarocci, G., Belleville, S., & Enns, J. (2003). Locally oriented perception with intact global processing among adolescents with high-functioning autism: evidence from multiple paradigms. *Journal of Child Psychology and Psychiatry, 44,* 904–913.

Moyer, R. S., & Landauer, T. K. (1967). Time required for judgements of numerical equality. *Nature, 215,* 1519–1520.

MTA Cooperative Group (2004). National Institute of Mental Health multimodal treatment study of ADHD follow-up: Changes in effectiveness and growth after the end of treatment. *Pediatrics, 113*(4), 762–769.

Mundy, P. (2003). Annotation: The neural basis of social impairments in autism: The role of the dorsal medial-frontal cortex and anterior cingulate system. *Journal of Child Psychology and Psychiatry, 44,* 793–809.

Muter, V., Hulme, C., Snowling, M. J., & Stevenson, J. (2004). Phonemes, rimes, vocabulary, and grammatical skills as foundations of early reading development: Evidence from a longitudinal study. *Developmental Psychology, 40,* 663–681.

Muter, V., Taylor, S., & Vargha-Khadem, F. (1997). A longitudinal study of early intellectual development in hemiplegic children. *Neuropsychologia, 35,* 289–298.

Nathan, E., Stackhouse, J., Goulandris, N., & Snowling, M. J. (2004). The development of early literacy skills among children with speech difficulties: A test of the "Critical Age Hypothesis". *Journal of Speech, Language and Hearing Research, 47,* 377–391.

Nation, K. (1999). Reading skills in hyperlexia: A developmental perspective. *Psychological Bulletin, 125*(3), 338–355.

Nation, K., & Penny, S. (2008). Sensitivity to eye gaze in autism: Is it normal? Is it automatic? Is it social? *Development and Psychopathology 20,* 79–97.

Nation, K., & Snowling, M. J. (1997). Assessing reading difficulties: the validity and utility of current measures of reading skill. *British Journal of Educational Psychology, 67,* 359–370.

Nation, K., & Snowling, M. J. (1998a). Semantic processing and the development of word recognition skills: Evidence from children with reading comprehension difficulties. *Journal of Memory and Language, 39,* 85–101.

Nation, K., & Snowling, M. J. (1998b). Individual differences in contextual facilitation: Evidence from dyslexia and poor reading comprehension. *Child Development, 69,* 996–1011.

Nation, K., & Snowling, M.J (1999). Developmental differences in sensitivity to semantic relations among good and poor comprehenders: evidence from semantic priming. *Cognition, 70,* B1–B13.

Nation, K., & Snowling, M. J. (2000). Factors influencing syntactic awareness in normal readers and poor comprehenders. *Applied Psycholinguistics, 21,* 229–241.

Nation, K., Adams, J. W., Bowyer-Crane, C. A., & Snowling, M. J. (1999). Working memory deficits in poor comprehenders reflect underlying language impairments. *Journal of Experimental Child Psychology, 73,* 139–158.

Nation, K., Clarke, P., Marshall, C., & Durand, M. (2004). Hidden language impairments in children: parallels between poor reading comprehension and specific language impairment? *Journal of Speech, Language and Hearing Research, 47,* 199–211.

Nation, K., Snowling, M. J., & Clarke, P. (2007). Dissecting the relationship between language skills and learning to read: Semantic and phonological contributions to new vocabulary learning in children with poor reading comprehension. *Advances in Speech-Language Pathology, 9*(2), 131–139.

National Reading Panel (2000). *Report of the National Reading Panel: Reports of the subgroups.* Washington, DC: National Institute of Child Health and Human Development Clearing House.

National Research Council (2001). *Educating children with autism.* Washington, DC: National Academy Press.

Neale, M. D. (1989). *The Neale Analysis of Reading Ability: Revised British edition.* Windsor, UK: NFER.

Neale, M. D. (1997). *Analysis of Reading Ability (NARA II).* Windsor: NFER Nelson.

Neale, M., & Kendler, K. (1995). Models of comorbidity for multifactorial disorders. *American Journal of Human Genetics, 57,* 935–953.

Newbury, D., Bishop, D., & Monaco, A. P. (2005). Genetic influences of language impairment and phonological short-term memory. *Trends in Cognitive Sciences, 9,* 528–534.

Nicolson, R. I., & Fawcett, A. J. (1990). Automaticity: A new framework for dyslexia research? *Cognition, 35,* 159–182.

Nicolson, R. I., Fawcett, A. J., & Dean, P. (2001). Developmental dyslexia: The cerebellar deficit hypothesis. *Trends in Neurological Sciences, 24,* 508–511.

Nigg, J. T., Willcutt, E. G., Doyle, A. E., & Sonuga-Barke, E. J. S. (2005). Causal heterogeneity in attention-deficit/hyperactivity disorder: do we need neuropsychologically impaired subtypes? *Biological Psychiatry, 57,* 1224–1230.

Nittrouer, S. (1999). Do temporal processing deficits cause phonological processing problems? *Journal of Speech, Language and Hearing Research, 42*(4), 925–942.

Norbury, C. F. (2005). Barking up the wrong tree? Lexical ambiguity resolution in children with language impairments and autistic spectrum disorders. *Journal of Experimental Child Psychology, 90*(2), 142–171.

Norbury, C. F., & Bishop, D. V. M. (2002). Inferential processing and story recall in children with communication problems: A comparison of specific language impairment, pragmatic language impairment, and high functioning autism. *International Journal of Language and Communication Disorders, 37,* 227–251.

Norbury, C. F., & Bishop, D. V. M. (2007). Inferential processing and story recall in children with communication problems: A comparison of specific language impairment, pragmatic language impairment and high-functioning autism. *International Journal of Language and Communication Disorders, 37,* 227–251.

Nunes, T., & Bryant, P. (1996). *Children doing mathematics.* Oxford: Blackwell.

Oakhill, J. (1982). Constructive processes in skilled and less-skilled comprehenders' memory for sentences. *British Journal of Psychology, 73,* 13–20.

Oakhill, J. (1983). Instantiation and memory skills in children's comprehension of stories. *Quarterly Journal of Experimental Psychology, 34A,* 441–450.

Oakhill, J. (1984). Inferential and memory skills in children's comprehension of stories. *British Journal of Educational Psychology, 54,* 31–39.

Oakhill, J., & Patel, S. (1991). Can imagery training help children who have comprehension problems? *Journal of Research in Reading, 14,* 106–115.

Oatley, K., & Jenkins, J. M. (1996). *Understanding emotions*. Oxford: Blackwell Publishers.

Oberman, L., & Ramachandran, V. (2007). The simulating social mind: The role of the mirror neuron system and simulation in the social and communicative deficits in autism spectrum disorders. *Psychological Bulletin, 133*, 310–337.

Oetting, J. B., Rice, M. L., & Swank, L. K. (1995). Quick Incidental Learning (QUIL) of words by school-age children with and without SLI. *Journal of Speech and Hearing Research, 38*, 434–445.

O'Hare, A. E., Brown, J. K., & Aitken, K. (1991). Dyscalculia in children. *Developmental Medicine and Child Neurology, 4*(33), 356–361.

Oie, K. S., Kiemel, T., & Jeka, J. J. (2002). Multisensory fusion: Simultaneous re-weighting of vision and touch for the control of human posture. *Cognitive Brain Research, 14*(1), 164–176.

Oliver, B., Harlaar, N., Hayiou-Thomas, M. E., Kovas, Y., Walker, S. O., Petrill, S. A., et al. (2004). A twin study of teacher-reported mathematics performance and low performance in 7-year-olds. *Journal of Educational Psychology, 96*(3), 504–517.

Olson, R. K., Datta, H., J, G., & DeFries, J. C. (1999). A behavior–genetic analysis of reading disabilties and component processes. In R. M. Klein & P. McMullen (Eds.), *Converging methods for understanding reading and dyslexia* (pp. 133–152). Cambridge, MA: MIT Press.

Oney, B., & Goldman, S. R. (1984). Decoding and comprehension skills in Turkish and English: Effects of the regularity of grapheme–phoneme correspondences. *Journal of Educational Psychology, 76*(4), 557–568.

Oosterlaan, J., Logan, G., & Sergeant, J. (1998). Response inhibition in AD/HD, CD, comorbid AD/HD+CD, anxious and control children: A meta-analysis of studies with the stop task. *Journal of Child Psychology and Psychiatry, 39*, 411–425.

O'Riordan, M. A., Plaisted, K. C., Driver, J., & Baron-Cohen, S. (2001). Superior visual search in autism. *Journal of Experimental Psychology: Human Perception and Performance, 27*, 719–730.

Ozonoff, S., Pennington, B. F., & Rogers, S. J. (1991). Executive function deficits in high-functioning autistic individuals: Relationship to Theory of Mind. *Journal of Child Psychology and Psychiatry, 32*, 1081–1105.

Palladino, P., Cornoldi, C., De Beni, R., & Pazzaglia, F. (2001). Working memory and updating processes in reading comprehension. *Memory and Cognition, 29*, 344–354.

Paracchini, S., Scerri, T., & Monaco, A. P. (2007). The genetic lexicon of dyslexia. *Annual Review of Genomics and Human Genetics, 8*, 57–79.

Pascoe, M., Stackhouse, J., & Wells, B. (2006). *Persisting speech difficulties in children*. Chichester: Wiley.

Passolunghi, C. M., & Siegal, L. S. (2001). Short-term memory, working memory, and inhibitory control in children with difficulties in arithmetic problem solving. *Journal of Experimental Child Psychology, 80*, 44–57.

Passolunghi, C. M., & Siegal, L. (2004). Working memory and access to numerical information in children with disability in mathematics. *Journal of Experimental Child Psychology, 88*, 348–367.

Patel, T. K., Snowling, M. J., & De Jong, P. F. (2004). Learning to read in Dutch and English: A cross-linguistic comparison. *Journal of Educational Psychology, 96*, 785–797.

Patton, P., Belkacem-Boussaid, K., & Anastasio, T. J. (2002). Multimodality in the superior colliculus: an information theoretic analysis. *Cognitive Brain Research, 14*(1), 10–19.

Paul, R. (2000). Predicting outcomes of early expressive language delay: Ethical implications. In I. V. M. Bishop (Ed.), *Speech and language impairments in children: Causes, characteristics, intervention and outcome* (pp. 195–209). Hove, UK: Psychology Press.

Paul, R., Hernandez, R., Taylor, L., & Johnson, K. (1996). Narrative development in late talkers. *Journal of Speech and Hearing Research, 39*, 1295–1303.

Paulesu, E., Demonet, J.-F., Fazio, F., McCrory, E., Chanoine, V., Brunswick, N., et al. (2001). Dyslexia: Cultural diversity and biological unity. *Science, 291*, 2165–2167.

Paulesu, E., Frith, U., Snowling, M., Gallagher, A., Morton, J., Frackowiak, F. S. J., et al. (1996). Is developmental dyslexia a disconnection syndrome? Evidence from PET scanning. *Brain, 119*, 143–157.

Pearl, J. (2000). *Causality*. Cambridge, UK: Cambridge University Press.

Pellicano, E., Gibson, L., Maybery, M., Durkin, K., & Badcock, D. (2005). Abnormal global processing along the dorsal visual pathway in autism: A possible mechanism for weak visuospatial coherence? *Neuropsychologia, 43*, 1044–1053.

Pellicano, E., Maybery, M., Durkin, K., & Maley, A. (2006). Multiple cognitive capabilities / deficits in children with an autism spectrum disorder: "Weak" central coherence and its relationship to theory of mind and executive control. *Development and Psychopathology, 18*, 77–98.

Pelphrey, K. A., Morris, J. P., & McCarthy, G. (2005). Neural basis of eye gaze processing deficits in autism. *Brain, 128*(5), 1038–1048.

Pennington, B. F. (2002). *The development of psychopathology: Nature and nurture*. New York: Guildford Press.

Pennington, B. F. (2006). From single to multiple deficit models of developmental disorders. *Cognition, 101*, 385–413.

Pennington, B. F., & Lefly, D. L. (2001). Early reading development in children at family risk for dyslexia. *Child Development, 72*, 816–833.

Pennington, B. F., & Ozonoff, S. (1996). Executive function and developmental psychopathology. *Journal of Child Psychology and Psychiatry, 37*, 51–87.

Pennington, B. F., & Smith, S. D. (1988). Genetic influences on learning disabilities: An update. *Journal of Consulting and Clinical Psychology, 56*(6), 817–823.

Pennington, B. F., Filipek, P. A., Lefly, D., Chhabildas, N., Kennedy, D. N., Simon, J. H., et al. (2000). A twin MRI study of size variations in the human brain *Journal of Cognitive Neuroscience, 12*(1), 223–232.

Pennington, B. F., Grossier, D., & Welsh, M. C. (1993). Contrasting cognitive defects in attention deficit hyperactivity disorder vs. reading disability. *Developmental Psychology, 29*, 511–523.

Pennington, B. F., van Orden, G. C., Smith, S. D., Green, P. A., & Haith, M. M. (1990). Phonological processing skills and deficits in adult dyslexic children. *Child Development, 61*, 1753–1778.

Perfetti, C. A., Landi, N., & Oakhill, J. (2005). The acquisition of reading comprehension skill. In M. J. Snowing & C. Hulme (Eds.), *The science of reading: A handbook* (pp. 227–247). Oxford: Blackwell.

Perfetti, C., Marron, M., & Foltz, P. (1996). Sources of comprehension failure. Theoretical perspectives and case studies. In C. Cornoldi & J. Oakhill (Eds.), *Reading comprehension difficulties: Processes and intervention* (pp. 137–165). Mahwah, NJ: Lawrence Erlbaum Associates.

Perner, J., & Leekham, S. R. (2008). The curious incident of the photo that was accused of being false: Issues of domain specificity in development, autism, and brain imaging – Festschrift for Uta Frith. *Quarterly Journal of Experimental Psychology, 61*, 76–89.

Petrill, S. A., Deater-Deckard, K., Schatsneider, C., & Davis, C. (2005). Measured environmental influences on early reading: Evidence from an adoption study. *Scientific Studies of Reading, 9*, 237–259.

Piek, J. P., & Coleman-Carman, R. (1995). Kinaesthetic sensitivity and motor performance of children with Developmental Coordination Disorder. *Developmental Medicine and Child Neurology, 37*, 976–984.

Piek, J. P., & Skinner, R. A. (1999). Timing and force control during a sequential tapping task in children with and without motor coordination problems. *Journal of the International Neuropsychological Society, 5*, 320–329.

Pine, J., & Lieven, E. (1997). Slot and frame patterns and the development of the determiner category. *Applied Psycholinguistics, 18*, 123–138.

Pinker, S. (1979). Formal models of language learning. *Cognition, 7*, 217–283.

Pinker, S. (1994). *The language instinct.* London: Penguin Press.

Pitcher, T., Piek, J. P., & Hay, D. (2003). Fine and gross motor ability in males with ADHD. *Developmental Medicine and Child Neurology, 45*, 525–535.

Pitchford, N. J., Funnell, E., de Haan, B., & Morgan, P. S. (2007). Right hemisphere reading in a case of developmental deep dyslexia. *Quarterly Journal of Experimental Psychology, 60*, 1187–1196.

Plaisted, K., O'Riordan, M., & Baron-Cohen, S. (1998). Enhanced visual search for a conjunctive target in autism: A research note. *Journal of Child Psychology and Psychiatry, 39*, 777–783.

Plaut, D. C. (1997). Structure and function in the lexical system: insights from distributed models of word reading and lexical decision. *Language and Cognitive Processes, 12*(5/6), 765–805.

Plaut, D. C., McClelland, J. L., Seidenberg, M. S., & Patterson, K. (1996). Understanding normal and impaired word reading: Computational principles in quasi-regular domains. *Psychological Review, 103*, 56–115.

Plomin, R., & Kovas, Y. (2005). Generalist genes and learning disabilities. *Psychological Bulletin, 131*(4), 592–617.

Plomin, R., DeFries, J. C., McClearn, G. E., & Rutter, M. (1997). *Behavioral genetics* (3rd ed., Vol. 3). New York: W. H. Freeman.

Polatajko, H. J., & Mandich, A. D. (2004). *Enabling occupation in children: The Cognitive Orientation to daily Occupational Performance (CO-OP) approach.* Ottawa: CAOT Publications.

Polatajko, H. J., Law, M., Miller, J., Schaffer, R., & McNab, J. (1997). The effect of sensory integration program on academic achievement, motor performance and self-esteem in children identified as learning disabled: Results of a clinical trial. *Occupational Therapy Journal of Research, 11*, 156–176.

Polatajko, H. J., Macnab, J. J., Anstett, B., Malloymiller, T., Murphy, K., & Noh, S. (1995). A clinical trial of the process-oriented treatment approach for children with Developmental Co-ordination Disorder. *Developmental Medicine and Child Neurology, 37*, 310–319.

Popper, K. (1980). Evolution. *New Scientist, 87*, 611.

Premack, D., & Woodruff, G. (1978). Does the chimpanzee have a theory of mind? *Behavioral and Brain Sciences, 4*, 515–526.

Price, C. J., & McCrory, E. (2005). Functional brain imaging studies of skilled reading and developmental dyslexia. In M. J. Snowling & C. Hulme (Eds.), *The Science of reading: A handbook* (pp. 473–496). Oxford: Blackwell.

Pring, L. (2007). *Autism and blindness: Research and reflections*. London: Whurr Publishers.

Pring, L., Hermelin, B., & Heavey, L. (1995). Savants, segments, art and autism. *Journal of Child Psychology and Psychiatry, 36*(6), 1065–1076.

Prior, M. (2004). *Learning and behavior problems in Asperger syndrome*. New York: Guilford Press.

Quay, H. C. (1988). *The behavioral reward and inhibition system in childhood behavior disorder. Attention deficit disorder* (Vol. 3). Oxford: Pergamon Press.

Raberger, T., & Wimmer, H. (2003). On the automaticity/cerebellar deficit hypothesis of dyslexia: Balancing and continuous rapid naming in dyslexic and ADHD children. *Neuropsychologia, 41*, 1493–1497.

Rack, J. P., Snowling, M. J., Hulme, C., & Gibbs, S. (2007). Commentary: No evidence that an evidence-based treatment programme (DDAT) has specific benefits for children with reading difficulties. *Dyslexia, 13*, 97–104.

Rack, J. P., Snowling, M. J., & Olson, R. K. (1992). The nonword reading deficit in developmental dyslexia: A review. *Reading Research Quarterly, 27*, 29–53.

Raitano, N. A., Pennington, B. F., Tunick, R. A., Boada, R., & Shriberg, L. D. (2004). Pre-literacy skills of subgroups of children with phonological disorder. *Jounal of Child Psychology and Psychiatry, 45*, 821–835.

Ramani, G. B., & Siegler, R. S. (2008). Promoting broad and stable improvements in low-income children's numerical knowledge through playing number board games. *Child Development, 79*, 375–394.

Ramus, F. (2004). Neurobiology of dyslexia: A reinterpretation of the data. *Trends in Neurosciences, 27*(12), 720–726.

Rapin, I., & Allen, P. (1987). *Developmental dysphasia and autism in pre-school children: characteristics and subtypes*. Paper presented at the First International Symposium on Speech and Langugae Disorders in Children, London.

Rapport, S., & Wright, T. (1963). *Science: Method and meaning*. New York: New York University Press.

Rasmussen, P., & Gillberg, C. (2000). Natural outcome of ADHD with developmental coordination disorder at age 22 years. *Journal of the American Academy of Child and Adolescent Psychiatry, 39*, 1424–1431.

Read, C., Zhang, Y., Nie, H., & Ding, B. (1986). The ability to manipulate speech sounds depends on knowing alphabetic writing. *Cognition, 55*, 151–218.

Reed, M. A. (1989). Speech perception and the discrimination of brief auditory cues in reading disabled children. *Journal of Experimental Child Psychology, 48*(2), 270–292.

Reiersen, A., Constantino, J., Volk, H., & Todd, R. (2007). Autistic traits in a population-based ADHD twin sample. *Journal of Child Psychology and Psychiatry, 48*, 464–472.

Reiss, A. L., Mazzocco, M. M. M., Greenlaw, R., Freund, L. S., & Ross, J. L. (1995). Neurodevelopmental effects of X monosomy. A volumetric imaging study. *Annals of Neurology, 38*, 731–738.

Reitveld, M., Hudziak, J., Bartels, M., van Beijsterveldt, C., & Boomsma, D. (2004). Heritability of attention problems in children: Longitudinal results from a study of twins age 3 to 12. *Journal of Child Psychology and Child Psychiatry, 45*, 577–588.

Rescorla, L., Roberts, J., & Dahlsgaard, K. (1997). Late talkers at 2: Outcome at age 3. *Journal of Speech, Language and Hearing Research, 40*(3), 556–566.

Rice, M. L. (2000). Grammatical symptoms of specific language impairment. In D. Bishop & L. Leonard (Eds.), *Speech and language impairments in children: Causes, characteristics, intervention and outcome* (pp. 17–34). Hove, UK: Psychology Press.

Rice, M. L., & Wexler, K. (1996). Toward tense as a clinical marker of specific language impairment in English-speaking children. *Journal of Speech and Hearing Research, 39,* 1239–1257.

Rice, M. L., Oetting, J. B., Marquis, J., Bode, J., & Pae, S. (1994). Frequency of input effects on word comprehension of children with specific language impairment. *Journal of Speech and Hearing Research, 37,* 106–122.

Rice, M. L., Taylor, C. L., & Zubrick, S. R. (2008). Language outcomes of 7-year-old children with or without a history of late language emergence at 24 months. *Journal of Speech, Language and Hearing Research, 51*(2), 394–407.

Rice, M. L., Wexler, K., & Cleave, P. L. (1995). Specific language impairment as a period of extended optional infinitive. *Journal of Speech and Hearing Research, 38,* 850–863.

Rice, M. L., Wexler, K., & Hershberger, S. (1998). Tense over time: The longitudinal course of tense acquisition in children with specific language impairment. *Journal of Speech and Hearing Research, 41*(6), 1412–1431.

Rice, M. L., Wexler, K., & Redmond, S. M. (1999). Grammaticality judgments of an extended optional infinitive grammar: Evidence from English-speaking children with specific language impairment. *Journal of Speech, Language and Hearing Research, 42,* 943–961.

Richardson, U., Leppänen, P., Leiwo, W., & Lyytinen, H. (2003). Speech perception differs in infants at familial risk for dyslexia as early as six months of age. *Developmental Neuropsychology, 23,* 385–394.

Ricketts, J., Nation, K., & Bishop, D. V. (2007). Vocabulary is important for some, but not all reading skills. *Scientific Studies of Reading, 11,* 235–257.

Risi, S., Lord, C., Gotham, K., Corsello, C., Chrysler, C., Szatmari, P., et al. (2006). Combining information from multiple sources in the diagnosis of autism spectrum disorders. *Journal of the American Academy of Child and Adolescent Psychiatry, 45,* 1094–1103.

Rittle-Johnson, B., & Siegler, R. S. (1998). The relation between conceptual and procedural knowledge in learning mathematics. In C. Donlan (Ed.), *The development of mathematical skill* (pp. 75–110). Hove, UK: Psychology Press.

Rizzolatti, G., & Craighero, L. (2004). The mirror-neuron system. *Annual Review of Neuroscience, 27,* 169–192.

Rizzolatti, G., Fadiga, L., Gallese, V., & Fogassi, L. (1996). Premotor cortex and the recognition of motor actions. *Cognitive Brain Research, 3*(2), 131–141.

Rizzolatti, G., Luppino, G., & Matelli, M. (1998). The organization of the cortical motor system: New concepts *Electroencephalography and Clinical Neurophysiology, 106,* 283–296.

Robertson, I., Ward, T., Ridgeway, V., & Nimmo-Smith, I. (1994). *Test of Everyday Attention (TEA).* Suffolk, UK: Thames Valley Test Company.

Rochelle, K., & Talcott, J. (2006). Impaired balance in developmental dyslexia? A meta-analysis of contending evidence. *Journal of Child Psychology and Psychiatry, 47,* 1159–1166.

Rogers, S. J., & Vismara, L. A. (2008). Evidence-based comprehensive treatments for early autism. *Journal of Clinical Child and Adolescent Psychology, 37*(1), 8–38.

Romani, C., Ward, J., & Olson, A. (1999). Developmental surface dysgraphia: What is the underlying congitive impairment? *Quarterly Journal of Experimental Psychology, 52,* 97–128.

Roodenrys, S., Hulme, C., & Brown, G. (1993). The development of short-term memory span: Separable effects of speech rate and long-term memory. *Journal of Experimental Child Psychology, 56,* 431–442.

Ropar, D., & Mitchell, P. (1999). Are individuals with autism and Asperger's syndrome susceptible to visual illusions? *Journal of Child Psychology and Psychiatry, 40,* 1283–1293.

Rourke, B. P. (1989). *Nonverbal learning disabilities. The syndrome and the model.* New York: Guilford Press.

Rourke, B. P. (1995). *Syndrome of nonverbal learning disabilities: Neuro-developmental manifestations*. New York: Guildford Press.

Rousselle, L., & Noël, M.-P. (2007). Basic numerical skills in children with mathematics learning disabilities: A comparison of symbolic vs non-symbolic number magnitude processing. *Cognition, 102*, 361–395.

Rubia, K., Taylor, E., Smith, A. B., Oksannen, H., Overmeyer, M. D., & Newman, S. (2001). Neuropsychological analyses of impulsiveness in childhood hyperactivity. *British Journal of Psychiatry, 179*, 138–143.

Rumbaugh, D., Savage-Rumbaugh, S., & Hegel, M. (1987). Summation in the chimpanzee (Pan troglodytes). *Journal of Experimental Psychology: Animal Behavior Processes, 13*, 107–115.

Russell, J., Mauthner, N., Sharpe, S., & Tidswell, T. (1991). The 'windows task' as a measure of strategic deception in preschoolers and autistic subjects. *British Journal of Developmental Psychology, 9*, 331–349.

Rust, J. (1996). *Wechsler objective numerical dimensions*. London: Psychological Corporation.

Rutter, M. (2002). The interplay of nature, nurture, and developmental influences: The challenge ahead for mental health. *Archives of General Psychiatry, 59*, 996–1000.

Rutter, M. (2005a). Environmentally mediated risks for psychopathology: Research strategies and findings. *Journal of the American Academy of Child and Adolescent Psychiatry, 44*, 3–18.

Rutter, M. (2005b). *Genes and behavior*. Oxford: Blackwell.

Rutter, M. (2006). Implications of resilience concepts for scientific understanding. *Annals of the New York Academy of Sciences, 1094*, 1–12.

Rutter, M., & Maughan, B. (2002). School effectiveness findings 1979–2002. *Journal of School Psychology, 40*, 451–475.

Rutter, M., & Maughan, B. (2005). Dyslexia: 1965–2005. *Behavioural and Cognitive Psychotherapy, 33*, 389–402.

Rutter, M., & Mawhood, L. (1991). The long-term psychosocial sequelae of specific developmental disorders of speech and language. In M. Rutter & P. Casaer (Eds.), *Biological risk factors for psychosocial disorders* (pp. 233–259). Cambridge, UK: Cambridge University Press.

Rutter, M., & Redshaw, J. (1991). Annotation: Growing up as a twin: Twin–singleton differences in psychological development. *Journal of Child Psychology and Psychiatry, 32*(6), 885–895.

Rutter, M., & Yule, W. (1975). The concept of specific reading retardation. *Journal of Child Psychology and Psychiatry, 16*, 181–197.

Rutter, M., Anderson-Wood, L., Beckett, C., Bredenkamp, D., Castle, J., Groothues, C., et al. (1999). Quasi-autistic patterns following severe early global privation. *Journal of Child Psychology and Psychiatry, 40*, 537–549.

Rutter, M., Bailey, A., & Lord, C. (2003). *SCQ: The Social Communication Questionnaire. Manual*. Los Angeles, CA: Western Psychological Services.

Rutter, M., Caspi, A., Fergusson, D., Horwood, L. J., Goodman, R., Maughan, B., et al. (2004). Sex differences in developmental reading disability: New findings from 4 epidemiological studies. *Journal of the American Medical Association, 291*, 2007–2012.

Rutter, M., Kim-Cohen, J., & Maughan, B. (2006). Continuities and discontinuities in psychopathology between childhood and adult life. *Journal of Child Psychology and Psychiatry, 47*, 276–295.

Rutter, M., LeCouteur, A., & Lord, C. (2003). *Autism Diagnostic Interview – Revised*. Los Angeles, CA: Western Psychological Services.

Sampson, G. (2005). *The 'language instinct' debate*. London: Continuum International.

Scarborough, H. S. (1990). Very early language deficits in dyslexic children. *Child Development, 61*, 1728–1743.

Scarborough, H. S., & Dobrich, W. (1990). Development of children with early delay. *Journal of Speech and Hearing Research, 33*, 70–83.

Schachter, R., & Logan, G. D. (1990). Impulsivity and inhibitory control in normal development and childhood psychopathology. *Developmental Psychology, 26*, 710–720.

Schoemaker, M. M., Niemeijer, A. S., Reynders, K., & Smits-Engelsman, B. (2003). Effectiveness of neuromotor task training for children with developmental coordination disorder: A pilot study. *Neural Plasticity, 10*(1/2), 155–163.

Schoemaker, M. M., van der Wees, M., Flapper, B., Verheij-Jansen, N., Scholten-Jaegers, S., & Geuze, R. H. (2001). Perceptual skills of children with developmental coordination disorder. *Human Movement Science, 20*(1/2), 111–133.

Schopler, E., Reichler, R., & Rochen-Renner, B. (1998). *The Childhood Autism Rating Scale (CARS)*. Los Angeles: Western Psychological Services.

Scientific Learning Corporation (1997), Retrieved August 31, 2008 from http://www.scilearn.com/

Scoville, W. B., & Milner, B. (1957). Loss of recent memory after bilateral hippocampal lesions. *Journal of Neurology, Neurosurgery and Psychiatry, 20*, 11–21.

Sebat, J., Lakshmi, B., Troge, J., Alexander, J., Young, J., Lundin, P., et al. (2004). Large-scale copy number polymorphism in the human genome. *Science, 305*, 525–528.

Seidenberg, M. S., & McClelland, J. (1989). A distributed, developmental model of word recognition. *Psychological Review, 96*, 523–568.

Seigneuric, A., & Ehrlich, M.-F. (2005). Contribution of working memory capacity to children's reading comprehension: A longitudinal investigation. *Reading and Writing, 18*, 617–656.

Seigneuric, A., Ehrlich, M. F., Oakhill, J. V., & Yuill, N. (2000). Working memory resources and children's reading comprehension. *Reading and Writing, 13*, 81–103.

Semel, E. M., Wiig, E. H., & Secord, W. (1992). *Clinical evaluation of language fundamentals – revised*. San Antonio: Psychological Corporation.

Sergeant, J. A. (2005). Modeling attention-deficit/hyperactivity disorder: a critical appraisal of the cognitive-energetic model. *Biological Psychiatry, 57*, 1248–1255.

Sergeant, J.A., & van der Meere, J. (1988). What happens after a hyperactive child commits an error? *Psychiatry Research, 24*, 157–164.

Sergeant, J. A., Oosterlaan, J., & van der Meere, JJ (1999). Information processing and energetic factors in attenton deficit/hypoeractivity disorder. In H. C. Quay & A. Hogan (Eds.), *Handbook of disruptive behaviour disorders* (pp. 75–104). New York: Plenum Press.

Serniclaes, W., Van Heghe, S., Mousty, P., Carré, R., & Sprenger-Charolles, L. (2004). Allophonic mode of speech perception in dyslexia. *Journal of Experimental Child Psychology, 87*, 336–361.

Service, E. (1992). Phonology, working memory and foreign-language learning. *Quarterly Journal of Experimental Psychology, 45A*(1), 21–50.

Seymour, P. H. K. (2005). Early reading development in European orthographies. In M. J. Snowling & C. Hulme (Eds.), *The science of reading: A handbook* (pp. 296–315). Oxford: Blackwell.

Seymour, P. H. K., & Elder, L. (1986). Beginning reading without phonology. *Cognitive Neuropsychology, 1*, 43–82.

Shager, M., Demetriou, A., & Pervez, M. (1986). *The structure and scaling of concrete operational thought: Three studies in four countries and only one story*. Unpublished manuscript.

Shah, A., & Frith, U. (1983). An islet of ability in autistic children: A research note. *Journal of Child Psychology and Psychiatry, 24,* 613–620.

Shalev, R. S., Manor, O., Kerem, B., Ayali, M., Badichi, N., Friedlander, Y., et al. (2001). Developmental dyscalculia is a familiar learning disability. *Journal of Learning Disabilities, 34*(1), 59–65.

Shallice, T. (1988). *From neuropsychology to mental structure.* Cambridge, UK: Cambridge University Press.

Shankweiler, D., Liberman, I. Y., Mark, L. S., Fowler, C. A., & Fischer, F. W. (1979). The speech code and learning to read. *Journal of Experimental Psychology: Human Learning and Memory, 5,* 531–545.

Share, D. L., McGee, R., McKenzie, D., Williams, S., & Silva, P. A. (1987). Further evidence relating to the distinction between specific reading retardation and general reading backwardness. *British Journal of Developmental Psychology, 5,* 35–44.

Share, D. L., Moffitt, T. E., & Silva, P. A. (1988). Factors associated with arithmetic-and-reading disability and specific arithmetic disability. *Journal of Learning Disabilities, 21,* 313–320.

Shaywitz, B. A., Fletcher, J. M., Holahan, J. M., & Shaywitz, S. E. (1992). Discrepancy compared to low achievement definitions of reading disability: Results from the Connecticut longitudinal study. *Journal of Learning Disabilities, 25*(10), 639–648.

Shaywitz, S. E., Escobar, M. D., Shaywitz, B. A., Fletcher, J. M., & Makugh, R. (1992). Evidence that dyslexia may represent the lower tail of a normal distribution of reading ability. *New England Journal of Medicine, 326,* 145–150.

Shaywitz, S. E., Shaywitz, B. A., Pugh, K. R., Fulbright, R. K., Constable, R. T., Mencl, W. E., et al. (1998). Functional disruption in the organization of the brain for reading in dyslexia. *Proceedings of the National Academy of Sciences of the USA, 95,* 2636–2641.

Sherman, D. K., McGue, M. K., & Iacono, W. G. (1997). Twin concordance for attention deficit hyperactivity disorder: A comparison of teachers' and mothers' reports. *American Journal of Psychiatry, 154*(4), 532–535.

Sherrington, C. (1906). *The integrative action of the nervous system.* New York: Charles Scribner.

Shipley, B. (2000). *Cause and correlation in biology.* Cambridge, UK: Cambridge University Press.

Shrout, P., & Bolger, N. (2002). Mediation in experimental and nonexperimental studies: New procedures and recommendations. *Psychological Methods, 7,* 422–445.

Siegler, R. S. (1988). Strategy choice procedures and the development of multiplication skill. *Journal of Experimental Psychology: General, 117*(3), 258–275.

Siegler, R. S., & Shrager, J. (1984). Strategy choice in addition and subtraction: How do children know what to do? In C. Sophian (Ed.), *Origins of cognitive skills* (pp. 229–293). Hillsdale, NJ: Lawrence Erlbaum Associates.

Silani, G., Frith, U., Demonet, J.-F., Fazio, F., Perani, D. C., Price, C., et al. (2005). Brain abnormalities underlying altered activation in dyslexia: A voxel based morphometric study. *Brain, 128,* 2453–2461.

Sims, K., & Morton, J. (1999). Modelling the training effects of kinaesthetic acuity measurement in children. *Journal of Child Psychology and Psychiatry, 39*(5), 731–746.

Sims, K., Henderson, S. E., Hulme, C., & Morton, J. (1996). The remediation of clumsiness. An evaluation of Laszlo's kinaesthetic approach. *Developmental Medicine and Child Neurology, 38,* 976–987.

Skuse, D. (1993). Extreme deprivation in childhood. In D. Bishop & K. Mogford (Eds.), *Language development in exceptional circumstances* (pp. 29–46). Hove, UK: Lawrence Erlbaum Associates.

Skuse, D. (2001). Endophenotypes and child psychiatry. *British Journal of Psychiatry, 178,* 395–396.

Skuse, D., Warrington, R., Bishop, D., Chowdhury, U., Lau, J., Mandy, W., et al. (2004). The Developmental, Dimensional and Diagnostic Interview (3Di): A novel computerized assessment for autism spectrum disorders. *Journal of the American Academy of Child and Adolescent Psychiatry, 43,* 548–558.

SLI Consortium (2002). A genome wide scan identifies two novel loci involved in specific language impairment. *American Journal of Human Genetics, 70,* 384–398.

SLI Consortium (2004). Highly significant linkage to SLI1 locus in an expanded sample of individuals affected by Specific Language Impairment (SLI). *American Journal of Human Genetics, 94,* 1225–1238.

Smith, T., Groen, A. D., & Wynn, J. W. (2000). Randomized trial of intensive early intervention for children with pervasive developmental disorder. *American Journal of Mental Retardation, 105,* 269–285.

Smits-Engelsman, B. C. M., Wilson, P. H., Westenberg, Y., & Duysens, J. (2003). Fine motor deficiencies in children with developmental coordination disorder and learning disabilities: An underlying open-loop control deficit. *Human Movement Science, 22(4/5),* 495–513.

Smyth, M. M., & Mason, U. C. (1997). Planning and execution of action in children with and without developmental coordination disorder. *Journal of Child Psychology and Psychiatry, 38,* 1023–1037.

Snowling, M. J. (1981). Phonemic deficits in developmental dyslexia. *Psychological Research, 43,* 219–234.

Snowling, M. J. (2000). *Dyslexia* (2nd ed.). Oxford: Blackwell.

Snowling, M. J. (2006). Nonword repetition and language learning disorders: A developmental contingency framework. *Applied Psycholinguistics, 27,* 587–591.

Snowling, M. J. (2008). Specific disorders and broader phenotypes: The case of dyslexia. *Quarterly Journal of Experimental Psychology, 61,* 142–156.

Snowling, M. J., & Frith, U. (1986). Comprehension in 'hyperlexic' readers. *Journal of Experimental Child Psychology, 42,* 329–415.

Snowling, M. J., & Hulme, C. (1994). The development of phonological skills in children. *Philosophical Transactions of the Royal Society B, 346,* 21–26.

Snowling, M. J., & Hulme, C. (2005). Learning to read with a language impairment. In M. J. Snowling & C. Hulme (Eds.), *The science of reading: A handbook* (pp. 397–412). Oxford: Blackwell.

Snowling, M. J., & Hulme, C. (2006). Language skills, learning to read and reading intervention. *London Review of Education, 4,* 63–76.

Snowling, M. J., Adams, J. W., Bishop, D. V. M., & Stothard, S. E. (2001). Educational attainments of school leavers with a preschool history of speech-language impairments. *International Journal of Language and Communication Disorders, 36(2),* 173–183.

Snowling, M. J., Bishop, D. V. M., & Stothard, S. E. (2000). Is pre-school language impairment a risk factor for dyslexia in adolescence? *Journal of Child Psychology and Psychiatry, 41,* 587–600.

Snowling, M. J., Bishop, D. V. M., Stothard, S. E., Chipchase, B., & Kaplan, C. (2006). Psycho-social outcomes at 15 years of children with a pre-history of speech-language impairment. *Journal of Child Psychology and Child Psychiatry, 47,* 759–765.

Snowling, M. J., Bryant, P. E., & Hulme, C. (1996). Theoretical and methodological pitfalls in making comparisons between developmental and acquired dyslexia: Some comments on A. Castles and M. Coltheart (1993). *Reading and Writing, 8,* 443–451.

Snowling, M. J., Chiat, S., & Hulme, C. (1991). Words, non-words and phonological processes: some comments on Gathercole, Willis, Emslie and Baddeley. *Applied Psycholinguistics, 12*, 369–373.

Snowling, M. J., Gallagher, A., & Frith, U. (2003). Family risk of dyslexia is continuous: Individual differences in the precursors of reading skill. *Child Development, 74*, 358–373.

Snowling, M. J., Goulandris, N., Bowlby, M., & Howell, P. (1986). Segmentation and speech perception in normal and dyslexic readers. *Journal of Experimental Child Psychology, 41*, 409–507.

Snowling, M. J., Muter, V., & Carroll, J. M. (2007). Children at family risk of dyslexia: A follow-up in adolescence. *Journal of Child Psychology and Child Psychiatry, 48*, 609–618.

Snowling, M. J., Van Wagtendonk, B., & Stafford, C. (1988). Object-naming deficits in developmental dyslexia. *Journal of Research in Reading, 11*, 67–85.

Sodian, B., & Frith, U. (1992). Deception and sabotage in autistic, retarded and normal children. *Journal of Child Psychology and Psychiatry, 33*(3), 591–605.

Solanto, M. V., Arnsten, A. F. T., & Castellanos, E. X. (2001). *Stimulant drugs and ADHD.* Oxford: Oxford University Press.

Sonuga-Barke, E. J. S. (2002). Psychological heterogeneity in AD/HD – a dual pathway model of behaviour and cognition. *Behavioural Brain Research, 130*(1/2), 29–36.

Sonuga-Barke, E. J. S., Taylor, E., & Heptinstall, E. (1992). Hyperactivity and delay aversion – II. The effect of self versus externally imposed stimulus presentation periods on memory. *Journal of Child Psychology and Psychiatry, 33*, 399–409.

Sonuga-Barke, E. J. S., Taylor, E., Sembi, S., & Smith, J. (1992). Hyperactivity and delay aversion – I. The effect of delay on choice. *Journal of Child Psychology and Psychiatry, 33*, 387–398.

Sophian, S. (1998). A developmental perspective on children's counting. In C. Donlan (Ed.), *The development of mathematical skills* (pp. 27–46). Hove, UK: Psychology Press.

Spencer, T., Biederman, J., Madras, B., Faraone, S., Dougherty, D., Bonab, A., et al. (2005). In vivo neuroreceptor imaging in attention-deficit/hyperactivity disorder: A focus on the dopamine transporter. *Biological Psychiatry, 57*, 1293–1300.

Sperber, D., & Wilson, D. (1995). *Relevance: communication and cognition* (2nd ed.). Oxford: Blackwell.

Spinath, F. M., Price, T. S., Dale, P. S., & Plomin, R. (2004). The genetic and environmental origins of language disability and ability. *Child Development, 75*, 445–454.

Stanovich, K. E. (1994). Does dyslexia exist? *Journal of Child Psychology and Psychiatry, 35*(4), 579–595.

Stanovich, K. E., & Siegel, L. S. (1994). The phenotypic performance profile of reading-disabled children: A regression-based test of the phonological-core variable-difference model. *Journal of Educational Psychology, 86*, 24–53.

Stanovich, K. E., Siegel, L. S., & Gottardo, A. (1997). Converging evidence for phonological and surface subtypes of reading disability. *Journal of Educational Psychology, 89*, 114–127.

Stark, R. E., Bernstein, L. E., Condino, R., Bender, M., Tallal, P., & Catts, H. (1984). Four-year follow-up study of language impaired children. *Annals of Dyslexia, 34*, 49–68.

Stein, C. M., Schick, H., Terry Taylor, L., Shnberg, C., Millard, A., Kundtz-Kluge, K., et al. (2004). Pleiotropic effects of a chromosome 3 locus on speech-sound disorder and reading. *American Journal of Human Genetics, 74*, 283–297.

Stevenson, J., & Fredman, G. (1990). The social environmental correlates of reading ability. *Journal of Child Psychology and Psychiatry and Allied Disciplines, 31*, 681–698.

Stone, C. A., & Sobel, M. E. (1990). The robustness of estimates of total indirect effects in covariance structure models estimated by maximum likelihood. *Psychometrika, 55*, 337–352.

Stothard, S. E., & Hulme, C. (1992). Reading comprehension difficulties in children: The role of language comprehension and working memory skills. *Reading and Writing, 4*, 245–256.

Stothard, S., & Hulme, C. (1995). A comparison of reading comprehension and decoding difficulties in children. *Journal of Child Psychology and Psychiatry, 36*(3), 399–408.

Stothard, S. E., Snowling, M. J., Bishop, D. V. M., Chipchase, B., & Kaplan, C. (1998). Language impaired pre-schoolers: A follow-up in adolescence. *Journal of Speech, Language and Hearing Research, 41*, 407–418.

Stromswold, K. (2001). The heritability of language: A review and meta-analysis of twin, adoption, and linkage studies. *Language Acquisition, 77*, 647–723.

Stroop, J. R. (1935). Studies of interference in serial verbal reactions. *Journal of Experimental Psychology, 18*, 643–662.

Sugden, D. (2007). Current approaches to intervention in children with developmental coordination disorder. *Developmental Medicine and Child Neurology, 49*, 467–417.

Sugden, D., Chambers, M., & Utley, A. (2006). *Leeds Consensus Statement: Developmental coordination disorder as a specific learning difficulty*. Leeds: DCD-UK/Discovery Centre.

Swan, D., & Goswami, U. (1997a). Phonological awareness deficits in developmental dyslexia and the phonological representations hypothesis. *Journal of Experimental Child Psychology, 60*, 334–353.

Swan, D., & Goswami, U. (1997b). Picture naming deficits in developmental dyslexia: The phonological representations hypothesis. *Brain and Language, 56*(3), 334–353.

Tager-Flusberg, H. (1991). Semantic processing in the free recall of autistic children – further evidence for a cognitive deficit. *British Journal of Developmental Psychology, 9*, 417–430.

Tager-Flusberg, H. (2001). Understanding the language and communicative impairments in autism. In L. M. Glidden (Ed.), *International review of research in mental retardation: Autism* (pp. 185–205). San Diego, CA: Academic Press.

Tager-Flusberg, H., & Joseph, R. (2003). Identifying neurocognitive phenotypes in autism. *Philosophical Transactions of the Royal Society B, 358*, 303–314.

Tallal, P. (1980). Auditory-temporal perception, phonics and reading disabilities in children. *Brain and Language, 9*, 182–198.

Tallal, P., & Piercy, M. (1973). Developmental aphasia: impaired rate of non-verbal processing as a function of sensory modality. *Neuropsychologia, 11*, 389–398.

Tallal, P., & Piercy, M. (1974). Developmental aphasia: Rate of auditory processing and selective impairment of consonant perception. *Neuropsychologia, 12*, 83–93.

Tallal, P., & Stark, R. E. (1982). Perceptual/motor profiles of reading impaired children with or without concomitant oral language deficits. *Annals of Dyslexia, 32*, 163–176.

Tallal, P., Miller, S. L., Bedi, G., Byma, G., Wang, X., Nagarajan, S. S., et al. (1996). Language comprehension in language-learning impaired children improved with acoustically modified speech. *Science, 271*, 81–84.

Tannock, R. (1998). Attention deficit hyperactivity disorder: Advances in cognitive, neurobiological, and genetic research. *Journal of Child Psychology and Psychiatry, 39*, 65–99.

Taylor, E. (2006). Hyperkinetic disorders. In C. Gillberg, R. Harrington, & H.-C. Steinhausen (Eds.), *A clinician's handbook of child and adolescent psychiatry* (pp. 489–521). Cambridge, UK: Cambridge University Press.

Taylor, E. & Sonuga-Barke, E. J. S. (2008). Disorders of attention and activity. In M. Rutter, D. Bishop, D. Pine, S. Scott, J. S. Stevenson, E. A. Taylor, & A. Thapar (Eds.), *Rutter's child & adolescent psychiatry* (5th ed., pp. 521–542.). Oxford, UK: Wiley-Blackwell.

Taylor, E., Schachar, R., Thorley, G., & Wieselberg, M. (1986). Conduct disorder and hyperactivity: I. Separation of hyperactivity and antisocial conduct in British child psychiatric patients. *British Journal of Psychiatry, 149*, 760–767.

Temple, C. M. (1989). Digit dyslexia: A category-specific disorder in developmental dyscalculia. *Cognitive Neuropsychology, 6*(1), 93–116.

Temple, C. M. (1991). Procedural dyscalculia and number fact dyscalculia: Double dissociation in developmental dyscalculia. *Cognitive Neuropsychology, 8*(2), 155–176.

Temple, C. M., & Carney, R. A. (1993). Intellectual functioning of children with Turner syndrome: A comparison of behavioural phenotypes. *Developmental Medicine and Child Neurology, 35*, 691–698.

Temple, C. M., & Marshall, J. (1983). A case study of a developmental phonological dyslexia. *British Journal of Psychology, 74*, 517–533.

Temple, C. V. (1997). *Developmental cognitive neuropsychology*. Hove, UK: Psychology Press.

Temple, E., & Posner, M. I. (1998). Brain mechanisms of quantity are similar in 5-year-olds and adults. *Proceedings of the National Academy of Sciences of the USA, 95*, 7836–7841.

Temple, S. M., & Sherwood, S. (2002). Representation and retrieval of arithmetical facts: Developmental difficulties. *Quarterly Journal of Experimental Psychology, 55A*(3), 733–752.

Thapar, A., Langley, K., Asherson, P., & Till, M. (2007). Gene–environment interplay in attention-deficit hyperactivity disorder and the importance of a developmental perspective. *British Journal of Psychiatry, 190*(1), 1–3.

Thelen, E. (1995). Motor development: A new synthesis. *American Psychologist, 50*(2), 79–95.

Thomas, M. (2005). Characterising compensation. *Cortex, 41*, 434–442.

Thorpe, K., Rutter, M., & Greenwood, R. (2003). Twins as a natural experiment to study the causes of mild language delay: II: Family interaction risk factors. *Journal of Child Psychology and Psychiatry, 44*(3), 342–355.

Tomasello, M. (2000). Acquiring syntax is not what you think. In D. V. M. Bishop & L. B. Leonard (Eds.), *Speech and language impairments in children* (pp. 1–16). Hove, UK: Psychology Press.

Tomasello, M. (2003). *Constructing a language: A usage-based theory of language acquisition*. Cambridge, MA: Harvard University Press.

Tomblin, J. B., & Buckwalter, P. (1998). The heritability of poor language achievement among twins. *Journal of Speech and Hearing Research, 41*, 188–199.

Tomblin, J. B., Freese, P. R., & Records, N. L. (1992). Diagnosing specific language impairment in adults for the purpose of pedigree analysis. *Journal of Speech and Hearing Research, 35*, 832–843.

Tomblin, J. B., Records, N. L., Buckwalter, Zhang, X., Smith, E., & O'Brien, M. (1997). Prevalence of specific language impairment in kindergarten children. *Journal of Speech and Hearing Research, 40*, 1245–1260.

Tomblin, J. B., Records, N. L., & Zhang, X. (1996). A system for the diagnosis of specific language impairment in kindergarten children. *Journal of Speech and Hearing Research, 39*, 1284–1294.

Tonnquist-Uhlen, I. (1996). Topography of auditory evoked long-latency potentials in children with severe language impairment: The T-complex. *Acta Oto–Laryngologic (Stockholm) 689*, 680–689.

Toplak, M., Dockstader, C., & Tannock, R. (2006). Temporal information processing in ADHD: Findings to date and new methods. *Journal of Neuroscience Methods, 151*, 15–29.

Torgesen, J. K. (2001). The theory and practice of intervention: Comparing outcomes from prevention and remediation studies. In A. Fawcett & R. Nicolson (Eds.), *Dyslexia: Theory and good practice* (pp. 185–201). London: David Fulton Publishers.

Torgesen, J. K., Alexander, A. W., Wagner, R. K., Rashotte, C. A., Voeller, K., Conway, T., et al. (2001). Intensive remedial instruction for children with severe reading disabilities: Immediate and long-term outcomes from two instructional approaches. *Journal of Learning Disabilities, 34*, 33–58.

Tramo, M. J., Shah, G. D., & Braida, L. D. (2002). Functional role of auditory cortex in frequency processing and pitch perception. *Journal of Neurophysiology, 87*, 122–139.

Treiman, R., & Breaux, A. M. (1982). Common phoneme an overall similarity relations among spoken syllables: Their use by children and adults. *Journal of Psycholinguistic Research, 11*(6), 569–598.

Tunmer, W. E. (1989). The role of language related factors in reading disability. In D. Shankweiler & I. Y. Liberman (Eds.), *Phonology and reading disability: Solving the reading puzzle. International Academy for Research in Learning Disabilities Monograph* (pp. 91–132) Ann Arbur: University of Michigan Press.

Turner, M. A. (1999). Generating novel ideas: Fluency performance in high-functioning and learning disabled individuals with autism. *Journal of Child Psychology and Psychiatry, 40*, 189–201.

Turner, D. C., Blackwell, A. D., Dowson, J. H., McLean, A., & Sahakian, B. J. (2005). Neurocognitive effects of methylphenidate in adult attention-deficit/hyperactivity disorder. *Psychopharmacology, 178*(2), 286–295.

Ullman, M. T., & Pierpont, E. I. (2005). Specific language impairment is not specific to language: The procedural deficit hypothesis. *Cortex, 41*, 399–433.

Valdois, S., Bosse, M.-L., & Tainturier, M.-J. (2004). The cognitive deficits responsible for developmental dyslexia: Review of evidence for a selective visual attentional disorder. *Dyslexia, 10*, 339–363.

van Dellen, T., & Geuze, R., H. (1990). Motor response processing in clumsy children. *Journal of Child Psychology and Psychiatry, 29*(4), 489–500.

van den Broek, P., Young, M., Tzeng, Y., & Linderholm, T. (1999). The landscape model of reading: Inferences and the on-line construction of a memory representation. In I. van Oostendorp & S. R. Goldman (Eds.), *The construction of mental representations during reading* (pp. 71–98). Mahwah, NJ: Lawrence Erlbaum Associates.

van der Lely, H. K. J. (1994). Canonical linking rules: Forward versus linking in normally developing and specifically language-impaired children. *Cognition, 51*, 29–72.

van der Lely, H. K. J. (2005). Domain-specific cognitive systems: Insight from Grammatical-SLI. *Trends in Cognitive Science, 9*, 53–59.

van der Lely, H. K. J., & Harris, M. (1990). Comprehension of reversible sentences in specifically language impaired children. *Journal of Speech and Hearing Disorders, 55*, 101–117.

van der Lely, H. K. J., & Stollwerk, L. (1997). Binding theory and specifically language impaired children. *Cognition, 62*, 245–290.

van der Lely, H. K. J., Rosen, S., & McClelland, A. (1998). Evidence for grammar specific deficit in children. *Current Biology, 8*(23), 1253–1258.

van Harskamp, N. J., & Cipolotti, L. (2005). Cognitive and social impairments in patients with superficial siderosis. *Brain, 128*, 1082–1092.

Van Ijzendoorn, M. H., & Bus, A. G. (1994). Meta-analytic confirmation of the nonword reading deficit in developmental dyslexia. *Reading Research Quarterly, 29*, 266–275.

Van Orden, G. C., Pennington, B. F., & Stone, G. O. (2001). What do double dissociations prove? *Cognitive Science, 25*, 111–172.

van Weerdenburg, M., Verhoeven, L., & van Balkom, H. (2006). Towards a typology of specific language impairment. *Journal of Child Psychology & Psychiatry, 47*, 176–189.

Vargha-Khadem, F., Watkins, K. E., Price, C. J., Ashburner, J., Alcock, K., & Connelly, A., et al. (1998). Neural basis of an inherited speech and language disorder. *Proceedings of the National Academy of Science USA, 95*, 12695–12700.

Vellutino, F. R. (1979). *Dyslexia: Research and Theory*: MIT Press.

Vellutino, F. R., Scanlon, D. M., & Spearing, D. (1995). Semantic and phonological coding in poor and normal readers. *Journal of Experimental Child Psychology, 59*, 76–123.

Viding, E., & Frith, U. (2006). Genes for violence lurk in the brain. Commentary. *Proceedings of the National Academy of Sciences, 103*, 6085–6086.

Visser, J., Geuze, R. H., & Kalverboer, A. F. (1998). The relationship between physical growth, level of activity and the development of motor skills in adolescence: Differences between children with DCD and controls. *Human Movement Science, 17*, 573–608.

Volkmar, F. R., Lord, C., Bailey, A., Schultz, R., & Kiln, A. (2004). Autism and pervasive developmental disorders. *Journal of Child Psychology & Psychiatry, 45*, 135–170.

von Hofsten, C., & Rosblad, B. (1988). The integration of sensory information in the development of precise manual pointing. *Neuropsychologia, 26*(6), 805–821.

Waddington, C. (1966). *Principles of development and differentiation*. New York: MacMillan.

Wagner, R. K., Torgesen, J. K., & Rashotte, C. A. (1994). Development of reading-related phonological processing abilities: Evidence of bi-directional causality from a latent variable longitudinal study. *Developmental Psychology, 30*, 73–87.

Walker, I., & Hulme, C. (1999). Concrete words are easier to recall than abstract: Evidence for a semantic contribution to short-term serial recall. *Journal of Experimental Psychology: Learning, Memory, and Cognition, 25*, 1256–1271.

Wann, J. P., Mon-Williams, M., & Rushton, K. (1998). Postural control and co-ordination disorders: The swinging room revisited. *Human Movement Science, 17*(4–5), 491–513.

Warrington, E., & Shallice, T. (1969). The selective impairment of auditory verbal short-term memory. *Brain, 92*, 885–896.

Watkins, K., Vargha-Khadem, F., Ashburner, J., Passingham, R., Connelly, A., Friston, K. J., et al. (2002). MRI analysis of an inherited speech and language disorder: structural brain abnormalities. *Brain, 125*, 465–478.

Wechsler, D. (1974) *Wechsler Intelligence Scale for Children-Revised*. New York: The Psychological Corporation.

Wechsler, D. (1993). The Wechsler Objective Reading Dimensions. New York: The Psychological Corporation.

Westen, D., Novotny, C., & Thompson-Brenner, C. (2004). The empirical status of empirically supported psychotherapies: Assumptions, findings, and reporting in controlled clinical trials. Psychological Bulletin, 130, 631–663.

Wexler, K. (1994). *Optional Infinitives, head movement, and economy of derivations*. Cambridge: Cambridge University Press.

Whalen, J., McCloskey, M., Lindemann, M., & Bouton, G. (2002). Representing Arithmetic Table Facts in Memory: Evidence from Acquired Impairments. *Cognitive Neuropsychology, 19*(6), 505–522.

White, S. (2006). *Subtypes in the autism spectrum: relating cognition to behaviour*. Unpublished PhD, University College London, London.

Whitehouse, A. J. O., Barry, J. G., & Bishop, D. V. M. (2007). The broader language phenotype of autism: A comparison with specific language impairment. *Journal of Child Psychology and Psychiatry 48*(8), 822–830.

Whitehurst, G. J., & Lonigan, C. J. (1998). Child Development and Emergent Literacy. *Child Development, 69*(3), 848–872.

Wiegersma, P. H., & Van der Velde, A. V. (1983). Motor Development of Deaf Children. *Journal of Child Psychology and Psychiatry, 24*(1), 103–111.

Wilcox, A. L., & Polatajko, H. J. (1993). Verbal self-guidance: A treatment technique for children with developmental coordination disorder. *Canadian Journal of Occupational Therapy, 60* (Conference Supplement), 20.

Willcutt, E., & Pennington, B. (2000). Comorbidity of reading disability and attention-deficit/ hyperactivity disorder: Differences by gender and subtype. *Journal of Learning Disabilities, 33*, 179–191.

Willcutt, E. G., Doyle, A. E., Nigg, J. T., Faraone, S. V., & Pennington, B. F. (2005). Validity of the executive function theory of attention deficit/hyperactivity disorder: A meta-analytic review. *Biological Psychiatry, 57*, 1336–1346.

Willcutt, E. G., Pennington, B. F., Boada, R., Tunick, R. A., Ogline, J., Chhabildas, N. A., et al. (2001). A comparison of the cognitive deficits in reading disability and attention-deficit/hyperactivity disorder. *Journal of Abnormal Psychology, 110*, 157–172.

Willcutt, E. G., Pennington, B. F., Chhabildas, N. A., Olson, R. K., & Hulslander, J. L. (2005). Neuropsychological analyses of comorbidity between RD and ADHD: In search of the common deficit. *Developmental Neuropsychology, 27*, 35–78.

Willcutt, E., Pennington, B., & DeFries, J. (2000). Twin study of the etiology of comorbidity between reading disability and attention-deficit/hyperactivity disorder. *American Journal of Medical Genetics, 96*(3), 293–301.

Willcutt, E., Pennington, B., Smith, S. D., Cardon, L. R., Gayan, J., Knopik, V., et al. (2002). Quantitative trait locus for reading disability on chromosome 6p is pleiotropic for attention-deficit/hyperactivity disorder. *American Journal of Human Genetics (Neuropsychiatric Genetics), 114*, 260–268.

Williams, J. H. G., Whiten, A., Suddendorf, T., & Perrett, D. I. (2001). Imitation, mirror neurons and autism. *Neuroscience and Biobehavioral Reviews, 25*(4), 287–295.

Willoughby, M. (2005). Developmental course of ADHD symptomotalogy during the transition from childhood to adolescence: A review with recommendations. *Journal of Child Psychology and Psychiatry, 44*, 88–106.

Wilson, A. J., & Dehaene, S. (2007). Number sense and developmental dyscalculia. In D. Coch, G. Dawson & K. W. Fischer (Eds.), *Human behavior learning and the developing brain: Atypical development* (pp. 212–238). New York: Guilford Press.

Wilson, A. J., Revkin, S. K., Cohen, D., Cohen, L., & Dehaene, S. (2006). An open trial assessment of "the number race", an adaptive computer game for remediation of dyscalculia. *Behavioral and Brain Functions, 2*(20), 1–16.

Wilson, B., Alderman, N., Burgess, P. W., Emslie, H., & Evans, J. J. (1996). *The Behavioural Assessment of the Dysexecutive Syndrome (BADS)*. Suffolk, UK: Thames Valley Test Company.

Wilson, B., Kaplan, B., Crawford, S., Campbell, A., & Dewey, D. (2000). Reliability and validity of a parent questionnaire on childhood motor skills. *American Journal of Occupational Therapy, 54*, 484–493.

Wilson, P. (2005). Practitioner review: Approaches to assessment and treatment of children with DCD. *Journal of Child Psychology and Psychiatry, 46*(8), 806–823.

Wilson, P. (2006). Shaping up movement intervention research. In D. Sugden, M. Chambers, & A. Utley (Eds.), *Leeds Consensus Statement: Developmental coordination disorder as a specific learning difficulty*. Leeds: DCD-UK/Discovery Centre.

Wilson, P., & McKenzie, B. (1998). Information processing deficits associated with developmental coordination disorder: A meta-analysis of research findings. *Journal of Child Psychology and Psychiatry, 39*, 829–840.

Wimmer, H. (1996). The non-word reading deficit in developmental dyslexia: Evidence from children learning to read German. *Journal of Experimental Child Psychology, 61*, 80–90.

Wimmer, H., & Goswami, U. (1994). The influence of orthographic consistency on reading development: Word recognition in English and German. *Cognition, 51*, 91–103.

Wimmer, H., & Perner, J. (1983). Beliefs about beliefs: Representation and constraining function of wrong beliefs in young children's understanding of deception. *Cognition, 13*, 103–128.

Wimmer, H., Mayringer, H., & Landerl, K. (1998). Poor reading: A deficit in skill-automatization or a phonological deficit? *Scientific Studies of Reading, 2*(4), 321–340.

Windfuhr, K. (1998). *Verbal learning, phonological processing and reading skills in normal and dyslexic readers*. Unpublished PhD thesis, University of York.

Windfuhr, K., & Snowling, M. J. (2001). The relationship between paired associate learning and phonological skills in normally developing readers. *Journal of Experimental Child Psychology, 80*, 160–173.

Wing, L. (1980). Childhood autism and social class: A question of selection? *British Journal of Psychiatry, 137*, 410–417.

Wing, L., & Gould, J. (1979). Severe impairments of social interaction and associated abnormalities in children: Epidemiology and classification. *Journal of Autism and Developmental Disorders, 9*, 11–29.

Wing, L., & Potter, D. (2002). The epidemiology of autistic spectrum disorders: Is the prevalence rising? *Mental Retardation and Developmental Disabilities Research Reviews, 8*(3), 151–161.

Wise, B. W., Ring, J., & Olson, R. K. (1999). Training phonological awareness with and without explicit attention to articulation. *Journal of Experimental Child Psychology, 72*, 271–304.

Witkin, H., Oltman, P., Raskin, E., & Karp, S. (1971). *Children's Embedded Figures Test*. Palo Alto: CA: Consulting Psychologists Press.

Witton, C., Talcott, J. B., Hansen, P. C., Richardson, A. J., Griffiths, T. D., Rees, A., et al. (1998). Sensitivity to dynamic auditory and visual stimuli predicts nonword reading ability in both dyslexic and normal readers. *Current Biology, 8*, 791–797.

Witton, C., Stein, J. F., Stoodley, C. J., Rosner, B. S., & Talcott, J. B. (2002). Separate influences of acoustic AM and FM sensitivity on the phonological decoding skills of impaired and normal readers. *Journal of Cognitive Neuroscience, 14*(6), 866–874.

Wolf, M., & Bowers, P. G. (1999). The double-deficit hypothesis for the developmental dyslexias. *Journal of Educational Psychology, 91*(3), 415–438.

Woodcock, R., McGrew, K., & Mather, N. (2001). *Woodcock-Johnson® III NU Complete*. Itasca, IL: Riverside Publishing.

Woodruff, G., & Premack, D. (1981). Primitive mathematical concepts in the chimpanzee: Proportionality and numerosity. *Nature, 293*, 568–570.

World Health Organization (1992). *International statistical classification of diseases and related health problems* (Vol. 1, ICD-10). Geneva: World Health Organization.

World Health Organization (1993). *The ICD-10 classification for mental and behavioural disorders: Diagnostic criteria for research*. Geneva: World Health Organization.

Wright, B. A., Lombardino, L. J., King, W. M., Puranik, C. S., Leonard, C. M., & Merzenich, M. M. (1997). Deficits in auditory temporal and spectral resolution in language-impaired children. *Nature, 387*, 176–178.

Wright, H., & Sugden, D. (1996). A two-step procedure for the identification of children with developmental co-ordination disorder in Singapore. *Developmental Medicine and Child Neurology, 38,* 1099–1105.

Wright, S. (1920). The relative importance of heredity and environment in determining the pie-bald pattern of guinea pigs. *Proceedings of the National Academy of Science, 6,* 320–332.

Wright, S. (1921). Correlation and causation. *Journal of Agricultural Research,* 20, 557–585.

Wulfeck, B., & Bates, E. (1995). *Grammatical sensitivity in children with language impairment.* San Diego: Center for Research in Language, University of California.

Wynn, K. (1992). Children's acquisition of the number words and the counting system. *Cognitive Psychology,* 24(2), 220–251.

Xu, F., & Spelke, E. S. (2000). Large number discrimination in 6-month-old infants. *Cognition,* 74(1), B1–B11.

Xu, F., Spelke, E. S., & Goodard, S. (2005). Number sense in human infants. *Developmental Science,* 8(1), 88–101.

Yuill, N., & Oakhill, J. (1988). Effects of inference training on poor reading comprehension. *Applied Cognitive Psychology,* 2, 33–45.

Yule, W., Rutter, M., Berger, M., & Thompson, J. (1974). Over and under achievement in reading: Distribution in the general population. *British Journal of Educational Psychology,* 44, 1–12.

Zammit, S., Allebeck, P., Andreasson, S., Lundberg, I., & Lewis, G. (2002). Self reported cannabis use as a risk factor for schizophrenia in Swedish conscripts of 1969: Historical cohort study. *British Medical Journal,* 325(7374), 1199.

Zelazo, P. D., & Muller, U. (2000). Executive function in typical and atypical development. In U. Goswami (Ed.), *Handbook of cognitive development* (pp. 445–469). Oxford: Blackwell.

Zelazo, P. D., Carter, A., Reznick, J. S., & Frye, D. (1997). Early development of executive function: A problem-solving framework. *Review of General Psychology,* 1, 198–226.

Zelazo, P. R., Zelazo, N. A., & Kolb, S. (1972). Walking in the new-born. *Science,* 177, 1058–1059.

Zwaigenbaum, L., Bryson, S., Rogers, T., Roberts, W., Brian, J., & Szatmari, P. (2005). Behavioral manifestations of autism in the first year of life. *International Journal of Developmental Neuroscience,* 23(2/3), 143–152.

Subject Index

Author Index